W9-CPA-834

Small Business:
An Entrepreneur's Business Plan

9e

Gail P. Hiduke
Saddleback College

J. D. Ryan
Emeritus, Irvine Valley College

CENGAGE

Australia • Brazil • Mexico • Singapore • United Kingdom • United States

Small Business: An Entrepreneur's Business Plan, Ninth Edition
Gail P. Hiduke and J. D. Ryan

Senior Vice President, LRS/Acquisitions & Solutions Planning: Jack W. Calhoun

Editorial Director, Business & Economics: Erin Joyner

Senior Acquisition Editor: Michele Rhoades

Developmental Editor: Ted Knight

Editorial Assistant: Tamara Grega

Market Development Manager: Jonathan Monahan

Marketing Coordinator: Michael Saver

Brand Manager: Robin LeFevre

Executive Marketing Communications Manager: Jason LaChapelle

Art and Cover Direction, Production Management, and Composition: PreMediaGlobal

Media Editor: Rob Ellington

Rights Acquisition Director: Audrey Pettengill

Rights Acquisition Specialist, Text and Image: Amber Hosea

Manufacturing Planner: Ron Montgomery

Cover Image: © iStockphoto/Image Source

© 2014, 2009 Cengage Learning, Inc.

ALL RIGHTS RESERVED. No part of this work covered by the copyright herein may be reproduced, transmitted, stored, or used in any form or by any means graphic, electronic, or mechanical, including but not limited to photocopying, recording, scanning, digitizing, taping, Web distribution, information networks, or information storage and retrieval systems, except as permitted under Section 107 or 108 of the 1976 United States Copyright Act, without the prior written permission of the publisher.

For product information and technology assistance, contact us at
Cengage Customer & Sales Support, 1-800-354-9706

For permission to use material from this text or product, submit all requests online at **www.cengage.com/permissions**
Further permissions questions can be e-mailed to
permissionrequest@cengage.com

Library of Congress Control Number: 2012948803

ISBN-13: 978-1-285-16995-8

ISBN-10: 1-285-16995-6

Cengage
20 Channel Center Street
Boston, MA 02210
USA

Cengage is a leading provider of customized learning solutions with office locations around the globe, including Singapore, the United Kingdom, Australia, Mexico, Brazil, and Japan. Locate your local office at: **www.cengage.com/global**

Cengage products are represented in Canada by Nelson Education, Ltd.

To learn more about Cengage platforms and services, register or access your online learning solution, or purchase materials for your course, visit **www.cengage.com**.

Printed in the United States of America
Print Number: 05   Print Year: 2019

brief contents

Image_Source/iStockphoto.com

Image_Source/iStockphoto.com

contents

Image_Source/iStockphoto.com

preface

Welcome to the ninth edition of *Small Business: An Entrepreneur's Business Plan.* We created our book for the thousands of dreamers like you who want to create their own ventures. Most first-time entrepreneurs start out with little more than an idea. By combining your talents, passions, and ideas with a practical approach, we will show you how to take your idea and form it into a functional Business Plan and succeed.

Every great adventure begins with a map; thus, this book serves as your map and navigator. The Action Steps provide you with direction and tasks to accomplish along the way, while the vignettes provide a firsthand look at the trials, tribulations, and successes of fellow entrepreneurs.

In completing the Action Steps, you will learn how to develop a Business Plan from the inception of an idea to identifying and locating Target Customers and determining how to market to them successfully. Hold on tight, fasten your seatbelt and prepare to embark on your great entrepreneurial adventure!

■ ORGANIZATION

Target the Chapters that Call to You

The Action Steps are spaced out across 15 chapters, from Chapter 1, "Your Great Adventure," to Chapter 15, "Pull Your Plan Together."

- Chapters 1, 2, and 3 ask you to focus on yourself and your ideas, while also researching trends and future opportunities. If you are just exploring entrepreneurship, concentrate first on these chapters and the accompanying Action Steps. Remember, you are designing not only your Business Plan but also your life plan.
- Chapters 4, 5, and 6 help you locate several of the keys to success in small business: your Target Customer, knowledge of your competition, gaps in the marketplace, and finding the right location.
- Chapter 7 helps you reach out to your Target Customer with the vast array of promotional tools.
- Chapter 8 plunges you into numbers—determining how much you will need to start up and how much you will need to keep going. Chapter 9, "Shaking the Money Tree," helps you find the money to take your dream from the drawing board to reality.
- Chapter 10 focuses on copyrights, trademarks, and patents to help you keep control of your intellectual property. This is especially helpful if you are a creative person trying to peddle an invention or sell a book.
- Chapter 11 helps you build a winning team to accomplish your dreams.
- Chapter 12 guides you through insurance, taxes, and ethical dilemmas.
- Chapter 13 offers tips and advice if you want to purchase an ongoing business. If you want to join the franchise movement, read Chapter 14 first. There are franchisees around every corner in the United States, but not all of them are happy with their lot. If your goal is to be a happy franchisee,

complete a Business Plan for your specific franchise location to determine if it will live up to the hype.

- Chapter 15 asks you to gather all of your Action Steps together to formulate the basis of your Business Plan—your business's launching document.
- Appendix A is a Fast-Start Plan which works for a small business comprised of an owner with no or few employees, or where additional work is contracted out and the loss of investment will not sink the ship. Consider completing a Fast-Start Plan early on to determine if your idea warrants you going forth.
- Appendix B showcases Annie's Business Plan Proposal for a chocolate and candy store located at Sea World.
- Appendix C contains forms to assist you in your entrepreneurial planning: personal budget, Small Business Administration loan forms, and other helpful and time saving documents.

■ KEY FEATURES

Action Steps

More than 70 Action Steps take you through every phase of a start-up, from the initial dream to developing marketing and distribution strategies and finally to building and implementing the completed Business Plan.

Entrepreneurial Vignettes

Throughout the text we present you with case studies full of strategies and real-world applications that provide insight into entrepreneurial minds and ventures. We have modified many of the stories for simplicity and clarity. Many of the vignettes are based on entrepreneurs who have shared their stories over the years.

Business Plans

Featured Business Plans include *Yes, We Do Windows: A Fast-Start Plan* (located in Appendix A), applicable for very small businesses requiring minimal capital, and *Annie's* (found in Appendix B), an in-depth Business Plan Proposal for a chocolate store to be located at Sea World.

Entrepreneurial Links

Recognizing that the entrepreneurial life can be lonely and scary at times, we encourage you to reach out to available community, government, and entrepreneurial resources for support, guidance, and direction. From Stanford University entrepreneurial podcasts to the Angel Capital Association, we encourage you to seek out like-minded individuals dreaming the same dream as you and organizations that will foster your dream.

Global Resources

To encourage entrepreneurs to reach beyond the U.S. market, we provide global statistics and resources throughout the text.

Passion

In each chapter we highlight a passionate entrepreneur, one who exhibits his or her enthusiasm for products, locations, or markets. Not all entrepreneurs are passionate solely about money; in fact, few are. Many are driven by their dedication to help others. Thus, we highlight entrepreneurs like Melissa Marks Papock, founder of Cabana Life, who developed a line of sun-protective clothing for women and children after being diagnosed with melanoma. And another passionate entrepreneur, Eileen Parker, founder of Cozy Calm, a firm that provides weighted blankets for people with sensory processing issues.

■ NEW AND REVISED FOR THE NINTH EDITION

New resources and websites have been added throughout the chapters. Approximately 40 percent of the entrepreneurial vignettes, Entrepreneurial Resources, Passionate Entrepreneurs, and Global Village highlights have been updated or replaced with new information.

To reflect the changes in our society, we have highlighted social and hybrid entrepreneurs throughout the book, such as Gabrielle Palermo, one of the founders of G3Box whose firm focuses on "the conversion of steel shipping containers into low-cost, modular, and mobile medical clinics."

Chapters 2 and 3 highlight many new trends and opportunities for entrepreneurs. We feature such hot topics as water shortages, rising natural resource prices, and the mobile generation. We also explore such large and forceful markets as aging baby boomers, millennials, and the iGeneration.

Chapters 4 and 6 expand the use of data for product positioning and location decisions. Competitive analysis and strategy have been expanded in Chapter 5, allowing the reader to utilize the research information gained in Chapters 2 through 4 and develop more thorough, competitive plans and strategies to meet his or her Target Customers' needs.

We discuss the melding of promotion, distribution, and location decisions as the web's impact is part of almost all entrepreneurial decisions today.

Chapter 10 has the most current information available on patents, trademarks, and copyrights.

Chapters 13 and 14 recognize and address the large number of entrepreneurs who decide to purchase an ongoing business or franchise. We have included more in-depth information on franchise brokers, as well as social networking franchising websites.

■ PLANNING FOR SUCCESS

The reason we wrote this book was to provide you with a Business Plan workbook. We supply the steps, and you supply the effort and hard work to chart a course for your dream business. Writing a Business Plan sharpens your focus. When you sharpen your focus, you see more clearly. Seeing more clearly raises your confidence. In the big world of small business, as in life, confidence helps you keep going when the going gets tough. There is an adage in the business world: If you fail to plan, then you are planning to fail.

Before you write a Business Plan, you should study the form. From the outside, a Business Plan looks like a stack of paper: for the short plan it is a thin stack; for the long plan, it is a thick stack bound together to look like a book. However thick the stack, your plan will be a document with a beginning, middle, and end. But in reality your plan has no end point; as our world moves so rapidly today your Business Plan will become a living and ever-evolving document.

There are two good plans in this book that serve as a guide and many more good plans floating out there in cyberspace for you to pursue, and we lead you to those. We have tried to provide current material, but Internet sites will come and go, and government programs will take new forms. Because of the dynamic nature of business today, we urge you to keep current by checking both the Internet and our website for their vast resources at *http://academic.cengage .com/management/ryan*.

Because laws and tax issues are constantly in flux, always consult your legal counsel and tax advisors rather than relying only on the material contained in this text or on any Internet site. All forms have been provided as examples only and should not be used without benefit of legal counsel. Our society is highly litigious, and you must be diligent if you want to stay out of court. Never skimp on legal fees!

We hope you open one of the three entrepreneurial doorways: starting your own business from scratch, franchising, or buying a business. We encourage you to find success along with over 200,000 fellow budding entrepreneurs who have followed the Action Steps provided. Good luck!

■ INSTRUCTOR'S RESOURCE MATERIALS

Instructor's Manual and Test Bank

The Instructor's Manual includes teaching aids such as learning objectives, lecture outlines, and suggestions for guest speakers and class projects. The Test Bank is full of true/false, multiple-choice, and short-answer questions.

Voxant Newsroom Videos

Video segments from Voxant's Newsroom are located at *http://academic.cengage.com/management/ryan* and include content from major content providers, such as CBS and Reuters. Questions for each video are included in the Instructor's Manual.

PowerPoint Slides

The PowerPoint presentation is colorful and varied and was designed to hold students' interest and reinforce each chapter's main points. The PowerPoint presentation is available only on the website.

Website

Visit our website at *www.CengageBrain.com*, where you will find a complete listing of the "Entrepreneurial Links" and margin definitions found in the text; links on management topics, careers, and time management; and other valuable resources for both the instructor and student.

Accessing CengageBrain

1. Use your browser to go to www.CengageBrain.com.
2. The first time you go to the site, you will need to register. It's free. Click on "Sign Up" in the top right corner of the page and fill out the registration information. (After you have signed in once, whenever you return to CengageBrain, you will enter the user name and password you have chosen and you will be taken directly to the companion site for your book.)
3. Once you have registered and logged in for the first time, go to the "Search for Books or Materials" bar and enter the author or ISBN for your textbook. When the title of your text appears, click on it and you will be taken to the companion site. There you can chose among the various folders provided on the Student side of the site. NOTE: If you are currently using more than one Cengage textbook, the same user name and password will give you access to all the companion sites for your Cengage titles. After you have entered the information for each title, all the titles you are using will appear listed in the pull-down menu in the "Search for Books or Materials" bar. Whenever you return to CengageBrain, you can click on the title of the site you wish to visit and go directly there.

CourseMate

Make the grade with CourseMate + LivePlan! This interactive website helps you make the most of your study time by accessing everything you need to succeed online in one convenient place, while producing a high-impact business plan good enough to present to investors. LivePlan business plan software from Palo Alto Software is automatically included with this version of MANAGEMENT CourseMate, giving you the ability to collaborate with your classmates, receive video guidance along the way, and produce a complete professional business plan. LivePlan software is used by real entrepreneurs. MANAGEMENT Course-Mate also provides an interactive eBook automatically, that gives you the option to save money by going all digital (with the option to upgrade to print at any time for a discount). Numerous interactive learning tools, such as quizzes, flash-cards, videos, and more, help you master today's management concepts.

Acknowledgments

First and foremost we want to thank the thousands of entrepreneurs we have met whose grit, determination, passion, and hard work have served as an inspiration to us. Many of their personal stories have been woven throughout this book. In addition, we have attempted to address many of the problems and issues they have faced. Thus, many of the stories throughout the text are composites of entrepreneurs we have met in our journeys.

Jan Galati, an entrepreneurial accountant, reviewed and improved Chapter 8 and provided steady support and guidance throughout the text. Larry Drummond, a senior human resource professional, provided insight and his expertise for Chapter 11. Pat Perkowski, owner of Fashion Forward Productions, edited and greatly enhanced many of the chapters based on her 25 years as an entrepreneur. Doris Weinbaum, whose business was for sale and sold during the writing of the text, offered great insight for Chapter 14. Additional readers, Kelsey Galati, Danny Doyer, and Kaitlin Galati, budding entrepreneurs, and students, revised and enhanced many of the chapters.

Casey Campbell's steady mood, excellent research capabilities, and organizational skills supported the successful completion of the text. I am incredibly indebted to him and appreciate his efforts more than I can say.

Without the support, patience, and love from my sons, the journey would not have been as easy or as sweet. I also want to thank my parents, Andrew and Carolyn Hiduke, for raising me and teaching me the importance of "hard work and commitment".

Many say it "takes a village to raise a child." Well I say it "takes a village to write a book" and I am forever grateful for my village.

We also want to extend a thank-you to the reviewers whose insightful comments helped to shape this edition:

Lou Firenze	*Northwood University–Midland*
Mark Zweig	*University of Arkansas–Fayetteville*
Cathy Lewis-Brim	*Warner Southern College*
Carol Carter	*Louisiana State University*
Dennis Pitta	*University of Baltimore*

I appreciate all the efforts of Michele Rhoades and my Developmental Editor, Ted Knight, who has guided me throughout the process, easing my fears, prodding me, and most importantly supporting me.

Gail Hiduke

Image_Source/iStockphoto.com

Your Great Adventure
Exploring the Right Fit

Learning Objectives

- Discover the right complementary entrepreneurial fit for you.

- Begin filling your Adventure Notebook with ideas and information to build Business Plan.

- Understand how to use text and access vast entrepreneurship resources.

- Review the three doorways to entrepreneurship.

- Identify various entrepreneurial types.

- Determine why today's economic and technology climate is an advantageous time to start a business.

- Understand your financial and family situation.

- Make bold assessment of your personal strengths and weaknesses.

- Brainstorm a clear picture of success in small business.

- Investigate the practices of financially successful businesses in your community. Evaluate those who did not succeed—what contributed to their failure? For those who succeeded—what contributed to their success?

- Expand your knowledge of small business through interviewing small-business owners.

- Design your own entrepreneurial lifestyle to include your realistic expectations of the time and energy you are committed to devote to your vision as an entrepreneur.

ACTION STEP 1

Adventure Notebook

If you are a typical creative thinker and entrepreneur, you probably write 90 percent of your important thoughts on the back of an envelope or enter them on a tablet or smartphone. That might have been okay in the past, but now that you are doing this for real, becoming organized with the right tools is paramount. Storing information can be done with an organizer or desktop folders for your ideas and Business Plan. This data becomes your **Adventure Notebook**. Keep track of small items such as articles, advertisements, and business cards. Your Adventure Notebook will become the heart of your Business Plan, and it should include:

1. Twelve-month calendar
2. Appointment calendar with reminders on your smartphone, as missing an appointment can impact your success
3. List of priorities
4. All Action Steps with #5 in front
5. An idea list—continue to add items to this throughout your search
6. A "new eyes" list for keeping track of successful and not-so-successful businesses you come across, plus notes about the reasons for their success or failure
7. A list of possible team members
8. Articles and statistics you gather that serve as supportive data for your Business Plan
9. A list of helpful websites
10. A list of experts who might serve as resource people when you need them, such as lawyers, CPAs, bankers, successful businesspeople, and so on
11. A list of potential customers
12. A list of names and phone numbers of contacts for goods and services

Entrepreneur A visionary self-starter who loves the adventure of a new enterprise and is willing to risk his or her own money

Adventure Notebook Dream to reality with collection of Action Steps and information

Action Steps Activities to prepare you to write a Business Plan

Business Plan A working blueprint outlining finances and direction for a new start-up or expansion

---

Life is short, and you only go around once. Make sure you are achieving what you want, having fun, making money, and being the best person you can be. How do you do that? Some people do it by going into business for themselves and if you are thinking about owning your own business, this book is for you.

Try this line of thought: What do you want to be doing in the year 2020? In 2030? What is the best course of action for you right now? What might be the best business for you? What are your strengths? What do you want out of life? What are your dreams? And most of all, what are your passions?

This is the age of the **entrepreneur.** According to the Small Business Administration (SBA), *http://www.sba.gov,* there are 27 to 30 million small businesses out there. Each year, according to the Kauffman Foundation, a leading supporter of entrepreneurship, more than a half a million new businesses are started.

If you are thinking about starting a small business, you are among the 6 million budding entrepreneurs currently dreaming the same dream. Statistics from the Entrepreneurial Research Consortium show that one in three U.S. households has been involved in small business. Most new jobs in the private sector are created by firms with fewer than 20 employees. According to the SBA, small businesses hire 40 percent of high tech workers and surprisingly produce 13 times more patents per employee than large firms.

Yes, it is a great time to be an entrepreneur. You could have the time of your life.

■ BUILDING YOUR ROAD MAP

If you follow the Action Steps throughout the book, you are on your way to building a successful venture. Beginning with Action Step 1, the book will guide you through the bustling marketplace—through trends, Target Customers, and promotions; through shopping malls, spreadsheets, websites, and hushed gray bank buildings; through independent businesses that are for sale; through franchise opportunities—all the way to your own new venture and Business Plan (Figure 1.1).

We supply the Action Steps, and you supply the effort to chart your course. Writing a Business Plan sharpens your focus. When you sharpen your focus, you see more clearly. Seeing more clearly raises your confidence. In business, as in life, confidence helps you keep going when the going gets tough. And it will!

Before you write a Business Plan, you should study the form. From the outside, a Business Plan looks like a stack of paper; for the short plan (Appendix A) it is a thin stack; for the long plan (Appendix B), it is a thick stack bound together to look like a book. However thick the stack, your plan will be a document with a beginning, middle, and end and should remain a living, breathing, and ever evolving document. Don't put it on a shelf. Keep it on your desk and revise, revise, and revise—in the planning stage and more importantly, when you become operational.

Target the Chapters That Call to You

The Action Steps are spaced out across 15 chapters, from Chapter 1, "Your Great Adventure," to Chapter 15, "Pull Your Plan Together."

figure **1.1**

Entrepreneurial Road Map

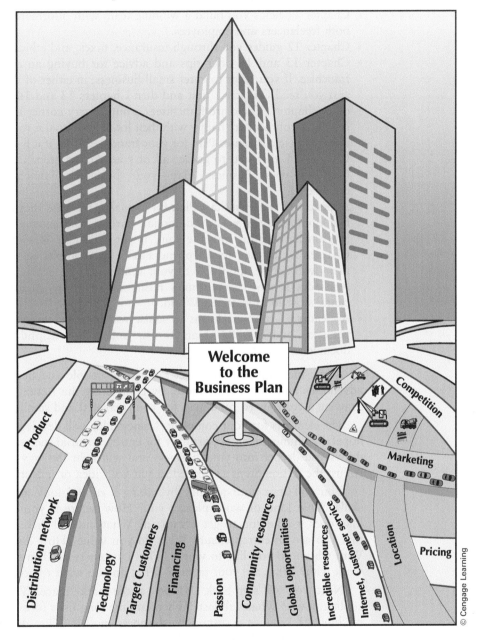

- Chapters 1, 2, and 3 help you focus on yourself and your ideas; they explain how to develop and test your ideas in the marketplace before you risk your money. If you are exploring entrepreneurship, concentrate on these chapters and the accompanying Action Steps. Remember, you are designing not only your Business Plan but also your life plan.
- Chapters 4, 5, and 6 help you locate several of the keys to success in small business: your Target Customer, the right location, and gaps in the marketplace.
- Chapter 7 helps you reach out to your Target Customer with promotional tools.
- Chapter 8 plunges you into numbers—how much you will need to start up and how much you will need to keep going. Chapter 9, "Shaking the Money Tree," helps you find the money to take your dream from the drawing board to reality.

- Chapter 10 focuses on copyrights, trademarks, and patents to help you control your intellectual property. This is especially helpful if you are a creative person trying to peddle an invention, App, or book.
- Chapter 11 helps you build a winning team with information on the hiring of both freelancers and employees.
- Chapter 12 guides you through insurance, taxes, and ethical dilemmas.
- Chapter 13 and 14 offer tips and advice for buying an existing business or franchise. If you want to enter small business, in either of these ways, we suggest you read Chapter 1 first and then Chapters 13 and 14 before reading the other chapters. There are franchisees around every corner in the United States, but not all of them are happy with their lot. If your goal is to be a happy franchisee, complete a Business Plan for your franchise to see if it lives up to the hype.
- Chapter 15 asks you to gather all of your Action Steps together to form the basis of your Business Plan—your business's launching and working document.
- Appendix A is a Fast-Start Plan for a smaller business that has an owner with few employees, or where additional work is contracted out and the loss of investment will not sink the ship. If your business is a microbusiness, read Chapter 1 and then read Appendix A before completing the Action Steps as many will not be applicable to your venture.
- Appendix B showcases Annie's Business Plan Proposal for a chocolate and candy store located at Sea World.
- Appendix C contains forms to assist you in your entrepreneurial planning: personal budget, SBA loan forms, and other helpful and time saving documents.

Microbusiness Very small business in terms of employees but not necessarily revenue

Along the way you will meet fascinating people and hopefully, have a few adventures and fun. Furthermore, by completing the Action Steps, you will be drawing a customized road map for your personal and small-business success.

The elements for your complete Business Plan will develop along the way and hopefully illuminate an opportunity for entrepreneurial success. Each Action Step draws you deeper into your business and will light the way to your final plan. Adjust the Action Steps as needed to suit your idea or industry.

You will start your journey by taking a careful look at yourself and your skills. What kind of work pleases you? How secure is your present job? How long does it take you to get organized? What internal drive makes you believe that you are an entrepreneur? What do you value? How do you like to work? With whom do you like to work? What customers or clients would you like to work with? What are your talents? What do you want to accomplish?

Next, you will step back and look at the marketplace. What is hot? What is cooling down? What will last? Where are the long lines forming? What are people buying? What is a sustainable business model? What distinguishes the up-and-comers from the down-and-outers? You will brainstorm a business that will fit into an industry niche, toss around numbers to get a feel for how they turn into profits, and keep having fun.

Brainstorm Unlock your brain to possibilities

Then it will be time to profile your Target Customer, assess the competition, figure out clever promotional strategies, test your product, and scout locations. By that time, you will know where you are going, and you will feel that you are in control of your own destiny.

Next, you will move on to pricing structures, cash-flow statements, distribution strategies, and building a winning team. By the time you reach Chapter 15, you will have gathered enough material to write a complete Business Plan for showcasing your business to the world—that is, to bankers, vendors, lenders, venture capitalists, credit managers, key employees, family, and friends.

Your finished plan will be a working and ever-evolving document for your business. It will provide a walk-through of your industry, generate excitement in potential investors, demonstrate your competence as a thoughtful planner, and underline the reasons customers will clamor for your product or service. Your plan will also serve as a means of channeling your creative energies.

We are all familiar with the entrepreneurs who started businesses with an idea written on the back of a napkin in a restaurant and were funded by wealthy venture capitalists before ever writing a Business Plan. But realistically, most entrepreneurs need to do research to start their business.

In the fast-paced technology field many companies have begun and sold for billions without showing any profit and oftentimes not even knowing what their revenue model would be when they started. The truth is for many highflying firms there are few metrics, distribution models evolve daily, and competition pops up overnight. Thus, for those firms developing a Business Plan poses huge challenges as support data is not available. If you are entering one of these areas, you will need to keep abreast of changes on a daily basis in your industry and be willing to change your plan at a moment's notice.

Revenue model Form business will take to generate sales, income and profits

Although the text takes you from marketing to location choice to pricing, the reality is that all of the steps of the Business Plan will force you to revise your initial assumptions as you test out your ideas in the marketplace. And even though the Action Steps appear to be separate, the information you gain from each step must be integrated into your evolving Business Plan. Map out your strategy in numbers and words for your plan and realize they will continue to evolve throughout the start-up phase into the future.

We call it a road map, but think of it as a Los Angeles road map; always changing, with roadblocks, traffic jams (too many competitors), and fortunately new roads and thus opportunities for you! The book serves as a guidebook to a Business Plan, but we recognize the vast changes and encourage you to always use outside information and links to keep abreast of changes so you will know when new roads are opening.

One reason you are reading this book is that you are creative. You like to build, to pull things together, to plant seeds and watch things grow, to develop projects, to produce. When your mind is racing, you probably come up with more ideas than you can process. That is when you need a plan to keep your entrepreneurial energies on track while the creative steam rises. Perhaps you have always dreamed of working for yourself and being your own boss. Well, you can realize that dream—*if you are prepared*.

Preparing yourself takes time, energy, and the willingness to reach out to the larger business community within which you will operate. Once you begin, and once you possess basic knowledge about your industry and markets, you will reach out to entrepreneurs, associations, inventors' forums, and website communities.

Throughout the text, we highlight many Entrepreneurial Resources—websites, books, associations, and programs that provide excellent sources of information and assistance usually available at no or low cost, which are only the tip of the iceberg. One of this chapter's Resources highlights several student entrepreneurial organizations which offer college students an opportunity to learn and grow with others on their campus. Show your tenacity and search out the best sources for yourself and your business. You will be glad you did.

Key Points from Another View at the end of each chapter represent additional entrepreneurial insight to guide you in your quest and provide support for your endeavors. All feature boxes and Key Points are integral parts of each chapter.

We hope to kick-start our readers into thinking internationally by highlighting global information within the Global Village boxes. The opportunities are limitless, yet few entrepreneurs take the global path. Be a pioneer in your industry or market, and reach out to the almost 7 billion people who live outside the United States. With today's technology, reaching across the ocean is as easy as reaching across the table. Do your homework and you may find a global business a viable option.

Prepare yourself for long and oftentimes very lonely workdays. You *are* the business oftentimes; so you will have very little down time. Limited resources do not allow for additional personnel. You will have to deal with physical and mental stress, crashing hard drives, loan turndowns, and so on as part of your life early in your business. Your personal vision will have to drive you through the tough times if you are to succeed.

Thus throughout the text and especially in the Passion features, we have highlighted entrepreneurs who are passionate about their products and services, employees, markets, or ideas and dreams. Read their stories and search your soul. Believe in yourself and your passions, because those beliefs and hard work lead to entrepreneurial success. Answer the questions in the following passion features. And begin to ask yourself, Do I truly have what it is going to take? Am I willing to take calculated risks and follow my passions?

■ JUMP-START WITH ENTREPRENEURIAL LINKS

The Internet's resources are limited only by the amount of time you have available. As you work through the text and Action Steps, you will access a wealth of information, ask questions of experts, communicate with fellow entrepreneurs, and discover marketing and financial resources on the Internet. Throughout the text, we will highlight many useful sites and encourage you to reach out further with Twitter, Facebook, and LinkedIn.

Resources for entrepreneurs continue to grow each day but below we list some of our favorite sites.

Web Link Starting Points

- Fast Company *http://www.fastcompany.com*
- Inc. *http://www.inc.com*
- Entrepreneur *http://www.entreprenur.com*
- Sprouter *http://www.sprouter.com*
- Ewing Marion Kauffman Foundation *http://www.kauffman.org*
- Under30Ceo *http://www.under30ceo.com*
- Small Business Administration *http://www.sba.gov*
- National Federation of Independent Business *http://www.nfib.com*
- Startup America Partnership *http://www.s.co*
- Alltop *http://www.alltop.com*

As you move through the phases of the book, addressing personal assessment, trends, product development, social media, distribution, number crunching, legal issues, and writing a plan, we encourage you to expand your information by exploring web resources at each step of your Business Plan.

Also, the web offers numerous examples of Business Plans—some free, some for sale—on how to blueprint your business.

This book, online sources, and fellow entrepreneurs will show you how to sharpen your vision so that you can write your personal Business Plan you need to succeed in a fast-changing world. To jump-start each day and keep your entrepreneurial focus, sign up for daily updates from the many sites above and ones specifically aimed at your industry. Also, consider watching and learning daily from interviews with the greatest entrepreneurs at websites such as Inc., Fast Company, and Stanford's Entrepreneurship Corner.

The chapter's Entrepreneurial Resource highlights Start-up Tools from Stanford University Professor, Steve Blank's website. Blank's book, *The Startup Owner's Manual: The Step-by-Step Guide for Building a Great Company* and his course at Stanford are leading the "lean start-up" revolution, which

—figure **1.2**

Basic Business Plan Outline

SBA Elements of a Business Plan

Agenda should include an executive summary, supporting documents, and financial projections. Although there is no single formula for developing a business plan, some elements are common to all business plans. They are summarized in the following outline:

1. Cover sheet
2. Statement of purpose
3. Table of contents

I. The Business
   A. Description of business
   B. Marketing
   C. Competition
   D. Operating procedures
   E. Personnel
   F. Business insurance
II. Financial Data
   A. Loan applications
   B. Capital equipment and supply list
   C. Balance sheet
   D. Break even analysis
   E. Pro-forma income projections (profit and loss statements)
   F. Three-year summary
   G. Detail by month, first year
   H. Detail by quarters, second and third years
   I. Assumptions upon which projections were based
   J. Pro-forma cash flow
III. Supporting Documents
   A. Tax returns of principals for the last three years and personal financial statements (all banks have these forms)
   B. For franchised businesses, a copy of franchise contract and all supporting documents provided by the franchisor
   C. Copy of proposed lease or purchase agreement for building space
   D. Copy of licenses and other legal documents
   E. Copy of resumes of all principals
   F. Copies of letters of intent from suppliers

Sample Plans

One of the best ways to learn about writing a business plan is to study the plans of established businesses in your industry.

Source: For more information, see *http://www.sba.gov/smallbusinessplanner/plan/writeabusinessplan/SERV_WRRITINGBUSPLAN.html*. (Accessed January 10, 2008).

recognizes and addresses that "Customer development operates at different speeds for web/mobile startups versus products sold through physical channels as web products obtain feedback faster."

Knocking at the Entrepreneurial Doors

There are three doorways to small-business ownership. Doorway 1 is buying an ongoing business: You search, locate a business that you like, and buy it. Sounds pretty easy, doesn't it? A business broker will make it sound even easier, so beware!

Doorway 2 is buying a franchise: You find a logo you like—one with national visibility—and buy it. In exchange for your money, the franchisor may or may not supply you with inventory, advice, training, buying power, a shorter learning curve, and a product or service that is well known in the marketplace. Sounds pretty easy, doesn't it? A slick franchisor will make it sound even easier. In addition to franchising, many more individuals will reach out and become part of multilevel marketing business opportunities.

Multilevel marketing Salesperson receives commissions on personal sales and sales of those they recruit

Doorway 3, is starting a new business, one that is compatible with your interests, skills, and passions that are also backed up by careful research that demonstrates strong customer need, willingness, and ability to purchase.

Entering the world of small business by any of these doorways demands a carefully designed Business Plan—words and numbers written out on paper that guide you through the gaps, competition, bureaucracies, products, and services.

What About These Three Doorways?

Many entrepreneurs enter the world of small business by buying an existing business or investing in a franchise operation. Upon gaining some business experience, many of these individuals decide to start a totally new business from scratch. Few entrepreneurs are happy with just one business. They start up, they sell, and they start up again.

No matter which doorway you choose, you will need a Business Plan. If you buy an ongoing business, you may inherit the seller's Business Plan. However, it is advisable to write one of your own. Ask the seller, again and again if necessary, for the data you need to begin writing your own plan before you finalize the sale. Do not take any figures as facts without investigating: Do your own research. Check out the seller's claims of huge potential profits and endless goodwill before you commit to a purchase.

If you invest in a franchise, you will be buying a Business Plan from the franchisor. But until you see it, you will not know for certain what additional research is needed to determine how the franchise will fit with your local customers and community.

Writing a Business Plan is a lot cheaper than plunking down money on a franchise that may not be successful. If you start your own business through any of the three doorways, a Business Plan is an absolute must. That plan stands between you and success or failure.

Your life needs focus and purpose. Wanting security, honesty, excitement, substance, and success are a natural part of your makeup. Deciding which road to take will be worthwhile if you keep your eyes and ears wide open.

Personal financial security obtained by employment in large companies continues to wane. Many people are recognizing that self-reliance through one of the

Entrepreneur's Resource

Steve Blank's Startup Tools @ steveblank.com
A treasure trove of hundreds and hundreds of resources and links awaits you! The following are only a tip of Blank's iceberg!

- Founding/Running a Startup Advice
- Market Research
- Web Prototyping, Testing, and Building Tools
- Entrepreneurial Groups
- BusinessModel Canvas/Customer Development Tools
- Website Setup
- "How Big is the Market" Tools
- "Do I Contact Customers?" Tools
- Product Launch Tools
- Traditional Media
- SEO and Analytics Tutorials
- Analytics Tools
- Search Engine Optimization Tools
- Online Marketing Suites
- E-mail Blasting
- Surveys
- Collaboration
- On-line Communities
- Website Tools
- Cloud Services and Tools
- Project Management
- Find a Co-founder
- Market Research Resources Online
- Advice on Raising Startup Capital

Blank's links will be of special interest and assistance to readers who are developing web or cloud based businesses.

three doorways often provides the most secure and rewarding career option. The text is written to help you take control of your business and personal life and also prepare you to enter one of the three doorways.

■ THE AGE OF THE ENTREPRENEUR

If the business world is changing faster and faster—revving up like a high-speed motor—what do you do? If life is not what you imagined it would be when you were in high school, what do you do? If the big firm you targeted as your dream employer is busy downsizing, if the job you trained for is now obsolete, if the position you now have is spoiled by office politics—what do you do?

If you have a great idea for a product but your employer does not believe in it, what do you do? If you have found a great location for a small, unique restaurant on your last vacation to Sun Valley, what do you do? If you saw a great product on your trip to Hungary and think it would sell well in Cedar Falls, Iowa, what do you do?

The answer is: Start up a business. Figure out who you are and what you want from life. Think with your pencil and spreadsheets while you figure out how much you are willing to pay for the "good life." How much time are you willing to spend? How much money? How much sweat? How much risk can you handle?

What Type of Entrepreneur Do You Want to Be?

For some, becoming an entrepreneur is a lifelong dream; for others, it is buying a job. It is the excitement of an unlimited income or a way to pay the bills. It is the dream of never having a boss or the dream of being the boss. It is the desire to leave a legacy, the joy of producing the perfect product, an opportunity to change the world. Becoming an entrepreneur is manifesting the desire to live out your dreams and passions.

Three types of entrepreneurs designated by Rishi Anand, Founder and Managing Director of VentureGiant.com, follow:

1) The Lifestyle Entrepreneur:

This is someone who has decided to build a business to make a living and to satisfy his or her own personal motivations. This entrepreneur would like to create a successful company—but building a company to be listed on the NASDAQ would definitely NOT be a driving force. Instead this entrepreneur would be more likely to be "income statement affluent" over any of the other types of Entrepreneurs listed—and the choice of businesses he or she would choose to be involved with would generally be non-scalable, but usually cash generative businesses.

2) The Empire Builder:

This particular entrepreneur would be classed as "balance sheet affluent." This entrepreneur buys—but does not easily sell, usually stubbornly choosing to go "long" on all of his investments and business decisions. This entrepreneur would not really consider selling or exiting from his company, unless it was absolutely essential or involved members of the board physically dragging him/her out of their presidential chair.

3) The Serial Entrepreneur:

It is fair to state that this entrepreneur's main motivation will be the cash payout on the exit or sale of their venture so that they are able to move on and build their next company.

Source: Rishi Anand, "What Type of an Entrepreneur Are You?" Under30CEO, March 27, 2012, from *http://under30ceo.com/what-type-of-an-entrepreneur-are-you*. Reprinted with permission.

ACTION STEP 2

Why Do I Want to Be an Entrepreneur?

1. Review your current job situation. Are you happy? Are you excited about going to work each day? Is there something else you would rather be doing? If money were no object, what would you do?

2. In your Adventure Notebook, make a list of all the reasons why you want to become an entrepreneur.

3. Assess how those reasons will fit into your desired personal, family, financial, and professional life-styles and your social, spiritual, and ego needs. Spend a few minutes now and many, *many* hours throughout the next few months reviewing how various businesses fit into your prioritized list. What doesn't fit? What does?

4. Make a list of all the reasons you do not want to become an entrepreneur. Review the list. What can you do to minimize these issues? When you honestly review the advantages and disadvantages of being an entrepreneur, you will see that they often are flip sides of each other. For example, many people want to become entrepreneurs to be their own boss only to find out they now have many bosses—employees, customers, suppliers, and investors.

5. Be sure to look realistically at your lists and keep refining them as you seek fulfillment of your passions and dreams. As you explore various businesses, continue to return to your answers, and focus on whether your selected business ideas will meet your personal goals as well as your entrepreneurial focus and passion.

Social entrepreneur Solving a social problem through entrepreneurship

Intrapreneur Entrepreneur within a large corporation

In addition to the types above, there are many other types of business owners including reluctant entrepreneurs, who come to owning their own businesses oftentimes out of necessity, such as Bernard's McGraw founder of Bernard's Creole Kitchen:

After Hurricane Katrina's devastation in New Orleans, Bernard, his wife, and six sons evacuated to Texas. Back home, Bernard had been catering manager for the Bayou Baglery, which closed after the hurricane. With no home or job to return to in New Orleans, Bernard decided to set his family's roots down in San Antonio, and do what he knows best: Creole Cooking.

Bernard's first restaurant was in a run-down shack on the city's Southside. He soon had a loyal following, as word spread about his delicious food. He won the San Antonio Critic's Choice Award, the Blue Plate Award, and the Talk of the Town Award.

While studying Biblical Theology at The Baptist University of the Americas, Bernard finally received the break he deserved. The college asked him to relocate "Bernard's Creole Kitchen" in their dining area.

Bernard decided to formally finance his business with a loan from ACCION Texas-Louisiana and start building his credit. With his $4,265 loan, he stocked his new location with supplies and hired three part-time employees. He now has a guaranteed amount of 85 students a day (plus additional students without meal plans who pay cash), and a restaurant with a seating area for his regular customers.

Bernard remembers the love and generosity he received during the struggle of starting a new life with less than a suitcase of belongings. Even with his demanding schedule of running a business, Bernard has still found time during his days off to feed homeless people with a program he started, "Gumbo Under the Bridge".

Source: Accion. From *www.accion.org/page.aspx?pid=4014*, (Accessed May 14, 2012). Reprinted with permission.

Others become accidental entrepreneurs, such as the thousands of individuals who have solved a problem by writing an App and found themselves in business! Josie Rietkerk, owner of Caterinas, opened her first retail store to keep an eye on her three teenagers. Now those teens are grown and two of them help run four stores. Chris McCormack, planted a vegetable garden for his parents and soon had a business building and planting gardens for others. These are the good type of accidents, though some are way more profitable than others!

Striving to solve societal problems through entrepreneurship and affect sustainable social change propels social entrepreneurs like Dale Partridge and Aaron Chavez, founders of Sevenly:

Confronting their own lack of activism and the need for social change, they dreamed of motivating people to care about the plight of those less fortunate.

Convinced that people would take action if given the means, they established Sevenly to address seven causes: hunger, water, slavery, aid, disaster, medical and poverty.

They donate $7 from every fair trade T-shirt purchase to its charity partner of the week; it raised $175,000 in its first six months of operation. Every week, Sevenly partners with a different charity, creating a special T-shirt that represents their cause. Eighty-five percent of its sales are driven from social media, which Sevenly credits with its success.

Source: Elaine Murphy & Sarah Vaughn, "40 UNDER 40: Dale Partridge & Aaron Chavez," 01 May 2012, *www.ocmetro.com*, (Accessed May 14, 2012). Reprinted with permission.

One more type of entrepreneur—an intrapreneur—is actually born within an organization. With 3M's Art Fry and Spencer Silver, creators of the Post-It note, being two of the most famous intrapreneurs. The men took advantage of 3M's "bootlegging" policy, which encourages 3M employees to use 15 percent of their time to develop their own ideas.

Your job situation can change quickly; your life situation may change or your personal desires may change. Thus, you may be become any one of the above type of entrepreneurs. Take a moment now and complete Action Step 2 as you delve into your entrepreneurial motives.

■ REV UP

Small companies, those with fewer than 100 employees, employ over half of the private-sector workers in the United States. Start-ups produce new jobs, and these jobs are created by an absolutely unique partnership—the marriage of money, risk, and hard work. The money comes from savings, friends, family, credit cards, second mortgages, bank loans, angels and venture capitalists.

Hard work, faith, and passion come from the driving force of the entrepreneur and from those who trust the entrepreneur. Entrepreneurship should grow and blossom with the fields—biotechnology, nanotechnology, surveillance technology, organic agriculture, green technology, and others—so they are ripe and ready for the harvest. Plant early.

You are in the Age of the Entrepreneur and money and your birthdate are no longer barriers. In fact, "According to the Global Entrepreneurship Monitor, people over the age of 35 made up 80 percent of the total entrepreneurship activity in 2009."

Ready to Start?

First, you need to become organized, starting with your Adventure Notebook in Action Step 1. Some people believe organization stifles creativity. Jan Wilkes was like that until she saw the value of using her Adventure Notebook in developing a new Internet travel business—Romantic California Escapes.

Romantic California Escapes—From Adventure Notebook to Internet Travel Business

During her five years working as a travel agent for three different travel agencies, Jan kept records, listing what seemed to be important elements of the travel business, her contacts, news and magazine articles, ideas, competitors' ads, websites, and business cards. Her Internet guru friend, Pat Perk, tired of working for other people, enthusiastically agreed to be her partner in starting up a new company of their own.

After reviewing her notes, Jan looked for a gap in the marketplace. She realized that many of her clients were looking for short breakaway escapes. With both husband and wife working full-time, week-long escapes were more and more difficult for her clients. Therefore, Pat suggested to her partner that they tap into the Internet by focusing on using websites that offered weekend discounts on cars, hotels, and airfares within California.

After extensive research, Jan and Pat repackaged these deals into great California weekend escapes. By adding extras such as dinners, flowers, theater tickets, and limousine services, Romantic California Escapes emerged. The extras added value to the trips and removed all the planning hassles that busy couples today have little time or inclination for.

Next, Jan and Pat determined how best to reach their market. They were fortunate in that Jan had retained most of her past clients' phone numbers, home addresses and email addresses. She and Pat sent email postcards of beautiful California scenes announcing their new online service. Upon registering online for weekly emails potential customers were offered a chance to win a wonderfully romantic trip to Big Sur's Post Ranch Inn, one of the most exclusive private resorts in California. Surprisingly, 30 percent responded. Once online, respondents were asked to fill out detailed questionnaires about their travel desires for weekend escapes.

Knowing most of her customers on a personal basis, Jan decided to pick up the phone and spent three weekends touching base with each of her clients. They were thrilled with her business idea and provided feedback, which improved her original business idea. In today's high-tech world, oftentimes, personal touch works really well as it is unexpected and greatly appreciated.

Every Tuesday at 5 p.m., Romantic Escapes tweeted, e-mailed, and posted their weekend escapes on Facebook. Thus, Wednesday through Friday, Jan and Pat were busy booking trips as many personal emails went out to customers as well as general listings. Within six months, they were profitable and clients quickly became repeat clients. Sales rapidly increased due to strong word of mouth and Facebook, where clients were encouraged to post travel photos. Romance was in the air, and money was in the bank for Pat and Jan.

By completing the Action Steps in the text, we hope you will find a profitable niche in the marketplace like Pat and Jan.

Why Today Is the Day to Begin Your Venture

Technology today allows budding entrepreneurs to appear on equal footing with the big guys. With tools such as cloud computing, web development online tools, web analytics, access to affordable phenomenal software developers, software for sales and project management, one can literally begin a business overnight if one chooses. Barriers to entry aren't just falling; they no longer exist for many types of new ventures.

With Skype and smartphones, we increase our productivity and can operate anywhere anytime. One entrepreneur just spent six weeks vacationing in Europe with her children, pulling into a café for a latte and a few hours of work each day.

Word of mouth, while always one of the most important forms of marketing, is on hyper speed with social media propelling startups. Client contact and customer development are enhanced by two-way conversations held online. Developing your web content to advertise, woo, and maintain customers is easier than ever as design freelancers and coders from around the world are just a click away.

PayPal and Square allow for payment collection ease beyond belief. Allowing entrepreneurs to collect funds immediately any place any time!

The changing world and economy open endless possibilities and technology opens the gates wide for entrepreneurs to act now! Follow one writer's quest to be an entrepreneur using technology, hard work, and intuition.

Marketer to Writer

When she turned 30, Sally Honeycutt Binson took a good look at her life. Sally lived in Charleston, South Carolina; she had a fine job as a marketing director of a restaurant chain and earned a good salary. Her home—sunny with a view of the water—was wonderful. But Sally paid a price for the "good life" with endless meetings, squabbles with her boss, and lots of air miles.

To plot her future, Sally drew a mind map (Figure 1.3). When she put herself inside a bubble in the center of the page, she did not get anywhere. When she added "writing" inside a bubble, she found a new career: writer. Sally had a degree in English literature and read constantly. Knowing she wanted to write full-time eventually, Sally created a home office and began to write. Her first efforts were rejected by agents and publishers.

Sally then researched her local bookstore and Amazon listings and was struck by how large the romance, mystery, and science-fiction sections were. Using her marketing background, she took a few bookstore managers to lunch and asked: What was selling? What did readers want? What did editors want? Which books received the most promotion? She also spent many hours researching books, reviews, and readership statistics online at Amazon and Powell's.

Armed with information about book sales and target readers, Sally enrolled in a writing course at her local community college. The instructor was a published author. With his guidance, Sally studied the mystery genre.

Before she began writing her second book, Sally checked out websites for anything related to mystery. At MysteryNet.com she found a site for mysteries with information on writing, selling, readers' groups, and webzines. Sally joined two organizations: Mystery Writers of America and Sisters in Crime. A contact from Sisters in Crime connected Sally to several literary agents.

A Book Is a Product

Before she developed her product, she engaged in intensive research and development (R&D) by analyzing ten mystery novels. Using the analytical techniques she learned

— figure **1.3**

Mind Map for Mystery Writer Sally Honeycutt Binson

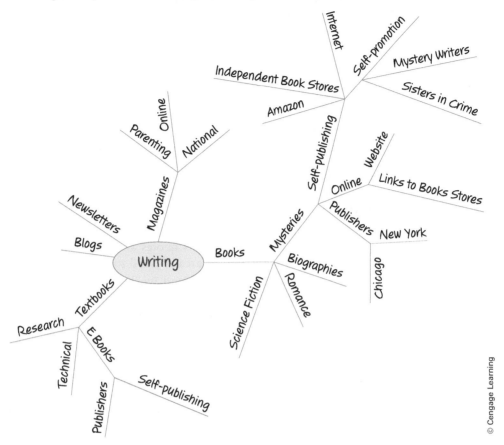

© Cengage Learning

in her writing class, Sally discovered the secret of mystery writing: conceal and then reveal. Following her instructor's advice, the setting of her first mystery was a location Sally was familiar with: an island off the coast of South Carolina. Because she could relate easily to her own gender's thinking patterns, Sally's main characters were female: the sleuth, the victim, and the killer.

In one year, Sally had a manuscript. Although her agent connections through Sisters in Crime did not work out, Sally did find an agent through the Internet and mailed a plot outline and the first three chapters. The agent sold the book to a publisher. And when the royalty checks were enough to provide her with six months' financial security, Sally tendered her resignation. By then, her second book was underway: **Murder on Amelia Island.**

■ WHAT IS YOUR CURRENT FAMILY AND FINANCIAL PICTURE?

You've looked at why you want to be an entrepreneur in this dynamic time, now you need to assess your current financial situation to prepare for your future as one by completing Action Step 3. What are you worth? What money do you have access to? Is your family dreaming the same dream as you? If so, great. If not, ask what they *are* willing to do to help and what *are* they willing to give up?

An essential element to achieving a successful entrepreneurial lifestyle is family support. Spend a great deal of time understanding the realistic demands on you and your family from both time and financial standpoints.

ACTION STEP 3

Review Your Financial and Family Picture

Sit down with your family to discuss how starting your own business may affect the family's financial future. Complete the Personal Financial Statement and Personal Budget, which can be found in Appendix C. You will need these figures later to determine your financial needs and also to assess the financial contribution you will be able to make to your business.

After completing the above, consider the following:

1. Can I live on less? How much less?
2. What can I cut from my budget? Go through each line item in the budget to assess where you can cut expenses.
3. How long can I continue to cut my budget before I feel too deprived? How long before my family feels deprived?
4. Your personal financial statement will show your assets and liabilities. Which of your assets can you access easily and turn into cash and what amount of your net worth (assets minus liabilities) are you willing to put at risk?
5. Discuss with your family the time and money sacrifices that will be involved in developing your new venture.
6. Meet with a fee-only financial planner and your accountant to discuss your unique financial issues if needed.

A business is a living, breathing entity, and it takes time for the golden egg to hatch. Be prepared to wait awhile.

The following websites will assist you in preparing budgets and will answer many questions about financial planning issues.

LearnVest
Mint
Kiplingers
Money

Review your current financial picture. Complete the personal financial statement and budget in Appendix C and use Mint.com to track your expenditures. Sit down with your family and review how to reduce expenses. For many, short-term financial pain is worth long-term gain; for others, it is not.

If you are risking a large sum of family money and/or giving up a substantial salary, consider meeting with a professional financial planner first. Fee-only planners will meet with you to discuss your situation without the pressure to purchase financial products. In addition, a planning meeting with your accountant may also prove very helpful, as some businesses can be structured to provide tax breaks.

A major impediment to entrepreneurship is the ability to obtain affordable health insurance for you and your family. This issue should not be taken lightly and should be addressed *before* you take the leap. Check out COBRA insurance from your current employer, your spouse's insurance, associations' insurance offerings, and private health insurance through an HMO or PPO.

Also, look into policies with lower rates that provide catastrophic coverage. eHealthInsurance online provides quotes and if you are a healthy 25 year old, your premiums may be in the area of $100 to $200 a month.

Many entrepreneurs have found working 20 hours a week at one of the few firms that provide insurance to part-time employees is one alternative. For others, their spouse carries a family policy. You must be willing to be creative and work hard on this important area to protect yourself and your family. New laws impacting health insurance will be implemented over the next few years so stay abreast of changes and for further information read Chapter 12.

Believing in your dreams is an important part of being an entrepreneur. Your goals and love of what you do will make the sacrifices worth it as you reach for the possibilities. Living at home for an extra year to save cash, working a part-time job to support your fledgling business, or moving to a less-expensive area of the country all become realistic options if you believe in your own dream.

Amilya Antonetti, founder of Soapworks, and her husband were willing to leave their jobs, sell their home, and risk everything for their dream of providing hypoallergenic, nontoxic cleaning products. Remember that most start-up businesses fail due to lack of adequate cash flow and funding. So, what are you willing to give up for your dream so you will have the funds to make your dream a reality?

Besides insurance and financial planning, you need to be aware of your credit score and its implications for borrowing. Please review the information in Chapter 9 dealing with credit and your credit score.

◼ WHAT DOES IT TAKE TO BE AN ENTREPRENEUR?

To find out if you have what it takes, first profile yourself as an entrepreneur in Action Step 4, and complete the questionnaire in the Passion feature. You will not be a perfect fit on any questionnaire, because there is no such thing.

The assessment tools in Action Step 4 and others online address many issues to consider before entering the world of entrepreneurship. Take time to explore these issues and share your responses and concerns with those who know you well and want the best for you.

Entrepreneurship requires persistence, hard work, commitment, reliability, decisiveness, risk, and failure management. As an entrepreneur, your challenges will include balancing family and work, maintaining focus, reaching emotional

PASSION

Do You Have the Passion to Be an Entrepreneur?

There is no one "perfect" entrepreneurial set of traits, but there certainly are traits along with the inner strength to believe in yourself and your passions, which are important to your success. Take some time to answer the following questions honestly.

1. Do you truly believe in your ideas?
2. Are you organized?
3. Can you handle pressure and stress?
4. Are you a reasonable risk taker?
5. Are you creative and can you share your creative excitement with others?
6. Can you make lemonade out of lemons and roll with the punches?
7. Do you dread routine days?
8. Are you self-confident?
9. Are you reliable and ready to work really hard?
10. Are you willing to fight for what you believe in?
11. Are you able to make decisions on your own?
12. Are you comfortable working with new people and new ideas?
13. Are you a self-starter?
14. When you loose, can you deal with it and move on?
15. Can you control your emotions and temper?
16. Do you have a need to achieve?
17. Can you laugh at yourself?
18. Are you disciplined?
19. Do you have lots of ideas and see solutions to problems?
20. Can you live without perfection and external recognition?

Be passionate about your products or services and employees and you will be one step closer to entrepreneurial success.

© Cengage Learning 2014

ACTION STEP 4

Self-Assessment

Complete the questionnaires in Table 1.1 and the Passion feature. With your entrepreneurial juices flowing, go online and access: the SBA's Small Business Readiness Assessment Tool and the University of Pennsylvania's Authentic Happiness site for several different character and strengths tests, Afterwards, you should be able to answer the following questions:

1. What are your personal strengths?
2. What skills have you acquired through the years?
3. What are you good at doing?
4. What makes you happiest?
5. What type of businesses might offer you the fulfillment you desire?
6. What personality traits will help you in your own business?
7. What personality traits might hinder you in your own business?
8. What do you value?
9. What are your financial dreams?
10. What are your passions?

In Action Step 5, you will be pulling together all your information. Keep your information current and continue to refine your answers as you continue to work on your Business Plan and talk to others.

---

and monetary goals, and dealing with the initial exhaustion, loneliness, and stress inherent in almost any entrepreneurial venture.

In addition to a strong work ethic and the ability to handle stress, an entrepreneur must possess basic business skills. Looking ahead you will need to assess your strengths and weaknesses in the areas of sales, marketing, financial planning, accounting, personnel management, technology, and so on, as shown in Table 1.1.

If you find yourself questioning your abilities in any one area, search out college classes, books, online classes, and mentors to fill your skill gaps before making the entrepreneurial leap. Also, the Key Points from Another View feature at the end of the chapter explores the various roles you will play as an entrepreneur.

Wearing many hats is a challenge but necessary for almost all early entrepreneurs. Woody Stingley, founder of an industrial products firm, shared how during his first year in business he worked all evening developing new products, slept in his office for a few hours, woke up washed his face, put a clean shirt and tie on and called on customers all day. Just to repeat again and again. Many years later Woody was *very* happy he had worked so hard early on!

Exploring your passions and needs in this first chapter starts you on the Business Plan journey. To obtain the most from this text requires that you complete the Action Steps immersing yourself in a new and exciting venture. Even if you do not end up following through with your Business Plan, you will have learned the process.

table 1.1

Strengths and Weaknesses Skill Checklist

The chart below will help you identify your strengths and weaknesses and will give you a better idea of whether you are ready to become a small-business owner. Examine each of the skills areas listed in the chart. Ask yourself whether you possess some or all of the skills listed. Rate your skills in each area by circling the appropriate number, using a scale of 1 through 5; use 1 for low, 2 for between low and medium, 3 for medium, 4 for between medium and high, and 5 for high.

Skills	Rating				
	Low		Medium		High
Sales					
• pricing					
• tracking competitors buying					
• sales planning					
• negotiating					
• direct selling to buyers	1		2	3	4 5
• customer service follow-up					
• managing other sales reps					
• tracking competitors					
Marketing					
• advertising/promotion/public relations					
• annual marketing plans					
• media planning and buying					
• advertising copy writing					
• social media marketing strategies	1		2	3	4 5
• distribution-channel planning					
• pricing					
• packaging					
Financial Planning					
• cash-flow planning					
• monthly financials					
• bank relationships	1		2	3	4 5
• management of credit lines					
Accounting					
• bookkeeping					
• billing, payables, receivables					
• monthly profit and loss statements/balance sheets	1		2	3	4 5
• quarterly/annual tax preparation					
Administrative					
• scheduling					
• payroll handling	1		2	3	4 5
• benefits administration					
Personnel Management					
• hiring employees					
• firing employees					
• motivating employees	1		2	3	4 5
• general management skills					
Personal Business Skills					
• oral presentation skills					
• written communication skills					
• computer skills					
• word-processing skills	1		2	3	4 5
• fax and e-mail experience					
• organizational skills					

(continued)

————————table **1.1**

Strengths and Weaknesses Skill Checklist *(continued)*

Intangibles

• ability to work long and hard					
• ability to manage risk and stress					
• family support	1	2	3	4	5
• ability to deal with failure					
• ability to work alone					
• ability to work with and manage others					

Total

After rating yourself in each area, total up the numbers and apply the following rating scale:

- If your total is less than 20 points, you should reconsider whether owning a business is the right step for you.
- If your total is between 20 and 25, you are on the verge of being ready, but you may be wise to spend some time strengthening some of your weaker areas.
- If your total is above 25, you may be ready to start a new business.

Source: Reproduced with permission from CCH Business Owner's Toolkit™, *http://www.toolkit.cch.com*, published and copyrighted by CCH Tax & Accounting.

One never knows when the entrepreneurial passion will start to burn again, and when it does, you will know the process and be able to follow your dream through with a Business Plan. Keep your mind open as opportunities abound.

"Successful founders can be gregarious or taciturn, analytical or intuitive, risk averse or thrill seeking," according to Amar Bhide (Harvard School of Business), who also believes that there is no "ideal" entrepreneurial personality. Thus, one sees Mark Zuckerberg, Steve Jobs, Richard Branson, and Bill Gates, all wildly successful but absolutely not all the same personality!

The entrepreneur who succeeds is one who works incredibly hard. But Jeff Bezos has joked in the case of Amazon.com's success, "half of it was timing, half of it was luck, and the rest of it was brains. The fact of the matter is, the odds are stacked against any start-up. Heavily so. There's a huge amount of luck and timing involved."

Entrepreneurial Success

Starting a business allows you to design your own successful lifestyle, which Action Step 5 asks you to do. Warren Bennis and Patricia Ward Biederman, authors of *Organizing Genius* (Perseus Books), developed a four-question test aimed at anyone seeking success. The questions are:

1. Do you know the difference between what you want and what you are good at?
2. Do you know what drives you and what gives you satisfaction?
3. Do you know what your values and priorities are, what your organization's values and priorities are, and can you identify the differences between the two?
4. Having measured the differences between what you want and what you are able to do, between what drives you and what satisfies you, and between your values and those of your organization, are you able to overcome those differences?

Source: Fast Company, *http://www.fastcompany.com/magazine/09/one.html* (Accessed May 9, 2012).

Bennis concludes that the key to success is identifying talents unique to you and then finding the right arena in which to use them. Many entrepreneurial

ACTION STEP 5

"Inc. Yourself"

Mind map your way to a picture of what you want you to become, your product—yourself. There is no such thing as a wrong idea or a wrong direction. So far you have looked at why you want to be an entrepreneur and what success means to you, and you have reviewed your skills, accomplishments, and passions. It is now time for you to mind map the life *you* want.

1. Review your answers to Action Steps 2 through 4 and define success for yourself by reviewing the checklist below and also add any additional items that signify success to you.

Success Checklist

A. Do you measure success in dollars? If so, how many?
B. What other ways do you measure success?
   - Being able to enjoy a certain lifestyle
   - Dealing with friendly customers who appreciate your service
   - Power, recognition, and/or fame
   - Being able to live and work where you want
   - Providing employment and training for others
   - Being the best business in your area
   - Having time to enjoy your children and hobbies
   - Participating in teamwork
   - Building a legacy
   - Early retirement
   - Making people's lives safer and better
   - Helping others directly or indirectly

2. Draw a circle in the middle of a piece of paper. Write your name inside the circle. Close your eyes for a few minutes, and allow your imagination to take over. Think of yourself as a product. In 5 to 10 years, where and what do you want to be? What do you want—personally, socially, spiritually, financially, and as a lifestyle—and what are your material wants and needs?

(continued)

(continued)

You can predict your future as well as anyone else; mesh the information with your imagination and go for it! Others may be able to predict but only you can make it happen. Your final mind map should represent your desired entrepreneurial and personal lifestyle.

leaders suggest that successful ventures come when our passions coincide with customer needs and ability to purchase.

Success is personal and subjective, whereas income and return on investments are measurable. Success wears many faces. You need to think about this as you start your adventure, because being an entrepreneur is the best chance you will have at defining your personal and professional success.

Review the following Top 10 Success Factors for Entrepreneurs and complete Action Step 5 to discover your personal success factors.

Top 10 Success Factors for Entrepreneurs

From Naveen Jain, CEO of Intellius

I've been an entrepreneur most of my adult life and, recently, I've begun thinking about what it takes to become successful as an entrepreneur—and how I would even define "success." I've given a lot of talks over the years on the subject of entrepreneurship. The first thing I find I have to do is to dispel the persistent myth that entrepreneurial success is *all* about innovative thinking and breakthrough ideas. I've discovered that entrepreneurial success usually comes through *great execution*, simply by doing a superior job of doing the blocking and tackling. But what else does it take to succeed as an entrepreneur and how should an entrepreneur define success? Here's what I came up with:

1. Be passionate. You must be passionate about what you're trying to achieve. That means you're willing to sacrifice a large part of your waking hours to the idea you've come up with. Your passion will ignite the same intensity in the others who join you as you build a team. And with passion, both your team and your customers are more likely to truly believe in what you are trying to do.
2. Maintain focus. Great entrepreneurs focus intensely on an opportunity where others see nothing. This focus and intensity helps to eliminate wasted effort and distractions. Most companies die from indigestion rather than starvation. Companies suffer from doing too many things at the same time rather than doing too few things very well. Stay focused on the mission.
3. Work hard. Success only comes from hard work. There is no such thing as overnight success; behind every "overnight success" lies years of hard work and sweat. People with luck will tell you there's no easy way to achieve success—and that luck comes to those who work hard. Focus on things you can control; stay focused on your efforts and let the results be what they will be.
4. Enjoy the journey. The road to success is going to be long, so remember to enjoy the journey. Everyone will teach you to focus on goals, but successful people focus on the journey and celebrate the milestones along the way. Is it worth spending a large part of your life trying to reach the destination if you didn't enjoy the journey? Won't your team also enjoy the journey more as well? Wouldn't it be better for all of you to have the time of your lives *during* the journey, even if the destination is never reached?
5. Trust your gut instinct. There are too many variables in the real world that you simply can't put into a spreadsheet. Spreadsheets spit out results from your inexact assumptions and give you a false sense of security. In most cases, your heart and gut is still your best guide. We've all had experiences in business where our heart told us something was wrong while our brain was still trying to use logic to figure it all out. Sometimes a faint voice based on instinct is far more reliable than overpowering logic.
6. Be flexible but persistent. Every entrepreneur has to be agile, continually learning and adapting as new information becomes available. At the same time, you have to remain devoted to the cause and mission of your enterprise. That's where that faint voice becomes so important, especially when it is giving you early warning signals that things are off-track. Successful entrepreneurs find the balance between listening to that voice and staying persistent in driving for success—because sometimes success is waiting right across from the transitional bump that's disguised as failure.
7. Rely on your team. It's a simple fact: no individual can be good at everything. Everyone needs people around them who have complementary skill sets. It takes a lot of soul searching to find your own core skills and strengths. After that, find the smartest people you can who *complement* your strengths. It's tempting to gravitate toward people who are like you; the trick is to find people who are not like you but who are good at what they do—and what you can't do.
8. Focus on execution. Unless you are the smartest person on earth, it's likely that many others have thought about doing the same thing you're trying to do. Success doesn't necessarily come from breakthrough innovation, but from flawless execution. A great strategy alone won't win a game or a battle; the win comes from

basic blocking and tackling. No matter how much time you spend perfecting your business plan, you still have to adapt according to the ground realities. You're going to learn a lot more useful information from taking action rather than hypothesizing.

9. Have integrity. I can't imagine anyone ever achieving long-term success without having honesty and integrity. These two qualities need to be at the core of everything we do. Everybody has a conscience, but too many people stop listening to it. There is always that faint voice that warns you when you are not being completely honest or even slightly off track from the path of integrity. Be sure to listen to that voice.

10. Give back. Success is much more rewarding if you give back. By the time become successful, lots of people will have helped you along the way. You'll learn, as I have, that you rarely get a chance to help the people who helped you because in most cases, you don't even know who they were. The only way to pay back the debts we owe is to help people we can help—and hope they will go on to help more people. It's our responsibility to do "good" with the resources we have available.

You might do all of the above and will wonder "but am I successful?" Success, of course, is very personal; there is no universal way of measuring success. What do successful people like Bill Gates and Mother Teresa have in common? On the surface it's hard to find anything they share, and yet both are successful. I personally believe the real metric of success isn't the size of your bank account. It's the number of people in whose lives you are able make a positive difference. This is the measure of success we need to apply while we are on our journey to success.

Naveen Jain is a philanthropist, entrepreneur and a technology pioneer. He is a founder and CEO of Intelius, chairman of education & global development at XPrize foundation and on the board of trustees at Singularity University. Previously, he was the founder and CEO of InfoSpace, and a senior executive at Microsoft Corporation. Among his achievements are: Ernst & Young Entrepreneur of the Year; Albert Einstein Technology Medal for pioneers in technology; "Top 20 Entrepreneurs" by Red Herring; "Six People Who Will Change the Internet" by Information Week.

Source: "The Top 10 Success Factors for Entrepreneurs" by Naveen Jain, CEO of Intelius, CBS NEWS. Reprinted with permission.

GLOBAL**VILLAGE**

World Economic Data to Ponder

From World Development Indicators Database, World Bank 2010 Data

Country (215 listed)	PPP/US Dollars*	World Rank
Luxembourg	$63,850	4
Macao SAR, China	$57,120	6
United States	$47,020	18
Japan	$34,790	35
Czech Republic	$23,620	62
Chile	$13,890	85
China	$7,570	118
India	$3,560	153
Sudan	$2,020	176
Haiti	$1,110	196
Malawi	$850	206

PPP is purchasing power parity: an international dollar has the same purchasing power over Gross National Income (GNI) as a U.S. dollar has in the United States.

(continued)

(continued)

According to the recent World Bank Development Data Group, approximately one-sixth of the world's people produce 78 percent of the world's goods and services and receive 78 percent of the world's income—an average of $70 a day. About 50 percent of the world's population lives on less than $2.50 a day.

As you venture around the world as a potential global entrepreneur, you need to be aware of the economic conditions that will preclude selling medium- and high-ticket items in many countries. Considering the statistics above, you will recognize that a huge market for basic products and services, clean water, electricity, communications, and infrastructure exists throughout the world.

The global entrepreneur will view the above statistics as an opportunity, not a threat, to their business ventures. How can you take advantage of the opportunities in Uganda, Indonesia, India, or Kenya? Half of U.S. exporters employ fewer than five people, so explore and find the right business for you. The possibilities are endless.

Based on 2010 Data.

Source: *http://www.data.worldbank.org*, (Accessed May 9, 2012).

Entrepreneur's **Resource**

Share and Develop Your Passions with Others

Entrepreneurial Student Campus Organizations

Joining a student organization is an excellent way to build valuable contacts and expand your business knowledge. However, more important is joining with others who are dreaming the same dream and learning the ropes from others who have made a similar climb. If your college does not have one of these organizations, be entrepreneurial and develop a chapter on your campus:

Collegiate Entrepreneurs Organization (*http://www.c-e-o.org*)

Group seeks to inform, support, and encourage college students' entrepreneurial ventures, serving over 30,000 students in over 240 collegiate organizations.

Students in Free Enterprise (*http://www.sife.org*)

International nonprofit organization with presence on over 1,600 college campuses in 39 countries who awards over $1,000,000 in prize money each year.

National Collegiate Inventors & Innovators Alliance (*http://www .NCIIA.org*)

Group presents entrepreneurship workshops for technology-oriented ventures on college campuses working with students to bring product concepts to commercialization. The Alliance links program participants with technology professionals and offers annually $2 million in grants to student projects. Students are also taught how to develop projects capable of attracting future angel and venture capital funding.

The three organizations above are just the start. Seek out others, especially those within engineering and medical programs.

Defining Business Success and Doing Quick and Dirty Numbers

Thinking about business success can be stimulating and enlightening. What makes a business successful or unsuccessful? How do you measure success? How do your friends measure success? Action Step 6 will help you discover businesses which appear successful.

You and your friends can merely speculate about which businesses are actually doing well financially or building a scalable business. Only a detailed examination of each business's books and potential will give the whole picture, but we urge you to exercise your marketplace intuition. For example, next time you dine out, try to estimate:

- The number of customers in the restaurant
- The total number of customers the restaurant serves each day
- The average price per meal
- The number of employees in the front and in the kitchen
- The number of cars in the parking lot at different times of the day
- The approximate cost of the food on your plate
- The cost of advertising
- The overhead cost, which would include utilities and rent

Next, multiply the average per-meal price by the total number of daily customers. Perform your estimates on different days of the week and at different hours, and do this type of analysis for other businesses you patronize. Soon you will have the feel for which businesses are losing customers and which are winning them. Success factors will begin to emerge. Adjust the questions above to fit your industry and also anytime you need to make adaptations throughout the Action Steps.

Now, attempt to develop a business's profit profile. In the course of your interviews (see Action Step 7), try to ascertain key numbers, such as gross sales, cost of goods sold, rent, salaries (owner, management), and how much is spent on marketing (advertising, commissions, promotions, and so on). Estimate the other expenses and arrive at a range that will give you perspective when the time comes to work with your own numbers.

For example, suppose a business has $500,000 in sales. The cost of goods sold (COGS) averages 53 percent, rent is $2000 a month, and total salaries are 15 percent of gross sales. The company spends 6 percent of their gross on marketing. Based on these numbers, you can estimate benefits, including FICA (social security) costs, at 20 to 30 percent of salaries; other expenses—supplies, utilities, accounting, legal, auto, entertainment, and so on—also can be estimated at 8 to 12 percent. Combining what you have been given with your estimates yields the profit profile.

On the high side, the profit profile is slightly better than 10 percent, or $51,000. On the low side, it is slightly below 5 percent, or $23,500. (That $23,500 may not be as low as it appears if the owner has already taken a salary, auto, and entertainment expenses.) Taxes would still be owed.

	High Side	Low Side
Sales	$500,000	$500,000
COGS (53% of sales)	$265,000	$265,000
Gross Profit	$235,000	$235,000
Marketing (6%)	$30,000	$30,000
Salaries (15%)	$75,000	$75,000
FICA/benefits	$15,000	$22,500
Rent ($2000/mo.)	$24,000	$24,000
Other expenses	$40,000	$60,000
Net profit before taxes	$51,000	$23,500

ACTION STEP 6

Survey Your Friends About Business Success

1. The next time you are at a party or with a group of your colleagues and there is a lull in the conversation, ask them for three to five small businesses they perceive as successful. Then discuss what signs indicate their success and what the reasons behind the success are. If this cannot be done in person, e-mail 10–20 individuals for their responses.
2. Group the negative thinkers together in a "devil's advocate" group, and have them list unsuccessful businesses and point out the reasons why those firms are losing.

As you continue to assess businesses in your selected industry and other industries, you will begin to recognize success and failure factors that are constant throughout. Stay sharply tuned to successful enterprises. Do not be reluctant to stay alert to the facts before you.

Scalable business Ability of business to function as firm grows rapidly

Cost of goods sold (COGS) Expenses directly attributable to production

ACTION STEP 7

Interview Entrepreneurs

1. Interview at least three people who are self-employed, with at least one in your area of interest. If you are a potential competitor, you may need to travel to find an interview subject willing to help you.

    Successful entrepreneurs love to tell how they achieved success. Be up front about the type of information you need and why you want it. Then make appointments with them at their convenience. Look for the passion behind their success. Face to face interviews will always produce the best information. However, if you cannot accomplish this, use the phone or email.

2. Prepare for your interviews by making a list of open-ended questions which leave room for embellishment. Some suggestions are:

   - What were your first steps?
   - How did you arrange financing?
   - If you had it to do all over again, what would you do differently?
   - How large a part does creativity play in your business?
   - What are your tangible and intangible rewards?
   - What was your best marketing technique?
   - What portion of gross sales do you spend on advertising?
   - Did you hire more employees than you originally expected?
   - What makes your business unique?
   - How do you use social media?
   - Did you write a Business Plan? If not, do you wish you did?
   - Are gross profits what you expected them to be?
   - Would you do it again?

Depending on how you relate to your subject, you might be able to think of these first interviewees as sources of marketplace experience. They may provide you with contacts for later recommendations you will need for a—lawyer, accountant, banker, insurance agent, and so on.

    It helps to take notes during interviews. The information will begin to assemble into patterns sooner than you think. Be sure to send a handwritten thank-you note. Your entrepreneur will be shocked and you will be remembered!

(continued)

Looking at the profit potential of any business is absolutely essential, because many entrepreneurs fall in love with an idea or a product and do not take the time to see if the venture first would be profitable. Without profits your venture will be very short lived.

Do not wait until you have developed a product, planned distribution, and completed marketing strategies to run numbers. Many entrepreneurs tell us, they don't like "numbers." Well, those numbers will keep the wolf from your door, so embrace them! *We encourage you to run "quick and dirty" numbers, like those above, all through the process of developing your Business Plan.*

You will need to make adjustments frequently. Do not be afraid to make changes if your data tells you to. Your goal is profit not protecting your ego.

Interviewing Successful Entrepreneurs

Action Step 7 encourages you to interview entrepreneurs primarily within your selected industry. As you continue to explore, we recommend you also interview your competitors, potential customers, distributors, suppliers, and wholesalers. Too much information never hurts, but too little usually does. Remember though, at some point you have to stop asking questions and leap forward! In some industries, that leap will come after a short time of research and in others only after 3 to 12 months of research.

■ SUMMARY

Throughout this chapter, you have reviewed your financial situation, personal goals, passions, strengths, and weaknesses, and you have worked on defining your desired new entrepreneurial lifestyle. Take the time to review your answers to these Action Steps with several people who know you well. Their input will be invaluable as you come to grips with the reality and challenges that face you in your entrepreneurial quest.

According to Jim Collins, author of *Built to Last*, it is best to look at developing a business that looks at the intersection of three circles: 1) what you are good at 2) what you stand for and 3) what people will pay you for. You have answered the first two with the action steps throughout this chapter that have asked you to search your soul, your pocketbook, and your family's needs and desires. In Chapter 2, you will be looking at your changing world for opportunities. In later chapters, you will discover the right target market: people who possess the dollars, authority, and willingness to purchase your product or service.

Your Adventure Notebook should be filling up now with information, concerns, and wonderful ideas. Entrepreneurship is difficult but rewarding for many. The risks and rewards can only be measured by each individual entrepreneur.

Earl Graves, Sr., founder of *Black Enterprise* says the secret of start-up success is a pit-bull-like refusal to give up: "You have to have a junkyard dog mentality." Before you open your own business, know yourself well, and ask yourself if you are a junkyard dog.

In addition to tenacity, a positive outlook will help drive your success. Jeff Bezos, founder of Amazon.com, was highlighted as one of the 25 Most Fascinating Entrepreneurs by *Inc.* magazine due to his outlook that "optimism is essential." During his interview, he said, "I believe that optimism is an essential quality for doing anything hard—entrepreneurial endeavors or anything else.

"That doesn't mean that you're blind or unrealistic, it means that you keep focused on eliminating your risks, modifying your strategy, until it is a strategy about which you can be *genuinely* optimistic.

"People think entrepreneurs are risk loving. Really what you find is successful entrepreneurs hate risk, because the founding of the enterprise is already so risky that what they do is take their early resources, the small amounts of capital that they have, whatever assets they have, and they deploy those resources systematically, eliminating the largest risk first, the second-largest risk, and so on, and so on."

Also, Bezos reminds, "You don't choose your passions, your passions choose you."

(continued)

Entrepreneurs love to talk about "their babies" and oftentimes share more than they should.

If you are in the technology field, link to Stanford University's Entrepreneurship Corner and daily watch interviews from the leading tech gurus such as Jack Dorsey-Square, Kevin Systrom-Instagram, and Reid Hoffman-LinkedIn. You will be inspired!

■ THINK POINTS FOR SUCCESS

Remember:

- We are entrepreneurs. Work is fun. We seldom sleep.
- Stay flexible.
- Change is accelerating everywhere, and change provides you with opportunities to follow your dreams.
- To find the doorway into your own business, gather data and keep asking questions. But make a decision!
- Sales propel your business forward.
- Get reckless on paper before you get reckless in the marketplace.
- Brainstorm.
- Draw mind maps.
- Confirm your venture with numbers and words.
- Write a Business Plan.
- Follow your passions.
- Leap! If you fall, get back up, recoup, and leap once more!

■ KEY POINTS FROM ANOTHER VIEW

Roles You'll Be Expected to Play

Here's a look at some of the roles you can expect to play in your own business:

- Tax collector — If you sell goods at the retail level, you're responsible for collecting a sales tax for various government entities; also, if you have employees, you're responsible for collecting payroll taxes from them.
- Manager/boss — If you have employees, you'll be responsible for all of the human resources-related functions, including recruiting, hiring, firing, and keeping track of all the benefits information; you'll be the one filling out all the insurance forms, answering employee questions and complaints, and making the decisions about whether you should change the benefits package you offer your employees.
- Sales/marketing/advertising executive — In addition to having to plan your marketing or advertising campaign, you'll have to carry it out; you may write advertising copy, do some preliminary market research, visit potential customers, and make sure existing customers stay happy; depending upon the type of business you own, you may have to join business groups, attend various breakfasts, lunches, and dinners, and just generally network with anyone who could help your business prosper.
- Accountant — Even if you have an accountant, you'll have to know a lot about accounting; you'll have to know which records to keep and how to keep them; if you don't have an accountant, you'll also have to prepare all of your tax forms, and you'll have to know how to prepare and interpret all of your own financial statements.
- Lawyer — Even if you have a lawyer, you'll have to know a lot about the law; if you don't have a lawyer, you'll have to prepare all of your own contracts and other documents and understand all of the employment laws if you have employees or want to hire someone.
- Business planner — As you own your business, you'll inevitably want to make changes, perhaps to expand the business or add a new product line; if you want to make a change, it'll be your responsibility to do it; you'll have to plan it and execute it, and you'll have to consider all of the ramifications of your decision.
- Bill collector — When customers don't pay, it'll be up to you to collect from them; you'll have to know what you can and can't do when collecting; you'll have to decide how best to collect from them and when to give up.
- Market researcher — Before you start your business, you'll have to find out who your customers are and where they're located; you may also have to conduct market research at various times during the life of your business, such as when you are considering introducing a new product.
- Technology expert — As a small business owner, you will probably come to depend upon your computer; you'll have to fix it when it breaks, install upgrades, and load software; you'll also have to keep up with the newest products and the latest changes in technology.
- Clerk/receptionist/typist/secretary — Even if you have clerical help, you'll inevitably do some filing,

answering the phone, and office organization. If you have someone else, for example, keep track of overdue accounts, you'll have to know how to do it so that you can teach them what to do.

Don't make the mistake of underestimating the number of hours involved in owning your own business. A person who spends 40 hours a week focused on his or her work will have to work a lot more hours as a business owner to get in 40 hours of activity directly relating to providing customers goods or services. And during the startup period, you'll probably be the busiest you'll ever be.

If your business operations are to be successful, you will have to be a "jack of all trades" and work hard and smart.

Source: Adapted from *http://www.toolkit.com/small_business_guide /sbg.aspx?nid=P01_0250* (Accessed January 10, 2008 May 8, 2012). Reproduced with permission from CCH Business Owner's Toolkit ™ (*http://www.toolkit.cch.com*) published and copyrighted by CCH Tax and Accounting.

■ ACTION STEPS

■ KEY TERMS

Image_Source/iStockphoto.com

Spotting Trends and Opportunities
Opening Your Eyes

Learning Objectives

- Develop your business intuition by training your eyes and ears to "sense" the future of market forces specific to customer needs.

- Understand the "big picture" and its effect on trends and opportunities.

- Learn to become your own futurist.

- Understand changing family structures and the impact on business.

- Gain an awareness of cultural changes as well as the splintering of the mass market.

- Research technological changes that will directly impact your industry.

- Begin to access the vast array of available secondary resources.

- Become excited about brainstorming techniques and embrace change.

- Learn how to conduct "new eyes" research by scanning your environment.

- Analyze the potential for small-business success by applying the life-cycle yardstick to industries.

Where can you find a business idea that produces a successful return on your dollar? One that fulfills your passions? One that will make you rich? One that will make you a household name in your industry? One that will fulfill your dreams? What are the best ventures for you to pursue today?

Only you can answer these questions, because the best choice for you is one that you will enjoy, and one that can support you financially in the short term and the long term. The experiences, passions, skills, and aptitudes that are unique to you, combined with your temperament, should be in the forefront as you seek the best business choice. The Action Steps in the first chapter were designed to help you discover your personal uniqueness: Who are you? What are your skills? What special knowledge, skills, or expertise do you have that sets you apart from the pack? The Action Steps in Chapter 2 and 3 are targeted toward researching and evaluating opportunities, which mesh with your desires and uniqueness.

■ OPENING YOUR EYES AND MIND TO VAST OPPORTUNITIES

Look around, and check out the new businesses in your town and online. Which new firms are succeeding in your selected industry? What new target markets are developing? What could you sell on the Internet? How can you meet the needs of the aging baby boomers? What about the needs of the echo boomers/millennials and the iGenerations? What desires for products or services do you have? What needs do your friends have? Is there a product you could repurpose? Are there any products you could combine to increase their individual value? Can you take a product or service and make it more "sustainable"? Any new avenues or channels to sell your product?

But before you begin looking at demographic, economic, and technological trends, we want you to be aware that you have the resources, knowledge, and ideas to start a business if necessary right now.

Not everyone has a nest egg or a rich uncle. Most millionaires are self-made, and not a product of inherited wealth. Most entrepreneurs are just regular people who are committed to the time, energy, and devotion needed to launch and grow a thriving business.

After completing Action Step 8 (which asks you to assume you have $1,000, a phone, and a working car or truck), you may discover an opportunity you never recognized before; at the least, you will have a list of business opportunities ready and waiting for the next friend who complains about not having any money.

Your list can show the way to dollars. As fledgling entrepreneurs have shared their lists, we have seen light bulbs go on. One student with less than $100 started an incredibly successful window-washing business. Two students joined together using their interior design skills to offer computerized aided interior designs in addition to their monthly trips to the Furniture Mart with their clients. And yet another offered personal training and time 'shooting hoops' to overweight teenage boys, who he discovered benefited more from having someone to talk to than the exercise.

As you progress through the chapters, you will be building a Business Plan quite likely for another business. But by completing Action Step 8 you may find your dream business and if not, you'll at least know how to make money if you lose your job tomorrow.

Chapter 2 is designed to help you recognize opportunities in market segments so you can define the gaps in the marketplace. You want to be sure 1) your business provides a solution to a problem, 2) that people are willing to pay for it (not

---

Target market Segment of a market most likely to purchase the product or service. Possesses desire, dollars, and authority

Baby boomers Persons born between 1946 and 1963

Echo boomers Persons born between 1977 and 1994

Millennials Persons born between 1977 and 1994

iGeneration Persons born after 1994

Demographic Quantifiable data on population, race, age, education, income, gender

Market segments Identifiable slices of a larger market

just say they are willing but actually purchase!), and 3) you enter the market-place from a position of strength. Now is the time to look at our changing world and your selected industry to spot trends and opportunities.

Be a trend spotter and ride your way to a successful business. Do not forget to add blood, sweat, tears, energy, enthusiasm, money, and passion to your good idea. When we began working with entrepreneurs some 25 years ago, we handed out sage advice: "Just find a need and fill it."

Now we say, "Examine the marketplace thoroughly for flaws and opportunities, and use technology to keep track of your customer's needs continually." We also used to say, "If you're doing business now the same way you did two years ago, you're probably doing many things wrong." Now we say, "If you're doing business today the same way you did three months ago, revise your plan."

Use your marketplace radar to choose a growth segment of a growth industry and ride the crest of the wave. Choosing the hot growth sector is usually the right way to begin before the trend turns down. Occasionally, however, the trend sours quickly.

If you are already in a small business, or thinking about opening one, make it easy on yourself by first identifying industries in the growth phase of their life cycle. Play "marketplace detective."

Twenty years ago, you could ride a trend for 5 to 10 years; now that time is greatly compressed reaching a profit sooner rather than later is essential for continuing your business. Many businesses today are testing their ideas in the marketplace before actually launching their business and we highly suggest you test the market as soon as possible in developing your venture.

When you focus in on a particular business, do you sense growth over the long term? Or is it involved with a fad that will not last? For your business, you want a growth industry that will generate new customers quickly, allowing you to build a repeat customer base.

As a small-business owner, one of the things you must have going for you is fast footwork, so you can adjust to change quickly; it is one of your best weapons in the marketplace. But you can benefit from fast footwork *only if you operate from a position of knowledge*; keep your eyes open and ears tuned to the marketplace. We recommend you follow your competition constantly while keeping abreast of the broad changes in society and technology.

Look before you leap. Brainstorm with your family, friends, colleagues, and competitors; and, most importantly, interview and truly *listen* to your potential customers. Study the marketplace. Read industry journals. Sign up for blogs, use Twitter, RSS feeds, newsletters, etc. Utilize resources at your local entrepreneurship center (see Entrepreneurial Resource) to help guide you in your search as well.

Develop and use your new eyes. With trained eyes, you will be able to see the big picture. When conducting your research, start with the big picture and work down into your industry and then your competitors and specific marketplace. To jump-start your brain, complete Action Step 9. You may not open a business after taking this class or reading this text. However, by keeping an open mind to new information and training your intuition over the next few years, an incredible opportunity may be placed in front of you and you will be prepared to act. Allow yourself to dream.

It's a Dynamic World

- Satellites and mobile communications create a global neighborhood with endless opportunities. Mobile phones are exploding throughout Africa, opening markets that only a few months ago were closed to business opportunities.
- Health care technology changes at lightning speed. For many we are extending life. However, we desperately need to deal with chronic problems: heart disease,

ACTION STEP 8

$1,000 and a Working Vehicle

Off the top of your head, Are you able to think of a business to start with little capital and no employees? Place yourself in the position of having to make money within one week. You *have* to start a business, and you have $1,000; a working car or pickup truck; an apartment, garage, or dorm room; and a smartphone. Remember, the business must be legal! What will it take to make the first move and get you started?

1. Ask friends what they need. Drive through local neighborhoods and towns. Jump on the Internet. Read local papers in other areas. Find out what other people are accomplishing with what appears to be a small investment. What did you find? What opportunities can you explore further?
2. Can you purchase products at a warehouse to resell online? If you have time, visit a swap meet and explore online selling at eBay, Craigslist, or Yahoo.
3. Could you tap a skill you already possess? For example, could you be a foreign language tutor?
4. Compile a list of all the business opportunities you have discovered and share them with your friends, colleagues, and potential customers. What are they willing to pay for your products and services? How often would they purchase? Who are your competitors?
5. Use the Fast-Start Business Plan in Appendix A to launch.

P.S.: Apple Computer started with $1,350. Dell Computer started with $1,000. Nike started with $1,000.

P.P.S.: Walt Disney started in his garage!

Life cycle The progression through stages—from birth to death—of a product, business, service, industry, location, target market, and so on

New eyes Observation with intuition

ACTION STEP 9

Opening Your Mind to New Information

Don't Just Think Out of the Box, Get Out of Your Box!

Your community and workplace are your normal marketing labs. But it is time to open your mind to unfamiliar territory and any new information that is available, which may lead you down some interesting paths where new opportunities lie. Leave your information comfort zone. Time to head out! Do not start this step on the Internet. Get some fresh air and generate energy for your vision.

1. **First stop**: large bookstore (if you can find one!) with lots of magazines. Select and read five distinctly different magazines that you have never read before. What did you learn? Did you read about target markets and products that you did not know existed? What additional opportunities exist? Next, review the top ten bestsellers in the following categories: fiction, nonfiction, children's, trade, and paperbacks. What do they tell you about your current world? Did you see any new genres you didn't know existed?

2. **Second stop**: Twitter and iTunes. What's hot? What's not? What's trending up and down? Opportunities for you?

3. **Third stop**: local mall. What new stores are opening? Which department store has the best service? Highest prices? Best selection? Which restaurants are hot? Where are the longest lines? Do you want to compete in any of these arenas?

4. **Fourth stop**: your favorite store. Compile a list of all the products and services that were not there one year ago; if you are visiting a computer store, shorten the time to two to three months. Can you guesstimate **shelf velocity**? What's hot? What's not? How will this store fair in light of Internet competition?

5. **Fifth stop**: your television set. Spend one hour watching *CNN World Report*. Make a list of the stories. Did any surprise you? Did you spot any opportunities? What problems need to be solved?

6. **IDEO**, **TrendHunter**, **TechCrunch**, **Science**: Log on and stretch

(continued)

Entrepreneur's **Resource**

Entrepreneurship Centers

Throughout the United States, more than 200 entrepreneurship centers are ready, willing, and able to help you start up or expand your venture. Many of the centers are headquartered at universities and may include Small Business Development Centers (SBDCs), Small Business Innovation Research Centers (SBIRs), incubators, accelerators, innovation institutes, and franchise management institutes.

Centers serve the needs of their respective communities and thus their offerings are quite variable. Inexpensive or free workshops, consulting, short-term coursework, competitions, degree programs, and specialized programs are available.

To locate a center in your area, log on to the web and complete a search under entrepreneurship centers, institutes, etc. Several entrepreneurship centers are highlighted below.

Coleman Entrepreneurship Center

College of Commerce
DePaul University
Chicago, IL 60604

Programs and activities: Provides a customizable program, Blueprint, to connect you to Chicago's startup community or help aggressively start a business. They will be with you at every step. Located in the heart of Chicago where some of the city's finest entrepreneurs are at the student's disposal as mentors, ready to guide every step of the way. The Center also offers DePaul Net Impact, an entrepreneurial group whose focus is on sustainable businesses and the Center for Creativity and Innovation.

Entrepreneurship Center

Miller College of Business
Ball State University
Muncie, IN 47306

Programs and activities: Entrepreneurs in Residence program, Military 2 Market program, participation in national and international business plan competitions, Entrepreneurial Disney Experience. Collegiate Entrepreneurs Organization, student consulting for emerging and growing ventures.

Center for Entrepreneurship

Appalachian State University
Transportation Insight Center for Entrepreneurship
Boone, NC 28608

Programs and activities: Association of Student Entrepreneurs, The Carole Moore McLeod Entrepreneur Summit for 40 entrepreneurs each year, mentoring provided by local entrepreneurs, free workshops offering business start-up, capital formation, and intellectual property workshops.

high blood pressure, and diabetes which are so devastating and costly. What opportunities do you see in helping people practice healthy lifestyles or cope with chronic diseases?

- Business operates 24/7. We are always online and the store is always open online. Individuals are always on too! Are there any businesses which will capitalize on the need to escape for the "always connected"?
- Technology creates incredible opportunities in manufacturing and distribution.
- Competition is everywhere and more intense than ever. With mobile tracking and mobile price comparison apps, stakes become even higher.

- A world of 7 billion today exploding to a world of 9 billion by 2050 (see Global Village). Threats and opportunities abound!

■ ENVIRONMENTAL VARIABLES

Changes within the business and social world occur within five major environmental variables. Your challenge is threefold: 1) to constantly be aware and follow the big picture, which consists of the five major variables; 2) to recognize the changes occurring within each variable; and 3) to identify solutions for problems as changes occur. The five major environmental variables are:

1. Technology: biotechnology, sustainability, energy sources development, nanotechnology, personal genomics, water shortages

(continued)

yourself as you explore new technologies. What's innovative? What problems are companies working on? What additioinal problems need to be solved?

7. **Final stop**: stay logged in. For at least two to four hours, surf topics you know *nothing* about. What did you learn? What opportunities did you find? What surprised you?

Your brain should now be in high gear—and suffering from information overload! Use what you have learned as you continue to explore opportunities and every few months do this exercise again so you will always expose yourself to new ideas!

Shelf velocity The speed at which a product moves from storage to shelf to customer

GLOBAL**VILLAGE**

Why Go Global? Look at the Numbers!

Total Population of the Continents

continent	population (in thousands)(est.)					
	1950	1975	2000	2010	2025	2050
Africa	227,270	418,765	819,462	1,033,043	1,400,184	1,998,466
Asia	1,402,887	2,379,374	3,698,296	4,166,741	4,772,523	5,231,485
Europe	547,460	676,207	726,568	732,759	729,264	691,048
Latin America and the Caribbean	167,307	323,323	521,228	588,649	669,533	729,184
Northern America	171,615	242,360	318,654	351,659	397,522	448,464
Oceania	12,807	21,286	31,160	35,838	42,507	51,338
World	2,529,346	4,061,317	6,115,367	6,908,688	8,011,533	9,149,984

source: UN Statistics Division, Department of Economic and Social Affairs. "World Population Prospects: The 2008 Revision".
note: future estimates are based on a medium fertility variant of population growth.

Total Population of the Continents by percentage

continent	population (est.)					
	1950	1975	2000	2010	2025	2050
Africa	8.99%	10.31%	13.40%	14.95%	17.48%	21.84%
Asia	55.46%	58.59%	60.48%	60.31%	59.57%	57.17%
Europe	21.64%	16.65%	11.88%	10.61%	9.10%	7.55%
Latin America and the Caribbean	6.61%	7.96%	8.52%	8.52%	8.36%	7.97%
Northern America	6.78%	5.97%	5.21%	5.09%	4.96%	4.90%
Oceania	0.51%	0.52%	0.51%	0.52%	0.53%	0.56%
World	100.00%	100.00%	100.00%	100.00%	100.00%	100.00%

source: UN Statistics Division, Department of Economic and Social Affairs. "World Population Prospects: The 2008 Revision".
note: future estimates are based on a medium fertility variant of population growth.

(continued)

(continued)

Our world has grown from 3 billion to over 7 billion people in only 45 years. Asia and Africa combined are predicted to comprise 80 percent of the population in 2050! According to *The Economist*, Ethiopia, Mozambique, Tanzania, Congo, Ghana, Zambia, and Nigeria are seven of the top 10 world's fastest-growing economies.

"The increase in the world population over the next 40 years is equivalent to the total world population in 1950." Less than 1 in 20 people in the world live in North America today, and only 1 in 25 will in 2050. Is it any wonder why huge multinational firms are heading off to the rest of the world? You can too!

Which products and services will those who live outside of the developed countries need? What resources are available? What cultural, financial, environmental, and legal obstacles must be overcome to meet the needs of 2050's estimated 9 billion people, two thirds of whom will live in urban areas?

Potential international customers are being born each minute, and so are potential international entrepreneurs. According to Nielsen, "Over a three-year period, emerging market innovation increased by 100%, driven by Africa (+131 percent growth) and BRIC countries (Brazil, Russia, India, and China) (+173 percent growth)."

Nielsen also reports, "According to the International Monetary Fund, more than half of global purchasing power resides in emerging markets, where Gross Domestic Product is expected to grow at a rate 50% greater than developed markets from 2011 to 2016."

Could it be time for you to search out opportunities overseas? If so, begin your research on specific countries with two federal government websites and resources:

U.S. Department of State: *Fact Sheets* replacing *Background Notes*: Factual publications that contain information on all the countries of the world with which the United States has relations. They include facts on each country's land, people, history, government, political conditions, economy, and focus on U.S. relations within each country.

CIA Word Factbook: Provides country-specific demographic, government, economic, and infrastructure information for 267 countries.

In addition to Internet resources, search out federal and state trade offices, local colleges with international programs, consulates, embassies, and international chamber of commerce organizations.

Source: *http://www.geohive.com/earth/pop_continent.aspx*

2. Competition: deregulation and regulation, impact of "big box stores" (Costco, Home Depot), Internet, mobile technology, international (covered in depth in Chapter 5)
3. Social/cultural: immigration, single households, single parents, religion, ethnic shifts, aging population (covered more in Chapters 3 and 4)
4. Legal/political: who is in power, tax laws, changing rules (international, federal, state, and local) (covered throughout text)
5. Economics: recessions, inflation, down-shifting of middle class, cost of housing, food, energy

Each change in the environmental variables and the subsequent trends affect how products are manufactured, marketed, and delivered to customers. How can you capitalize on the changes?

To keep abreast of environmental changes read *Newsweek, Time, TechCrunch, The Economist, Wired*, and *Fast Company and others*. Peruse your industry journals and websites and begin to learn how to spot changes.

In addition, the World Future Society (WFS) constantly scans the environment for trends and predicts the future. Figure 2.1 lists 10 forecasts WFS views as "significant probable developments that deserve wide attention." Combine the

figure **2.1**

The Futurist's Top Ten Forecasts for 2012 and Beyond

THE FUTURIST magazine examines key developments in technology, the environment, the economy, international relations, etc., in order to paint a full and credible portrait of our likely future. Each year since 1985, the editors of *THE FUTURIST* have selected the most thought-provoking ideas and forecasts appearing in the magazine to go into our annual Outlook report. Over the years, Outlook has spotlighted the emergence of such epochal developments as the Internet, virtual reality, and the end of the Cold War. The forecasts are meant as conversation starters, not absolute predictions about the future.

The Society hopes that this report—covering developments in business and economics, demography, energy, the environment, health and medicine, resources, society and values, and technology—will assist its readers in preparing for challenges and opportunities.

1. Learning will become more social and game-based, and online social gaming may soon replace textbooks in schools. The idea that students learn more when they are engaged—as they are when playing games—is helping educators embrace new technologies in the classroom. In addition to encouraging collaborations, games also allow students to learn from their mistakes with less fear of failing.
2. Commercial space tourism will grow significantly during the coming decade. By 2021, there will be 13,000 suborbital passengers annually, resulting in $650 million in revenue. Many companies are currently working to make commercial space flight a viable industry, according to Melchor Antuñano, director of the FAA Civil Aerospace Medical Institute.
3. Nanotechnology offers hope for restoring eyesight. Flower-shaped electrodes topped with photodiodes, implanted in blind patients' eyes, may restore their sight. The "nanoflowers" mimic the geometry of neurons, making them a better medium than traditional computer chips for carrying photodiodes and transmitting the collected light signals to the brain.
4. Robotic earthworms will gobble up our garbage. Much of what we throw away still has value. Metals, petroleum, and other components could get additional use if we extracted them, and robotic earthworms could do that for us. The tiny, agile robot teams will go through mines and landfills to extract anything of value, and then digest the remaining heaps into quality top soil.
5. The dust bowls of the twenty-first century will dwarf those seen in the twentieth. Two giant dust bowls are now forming, in Asia and in Africa, due to massive amounts of soil erosion and desertification resulting from overgrazing, over-plowing, and deforestation, warns environmental futurist Lester R. Brown.
6. Lunar-based solar power production may be the best way to meet future energy demands. Solar power can be more dependably and inexpensively gathered on the Moon than on Earth. This clean energy source is capable of delivering the 20 trillion watts of power a year that the Earth's predicted 10 billion people will require by mid-century.
7. Machine vision will become available in the next 5 to 15 years, with visual range ultimately exceeding that of the human eye. This technology will greatly enhance robotic systems' capabilities.
8. Advances in fuel cells will enable deep-sea habitation. Fuel cells such as those currently being developed for automobiles will produce electricity directly, with no toxic fumes. This advance will eventually make it easier to explore and even colonize the undersea world via extended submarine journeys.
9. Future buildings may be more responsive to weather fluctuations. "Protocell cladding" that utilizes bioluminescent bacteria or other materials would be applied on building facades to collect water and sunlight, helping to cool the interiors and produce biofuels. The protocells are made from oil droplets in water, which allow soluble chemicals to be exchanged between the drops and their surroundings.
10. The end of identity as we know it? It may become very easy to create a new identity (or many identities) for ourselves. All we will have to do is create new avatars in virtual reality. Those avatars will act on our behalf in real life to conduct such high-level tasks as performing intensive research, posting blog entries and Facebook updates, and managing businesses. The lines between ourselves and our virtual other selves will blur, to the point where most of us will, in essence, have multiple personalities.

Source: "THE FUTURIST Magazine Releases its Top Ten Forecasts for 2012 and Beyond." Originally published on *www.wfs.org*. Used with permission from the World Future Society.

research, ideas and stats from this chapter as well as your own answers to the Action Steps to begin to identify needs and opportunities.

■ CHANGING HOUSEHOLD STRUCTURES AND DEMOGRAPHICS

How does your world differ from the world your parents experienced? How does your younger siblings' world differ from yours? How will your children's world differ from yours? You may recognize how your world differs from your parents and siblings. However, the real business opportunities will result when you focus on how your children's world will differ from yours. Figure 2.2 highlights some of the generational differences between the age groups. As you review these differences, stop for a moment and think how the behavior of each generation varies, in regards to communication styles, education, and to how they view technology, life, love, work, and family.

figure **2.2**

Comparing Generations

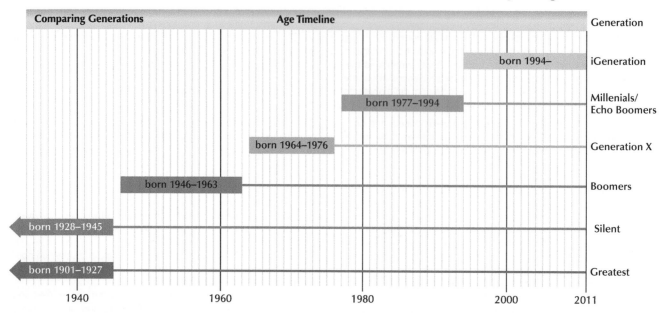

Comparing Generations	Age Timeline	Generation

born 1994–   iGeneration

born 1977–1994   Millenials/Echo Boomers

born 1964–1976   Generation X

born 1946–1963   Boomers

born 1928–1945   Silent

born 1901–1927   Greatest

1940   1960   1980   2000   2011

Consider how these changes affect buying behavior, lifestyles, and services and products desired and required.

1. 51% of adults 18 or older were married in 2012. In 1960, 72% of adults were married.

2. In 1960, the average of first marriages was 22.8 for men and 20.3 for women. In 2010, the average ages were 28.7 and 26.5.

3. In 2011, the U.S. birthrate recorded its lowest birthrate ever. In 1950, family size of four or more children was common, today common is one child or no child.

4. 42% of all U.S. children in 2010 were born outside of marriage.

5. In 1985, almost equal number of men and women graduated from college. However, in 2009, 685,000 men graduated from college and 918,000 women graduated.

6. In 1940, 5% of people 25 and over graduated from college. By 2010, that percentage has risen to 24%. Today 80% of those over 25 have graduated from high school and in 1940 that percentage was 24.5%.

Demographic shifts above and below as well as many others taking place will have a profound effect on your future customers and future employees. Consider these shifts and others as you move forward with your dream.

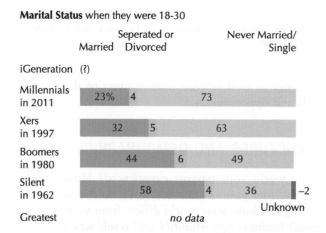

Marital Status when they were 18-30

	Married	Seperated or Divorced	Never Married/Single
iGeneration	(?)		
Millennials in 2011	23%	4	73
Xers in 1997	32	5	63
Boomers in 1980	44	6	49
Silent in 1962	58	4	36	–2 Unknown
Greatest	*no data*		

Source: © Cengage Learning 2014. Based on data from U.S. Census and *www.pewsocialtrends.org*.

The traditional American family, married with children, has slipped to a new low of one in five households. Also, the number of households headed by women has doubled in 30 years. And single member households are higher than ever.

The opportunities to serve the diverse family and household structures are vast: day care, after-school care, eldercare, recreation programs, food preparation, errand services, and college-planning programs. If you compile a list of all the services Phil and Claire Dunfey (of the Emmy-winning comedy, *Modern Family*) provide to keep their household running, you will discover many service-oriented businesses today providing those services—and more—to families and individuals who can afford outside assistance to keep their households running.

Who else is in need of the Dunfey's services? The elderly? Single parents? The disabled? The chronically ill? Grandparents raising grandchildren? Couples who both work? All of these groups are ability and/or time starved. In fact, many say real wealth today is *time*. Service businesses generated 46 percent of 2011 GDP, government services generated about 20 percent, and manufacturing 12 percent. People are thus buying time if they able. However, one needs to recognize that many of these groups may be time starved but they are also financially starved. For example, 49 percent of people in the United States do not have more than six months savings and about one out of six people receive food stamps. Thus, opening many opportunities for social entrepreneurs to provide services and help solve these issues. For example, for cash strapped individuals multi-generational households and shared housing may be options that social entrepreneurs could capitalize on.

Do you see a need for a service? Do any of your friends or colleagues have the same need? Are people willing to pay for this service? If so, what will they pay? Can you provide this service and get the word out? If you answered yes, go for it!

In many instances, service-oriented businesses can begin out of the home with low capital investment, few or no employees, and a great idea that fills a need. According to Andrew Carnegie, *"Making money shouldn't be your first goal. Fill a need, and if you're good enough at it, the money will come."*

Today people are marrying later, having fewer children. having them later in life, and remarrying and reformulating new families with greater frequency. Twenty-one percent of homes today are purchased by single women, something almost unheard of just 30 years ago. Figure 2.3 breaks down household family

---

figure **2.3**

Household Makeup 2010 U.S. by Type and Gender and Percent Change 2000–2010

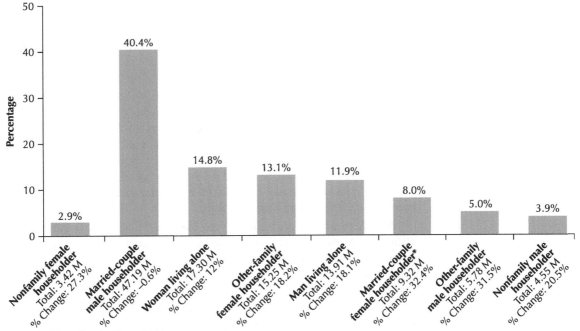

*Householder = head of household

Source: Data from Advertising Age, October 17, 2011, page 36 structures based on the 2010 Census and compares them to the 2000 Census. Family structures are changing along with the jobs we hold today and our lifestyles.

New York Times writer Christopher Caldwell stresses that we are not moving to a service economy, we are already there: "According to the Bureau of Labor Statistics, the U.S. now has more choreographers (16,340) than metalcasters (14,880), and more people make their livings shuffling and dealing cards in casinos (82,960) than running lathes (65,840). There are three times as many security guards (1,004,130) as machinists (385,690). Whereas 30 percent of Americans worked in manufacturing in 1950, fewer than 9 percent do now."

Education and training will play a leading role in preparing and retraining the workforce. Thus, opening many opportunities for tutoring services, instructors, educational software developers, career planners, and test-preparation services. Also, we will continue to see online education programs skyrocketing as overcommitted individuals find it difficult to attend and afford traditional learning programs. Free online education will challenge and compete with major universities for students. Udacity, edX, and Coursera are three firms leading the charge with top schools such as Princeton, Stanford, University of Michigan, Harvard, Penn, and MIT signed up. Over 100,000 students from throughout the world signed up for Stanford's first three free online computer related courses! Checkout these free online entrepreneurial courses.

Generation Y Individuals born between 1977 and 1994

It is estimated that Generation Y individuals will have more than 10 different careers in their work lives. Training and retraining will be part of their lives, and hopefully can be provided by creative entrepreneurs and learning mediums.

Ken Dychtwald, a leading researcher on the baby boomers, predicts that each generation will follow a "Cyclic Life Plan where people in the future will learn, work, relax, learn some more, work in a different role, play differently, go back to school, work in a new calling."

Immigration will play a leading role in the future growth of the United States. According to the Pew Research Center, "If current trends continue, the population of the United States will rise to 438 million in 2050, up from 296 million in 2005, and 82 percent of the increase will be due to immigrants arriving from 2005 to 2050 and their U.S.-born descendants." Opportunities abound to meet the social and business needs of the changing consumers and the workforce. See Table 2.1 to view the population changes by racial and ethnic groups. What opportunities do you see in these changes?

The Pew Research Center's U.S. Population Projections: 2005–2050 notes a startling fact on the nation's future "dependency ratio," the number of children and elderly compared with the number of working-age Americans. There were 59 children and elderly people per 100 adults of working age in 2005. That will rise to 72 dependents per 100 adults of working age in 2050. With this study in hand, one can recognize the potential labor shortage and the wealth of opportunity, along with the need to increase productivity through the use of technology. Who will take care of the frail elderly and the small children when there are so few potential employees?

Are there any opportunities here for you? Each change and trend in our society represents threats and opportunities to current and future businesses. If current businesses do not expand and change, new businesses will move in. Your firm's success depends on *you* recognizing changes and capitalizing on them.

What opportunities can you envision from the above information? What gaps are in the marketplace that you can fill? How can you help these table 2.1

America Is Changing

Pew Research Center Publications
Immigration to Play Lead Role In Future U.S. Growth

By Jeffrey Passel and D'VeraCohn, Pew Research Center

February 11, 2008

Executive Summary

If current trends continue, the population of the United States will rise to 438 million in 2050, from 296 million in 2005, and 82% of the increase will be due to immigrants arriving from 2005 to 2050 and their U.S.-born descendants, according to new projections developed by the Pew Research Center.

Of the 117 million people added to the population during this period due to the effect of new immigration, 67 million will be the immigrants themselves and 50 million will be their U.S.-born children or grandchildren.

U.S. Population 1960–2050
Share of total, by racial and ethnic groups

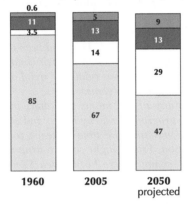

☐ White   ☐ Hispanic   ■ Black   ■ Asian

Among the other key population projections:

- Nearly one in five Americans (19%) will be an immigrant in 2050, compared with one in eight (12%) in 2005. By 2025, the immigrant, or foreign-born, share of the population will surpass the peak during the last great wave of immigration a century ago.
- The major role of immigration in national growth builds on the pattern of recent decades, during which immigrants and their U.S.-born children and grandchildren accounted for most population increase. Immigration's importance increased as the average number of births to U.S.-born women dropped sharply before leveling off.
- The Latino population, already the nation's largest minority group, will triple in size and will account for most of the nation's population growth from 2005 through 2050. Hispanics will make up 29% of the U.S. population in 2050, compared with 14% in 2005.
- Births in the United States will play a growing role in Hispanic and Asian population growth; as a result, a smaller proportion of both groups will be foreign-born in 2050.
- The non-Hispanic white population will increase more slowly than other racial and ethnic groups; whites will become a minority (47%) by 2050.
- The nation's elderly population will more than double in size from 2005 through 2050, as the baby boom generation enters the traditional retirement years. The number of working-age Americans and children will grow more slowly than the elderly population, and will shrink as a share of the total population.

The Center's projections are based on detailed assumptions about births, deaths and immigration levels—the three key components of population change. All these assumptions are built on recent trends. But it is important to note that these trends can change. All population projections have inherent uncertainties, especially for years further in the future, because they can be affected by changes in behavior, by new immigration policies, or by other events. Nonetheless, projections offer a starting point for nderstanding and analyzing the parameters of future demographic change.

The Center's report includes an analysis of the nation's future "dependency ratio"—the number of children and elderly compared with the number of working-age Americans. There were 59 children and elderly people per 100 adults of working age in 2005. That will rise to 72 dependents per 100 adults of working age in 2050.

Source: "Immigration to Play Lead Role In Future U.S. Growth," by Jeffrey Passel and D'Vera Cohn, Pew Research Center, February 11, 2008
http://pewresearch.org/pubs/729/united-states-population-projections, (Accessed April 25, 2008).

ACTION STEP 10

Changes = Trends = Opportunities

Pick up the last six issues of *The Economist, Time, and The Wall Street Journal*—your local library should have copies. While reading keep in mind your research from Action Step 9. Yes, you can do this online but you will concentrate better if you can really look at *all* the articles and start to see some patterns. If you own the magazines, rip the articles and stack them. What is happening in the world? Fill in the chart with the areas that are changing within each environmental variable.

If you are fortunate and have done your research, you will spot changes before trends start to develop. Being at the forefront of trends has made business-savvy people rich. Remember when the biotechnology industry began? How about smartphones? How about Facebook? If you had spotted opportunities within these technologies, hopped on board, and rode the opportunities to success, where would you be today?

Under each of these factors will be many changes and trends, which will bring threats to some industries and opportunities to others. All you need to do is find one opportunity!

Social/cultural
    Changes:
        Trends
            Opportunities:
Competition
    Changes:
        Trends:
            Opportunities:
Technology
    Changes:
        Trends:
            Opportunities:
Legal/political
    Changes:
        Trend:
            Opportunities:
Economics
    Changes:
        Trends:
            Opportunities:

families? What services and products can you provide for them? The changing family is only one social change; there are many others, such as people living longer and healthier lives, rising incomes and falling incomes, younger children with large spendable incomes and greater influence on family buying habits, and so on. What other changes do you see? What opportunities open up?

Follow how one entrepreneur parlayed his love of chess into a business focusing on after-school programs for the children of time-deprived working parents.

Checkmate!

Chess had changed Sammy Doyle's life, and he wanted to change others' lives too. At most grade schools, chess is not considered a trendy game. But Sammy knew he could make chess cool. After graduating from college, he worked with local elementary schools, volunteering his time to teach chess with four free, half-hour lessons. After providing incredibly fun lessons—bishops being conked on the head, three-foot-tall chess pieces, double chessboards, and lots of laughter—Sammy was ready to launch after-school chess classes at $10 per class per child. In some schools more than 30 percent of the kids took his classes, and currently, several thousand children are involved in his programs.

Yes, Sammy wrenched kids away from PlayStation 3, the Internet, and texting! Parents were thrilled. They had been looking for an activity without a joystick or keyboard that would challenge their children's minds. Few envisioned chess would be the answer. Sammy was riding the trend of parents seeking alternatives to television, computers, and video games.

Many of the moms and dads in the upscale community where Sammy lived were programmers, engineers, and scientists who had played chess as children but could not find the time to teach their own kids. Sammy came to the rescue. In addition, Friday-night chess tournaments, traveling chess teams, chess camps, and chess champs were born when Sammy Doyle listened to his customers—parents and kids.

Sammy started his business for less than $1,000. Can you do the same? Action Step 8 asks you to explore business opportunities open to you if you have only $1,000, a working car or pickup truck, and a phone. In good times and bad times, there are *always* opportunities to make money.

■ BOOMER EXPLOSION

Europe on $5 a day, Beach Boys, Beatles, Twiggy, bell-bottom pants, Viet Nam War, Berlin Wall, Sputnik, man on the moon, peace, and driving VW bugs and Ford Mustangs are all identified with the baby boomers. Today those over 65 make up 13 percent of our population. However, over the next 19 years *10,000 baby boomers a day will turn 65!* Thus, by 2031, 20 percent of the U.S. population will be over 65.

Baby boomers, a major economic and social force in our society for decades (see Figure 2.4), are aging, much to their dismay. As they approach their late 50s and 60s, they are redefining aging and retirement. What products and services will they need and want? Where will they buy them? How can you reach them?

Between the end of World War II and 1965, 78 million baby boomers were born, and they now control over 70 percent of the financial assets in America. In addition, they account for over 50 percent of discretionary income. They are a major gorilla in the marketplace impacting almost every industry. They purchase over 41 percent of all cars and over 48 percent of all luxury cars. Looking at traveling, health care, investing, saving, planning for retirement, investing in second homes, and reinventing retirement, their impact and dollars provide incredible business opportunities. Figure 2.4 highlights the past changes of the baby boomers. Your goal is to identify and capitalize on future changes and thus

——————————————————————————————— figure **2.4**

Boomer Impact

Where Boomers Have Been

- Boomers didn't just eat food—they transformed the snack, restaurant, and supermarket.
- Boomers didn't just wear clothes—they transformed the fashion industry.
- Boomers didn't just buy cars—they transformed the auto industry.
- They didn't just date—they transformed sex roles and practices.
- They didn't just go to work—they transformed the workplace.
- They didn't just get married—they transformed relationships and the institution of marriage.
- They didn't just borrow money—they transformed the debt market.
- They didn't just go to the doctor—they transformed health care.
- They didn't just use computers—they transformed technology.
- They didn't just invest in stocks—they transformed the investment marketplace.

Where Boomers Are Headed

The rising "age wave" will continue to produce many demographically motivated revolutions in the consumer marketplace. As the boomers pass through their middle years and on to maturity, five key factors will reshape supply and demand:

1. Concern about the onset of chronic disease and boomers' desire to do whatever is possible to postpone physical aging.
2. Increasing amounts of discretionary dollars—for some but not all—as a result of escalating earning power, inheritances, and return on investments.
3. Entry into new adult life stages including empty nesting, care giving, grandparenthood, retirement, widowhood, and retirement—each with its own challenges and opportunities.
4. A psychological shift from acquiring more material possessions toward a desire to purchase enjoyable and satisfying experiences.
5. The continued absence of "disposable time" due to complex lifestyles.

Source: Ken Dychtwald, "The Age Wave Is Coming," *http://www.agewave.com/agewave.shtml* (Accessed February 8, 2005). Courtesy of Age-Wave.com, 2004.

opportunities. The *Business Journal of Phoenix* cited a Robert Half International survey of 150 senior executives working within the nation's largest companies and found the executives considered, "the retirement of baby boomer employees to have the greatest impact on the workplace in the next generation". Although, many boomers will need to work full or part-time in retirement due to their losses in real estate and the stock market.

By 2030 half of all U.S. adults will be 50 or older. According to many sources, the boomers will *not* "go gently into that good night." They will fight the aging process with every dollar they have available. Ken Dychtwald, founder of AgeWave, a consulting firm guiding Fortune 500 companies and government groups reaching out to boomers, explains where the baby boomers have been and where they are headed in Figure 2.4. Dychtwald also notes that "two thirds of people in the history of the world who have lived past age 65 are still alive today!" And as these boomers look toward their final years, they make clear that they fear going into a nursing home three times more than they fear dying. Thus, you see massive growth in home healthcare monitoring and assistance. Also, the opportunities for service and housing industries are limitless.

Large companies are reaching out to these "older adults," (who don't like the term "senior citizens"), with larger printing on packaging, ergonomically adjusted packaging, adjusted lighting and shelving in stores, and redesigned appliances. Style has always been important to boomers and it will continue to be as they age as well. Think Chico's clothing for women.

One cannot look at past generations to predict the buying habits of this group. Boomers are wealthier, more educated, with fewer children, and are in "new family" structures and more often living alone. Firms are going right to the source, asking boomers what they want.

Boomer research conducted by Pulte Homes/Del Webb, a premier developer of retirement communities, showed not only a need for retirement communities in sunny climates, but also the need for communities in the East and Midwest to serve boomers who choose to retire closer to home. Many of these new homes are being built with "universal design" features, such as varying counter heights, walk-in showers, and wheelchair accessible doorways, allowing individuals to stay in their own homes longer. Capitalizing on this market, Anne Vater of Vater Construction of Crown Point, Indiana, became a Certified Aging In Place Specialist (CAPS)™ and Certified Green Professional through the National Association of Home Builders (NAHB). Anne and Eric Vater built a green universal designed home to show prospective clients that such homes could be functional as well as beautiful. Vater Construction also retrofits homes using universal design features for those who choose to age in place.

In addition to large retirement communities, creative living environments are being built to meet the boomers needs with co-housing projects and shared living arrangements with dual master suites. Some boomers have decided to forego a home anywhere and are spending their "golden years" cruising 365 days a year! Some cruise for as little as $100 a day per person, which is less than living in an assisted living center.

Now scrutinize boomers—from the top of their heads to the bottom of their feet—to determine if you can develop products or services to make money. Brainstorm away! If you are 20-something, look at your parents and grandparents; if you are 40-something, look in the mirror. Be as creative and wild as you can be. The following should help get you started:

- Hair: Toupees, hair implants, wigs, great hats, special sunscreen for bald spots, graying gracefully
- Eyes: Eye drops, cool magnifiers, trifocals, refractive surgery, eyelid lifts, eyelash growth enhancers, reading sunglasses, drugs for macular degeneration, vitamins for eye health
- Face: Plastic surgery, skin creams, Botox, laser resurfacing, skin cancer checkups, facial exercise classes, facial massages, makeup formulated for aging skin, creams for brown spots

Every doctor, dentist, lawyer, accountant, travel agent, and financial planner waits in the wings for boomers to break down the door. Estate planners, trust attorneys, and eldercare attorneys are presenting workshops everywhere to capture this exploding marketplace's dollars.

The "sandwich generation," those who both care for teenagers and elderly parents, are in special need of help as they are overwhelmed with responsibilities and time pressures. Those boomers, who are watching their parents' health decline and subsequent deaths, will definitely be involved in changing healthcare delivery at the end of life.

In addition to being responsible for children and parents, many boomers are also raising grandchildren, opening up an entire new market for assistance. Unfortunately, many of these grandparents are financially strapped and thus they may need many services but not have the funds to pay.

Another segment developing for the first time due to our extended life span consists of elderly people caring for the frail elderly. Support systems are weakened as many elderly have outlived their family members, or no longer have the support of children, grandchildren, or siblings near by.

Those over 85 are the fastest growing segment of the population. Today there are over 500,000 centenarians alive in the world and the number is growing at 7 percent a year! The need for assistance is vast; just make sure you don't use the word "old" when selling your services to the aging baby boomers!

AARP The Magazine (formerly *Modern Maturity*), the largest distributed subscription magazine targeted at those over age 50—and distributed free to American Association of Retired Persons (AARP) members as part of their membership dues—may have one of the hottest websites of the future. Legally, politically, and economically, those over age 50 have always been a strong force. With the power of the Internet, social, political, and economic change are not only possible but also inevitable.

Boomers are using their power to enter entrepreneurship at the highest rate of any age group. Downsizing in corporations and declining traditional pension plans have left many boomers with the financial need to work. However, for others the desire to continue to be productive comes from healthy aging in which many boomers are looking at 30 to 40 years ahead of them. The rising age requirement to collect full social security benefits also plays into the growth of boomer entrepreneurship.

Middle class Americans lost 40 percent of their net worth over the last 5 years and fewer receive traditional pensions forcing many to continue to work beyond their desired retirement date. Thus, Art Koff, realizing this need, launched RetiredBrains.com.

As the boomers age, will they all be alike? Not according to Yankelovich's MindBase, a marketing tool created to answer the questions "Who will buy?" and "Why?" There are two major groups of older people: One group is the Renaissance Masters, "financially secure individuals who are vitally connected to community and to life ... upbeat about their future, and (who) remain interested in personal development."

The other group is the Maintainers, "mature individuals who use the past as their point of reference. The Maintainers group is sedentary and resource constrained." In addition, Yankelovich further segments each of these groups based on attitudes, personalities, values, and motivations. The opportunities to capitalize on the needs of older people are vast, but do not make the assumption that they are all the same. Also, recognize that 35 percent of those over 65 today rely solely on Social Security for their income. Although their needs are not the same as the top 10 percent of retirees, there are still many opportunities in this market as well.

Not only is the U.S. population aging rapidly, but throughout the rest of the developed world as well. Here are a few projects being developed abroad to combat some of the issues of loneliness and reduced income:

- Mensheds in Australia by a charity working with seniors at risk of loneliness or isolation by building communal sheds.
- Fureal Kippu in Japan is developing a system of local alternative currencies aimed at getting people to care for elderly people. For example, one currency unit earned looking after an elderly neighbor could be spent on a volunteer visiting one's own elderly relatives.
- The Good Gym in the UKwhich pairs runners or joggers with isolated elderly individuals-people do a run but pop in for a five-minute chat with somebody along the route.
- Aconchego in Portugal, a project that links elderly people at risk (and with a spare room) with younger people, such as students who need a room.

Source: *Financial Times* (UK) magazine 23-24 July 2011, Special Report on the Future, (Accessed June 17, 2012).

Where will you find additional opportunities to serve the boomers? Open your eyes, research, look at statistics and projections, ask questions, and listen. Visit social media sources and read what people are complaining about. Search out solutions to their problems. The answers are there.

■ MILLENIALS RISING

"This is the first generation to grow up digital—coming of age in a world where computers, the Internet, video games, and smartphones are common, and where expressing themselves through these tools is the norm. Given how present these technologies are in their lives, do young people act, think, and learn differently today? And what are the implications for education and for society?" commented President Jonathan Fanton of the MacArthur Foundation, one of the nation's largest private philanthropic foundations. And we ask you: What are the implications for entrepreneurs?

The device the millennials, the techno-savvy generation, "cannot live without" is the cell phone or preferably the smartphone. Your challenge will be to meet the millennials where they shop, search, travel, play, and learn.

Millennials Persons born between 1977 and 1994

Millennials are experiencing one of the longest and deepest recessions since the Great Depression and it is changing their working and buying patterns. In 2012, 37 percent of 18- to 29-year olds were underemployed or out of the workforce. Thus many millenials who were brought up having a lot of "things," no longer can afford them; but the desire still burns. And their needs are being met by the new "sharing economy".

According to Rachel Botsman, co-author of *What's Mine is Yours: The Rise of Collaborative Consumption* the sharing economy has grown out of consumers' comfort with technology. Bartering, renting, peer to peer lending and sharing are all made possible on a large scale today.

Again, neighborhood sharing has always been a part of the world, but never before have we had the technology to provide the platforms for unknown parties to collaborate with ease and security. With Pinterest, Facebook and LinkedIn profiles, we can basically know our "neighbor" providing us the trust factor we need. Millenials are comfortable sharing their private information so it isn't that big a leap for them to share their "things." *Fast Company* recently listed a number of firms helping others build a "sharable life". A few of the examples follow:

Zimride.com A program for organizations to use to facilitate ride-sharing for their students and/or employees.

Thredup.com A unique marketplace for parents to swap their children's toys and clothes.

AirBnB.com A marketplace to list rooms, homes, couches, and boats to rent from private parties.

Gobble.com "Instead of the restaurant around the corner, Gobble taps local chefs" to prepare and deliver meals in the Silicon Valley.

Relayrides.com "Rent cars from people in your community. Nationwide car sharing. Insurance included."

What else will millenials be willing to share? If you can answer this question, congratulations as you may be on your way to a billion dollar business!

Not all millenials fit into the following stereotype, but many do: they seldom read newspapers, watch TV at a scheduled time, listen to radio news, and typically do not own a land-line phone; they watch movies and TV shows primarily on laptops, tablets, or phones, and spend hours a day with social media; they are less religious and more educated than any generation, and more cautious of others due to 9-11; only 6 in 10 were raised by both parents, but they get along with parents on a more equal footing than past generations; they multitask, live in more urban environments, marry later, have fewer or no children, sleep with cell phones and check Facebook and texts before rising.

When viewing the figures and the information above, what new products and services can you think of to provide millenials as they enter college, the workforce, rent homes, start families, and purchase homes? One creative business, Grubwithus, invites users to visit their webpage, check out local restaurants offering fixed price dinners, pay in advance online, and join other strangers for dinner. Tired of being online? Grab dinner with others!

A Nickelodeon study concluded that millennials have "more choices, more freedom, and more empowerment possibly than any other generation." However, with all these opportunities and information also comes confusion and indecision. Problem=opportunity=solution—Check out how one firm found a solution to this problem by developing the website *www. justbuythisone.*

In addition, Miami University entrepreneurship professor Jay A. Kayne notes millennials "have an aversion to being ordinary." Marketing to millennials requires you prove that your product or service is relevant to their lives more so than for h past generation. And you will need to be constantly aware of changing technologies and communication patterns of the millennials. Not only will millennials play a significant role in the workforce, but we believe their impact through entrepreneurship activities will be even stronger.

■ iGENERATION ALWAYS CONNECTED

According to Ms. Finlayson, Fuse Marketing's Director of Agency Insights, the iGeneration, those children born after 1994, "Are not just comfortable with technology, *they're uncomfortable without it.* Influence with and over each other is extremely important, and while that's not terribly different than it was before, it's much more widespread because of social media. So many of them now find out about bands, brands of jeans, or snack foods from each other on social media."

The iGeneration, also known as GenZ and Generation C (for connected), have tremendous influence over their parents' buying behavior as well as their friends. The tween market currently is around $30 billion but they are said to have influence over $150 billion when family purchasing is considered.

They conduct their lives through texting and use of apps for everything. According to Nielsen, the iGeneration spends almost twice as much time connected as other generations, on average spending almost eight hours a day living in their techno cocoon. Always on, always available, with very little down time.

ACTION STEP 11

Spotting Trends in Your Selected Target Markets

1. Select a target market of your choice—millennials, healthy and active seniors, frail and elderly, soccer kids, iGeneration, or any other. Search the net for statistics and information. Start with census data at *http://www.census.gov.*

2. Using your statistics, intuition, and knowledge of the target market, work back through the chapter's baby boomer starting points and go through a day in the life of your selected target market. Next, interact with the social media they use. What trends do they identify with? What products and services do they desire? How can you best meet their needs? Start asking questions of your Target Customer and truly listen. Constantly ask "why" to reach true motivations and behaviors.

3. Next, review the list of products, ideas, and services baby boomers identified with. Compile a similar list for your Target Customer. As you continue through this book, you will learn how to further refine your target market and spot problems and opportunities.

PASSION

Build Your Future, Inc.

Redefining a Life and Living with Passion

For years Patti Moir dreamed of her *own* business with her *own* schedule, her *own* office, and her *own* clients. When she turned 55, Patti knew it was time for her to spread her wings and fly into a new life, where she would not only help high school students build their futures but also build her own new future. It would be a future that would include time for herself, her grandchildren, exercise, golf, and most of all time to enjoy the few sun-filled days in Lake Oswego, Oregon.

Patti was passionate about finding balance for her life. After passionately teaching, tutoring, and counseling for more than 30 years and with a secure pension in hand, Patti's vast experience and counseling reputation at one of the leading high schools in the country spurred her to open an educational college counseling service business.

Patti's passion for helping millenials and the iGeneration find their way through the college-planning process is a welcome relief to parents and teens. With the National Association for College Admission Counseling reporting a 315 to 1 student to counselor ratio, the trend toward stiffer admissions requirements, and a much more competitive atmosphere, many parents and teens require a specialist like Patti to maneuver through the admission maze. Patti has definitely found her passion for sunlight and students, and as a side benefit, has increased her income substantially.

Students and parents thank her for the personal attention she provides and for truly listening to their needs during their meetings. Also, they often express their appreciation that her office is a computer and Internet free zone.

© Cengage Learning

Social networking increases the "It's all about me" attitude. Privacy is a non-issue as they have been exposed on the net since utero, as many of their digital footprints started with their first ultrasound posted by their parents on Facebook.

They understand they are being marketed to at all times through all their portals. Mobile marketing is not new, they don't know a life without it. Thus, entrepreneurs have to be creative; constantly designing unique products and services and new ways to break through to them.

■ THE SPLINTERING OF THE MASS MARKET

Today's consumers are informed, individualistic, and demanding. Their buying habits are often difficult to isolate, because they tend to buy at several levels of the market. For example, high-fashion, high-income consumers may patronize upscale boutiques but buy their household appliances at Wal-Mart. They may shop at Williams-Sonoma for specialty Sprinkles cake mixes but buy their flour in bulk at Costco.

For the consumer, three key factors have splintered the mass market:

1. A shrinking middle class: The middle class lost 40 percent of their financial net worth during the past five years. Incomes have stagnated and most of the growth shown over the past years has been attributed to two income households, and as we have said before those households are shrinking. In 2012, about 22 percent of all children in the United States lived below the federal income guidelines for poverty, which is approximately $22,300 for a family of four. Incomes for most have stagnated at 1997 levels (see Figure 2.5). According to the Federal Reserve, the average American has total household debt equal to 109 percent of his or her annual after-tax income. Forty-nine percent of Americans would not have enough cash to cover three months of their living expenses and 28 percent do not have *any* money saved. However the top .1 percent of Americans' wealth has grown tremendously. As the middle class shrinks we are seeing two distinct marketing strategies developing to reach customers at both ends of the population, think Tiffany's and Dollar General.

2. Ethnic groups shifting and growing throughout the United States: According to census data, 50 percent of the country's over 36 million Hispanics reside

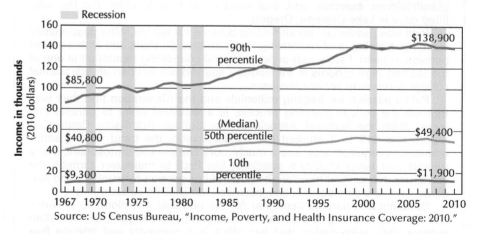

figure **2.5**

Real U.S. Household Income at Selected Percentiles

Source: US Census Bureau, "Income, Poverty, and Health Insurance Coverage: 2010."

Source: U.S. Census Bureau, Current Population Survey, 1968 to 2011 Annual Social and Economic Supplements. From *http://www.census.gov/newsroom/releases/pdf/2010_Report.pdf* (Accessed December 4, 2012).

in California and Texas.Hawaii, New York, and California are the home of half of the over 12 million Asians in the United States. Over 70 percent of Blacks live in the South and the Northeast. The greater Los Angeles area, already the most ethnically diverse population in the world, has television stations available in Korean, Spanish, Chinese, Farsi, and Vietnamese. In one Orange County, California school district, the students speak more than 50 languages. Previously ethnic groups have been geographically concentrated. However, ethnic diversity is expanding throughout the United States (see Table 2.1).

3. Living arrangements are changing and evolving: Only 51 percent of adults are married today and 28 percent of all households have just one person. The percentage of people living by themselves has doubled since 1960. In some of the larger cities like Atlanta and Denver, 40 percent of the population lives alone; that figure climbs to 48 percent in Washington, D.C.

   Forty-one percent of all children born today are born to unwed mothers, and for those having children under 30 that rate increases to 53 percent. Only one-third of these families include the support of a live-in partner.

   Unmarried couples without children make up 6 percent of U.S. households and financial planners and lawyers are reaching out to them to serve their specific needs.

   Another huge change is the number of young people between the ages of 25 and 34 living with their parents: 19 percent of men and 10 percent of women. The cost of housing and the recession have seen more and more boomerangers seeking the security of their family homes.

   Multigenerational families are growing with 4.4 million households today comprising three or more generations. Some homebuilders are now building homes specifically for this target market as the multigenerational household spreads from lower to upper class families. The growth of this market is both made out of choice and out of necessity as younger people cannot find jobs and older people need assistance.

   Also, 4.9 million children (7 percent) today are being raised by grandparents and 1.9 million children (2.5 percent) are raised by other relatives. Again the economy and personal issues have brought many children into "other than parent headed households." (Figure 2.3)

If you look with new eyes, you can see additional major segments emerging, growing, and becoming more powerful: such as healthy and active 90-year-olds and the rising Hispanic middle class. Your goal should be to look at all these trends and discover the opportunities to meet the needs of the changing markets.

Today's technology allows us to define ever-smaller target markets or market niches. With the power of the Internet and the right software, we achieve one-to-one target marketing. If you order product B, and 50 percent of customers who order product B also order product Z, information or an advertisement for product Z will pop up on your screen automatically—basically, a salesperson or marketer in a box. Amazon's incredible software provides an excellent example of one-to-one marketing and sales promotion, presenting a challenge to bricks-and-mortar stores. However, while many voiced the demise of brick-and-mortar stores 15 years ago, we now see eBay, Social Living, and Google all planning to open retail stores. Apple's successful example is luring them. Reality is we still like to touch what we buy and we still do enjoy physical social contact!

Take time now to explore your chosen target market, and to spot the emerging trends and opportunities further, by completing Action Steps 10 and 11.

■ FRANCHISES RESPOND TO SOCIAL AND CULTURAL CHANGES

Take a look at the top 10 new franchises for 2012 according to *Entrepreneur* magazine, and see how they are meeting the needs of a changing society with health and beauty consciousness reigning.

Entrepreneur Magazine's Top Ten New Franchises for 2012

1. No Mas Vello (laser hair removal)
2. Complete Nutrition (weight loss and nutrition products)
3. Yogurtland Franchising Inc. (self-serve frozen yogurt)
4. ShelfGenie Franchise Systems LLC (custom shelving and accessories for cabinets/pantries)
5. The Senior's Choice Inc. (assisted living and health care staffing services)
6. CPR-Cell Phone Repair (personal electronics repairs and sales)
7. Get in Shape for Women (small group personal training for women)
8. Signal 88 Security (private security guard and patrol services)
9. Menchie's (frozen yogurt)
10. Smashburger Franchising LLC (hamburgers)

Source: *Entrepreneur* Magazine's 2012 Franchise 500, *http://www.entrepreneur.com/franchises/rankings/topnew-115520/2012,-1.html* (Accessed June 10, 2012).

The following list includes *Entrepreneur's* fastest-growing franchises for 2012 based on straight growth in the number of franchises verified in *Entrepreneur's 33rd Annual Franchise 500* listing. With two of the leading franchises being tax services, one recognizes the complexity of our tax system and with three commercial cleaning services one wonders, "Has everyone laid off their janitorial staffs?"

According to *Entrepreneur,* "The following list is not intended to endorse any particular franchise but simply to provide a starting point for research."

Entrepreneur Magazine's Top Ten Fastest-Growing Franchises for 2012

1. Stratus Building Solutions (commercial cleaning)
2. Subway (submarine sandwiches and salads)
3. CleanNet USA Inc. (commercial cleaning)
4. Vanguard Cleaning Systems (commercial cleaning)
5. H&R Block (tax preparation and electronic filing)
6. Dunkin' Donuts (coffee, doughnuts, baked goods)
7. Chester's (quick-service chicken restaurant)
8. Liberty Tax Service (individual and online tax prep)
9. 7-Eleven Inc. (convenience store)
10. Anytime Fitness (fitness center)

Source: *Entrepreneur* Magazine's 2012 Franchise 500, *http://www.entrepreneur.com/franchises/rankings/fastestgrowing-115162/2012,-1.html* (Accessed June 10, 2012).

■ INFORMATION EXPLOSION

If some days you feel like you are on information overload, you are! The average person today receives more information from their big-city Sunday newspaper than a person living during the Middle Ages received in an entire lifetime. The wants and needs of the American consumer are screaming, "Faster!"

Active millenials do not take their tents to the mountains and veg out for the week. They take their mountain bikes and mountain climbing equipment. They plan their vacations with TripAdvisor, find the best climbing sites, jump in the Prius with their playlists, find food on the way using Yelp, and use a GPS system to guide them to their destinations. No vegging out is allowed at any point. And REI, a major outdoor retailer, is there to meet their needs.

Instead of turning to maps to find our way, we turn on our iPhones. Instead of calling a friend for a restaurant recommendation, we text a friend, ask for a recommendation on Facebook or Twitter, or scan reviews as we walk down the street. Instead of calling a travel agent, we log on to Fodor's or Couchsurfing, and instead of calling a doctor, we log on to Web MD. With all this information at our fingertips, we are overloaded and sometimes overwhelmed with our options. If we have a question, we post on Quora. If we want to meet people, Meetup is the answer. If we want others to evaluate our ideas, EdisonNation is there. We *need* personal information managers. Could that be a potential service business?

Our private lives and work lives are converging. With technology, our workplaces can be in contact with us 24/7 wherever we are in the world. We spend more time working and seem accessible at all time providing added stress.

Each change and stress becomes an opportunity for the enterprising entrepreneur. How can you help your customer manage work-life stress? How can you help your customers manage information overload when purchasing from you? And how can you manage the appropriate amount of contact and use of mediums with your customer?

Have some fun now with a group of people and complete Action Step 12. Remember, the more problems you spot, the more opportunities arise. With each problem, you move one step closer to your Business Plan.

■ TECHNOLOGY REVOLUTION

Where does one start when talking about the revolution and where it will all lead? Wherever it leads, the opportunities are unbounded. As we look to the future, we will be less interested in technology per se but more interested in how it will improve our lives, health, and companies. Review Figure 2.6 to gain an idea of the types of firms in health care, information technology, and clean technology, which leading venture capitalists are funding. These firms tend to be on the leading edge of technology much like the researchers from the MIT Lab whose projects follow. Looking at the problems these companies are trying to solve, hopefully will spur your creativity. Envision how your skills and knowledge can be used to help solve these problems and others such as clean water, food shortages, and homes for the billions who will be joining us soon.

Twenty-two percent of our income is spent on health care today, whereas in 1950 less than 8 percent was devoted to it. As people live longer the cost of health care continues to rise. Caring for those with Alzheimer's is estimated at $200 billion for 2012. Thus, if you are able to help the 5.4 million Americans living with Alzheimers by providing care, products, technology, food, or services to those suffering and their family members you may have landed on your golden opportunity.

Monitoring blood pressure, blood sugars, medications, weight, etc. are all being done today through in home and wearable technology, thus reducing

ACTION STEP 12

Have Fun Identifying Problems and Opportunities

1. Gather a group of your friends or colleagues and ask them about their wants and needs. It is likely that you will discover gaps in the marketplace. Do not judge the answers you receive; you are only seeking information, and the more ideas you generate, the better. Adapt the following questions to fit your market:
   - What frustrates you most about your daily life? Banking? Dating? Buying a car? Grocery shopping? Clothing shopping? Buying textbooks? Registering for class? Eating out? Relaxing? Exercising?
   - What products or services do you need or want but cannot find?
   - What products or services would enhance your quality of life?
   - How could you increase your productivity without working more hours?
   - What would make you happy?
2. If you are dealing with a nonconsumer product or service, change the questions to fit your market. Make a list of the gaps that the group identifies, then project the list out as far as you can into the marketplace and respond to the wants, needs, and frustrations of your friends.
3. Are the needs local, national or global in scope?

figure 2.6

Venture Capital Creates and Funds New Industries

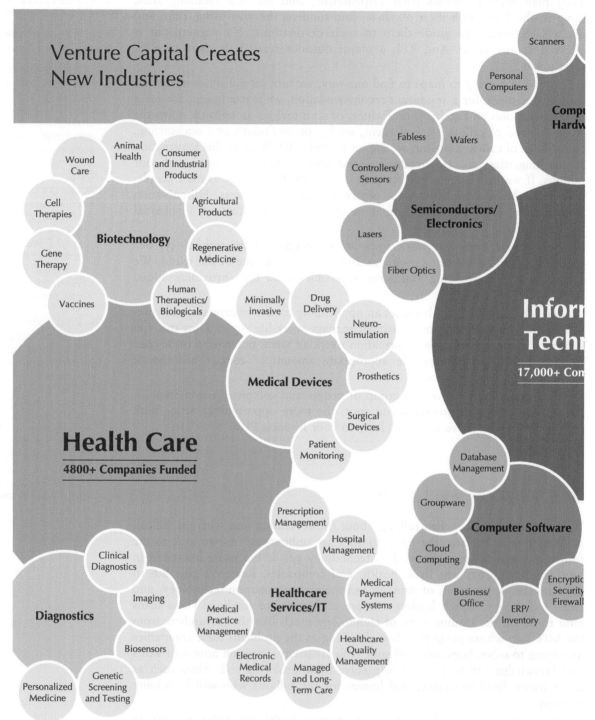

Venture Capital Creates New Industries

Biotechnology
- Animal Health
- Wound Care
- Consumer and Industrial Products
- Cell Therapies
- Agricultural Products
- Gene Therapy
- Regenerative Medicine
- Vaccines
- Human Therapeutics/ Biologics

Semiconductors/ Electronics
- Fabless
- Wafers
- Controllers/ Sensors
- Lasers
- Fiber Optics

Computer Hardware
- Scanners
- Personal Computers

Medical Devices
- Minimally invasive
- Drug Delivery
- Neuro-stimulation
- Prosthetics
- Surgical Devices
- Patient Monitoring

Information Technology
17,000+ Companies

Health Care
4800+ Companies Funded

Diagnostics
- Clinical Diagnostics
- Imaging
- Biosensors
- Personalized Medicine
- Genetic Screening and Testing

Healthcare Services/IT
- Prescription Management
- Hospital Management
- Medical Payment Systems
- Medical Practice Management
- Healthcare Quality Management
- Electronic Medical Records
- Managed and Long-Term Care

Computer Software
- Database Management
- Groupware
- Cloud Computing
- Business/ Office
- ERP/ Inventory
- Encryption Security Firewall

the number of visits to the doctor and allowing nursing personnel to keep in touch and offer help over the phone or computer. In the coming years, technology will not only be used to extend our lives but for managing our health, distribution of services, and the management of tests and medicines. In some instances, we have even seen low-cost medical options

figure **2.6**

Venture Capital Creates and Funds New Industries *(continued)*

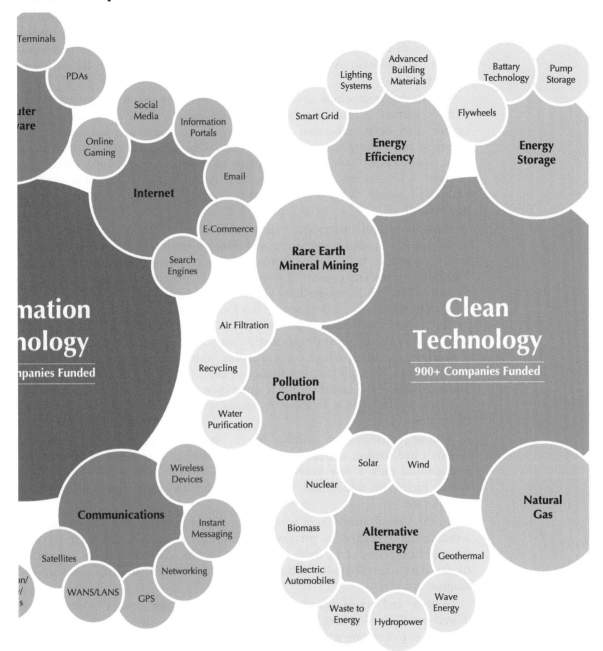

Throughout its history, venture capital investment has built entire industry sectors by funding ground breaking innovations. From biotechnology to information technology to clean technology, thousands of startups have been brought to life, improving the way we live and work each day.

Source: Venture Impact: The Economic Importance of Venture Backed Companies to the U.S. Economy, 2011, Pages 6–7. Retrieved from *http://www.nvca.org/index.php?option=com_content&view=article&id=255&Itemid=103*. Reprinted with permission.

developed for third-world countries brought back to the United States for implementation.

The Human Genome Project mapped the 30,000 genes that make up human DNA. But now the quest is on to discover the roles hundreds of thousands of proteins and 10,000 microbes play in making us human.

Possibilities for products and services are mind-boggling and will come at an incredible pace. Will we have our DNA mapped to plan our future careers or determine which sports or arts we are best suited for? What about personality traits? Instead of marriage counseling will we opt for DNA testing to see if we are compatible? Will our DNA information be used to deny health insurance or offer us cut rates on life insurance? How far will we go to customize our children? And will there be franchised centers on every corner to help us?

Embedded microchips are common in veterinary medicine, giving veterinarians instant access to a pet's medical history. Will it be long before people also have embedded microchips? These chips are becoming more common in clothing and medical devices. One restaurant recently encouraged customers to have embedded chips so that they could automatically be charged for food and drinks. Can you discover any other new uses for embedded chips? What about in appliances? Clothing? Furniture? Sports equipment?

Computers and smartphones have changed every facet of modern life. We rarely reach a human being when we contact a business. When frustrated, we send an e-mail or text. Computer-to-computer communication is now a way of life. Handwritten letters seem to be a thing of the past. As technology continues to impact our lives, consider how Google glasses will impact our lives? Just for a moment realize that it will not be too long before billions of people in third-world countries will carry a phone or tablet computer that provides instantaneous access to people and information anywhere in the world. Today people throughout the world who have no running water and no access to health care, have iPhones. With all that knowledge at the fingertips of billions, can you or anyone imagine the future? Take a quiet moment to really think and imagine this new world, as it is in those moments when we imagine that ideas come to fruition.

Online collaboration within design, startups, science, publishing and research are fueling entrepreneurial imaginations. This non-hierachial manner ignored only a few years ago is opening opportunities throughout the world fueled by millennials openness to sharing ideas and willingness to collaborate.

In the United States there is some backlash stirring against technology and social media in regards to privacy and security issues. Also, will there possibly be opportunities to serve those who yearn for the warm and fuzzy encounters of the past where humans actual physically interacted, smiled, touched, and laughed together?

Author and social scientist Sherry Turkle, in her newest book, *"Alone Together: Why We Expect More from Technology and Less From Each Other,"* explores our growing tendency to rely on technology above human interactions and asks where it is all headed. What impact will technology have on your business?

Keep up on technology news by watching technology-oriented programming, reading *Forbes ASAP* and *Scientific American,* and checking out MIT's, Stanford's and Caltech's websites. Also, watch TED or Big Think talks on technology.

MIT's Media Lab site brought up a phenomenal array of research projects below, which provide insight into how technology is addressing major problems. Read through this list, visit the site and explore projects you are interested in for more information and then sit back and ask yourself, 1) What does all this mean for the future? and 2) How can I capitalize on this information?

MIT Media Lab Research Groups and Projects

The Media Laboratory at MIT (*http://www.media.mit.edu/research/groups-projects*) provides an exceptionally rich environment for exploring basic research and applications at the intersection of computation, technology, social behavior, science, medicine, and the arts, among other areas. Among the twenty plus research projects currently ongoing at the Media Lab:

* How new technologies can help people better communicate, understand, and respond to information.
* How technology can be used to enhance human physical capability.
* How new strategies for architectural design, mobility systems, and networked intelligence can make possible dynamic, evolving places that respond to the complexities of life.
* How to create technical and social systems to allow communities to share, understand, and act on civic information.
* How digital and fabrication technologies can radically transform the design and construction of objects, buildings, and systems.
* How radical new collaborations will catalyze a revolution in health.
* How sensing, understanding, and new interface technologies can change everyday life, the ways in which we communicate with one another, storytelling, and entertainment.
* How to build socially engaging robots and interactive technologies that provide people with long-term social and emotional support to help people live healthier lives, connect with others, and learn better.
* How sensor networks augment and mediate human experience, interaction, and perception.
* How software can act as an assistant to the user rather than a tool, by learning from interaction and by proactively anticipating the user's needs.
* How speech technologies and portable devices can enhance communication.
* How to engineer intelligent neurotechnologies to repair pathology, augment cognition, and reveal insights into the human condition.
* How to design seamless interfaces between humans, digital information, and the physical environment.

Source: **MIT Media Lab**, *http://www.media.mit.edu/research/groups-projects* (Accessed June 10, 2012).

The future of integrating science into all areas of our lives as shown above through the innovative and creative ideas of MIT researchers proves that the future holds incredible improvements for our lives. Universities throughout the world are actively commercializing their pure research into useable products.

With artificial body parts and transplanted organs an everyday occurrence, will cancer, Parkinson's, Alzheimer's, and heart disease become distant memories because of advances in biotechnology? If these diseases were cured, what could you do with the empty doctor's offices? Medical buildings? Equipment? Surgeons provide online instructions in real time to operating rooms throughout the world. When a patient's chest is open and a surgeon must cut in a precise spot, an online surgeon is ready to assist—not only for his own patients in town, but also for doctors and patients in places like Bolivia. Microsurgery and laser surgery today are also reducing hospital stays and stand-alone surgicenters are growing to accommodate these surgeriesAmputees benefit from the use of incredible new materials and design capabilities spurred on by the need for prosthetics for Iraq and Afghanistan veterans. Technology continues to revolutionize the lives of the disabled, and the future holds even more promise.

Clean and green technologies firms are growing quickly as we deal with the energy and water crises, which are developing here and around the world. Below is a listing of key green technologies:

Energy: solar, wind, smart grid devices and networks, energy storage, and infrastructure

ACTION STEP 13

Investigate New Technologies

If you are a tech expert, share your insights with others to bring them up to speed. Technology affects every aspect of small business today—distribution, marketing, products, and so on. So if you are not tech savvy, it is time to get up to speed.

1. Read several copies of *Wired, Fast Company, The Futurist, Science,* or other tech industry magazines of your choice. Find 5 to 10 articles on technologies that amaze you. Watch a few TED talks on technology. What new technologies did you find? What new opportunities did you discover?
2. Share your findings with others. Remember a technological breakthrough in one industry will often lead to a breakthrough in another industry.
3. Log on to research university websites, such as the MIT site noted in this chapter. If you have selected an industry already to be part of, search out the schools that perform research in that industry and read through the sites. What did you discover? What ideas or research can you follow up on?

With information in hand, you will be better prepared to focus on the opportunities afforded by these changing technologies. As you go forth with your business idea, never stop reading. Always be aware and continually follow emerging technologies.

Market research Collection and analysis of data pertinent to current or potential viability of a product or service

Secondary research Reading and using previously published (primary) research

Materials & Manufacturing: bio-based materials, green building materials, and reuse and recycling

Specialized Suppliers and Supporting Industries: environmental testing and mitigation, contract manufacturing, engineering and design services

Transportation: hybrid and all-electric vehicles, advanced batteries, electric rail and transportation infrastructure

Water: energy-efficient desalination, water recovery & capture, and new filtration membranes

Looking at the above list and other industries from Figure 2.6, what opportunities do you foresee for your community? What products or services might you be able to develop or provide to these leading edge firms? What products and services will become obsolete? How will our jobs and lives change? We ask you not only to follow technology but to take chances and explore the incredible possibilities.

Some individuals make a business of trend watching. Among these are leading trend watchers are Joi Ito, Director of the MIT Media Lab; Ann Mack, Director of Trend Spotting at the JWT advertising firm; and Ken Dychtwald, founder of AgeWave, an expert in the aging population (see Figure 2.4). In addition, every leading-edge technology has experts who follow the trends, such as Mary Meeker, an Internet analyst and venture capitalist for Kleiner Perkins Caulfied Byers. In her state of the Internet report she observed "how technology has compelled businesses to 're-imagine' their products and services and how they deliver value. She expects the magnitude of upcoming change will be breathtaking as we reach near ubiquitous high-speed Internet access in the developed world, and benefit from unprecedented global technology innovation, the availability of inexpensive devices, access and services as well as vastly accelerated reach."

Locate your "industry gurus" and read *everything* they write. In addition to individual technology watchers, major market research firms McKinsey and Nielsen provide extensive studies, many of which are available on the Net. Complete Action Step 13 now, which asks you to explore new technologies in depth.

■ INFORMATION IS EVERYWHERE

It is hoped that the information presented so far has your creative juices flowing. If you want to learn more and explore several opportunities and potential markets, you will need market research, creativity, and intuition to discover the right opportunity for you. Conducting secondary research is easier with the advent of the greatest information data bank ever at your fingertips—the Internet.

Research data previously available only to large corporations with big R&D budgets are now available to you free, or for only a few dollars. Many large research organizations publish "White Papers," which are overviews of their research, offered in hope that you will purchase their more in depth reports. These White Papers offer a great deal of insight and provide great starting points to learn about various industries and markets. If you keep your eyes wide open, your intuition and creativity will blossom.

Secondary Research

Researching industries and markets takes three forms: secondary, primary, and "new eyes" research. Secondary research should be your starting point. When you read what someone else has discovered and published, you are carrying out secondary research.

Keeping your eyes open not only to your industry but to other industries is vital. Also, ideas and research currently being explored within one function of a company can be adapted into another function, such as computer software. Reinventing the wheel is not necessary for entrepreneurs to succeed. One can choose to improve the wheel's looks, speed, function, or to reduce the cost—all can be highly lucrative.

Conducting thorough secondary research will prepare you to perform targeted primary research, because you will be better prepared to ask focused questions and thus get to the heart of any issue in less time. Also, by continuing to flood your brain with information, you will start to build your intuition; then your "new eyes" will work even better.

Contact trade associations such as the National Restaurant Association (Figure 2.7) for industry, supplier, distributor, and customer information. Trade associations conduct marketing and product research, provide conferences, publish trade journals, offer books, and online classes. Many associations have well trained staff available to talk with individuals about building and growing their businesses.

Trade associations Dedicated to meeting member needs within a specific industry

Trade journals Narrowly focused publications for specific industry or activity

They may also provide data to project how much money one can expect to net in their industry and provide benchmarks regarding costs. We encourage you to check your assumptions all along the way as you research your venture. Data from associations will help you determine if you are on the right track financially. Good research techniques here will save lots of footwork and you should never underestimate the information available through associations. Their primary goal is the success of their members, so they listen and are attuned to their members' information needs.

Early on in your research, national and local association chapters often can provide you with invaluable personal contacts for further primary research. Many associations offer student memberships at a reduced cost providing access to their websites and specialized research. Also, take time to ask people in your industry which associations they belong to and which magazines, journals, Twitter feeds, newsletters, and websites they use.

Next, move online to *ipl2* to find magazines that reach your target market and trade journals in your industry. Magazines develop media kits (see Chapter 4), many available online, which provide statistics on their readership for their advertisers. This is one of the quickest ways to get a read on the marketplace. Reading magazines and media kits will show you competitive products, interests shared by your customers, and industry and product trends; and also will provide extensive demographic, psychographic, and usage information.

Media kits Readership profiles, ad information, and market research developed by magazines for use by potential advertisers

Psychographic Descriptive information on values, attitudes, and lifestyles

Sometimes highly technical journals are not easy to locate or access online. If this is the case, ask your library to help you locate the corporate libraries within your local area and industry. Many corporate libraries will allow individuals access to their facilities upon request. In addition, their trained librarians can be an invaluable resource, not only in locating information but in searching out people within their corporations who are conducting research applicable to your business venture. If you do not have access to a good library, contact *ipl2* for their free online librarian help desk.

To gain access to government statistics, local, state, and federal, log on to USA.gov (see Entrepreneurial Resource) where Census data, demographics, environmental data, health and nutrition, etc. will be at your fingertips.

In fact, as you begin your collection of relevant data, you would also do well to locate the best research librarian in your college or local library. In many universities, individual libraries exist within certain specialties, such as pharmacy or biomedical engineering. In larger urban areas, individual city or county library branches are designated as business research libraries.

figure **2.7**

National Restaurant Association

National Restaurant Association

ACTION STEP 14

Launch Your Industry Research

1. Locate the names of trade associations your business would be part of and make note of the addresses, phone numbers, and websites. Contact the associations and request information. Because you are a potential member, they should send you an enormous amount of information and provide membership details. If you mention you are a student conducting research, they may be surprisingly helpful and may even offer student memberships. Also, to enhance your research, contact associations your suppliers and customers may belong to. Combining this information will provide you with an incredible amount of data to sift through.

2. Locate a local chapter of a national association relevant to your business and attend a local meeting as a guest or student.

3. Locate magazines or journals within 1) your selected industry, 2) journals that reach your **Target Customers**, and 3) magazines or journals for your suppliers. Once you have located the material, spend time and start reading for as long as you can! Information is power.

4. Read the magazine/journals media kits online. The information will provide good solid basic information. Complete this Action Step before moving on; as you will need the information to complete the Action Steps in Chapters 3 through 5.

Target Customers Persons who have the highest likelihood of buying your product or service

Also, log on to university websites to discover faculty members conducting research, which may be applicable to your business venture. In fact, you may find out the university offers an incubator for new businesses and your idea might be one they are interested in. Throughout the chapters, we will be introducing you to many additional secondary sources, but it is now time to begin your secondary industry research with Action Step 14.

Entrepreneur's Resource

USA.gov

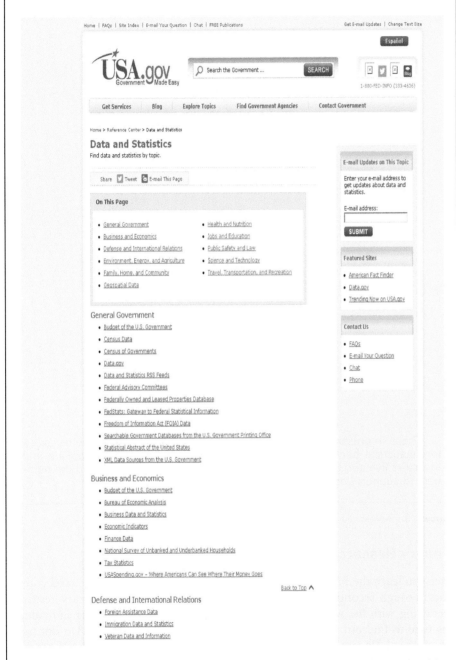

Historical and current economic and financial data are available along with Consumer Price Index (CPI), housing, employment, manufacturing, economic policy, and general economic indicators.

In addition to the excellent resource above, log on to *http://catalog.gpo.gov* to locate your local Federal Depository Library where you will be able to search through government publications either online or on site with trained librarians.

(continued)

(continued)

Environment, Energy, and Agriculture
- Agriculture Statistics
- Chemical Substance Inventory
- Climate Data
- Energy Statistics
- Environmental Data
- Geologic Maps Database
- Open Energy Info
- Pesticide Data

Back to Top ∧

Family, Home, and Community
- Aging Statistics
- American FactFinder: Facts About Your Community
- Child and Adolescent Health Data
- Child and Family Statistics
- Genealogy and Family History Research
- Genealogy Resources, by State
- Immigration Data and Statistics
- Population Clock – U.S. and World
- State and County Quick Facts from the U.S. Census Bureau

Geospatial Data
- Geo.Data.gov
- GeoPlatform.gov

Back to Top ∧

Health and Nutrition
- Child and Adolescent Health Data
- Health and Human Services Data and Statistics
- Health Statistics
- National Center for Health Workforce Analysis: Area Resource File
- Public Health Data

Jobs and Education
- Education Data
- Labor Statistics
- National Center for Health Workforce Analysis: Area Resource File

Back to Top ∧

Public Safety and Law
- Crime and Justice Statistics

Science and Technology
- Federal Research and Development Projects
- Science Accelerator
- Scientific Data

Travel, Transportation, and Recreation
- Transportation Statistics
- Travel and Tourism Statistics

Back to Top ∧

Page Last Reviewed or Updated: November 20, 2012

Stay Connected to USA.gov   Mobile   RSS   Get E-mail Updates

Home | About Us | Contact Us | Website Policies | Privacy | Link to Us

USA.gov is the U.S. government's official web portal.

> These impressive collections of data are easy to use and provide excellent statistical back-up data for a Business Plan. Remember, bankers and investors live and die by numbers, and this is where you may find the numbers to support your business ideas and dreams.

Courtesy of USA.gov

Source: *http://www.usa.gov/Topics/Reference-Shelf/Data.shtml*

Primary Research

After you learn the basics about your industry, customers, suppliers, and competitors through secondary research, you are ready to conduct primary research, interacting with the world directly by talking with and interviewing individuals. It is time to find out exactly what your potential customer wants: Do not make assumptions! Do not give them what *you* want to give them—*give them what they want and will pay for.*

Below are a few sample questions. However, you will need to formulate your own questions to fit your industry and market. The more people you interview, the more targeted and refined your questions should become. Ask away and truly listen:

- What brands do you wish your favorite clothing store would carry?
- How likely are you to use your smartphone to keep track of your eating habits?
- How much do you usually spend each month on fast-food meals?
- How would your ideal automobile dealer behave?

- What would you not buy on the Internet? Why not? What could a firm provide to change your mind?

Ask vendors and suppliers: What advertising works best in businesses like ours? What products are hot? What services are being offered? What are the biggest problems for suppliers in the industry?

Ask small-business owners: With whom do you bank? Where did you obtain your first financing? What percentage of sales do you spend on advertising? How do you deal with shipping charges? How do you encourage repeat customers?

New Eyes Research

New eyes research provides a variety of fresh ways to look at a business. Based on your knowledge, experience, and intuition, play detective. You might become a "mystery shopper" to check out your competition. You might sit in your car and take telephoto pictures of a business you are thinking about buying; when Target Customers appear, snap their picture so that you can profile them later. Stand in a supermarket aisle and, trying not to look nosy, observe what is in a person's shopping cart. For example:

Hamburger + chips + Popsicles + apples + *Redbook* = busy family with young active children; probably driving a van or SUV

Protein bars + salmon + *Runner's World* + *GQ* + asparagus + pesto = Single man who is athletic, clothes- and weight-conscious, and probably likes to cook

Another option is to snoop through Pinterest, Facebook or LinkedIn profiles of your potential Target Customers. Profiling your Target Customer is necessary for you to gain a handle on your customers' needs and wants. Profiling will be covered thoroughly in later chapters, but start training your observation faculties by completing Action Step 15.

New eyes research is fun. Combined with books, magazines, trade journals, publications (*The Wall Street Journal*, for example), and talking to people, it will lead you all the way to your Business Plan. And the Business Plan will either lead you to success or show you that your idea is not worth any more of your time.

Train your mind. Remain open to new ideas, technology, information, statistics, people, and a rapidly changing world. Observe everything. Keep your ideas together in a notebook, computer or your phone. The more ideas that pour in, the more likely you are to find the right fit for you and your target market. Alex Rusch, the founder of the largest audio-books firm in Switzerland, RuschVerlag, said he kept a notebook, and when he had 200 ideas, he sat down and reviewed them all before launching his firm. Chapter 3 will help you sort through your ideas.

■ THE BIG PICTURE

A Business Plan begins with the "big picture"—the industry overview. Industries go through life cycles. Products and services within industries also progress through the stages of the cycle: embryo, growth, maturity, and decline. At the same time, target markets experience major cyclical changes. The industry overview in your Business Plan helps you gain perspective on your niche and helps readers, lendors, or investors, understand why you have chosen to pursue this particular segment of the market at this particular time.

To be successful in small business, you need to know what business you are really in and where your business is situated in its life cycle. Entrepreneurs tend to be in a big hurry. They want to push on, to get on with it, to throw open the doors to

ACTION STEP 15

Just for Fun Start to Decode

1. Use your "new eyes" to uncover the lifestyle of your customer by analyzing the contents of a supermarket shopping cart. Play detective the next time you are in a supermarket and make some deductions about lifestyles as you observe the behaviors of shoppers.

2. Give each subject a fantasy name, perhaps associated with a product (Chad Cereal, Steve Steak, and Sally Sugar) so that you can remember your insights. What can you deduce about each shopper's lifestyle? What do their shoes say? Their clothes? Their jewelry? Their hairstyle? Their car?

3. Put these deductions together with a demographic checklist (sex, age, income, occupation, socioeconomic level), and then decide if any of these shoppers are potential Target Customers for your business.

4. Trained marketers look for a category of buyer known as a "heavy user." A heavy user of apples would eat 7 to 10 apples a week. A heavy user of soda would drink four a day. A heavy user of airlines—called a "frequent flyer"—flies 10 to 30 times a year. Can you determine who the heavy users are in your business?

5. If you don't want to go out, you can also complete the assignment using Pinterest, Facebook or LinkedIn profiles, where people have become open books!

Niche A small, unique slice of an industry segment; potential slice of industry market share customers, and read the bottom line—and that is not all bad. But before you charge into the arena, step back and examine what is going on in your industry segment.

Where are the lines forming? In what part of your community do you see "Going Out of Business" signs? Where are the start-ups? What is hot? What is cooling down? Which business segments will still be thriving three years from now? If you opened the doors of your new business today, how long would it be before your product or services were no longer valuable or wanted?

Let us back up and view the broader picture. Before the Industrial Revolution, most people were self-employed. Farmers and sheepherders were risk takers because they had to be; there were few other options. The family functioned as an entrepreneurial unit.

Today's growth of megacorporations should not be viewed as a threat to the small venture but as an opportunity. First, most large corporations are dependent on small business to produce support products and services. Second, bigger is not always better. Many small businesses—even those whose markets are expanding rapidly—are barely noticed by large corporations. And therein lays opportunity! If you are lucky, you will hit on an idea for a great business and be bought out for millions by Mark Zuckerberg or the next billionaire!

So look before you leap. Brainstorm with your family, friends, colleagues, and suppliers. Interview potential customers; they will tell you what they want and need. If you have done your research, your new eyes will be in full gear, and you will be able to recognize the opportunities and understand the risks. Continue to study the marketplace with your new eyes and never stop reading or talking. Time to follow how one partnership pursued their dream after researching their market.

■ MIND MAPPING YOUR WAY INTO SMALL BUSINESS

Snowboard Express

Annie and Valerie loved to snowboard. For seven years, they snowboarded every chance they had—Mammoth, Vail, Tahoe, Bend, and Park City. They kept looking for ways they could make a living snowboarding. At school Annie and Valerie discovered the technique of mind mapping [see Figure 1.3]—a method of note taking using clusters and bubbles—to let information flow along its own course. Maybe they could mind map their way into the snowboarding business!

In the center of a large sheet of paper they wrote "snowboarding." In a bubble next to "snowboarding" they wrote "travel." Momentum built up. They wrote "segments," "beginners," "preteens," "teens," "college students," and "families." Then they wrote "clothes and accessories," "gloves," "pants," "jackets," "goggles," "boots," and "socks." Then they let their imaginations go even further and wrote "The Alps," "Vermont," "California," "Utah," "Chile," "contests," "lessons," "trips," "fun," "tricks", "exciting," "skateboarders," "transportation," "buses."

"This is great fun!" Annie said.

"This smells like money and fun!" Valerie exclaimed.

The two friends kept on mapping until they developed an idea for their business— Snowboard Express—roundtrip weekend bus transportation to mountain ski resorts from five local pickup points surrounding Salt Lake City. Different resorts were selected each weekend.

Two or three weeks after they began booking their trips, they went back to their mind map and the words "clothes and accessories" jumped out at them. They went to one of the major snowboard clothing manufacturers and bought out their seconds and sold them all to Snowboard Express customers at 100 percent over cost within four weeks.

After they had been in business for only two months, a few women asked if Valerie and Annie could provide weekday trips so they could have the mountains to themselves while their children were in school—and a new market segment was uncovered, and a gap was filled. They listened to their customers and began "Slope Thursdays."

Sometime in April, the riders began asking what Annie and Valerie were going to do for the summer. They responded by asking, "What are you doing this summer?" The answer they kept hearing was, "I'm going mountain biking." Valerie and Annie were off to explore the regional mountain bike trails. Afterward they talked to their bus drivers to determine how they could transport the bikes on the buses. With their answers in hand, market research completed, and bike racks ordered, "Mountain Bike Express" was born. Annie and Valerie found listening to their customers was the key to their year round success.

■ BRAINSTORMING TECHNIQUES

In addition to mind mapping with a partner, you can gather a group of people together for a simple exchange of ideas, which can later lead to mind mapping sessions. If you gather around you people with spark, creativity, wit, positive attitudes, knowledge, and good business sense, the results will almost always surprise you.

Invite people who bring different ideas, backgrounds, and experience to the table. Incredible solutions to problems are found oftentimes when two very different disciplines combine. Don't be afraid to ask some people who are "wild cards," just make sure you have the ability to control the situation if they try to take over. Encourage off the wall and "out of the box" thinking.

Appreciate the "idea" person. It is difficult to imagine new ventures without several idea people. Encourage a dialog for your benefit as well as those with the new ideas. You may be the one to bring the focus back to reality keeping this person as part of the team. Train yourself to avoid negative reactions when brainstorming as this can affect the energy generated by those participating.

With limitless possibilities, the trick is to structure brainstorming sessions in a way that maximizes creativity. You want members to encourage each other, to be able to stretch their minds, and to set their competitive instincts aside.

Also, you want members who are willing to critique and challenge others, as you are working to find solutions to problems and those critiques and questions will redefine the problem and refine the solutions. Work hard to assure your brainstorming session does not become a groupthink where everyone is following the leader. That is the opposite of what you are aiming for.

A few more suggestions follow.

When Gathering Participants and Planning Your Meeting

1. Find imaginative people who stretch their minds and who can set their competitive instincts aside for a while.
2. Remember, you are not implementing yet. Judgment will kill a session but questions will not.
3. Find a neutral location and eliminate interruptions. If you cannot meet physically together, use Skype or GotoMeeting.com.
4. Encourage members of the group to reinforce and believe in each other and also to challenge.
5. Consider recording a brainstorming situation. If not, have someone record the group's ideas on a laptop or flip chart.
6. Pick a time that is convenient and not rushed to make it relaxed for all involved.
7. Invite 5 to 10 people; some will drop out, and you should allow for no-shows.
8. Schedule the starting time. Relax and begin after about a half-hour.

9. Allow time for self-introductions in terms of accomplishments, problems, activities, and interests. Tell participants not to be modest. They are winners, and they want to be seen as winners.

10. Encourage everyone to *listen* to the other members.

11. Silence is good. It means people are thinking. Try not to fill every moment with talking.

12. Laugh and enjoy the process.

Additional Tips

• Have everyone arrive with a business idea or a problem that needs to be solved.

• Before the close of the first meeting, cast a vote to select two or three hot ideas and ask participants to prepare a one-page checklist summarizing and analyzing the ideas. Ask them to share with others. Request the participants to work on the ideas for a week and meet back.

• Brainstorm the hot ideas further by fleshing the ideas out and coming up with business ideas and markets. Make it clear the basic purpose is to get energy and ideas rolling.

• The best brainstorming sessions occur when you connect brain-to-brain with other creative, positive people; it helps remind you that you've still got it. Brain energy is real, and you need to keep tapping it.

• Great snacks keep the troops fortified!

■ LIFE-CYCLE STAGES

Economically, socially, technically, and financially, our world is changing at incredible speed. The world is at warp speed—a revolution. Satellites circle the globe bringing mobile phones and computing to the most remote regions of Asia and Africa. Smartphones change the way we shop, pay for goods, and locate products, services, and people. China, India, and Indonesia explode with entrepreneurs. Opportunities abound.

Review past Action Steps and make a list of all the trends, products, services, and markets you unearthed. Divide these into four groups according to their current stage in the life cycle (Figure 2.8). If a trend is just beginning and is in its formative stage, label it *embryo*. If it is exploding, label it *growth*. If it is no longer growing and is beginning to wane, label it *mature*. If it is beyond maturity and feeling chilly, label it *decline*. Think through these life-cycle stages often. Everything changes—products, needs, marketing, distribution channels, target markets, technology, and neighborhoods. Complete Action Step 16 to explore life-cycles.

Market signals are everywhere—on Craigslist, in the queues at the theater, in the price slashing after Christmas, and in discount coupons and Groupons, rebates, closings, failed and successful IPOs, and grand openings.

Which items have you seen go through their life cycle from upscale to deep discounts? Or just from upscale to mainstream at Target—such as Missoni. Looking at the life-cycle diagram, you can see that the auto industry as a whole is very mature. Nonetheless, some of its segments remain promising; for example, car sharing and mini, electric, and hybrid vehicles.

Today, product life cycles are measured in terms of months and years rather than decades and generations. Few of us today could imagine life without smartphones. What will be the next big thing we will not be able to live without?

Rapid technical and societal changes offer great opportunity but also pose increased risk if you make the wrong decision. The market no longer allows you years to test and prove your product or idea.

ACTION STEP 16

Match Trends with Life-Cycle Stages

1. Throughout this chapter, you have discovered many trends, new products, and services and problems to solve. Pull out your notes and past Action Steps. Review Figure 2.8 and draw a life-cycle chart, and place the trends, products, and services you have found in their appropriate stages. How many lie in the embryo/birth stage? In the growth stage? In the maturity stage?

2. It is now time to move forward and to try to discover possible opportunities within the embryo or growth stage. What new opportunities exist? Which would you like to explore further?

If you are entering the embryo stage, be prepared to "beat the pavement" for new business. If you are entering a mature or declining market, be ready to meet and beat the competition head on.

— figure **2.8**

Life-Cycle Stages and Products

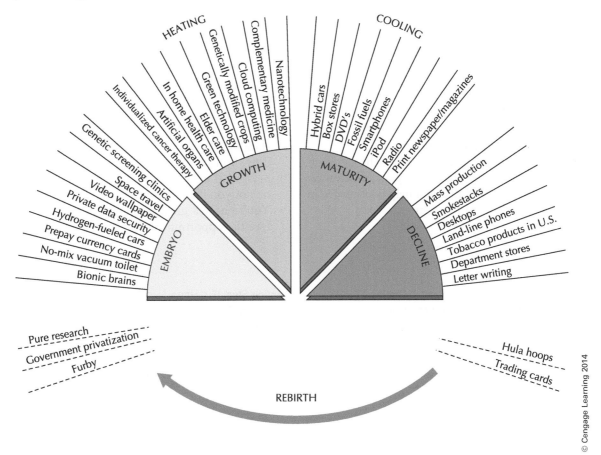

© Cengage Learning 2014

■ **SUMMARY**

We have asked you to look at trends in hopes that you can begin to spot opportunities. Almost every industry is changing constantly today. One cannot listen to the news or read without hearing daily of changes in the health care, education, manufacturing, retailing, auto, and energy areas. If you truly keep your eyes open and are willing to listen, you will find an area, which will provide you the opportunity to create a successful venture.

Information on trends surrounds you—on TV, on the Internet, on the freeways, in the headlines and classifieds, at government agencies, and in the many trade associations. This information provides you with the big picture if you know how to look for it. We have also provided you with current resources to continue your research.

For your Business Plan, you will need to demonstrate your knowledge and understanding of the business opportunity you will pursue. Investors look for opportunities within growth segments of growth industries, and you should too. Investors look for solid data supporting your business idea. Be sure to file any hard data you locate and include it in the appendices of your Business Plan.

You looked at who you are and what you wanted in Chapter 1. You became a trend spotter in this chapter. Now it is time for you to put your research and ideas together to generate the right opportunity for you as you continue to pursue opportunities in Chapter 3.

■ THINK POINTS FOR SUCCESS

- The most valuable tool you have for charting trends is new-eyes research combined with extensive secondary and primary research.
- Keeping your eyes open, not only to your selected industry but also to developments in other industries that may impact yours, will keep you one step ahead.
- The life-cycle yardstick helps you discover a growth industry, decide what business you're really in, and uncover promising gaps and segments.
- Trends don't usually develop overnight. The signs are out for all to read months, sometimes years, in advance.
- Try to latch on to a trend that will help you survive in style for the next three to five years.

- Don't assume that because you have caught one trend, that another one won't nip at your heels down the road.
- Once you determine your market segment, focus your research. Save time and money by first accessing valuable resources, such as trade associations, periodicals, websites, blogs, etc.
- Read everything you can and talk to everyone you can. The opportunities will appear endless.
- Trends are like customers. You can spot some by standing outside and others by staring through a window. Still others won't show up until you're in business, working and sweating away, wondering whether or not you'll make it.
- You're now a great trend spotter, so it's time to analyze the opportunities you have unearthed.

■ ACTION STEPS

■ KEY TERMS

Image_Source/iStockphoto.com

Opportunity Selection
Filtering Your Ideas

Learning Objectives

- Incorporate personal goals with your business objectives and match them with one of the many opportunities in the marketplace.

- Build on a positive and unique thrust for your business.

- Gain insight into markets using the life-cycle yardstick.

- Discover how problems can be turned into opportunities.

- Understand how to use the North American Industrial Classification System (NAICS).

- Research your favorite industry using secondary and primary data.

- Discover the incredible association and trade show resources at your fingertips.

- Narrow your industry and target market research until viable gaps appear.

- Brainstorm creative solutions with mind mapping.

- Use a matrix grid for blending your objectives with your research findings to produce a portrait of a business.

- Listen to your customers' needs and define your business to meet their needs. Explore IDEO's "design thinking"

- Begin to develop your "elevator speech."

- Conduct a feasibility analysis.

As you head toward one of the three doorways to small business, you may feel overcome with ideas. Hopefully, you are also feeling inspired, exhilarated, encouraged, and ready for the challenge.

Opportunities exist that were unheard of two years ago and, in some instances, 24 hours ago. The speed of change is overwhelming. If you have done the research in Chapter 2, you understandably are experiencing information overload. As a creative, wound-up, and ready-to-take charge person, unless you live vigorously for 200 years, you will never be able to follow up on all the changing trends, markets, and ideas you have discovered. So this chapter will help you sort through the opportunities.

What you need is a filtering system, something like a wine press or a Mouli mill (the kitchen machine that turns apples into applesauce) to get rid of peels (segments that are not growing), stems (markets where barriers to entry are too high), and seeds (opportunities that do not mesh with your personal objectives).

After completing the Action Steps in Chapters 2 and 3, you will have gained invaluable information and identified several well-defined business opportunities, moving you one step further along on your Business Plan.

■ WELCOME TO OPPORTUNITY SELECTION

Conducting research will help you exploit gaps, which are untapped opportunities in the marketplace. Research also shows you what new skills you need to develop. It opens up the world and helps you then focus the power of your mind on a particular segment and opportunity. We also suggest you always remain open to exploring global opportunities, such as Gabriele Palermo's firm G3Box (see Global Village) which developed a creative and cost-effective utilization of shipping containers for medical clinics in poverty stricken areas of Africa.

If you have been completing each Action Step as you read through this book, you are now ahead of the game. If you have not been completing the Action Steps, you will need to go back and finish them in order to move forward. To achieve effective opportunity selection:

1. Keep personal and business objectives in mind throughout the filtering process.
2. Learn more about your favorite industry looking at the growth areas.
3. Identify three to five promising concepts.
4. Through research, identify problems that need solutions.
5. Brainstorm looking at product design, distribution, Target Customers, technology, and competition amongst others for areas needing improvement.
6. Mesh possible solutions with your personal and financial objectives.
7. Complete a quick feasibility analysis to determine which ideas you should proceed with and concentrate on the most promising opportunities.

At this point you are beginning your plan. The marketplace is open, filled with excitement and confusion. The most important thing is not to lose your momentum. As you learn more you will build your confidence, and confidence helps you win.

Opportunity selection is like a huge funnel equipped with a series of filters (Figure 3.1). You pour everything into the funnel: goals, personality, problems,

figure **3.1**

Opportunity Selection Funnel

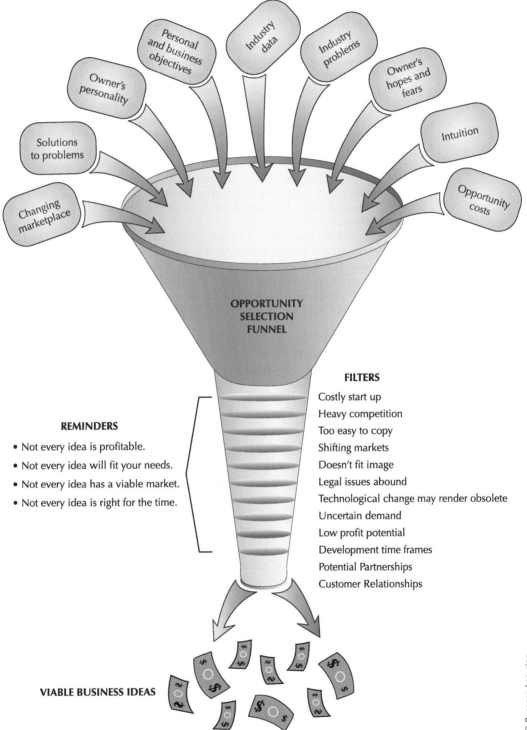

Personal and business objectives

Industry data

Industry problems

Owner's personality

Owner's hopes and fears

Solutions to problems

Intuition

Changing marketplace

Opportunity costs

OPPORTUNITY SELECTION FUNNEL

FILTERS

Costly start up
Heavy competition
Too easy to copy
Shifting markets
Doesn't fit image
Legal issues abound
Technological change may render obsolete
Uncertain demand
Low profit potential
Development time frames
Potential Partnerships
Customer Relationships

REMINDERS

- Not every idea is profitable.
- Not every idea will fit your needs.
- Not every idea has a viable market.
- Not every idea is right for the time.

VIABLE BUSINESS IDEAS

© Cengage Learning

hopes, fears, industry data, research, and intuition. And, after you narrow the choices, viable business ideas filter through to the bottom. Carrying out this process gives you the knowledge of where you are going. Knowledge is power.

Use this filtering process not just at this step, but also throughout the building of your Business Plan. Through your research add additional variables which are pertinent to you. As you gather information in each chapter, come back to the filter to determine if your idea is still filtering through. You are looking for the best fit for you. This filter serves as a reminder that not all ideas are feasible or profitable.

International Freelancer and Soloist

After Eric Duke graduated from law school, he freelanced as a lawyer while planning his wedding and year-long European and Asian honeymoon with his fiancée, Veronica, who had just earned her engineering degree from the University of Minnesota. While planning the trip, Eric and Veronica realized their true dream was to live overseas for several years. They figured now was the time to experience overseas living— no children, no car payments, and no mortgage.

While researching the overseas job market, Eric and Veronica recognized that continuing to freelance might be the best choice for them both. Eric spent a great deal of time online researching opportunities. One day he found an article about a nearby conference for private investors interested in overseas investment opportunities. Eric signed up, and after paying $2,500 was ready to begin his primary research as he had completed his secondary research online and was prepared for the next phase.

At the conference, he came into contact with 50 investors and companies from around the world. Eric made the best use of every meeting and break by finding out each person's interests and needs. His ability to put people at ease was a natural part of his personality, a strength he utilized effectively. By the end of the conference, he had set up three meetings. In addition, Eric had a handshake deal with a Greek investor and an idea for another potential client for an international office in Paris.

Eric's degree from the University College London and his international travels, combined with his online secondary research before the meeting all paid off! This was $2,500 well spent! Eric's goals were always clear, and thus he was able to take advantage of the conference and respond to potential clients' questions. Although it may seem that some people fall into opportunities, most "lucky" people are fully prepared. As many entrepreneurs say, "Preparation is the key to success!"

If you are looking for an opportunity like Eric, check on Meetup.com for a wide range of meet-ups, or check your local business journal. You will be surprised at the opportunities you may find. As always, we encourage you to meet face to face with others to gather the best information.

Before you begin your industry research, review Action Step 5, which asked you to "Inc. Yourself." Think back to what is important to you as Eric Duke did. Keep this portrait in the front of your mind at all times. Stay focused on what you want your life and your business to become. As you begin to explore the vast opportunities within your selected industry, you will discover that some will mesh better than others. Making your business work for you and your customers will bring the most satisfaction. Maintain your business objectives, personal skills, passions, and strengths as you begin to follow the unending research threads. There is no such thing as being over prepared unless it stops you from moving forward.

■ INDUSTRY RESEARCH

Searching for trends in Chapter 2, you probably found several industries that sounded interesting. Next, you will be brainstorming, mind mapping, funneling, and matrixing ideas and opportunities throughout this chapter. It is time now to focus in on one industry in more depth and, by the end of the chapter; you may be able to begin to define your main business idea.

The industry that interests you most might be genetics, robotics, infotainment, food service, travel, education, publishing, construction, manufacturing, or developing apps for one or more of these industries. Select an industry or area you can maintain an interest in and passion for.

If you are not ready to start a business but are taking the class in hopes that someday you might be, follow through on all the Actions Steps by selecting an idea most appealing to you at this time. Learning the business planning process is key. Thus, in a few years when you *are* ready to start your venture you will know the steps and the process. The technologies, websites, distribution channels, and marketing mediums will change but the fundamentals of entrepreneurship and making money will be the same.

As you moved through your favorite industry collecting information from your previous Action Steps, what problems did you find? What are the solutions? How can you explore these further?

While Chapter 2 focused on the broader picture—trends and problems—the focus of Chapter 3 is on the industry and opportunity you select. Cabana Life's founder Melissa Papock (see the Passion box) needed to find a solution to her desire to be in the sun *and* her need for skin protection. In searching for a solution, she found a way to produce 100 percent protective clothing using patented technology sun protection fabric, and she developed Cabana Life.

Melissa combined the sense of fashion she developed while working in merchandising, her desire for alternative sun protective clothing, and her entrepreneurial drive. Her industry research led her to develop an entire line of clothing and accessories. In Melissa's case, she knew her target market's needs and researched the industry to determine how to meet those needs in light of current and potential competition.

After researching your industry in this Chapter, you will move to Chapter 4 where you will profile your specific target market, and Chapter 5 where you will further identify and analyze your competition. In Chapter 5 you will also be introduced to Touchpoints, which focus on each contact your customer has with your product or service either directly or indirectly. As you complete Action Step 28, additional gaps in the marketplace may emerge from one of these touchpoints.

With melanoma growing rapidly, especially among young adults, Melissa recognized a problem and identified the market. As Vinad Khosla of Kleiner Perkins Caufield & Byers shares, "Any big problem is a big opportunity. If there is no problem, there is no solution and no reason for the company to exist. No one will pay you to solve a problem that doesn't exist."

You are now looking for an accurate picture of opportunities in your selected industry. If you will be conducting in depth technology research within your chosen industry, the resources from the Small Business Innovation Research (SBIR) offices (see Entrepreneurial Resource and Chapter 9) may prove beneficial in providing grants to help fund research and commercialize your product.

Conducting secondary and primary research does not eliminate risk, but it definitely reduces it. You need to learn what is breaking, what is cresting, and what is cooling down. You also need to be aware of potential industry changes on the horizon. Action Step 14 in Chapter 2 asked you to start researching by finding at least one association and one periodical associated with a selected industry. Now it is time to explore your selected industry in greater depth:

- What role is technology playing in the industry?
- What changes in technology may affect the future of the industry?
- Who are the key players?
- What are the trends both positively and negatively?
- Are there barriers to entry? If so, what are they?
- What are the niches?
- Where are the gaps?
- What is the cost of positioning yourself?
- Are there distribution channels changing?

Positioning Where a firm or product lies in the buyer's mind compared to other products

PASSION

Malignant Melanoma Drives Entrepreneur

Cabana Life

"After being diagnosed with a malignant melanoma at age 26, the deadliest form of skin cancer, I discovered something very important about the clothing that I thought was protecting me. Ordinary, lightweight clothing is often the equivalent of SPF 5! That is when my doctor informed me that sun protective clothing exists. I wondered why I hadn't heard of sun protective clothing, but when I saw the available options, I knew exactly why.

"Sun protective clothing is only helpful if you wear it, and I realized there was a need to develop *stylish*, UPF clothing for my fellow fashion-conscious friends.

"So with the help of my loving husband (who also battled skin cancer), we formed Cabana Life. Our growing family has helped fuel our desire to protect and educate children and parents alike.

"Trust me, I never expected to hear the 'C' word, and at such a young age! But if we can use our experiences help you protect yourself or loved ones, we've accomplished our goal.

"Cabana Life combines fashion with function by offering stylish clothing with 50+ UV protection through patented technology. The collection offers a variety of beach-essentials including rashguards, bathing suits, hats, coverups, tunics, shirts, and pants for boys, girls, women and men."

"Cabana Life is a socially-conscious company that strives to increase skin cancer education through numerous strategic partnerships with nonprofit organizations such as Huntsman Cancer Institute, the Skin Cancer Foundation, Melanoma Research Alliance, Women's Dermatologic Society, Shade Foundation, and many others."

Source: *http://www.cabanalife.com* (Accessed June 22, 2012).

- Who are the industry leaders? What makes each successful?
- What is required to succeed?
- Can the market handle another player?
- Is the industry regulated? Are any new regulations coming down the pike?
- How long does it take to bring a product to market?
- What role does the Internet play in marketing and distribution?
- Can target customers be reached affordably?
- How is social media used within the industry?
- Can my firm offer additional product or service benefits, which the customer is willing to pay for?
- What role does international competition play in the industry?

Later, after you have gathered data, you can use these and other emerging questions as filters for the Opportunity Selection Funnel (see Figure 3.1). In addition, you are building background information and statistical data for your Business Plan. Remember, bankers and investors want to see back-up data; your research should provide facts and figures that demonstrate the need for your product or service in your selected industry or area.

One of the reasons you were asked to look at the big picture in Chapter 2 was to be sure you kept your eyes open to technology and changes throughout the business world. For example, publishers continually keep an eye out on the progress of e-books and apps. And as tablets and smartphones become cheaper and printers become faster, potential for even greater change exists in the book market. What will be the future for textbook manufacturers, local and chain bookstores, writers, graphic artists, and paper manufacturers? Change is inevitable; view threats as opportunities. Keep your eyes wide open, or be left in the dust!

Find an industry segment where there is room for growth. In addition to growth, look for industry breakthroughs. What in your selected industry or segment is really screaming? Early computer memory banks filled large rooms and read data from punched cards. The first industry breakthrough was the printed circuit, the second was the microchip processor, the third was the Internet, and the fourth is mobile technology. What will be the fifth? What breakthroughs are now occurring in your selected industry? Does your business idea capitalize on the latest advances in technology, innovation, and imagination?

Breakthrough A new way through, over, under, or around an obstacle

Entrepreneur's Resource

Small Business Innovation Research (SBIR) and Touch Graphics

A Win-Win Situation

Like many entrepreneurs, Steven Landau studied a field that ended up having nothing to do with the one he ultimately pursued. An architect by training, after graduating from Harvard's Graduate School of Design, he went to work in New York. Here, he "discovered that I really had a bent for invention." He met up with a professor from the City University of New York who was blind, and, in 1997, a business was born making educational materials accessible for people with visual impairments.

Owing to a small market size and the limited purchasing power of its target audience, disability companies aren't ideal clients for venture capitalists. Instead, Landau turned to the SBIR Program for what he describes as an R&D injection (the first of six grants). That boost proved to be vital. "We would not exist without SBIR," he says. "There's no question about that. It has been the central enabling tool that's permitted us to generate intellectual property. SBIR has been the key to everything we've done."

With SBIR support from the Department of Education, Touch Graphics has commercialized a plethora of products that now are in use throughout the United States and elsewhere. Its flagship creation, the patented Talking Tactile Tablet, acts as a "viewer" for raised-line graphic pictures and illustrations—anything from a pie chart to a map of Washington, DC, to a diagram of a neuron. As a user touches these things, he hears a description that explains what he's looking at.

As of 2010, over 800 tablets have been sold and dozens of applications developed. Currently, Touch Graphics is developing a cheaper version for emerging markets such as Brazil, India, Turkey, Russia, and Indonesia, as well as a Talking Tactile Pen, which it describes as a "a new system for audio-tactile interactive computing."

"Some of our users are exceptionally bright and driven," Landau points out. "They just need tools to overcome their barriers." Manufacturing and marketing these tools affirms for Landau that he made the right career decision."

The Small Business Innovation Research (SBIR) program is a highly competitive program that encourages domestic small businesses to engage in Federal Research/Research and Development (R/R&D) that has the potential for commercialization. Through a competitive awards-based program, SBIR enables small businesses to explore their technological potential and provides the incentive to profit from its commercialization. By including qualified small businesses in the nation's R&D (research and development) arena, high-tech innovation is stimulated and the United States gains entrepreneurial spirit as it meets its specific research and development needs.

Source: *sbir.gov/success-story/sbir-and-touch-graphics-win-win-situation*, (Accessed June 22, 2012).

ACTION STEP 17

Research Your Selected Industry Segment through Secondary Data

1. Which industry segments really attract you?
2. What magnetic pull seems most attractive when combined with your strengths? To help you get started, recall what you discovered in Action Steps 8, 9, 11, 12, 13, and 15. Keep your views wide-angled by looking at two or three segments that you find especially promising and interesting.
3. After you have decided on your segment, research it in depth. Organize your research by categorizing trends, target markets, **competition,** industry breakthroughs, and **market share.** For now, while looking for opportunities, focus primarily on the industry segment and its changes, and be sure to file or bookmark all extraneous data for upcoming Action Steps.
4. If you are working alone, write an industry overview. If you are working with a team, have each team member write an overview, and then meet to hash out your final draft after you have shared your perspectives.

This is a never-ending Action Step. As once you are in business, you must continually remain diligent tracking all aspects of your target market. Now that your money and your business are on the line it is imperative to your firm's success!

Growth industry Annual sales increase well above average

Competition A contestant in the same arena who is fighting for the customers' dollars

Market share Percentage of total available market

■ CONDUCTING SECONDARY RESEARCH FOR YOUR SELECTED INDUSTRY

Chapter 2 introduced secondary, primary, and new-eyes research. You may have stumbled across a wonderful opportunity with your new eyes, and now it is time to develop industry-specific knowledge. Is someone else already conducting a similar business? Is there a market? Are you in a growth industry? Will enough people pay for your product or service? What do you need to know before jumping in? The first place to start is with secondary research. If you are lucky, it will provide you with excellent free background information from which to do further primary research. When researching your industry, you need to understand how to use NAICS/SIC codes.

Industry Research Using NAICS/SIC Codes

Almost all government statistics, business research, and tracking use the North American Industry Classification System (NAICS). NAICS (pronounced "nakes") replaces the U.S. Standard Industrial Classification (SIC) system and provides comparable statistics for businesses throughout North America. To locate your selected industry's NAICS code, and those of your potential customers and suppliers, refer to the government's NAICS manual—available at your library—or online at *http://www.naics.com.*

NAICS is a numerical system that assigns a number to almost every identifiable industry. The structure of the new system and an example follow:

XX Industry sector (20 major sectors)
XXX Industry subsector
XXXX Industry group
XXXXX Particular type of industry
XXXXXX U.S., Canadian, or Mexican national specific industry

North American Industry Classification System

An example of this coding system follows:

31 Manufacturing
315 Apparel Manufacturing
3151 Apparel Knitting Mills
31511 Hosiery and Sock Mills
315111 Sheer Hosiery Mills
315119 Other Hosiery and Sock Mills
31519 Other Apparel Knitting Mills
315191 Outerwear Knitting Mills
315192 Underwear and Nightwear Knitting Mills
3152 Cut and Sew Apparel Manufacturing
31521 Cut and Sew Apparel Contractors
315211 Men's and Boys' Cut and Sew Apparel Contractors
315212 Women's and Girls' Cut and Sew Apparel Manufacturing
31522 Men's and Boys' Cut and Sew Apparel Manufacturers
315221 Men's and Boys' Cut and Sew Underwear and Nightwear Manufacturing
315222 Men's and Boys' Cut and Sew Suit, Coat, and Overcoat Manufacturing
315223 Men's and Boys' Cut and Sew Shirt (except Work Shirt) Manufacturing
315224 Men's and Boys' Cut and Sew Trouser, Slack, and Jean Manufacturing
315225 Men's and Boys' Cut and Sew Work Clothing Manufacturing
315228 Men's and Boys' Cut and Sew Other Outerwear Manufacturing

NAICS and SIC codes help you:

- Discover what industry you are in for statistical purposes.
- Define industry bounderies.
- Locate customers, suppliers, manufacturers, and competitors.
- Access the number of potential customers and potential market.
- Reach out to other industries thoughtfully and systematically.
- Track customer sales by industry or segment.

Once you have located all necessary NAICS codes, you are ready to begin your industry research. Action Steps 17 and 18 should be reviewed now and worked on throughout the chapters. However, if you are involved in a rapidly growing area, NAICS codes may not be of great use. Thus, you may need to adjust these Action Steps to work for your industry.

Trade Associations

One of your most important secondary research stops should be the trade associations within your selected industry as well as the industries of your customers and suppliers, as introduced in Chapter 2. Throughout the text, we have highlighted many of the resources available through one association, the National Restaurant Association (NRA), which represents the restaurant and hospitality industry. We have done so to encourage you to seek out your industry associations who will provide low cost information and resources. Your venture's success is important to them as they want to grow their industry by assisting and stimulating new ventures.

Do you want to know what the industry experts think the latest trends will be? Do you want an in-depth analysis of the industry? What about information concerning workforce trends and the emerging restaurant consumer? Need statistics on sales by a restaurant group? If so, the NRA will happily sell you their yearly *Restaurant Industry Forecast* (Figure 3.2) for $200. However, you also

ACTION STEP 18

Determine NAICS Code

1. Find the NAICS codes for your:
   a. Industry segment (for example, retail candy store)
   b. Suppliers
   c. Wholesalers
   d. Customers (if applicable)
2. Determine through your research the size of your market in dollars and volume.
3. What percentage of the market would you need to capture to make your venture profitable?
   a. Is that possible?
   b. Is it probable?
4. Locate future sales projections for your industry.
   a. What is the growth rate?
   b. Are you in a **growth segment** which you can capitalize on?

Growth segment An identifiable slice of an industry that is expanding more rapidly than the industry as a whole

---

— figure **3.2**

2012 Restaurant Industry Forecast: Table of Contents

The National Restaurant Association is pleased to provide the *2012 Restaurant Industry Forecast*, our 43rd annual profile of restaurant-industry opportunities and challenges for the year ahead. The research and insights are based on analysis of the latest economic data, as well as extensive surveys of restaurateurs and consumers.

The National Restaurant Association will closely monitor incoming industry and economic data in the months ahead and provide updates to this *Forecast* at www.restaurant.org/research.

The *2012 Restaurant Industry Forecast* was prepared by the National Restaurant Association Research and Knowledge Group:

Hudson Riehle
Senior Vice President, Research and Knowledge

Bruce Grindy
Chief Economist

Tim Smith
Art Director

Annika Stensson
Public Relations

Jennifer Batty
Editor

NATIONAL RESTAURANT ASSOCIATION®

1200 17th St., NW, Washington, DC 20036
(800) 424-5156 I www.restaurant.org

© 2012 National Restaurant Association

ISBN 978-1-931400-74-9

Thank you to our National Restaurant Association *2012 Restaurant Industry Forecast* sponsor:

Yield. Ease. Sustainability.

Inside

Source: *www.restaurant.org*, National Restaurant Association, 2012.

could join the association at the student rate of $75 and access the report for free. Locate your associations and then read and learn about the industry from the inside and out before you make the leap.

Secondary information, such as the *Forecast*, always provides a starting point for your research. For example, after reading a report on national and statewide trends in food and menu prices, your primary research on specific trends and pricing in your local area will be much easier to conduct. Your questions to those in the industry will now become focused, targeted, and productive. Secondary information sharpens intuition as well. From the following highlights of the NRA's 2012 *Forecast*, you also will gather insight into future opportunities:

• The restaurant industry will continue to fuel U.S. employment in the year ahead as the nation's second largest private sector employer. Overall restaurant industry employment will reach 12.9 million in 2012, representing 10 percent of the total U.S. workforce.

• In 2012, the National Restaurant Association expects the restaurant industry to add jobs at a 2.3 percent rate, a full percentage point above the projected 1.3 percent gain in total U.S. employment. Restaurant job growth is expected to outpace the overall economy for the 13th straight year.

• Wholesale food prices posted their strongest annual increase in more than three decades in 2011. In 2012, prices are expected to continue to increases for some commodities, while price pressures will ease for others. As one-third of sales in a restaurant go toward food and beverage purchases, fluctuations in food prices are significant to a restaurant's bottom line.

• There is substantial pent-up demand for restaurant services, with 2 out of 5 consumers saying they are not using restaurant as often as they would like. With the right incentives, that demand can translate into sales.

• Nearly 4 in 10 consumers say they'd be likely to use an electronic ordering system and menus on tablet computers at tableservice restaurants. About half said they would use at-table electronic payment options and a restaurant's smartphone app to view menus and make reservations.

• At quickservice restaurants, about 4 out of 10 consumers say they would place online orders for takeout, use in-store self-service ordering kiosks, and use smartphone apps to look at menus and order delivery.

• Nearly three-quarters of consumers say they are more likely to visit a restaurant that offers locally produced food items, and more than half of all restaurants currently offer locally sourced produce.

• Nearly three-quarters of consumers say they are trying to eat healthier now at restaurants than they did two years ago, and a majority of restaurants agree that customers are ordering more such items.

Looking at the information above, what opportunities in the restaurant or food industry do you see? Read between lines, question what you read, call and discuss with the people at association headquarters, and begin to formulate questions for others as you step out.

Dealing with an industry that employs millions of people and encompasses hundreds of thousands of businesses leads the NRA to spend an incredible amount of money and time developing products, information, and services for their member organizations, as do most large associations. For example, they provide members access to an information service professional, who aids members in their search for hiring practice information, legal changes, statistical data, and financial information. In exchange for this and numerous other services, a typical Idaho restaurant with sales of $500K to $1 million would pay would pay around $500 yearly in NRA and Idaho Lodging and Restaurant Association membership fees.

In reviewing the information from the *Forecast*, you will see that there may be untapped food markets or a niche you never knew existed, such as community centers, colleges, clubs, prisons, and recreational camps. What about in-transit restaurant services and commercial cafeterias? Your key to locating and tapping markets may lie within the data and the human sources at your respective associations.

For specific training opportunities, associations present online courses, classes and workshops which help entrepreneurs get up and running quickly and efficiently, saving time, money, sweat, and tears.

Seminars and workshops are offered locally, statewide, or regionally. In addition, many associations offer start-up manuals with incredibly detailed and well-researched advice and information. Some "would-be" entrepreneurs can be arrogant and will not take advice from others. Do not make this mistake! Developing expertise takes time, energy, and money. Be open and willing to learn from others. Ideas and solutions come from many sources and you can learn from others' successes and failures.

To estimate gross sales, profit, and operating expenses, Restaurant.org provides a yearly *Industry Operations Report*, which can be purchased for $60 by members and $125 by non-members. In addition, at the NRA site one can learn about opening up a restaurant by surfing subjects such as catering, décor, food safety, and technology. With only a few clicks you can find a how-to series, a buyers' guide, and lists of associations, magazines, books, and websites to continue your research. One wonders why anyone would open a restaurant without stopping here first.

Do you know about the Juice and Smoothie Association? How about the American Correctional Foodservice Association? If you are producing frozen foods, the American Frozen Food Institute is there to serve you. These and about 100 more associations are linked through Restaurant.org.

In addition to associations, outside publications are an incredible source of information on retailers, wholesalers, consumers, and your competition. Restaurant.org links to over 100 restaurant, foodservice, and hospitality industry publications (Figure 3.3) such as *El Restaurante Mexicano*, a bilingual magazine for Mexican, Tex-Mex, Southwestern, and Latino Restaurants, and *Restaurant Startup and Growth*, a monthly magazine focusing on new ventures.

Tracking the latest food industry changes is easier with Restaurant.org's news webpage. Recent headlines included information on health plans for small businesses, organic/natural foods, and minority restaurant operators. Keeping up on food safety, nutrition, and commodity prices would be a full-time job, but with the site's webpage devoted to these issues, you can be assured you are receiving the latest information. Since government and legal issues have a major impact on food service, the site will also keep you abreast of employment laws and potential regulatory changes. Direct links to state and local resources are also included.

A challenge for many start-up restaurants is locating suppliers. Through the Restaurant.org website, you will be able to access thousands of providers in over 800 categories. The National Restaurant Association (NRA) is representative of many of the incredible organizations that strive to help make their members' businesses strong and successful, as well as encourage them to respond to environmental changes to maintain their viability and profitability. It is now time for you to continue to explore your industry in depth through Action Steps 17-19. Start your search for information with the best associations that deal with your venture and maybe you will be fortunate enough to find a goldmine like Restaurant.org.

figure **3.3**

Restaurant, Foodservice and Hospitality Industry Publications

Restaurant, Foodservice and Hospitality Industry Publications

This list is a sample of the foodservice publications available and is intended to be a useful resource for restaurant-industry professionals. For questions about this list or to add another publication, please contact media@restaurant.org.

NATIONAL RESTAURANT ASSOCIATION PUBLICATIONS

Washington Report — newsletter published once a month
Restaurant.org news — online news highlights
Research News & Numbers — trends, facts and figures
Restaurant TrendMapper — analysis of economic news

FOODSERVICE PUBLICATIONS — BROAD INDUSTRY COVERAGE

My Foodservice News — 740-345-5542 phone, 740-345-5557 fax
Nation's Restaurant News — weekly, 800-944-4676 circulation, 212-756-5188 editorial
Restaurant Business — monthly, 847-763-9627 circulation, 646-708-7319 editorial
Restaurant Hospitality — monthly, for the full-service restaurant market, 866-505-7173 circulation, 913-514-3621 fax
Restaurants & Institutions — monthly, 800-446-6551 circulation, 630-288-8204 editorial
Slammed Magazine — monthly, 617-422-0404

FOODSERVICE PUBLICATIONS - SPECIALTY TOPICS

Asian Restaurant News — for Asian-themed restaurants
Bartender Magazine — for and about bartending
Beverage World — beverage production and distribution, monthly, 847-763-9627 circulation, 646-708-7301 editorial
Bon Appetit — food and entertaining, 800-765-9419
Cheers — for fullservice restaurant and bar operators serving alcohol, 203-855-8499
Chef — the "idea" magazine for American chefs, 888-545-3676 ext. 10 circulation, 312-849-2220 editorial
Chinese Restaurant News — serves American-Chinese restaurants in North America
Club Management — official magazine of the Club Managers Association of America, 314-961-6644
Cooking For Profit — kitchen operations, 920-923-3700
Cooking Light — healthy cooking and living, 205-445-6000
Cornell Hospitality Quarterly — 888-437-4636 circulation, 607-255-3025 editorial

Source: *restaurant.org/tools/magazines/National* Restaurant Association.

Trade Shows

Another way to research your selected industry is to attend trade shows—events at which manufacturers and service providers in a common industry demonstrate their wares to potential distributors, wholesalers, and retailers. While there, research your competition, pick up literature, talk to everyone you can, and

GLOBAL**VILLAGE**

Entrepreneur® Magazine's College Entrepreneur of 2011
Gabrielle Palermo

G3Box

Two professors at Arizona State University posed a challenge to their engineering students: Come up with a function for the numerous used shipping containers abandoned at ports around the world. For Gabrielle Palermo and three of her classmates, crafting a solution to this problem has evolved into not only a compelling model of adaptive reuse, but possibly a lifelong career.

From the roots of that classroom project, Palermo, a junior studying biomedical engineering, and her partners—mechanical engineering senior Billy Walters and mechanical engineering master's students Susanna Young and Clay Tyler—have started G3Box, a company that aims to convert the deserted or decommissioned steel containers into medical clinics that can be deployed around the world.

Many companies use shipping containers that end up languishing at their end locations due to the high cost of returning them to their points of origin. Palermo says the team's thinking immediately turned to ways to convert the containers into something that could help people.

Young and Tyler began working with the idea of turning the 160- or 320-square-foot containers into maternity clinics for use in developing countries with high maternal mortality rates. Palermo and Walters, meanwhile, had been working with Payson, Ariz.-based disaster-relief organization Telehelp on improving container clinics that had been deployed in Haiti after the 2010 earthquake but were found to have insufficient insulation and ventilation. The four students came together to form G3Box—the name comes from "generating global good"—with the idea of designing their own clinics and selling them to nonprofits and nongovernmental organizations.

The modular, mobile medical units—outfitted with ventilation, insulation, power, potable water and any other services a customer might request—can be used by hospitals or organizations that would like to expand existing facilities, or can be easily transported to disaster zones for use as temporary clinics. G3Box plans to function as a hybrid for-profit company and nonprofit foundation.

The students have raised $4,000 from ASU's Innovation Challenge and another $10,000 in seed funding from the school's Edson Student Entrepreneur Initiative. The team is working on a prototype maternity clinic, in a container donated by Swift Transportation, and hopes to deploy it this summer in Kenya, as part of a partnership with Boulder, Colo.-based nonprofit Sustainable Resources. With the $5,000 in prize money from the Entrepreneur of 2011 Awards, the students hope to obtain their second container and build a prototype disaster-relief clinic.

"We feel that medical clinics are the biggest need right now," Palermo says, adding that the containers could eventually be used for "any type of social work around the world: classrooms, food distribution units, dental offices—basically anything someone wants."

The containers, which cost $12,000 to $18,000 to build (the high end of the range includes solar panels), will initially be constructed in the U.S. and delivered to areas of need, but the hope is to eventually have assembly sites near international ports, particularly in Africa.

For Palermo, what started as a student project has the potential to turn into a dream job. "When I started college I didn't really think I was going to be growing a business," she says. "Doing G3Box for my future career or starting up other companies that focus on social good is my passion now."

Source: Carolyn Horwitz, "Meet the Entrepreneur of 2011 Award Winners," Entrepreneur Magazine, 21 December 2011. Copyright © 2012 Entrepreneur Media, Inc. 1212:SH soak it all in. Most trade shows are open only to people within the industry. If you cannot gain access as a member of the trade, ask if you can attend for a guest or student fee; if that is not possible, network your way to a friend or acquaintance that may take you as a guest.

Over 500 firms presented their wares and services at The WasteExpo 2012 Conference and Trade Show, attended by over 8,000 people. For four days in May, the Las Vegas Convention Center teemed with sellers trying to capture the eyes and ears of buyers from throughout the world. Product and service providers reached out to those involved in the over $45 billion solid waste and recycling market and for those plying the aisles opportunities were everywhere. When visiting a trade show observe, talk to everyone, ask questions and most importantly *listen*.

In addition to all the exhibits, over 20 wide-ranging, free educational workshops and programs were offered such as the following:

- Avoid Greenwashing in Reporting Sustainability
- Melted and Crushed; Plastic, Glass and Metal Markets
- Bad Stuff in Trash: Dealing with Worker Exposure
- E-fficient E-recycling
- Hybrid Trucks: Market Analysis and Forecast

To locate trade shows for your industry, log on to the Trade Show News Network database, which can be searched by event name, industry, date, city, state, and country. You will be hyperlinked to one of the thousands of trade shows held throughout the world each year. In addition, the website will help you locate trade show suppliers for over 50 product categories, such as tents, lighting, traffic builders, and trade show bags to use when you are ready to sponsor your own tradeshow booth.

Additional Secondary Resources for Research and Opportunity Gathering

- Newspapers: Several trend watchers monitor more than 6,000 regional and daily newspapers. Follow their lead and study local newspapers for business and other news. Thousands of daily, weekly, national, and college papers as well as magazines are linked at NewsLink. If you are exploring a service business, research other towns' papers to see if someone is currently providing such a service; phone the owners, and ask good questions. Remember, people love to talk about their "babies."
- Magazines and trade journals: Reviewing magazines keeps you up to date. The ads tell you what is hot and where the money is flowing and many articles look toward the future. For the broadest in world coverage, consider reading *The Economist* and the *Wall Street Journal*.
- Banks: Banks make money by loaning money. Large corporate banks have staffs of economists, marketing experts, and others who research and write forecasts and reports on economic trends. Check online for these reports.
- Brokerage firms: These service-oriented companies have staff analysts who survey specific industries. The analysts gather earnings statistics, attend corporate and stockholder meetings, read annual reports, and publish reports about individual companies and industry overviews. These reports, which predict the direction an industry is taking, are available to clients of the firms and are sometimes available at libraries. Contact the report authors for further information and insight as often they are written with a rosy outlook but upon digging you may discover otherwise. If you are lucky, an expert may point you in the direction of a new opportunity.
- Planning offices: Cities and counties employ planners to chart and plan future growth. Check city and county offices' listings to access these offices. For the best service, you will need to visit the office, make friends with the staff, and

be pleasant and patient. If you are planning a retail establishment or a manufacturing facility, these visits are essential. You also may need to attend city council meetings, or at least read all of the meeting minutes to be aware of upcoming changes and long-range planning.

- Reports from colleges and universities: State universities publish annual and semiannual reports on economic conditions in the states where they are established. Private institutions of higher learning with special interests also publish research reports. Cutting-edge leaders in their fields conduct a vast amount of technical research at universities throughout the world. Also, search directly on the Internet for experts in your field and e-mail them with questions.
- Real estate firms: Large commercial and industrial real estate firms have access to developers' site research. The more specific your request, the easier it will be for these firms to help you. Familiarize yourself with the dynamics of the area. Which firms are going into business? Which firms are relocating? Where is expansion occurring? Making friends with an industry insider will help you gain access to this information.
- SBA: The Small Business Administration site provides excellent access to thousands of resources, including franchising, financing, start-up costs, and federal and state programs.
- Chambers of Commerce: Check your local Chamber for research and contacts.
- Bureau of Labor Statistics: Economic and employment statistics can be obtained in hard copy or downloaded.
- Websites: To locate industry information on the Internet, begin searching under your selected industry and follow the never-ending thread. Delve into competitors', suppliers', and potential customers' websites for information. Chapter 5 covers researching competitors.
- Standard & Poor's Industry Surveys may be accessed online at their website: This site provides an overall review of 50 North American industry and 10 global industry groups.
- Company directories: Hoover's, Dun & Bradstreet, and ThomasNet to locate competitors, sources, and customers.
- Information databases and sources: ABI/INFORM, Standard & Poor's NetAdvantage, Wall Street Journal Index, Small Business Sourcebook—all are excellent starting points.
- Private Database Vendors: Gfk MRI, Easy Analytic Software (EASI), and Claritas are a few, but there are many more.
- Online communities and message boards: Keep abreast of all those who are working in the industry through blogs, online newsletters, YouTube, Facebook, Twitter, RSS feeds, Quora, LinkedIn, and the ever present and helpful Google. Many of these sites and others will allow you to post queries and ideas and will respond with answers and feedback.
- Other: Research on Main Street and Stanford's Steve Blank's websites are two of the best sites to find additional up to date sources.

You never know what you will encounter while searching for information. Today, when you come upon an article it is easy to track down the writers and individuals highlighted within. Also, track down university researchers conducting cutting edge research and development in your industry through websites and journal articles. *Never* be afraid to reach out and don't forget a phone call or personal visit may help you far more. Sometimes, we forget the importance of one-on-one personal/professional relationships.

Virtual Communities

Locate an online community such as *http://www.foodonline.com*, a site providing a virtual vertical community and marketplace for professionals and vendors in the food equipment and ingredients industries. This website saves time in

Virtual community Online group of firms engaged in similar industry

locating products, supplier, and regulations, and it provides online chat rooms in which to locate additional information.

Locate your virtual community for access to thousands of experienced people, who can answer your questions. You do not have to recreate the wheel. As many others out there have been conducting business for years, so listen to their experiences and gain from their wisdom.

Foodonline.com also sends individual weekly and biweekly targeted newsletters for the beverage, dairy, food ingredients, and packaging industries, among others. These newsletters provide an easy way to keep up to date on the industry, new products, and your competitors.

Janet Shore, a successful entrepreneur, had only three days to complete a retail store proposal requiring only California food and gift products. After awarding Janet the contract, the mall owner inquired how she was able to pull the proposal together in three days. She enthusiastically replied, "Hard work, diligence, experience, and information!" Finding information so readily allows one to jump on opportunities.

Complete Action Step 19. Note: *If you are developing a product or service and need patent, copyright, or trademark information, read Chapter 10 before going further.*

ACTION STEP 19

Net Research Assignment

Action Step 19 asks you to complete several industry-specific research assignments. This Action Step will take you many hours to complete if done correctly and thoroughly.

1. Research at least three associations in your industry.
   a. What services do they offer? What classes and publications do they offer?
   b. What research can they provide?
   c. What is the cost to join? Where are their local meetings? When will you attend one?
2. Use *http://www.tsnn.com* to locate and research trade shows for your selected industry. Can you attend any of these? If so, when and where? And at what cost?
3. Using *http://www.newslink.org*, find publications where you can research your industry and customers. If you have a technical product, you will need to research it through specific databases found in the library and online.
4. Try to read at least four or five industry journals. This will be time well spent. If they are not readily available, locate someone in your desired line of business and ask if they will loan you copies.
5. Go to *http://www.census.gov* and begin to explore applicable census data. Future chapters will cover this in more depth.
6. Using Standard and Poor's, Hoover's, or Dun and Bradstreet, profile several of your competitors.
7. Locate virtual communities for your industry.

■ PRIMARY RESEARCH ON YOUR SELECTED INDUSTRY

After spending days, weeks, or months researching your favorite industry, whittle down the opportunities to two or three by using the Opportunity Selection Funnel (Figure 3.1) and the Action Steps throughout this chapter to help you.

Now get off the Internet and get out of the library! It is time to step out and talk directly with people involved in the industry: salespeople, developers, manufacturers, competitors, suppliers, and customers. By now you have developed a strong knowledge base and a million questions. Ask away, and take notes. Set your ego on the shelf. *Listen* to everything people say. Remember, your goal is to provide a service or product that your *market* needs and wants, not a product you want to give them.

Two southern California business partners were offered the opportunity to open a retail store in a great location. As they searched for a concept that would work in the location, they discovered that a children's clothing and toy store could be profitable.

The future owners then walked the streets and visited mall stores throughout their region discovering potential suppliers, pricing, product lines, and spending hours talking with children's clothing storeowners and customers. To their amazement, they found many customers willing and able to spend $75 to $100 on children's toys and untold amounts on children's clothing. Neither of the owners would be willing to spend this amount of money themselves for children's products, but they were not opening the store for themselves; they were opening it for their potential customers, who had high incomes and found the price points acceptable. By researching the market, they were able to make a decision based on facts, as opposed to their own instincts regarding consumer purchases.

Primary research can be conducted via telephone, online surveys such as Survey Monkey and Gutcheck, email, and face-to-face interviews as discussed in Chapter 2. Select research methods based on your needs, time, and available money. When conducting personal interviews, listen carefully and read between the lines. Ask intelligent follow-up questions. Keep asking *why*. One researcher suggests you ask "why" five times in an attempt to probe the psyche of your interviewee.

It is time to start sharing your business ideas with others, though it may be scary to do so. Action Step 20 will help you define your opportunity further. Many entrepreneurs are afraid to share their ideas for fear someone will steal them. It can happen. But if you do not share your idea, how can you turn it into a business? At some point, you must trust and go forth.

Online you may find a sample confidentiality agreement to use, which may make you feel more comfortable. Although, your lawyer should review any document you use.

■ INDUSTRY SEGMENTATION AND GAP ANALYSIS

Industry segmentation breaks down potential markets into as many "digestible" segments as possible, just as is done with NAICS codes. The more you learn about an industry, the better you will be at isolating opportunity gaps and seeing combinations of gaps that may constitute markets. Susan Johnson below explores the food industry to discover opportunities. This is the kind of thinking we want you to do in Action Step 21, another brainstorming and mind mapping activity. Have fun!

Susan's Healthy Gourmet

Susan Johnson, founder of Susan's Healthy Gourmet, searched for gaps and opportunities by taking a look at a major, far-reaching trend—the meal replacement market. People want fresh, high-quality food, but they do not want to cook. The "time bind" fueled this market change.

Frozen dinners have been available since 1953, but these cannot be compared to the freshly prepared, nutritionally balanced meals from Susan's Healthy Gourmet. These include shrimp pad Thai, mushroom ravioli, and salmon with artichoke and caper relish.

After coming home to face cooking one time too many, Susan realized that there had to be many other busy individuals hoping for a hot, wonderful healthy gourmet meal as they opened their front doors. With unemployment at less than 5 percent when she began her company, there were many others with the same need and available cash.

In researching her selected industry, Susan recognized that no one was producing fresh, made-from-scratch, calorie-controlled gourmet meals that met the guidelines of the American Heart Association, the American Cancer Society, and the American Dietetic Association. Others merely produced frozen meals, diet replacement drinks, take-out food, and so on.

Quality meals that were convenient and nutritionally balanced represented a gap Susan knew she could fill. With currently over 20 employees and a varied menu of 1 to 21 meals per week, Healthy Gourmet delivers to the home or to pick-up points twice a week. She has definitely developed a product and service that meets her customers' needs, as she has survived since 1996 and has recently been named the 2011 Family Business by the Orange County Business Journal amongst the many accolades her firm has received. She now has two other food businesses as well.

Susan's Healthy Gourmet is located in the heart of a growing, high-tech community whose demographics include young, highly educated, physically fit, and health conscious individuals and families.(Chapter 4 delves deeper into Susan's target market). Requests for diet fare led Susan to also include lower calorie options for breakfast, lunch, and dinner.

As she continues to meet the needs of the changing marketplace, she now offers a full vegetarian menu as well as kids' meals. Her latest additions include senior and diabetic meal packages.

Sixteen years after opening her doors, Susan is grossing more than she ever dreamed, serving over 250,000 meals a year throughout Los Angeles, San Diego, Orange County, and Riverside.

In business, one needs to segment markets and then differentiate products or services to meet the target market's needs. By requiring no minimum orders, Susan enabled busy people to access her products on their own terms without preset requirements.

ACTION STEP 20

Brainstorming Solutions

Time for creativity to come to the forefront! Brainstorm solutions with everyone you meet. If your business idea is fairly well developed, you should now be presenting it to people and asking them to brainstorm with you. If not, you should be working on developing an idea that meets people's needs—one they are willing to pay for.

You will generate better ideas and solutions now that you have completed your primary and secondary research. Have fun at this stage as you continue to explore your ideas. Write down everyone's input. You may want to record their responses. After brainstorming ideas, ask yourself the following questions:

1. Which niches can you own?
2. Which niches might be the most profitable?
3. Which niches will be easiest to reach?
4. What can you do to be unique?
5. How much are people willing to pay for your product/service?

Return to the Opportunity Selection Funnel (Figure 3.1). What additional filters could you add for your specific situation? Which potentially profitable ideas are filtering through?

Confidentiality agreement Deal between two or more parties not to disclose information

ACTION STEP 21

Mind Mapping Your Business

Narrow the Gaps; Watch Your Idea Emerge

Consider all the secondary and primary information you have gathered. Take out paper and pencil and start a few mind maps for several of the industries/ideas you have researched. Sketch out your mind maps focusing on specific opportunities. You need to stay with each segment until you know whether or not it will work for you.

Ideas will come together as you place opportunities next to each other. Through this exercise, you will be able to identify the most promising gaps in your selected industry.

Follow Susan's example and find and exploit gaps and develop products and services that fulfill the needs of the marketplace. Listen closely to your customers. They will lead you in the right direction.

Wrap your product around your target market through pricing, product development, marketing, advertising, and location. Many times, opportunities arise as new target markets can be served through technology, lower pricing, or the product can be offered in combination with another product or service.

When you write your Business Plan, explain why you have selected a particular industry segment, or gap and support your decision with hard data from your secondary and primary research. If you have chosen a promising segment and have communicated your excitement about it, you will have developed a "hook" for the banker, investor, or venture capitalist who will read your plan.

More Brainstorming for Possible Solutions

Brainstorming is a process used by many groups—think tanks, middle management, small businesses, and major corporations—to generate fresh ideas. The goal is to come up with many ideas, some that may seem far out or even erroneous, and then to see how concepts develop as momentum grows. The key to brainstorming is to reserve judgment initially so that creativity is not stifled.

What follows is a recap of a brainstorming session held by the founders of the Entrepreneurs' Computer Specialists when they began to transform problems into business opportunities. As you read, consider not only the information gathered but also the process involved.

Gamers' Dream

Three friends listed ideas for businesses that had come to them during the earlier steps of an opportunity selection process. One wanted to start a company to design computer game apps. Another, a graphic designer with game design experience, said he could certainly help with the artwork. Another wanted to design computer systems for entrepreneurs.

On a flipchart, Derek wrote "Design Computer Games apps."

"Here's another," Robert said. "Let's take over Apple!"

Phil yelled out, "Pre-Teens and video games!"

For a half-hour they transferred their ideas—game design, apps, retailing, end-user training, hardware and software system designs, computer repair, and consulting—onto the flip chart.

"Time for a break," Derek said.

When they came back from their break, Phil flipped to a clean sheet on the chart and proceeded to draw a mind map. As they developed the mind map, five areas emerged: entrepreneurial software design, game design and apps, gamers' paradise, retailing, and consulting.

Further refinements of the mind map brought gamers' paradise and game design into the foreground. All three men grew up playing video games and still were big fans and gamers. They also had many friends and nieces and nephews who were into gaming.

Excitement built up in the room as the ideas flowed, and soon all three friends were standing at the flip chart, adding their ideas and amendments to the mind map. As the brainstorming session wound down, they had identified two main areas to explore: game design and gamers' paradise.

The first area was game design. They could do this in their individual homes but felt if they were all together working, it would be more beneficial. Discussions led to developing games for the growing pre-teen, teen, and adult markets.

The second area was gamers' paradise, a place where people could come and work on the latest computers with the latest games, where the players could have parties or rent out the facility for their groups of friends.

Robert, who knew there were many parents concerned about gaming, thought maybe a safe place for pre-teens and teens could be offered for after-school and weekend gaming. They could charge an hourly fee or even sell memberships.

Phil said, "I want to design games, so being around my Target Customers would be great, and we could have testers in the other room if we set up a design studio in the back room of a facility."

There was a silence.

"So," Phil said, "We've got several options that look pretty good. How do we decide?"

"How about a matrix?" Derek suggested.

"A what?"

"It's a way of weighing what you really want. I learned about it from one of my inventor buddies. He called it an Opportunity Matrix."

"Let's try it," they said.

After you complete your brainstorming exercises as Derek and his team did, summarize your session so that you can identify the most useful ideas. Let us summarize what happened in their session:

1. Using the mind mapping device, the team identified problems and possible solutions.
2. They decided all ideas were good ideas.
3. The two ideas that looked best were gamers' paradise and designing game apps.
4. They asked whether they could do both at once, or if one would have to go on the back burner.

Matrix Analysis

Whereas some people like to use lists, mind maps, or opportunity funnels for arriving at conclusions, others prefer a more systematic numeric method. A matrix grid can provide a desired structure to serve as another type of filter. After you have brainstormed some possible solutions, you need to improve your focus on those solutions and evaluate them. The matrix grid in Figure 3.4 helped the gamers focus their energies and talents.

Matrix grid Measurement tool with which ideas are screened and evaluated in order to find solutions

figure **3.4**

Opportunity Matrix Grid for Future Gamers' Paradise

Ideas

Desires: Psychic rewards, Use team effectively, Profitable, Growth industry, Creativity, Capitalize on technology, Fun, adventure, excitement, TOTALS

Ideas: Design game and apps, Design computer systems, Retailing, Consulting, Software design, Computer repair

© Cengage Learning 2014

ACTION STEP 22

Develop Opportunity Matrix

Mesh Possible Solutions with Objectives

A matrix analysis helps you focus, especially if you are working with a group and have diverse objectives to satisfy. If you prepare a large grid and put it on the wall, all members of the team can participate.

1. Down the left side, list business goals brainstormed earlier. (Each person's will vary.)
2. Along the top, list the business opportunities you have discovered.
3. Select a rating system to use for evaluating the match of each possible solution with each objective. It could be a 10-point scale or a plus zero-minus system.

Plus (+) = 3
Zero (0) = 2
Minus (−) = 1

4. When you have rated all the combinations, find the total for each column. The totals will indicate your best prospects. The rest is up to you.

At their next meeting, the gamers rated each possible solution on the objectives, which they had designated earlier. On review, gamers' paradise and game design received the highest total of points from the group. The key people saw these as areas in which their teamwork skills within a fast-growing industry could be used best. In addition, the cost to develop a gamers' paradise was feasible, because Derek's family owned an empty office building with high street visibility and the rent would be very low.

There was no direct competition within 30 miles, and the team's enthusiasm and excitement about their idea ran high. In addition, one member suggested that as soon as they developed the gamers' paradise, it would not be long before they could begin to design games and apps as well.

In developing their business, they decided to:

Psychological cushion A unique, untouchable rung on the ladder in your Target Customer's mind

- **Build a psychological cushion:** *The founders would start a gamers' club. Anyone who joined for 6 to 12 months would have full access to a gaming computer and could reserve their time online. Discounts on facility rental would also be included, along with an opening game-day party invitation for members only when new games were released.*
- **Charge reasonable fees:** *Since the major market would be teens and pre-teens, charges would need to be reasonable and competitive with options such as movies.*
- **Stress fun in a safe environment:** *If gamers are having fun, they will play for hours and hours. With any luck, they will spread the word to all their fellow gamers via social media.*

Taking Stock

What have you learned about opportunity selection? Before you answer this, take a minute to rethink what you want to achieve with your business. If you feel a little uneasy about how fast you have run the last couple of laps, perhaps it is because you have not identified your industry or the right opportunity for you. If it does not feel like home, you should sense it now.

Have you used the Opportunity Selection Funnel from Figure 3.1? Have you whittled down the list from hundreds of trends to industry segments to the one opportunity that emerged through all your research? Does it feel like home? If so, you are ready to define your new business. If not, keep looking!

■ DESIGN THINKING

If you still do not have a strong business idea or are still searching for a problem to solve, visit OpenIDEO, an open innovation platform searching for solutions to some of the largest problems facing society. The open platform is currently addressing improving maternal health with mobile technology, affordable and safe e-waste disposal, increasing bone marrow donors, improving health in low income areas, and encouraging fresh food choices. Within these and many of the other problems they are researching, you may find an idea for a profit making business, a social entrepreneurship endeavor, or a hybrid venture such as G3Box (see Global Village).

OpenIDEO is sponsored by IDEO, one of the leading global design firms, "integrating the needs of people, the possibilities of technology, and the requirements for business success." As you read through IDEO's design thinking philosophy below, ask yourself, "How I can apply design thinking to my venture or use this thinking to come up with a new venture?"

IDEO's goal is to "deliver appropriate, actionable, and tangible strategies" while looking at desirability, viability, and feasibility. At the intersection of those three variables, one reaches innovative ideas (see Figure 3.5). Can you find innovative solutions to one of the many problems facing individuals, communities, and our world? If so, you may have a very successful venture in front of you. As one wise soul advises, "Find where your great joy meets the world's needs."

─────── figure **3.5**

Ideo Design Thinking

Design thinking is a deeply human process that taps into abilities we all have but get over-looked by more conventional problem-solving practices. It relies on our ability to be intuitive, to recognize patterns, to construct ideas that are emotionally meaningful as well as functional, and to express ourselves through means beyond words or symbols. Nobody wants to run an organization on feeling, intuition, and inspiration, but an over-reliance on the rational and the analytical can be just as risky. Design thinking provides an integrated third way.

The design thinking process is best thought of as a system of overlapping spaces rather than a sequence of orderly steps. There are three spaces to keep in mind: *inspiration*, *ideation*, and *implementation*. Inspiration is the problem or opportunity that motivates the search for solutions. Ideation is the process of generating, developing, and testing ideas. Implementation is the path that leads from the project stage into people's lives.

Under this system, IDEO uses both analytical tools and generative techniques to help clients see how their new or existing operations could look in the future—and build road maps for getting there. Our methods include business model prototyping, data visualization, innovation strategy, organizational design, qualitative and quantitative research, and IP liberation.

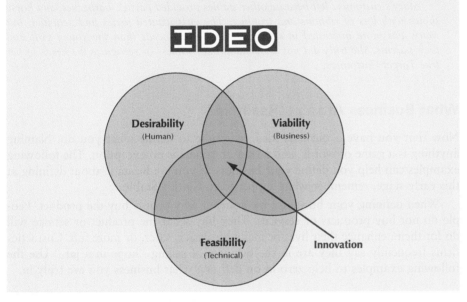

Source: Courtesy of IDEO, 2012. From *www.ideo.com/about/* (Accessed June 25, 2012).

■ DEFINE YOUR BUSINESS

Watch a carpenter framing a new house. He works close to the wood, nailing with quick strokes of his hammer. However, to get a view of the total house—the structure that will become someone's home—he must walk across the street. He has to step back from his detailed work to see the shape of the entire home. What business is the carpenter in? Is he in the nail-driving business, the framing business, or the home-building business? Or is he in the business of satisfying the age-old dream of home ownership?

Only by stepping back can you answer the very important question: What business am I in? You can move forward, once you know who your customers are and what internal and external needs your product or service is satisfying, Mary Clark's stable experience illustrates the importance of understanding exactly what business you are really in.

Clark's Stables

Mary Clark, a 30-year-old software engineer, had always been more interested in riding her prize-winning quarter horses than in programming. When her grandmother *died and left her $500,000, Mary made a down payment on a boarding stable and left the corporate world forever—or so she thought.*

The boarding stable was run down. It had stalls for 50 horses, but only 25 stalls were occupied. Mary did everything she could think of to make the place better for the horses. She spent $200,000 rebuilding, painting, and grading, which made Clark's Stables a very attractive place. She bought the highest quality feed and gave the horses the best care money could buy.

When owners began to move their horses to other stables after nine months, Mary could not understand why. She had not increased her fees, and she treated the horses like friends. After 12 months, only 6 paying customers remained. After 15 months, Mary was behind on her mortgage payments. In her 18th month, Mary sold the stable at a great loss. Luckily, she was able to return to her old programming job.

Mary had made the simple mistake of thinking horses were her customers. Her real Target Customers were young girls between the ages of 7 and 14 and their parents. Mary thought she was in the business of stabling horses. Actually, she should have seen that she was in the business of providing girls a fun, social activity, and offering parents a safe after-school activity for their daughters. The girls wanted fun, friends, training, and social events—and more importantly, to feel special.

Mary's customers left because other stables provided parties, barbecues, and horse shows with lots of ribbons and trophies. The girls wanted prizes and activities, but Mary was more interested in satisfying her horses' needs than the young girls and their parents. She truly did not understand her business or recognize the needs of her true Target Customers.

What Business Are You Really In?

Now that you have a business idea, it is time to define what you do. Naming anything is a game of words, and a small business is no exception. The following examples can help you define your business. If you are hesitant about defining at this early stage, remember what happened to Clark's Stable.

When defining your business, ask yourself why people buy the product. People do not buy products or services. They buy what the product or service will do for them: enhance their lives or make life easier, safer, or more fun. Cosmetics firms frequently say they are in the business of selling "hope in a jar." Use the following examples to help zero in on defining what business you are truly in.

If You Are a	Try Saying
Personal financial planner	"I'm in the peace-of-mind business."
Small-business teacher	"I'm in the dream-to-reality business."
Cosmetic plastic surgeon	"I'm in the do not-grow-old business."
Porsche dealer	"I'm in the ego-gratification business."
Gourmet cookware store	"I help people be Wolfgang Puck."
Personal trainer	"I keep people feeling young, fit, and sexy."
Coffeehouse owner	"I provide a place to relax and people watch."

Business definition A clear picture of the enterprise

Your business definition should be a work in progress as you further explore your target market and competition. Four of our favorite business definitions or mission statements follow:

Fast Company: "*Fast Company* is where best practice meets big ideas; new talent meets innovative tools; the emerging business community meets the emerging conversation about the future of business."

Deux Amis Needlepoint: "We believe there is nothing so beautiful as an exquisitely painted canvas or the enjoyment, satisfaction, and relaxation derived from fine handwork and stitching a lovely design with beautiful threads on fine canvas."

Chicken Soup: "We're selling stories that encircle the heart and penetrate the soul and cuddle up to make you feel better."

Travel + Leisure: "Travel + Leisure is the source for people who make travel their quest in life. Our authentic stories motivate readers, making us the catalyst for what is next and setting trends. Being the authority, we get there first."

Freestone Inn: "Splendid isolation" in Mazama, WA.

Sleeping Lady: "A stay inspired by nature" in Leavenworth, WA.

■ BEGIN TO DEVELOP YOUR ELEVATOR PITCH

Along with defining what business you are in you will also need to develop an elevator pitch, a brief 60-90 speech designed to hook your listener into responding, "Tell me more."

Elevator pitch Clear, concise description of your business idea

Most of the time the discussion on the elevator pitch comes at the end of a book or only in regards to raising money for a venture. But, we are asking you to look at it differently, by first defining your business in a few sentences and then flushing it out with enticing details to become your elevator pitch.

One of the most active venture capital organizations in the US, The Tech Coast Angels, sponsors a yearly "Fast Pitch" competition. Hundreds of applicants apply for one of 12 spots to present their fast pitch. Each entrepreneur receives private coaching and practice sessions for one month before the competition. 2012's winning pitch from Marty Metro Founder and CEO of Usedcardboardboxes.com follows: "Do you realize there is a 40 billion dollar industry right here in the United States that consists of cutting down trees to make cardboard boxes? And the real travesty is, most of those boxes are used once, then maybe recycled, but usually just thrown away. I run usedcardboardboxes.com.

We buy quality used boxes by the truckload from big companies like Kraft Foods and Proctor and Gamble. We then turn around and take those boxes to some of the other companies and consumers as an earth-friendly, low cost alternative to buying new. We're able to buy our boxes for just over the recycling rate, which is very low right now, and able to sell our boxes for the lowest price on the Internet, guaranteed.

We got our start back in 2006 when we were selling earth-friendly consumer moving kits around Los Angeles. In 2007, we did $600,000 in revenue. In 2008, we did $1.1 million. Today, usedcardboardboxes.com is the number one organic hit on Google, Yahoo, and MSN for the terms "used boxes." Last month, Walmart contacted us wanting to buy 100,000 boxes every two weeks for just one of their 117 distribution centers.

We're raising capital. We've already raised $500,000; we're raising another $250,000 in order to complete our business to business portal that allows us to connect our national supply, like Kraft Foods, with our national demand, like Walmart."

Source: *YouTube.com/watch?v=H_Yc412A1Fs*, (Accessed September 11, 2012).

At this point, your pitch will unlikely resemble as well-crafted and professionally developed pitch as Marty's. But as you continue to build your Business Plan, keep in mind that you should be working toward crafting as strong and focused pitch. You will want to impress not only future customers, but suppliers and—most important—potential investors with your pitch. If you stay focused, anytime anyone asks you what you do, you will have an instant well-formed answer (starting with either your business definition or the full fledged pitch).

Your pitch should be delivered in 75-90 seconds. Write and continually refine it as you develop your business idea. According to the late Louis Villalobos,

ACTION STEP 23

Define Your Business and Begin to Develop Your Pitch

1. Brainstorm what business you are really in. Let your mind play at this, and sum it up in one to three sentence. Remember your customers' comments when you were probing their psyches. Think benefits!

2. Next, think of yourself riding up 50 floors in an express elevator. You have 60–90 seconds to explain to a stranger what your business is about. What will you say? Can you dazzle him or her, so they will ask for more? Include your product or service's benefits, your target market, distribution, success to date, and why customers will buy from you. Review the information from Figure 3.6 and the examples in the text before you begin. Also, watch additional winning pitches from YouTube such as those from Shark Tank.

3. Review and refine your pitch one more time using Richard Koffler's rules:
   a. Show passion
   b. Show an understanding of the business and customers
   c. Offer industry perspective
   d. Add "magic dust"
   e. Tell who you are why you the need money

founder and director of the Tech Coast Angels, "To craft an effective pitch, identify your venture's key points and organize them into an effective story, edit to eliminate fluff, make each word serve a purpose, and then practice your delivery." Villalobos shared additional insight in Figure 3.6.

According to Richard Koffler, also a Tech Coast Angel, your pitch should "1) show passion, 2) show an understanding of the business and its customers, 3) offer industry perspective, 4) add 'magic dust,' and 5) tell who you are and why you need the money."

Complete Action Step 23 by revisiting the Opportunity Selections Funnel, narrowing your focus, and developing your business definition with a first draft of your pitch.

Being in business today is all about satisfying needs and providing benefits. You find a need, you satisfy it, and then you translate the results into a benefit for your customer. Create and develop your market niche or segment by changing your product or service as dictated by the customer. Marketing today emphasizes networking, creativity, associations, and partnerships; it requires:

1. Integrating customers' needs and desires and your strategies into the development of the product. Market needs drive the product or service.
2. Focusing your knowledge and experience on a specific and targeted customer segment or niche.
3. Creating customer, supplier, and even competitor relationships that will sustain and grow your customer base. Cooperation is the key.

Marketing encompasses everything a business does to move products and services from the manufacturer or provider to the customer so that the consumer is satisfied and the seller has met his or her objectives. Before moving further it is time to reassess your business idea with a feasibility analysis.

■ FEASIBILITY ANALYSIS

Before you invest time, money, passion, and energy into completing a full-scale Business Plan, it is time to reassess your idea and complete a short and honest feasibility analysis.

1. Review the environmental variables (technology, competition, social/cultural, legal/political and economic). How will each affect your business? What do you know? What don't you know?
2. Check your idea out with potential customers. Does it fly? If not, did they possibly give you a suggestion for what they would buy? What will they pay? Will they buy from you? How can you make customers "raving fans" so they will spread the word and grow your business? Did you have the courage to really listen? What value have you created for the customer? What makes your business unique? Does your product or service have a story you can capitalize on? What heart strings or purse strings are you able to pull on?
3. Review competitors honestly. (Chapter 5) Do not ignore their strengths. Step back and look at all the strengths, weaknesses, threats and opportunities in the marketplace you have uncovered. Which of these strengths and opportunities can you capitalize on? What, if anything, can you do to improve the areas of weakness? Are you prepared to handle the threats from competition and technology?
4. Does your business idea have "legs"? (will it last over time)
5. Have you tested the market to discover your Target Customer? Have you tested the product? Have you revised to meet needs and wants? (Read up

—figure **3.6**

Elevating Your Pitch

Nothing may have more impact on your chances of getting funded by angels or VCs than a great "elevator pitch"—the ability to capture an investor's interest quickly. Depending on the situation and context, "quickly" may be a few seconds, a minute, or a simple paragraph of text. Angels fund fewer than 5% of ventures that approach them; VC funds are even more selective, funding between 1-in-100 and 1-in-300. If you fail to ignite their interest immediately, investors will often tune out the rest of your presentation or relegate your plan to the "later" pile, which never gets read. Consider the following when crafting your elevator pitch.

1. **Grab them or lose them:** You may have a dynamite team, unassailable market niche, revolutionary product, disruptive technology. But investors may never hear of them. You must lead with the 4–6 points that differentiate your venture and that make it an attractive investment. The elevator pitch should be the first content slide in your PowerPoint, and the lead paragraph in your exec summary.

2. **Authors of best-selling novels understand:** Of the year or more that authors of best-sellers take to write one, about 10% of that time is spent on the first sentence, and another 10% on the balance of the first paragraph. Why? Because people go to the best-seller rack, take down a book, read the first sentence, and if that grabs them, read the rest of the paragraph, and if that grabs them they usually buy; but if either fails to engage them, they turn to the next book. Investors are like that.

3. **Say it in English for laypeople:** Unless your audience can explain your venture to someone else, you have lost them. Do you think investors ever tell their associates or spouses: "I saw this great venture today, but can't explain what they do"—they don't.

4. **Exclude fluff and hype:** Replace all superlatives ("unique," "revolutionary," "best," "fastest," etc.) with specifics; e.g. "priced 40% below market leader" is informative, whereas "lowest cost" says little. This is how Michael Moritz of Sequoia Capital puts it: "Factors like market size and intellectual property clearly play into our decisions, but there are no absolutes in the world of venture capital. The only thing that leaves me cold during a pitch from a startup is the use of the drop-dead words or phrases: 'synergy,' 'no-brainer,' and 'slam dunk.'"

5. **Relevance:** Avoid the unimportant (e.g., founded in May, offices in Los Angeles, Delaware C-Corporation). Make sure it's not only unique but relevant; that the names of all six founders start with 'J' may be unique, but it is hardly relevant.

6. **There is no pat answer:** Often I am asked what should be included in the elevator pitch, as if there were a standard set of points. Focus on what differentiates your venture and makes it an attractive investment. Below is a list of just a few of the items to consider:

Results (actual)	Team	Barriers to Entry and Niche to Dominate
• Cash flow	Spin-out from leader	Blocking patent
• Profit	Track record	Picket fence patents
• Revenues	Domain expertise	Exclusive agreements
• Sales	Tech wizard	Key customer(s)
• Bookings	Marketing guru	Vanity 800 number
• Key contacts	Sales star	Lead time
• Customers	Board	Regulatory permits
• Beta site(s)	Advisors	Trade secrets
• Proven concept	Degrees	

Source: Reprinted from "Suggestions and 6 Years of Winning Pitches" © 2007 Luis Villalobos, Founder and Board of Governors—Tech Coast Angels, with the permission of Luis Villalobos.

on testing your minimum viable product with blogger Eric Ries or read *The Startup Owner's Manual*.)

6. Have you reviewed sales and costs numbers? Roughly if you know your costs for a product are $10 each and your customers say they are only willing to pay $12.50. You need to reassess. Make sure the math works before proceeding.

7. Complete a fast-start Business Plan in Appendix A to begin to flesh out your ideas and see if they are feasible on paper, If not, regroup and see if you can

make changes that will increase the feasibility. If you can't, then maybe you need to move onto another idea. If your idea is financial feasible and fits with your ideals, move forward. If little money is needed to start, step out now and test your product in the marketplace and feel the success and build your business!

Bottom line (fill in the blanks): I sell (product/service) _____ with the benefit of (benefits) _____ to (Target Customer) _____ who I reach by (marketing medium) _____ and sell through (channels of distribution) _____ for (price) _____.

■ SUMMARY

You have located the industry that interests you, found a problem, provided a solution and conducted primary and secondary research. You have applied the life cycle to learn what stage the industry and products are in and have fore-casted how long it may take to make your business go. You have defined your business and gained a head start on your elevator pitch.

Looking back on the Opportunity Selection Funnel in Figure 3.1, review one more time your business and personal objectives to determine if the viable business ideas you have developed through your research fit as well as you need them to.

If you found your current skills and knowledge do not exactly guarantee success, you are sure of at least three things: you know where to acquire the skills and knowledge you need, you know how long it will take, and you are exploring the marketplace in every way you can.

You have brainstormed your business objectives and reviewed the interlocking concepts—life cycle, competition, and industry breakthrough and thus, your business idea is beginning to take shape.

According to Thomas Davenport, professor of information technology and management at Babson College, "All big ideas share at least one of three business objectives: improved efficiency, greater effectiveness, or innovations in products or processes. In a way, it's an exhaustive set of possibilities. You do things right, you do the right thing, or you do something new. Nobody wants to hear about a 'me too' business. Stress your differentiation and translate features into market-hungry benefits. It is important to prove you have an edge over the competition."

Be prepared for a chaotic and uncertain business environment. Learn to roll with the punches, expect rapidly changing markets and distribution channels, and be ready to explore and exploit new social media at all times. As an entrepreneur you will always be challenged and your life as an entrepreneur will never be dull. You will be defining and redefining your product and service constantly and your Business Plan will continue to evolve. Your survival depends on how you respond to opportunities.

■ THINK POINTS FOR SUCCESS

- Build your business around your likes, strengths, and passions while connecting with customers.
- Direct the power of your mind toward a particular industry segment through opportunity selection.
- Spend time early on learning about the industry, its major players, and its trends.

- Use all secondary data available so that when you move out to conduct primary data research, you will be in a position of knowledge and strength.
- Find a gap and take advantage of it. This is much easier and brings more success than being a "me too" competitor. If someone else owns the niche, find

another—unless you are willing to hold on and fight the competition with your deep pockets.

- Recognize that not all opportunities are equal.
- Acknowledge that not all opportunities can be profitable.
- Do not fall in love with a product or a market.
- Know that there has to be a compelling reason for the customer to change.
- Dare to be different in your approach.
- Define your business. Dazzle in 150 words or less. Make them beg for more.
- Complete a quick financial feasibility analysis to check to see if your idea has legs.
- Research! Research! Research! And never stop!

■ KEY POINTS FROM ANOTHER VIEW

The ABCs of Entrepreneurship

Article by: Harvey Mackay

I was recently asked by master marketer Jay Abraham to be on his radio program, "The Ultimate Entrepreneur" along with several others, including Stephen Covey and Mark Cuban. In that company, I knew I had my work cut out for me!

Let's start with the basics. What better way than to create the ABCs of entrepreneurship?

A is for ability. Entrepreneurs excel at identifying problems and solving them fast. They anticipate obstacles and opportunities.

B is for business plan. A good entrepreneur makes one before doing anything else.

C is for cash. Use it wisely, even if you're rolling in it.

D is for delegate. Decide what to outsource and delegate to others.

E is for ethics. If you have integrity, nothing else matters. If you don't have integrity, nothing else matters.

F is for failure. If you can survive it to fight again, you haven't failed.

G is for giving, because givers are the biggest gainers. If you truly believe in what you're doing, give it all you've got.

H is for humor. You are going to experience tough times, and humor helps pull you through.

I is for interpersonal relationships. Those with good people skills are able to adjust and survive as their business grows.

J is for journal, as in writing down your thoughts and ideas, as well as picking the brains of experts.

K is for knowledgeable. Successful entrepreneurs constantly update themselves on their products and industries.

L is for looking forward. A successful entrepreneur looks ahead, around corners and far into the future as possible.

M is for mentor. Find a "tiger." Retired professionals are a marvelous resource.

N is for never giving up. Amend plans if needed, but keep your eye on the prize.

O is for opportunities. Whether you see a need that is unfulfilled, a product that could be improved or a problem screaming for a solution, you are seeing an opportunity.

P is for passion. When you have passion, you speak with conviction, act with authority and present with zeal.

Q is for quantify. Your goals must be measurable, so it's necessary to have a standard to hold them to. You can't keep track of progress if you don't know where you want to go.

R is for risk. Entrepreneurs must be willing to take risks.

S is for self-survey. Do you really want to do this, or are you just trying to escape your problems? If you're going to be an entrepreneur, you have to believe in yourself.

T is for target audience. For your concept to succeed, you have to identify a realistic target audience, big enough to be profitable yet small enough for you to service it thoroughly.

U is for unflappable. Beyond the "don't sweat the small stuff" mentality, you need a level head and an open mind.

V is for veracity. The truth, the whole truth and nothing but the truth is what your employees and customers deserve from you.

W is for work hard—then work harder, until you get the results you are looking for.

X is for exercise regularly. (Pardon my spelling.) If you don't take care of yourself, you can't be at your best.

Y is for years, which is how long you may have to work to get your idea off the ground.

Z is for zookeeper. When you run the place, it's up to you to keep dangerous things in their cages while bringing visitors through the gates.

Mackay's Moral: Being an entrepreneur is a lot like the ABCs: Start at the beginning, follow through to the end.

Source: Harvey Mackay, "The ABCs of Entrepreneurship," April 5, 2012, from *http://harveymackay.com/column/the-abcs-of-entrepreneurship/*, (Accessed June 24, 2012). Reprinted with permission from nationally syndicated columnist Harvey Mackay, author of the New York Times #1 bestseller "Swim With The Sharks Without Being Eaten Alive."

■ ACTION STEPS

■ KEY TERMS

Image_Source/iStockphoto.com

Profiling Your Target Customer
Research to Discover Customer Needs

CHAPTER 4

Learning Objectives

- Understand the key to survival is knowing your Target Customer and providing a product or service that has real value to them.

- Identify primary and secondary Target Customers.

- Learn how to use media kits and online data to profile Target Customers.

- Understand how specific lifestyles, demographics, life stages, and social group factors impact individuals and their decisions.

- Explore various profiling systems.

- Profile Business to Business (B2B) customers.

- Interview, observe, and survey to gain insight into your Target Customer.

- Develop your customer-profiling ability into a reflex.

- Visualize your Target Customer by preparing a Target Customer collage.

- Constantly review and update information on your Target Customer.

Chapters 4 and 5 go together. Your best strategy is to read both chapters quickly, grasping the heavy connection between your Target Customer (Chapter 4) and competition and product differentiation (Chapter 5). Plan a second read of the chapters, taking notes, doing research, and completing the Action Steps for both chapters. Your Target Customer is the lifeblood of your business—your resource base.

You provide customers a product or a service they need, and in return they support your business by purchasing your product or service—and if you're lucky, spreading the word for you. Word of mouth is a timeless marketing tool. Your excellence will be rewarded as others learn of your services.

Competition occurs when someone else—another entrepreneur or corporation—wants your resource base enough to wage war. There are many ways this could occur, such as price reductions, marketing more specifically to your Target Customers' needs, or just promising a service that would result in the loss of your Target Customer.

It could be a quality or features war: The competitor has a superior product or better service and with various promotional campaigns makes sure everyone knows it! For example, your product is less environmentally sound, so the competition brings this to the attention of the public through their online blog postings, by having some of their Target Customers post on their Facebook updates, or they could use Twitter to spread the information.

The best defense against competition is to know your Target Customer and serve them well. Chapter 4 focuses on profiling your Target Customer through secondary, primary, and "new eyes" research.

By conducting ongoing market research you will:

- Minimize the risk of doing business
- Uncover opportunities
- Identify potential problems and solutions
- Be guided to customers
- Offer customers the solutions they need to their problems

The prime concerns covered in Chapter 3 can be summed up by two questions you asked yourself: "Do I have a product or service that is in a growth segment of a growth market?" and "Are my business goals consistent with my own personal goals?" By now we hope you have a solid idea of what business opportunities are right for you, since it is now time to establish whether there *is* a market for your products or services. If there *is* a market, are buyers willing to pay for your product or service? Can you reach them cost effectively? What is a reasonable way to determine a fair market value that promotes revenue and profit for your company and also is priced well for your customers? Chapter 5 will help you explore the competitive marketplace to determine if there is room for another player as well as the challenges that may occur.

■ THE POWER OF PROFILING

Understanding your Target Customer is your key to survival in small business. Profiling draws a "magic circle" around your Target Customer. Placing the customer in the center of that circle transforms the whole arena into a target at which to aim your product or service. Nothing happens without customers; every segment of your Business Plan must begin with complete knowledge of their wants and needs.

Profiling is also the instrument used to uncover the behavior modes of your customers. Generating profiles requires a combination of geographics; demographics, or statistical analysis; and psychographics, or firsthand intuitive insight and research into lifestyles, buying habits, patterns of consumption, and attitudes.

In this chapter, we focus on specific profiling techniques and resources that will give you an awareness of how to gain insight into that elusive customer.

It is often useful to ask prospective customers what one aspect of a product or service they would change. If you talk to enough people, a pattern will emerge that reveals a gap in the marketplace. Do not hesitate to ask for an honest review of your proposed product or service and encourage recommendations for improvement.

Effective market research can help you target promising, profitable niches and avoid stagnant ones. For example, a plumber who was ready to leave his day job with a construction company asked his friends what would make them more likely to use his plumbing services. Their replies were almost universal: "Will you come during evening or weekend hours, so I won't have to stay home from work?" In response, he called himself the "Off Hours Plumber" and worked from 4:00 to 9:00 p.m., Monday through Friday and all day Saturday, without charging overtime rates. He was an immediate success, because he had profiled his customers and found a market niche with his positioning. There is an old and true saying: "There are riches in niches."

Market niche A small, focused area of a market segment

Listening to the needs of their clients, two social workers devised an ingenious plan to help their clients who were unable to visit their loved ones in prison. This particular group had limited resources, no access to cars, and no access to any public transportation that served area prisons. Visits to husbands, wives, adult children, and siblings were therefore nearly impossible. Knowing frequent contact is necessary for future rehabilitation of the prisoners as well as keeping families together, they sought a solution.

Upon locating a used 15-passenger van, the social workers began Family Express: offering weekend roundtrips to one prison for $25 a passenger. Not only were they providing a service, they were also creating a community for their riders.

Developing long-term relationships and community beyond the product or service is essential in today's competitive marketplace. Customer loyalty and retention are the goals for firms practicing customer relationship marketing (CRM).

Customer relationship marketing The development of long-term, mutually beneficial, and cost-effective relationships with your clients.

With more than 2 million people in the U.S. prison and jail system today, the opportunity to serve the family needs of those incarcerated is unlimited. What other needs do you envision? How can you meet them?

One key question for any business idea is this: What is the "real" cost of providing the service or product? Your customer must be willing and able to pay the price you have determined is necessary for long-term success. We have suggested to you throughout these first four chapters to constantly do a "quick and dirty" back-of-the-envelope run on the numbers to check your concept as you develop your ideas. There are lots of great ideas—not all are profitable.

At times you may find that you are in a situation that prohibits adequate payment to cover basic costs. Often, an individual will decide to address the problem by developing a nonprofit organization.

Of the 600,000 prisoners released each year in the United States, the recidivism rate stands at 66 percent. Out of need and with determination and ingenuity, the entrepreneurial nonprofit organization Prison Entrepreneurship Program (PEP) has arisen. PEP, headquartered in Texas, provides entrepreneurship training to inmates and provides subsequent services as they transition back into the community. This unique program has reduced recidivism of their clients to only 5 percent. Additionally, 100 percent of their clients are employed within 90 days!

There are many market niches that have been ignored for far too long, many with simple needs that can be fulfilled by an entrepreneurial spirit. One of these many special niches could be the beginning of your success. Your goal is to determine a market niche and use data to build a profile of potential customers within a market segment.

Eileen Parker, highlighted below, chose to focus on the needs of people with autism and Sensory Processing Disorder by offering a weighted blanket, the Cozy Calm. The Autism Shop, a brick and mortar and online store in Minnesota also serves this niche market and describes itself as, "A one-of-a-kind Book & Toy Shop packed with merchandise and information for individuals with Autism Spectrum Disorder and the people who love, care for, and educate them."

 PASSION

The Success and Challenges of an Autistic Entrepreneur

It wasn't until six years ago that 46-year-old Eileen Parker learned she had autism. Born in Canada, Parker was non-verbal until the age of 5 and as an adult, has had a hard time holding down a job. She found routine office tasks difficult, from sitting in a chair to working on a computer to deciphering sound in a crowded space. When she was finally diagnosed, it felt like a weight had been lifted.

"It really explained a lot of things," says Parker, a resident of Minneapolis. "I also learned that in addition to autism, I have Sensory Processing Disorder, which means that input into my brain isn't processed correctly." But in 2008, Parker had a life-changing moment that would reverse her disappointing career path and lead her to build a unique and successful small business. A couple years after she was diagnosed, she went to see an occupational therapist. As part of Parker's treatment, the therapist covered her with a hospital-grade weighted blanket.

"I felt amazing the moment she put the blanket on me," Parker says. She says the blanket works on the body's sensory system, "overloading all sensory input so that all you feel is weight on the body. It causes feelings of relaxation within three to five minutes. I'd never had that before. It overrode all of my stress."

An Idea in Motion

Parker was so taken by the blanket's effect on her that she looked into buying her own. Her research revealed that most weighted blankets are homemade, which sparked the idea of starting her own commercial medical blanket company. "I wanted to make a blanket soft enough for people

(continued)

(continued)

with sensory issues, so I went through the patent process, worked with professional sewers, hired a few people, and founded Cozy Calm," she says. Cozy Calm is entirely online and sells to medical supply stores and hospitals. Parker says that the company has grown from $28,000 in sales in 2010 to more than $100,000 in 2011, with this year's numbers on a course "to triple that."

The Realities of Autism

As you might imagine, along with Parker's success also comes the numerous challenges of being an owner with autism. "I have a hidden disability that you can't physically see, which means people don't know how to work with it," she says. "I've had to educate my staff as to how my brain works." Social cues are especially difficult for Parker. She has a hard time picking up on conversational subtleties or deciphering the real meaning of a comment when it isn't apparent in speech. Parker admits that she doesn't always deal with her disability well. "The learning curve is incredible—and never-ending," she says.

Words of Wisdom

In talking about other businesspeople with disabilities, Parker says that being brave and trusting your entrepreneurial spirit are key components.

"I was so scared that people wouldn't accept me, but I've found people to actually be really supportive," she says.

Also, Parker suggests talking to and networking with other small business owners with disabilities to find out how they do it. Once she did some outreach she says she found that "there are a surprising number of entrepreneurs out there with autism."

For helpful resources, check out Global Network for Entrepreneurs with Disabilities.

Source: Katie Morell, "The Success and Challenges of an Autistic Entrepreneur." Copyright © 2012 American Express Company. All rights reserved. From *http://www.openforum.com/articles/the-success-and-challenges-of-an-autistic-entrepreneur*, story written by Katie Morell, (Accessed May 23, 2012). Reprinted with permission.

The Entrepreneurial Resource highlights the *Source Book of Multicultural Experts*, which leads you to many experts, statistics, and research surrounding various multicultural market niches. If your target market is in one of these areas seek out the experts early on.

When profiling your Target Customer, it is likely that several different prospective segments will be discovered. Further analysis will be required to focus on only the most worthy. These should then be separated by sales estimates, competitive factors, potential for repeat business, and the costs associated with reaching each segment.

Identifying the unmet needs of your market niche and clearly explaining the market potential for your concept can make or break a Business Plan. To accomplish this, first focus on your primary and secondary Target Customers, because these are the only customers that you can see right now. However, once you open your business, additional Target Customers may arrive on the scene that you never envisioned. Be prepared to refocus and take advantage of these new customers and opportunities. Change is the one constant in business and as an entrepreneur you must adapt to survive.

You are also going to have to think about whether you are going to sell directly to consumers or to businesses. These two areas are called business-to-consumer (B2C) marketing and business-to-business (B2B) marketing. B2B profiling is unlike the segmentation of consumer markets in that it is most effectively performed using geographic factors, customer-based

Entrepreneur's Resource

The Source Book of Multicultural Experts 2012/2013

As you focus on your target market, you may recognize the need for experts who have experience with your very specific Target Customers. The annual sourcebook will lead you to statistics, market experts, business leaders, and a deeper understanding of your market. The Source Book is published by Multicultural Marketing Resources, *http://www.multicultural.com.*

CONTENTS

About The Source Book of Multicultural Experts and Multicultural Marketing Resources, Inc.

Market and Special Sections

The African American Market

"The African American Market: Proven Urban Marketing Solutions" by Lafayette Jones, SMSi- Urban Call Marketing, Inc. and Sandra Miller Jones, Segmented Marketing Services, Inc.
African American Market Experts and Business Leaders
Asian American Market Experts and Business Leaders

The Asian American Market

"The Asian American Market: Looking Ahead from Census 2010" by Saul Gitlin, Kang & Lee Advertising

The Hispanic Market

"The Spanglish Generation: Tapping it to Grow and Conquer Market Share" by Eduardo Perez, PM Publicidad
Hispanic Market Experts and Business Leaders
Multicultural Market Experts and Business Leaders

Multicultural Market Research

"Multicultural Market Research: Breaking Out of the Old Marketing Research Box" by Michael Halberstam, Interviewing Service of America
Other Market Experts and Business Leaders

The Disability Market

"Disability Market – Connecting the Puzzle Pieces" by Tari Hartman Squire, EIN SOF Communications, Inc.

Direct Marketing

"Multicultural Marketing Strategies & Proper Identification" by Candace Kennedy, Ethnic Technologies, LLC

Listing by Industry Expertise

Alphabetical Listing by Company (with Contact Information & Profiles)

Source: MarketResearch.com. From *http://multicultural.com/sourcebook/source_book_multicultural_experts* (Accessed October 22, 2012). Reprinted with permission.

segmentation, company size, order size, and end-user applications and is covered later in the chapter.

The chapter assumes you are not in business yet and thus are discovering who your target market is. Once in business you will continue to learn about your customer and will have a significant amount of data points collected which will help you continually redefine your exact market. One of the reason businesses selling directly on the Internet are so successful is the amount of data collected on a minute by minute basis and the ability to change offerings based on that data.

Three Types of Target Customers

Entrepreneurs should watch for at least three Target Customer groups.

Primary: This Target Customer group is perfect for your business and could be a heavy user and constant source of revenue. They possess the resources to purchase your product; they have a need or desire, or you can create the need or desire for your product; and they have the authority to purchase the product. In addition, they can be reached through some form of advertising or promotion at a reasonable cost.

Secondary: This group almost slips away before you can focus the camera. Keeping good customer records will help you identify your secondary group and your primary group. Sometimes your secondary Target Customer group will lead you to a third customer who is invisible at first.

Invisible: These customers appear after you have the courage to open the doors and talk to whomever walks in, making them feel welcomed and appreciated.

© Cengage Learning

■ WHAT CAN WE LEARN FROM PUBLISHED SOURCES?

An easy way to understand the power of profiling is to analyze media sources that are aimed at different target markets. Although, we recognize that print media is declining, for many businesses it will be an important part of the promotion mix and analyzing their profiling techniques provides insight.

As shared earlier, web analytics provide much more detailed information since according to one source the "average Internet user will have 736 pieces of personal information collected every day."

Those data points include: phone numbers dialed, bills paid, e-mails sent, key words searched, groceries purchased, tolls, prescriptions, Internet searches and clicks, pictures taken, pictures searched, check ins, people searched for, people searching for you, videos watched and liked. These are just the tip of the iceberg. Marketers in the future will be tapping in to this exponentially exploding Cloud and data mining beyond our wildest comprehension at this point.

Robert Krulwich, NPR science correspondent, shared, "It's almost like there's an image of us accumulating in that Cloud that will become an ever more vivid copy, with information we wouldn't tell our best friends, our family or our spouse. But the Cloud knows."

Thirty years ago, there was usually only one bookstore owner in town and her brain was the cloud. She knew exactly what each of her customers wanted and would provide personal recommendations and reviews. She was in the business of one-to-one marketing just as Amazon.com is now when it recommends books to you online. The owner knew your preferences and so much about your life as you came in asking for books on Italy, childhood tantrums, marathon running, online dating, learning to play the guitar and discussing them with the owner on a monthly or weekly basis. In essence, Amazon.com has not created a new way to market, but is just adopting an old method of knowing the customer using today's technology.

The bookstore owner's brain has thus been replaced by a computer's review of your search and purchase history online along with the collective reviews and purchases of thousands of readers of a similar profile. Computer databases and the information they provide to online customers thus serve as salespeople today. Recently, Amazon.com sent an e-mail to clients who had purchased an author's first book, suggesting that they might also be interested in the author's second book. Local bookstores might send the same note to their hundreds of customers, but Amazon.com will be able to send an e-mail to millions. One can think of Amazon as the combined brain of all the bookstore owners in the U.S. coming together to offer products and services to customers.

The majority of media sources have conducted extensive research to develop demographic and psychographic profiles of their Target Customers. In many cases these profiles are available through media kits from the advertising departments. A media kit includes a copy of the magazine, a reader profile, distribution figures, a rate card (specifications for advertisements and costs), an editorial calendar (monthly proposed content schedule), and an audited bureau circulation statement (ABC statement). Usually kits can be found online.

Rate card A magazine's advertising prices and details for ad placements

If comparing the readers of three different entertainment magazines you might want to know: What brand of clothes do they wear? How much money do they spend on concerts? How much money do they spend on clubs? Where do they eat? What do they drive? What do they believe in? Where do they work? How much money do they make? What are their dreams?

The key here is to know which media sources your Target Customer reads, listens to, and watches. In-depth profiles from media companies are compiled for potential advertisers who are evaluating which advertising vehicle would best meet their Target Customer. So as you define your Target Customer, analyze the media they consume to delve into your customer's world.

Think of the differences and similarities among the readers of women's online and print magazines, such as *O, Redbook, Cosmopolitan,* and *Family Circle,* each aimed at a different segment of the women's market. What about the differences between the readers of *Sports Illustrated* and *ESPN The Magazine?*

In this chapter, we will focus primarily on magazines; Figures 4.1a and 4.1b highlight the readers of *Surfing* magazine and *Surfer's* online media readers. We could just as easily expand our discussion to include media analysis data for TV programs, radio stations, Internet sites, and, to a lesser extent, books and movies.

We often walk past magazines without giving them a glance. That is unfortunate, because magazines hold the answer to many questions about customers. One way to view a magazine is as a glossy cover wrapped around pages of advertisements and editorial copy. With new eyes, however, you can see that a mass-market magazine exists because it is a channel to the subconscious of a certain type of reader. That knowledge is power. What can you learn about target markets, consumption patterns, and buying power from the advertisements and feature articles in a magazine?

Put yourself in an analytical frame of mind, and begin by counting the advertisements. Then note the types of products that dominate the advertisements; these advertisements are probably aimed at the heavy users of those products. Next, study the models; they are fantasy images that the Target Customer is expected to identify with, aspire to, connect with, and remember. The activities pictured in the advertisements enlarge the fantasy, and the editorial links it to real life. A good advertisement becomes a slice of life—a picture that beckons the customer inside, toward the product.

figure **4.1a**

Surfing **Magazine Media Kit Information**

CIRCULATION & DISTRIBUTION

CIRCULATION NUMBERS

Circulation:	91,950*
Subscribers:	80,721
Newsstand:	10,354
Events/Promo:	875
Audience	643,000+**

GEOGRAPHIC DISTRIBUTION

West Coast:	41%
East Coast:	26%
Central US:	23%
Hawaii:	5%
International:	5%

DEMOGRAPHICS & PSYCHOGRAPHICS

DEMOGRAPHIC INFORMATION

Median age:	19
Average age:	21
Age range:	14-28
Female:	23%
Male:	77%
Under 21:	51%

PSYCHOGRAPHICS

Average years surfing: 8.9
Average surfing frequency: 12 days/month
Average amount spent on equipment: $820/year
Average amount spent on surf trips: $1,722
% of readers who shop for surf products at their local surf shops: 84%
Percent of readers who save their issue after reading it: 78%
HHI: $76,500

* JUNE 2012 ABC PUBLISHERS STATEMENT
** On average, 6 people other than the original recipient see each issue of SurfING. That means over 640,000 surfers read SURFING Magazine every month.

Source: Surfing Magazine Media Kit Information.

We took an issue of *Surfing* and did a new-eyes analysis for a board shorts manufacturer. After we looked at the articles and the advertisements, we completed a trial profile. We developed categories as we went along. (One of the nice things about new-eyes research is that you can expand the model as you collect data.) We looked for:

- Total number and size of advertisements, and models used
- Advertisements aimed at heavy users, the type of products that are advertised the most
- Large advertisements of two or more pages
- Lifestyle and demographics
- Main activities depicted in advertisements
- Content of magazine articles

Reviewing the Media Kit

The issue of *Surfing* we studied contained 138 pages with over 66 pages of advertisements. These advertisements, mostly full-page and two-page spreads,

figure **4.1b**

Digital Media

SURFERMAG.COM
Surfermag.com is the award-winning digital extension of the SURFER media package with an expanding viewership of over 320,000 unique visitors and 4 million page views per month. Everything you'd expect from the magazine is here, but the nature of the site allows us to go further. Features include exclusive video clips run on a state-of-the-art HD player, breaking news from every ocean on the globe, user message boards that draw 100,000 unique browsers a month, hi-definition photo galleries, blogs dedicated to the best writers and photographers in surf, and archival magazine content at your fingertips any time.

^ Back to Top

SURFER'S SOCIAL MEDIA
Boasting the biggest social media audience in action sports, SURFER reaches over 300,000 people every day through Facebook (277,000+ fans), twitter (52,000+ followers), and various other social streams. SURFER's brand recognition has allowed our social media reach to multiply 15 fold in the last calendar year alone. With no signs of slowing down, SURFER is influencing the way surf fans are consuming media.

How to get to SURFER:
Magazine / Digital Edition / Nook / Website / Flipboard

AGE:
Median: 25
15–30 yrs: 83%

SEX:
81% Male
19% Female

AVERAGE HOUSEHOLD INCOME:
$85,000

SITES STATISTICS
377,058 unique visitors and 4 million page views per month. Avg. visit: 5.5 min

ADVERTISING UNITS
Banner-728x90
Skyscraper-160x600
Box-300x250
Rich Media
Video Pre-Roll

Source: Surfing Magazine Media Kit Information.

covered almost 50 percent of the magazine. There were four main categories: clothing, surfboards, sunglasses, and shoes.

The advertisements predominantly depicted the surfer lifestyle. Professional surfers were showcased in several of the advertisements. The remaining models were primarily blond, surfer types between ages 18 to 25. Text, content, and advertisements almost meld together beautifully. In fact, it is oftentimes hard to discern which is editorial and which is advertising.

Next, we reviewed the *Surfing* media kit information (see Figure 4.1a), along with their website and magazine. From the following reader profile provided by *Surfing* magazine, the magazine's content, and what we know about their customer, we concur with *Surfing*'s customer profile:

They shun the pretension for innovation and excellence, astutely seeking both value and "the latest." Upwardly mobile, educated or being educated, idealistic, and stoked on their number-one passion (surfing), they are the first to try new maneuvers, new music, or new technologies they deem appropriate. Fashion and change leaders, they are the ones others turn to for advice.

The next step in profiling your Target Customer is to compare the profiles of the readers of all the magazines aimed at your target market to determine which best represents your customer. Look not only at demographics and psychographics but the spirit of the reader as well. Another surfing magazine editor defined his target reader as the "soul-surfer, one who lives to surf!" Complete Action Step 24 to focus more clearly on your Target Customer.

Changing Profiles

In the past we viewed segmentation of the market like taking a slice of a pie. Each business tried to aim their products at their slice, and slicing the pie was primarily based on demographic segmentation. As technology advanced and media outlets and marketing researchers conducted extensive studies on customers, we suggested to our readers that they try to aim for a single blueberry in a slice of blueberry pie. With the Internet and the explosion of relatively inexpensive independent target-market studies, we now suggest you aim for the seeds in the blueberry. If you add your intuition, demographics, geographics, psychographics, and extensive observation of your target market, you will accomplish one-to-one marketing: meeting the needs of the "seeds."

Society's fragmentation allows you to focus directly on the needs of your particular market segment. Rather than focusing only on demographic and geographic segmentation, you now also look for *lifestyle, social,* and *economic segments,* such as the differences between the purchases of 40-year-old first-time parents and the purchases of 40-year-old parents who have just sent their youngest child off to college. Below, LifeMatrix by NOP World (now part of Gfk MRI) identifies five parenting segments–each with their own set of financial needs, dreams, and outlooks.

- Dynamic duos—These are high-income parents who have digital-age lifestyles. They are extremely optimistic about the future and have high consumer confidence. They have many different drivers, though they are less likely to hold modesty, duty, obedience, and traditional gender roles as core values.
- Home soldiers—These are more traditional families with young children. These parents are home-centric, motivated by wealth, power, status, romance, and adventure. They are armchair warriors, more likely to dream of the perfect vacation than they are to travel.
- Priority parents—These are family-focused individuals with traditional values. Usually the parents of small children, they spend most of their time with their children and on family activities. Priority parents are fairly pessimistic about the financial outlook.
- Renaissance women—These are high-energy moms. They balance work and family and visit museums and cultural institutions with their children. They are motivated by freedom, creativity, curiosity, knowledge, and self-reliance. These women have an optimistic financial outlook.
- Struggling singles—These are single parents, very worried about money and making ends meet. They hold a very pessimistic view of their financial future. They aspire to have wealth, status, power, and possessions.

Source: NOP World, 2004.

With information like this, an entrepreneur can begin to understand the "soul" of their customer. By combining lifestage information, personal values, and lifestyles, entrepreneurs can begin to create products and messages that resonate with their target markets.

Use customer research data to focus on your customers, determine what products and services they want, and how to reach them with the right message at the right time. Then decide what pricing points will spur your customer to purchase from the ideal channel of distribution. To be successful, you will be manipulating these elements at start-up and throughout your business. As you continue to gather data on your customers you will be better able to meet their needs, which is key.

ACTION STEP 24

Media Kit Assignment—Target Customer

1. Choose five magazines or/and online sites you believe your Target Customer reads or visits. Many magazines have companion online sites and oftentimes present two separate analyses. (Return to Action Step 14 in Chapter 2 for the list you previously researched.)
2. Locate a media kit for each.
3. Compare the magazines and sites by first reviewing the content and the advertisements using your new eyes. Define who you believe the target market is for each.
4. Next, compare your new-eyes profile with the demographic and psychographic information provided. Then rank the five magazines from 1 to 5, with 1 being the magazine that best targets or represents your customer.

In the beginning, you may not be able to advertise in these magazines or on the sites due to cost, but you may very well be able to keep an eye on your competitors, and your target market, by following these sources.

One-to-one marketing Meeting customer needs on a personal and individual basis

One of the largest providers of lifestyle segmentation data, Nielsen, divides the U.S. market into 66 lifestyle groups, which are then grouped into 11 broader lifestage groups, as shown in Figure 4.2a, and social groups, as shown in Figure 4.2b.

As a marketing exercise, make several lists of restaurant chains, clothing stores, and car manufacturers (or your choice). Then study Figures 4.2a and 4.2b to determine which group or groups each of these firms may be targeting. Now take your business idea and the list of your competitors and determine which lifestage and social groups each is targeting.

Are there some arenas where competition is extremely challenging? Is there a group that no one is targeting? Where are the opportunities for you?

Sometimes offering the same product in a different *place* or at a different *price*, aiming your *promotion* differently, or changing the *product* slightly will allow you to compete in a slightly different arena.

Product differentiation Wrapping 4 P's, price, product, place, promotion around Target Customer.

Product differentiation includes changing any one or all four of these "P variables." Your goal is to wrap the four Ps around your target market as tightly as you can, and continue to change and rewrap as the target market, products, competition, and environment evolve.

From profiling your "blueberry seed" in Action Step 27 you will move into Chapter 5 where you will develop a competitive strategy aimed toward your well-developed "blueberry seed." Chapter 6 will help you select the best distribution strategies and Chapter 7 will help you promote your product while focusing on relevant demographic, geographic, and psychographic variables.

■ PROFILING IN ACTION

A native of Houston, Texas, Susan Johnson moved to California in 1994. With their children grown, she and her husband John decided to start a business and settle here permanently.

A family history of cancer and heart disease had made her very aware of the benefits of a healthy lifestyle. When she discovered that there was no one service offering prepared healthy meals for the home throughout Southern California, she decided to fill the niche by providing an effortless way for others to achieve a healthy diet. After much research she determined that Orange County was the most strategic location to accomplish her dream of serving all of Southern California. She opened her headquarters in Irvine in January 1996, with proven tested recipes approved by a dietitian, and custom computer programs that not only analyze the nutritional content of each meal, but also track the needs of her customers.

In January of 1998, Healthy Gourmet expanded to Los Angeles, and in May of 2000, Healthy Gourmet began service to San Diego. Susan's plan for Healthy Gourmet is to expand throughout the state of California, promoting good health to those whose goals include eating nutritious, great-tasting food. In the process, she's offering the convenience of eliminating the need for shopping, cooking, and clean up, thereby filling the need that's fueling today's trend toward home meal replacement.

2007 brought Susan's Healthy Kids and Family meals leading to 2008 where they added Senior, Diabetic, and Anti-Aging/Purification packages; making Susan's Healthy Gourmet the most versatile of the fresh, home replacement meal services.

Currently, Healthy Gourmet employs a full-time kitchen staff of 20 + to produce over 250,000 meals a year, with each order customized for its clients. Future plans include expanding the service through shipping to those areas unable to be serviced locally. Susan's dream to be able to provide meals to everyone who wants to enjoy the benefits provided by eating healthy is moving forward just as planned!

Source: Susan's Healthy Gourment, "Our History." From *http://www.susanshealthy gourmet.com/our_history.cfm*, (Accessed May 27, 2012). Reprinted with permission.

Let us review the secondary data resources currently available to aid someone like Johnson if she were to profile her target market today in Orange County.

figure **4.2a**

Nielsen PRIZM Lifestage Groups

PRIZM® Lifestage Groups

All 66 PRIZM segments are grouped into 11 broader Lifestage Groups, as shown by the color-coded chart below. Lifestage Groups capture a combination of three variables—affluence, householder age and whether there are children living at home. For example, the three Lifestage Groups that comprise Younger Years are, for the most part, young and childless households. What differentiates Lifestage Group Y1, Midlife Success, for Lifestage Group Y2. Young Achievers, is the level of affluence each has achieved at these younger ages.

Similarly, the four groups of segments that make up Family Life are likely to have children in common, while segments categorized as Mature Years are mostly empty-nesters. The most affluent Family Life segments fall into Lifestage Group F1, Accumulated Wealth, which includes Blue Blood Estates, Country Squires and Winner's Circle. The least affluent Family Life segments fall into Lifestage Group F4, Sustaining Families, which includes Family Thrifts, Bedrock America, Big City Blues and Low-Rise Living.

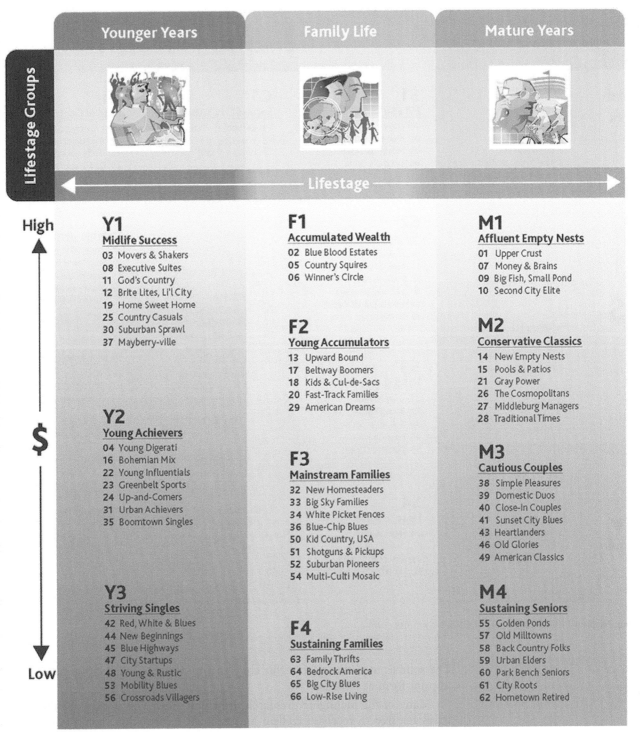

Younger Years   **Family Life**   **Mature Years**

Lifestage Groups

Lifestage

High

$

Low

Y1
Midlife Success
03 Movers & Shakers
08 Executive Suites
11 God's Country
12 Brite Lites, Li'l City
19 Home Sweet Home
25 Country Casuals
30 Suburban Sprawl
37 Mayberry-ville

Y2
Young Achievers
04 Young Digerati
16 Bohemian Mix
22 Young Influentials
23 Greenbelt Sports
24 Up-and-Comers
31 Urban Achievers
35 Boomtown Singles

Y3
Striving Singles
42 Red, White & Blues
44 New Beginnings
45 Blue Highways
47 City Startups
48 Young & Rustic
53 Mobility Blues
56 Crossroads Villagers

F1
Accumulated Wealth
02 Blue Blood Estates
05 Country Squires
06 Winner's Circle

F2
Young Accumulators
13 Upward Bound
17 Beltway Boomers
18 Kids & Cul-de-Sacs
20 Fast-Track Families
29 American Dreams

F3
Mainstream Families
32 New Homesteaders
33 Big Sky Families
34 White Picket Fences
36 Blue-Chip Blues
50 Kid Country, USA
51 Shotguns & Pickups
52 Suburban Pioneers
54 Multi-Culti Mosaic

F4
Sustaining Families
63 Family Thrifts
64 Bedrock America
65 Big City Blues
66 Low-Rise Living

M1
Affluent Empty Nests
01 Upper Crust
07 Money & Brains
09 Big Fish, Small Pond
10 Second City Elite

M2
Conservative Classics
14 New Empty Nests
15 Pools & Patios
21 Gray Power
26 The Cosmopolitans
27 Middleburg Managers
28 Traditional Times

M3
Cautious Couples
38 Simple Pleasures
39 Domestic Duos
40 Close-In Couples
41 Sunset City Blues
43 Heartlanders
46 Old Glories
49 American Classics

M4
Sustaining Seniors
55 Golden Ponds
57 Old Milltowns
58 Back Country Folks
59 Urban Elders
60 Park Bench Seniors
61 City Roots
62 Hometown Retired

Source: Nielsen PRIZM 2011 (*www.mybestsegments.com*).

figure **4.2b**

PRIZM NE Social Groups

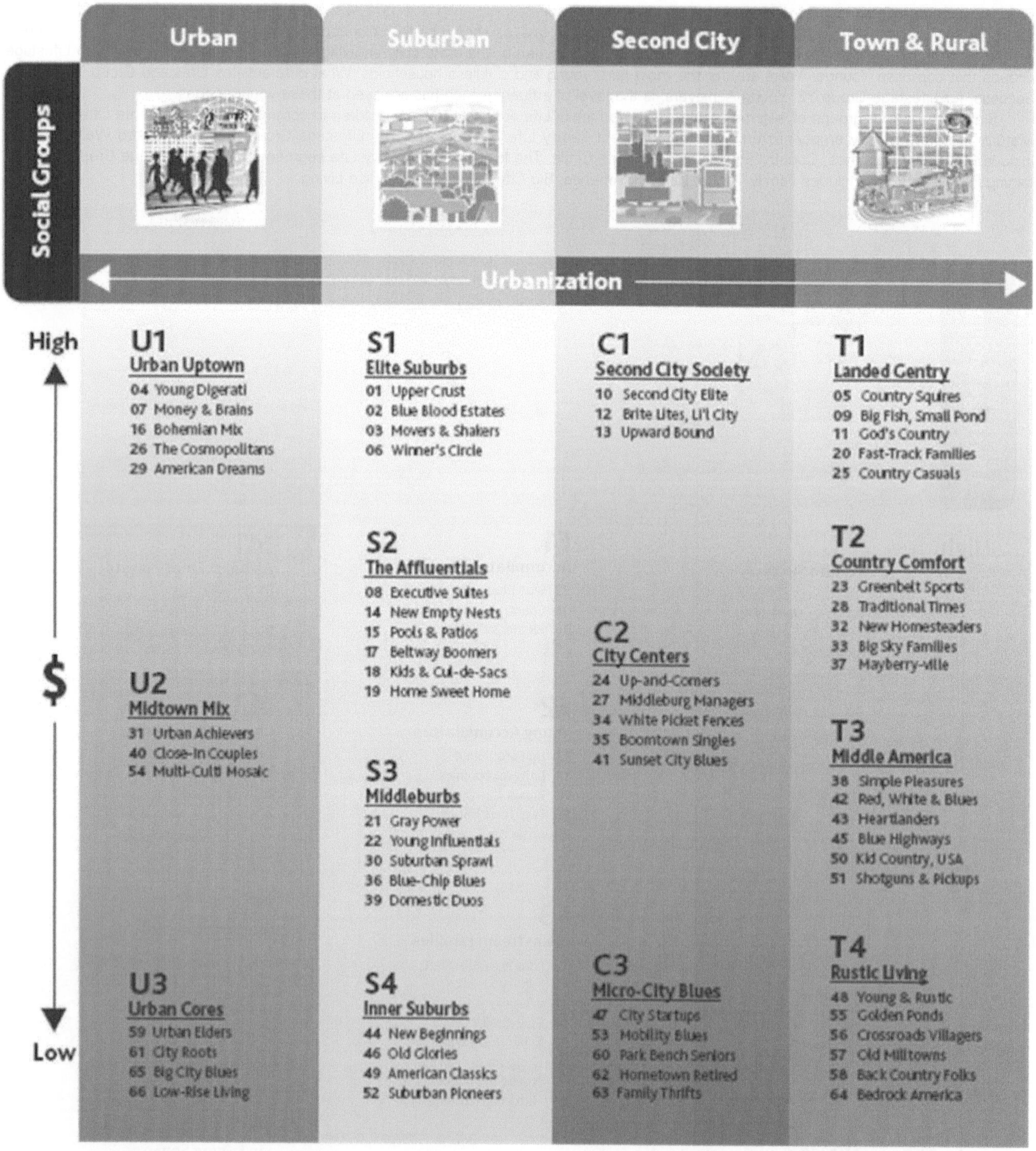

| Urban | Suburban | Second City | Town & Rural |

Social Groups

Urbanization

High

$

Low

U1
Urban Uptown
04 Young Digerati
07 Money & Brains
16 Bohemian Mix
26 The Cosmopolitans
29 American Dreams

U2
Midtown Mix
31 Urban Achievers
40 Close-In Couples
54 Multi-Culti Mosaic

U3
Urban Cores
59 Urban Elders
61 City Roots
65 Big City Blues
66 Low-Rise Living

S1
Elite Suburbs
01 Upper Crust
02 Blue Blood Estates
03 Movers & Shakers
06 Winner's Circle

S2
The Affluentials
08 Executive Suites
14 New Empty Nests
15 Pools & Patios
17 Beltway Boomers
18 Kids & Cul-de-Sacs
19 Home Sweet Home

S3
Middleburbs
21 Gray Power
22 Young Influentials
30 Suburban Sprawl
36 Blue-Chip Blues
39 Domestic Duos

S4
Inner Suburbs
44 New Beginnings
46 Old Glories
49 American Classics
52 Suburban Pioneers

C1
Second City Society
10 Second City Elite
12 Brite Lites, Li'l City
13 Upward Bound

C2
City Centers
24 Up-and-Comers
27 Middleburg Managers
34 White Picket Fences
35 Boomtown Singles
41 Sunset City Blues

C3
Micro-City Blues
47 City Startups
53 Mobility Blues
60 Park Bench Seniors
62 Hometown Retired
63 Family Thrifts

T1
Landed Gentry
05 Country Squires
09 Big Fish, Small Pond
11 God's Country
20 Fast-Track Families
25 Country Casuals

T2
Country Comfort
23 Greenbelt Sports
28 Traditional Times
32 New Homesteaders
33 Big Sky Families
37 Mayberry-ville

T3
Middle America
38 Simple Pleasures
42 Red, White & Blues
43 Heartlanders
45 Blue Highways
50 Kid Country, USA
51 Shotguns & Pickups

T4
Rustic Living
48 Young & Rustic
55 Golden Ponds
56 Crossroads Villagers
57 Old Milltowns
58 Back Country Folks
64 Bedrock America

Source: Nielsen PRIZM 2011 (*www.MyBestsegments.com*)

The sources used throughout this chapter are available both on the Internet and in print form at libraries.

Many of the highlighted research firms will allow you to tap into their databases for free to receive excellent and detailed information, but if you desire a great deal of in-depth and current information, you will need to pay a monthly or per-search fee. Oftentimes, this cost is relatively low in terms of the value it can provide to you. Also, in evaluating your Business Plan, many lenders expect demographic, geographic, and psychographic statistics to support your estimated Target Customer numbers. We have therefore included a sample of the services that provide such numbers.

For illustration purposes, we first focus on Susan's potential customers in Laguna Beach. Chapter 6 discusses additional issues in Susan's choice of physical location and provides more detail on geographic secondary information. Her initial research identified Orange County as an excellent location as a result of its high-income demographics, high level of dual-career couples, and propensity for large expenditures on restaurant meals. In addition, this location is centralized between Los Angeles and San Diego. Susan would be able to use the Orange County location as her main commissary kitchen, serving Los Angeles to the north and to San Diego going south.

Focusing on the demographics of their Laguna Beach customers, the first stop is U.S. Census data, *http://www.census.gov* (the last Census figures available are for 2010). You can also search the U.S. Census Bureau's American Fact Finder2 database (See Entrepreneurial Resource) by hundreds of different variables: education, employment, family household size, income, race, sex, age groupings, and so on.

If your area is one that is growing and changing rapidly, consider purchasing information from providers who project and measure changes within their own databases or by those firms who make projections based on the 2010 Census. In addition, information can be obtained through *http://quickfacts.census.gov*, where one can compare city, county, and state statistics, as shown in Table 4.1 where Laguna Beach is the focus.

Using SRDS's PRIZM NE lifestyle segmentation database provides additional insight into Healthy Gourmet's customers' psyches. PRIZM NE defines every zip code and drills down to zip code + 4, which is a geographical area that encompasses 10 to 12 households. PRIZM NE profiles focus on lifestyle, retail, financial, and media variables, and ConneXions focuses on the use of communications by each group. The five major clusters for Susan's 92625 neighborhood, in order, are: Executive Suites, Movers & Shakers, New Empty Nests, Pools & Patios, and Upper Crust, two of which are highlighted in Figure 4.3.

Primarily college graduates with median household incomes around $100,000, these customers enjoy traveling and driving very nice cars. Thus, her marketing and promotion materials should be focused specifically on meeting the needs of these time-strapped, health and status-oriented individuals.

Continuing on with the search for data brings us to VALS™ profiles developed by SRI and now operated by Strategic Business Insights (SBI), which focus on consumer psychological traits. A check of the VALS segmentation diagram (Figure 4.4) shows eight profiles: Innovators, Thinkers, Achievers, Experiencers, Believers, Strivers, Makers, and Survivors. According to SRI VALS:

> Consumers buy products and services and seek experiences that fulfill their characteristic preferences and give shape, substance, and satisfaction to their lives. An individual's primary motivation determines what in particular about the self or the world is the meaningful core that governs his or her activities. Consumers are inspired by one of three primary motivations: ideals, achievement, or self-expression. Consumers who are primarily motivated by ideals are guided by knowledge and principles. Consumers who are primarily motivated by achievement look for products and services that demonstrate success to their peers. Consumers who are primarily motivated by self-expression desire social or physical activity, variety, and risk.

Source: *http://www.sric-bi.com/VALS/types/shtml* (Accessed June 5, 2008).

table **4.1**

Laguna Beach/California QuickFacts U.S. Census Bureau

U.S. Census Bureau
State & County QuickFacts
Orange County, California

People QuickFacts	Laguna Beach	California
Population, 2011 estimate	NA	37,691,912
Population, 2010	22,723	37,253,956
Population, percent change, 2000 to 2010	–4.2%	10.0%
Population, 2000	23,727	33,871,648
Persons under 5 years, percent, 2010	3.3%	6.8%
Persons under 18 years, percent, 2010	16.1%	25.0%
Persons 65 years and over, percent, 2010	18.3%	11.4%
Female persons, percent, 2010	49.8%	50.3%
White persons, percent, 2010 (a)	90.9%	57.6%
Black persons, percent, 2010 (a)	0.8%	6.2%
American Indian and Alaska Native persons, percent, 2010 (a)	0.3%	1.0%
Asian persons, percent, 2010 (a)	3.6%	13.0%
Native Hawaiian and Other Pacific Islander, percent, 2010 (a)	0.1%	0.4%
Persons reporting two or more races, percent, 2010	2.9%	4.9%
Persons of Hispanic or Latino origin, percent, 2010 (b)	7.3%	37.6%
White persons not Hispanic, percent, 2010	85.7%	40.1%
Living in same house 1 year & over, 2006–2010	85.1%	84.0%
Foreign born persons, percent, 2006–2010	13.0%	27.2%
Language other than English spoken at home, pct age 5+, 2006–2010	12.0%	43.0%
High school graduates, percent of persons age 25+, 2006–2010	97.3%	80.7%
Bachelor's degree or higher, pct of persons age 25+, 2006–2010	63.0%	30.1%
Mean travel time to work (minutes), workers age 16+, 2006–2010	29.8	26.9
Housing units, 2010	12,923	13,680,081
Homeownership rate, 2006–2010	62.4%	57.4%
Housing units in multi-unit structures, percent, 2006–2010	26.8%	30.7%
Median value of owner-occupied housing units, 2006–2010	$1,000,001	$458,500
Households, 2006–2010	11,047	12,392,852
Persons per household, 2006–2010	2.06	2.89
Per capita money income in past 12 months (2010 dollars) 2006–2010	$83,998	$29,188
Median household income 2006–2010	$98,634	$60,883
Persons below poverty level, percent, 2006–2010	7.5%	13.7%

Business QuickFacts	Laguna Beach	California
Total number of firms, 2007	5,498	3,425,510
Black-owned firms, percent, 2007	S	4.0%
American Indian- and Alaska Native-owned firms, percent, 2007	S	1.3%
Asian-owned firms, percent, 2007	S	14.9%
Native Hawaiian and Other Pacific Islander-owned firms, percent, 2007	F	0.3%
Hispanic-owned firms, percent, 2007	S	16.5%
Women-owned firms, percent, 2007	25.9%	30.3%
Manufacturers shipments, 2007 ($1000)	NA	491,372,092
Merchant wholesaler sales, 2007 ($1000)	40,878	598,456,486
Retail sales, 2007 ($1000)	175,990	455,032,270
Retail sales per capita, 2007	$7,424	$12,561
Accommodation and food services sales, 2007 ($1000)	287,469	80,852,787

Geography QuickFacts	Laguna Beach	California
Land area in square miles, 2010	8.85	155,779.22
Persons per square mile, 2010	2,567.6	239.1

Source U.S. Census Bureau: State and County QuickFacts. Data derived from Population Estimates, American Community Survey, Census of Population and Housing, County Business Patterns, Economic Census, Survey of Business Owners, Building Permits, Consolidated Federal Funds Report, Census of Governments
Last Revised: Wednesday, 06-Jun-2012 17:02:00 EDT
Source: *http://quickfacts.census.gov/qfd/states/06/0639178.html*, (Accessed May 26, 2012).

—figure **4.3**

Sample Segments from PRIZM NE

nielsen | MyBestSegments

Home | ZIP Code Look-up | Segment Explorer | Learn More | Contact Us

Home > Nielsen PRIZM > Segment Details

2011 PRIZM Segmentation System

03 Movers & Shakers

Wealthy Middle Age w/o Kids

Movers & Shakers is home to America's up-and-coming business class: a wealthy suburban world of dual-income couples who are highly educated, typically between the ages of 35 and 54. Given its high percentage of executives and white-collar professionals, there's a decided business bent to this segment: members of Movers & Shakers rank near the top for owning a small business and having a home office.

Social Group: 04 Elite Suburbs
Lifestage Group: 01 Midlife Success

Snapshot | Neighborhood Demographics | Household Demographics | Lifestyles | Media | Premium

2011 Statistics
* US Households: 1,878,356 (1.61%)
* Median HH Income: $103,357

Lifestyle & Media Traits
* Order from J.Crew
* Attend NHL games
* Read Inc.
* Watch Saturday Night Live
* Land Rover Range Rover

Demographics Traits
* Urbanicity: Suburban
* Income: Wealthy
* Income Producing Assets: Elite
* Age Ranges: 35-54
* Presence of Kids: HH w/o Kids
* Homeownership: Mostly Owners
* Employment Levels: Management
* Education Levels: Graduate Plus
* Ethnic Diversity: White, Asian, Mix

US by County

This map highlights each County where Movers & Shakers households are found.

Top 5 Counties

Name	Index
Fairfax County, VA	703
Fairfax city, VA	631
Falls Church city, VA	627
Montgomery County, MD	491
Morris County, NJ	454

Legend

	%Comp	%Pen	Index
Quintile: 1	54.72	5.78	273
Quintile: 2	22.44	2.36	111
Quintile: 3	15.00	1.59	75
Quintile: 4	6.63	0.70	33
Quintile: 5	1.21	0.13	6

Source: Nielsen 2011

(continued)

Source: Nielsen PRIZM 2011 (*www.MyBestsegments.com*)

What motivates an individual to consume goods and services beyond age, income, and education? Energy, self-confidence, intellectualism, novelty seeking, innovativeness, impulsiveness, leadership, and vanity play critical roles. These personality traits, in conjunction with key

figure **4.3** ──────────────────────────────────

Sample Segments from PRIZM NE (continued)

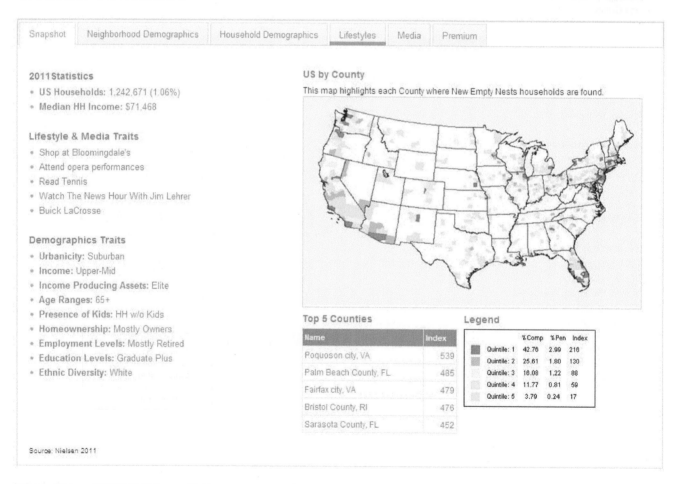

nielsen | MyBestSegments

| Home | ZIP Code Look-up | Segment Explorer | Learn More | Contact Us |

Home > Nielsen PRIZM > Segment Details

2011 PRIZM Segmentation System

14 New Empty Nests

Upper-Mid Mature w/o Kids

With their grown-up children recently out of the house, New Empty Nests is composed of upper-middle income older Americans who pursue active--and activist--lifestyles. Most residents are over 65 years old, but they show no interest in a rest-home retirement. This is the top-ranked segment for all-inclusive travel packages; the favorite destination is Europe.

Social Group: 05 The Affluentials
Lifestage Group: 09 Conservative Classics

| Snapshot | Neighborhood Demographics | Household Demographics | Lifestyles | Media | Premium |

2011 Statistics
- US Households: 1,242,671 (1.06%)
- Median HH Income: $71,468

Lifestyle & Media Traits
- Shop at Bloomingdale's
- Attend opera performances
- Read Tennis
- Watch The News Hour With Jim Lehrer
- Buick LaCrosse

Demographics Traits
- Urbanicity: Suburban
- Income: Upper-Mid
- Income Producing Assets: Elite
- Age Ranges: 65+
- Presence of Kids: HH w/o Kids
- Homeownership: Mostly Owners
- Employment Levels: Mostly Retired
- Education Levels: Graduate Plus
- Ethnic Diversity: White

US by County

This map highlights each County where New Empty Nests households are found.

Top 5 Counties

Name	Index
Poquoson city, VA	539
Palm Beach County, FL	485
Fairfax city, VA	479
Bristol County, RI	476
Sarasota County, FL	452

Legend

	%Comp	%Pen	Index
Quintile: 1	42.76	2.99	216
Quintile: 2	25.61	1.80	130
Quintile: 3	16.08	1.22	88
Quintile: 4	11.77	0.81	59
Quintile: 5	3.79	0.24	17

Source: Nielsen 2011

Source: Nielsen PRIZM 2011 (*www.MyBestsegments.com*)

demographics, and behavioral issues (see Key Points from Another View) combine together in forming consumers' buying decisions. Different levels of resources enhance or constrain a person's expression of his or her primary motivation.

—figure **4.4**

US Framework and VALS Types

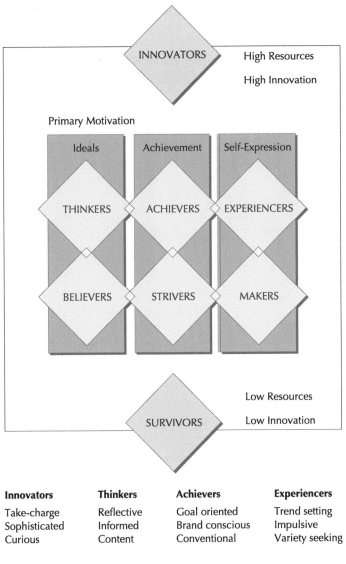

Innovators	Thinkers	Achievers	Experiencers
Take-charge	Reflective	Goal oriented	Trend setting
Sophisticated	Informed	Brand conscious	Impulsive
Curious	Content	Conventional	Variety seeking

Survivors	Believers	Strivers	Makers
Nostalgic	Literal	Contemporary	Responsible
Constrained	Loyal	Imitative	Practical
Cautious	Moralistic	Style conscious	Self-sufficient

Source: Strategic Business Insights.

Reading the following summary of an Innovator provides insight into one of the primary Target Customer profiles for Susan's Healthy Gourmet utilizing the VALS system (Figures 4.4 and 4.5).

Innovators are successful, sophisticated, take-charge people with high self-esteem. Because they have such abundant resources, they exhibit all three primary motivations in varying degrees. They are change leaders and are the most receptive to new ideas and technologies. Innovators are very active consumers, and their purchases reflect cultivated tastes for upscale niche products and services.

Image is important to innovators, not as evidence of status or power but as an expression of their taste, independence, and personality. Innovators are among the established and emerging leaders in business and government, yet they continue to

figure 4.5

Customer Insights

Demographic and Behavior Snapshots Highlight the Vibrancy of Using VALS™

Primary Motivation		Ideals		Achievement		Self-Expression		
	Innovators	Thinkers	Believers	Achievers	Strivers	Experiencers	Makers	Survivors
Psychological Descriptors	Sophisticated In Charge Curious	Informed Reflective Content	Literal Loyal Moralistic	Goal Oriented Brand Conscious Conventional	Contemporary Imitative Style Conscious	Trend Seeking Impulsive Variety Seeking	Responsible Practical Self-Sufficient	Nostalgic Constrained Cautious
	Percent of Innovators	Percent of Thinkers	Percent of Believers	Percent of Achievers	Percent of Strivers	Percent of Experiencers	Percent of Makers	Percent of Survivors
Total U.S.	10	11	16.5	14	11.5	13	12	12
Median age	45	56	52	41	28	24	46	70
Married	65	75	63	72	34	25	68	45
Work full time	72	55	47	70	52	55	59	13
Used Internet in past 30 days	98	88	61	93	70	85	68	29
Bought most recent vehicle used	39	37	50	45	59	53	59	44
Buy food labeled natural or organic	26	13	6	9	5	9	6	4
Walk for exercise	52	46	29	37	20	18	26	22
Played golf in past 12 months	18	16	6	15	7	10	7	3
Contribute to PBS/NPR	23	13	3	3	—	—	—	3
Media channel preference	Internet Print	Newspaper Internet	Television Radio	Internet Magazine	Radio Television	Magazine Internet	Radio Television	Television Newspaper

Source: VALS™/Mediamark Research & Intelligence, LLC Fall 2008

Source: Strategic Business Insights.

seek challenges. Their lives are characterized by variety. Their possessions and recreation reflect a cultivated taste for the finer things in life. Some of their favorite items are BMWs, *Wired*, sparkling water, and a rewarding experience.

Source: Strategic Business Insights (SBI); *www.strategicbusinessinsights.com/VALS.*

Refer to Figure 4.5 and review the characteristic attitudes, behaviors, and media habits of both the Innovators, who are Susan's customers, and the Strivers, who are not. Both of these VALS segments define adult consumers who have "different attitudes and exhibit distinctive behavior and decision-making patterns." Susan's customer profile sharpens when reviewing behaviors of her potential customers.

Susan once briefly described her primary customers as follows:

- Sophisticated
- Knowledgeable and concerned about their health
- Age 30 to 60
- Baby boomers who are in excellent shape and interested in retaining their health
- Professionals, entrepreneurs, and others who work very long hours and are active physically
- Highly educated
- Expect the best
- Purchase products to save time and energy and thus require high-level service and consistency

Susan has now had her business for 16 years. With her customer records, Susan now can determine exactly who her target market is. Information from her customer database probably led her to provide additional products for diabetics and the elderly. But for those just starting a business, the previous resources and others provide a good head start toward defining your initial Target Customers. Many more profiling systems are available online to use and purchase, we have only touched on a few to boost your search. By knowing your target market intimately, you will be far ahead of your competition. Continue to refine your profile as you work through the remainder of the chapter's Action Steps starting now with Action Step 25.

■ PROFILING BUSINESS TO BUSINESS (B2B) CUSTOMERS

Business-to-business markets include a wide range of customers that include government agencies, educational facilities, nonprofit organizations, as well as many industrial customers. Evaluate your customer based on demographics (size, geographic location), customer type, end-use application, and purchasing situation.

End-user profiling concentrates on how a product or service is used. Small firms often thrive in specific niches because larger firms may ignore small markets. Geographic profiling is used when customers are concentrated in a specific geographic area. Some examples include furniture makers in North Carolina, filmmakers in Vancouver, Canada, and biotechnology in San Diego. Such users have narrow and specific needs. If an industry leader is opening a plant in a different location, a new support business may do well in the area, as there will be less established competition.

Segmentation of business markets include the following:

- NAISC or SIC codes
- Sales revenue
- Number of employees
- End-use application
- Location
- Purchasing method (for example, low bid only or single sourcing)
- Credit risk
- Years in business
- Type of ownership (private, city, state, or federal government, nonprofit organizations)
- International versus U.S. sales
- Ability to reach decision maker
- Purchase decision: group or individual
- Economic and technological trends affecting industry
- Competitive nature of particular segments
- Barriers to entry into various segments

Use available secondary business information to help you:

- Check a firm's financial stability.
- Compare a firm's sales to its number of employees.
- Discover ownership of a firm or its subsidiaries.
- Locate specific companies.
- Search specific industries.
- Size up current and new markets by using multiple selection criteria.
- Search potential prospects or prospective employers in a targeted market.
- Identify decision makers so you can reach them directly.
- Identify and track competitors.

Chapter 5 contains information sources to track down business-to-business information. Hoover's, Dun and Bradstreet (D&B), ThomasNet, and infoUSA are just of few of the databases used to locate B2B customers. An abbreviated sample listing from ThomasNet appears in Figure 4.6. Also, throughout the text we have highlighted many government buyers who purchase billions of

ACTION STEP 25

Initial Customer Profile

1. Based on what you know to date, continue to profile your Target Customer using the following:
   - *Census*
   - *SRDS*
   - *Strategic Business Insights*
   - *Market Research.com*
   - *Experian*
   - *EASIdemographics*
   - Any additional databases that you can locate on the Internet or in the library

2. For B2B businesses, first access your customers' NAISC codes. Use sources you have already discovered as well as the following to profile your B2B clients:
   - *Hoovers*
   - *D&B*
   - *Edgar Online*
   - *Linkedin*
   - *Jigsaw*
   - *infoUSA*
   - *ThomasNet*

Also, search the library, association websites, and the Internet for directories that address your market. How large is the market in terms of numbers of customers? How large is the market in terms of potential sales? Who are the major players? List your top 10 prospects.

Focus on your Target Customer throughout the remainder of the chapter. As you recognize variables to add, or questions to be asked, jot them down. Action Steps 26 and 27 entail further profiling exercises.

figure **4.6**

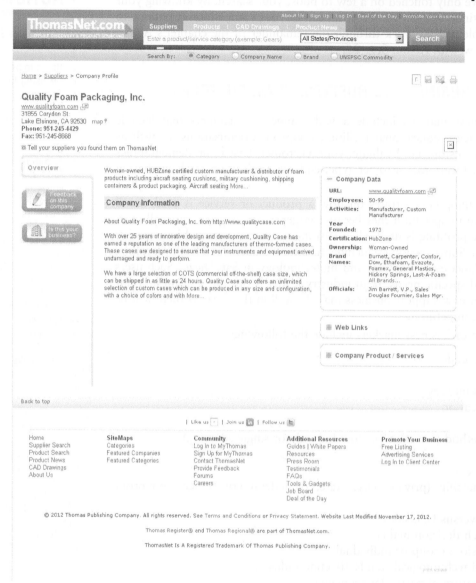

Source: Courtesy of *ThomasNet*.

dollars of products and services from civilian firms and encourage you to explore these markets.

In addition to the variables and information previously mentioned, personal traits of the individual buyers within each firm are important. Knowing the hobbies, activities, and lifestyles of the people to whom you are selling to may be as important as the listed demographic and geographic variables of the firms themselves. With LinkedIn and Facebook, gaining information and access to the right people is much easier than in past!

Relationships tend to be long term in B2B markets, and your ability to break into new markets may depend on your ability to break long-term relationships. Do *not* underestimate how difficult this may be.

■ PRIMARY RESEARCH IS ABSOLUTELY NECESSARY

Secondary sources of demographic and psychographic information, especially media sources, may provide enough data to form a fairly accurate profile of your Target Customer. Chances are, though, that you will need to test your profile against reality. Field interviews, surveys, and observation are three primary research tools that will provide you a more accurate profile of your Target Customer. Ben Gilad, leading competitive-intelligence researcher and author of *War Games: How Large, Small and New Companies Can Vastly Improve their Strategies and Outmaneuver the Competition* guides, "Only human sources can provide commentary, opinion, feelings, intuition, emotions, and commitment." Time for you to step out and meet your market!

Interviews Planned conversations by phone, mail, face-to-face, or on the Internet with another person or group of persons for the purpose of eliciting specific information

■ FIELD INTERVIEWS

Sometimes people enter into small businesses because of personal circumstances rather than an initial grand desire. Often they have to learn new skills and learn them fast. Fortunately, entrepreneurs tend to be bright, creative, and hardworking people. Jen Liong is a good example. When Jen discovered that she would have to work for herself, she quickly began to research her Target Customers by conducting field interviews.

Baby Store?

It was no secret that Jen Liong was distressed when her husband was transferred. She could not blame him for wanting the transfer; she would have wanted it, too. But Jen had a terrific job as regional manager of a full-line baby furniture and bedding store chain, and to keep both job and husband, she would have to commute more than 150 miles, 5 days a week. After many conversations and much soul searching, Jen and her husband decided to move to a lovely town with affordable housing near her husband's new workplace.

She missed her store, and it was hard living on one salary when they had gotten used to two. She also missed the excitement of retailing and customer contact. When Jen started to look for work, she found that her reputation had preceded her. The two local baby store owners knew of the chain where she had worked and were pretty sure that the only reason she wanted to work for them was to get a feel for the area so that she could open a store of her own and compete with them. This gave Jen an idea—to go ahead and compete with them. Their fear gave her confidence!

One thing Jen had learned on her way up the managerial and sales ranks was that it pays to know your customer. So, in the mornings after sending her children off to school, Jen would drive to various baby stores within a 60-mile radius of her town, and when customers came out of the local stores, she would strike up conversations with them and conduct casual interviews.

Being a mother helped her understand other mothers. She always dressed up a bit and asked obvious questions like:

- *What items did you buy?*
- *Was there anything you wanted and could not find?*
- *What do you like about this store?*
- *How close is this store to your home?*
- *Were the people helpful and courteous?*
- *How frequently do you shop here?*
- *At what other stores do you shop for baby items?*
- *What are your favorite parenting websites?*
- *What online stores do you purchase baby items from?*

Sometimes Jen parked in an alley to research the arrival and unloading of the delivery trucks. From experience she was able to estimate the store's purchases.

Jen developed a separate list of questions for pregnant women:

- *Have you had a baby shower?*
- *Which gifts did you like best?*
- *Which gifts seemed most useful?*

Entrepreneur's Resource

U.S. Census Bureau

AMERICAN FactFinder

Feedback   FAQs   Glossary   Help

MAIN   SEARCH   WHAT WE PROVIDE   USING FACTFINDER   English   Español

Your Selections

"Your Selections' is empty

Search using the options below:

Topics
(age, income, year, dataset, …)

Geographies
(states, counties, places, …)

Race and Ethnic Groups
(race, ancestry, tribe)

Industry Codes
(NAICS industry, …)

EEO Occupation Codes
(executives, analysts, …)

Quick Facts

Quick, easy access to facts about people, business, and geography.

Select the U.S. or a state to begin:

United States   GO

Popular Searches

- Decennial Census
- Population
- Poverty
- Housing
- Income

Your source for population, housing, economic, and geographic information

Quick Start

Enter search term(s) and click 'GO'

topic or table name   state, county or place (optional)

for   GO

○ topics ○ race/ancestry ○ industries ○ occupations

Or use the options on the left to begin your search

News and Notes   Sign up to receive New American FactFinder email updates

Nov 08, 2012

2011 Annual Survey of Manufactures (ASM) data are now available! The ASM provides sample estimates of statistics for all manufacturing establishments with one or more paid employees. Some key statistics include employment, payroll, supplemental labor costs, cost of materials consumed, operating expenses, value of shipments, value added by manufacturing, detailed capital expenditures, fuels and electric energy used, and inventories. more »

Oct 25, 2012

The 2009-2011 American Community Survey 3-year estimates are now available for cities, counties, and other geographic areas with populations of 20,000 or more. The 2009-2011 ACS 3-year data products are the first multiyear release to include the topic of Bachelor's Field of Degree. more »

Sep 27, 2012

Characteristics data for the population and housing units in urban and rural areas are now available from Summary File 1. The SF 1 urban/rural update provides data for individual urbanized areas and urban clusters, and the urban and rural portions (geographic components) of the Nation, regions, divisions, states, and more. Detailed tables P2 and H2 now provide the urban and rural population and housing unit counts, respectively, for all geographic entities. Detailed tables and quick tables, including a demographic profile, are available from SF 1. New Geographic Comparison Tables providing data for urban and rural areas will be released at a later date. New FTP files also are available. more »

Sep 27, 2012

Address Search

Find Census data by entering a street address.

View the American FactFinder Data Release Schedule

Download large volume data from the Census Bureau's FTP Site

A how-to guide for Building Deep Links into American FactFinder (PDF) is available

Reference Maps

Reference Maps show selected geographic boundaries for an area along with orienting features, such as roads.

United States   GO

Load Query

Use Load Query to restore a previously saved query

LOAD QUERY

Source: *http://factfinder2.census.gov/faces/nav/jsf/pages/index.xhtml*

- *What things are you buying before your baby comes?*
- *What things are you waiting to buy?*
- *How are you going to decorate the baby's room?*
- *What do you really need the most?*
- *What services would be most helpful to you?*

After completing 30 time-consuming interviews, Jen had an abundance of information along with her secondary research to make sound decisions concerning her Target Customer. She also learned how her potential customers viewed the strengths and weaknesses of her competition. Many times entrepreneurs look only for their competitors' weaknesses, but an entrepreneur can learn just as much from their competitors' strengths. Never underestimate the power of those strengths and the time and energy that went into developing them. Capitalize on the strengths of your competitors and take advantage of their weaknesses.

■ OBSERVING TARGET CUSTOMERS

Observing Using "new eyes" to learn about Target Customers

In addition to interviewing, Jen was involved in observing her customers. This is the least expensive but one of the most effective forms of market research. Put personal bias and intuition aside and truly observe your Target Customer. Take away all you know about your product or service and Target Customer and observe how your customer truly behaves—remember actions speak louder than words.

Several of Jen Liong's Target Customers shared that they bought all their children's clothing at upscale stores, but on observation she realized that more than half of the kids were dressed in Target and Wal-Mart clothing. People often say one thing but do another. Also, people do not always know why they make the purchasing decisions they make unless they spend some time thinking about their actions. They might not even recognize a need, but when presented with a new product or service based on your observations, it may be just what they wanted. Jen also observed the local stores focused on selling not only to mothers but also to the very large and lucrative market of doting grandmothers and aunts.

Use curiosity as you observe and interview. Ask as many open-ended questions as possible. When Jen Liong wrote down her interview responses, she also made notes of the following information:

- Makes and years of cars the women drove
- Attitudes toward their children
- Clothing worn by the children and their moms
- Types and brands of strollers
- Children's snacks
- Hairstyles and grooming of the mothers and children
- Amount spent on their own children versus gifts for others

In addition, Jen decided to check out the local playgrounds and snoop around. She took her friend's two small children, and off she went to ask questions. When Jen and her potential customers were surrounded by children in the park on a sunny day, the women opened up.

Jen combined the information she gathered from *http://www.census.gov*, *Standard Rates and Data Services Lifestyle Market Analyst* (SRDS), and VALS with her observations, interviews, and additional secondary data and was able to focus in on her target market.

To define their target market, a ladies specialty-clothing store considered hiring a marketing consultant. The first consultant proposed a lengthy research project at a cost of $4,000. The second consultant offered a $1,000 solution and asked the owner to pull together a list of the top 100 customers. With list in hand and after spending about 5 hours in the store observing, the consultant sat down with the top five saleswomen and together they were able to draw a circle around their Target Customer. The owner and salespeople knew from that point on who to put at the center of the dartboard. From that meeting, the buyers knew exactly who to buy for, and even the store's blog was reworked to meet the target market's needs and wants. The $3,000 saved was used to carry an additional line that the sales people believed, based on what they had observed, would sell quickly.

Where can you spend some time observing your Target Customer, and what will you ask them? In Chapter 5, when we research competition, we will return to interviewing and observing. Here, we will use another skill—surveying—to reach a more refined picture of a Target Customer.

■ SURVEYS

When Patti Hale, a budding entrepreneur, decided that she was going to work for herself, she quickly began to research Target Customers. The methods she chose were observation, interviewing, and surveying. You can do the same with your primary marketing research. Action Step 26 and Patti Hale's experience in the following paragraphs will guide you in conducting research for your potential business.

ACTION STEP 26

Interview and Observe Prospective Target Customers

Now that you have profiled your Target Customers using computer and media kit research, it is time for you to take a big step—to move from the world inside your head to the arena of the marketplace. It is time to rub elbows with the people who will be buying your product or service.

You know where your Target Customer hangs out, as well as his or her habits, income, lifestyle, personality, and buying patterns. You can guess this customer's dreams and aspirations. Now you are going to check out your assumptions directly by interviewing your potential Target Customers through additional research and observation.

1. First, observe your customer in the marketplace. Remember Jen Liong and the steps she took. Take notes as you simply observe.
2. Next, prepare for interviews. Develop questions in advance; most should be open ended and must call for more than just simple yes-or-no answers. Remember, the most important part of your research will be for you to keep an open mind. Your goal is to satisfy your customers' needs and thus you need to be open to *their* needs.
3. You may also conduct research by posting questions to newsgroups and social networks. Internet communities exemplify the free flow of information and you may find a very responsive group of people. Also, check out Survey Monkey, Ask Your Target Market, or Gutcheckit. com.

Designing and Conducting a Survey

A supervisor at a textile plant decided to leave her job and turn her love of food and people into a business: a restaurant. For some time, Patti had been developing her business skills. She had taken several courses in restaurant and bar management and an evening small-business course at a local college. In an attempt to gain a handle on her Target Customer, Patti read many studies on the dining habits of people in the Southeast. But how did these translate to her specific local market? Although the secondary research was very revealing, Patti could not risk her future on someone else's research and decided to do her own survey. She studied survey design and received advice from her professor, an experienced surveyor.

Patti considered surveying customers at Joe's Joint, one of the most popular eating spots in town. She often had a bite to eat there and got to know Joe, the owner, quite well. She told Joe about her plan to open a small restaurant some day and about how much she was learning in her small-business course. Patti convinced Joe to let her do a survey of his customers. After all, the price was right. Patti would do the survey free of charge and would give Joe the results—a classic win–win proposition.

Patti spent the next few days designing her survey method. How many customers should she survey? When should she do the survey? How should she conduct herself during the survey?

Next she developed the questions--How often do you eat out? How much do you spend with tax and tip included? What type of restaurants do you wish we had in town? Where do you go for special occasions? Where do you go for meals with your family? Date nights?

There was so much to do. She surveyed Joe's customers four evenings.

To Joe's surprise, customers wanted to fill out the questionnaire. To Patti's surprise, she overheard Joe explaining to someone that he thought it was about time he learned a bit more about what the customer wanted.

From her survey Patti determined that her target market saw no need or desire for additional restaurants in the town and in fact were actually cutting back on the amount they spent to eat out. This was a rude awakening for Patti. But at this point, she had only lost time and now could regroup and find another business idea, which might have more potential for profit.

■ MAKE CUSTOMER PROFILING A REFLEX

Profiling your customers will take time, energy, and diligent maintenance of future sales records. As you learn more and more about your customers, predicting their needs and wants will become easier. In addition, if you are fortunate, you will also uncover previously invisible customers who will emerge with needs that you have not anticipated. An alert entrepreneur will listen carefully to unexpected requests and be quick to respond to these opportunities, because a new market may be emerging. The following case is a typical example.

Invisible customer Surprise customer; usually a great find.

Some people go into business for themselves because they cannot work for someone else. Some are mavericks who do not like to take orders. Others are dreamers who love their own ideas. Still others, like Fred Bowers, have a physical handicap that makes them prefer self-employment to a job with a large firm. Sometimes customers "come out of the woodwork," as Fred's experience illustrates.

Soccer City's "Invisible Customers"

Fred Bowers had planned to be a career Marine until he was injured in a fall from a training helicopter. He could still walk, painfully, but his military career was finished. With a medical discharge in his pocket, Fred looked around for work, but none was to be found that would accommodate his disability.

"I'd always loved soccer," Fred said. "I'd been a pretty fair player, and my coaching experience had given me a good understanding of kids and their parents.

I thought there might be a place for a soccer specialty shop in our community, but before I went for financing, I spent several weeks checking it out."

Fred located 10 sporting-goods shops located within a 60-mile radius of his desired site and visited each. If he wished, for a small fee he could also access profiles, credit ratings, and credit reports on each of his potential competitors by conducting a search at Hoovers or D&B.

When Fred began profiling his Target Customers, he came up with two easy targets:

- *Primary target: male and female soccer players, age 4 to 12, and their parents*
- *Secondary target: male and female soccer players, age 13 to 18, and their parents*

He also gathered the following information:

- *Household income: $60,000 to $100,000 per year*
- *Level of parents' education: college degree*
- *Interests: sports, video games, movies, and music*
- *Automobiles: SUVs and Vans*

Then Fred segmented the youngsters into three groups: members of school soccer teams, members of American Youth Soccer Organization (AYSO) teams, and members of club and elite teams.

Because of Fred's knowledge of the game and helpful demeanor, his store prospered. Schools counted on him for an honest deal, and parents of players counted on his advice for equipment. "I had thought I'd just be selling products," Fred said. "What I was really doing was providing a service and playing therapist with parents and their children oftentimes."

After being in business a year, a third market began to emerge. The customers in this third group were adults, mostly foreign-born, from countries such as Great Britain, Mexico, and Brazil. They had grown up playing soccer and loved the game. To them, it was a fiercely fought national sport they loved to play. These heretofore-invisible customers would drive 50 to 75 miles to Fred's store for equipment they could not find elsewhere. Agreeing to sponsor several adult teams, his business continued to grow.

The next year, the local Boys and Girls Club started an indoor soccer league for 1,200 kids. Fred offered to sponsor all of the team photos. Needless to say, his business grew by supplying special indoor-soccer shoes and knee and shin pads. Fred now supplied AYSO and boys' high school soccer in fall, indoor soccer in winter, and girls' high school soccer in spring, and adult leagues that played primarily in spring and summer when fields were available.

"If I hadn't opened up, I wouldn't have known about the adult players. Now they make up at least 30 percent of my business. One day they weren't there; the next day they were. I like that. I like it a lot. It makes this whole adventure more interesting. Also, they really help with the cash flow, as the previous summers were awfully slow. In addition, keeping busy all year makes it much easier for me to be in the store day after day and to remain profitable."

■ VISUALIZING YOUR TARGET CUSTOMER

At this point, you have researched, surveyed, and observed your Target Customer. Now read how Louie Chen from Seattle was able to visualize his customer. Soon you will be able to do the same.

Louie Chen and His Dreams

Louie Chen, born in Seattle, grew up playing baseball but switched to tennis. This was a good choice because he became a professional and played on the tennis circuit for three years.

Worn down by constant travel, Louie Chen left the pro tour and returned to Seattle and a comfortable life as a stockbroker. He was a member of the chamber of commerce and several organizations for Asian Americans. Because of tennis, Louie did a lot of business at the country club. Louie was looking around for a new opportunity when he met Jiangli Chang, a recent immigrant to America.

ACTION STEP 27

Develop Target Customer Collage

Gather up all the information from the past three action steps. It is time to visualize your data.

1. Develop a collage—a composite image of your Target Customer. Look through magazines or online and select at least 30-45 pictures, phrases, and possibly statistics that represent your Target Customer's lifestyle.
2. Make a list of your customers' favorite television shows, movies, restaurants, activities, stores, radio stations, music, websites, magazines, and books and make the lists part of your collage. Creative types might consider doing a video to represent their Target Customer adding music.

Your collage should represent the demographics, geographics, and psychographics of your market. Use the research you have already conducted. If you haven't explored your competitors' Facebook fans, time to track back and snoop through the public profiles. Discover relationship status, political and religious views, education, employment, and a myriad of other interests. Also, use Pinterest and LinkedIn to access additional Target Customer interests.

After you complete the collage, hang it up near wherever you work on your Business Plan or make it your screensaver. Eat, sleep, and drink thinking about your Target Customer with the collage always in your line of sight as you prepare to hit the market with your product or service. As you develop your business, if you find you aimed incorrectly, correct the collage and your Target Customer definition and go forth again!

If you have a business-to-business product, complete your collage with NAISC/SIC codes, a list of 10 best prospects, pictures of the types of people you will be selling to, their lifestyles, and so on.

FOCUS! FOCUS! FOCUS!

Jiangli Chang, a middle-aged tennis player with a terrific backhand, was part of the Hong Kong exodus. He imported art from Japan and China. Jiangli expressed to Louie his difficulty in establishing a good banking relationship. Jiangli's problem started Louie Chen thinking. More and more Asians were coming to the Pacific Northwest. Recently, the Asian population in Washington had jumped 50 percent. With such growth, Louie Chen smelled opportunity. Louie enrolled in a local community college entrepreneurship course. His instructor was Grace Rigby, a marketing specialist, whose favorite tool was the Target Customer profile and collage.

"Profile your Target Customer. When you sleep, dream profiles. You'll have fun. You won't go wrong," Grace told him.

With Grace's help, Louie profiled his Target Customer. One of Grace's key teaching techniques was the Target Customer Collage.

"The collage combines all your data, interviews, surveys, and observations into a visual presentation," Grace said. "The idea is to clip pictures, statistics, phrases, and advertisements from magazines that represent your Target Customer. Then arrange all the pieces to form a collage. Hang the collage on the wall near your desk or make the collage online and use as your screensaver. When you find it difficult to write your Business Plan, focus on the collage. It should bring you right back into focus. Your sole purpose is to solve the needs and wants of your Target Customer."

Louie Chen's collage included the following pictures:

- *Six Asian men and women in business suits*
- *A private jet*
- *The Bank of Hong Kong*
- *Sushi*
- *An expensive leather briefcase and fine luggage*
- *Fine gold and diamond jewelry*
- *A laptop, Blackberry, and cellular phone*
- *An Asian man in shirtsleeves*
- *A man in a hardhat studying blueprints at a construction site*
- *An Asian man in golf gear teeing up at Pebble Beach*
- *Asian families traveling together*
- *Stock market tables*

The collage centered Louie on his Target Customer. Because he had an excellent credit history, a well-developed Business Plan, and a keen sense of his Target Customer, others were eager to finance Louie's bank. Louie chose the name Shangzai American Bank of Credit (SABC) for his bank and located it in the international district adjacent to downtown Seattle.

Specializing in the Asian market, Louie hired greeters such as Maryann Wu, who was fluent in Mandarin Chinese and Korean and spoke enough Japanese to get by. Maryann was studying Thai as well. She shook hands with customers and then directed them to a manager who spoke their native language or was very familiar with their country of origin.

One day while sitting at his desk, Louie saw an Asian male in his early fifties in the lobby. He wore an expensive tailored suit, carried a briefcase, and looked just like one of the men in his original collage. Louie hurried out of his office and greeted the gentleman, Sam Song, who subsequently deposited $1 million in his new SABC account.

Louie never stopped focusing on his Target Customer collage and had been adding to it during the past year in business. In fact, it was hanging in his office. But now he knew the person he wanted to celebrate with was Grace Rigby. Without Grace's insistence on focusing and refining his target market, he knew SABC would not have been a success.

Louie's Target Customer collage reflected business leaders, such as Sam Song. Customers who quite likely would be classified as Innovators on the VALS scale, with resources and deep interests in music and art. Louie found out later that one reason Sam Song immigrated to Seattle was for access to the Seattle Art Museum and the Pacific Northwest Ballet. It is now time for you to complete your own Target Customer collage following the instructions in Action Step 27. Start to visualize your customer. Keep the picture of your Target Customer in the forefront as you move into evaluating your competition and promoting your product.

■ SUMMARY

Before you open your doors, profile your Target Customer at least five times. After your doors are open, continue to gather data through surveys, interviews, sales information, Internet metrics, and observation. *Refine the profile continually.*

A profile combines demographic and geographic data (age, sex, income, education, residence, cultural roots, and so on) with psychographic insight (observations of lifestyle, buying habits, consumption patterns, attitudes, and so on). The magazines read and websites visited will also reveal a wealth of information about your Target Customers.

Questions you need to answer through profiling your Target Customer are:

1. Who are my Target Customers?
2. How can I best reach them?
3. What need will my product or service fill? (For example, landscaping is not just mowing grass and trimming shrubs. Its major selling points are enhancing the appearance and value of property and providing free time for homeowners.)
4. Where and how can I communicate my message with a minimum of confusion to my Target Customers?
5. What additional services do my Target Customers want?
6. What quality of service or product will meet my customers' desire?
7. What are they willing to pay?
8. Who else is after my customers?
9. Why do my customers act the way they do?
10. How can I build a long term relationship with my customers and encourage them to be raving fans and thus recruit new customers?

■ THINK POINTS FOR SUCCESS

- The term *psychographics* is derived from *psyche* and *graphos*, the Greek words for "life," or "soul," and for "written." Thus psychographics is the charting of your customer's life, mind, soul, and spirit.
- Segmenting is discovering the piece of the pie you should focus on. As you go deeper into your research, you will discover that perhaps you could reach the blueberries in the pie, and if you go further, you will reach the seeds—your true Target Customers. In essence, your collage developed in Action Step 27 should represent your blueberry seed. With

new technology, we may be able to reach the embryo of the seed!
- You can save a lot of time and money by using market research that has been conducted by others and such research should always be undertaken first.
- To discover your target market, use everything available: media kits, Internet metrics, demographic studies, lifestyle segmentations, and census data.
- Use NAISC or SIC codes to begin your research for B2B customers.
- Focus on your Target Customer.

■ KEY POINTS FROM ANOTHER VIEW

Your Customers Don't Make Rational Decisions

By Joe Hadzima with George Pilla

Behavioral economics and behavioral finance are some of the most fascinating areas of study today. The disciplines combine economics, finance, and psychology in ways that better model how consumers actually make

decisions. In general, the study of economics is based on theoretical models that only remotely resemble the complexities of the real world. These models assume that individuals behave like machines that always know what is in their best interest, always do what is in their best interest, have complete self-control, and only care about themselves.

That doesn't sound like anyone I know.

These models, on which many pricing decisions, investment decisions, and management decisions are based, leave out the "human element." Leaving out this element paints a two-dimensional picture of the world and doesn't provide the kind of actionable information of interest to business owners.

Behavioral economics, by including the study of psychology, adds the "human element" and can provide very valuable and actionable advice to business owners with respect to pricing and other important decisions. Let's take a closer look at the key elements of behavioral economics and how they apply to business decision-making.

First: Understand your customer's rules of thumb

Behavioral economics shows us that people make most of their decisions based on rules of thumb. A rule of thumb is an assertion that is true in many cases, but not in all cases. It also tends to be easy to remember and simple to apply. Common examples include:

- It's cheaper to buy a car than to lease one.
- You can get the best deals by shopping right after Christmas.
- Generics aren't as good as branded products.

There is some truth to these statements, but they absolutely do not apply to every circumstance. Yet once consumers internalize a rule of thumb, it is extremely difficult to convince them to change their minds.

Why not leverage these rules of thumb?

If your customers believe that shopping right after the Christmas holidays offers the best deals, then use that as an opportunity to sell higher margin products or to test new products and gauge the response. Even better, if your company can establish its own rule of thumb and spread it virally, it could be one of the most lucrative investments ever made.

Second: Frame your offering

Behavioral economics research also proves that *how* information is presented has a material impact on how consumers respond. Consumers, for example, respond more favorably to discounts when presented in percentage format instead of dollar format. An $18 entrée at a restaurant that is offered at 50 percent off will receive a greater response than advertising it as a $9 discount. Even though the economic benefit to the customer is identical, framing it as a percentage instead of a dollar amount will provide enhanced results.

Think about how many discounts and inventory clearance events your company has offered that didn't perform as expected. Did you frame the benefit correctly for your customers? Did you try different framing techniques and then compare the results? If not, then it would be highly advisable to do so next time.

Third: Markets are not efficient, so don't pretend they are

In an efficient market, identical products will sell at the same price because no one will pay more for something without justification. This, of course, assumes that buyers have perfect information about sellers and prices. It also assumes that all buyers value products in the same way. It doesn't take into account the individual perception that a consumer may have toward a product or service.

In the real world, it's clear that markets are not efficient. Consumers don't have perfect information and they don't value products identically. It's true that price comparison websites, group buying websites, and other online services have done much to enhance the amount of information available to buyers, but this is far removed from the "perfect" efficient market that economic models espouse.

The implications for the pricing of your products are enormous. Lower-priced competitors don't always have the advantage. For most businesses, it doesn't pay to be the lowest price competitor in the market. You just don't need to be.

Finally: People tend to act like sheep

Another key insight from behavioral economics is the fact that individuals do not always act individually. They are influenced by decisions made by their peers. Of the 7.5 million iPads that have been sold in the past six months, how many consumers bought one to take advantage of its functionality? How many bought it because all of their friends at work bought one? To Apple it may not make a difference why they buy, but the initial group of early adopters may have played a key role to complement Apple's great marketing and revolutionary product development.

If your company can build a trend around your product or service, then people will follow their peers and buy.

Mike Periu is the founder of EcoFin Media, LLC which develops financial training, financial education, entrepreneurship training and more to small business owners on television, radio, print and the internet. Over the past ten years he has started three companies and advised over 50 companies on financial strategies including fundraising.

Source: Mike Periu, "Your Customers Don't Make Rational Decisions." Copyright © 2012 American Express Company. All rights reserved. From *http://www.openforum.com/idea-hub/topics/managing/article/your-customers-dont-make-rational-decisions-1*, (Accessed May 30, 2012). Reprinted with permission.

■ ACTION STEPS

■ KEY TERMS

Image_Source/iStockphoto.com

Reading and Beating the Competition
Finding Marketplace Gaps

Learning Objectives

- Define competition in terms of size, growth, profitability, innovation, and market leaders.

- Discover your Target Customers' competitive touchpoints.

- Understand the value of positioning in relationship to competitors and Target Customers.

- Evaluate competitors using primary, secondary, and "new eyes" research.

- Develop skills to become the best marketplace detective you can be.

- Evaluate the competitive landscape broadly.

- Develop a competitor matrix.

- Create uniqueness to compete.

- Develop skills to become a lifelong scanner of the competitive landscape.

- Prosper in a rapidly changing competitive marketplace.

Only a few years ago, the subject of business competition conjured up warlike terms such as "beat the competition," "disarm your competitor," and "take a piece of their market." This market-sharing mentality assumed that when one went into business, one would take a piece of the action away from someone else. In an environment in which industries changed at a slow and predictable pace, the focus was aimed at attacking the competition—after all, there was little change going on, and this strategy seemed to be the only way to drum up new business.

The knowledge-based economy, technology, and the new, informed consumer have changed the way businesses view competition. Learning from and dancing with your competition is what the new economy is all about. Creating your own market niche and continually changing and improving your product or service as the customer dictates is the new goal. In many cases today, firms are creating new markets for products.

Competition is fiercely intense and constantly forces you to respond to market and industry changes at a lightning fast pace. To learn from some of the most successful entrepreneurs who thrive on competition and entering into new markets, listen to them daily at Stanford University's eCorner site (see Entrepreneurial Resource).

In the previous chapters, you learned about trend spotting, opportunity selection, and Target Customer profiling. We asked you to focus your business idea toward industry growth segments and customer needs. This chapter explains how your perceived competition can help you further define your specific niche—and it all starts with the customer. We recognize also that oftentimes you will enter into a mature market and offer steps to take in these markets as well.

Debbee and Steve Pezman, founders of *Surfer's Journal*, a high-quality, photograph-rich quarterly journal targeted to surfers older than 30, are guided by the following principle: "Identify your Target Customer, and serve them with a 'plus' that is hard to copy." As the Pezmans review new opportunities, they proceed only if they can answer "yes" to the following questions: "Is this a plus for our customer?" "Is this something our competitors will find difficult to copy?"

As you read through Chapter 5, completing the Action Steps and developing your business idea, continually ask the Pezmans' two questions to keep yourself on track and your customer in focus. Speed of information and change make being an entrepreneur more challenging, because products transition through the product life cycle so quickly. Take a moment to think about the following businesses: AOL, MySpace, and Digg. Consider how music has moved from records, eight-tracks, cassettes, CDs, Napster to iTunes. What's up next?

Roger D. Blackwell, independent consultant and professor of marketing at Ohio State University, shares:

> *There are too many companies chasing too few consumers, and the survivors are getting better and better at providing what consumers want. In the past*

many companies faced competition from great, average, and bad companies. But the bad and the average are being eliminated rapidly and we are left with only top-notch companies that are more likely to strive to have what the consumer wants. That puts pressure on all the surviving corporations, whatever their size, to conduct precise and speedy market research, so they can offer products that match consumers' desires sooner than the competition.

Product cycles have shortened in part because new products and product improvements have come from countrywide chains. A good idea in one part of the country quickly rolls out across the landscape. Local companies no longer have the luxury of waiting years before their competitors come up with better ideas. Now, new products that have been tested elsewhere—including other countries—quickly become competitive with local products. Honda, for example, has cut conception-to-production time from years to a matter of months. Technological advances in product design and development also have greatly sped up the pace of new product offerings.

Source: Joshua D. Macht, "The New Market Research," *Inc.*, *http://www.inc.com/magazine/ 19980701/964.html* (Accessed July 20, 2004). © 2004 Gruner + Jahr USA Publishing. First published in *Inc.* Magazine.

■ WHO IS YOUR COMPETITION?

Think back to Chapter 3, where we discussed defining your business, not in terms of products, but in terms of benefits—not selling a book per se, but selling information, enjoyment, or pleasant memories. If you choose to be an ice cream vendor, the thinking of the past would encourage you to list the vendors of all your competitors and pursue their business. In the new school of thought, your competition is anyone who currently provides or has the ability to provide the same benefit. If the benefit for your Target Customer is an afternoon treat, then your potential competitor is anyone who provides any number of treats.

Customers only have so many dollars, and everyone wants those dollars. Your customer could stop and buy specialty coffee drinks, yogurt, cupcakes, fruit smoothies, or cookies. All competing for your ice cream dollar. Other ice cream stores and yogurt stores in your area would be considered your primary or direct competitors, and the other businesses even grocery and convenience stores would be your indirect competitors.

Direct competitors Those companies or individuals that offer the same types of products or services, as perceived by your Target Customer

Indirect competitors Those companies or individuals that provide the same benefit, as perceived by your Target Customer

Never underestimate the power and influence of your indirect competitors. When exploring your competition, define it as broadly as possible at the beginning, and then work through the industry to identify direct and indirect competitors. Your competition is not necessarily who you think it is, although your views are important. *Your customers* truly define who the competition is, in terms of those who can best satisfy their needs and wants. How you solve their problems and make their lives easier will always be uppermost in your customers' minds.

Now, we want to introduce you to a third kind of challenge known as invisible competitors; that is, businesses that have the ability, capacity, background, and desire to compete if the sales and profits are evident. In a borderless, virtual environment, where you can order goods from as near as your next-door neighbor or from a place whose name you can't even pronounce, this type of invisible competition has become a real threat.

Invisible competitors People or businesses that have the capacity or desire to provide the same products, services, or benefits that you do

With Internet start-ups abounding, the ability to copy a site almost directly has proven very successful for the Samwer brothers of Germany, who have successfully copied Airbnb, eBay, and Groupon. According to one source, Airbnb took four years to develop and Wimdu, the copycat, took two months to develop! Warning, your invisible competitor may not be anywhere on your horizon and may only appear after you are successful. Power and money can move very quickly.

In a deep recession, customers may choose to withhold spending, thus, a "lack of cash" becomes your invisible competition. During the period of 2007-2010, "lack of cash" was a leading competitor for many tradespeople as homeowners became "do it yourselfers". "Lack of cash" won and many businesses closed their doors.

As you enter into your business, keep in mind that scanning your competitors is part of your daily business operation. No matter how hard you research, prepare, and monitor your competition, you *will* be surprised at how fast competitors will appear and affect your bottom line.

As you work through this chapter and complete your research, keep files containing relevant information on each of your competitors; at some point, you will be able to develop a Competitor Profile containing some of the elements presented in Figure 5.1 for each of your major competitors. Each entrepreneur will need to modify the profile to fit specific needs, issues, and goals while adding additional competitive variables for his or her respective industry and business model. Keep competitor files up to date as a matter of priority and never close your eyes to potential competition.

■ COMPETITIVE TOUCHPOINT ANALYSIS

As we have said before, people do not simply purchase products or services; they also buy what the products and services do for them. The customer's cry is: What's in it for me? How does your product make my life better, easier, more productive, and fun? How does it make me younger, sexier, or smarter? How does it reduce my costs and make me more profitable? To evaluate your competition, first you need to recognize what is of value to your customer.

Gather together a small group of your potential Target Customers for a "group think" on your competitors. Walk together through the entire experience your customers encounter with your competition. We like to call this process competitive touchpoint analysis. Each touchpoint represents a moment when the customer has contact with anything affiliated with the firm—advertising, products, website, public relations, receptionists, salespeople, or the store.

Competitive touchpoint analysis - Review of each time customer has contact with company

A restaurant owner or medical practice easily could develop a list of 150 touchpoints. Understand that at each touchpoint, the customer decides to go further or not with the sale. If they do purchase, their repeat purchases will be dependent on whether their needs at each touchpoint were satisfied. Web analytics today gauges how individuals use a site at many of these touchpoints and thus can adjust the site rapidly.

Compiling a touchpoints' list forces you to acknowledge your competitors' strengths and weaknesses. In addition, recognizing your competitors' strengths may indicate several areas where you should avoid competing, as the competition will be intense and take valuable time, energy and resources to succeed.

You will also discover several touchpoints that are absolutely necessary for success and which you must provide. List the touchpoints as defined by your Target Customers and ask them to rank their importance. Ask them which touchpoints are the non-negotiable ones. Then ask the following questions: Where do openings exist? Can you successfully compete in those openings? What needs are not being met? What area could you capitalize on? Where do

figure **5.1**

Elements of a Competitor Profile

Competitor Profile Elements

Searching for your competitive strengths and weaknesses requires identifying, classifying and tracking past, current and future actions of your competitors. Finding gaps in the competitive landscape will open up opportunities.

Use the following list as a guideline, adjusting for your competitive position, industry, and business.

Firm Identification:

Legal Name—informal or abbreviated versions. Note any parent company or subsidiaries, including globally (note any future plans for growth)

Contact Information—primary address, additional locations, Websites, email, phone, fax, LinkedIn

Company Organization—legal and organizational structure

Ownership—private or public, owners/percentages/involvement, note any proposed changes

Culture—beliefs, treatment of employees, customers, and suppliers, turnover of employees

History—length, successes, failures, expansions, brand loyalty

Environmental Forces:

Evaluate the firm's ability to respond to changes with the following forces: Social, cultural, legal, political, economic, and technology. Also, evaluate international issues regarding sales, manufacturing, distribution and marketing as well as the forces above.

Do any of your competitors have the strength to impact regulations and laws, which may allow them to gain a competitive advantage?

Assess supplier power, buying power, competitive rivalry, the threat of substitution and the threat of new entry as suggested by Michael Porter's Five Forces Analysis.

Credibility and Assets of the Firm:

Size, Stability, Reputation and Credibility—within industry, community, customers, suppliers, wholesalers

Proprietary Assets—Current and pending patents, trademarks, copyrights; trade secrets or processes, and brand names

Operational Capability:

Firm's Internal Resources and Abilities—1) employees (union, contract, shift, availability, experience) 2) facilities and equipment (age, technological advantages).

Outside Assets—relationships with subcontractors, wholesalers, and any strategic alliances or licensing deals.

Consider strongly any competitive operational advantages, such as economy or scale, low and or flexible overseas production, or engineering and technological expertise.

Product Design/Services and Innovation:

Product or Service—numbers, lines, quality, support, future product or services on horizon as well as R&D (research and development activities)

Design—strength of design team

Product life cycle—length of cycle and time to recoup costs

Strength of logo and brand recognition

Keep eyes on direct and indirect competition.

Revenue:

Sales and Market Share—watch for the gorilla in any market and also the sleepers whose sales are skyrocketing

Market Strategy:

Target Markets—primary, secondary, define specific target

Key Players:

Key Employees—management, engineering and design

Board of Directors—assess strength of board and involvement

Planned Additions to Management Team -look to Internet job listings and LinkedIn to follow ascertain movements

Finance Resources:

Items to Assess—cash flow, profit margins, balance sheet, income statements, inventory, cost of goods sold, return on investment (ROI), new capital investment

Look toward published financial statements if available. If not, gather industry averages through government and industry sources.

© Cengage Learning 2014

you see yourself being strong or weak? What images are your competitors projecting? What image will you project?

Recall Susan's Healthy Gourmet from Chapters 3 and 4. Let's walk through some possible touchpoints for Susan's customers. Keep in mind that many more touchpoints could be added to the following list:

- Clicks on Facebook ad: What is the quality of the banner advertisement? Is it professional? Is it directed to the right person? How many ads does the person probably see before responding?
- Responds to advertisement: How is the website designed? How easy is it to navigate? How easy is it to determine costs and programs? If the potential client has diet issues, how easy is it to find information? If the information cannot be located, can a client contact Susan's Healthy Gourmet? Is there a phone contact? If so, is the person who answers pleasant? How long does the customer wait on hold for a salesperson? Is the on-hold music appropriate? Is the salesperson knowledgeable and helpful? If the customer asks a question, which the salesperson cannot answer, how quickly does she receive a response? Is the program explained clearly? Are the customer's concerns addressed fully?
- Places order: Is the order form easy to fill out online and understand? Is the form attractive? Is delivery clear? Are alternatives clearly spelled out? Is ordering online easy and quick? Is there a real person to call if the customer has problems ordering online?
- Receives order: Is the correct order received at the right time and place? Is the meal attractively presented? Are heating directions clear? How does the meal taste?
- Calls to complain or change an order: How are complaint calls or changed orders handled? Are problems resolved in a timely fashion? Are follow-up calls made to ensure that the customer's problem has been rectified? Are clients treated with respect?

Discover the customer touchpoints in your business by completing Action Step 28. Later you will complete a competitor matrix to continue to evaluate your competitors. Once you have completed Chapters 6 and 7, return to Action Step 28 and refine your original answers.

To compete you need to stand out! Develop a distinctive competency. Own a niche or create a new market space. Success in business is not based merely on obtaining customers; true success is achieved by *retaining* customers. As you seek out your competitors' strengths, look for features that encourage customer loyalty. Keep reviewing your touchpoints, and aim for exceeding your competitors' offerings if this is within financial reason. Be consistent with your focus on the perceived *benefits* your customers receive.

If you truly listened to your potential customers as you completed the previous Action Steps, you may already be on your way to developing a profitable market niche. Niches may make you rich, but to maintain a profitable business over the long run, it is also important to build a reputation so customers will be consistently drawn in. This chapter enables you to dig even more deeply to develop a strategy and framework to compete as you put the pieces together from past Action Steps, such as trend spotting, identifying your Target Customer, and conducting competitive intelligence.

■ COMPETITIVE INTELLIGENCE

To further identify your direct, indirect, and invisible competitors, you need to conduct competitive intelligence (CI). The Society of Competitive Intelligence Professionals (SCIP) defines competitive intelligence as the "process of ethically

ACTION STEP 28

Evaluating Customer Touchpoints

Investigate your customer's perception of the competition and what benefits are important to him or her. As you look for a niche in the marketplace, you must review your competitors' actions, services, and products. Take a moment now to review Susan's Healthy Gourmet's Customer Touchpoints.

Work with a group of your potential Target Customers, and walk through the experience of purchasing your competitors' products. Make a long list (at least 60 to 80 items) of the touchpoints. Each facet of the entire product combines to make the jewel. The more you know about the jewel, the more you can make it shine.

1. After listing the touchpoints, ask Target Customers to select and rank their five most important touchpoints. As you review all your competitors' touchpoints, consider how you can equal or beat your competitors in these areas.
2. In what areas can you provide either real or perceived additional value for the customer?

Decide which facets are worth going head-to-head with, which are not worth dealing with, which are required by your customer, and which areas you can outperform your competition. Keep your touchpoints handy; you will return to them in Chapters 6 and 7. When writing your Business Plan, capitalize on the touchpoints that make you stand out in the crowd and are of most value and benefit to your customer.

Competitor matrix A grid used to get a clear picture of competitors' strengths, weaknesses, and other attributes

Distinctive competency Area of greatest strength in the marketplace

Competitive intelligence The process of analyzing information about your competitors, economy, customers, and applying to the future collecting, analyzing, and disseminating accurate, relevant, specific, timely, fore-sighted, and actionable intelligence regarding the implications for the business environment, competitors, and the organization itself. Intelligence is more than reading newspaper articles; it is about developing unique insight regarding issues within a firm's business environment. Note that the intelligence process generates insightful recommendations regarding *future* events for decision makers, rather than simply generating reports on the current competitive landscape. The process offers critical choices regarding future decisions that provide a desired competitive advantage."

Competitive intelligence is proactive, not reactive. Your major objective is to identify future customer needs and opportunities. The objective is *not* to eliminate your competitors but to *learn* and *benefit* from them as you develop and improve your specific niche or position in the marketplace. The following are 11 common goals of competitive intelligence:

1. Improve product features and customer benefits.
2. Improve customer service.
3. Find new ways to distribute product or service.
4. Improve advertising and promotions.
5. Develop more efficient production processes.
6. Reduce reaction and delivery time.
7. Add value to product or service.
8. Find new alliances and strategic partners.
9. Find new ways to grow current product or service.
10. Develop new product or service opportunities.
11. Add the human touch to your business.

Your competitive intelligence on the environmental factors, social/cultural, legal/political, economic, and technology from Chapters 2 and 3 will help you analyze the big picture. Chapter 4 looked at your Target Customers; and within this chapter, CI focuses on competition and its relationship to your Target Customers.

In the current business environment, competitor data is often free, instant, and easy to access. For example, if you want to produce noise cancelling earphones, visit Amazon and leading audio websites to read reviews. You will instantly learn about your competitors. Keep digging to learn which features need improvement and if there are any additional features customers desire in the future.

These reviews also provide you with the basis to formulate more complex questions for individual interviews, surveys, and focus groups as discussed in Chapter 4. In addition, you can jump online and read comments on the competitors' websites. Search Twitter for anything trending. By searching online, you will discover 1) what customers are saying 2) what third parties are saying 3) what companies and their employees are saying and 4) what industry insiders are sharing and questioning.

Use WeFollow or Listorium to find competitors, suppliers, engineers, or trend leaders to follow on Twitter. To manage Twitter information, Tweet-deck or Hootsuite may work for you. Stay abreast of the language used to describe your product and industry categories and make sure you know all of the Icons and sites where traffic is flowing, such as Twitter, Facebook, and LinkedIn.

If you want company or employee information, LinkedIn and LinkedIn Groups provide a treasure trove of information. Locate experts, see what questions are being asked, and you may find a niche within those questions—or at least ideas to follow up on. LinkedIn recently purchased Slideshare, another source of information, where you can locate presentations developed by your competitors and industry experts. You may discover some valuable secrets!

Google Alerts will keep you posted whenever your competitors, industry, or customers are mentioned. Years ago, there existed clipping services designed to cut out articles from hundreds of newspapers, magazines, and journals for clients. Today, two seconds on Google will provide that information for free. If you have complex items you want researched or tracked, consider hiring a programmer. Tell that person what you want and magically it will appear.

Compete, Quantcast, and Alexa track your competitors' online activities. Traffic, engagement, keyword and search metrics, demographic data, web rankings, referrals, and benchmarking are just a start of web analytics. Companies in this area are growing rapidly, so search for alternative web analytic firms who might specialize in your industry and/or Target Customer.

Depending on your business, you might need to monitor eBay, Pinterest, Yelp, TripAdvisor, or the many other online sites where your potential customers, shop, read reviews, or compare prices. Please note again that product development, distribution, location, and marketing are melding together as technology continues to effect vast and rapid change. Thus, you not only need to keep abreast of your industry but abreast of the business world in general.

For more insight into the importance of competitive intelligence, Fuld & Company, Inc., one of the leading intelligence firms, shares in Figure 5.2 what competitive intelligence is and what it is not.

Aim your competitive intelligence efforts at the environment, Target Customers, products, and competitors. Analyze the past but look to the future as you try discovering a niche in the marketplace. As eyeglass manufacturer, Warby Parker (see Key Points from Another View), found an opening to provide affordable stylish eyeglasses to the masses through their niche online business model.

■ CONTINUE SCOUTING THE COMPETITION

There are thousands of secondary sources to gather information in addition to the ones presented throughout the text. Although knowledge is power, action brings results. Evaluate your own style to determine if you have a tendency to overanalyze a situation. Too much information can lead one to analysis paralysis, and fear of failure can keep one stuck in a cycle of unproductivity. Are you afraid to make mistakes? If so, understand now you *will* make mistakes. The true entrepreneur chalks them up to experience, uses them as a tool to make better decisions in the future, and moves on not looking back.

Work from your strengths: which are built on knowledge. Awareness of your competitors' strengths and weaknesses will increase your confidence. Then you will succeed.

If you haven't yet scouted your competition by becoming a customer, it is time to do so: 1) review their websites and sign up for member loyalty programs, 2) visit their stores at several times of day, 3) call their 800-numbers, and 4) purchase items, pull them apart, investigate how they are made. Just as you asked your Target Customer questions about the buying process, ask yourself the same questions. But always remember, what is important to *your* customers is far more important than what you think is important! Listening is your secret weapon.

In researching your competition, look to government agencies that will lead you to information on public offerings, building permits, and registration for

figure 5.2

What Is Competitive Intelligence?

FULD&COMPANY
The Global Leader in Competitive Intelligence

Competitive Intelligence Is...	Competitive Intelligence Is Not...
1 Competitive Intelligence is information that has been analyzed to the point where you can make a decision.	**Competitive Intelligence is not spying.** Spying implies illegal or unethical activities. While spying does take place, it is a rare activity. Think about it; corporations do not want to find themselves in court, nor do they want to upset shareholders. For the most part, you will find spies in espionage novels, not in the executive suite.
2 Competitive Intelligence is a tool to alert management to early warning of both threats and opportunities.	**Competitive Intelligence is not a crystal ball.** There is no such thing as a true forecasting tool. Intelligence does give corporations good approximations of reality, near- and long-term. It does not predict the future.
3 Competitive Intelligence is a means to deliver reasonable **assessments.** Competitive intelligence offers approximations and best views of the market and the competition. It is not a peek at the rival's financial books. Reasonable assessments are what modern entrepreneurs such as Richard Branson, Bill Gates, and Michael Dell need, want, and use on a regular basis. They don't expect every detail, just the best assessment at the time.	**Competitive Intelligence is not database search.** Databases offer just that — data. Of course it is wonderful to have these remarkable tools. Nevertheless, databases do not massage or analyze the data. They certainly do not replace human beings who need to make decisions by examining the data and applying their common sense, experience, analytical tools, and intuition.
4 Competitive Intelligence comes in many flavors. Competitive intelligence can mean many things to many people. A research scientist sees it as a heads-up on a competitor's new R&D initiatives. A salesperson considers it insight on how his or her company should bid against another firm in order to win a contract. A senior manager believes intelligence to be a long-term view on a marketplace and its rivals.	**Competitive Intelligence is not the Internet or rumor chasing.** The Net is primarily a communications vehicle, not a deliverer of intelligence. You can find hints at competitive strategy, but you will also uncover rumors disguised as fact, or speculation dressed up as reality. Be wary of how you use or misuse the Net. Its reach is great, but you need to sift, sort, and be selective on its content.
5 Competitive Intelligence is a way for companies to improve their bottom line.	**Competitive Intelligence is not paper.** Paper is the death of good intelligence. Think face-to-face discussion or a quick phone call if you can, rather than paper delivery. Never equate paper with competitive intelligence. Yes, you must have a way to convey critical intelligence. Unfortunately, many managers think that by spending countless hours on computer-generated slides, charts and graphs, and footnoted reports, they have delivered intelligence. All they have managed to do is to slow down the delivery of critical intelligence. In the process, they have likely hidden the intelligence by over-analyzing it. Remember: Paper cannot argue a point — you can.
6 Competitive Intelligence is a way of life, a process. If a company uses CI correctly, it becomes a way of life for everyone in the corporation — not just the strategic planning or marketing staff. It is a process by which critical information is available for anyone who needs it. That process might be helped by computerization, but its success rests upon the people and their ability to use it.	**Competitive Intelligence is not a job for one, smart person.** A CEO might appoint one individual to oversee the CI process, but that one person cannot do it all. At best, the CI Ringmaster, the coordinator of the program, keeps management informed and ensures that others in the organization become trained in ways to apply this tool within each of their SBUs.

(continued)

—figure **5.2**

What Is Competitive Intelligence? *(continued)*

Competitive Intelligence Is...	Competitive Intelligence Is Not...
7 **Competitive Intelligence is part of all best-in-class companies.** High-quality, best-in-class corporations apply competitive intelligence consistently. The Malcolm Baldridge Quality Award, the most prestigious total quality award for American corporations, includes the gathering and use of external market information (a.k.a. CI) as one of its winning qualifications.	**Competitive Intelligence is not an invention of the 20th century.** CI has been around as long as business itself. It may have operated under a different name or under no name at all, but it was always present. Just review the story surrounding 19th century British financier Nathan Rothschild, who managed to corner the market on British government securities by receiving early warning of Napoleon's defeat at Waterloo. He used carrier pigeons, the e-mail of his day. He knew the information to watch and how to make sense of it; in the end, he used this intelligence to make a killing in the market.
8 **Competitive Intelligence is directed from the executive suite.** The best-in-class intelligence efforts receive their direction and impetus from the CEO. While the CEO may not run the program, he dedicates budget and personnel; most important, he promotes its use.	**Competitive Intelligence is not software.** Software does not in and of itself yield intelligence. The CI market is hot, and numerous software houses are producing products for the intelligence marketplace. Many more are repositioning existing software — in particular, data warehousing and data mining packages — for use in intelligence. Software has become an important weapon in the CI arsenal, but it does not truly analyze. It collects, contrasts, and compares. True analysis is a process of people reviewing and making sense of the information.
9 **Competitive Intelligence is seeing outside yourself.** Companies that successfully apply competitive intelligence gain an ability to see outside themselves. CI pushes the not-invented-here syndrome out the window.	**Competitive Intelligence is not a news story.** Newspaper or television reports are very broad and are not timely enough for managers concerned with specific competitors and competitive issues. If a manager first learns of an industry event from a newspaper or magazine report, chances are others in the industry already learned of the news through other channels. While media reports may yield interesting sources for the CI analyst to interview, they are not always the most timely, or specific enough for critical business decisions.
10 **Competitive Intelligence is both short- and long-term.** A company can use intelligence for many immediate decisions, such as how to price a product or place an advertisement. At the same time, you can use the same set of data to decide on long-term product development or market positioning.	**Competitive Intelligence is not a spreadsheet.** "If it's not a number, it's not intelligence." This is an unspoken, but often thought of, refrain among managers. "If you can't multiply it, then it is not valid." Intelligence comes in many forms, only one of which is a spreadsheet or some quantifiable result. My firm has completed numerous strategic assessments, where the numbers only address one aspect of the problem. Management thinking, marketing strategy, and ability to innovate are only three among a host of issues that rely on a wide range of subjective, non-numeric intelligence.

Leonard Fuld is president and founder of Fuld & Company, to a Cambridge, Massachusetts USA headquartered consulting firm with offices in London, Manila and Singapore and a pioneer in the field of competitive intelligence. Author of *The Secret Language of Competitive Intelligence* (Random House, 2006). In the past three decades, his firm has served over half the Fortune 500 in the United States, as well as many European companies.

Source: "What is Competitive Intelligence?" by Leonard M. Fuld President, Fuld & Company, Inc. Retrieved from *http://www.fuld. com/company/what-is-competitive-intelligence* (Accessed May 30, 2012). Reprinted with permission.

patents and trademarks. A company's goals, strategies, and oftentimes, technologies will be presented in the public records.

Talk with potential suppliers who will provide great insight into your competitors and the big picture. However, beware of and remember those suppliers who provide you with confidential information—as in the future they will provide the same information about you to your competitors.

Attend trade shows always asking open-ended questions, observing sales people and potential Target Customers, and investigating new products. And no one knows an industry's customers better than the salespeople. The more of your competitors' salespeople you encounter, the more you will learn.

ACTION STEP 29

Scouting Competitors and Finding Your Position on the Competitive Ladder

1. Complete secondary research on competitors. Do not worry if your list of competitors gets too long. The more competitors you detect, the more you can learn.

2. Using your touchpoints and past research, develop a competitor review sheet for each competitor as you begin to build your competitor profiles, as shown in Figure 5.1.

3. Start snooping: Evaluate competitors and rate them from 1 to 10. If you cannot move inside without blowing your mystery shopper disguise, send in a friend with your checklist, or make some telephone calls. You can elicit valuable information from a phone call prepared in advance. Interview everyone who will talk to you. Keep this Action Step handy; you will need it to complete Action Step 30.

Many trade shows require membership in their association to attend. If you are not yet a member, find someone who is and ask if you can come as their guest. If that is not available to you, hang out in the lobbies, coffee shops, and restaurants near the venue and ask questions of those you are sitting by. If you have done your research, carrying on a conversation with industry insiders should not be difficult.

Half the battle of succeeding is learning to understand the obstacles and to be on top of developments—to take advantage of all opportunities. The beauty of being an entrepreneur is being nimble enough to react quickly to change. However, you must understand the economy and your industry to know how best to react.

Even with all the research and knowledge, the key is to never underestimate your Target Customers' loyalty, fickleness, and resistance to change. Although in some areas, the desire for anything new will suffice—however, that is a tough business to maintain, as you receive little repeat business and constantly have to find new customers. Most of the time you must offer customers strong reasons to try your product and even stronger reasons to continue to use it.

Complete Action Step 29 to gain a foothold and improve your position on your customer's purchase ladder.

CI experts also suggest reviewing speeches, TV and radio programs, podcasts, blogs, government documents and research as well as attending workshops and conferences. Also, working with professional librarians may open up new avenues as well. Be careful when searching on the Internet: *Don't believe everything you read*. Unbiased and truthful data are often hidden or manipulated. Proceed with caution on making any decision based solely on Net info.

The importance of marketing research and CI is not the collection of the data but the processing of that data into information, analyzing so that it becomes knowledge, and then communicating that information to the decision makers. This process should be continual, encompassing all employees within your company.

Additional CI resources include industry research reports, which can be purchased through many resellers for example: Market Research.com, Research and Markets, and the Alacra Store. These sites provide research from more than 400 leading national and international research firms covering thousands of products and services. With free- and low-cost reports, you will find that many times, most of your secondary research has already been completed or at least the reports will provide you a head start.

Also, MarketResearch.com's free online research specialists will guide you to available appropriate and relevant research to purchase. As we have said before, keeping in touch with your trade or professional associations is essential, as is attending industry workshops and special meetings. Also consider accessing the fee-based services, as discussed in Chapter 3.

Sources such as the Science and Technical Information Network provide very detailed competitive information for a very low cost. College Internet sites will also lead you to researchers and programs in your area of expertise. Private database vendors are invaluable and necessary for anyone in a technical field.

Actively visiting and participating in online newsgroups, social networks, and blogs will help you unearth competitive nuggets. Make sure to spend a great deal of time on your competitors' and suppliers' websites. Presentations and papers by managers and researchers often can be accessed directly through company websites. Some researchers monitor company website job postings and infer the direction a technical company may be headed by combing through job specifications.

Looking outward, CI forces one to consider legal and political changes and their potential ramifications on future products and services. In addition, you must also always be scanning the world environment for ideas and competition. Use the *CIA*

FactBook, World Competitiveness Yearbook, http://www.export.gov, and other sources highlighted throughout the text to gather market intelligence and CI for your international business ventures. One way to keep competitive and to be able to sell internationally is to follow ISO standards (See Global Village).

Here are a few additional tips and tactics for scanning the competitive landscape mentioned in a Fast Compay article written in May 2012 by Michael Tchong (author of *Social Engagement* and founder of Social Revolution) and Richard Watson:

1. Every time you see something new happening, ask why it is happening-and how. And remember to question the answers you get. What are the upstart startups in your market doing? Are they all doing the same thing? Different things? Why?
2. Look for the patterns that link new ideas, attitudes and behavior. What's the same and what's different about the two new ideas? What do they share? Where do they contradict or diverge from one another? Why?
3. Watch for countertrends. If almost everyone is going one way and you see someone going in another direction, try to understand *why.* Perhaps they have seen an opportunity or challenge others have missed and you should follow in their footsteps.
4. Step back and look at the big picture regularly. Don't miss the big change or the big trend because you never raised your eyes from the micro-level.
5. Don't get swept away by short-lived fads. It's not always easy to tell a fad from a real trend, but keep questioning yourself at every step as you go along.
6. Finally, remember you don't have to reinvent *everything:* there is no need to forget or ignore the past or act as though it is completely irrelevant. If you closely study the history of products ad markets and also keep your eyes open to what is new and different today, then you will have the best foundation possible for determining what these products and markets will do in the future.

If you get all this right, there is good money to be made in second guessing the future. At the same time, good money can also be lost getting it wrong. And the really big money? Well, that does not come from following trends.

That comes from people with original ideas who *create* trends. People with the courage to build something—and then see if anyone will come. For everyone else, being a fast follower is probably the next best option.

■ SECONDARY RESEARCH SOURCES AND REPORTS

With the steps above in mind, continue to focus on your competitors and customers. The list of resources that follows, in addition to those previously presented, will assist you in secondary research. Two additional wonderful listings of resources can be found at Research on Main Street and Steve Blank's websites. Secondary research narrows your focus and prepares you for primary data searching.

Library and Internet References for Companies and Industries

To determine if the firm is publicly owned or privately owned/closely held:

- EDGAR Online

For international company information:

- D&B Principal International Business
- European Wholesalers & Distributors Directory

- World Trade Center Association World Business Directory
- Dun's Latin America's Top 25,000
- *World Trade* Magazine

For parent companies and subsidiaries:

- Directory of Corporate Affiliations
- D&B's America's Corporate Families
- Who Owns Whom: North America
- Guide to American Directories

For a company's type of business, executive officers, number of employees, and annual sales:

- Standard & Poor's Register of Corporations
- D&B's Million Dollar Directory
- Ward's Private Company Profiles
- Standard & Poor's Register of Corporations, Directors, & Executives
- Dun's Business Rankings
- Hoover's Billion Dollar Directory

For corporate background and financial data:

- Standard & Poor's Corporate Records
- Moody's Manuals
- Walker's Manual of Western Corporations

For company news:

- *Wall Street Journal* Online
- PR Newswire
- *Business Journals* website (access to 40 local business markets)

For specialized directories:

- Thomas Register of American Manufacturers
- Standard Directory of Advertising Agencies
- U.S.A. Oil Industry Directory
- Medical and Healthcare Marketplace Guide

For company rankings:

- Annual issues of Fortune, Forbes, Business Week, include Fortune 500, Global 500, America's Most Admired Companies, and the 100 Best Companies to Work For

Secondary sources may provide the most helpful future primary resource: access to the names and phone numbers of people involved in your industry and those who may have conducted research in your area. Now you have to be able to verify information and conduct interviews. You will be absolutely amazed at the incredible information people will share with you over the phone and through the Internet. Deal honestly with all of your contacts, and explain your reason for calling and requesting information; act responsibly and ethically.

Jan P. Herring, a former employee of the CIA ad current ower of Herring and Associates, wrote "Human Intelligence beats machine intelligence as most information never gets written down—it's just floating in people's heads." Thus, the only way to access human intelligence is to talk to people. Use your network and always look for opportunities to increase the size and extent of your network.

And always remember: The best information on your competitors comes from your customers. Be polite and don't put them in an awkward position. Say things like, "I know you have other choices. I appreciate your business and want it to continue. What am I and others doing that you most like/least

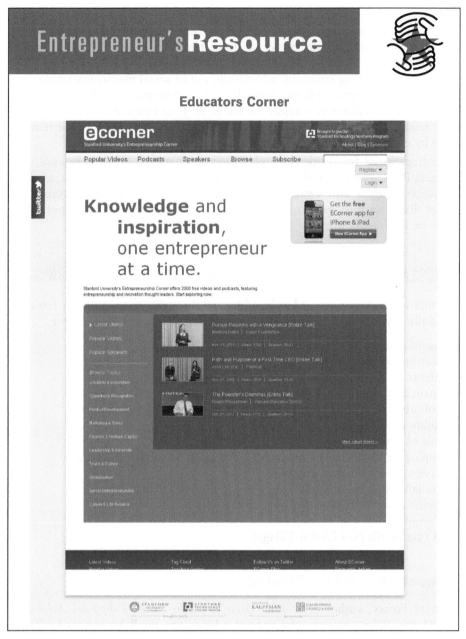

Educators Corner

Source: *http://ecorner.stanford.edu* (Accessed May 12, 2012).
Author's Note: Spend 15 minutes each day listening to the brightest entrepreneurial minds in the United States as they discuss globalization, marketing, financing, and opportunity recognition. Your entrepreneurial juices will flow!

like? What does my competition offer that you think I should also offer? What do you need that no one offers? What can we do to help each other grow and prosper?"

If your business or service is affordable, pay your friends and family members to purchase the products or services. Then discuss their experiences as well as yours. If they are purchasing from a website, sit down with them and watch how they maneuver through the site.

The more feedback you have, the better. Though, always be a little leery of your friends' and family's opinions. Some will only tell you what you want to hear, and others will be "Debbie Downers" and only remind you of the negatives. For true honesty, make sure you gather other opinions.

For each business, develop a competitor worksheet; it will become a competitor profile (see Figure 5.1), which includes all the important touchpoints and the competitor's business name, owner, address, telephone, e-mail address, Twitter, Facebook, length of time in business, estimated market share, Target Customer profile, image, pricing structure, advertising, use of social media, marketing, customer service, return policies, special order offerings, cleanliness, stocking, strengths, and weaknesses—adjust the list to fit your business. Take this part of your research seriously, because you are discovering your niche in the marketplace by evaluating your competitors.

Entrepreneurs frequently downplay their competitors. When you write your Business Plan, you will need to complete a thorough competitor section, explaining their strengths and weaknesses, and then you will need to convince your reader that your business can fill a niche left by these competitors. *Once again, never underestimate the power of your competitors.*

■ RESEARCH FOR MANUFACTURERS AND SCIENTIFIC FIRMS

The following areas may need to be addressed through your competitor research, especially if you are involved in a manufacturing or a scientific endeavor.

- Manufacturing facilities
- Distribution channels and facilities (in depth)
- Patents
- Financial strength
- Profitability
- Ability to acquire expansion capital
- Cost of production
- Employees (skilled sales force, great engineers, or software designers)
- Service reputation and availability
- Availability of spare parts
- Repair costs
- Warranties
- ISO standards (See Global Village)

Competition and Positioning

Michael Treacy, author of *Double Digit Growth: How Companies Achieve It No Matter What*, presents the natural advantages small businesses have and demonstrates how to capitalize on those advantages when competing with large companies. He distinguishes three value disciplines:

1. Operational excellence (e.g., Wal-Mart and Amazon)
2. Product leadership (e.g., Apple)
3. Customer intimacy (e.g., Nordstrom and Zappos)

No company can excel in all three, so focus on a value that differs from your major competitors and that you can realistically attain. A review of your customer touchpoints, competitor information, and completion of the competitor matrix at the end of the chapter will help you focus further on your distinctive competency in the marketplace.

Basically, competition is a game played out in customers' minds, where buying decisions are made. Inside customers' minds are many "ladders"—for products, services, sports figures, television programs, banks, and rental cars. To compete for a position at the top of one of these ladders, a business must first get a foothold and then wrestle with other businesses to improve its position. It is that simple.

GLOBAL**VILLAGE**

ISO in Brief

ISO (International Organization for Standardization) is the world's largest developer and publisher of International Standards.

ISO is a network of the national standards institutes of 164 countries, one member per country, with a Central Secretariat in Geneva, Switzerland that coordinates the system.

ISO is a non-governmental organization that forms a bridge between the public and private sectors. On the one hand, many of its member institutes are part of the governmental structure of their countries, or are mandated by their government. On the other hand, other members have their roots uniquely in the private sector, having been set up by national partnerships of industry associations.

Therefore, ISO enables a consensus to be reached on solutions that meet both the requirements of business and the broader needs of society.

Who Standards Benefit

ISO standards provide technological, economic, and societal benefits.

For businesses, the widespread adoption of International Standards means that suppliers can develop and offer products and services meeting specifications that have wide international acceptance in their sectors. Therefore, businesses using International Standards can compete on many more markets around the world.

For innovators of new technologies, International Standards on aspects like terminology, compatibility and safety speed up the dissemination of innovations and their development into manufacturable and marketable products.

For customers, the worldwide compatibility of technology that is achieved when products and services are based on International Standards gives them a broad choice of offers. They also benefit from the effects of competition among suppliers.

For governments, International Standards provide the technological and scientific bases underpinning health, safety, and environmental legislation.

For trade officials, International Standards create "a level playing field" for all competitors on those markets. The existence of divergent national or regional standards can create technical barriers to trade. International Standards are the technical means by which political trade agreements can be put into practice.

For developing countries, International Standards that represent an international consensus on the state of the art are an important source of technological know-how. By defining the characteristics that products and services will be expected to meet on export markets, International Standards give developing countries a basis for making the right decisions when investing their scarce resources and thus avoid squandering them.

For consumers, conformity of products and services to International Standards provides assurance about their quality, safety and reliability.

For everyone, International Standards contribute to the quality of life in general by ensuring that the transport, machinery, and tools we use are safe.

For the planet we inhabit, International Standards on air, water, and soil quality; on emissions of gases and radiation; and environmental aspects of products can contribute to efforts to preserve the environment.

Examples of the Benefits Standards Provide

Standardization of screw threads helps to keep chairs, children's bicycles, and aircraft together and solves the repair and maintenance problems caused by a lack of standardization that were once a major headache for manufacturers and product users.

Standards establishing an international consensus on terminology make technology transfer easier and safer. They are an important stage in the advancement of new technologies and dissemination of innovation.

(continued)

(continued)

Without the standardized dimensions of freight containers, international trade would be slower and more expensive.

Without the standardization of telephone and banking cards, life would be more complicated.

A lack of standardization may even affect the quality of life itself: for the disabled, for example, when they are barred access to consumer products, public transport and buildings because the dimensions of wheel-chairs and entrances are not standardized.

Standardized symbols provide danger warnings and information across linguistic frontiers.

Consensus on grades of various materials gives a common reference for suppliers and clients in business dealings.

Agreement on a sufficient number of variations of a product to meet most current applications allows economies of scale with cost benefits for both producers and consumers. An example is the standardization of paper sizes.

Standardization of performance or safety requirements of diverse equipment makes sure that users' needs are met while allowing individual manufacturers the freedom to design their own solution on how to meet those needs.

Standardized computer protocols allow products from different vendors to "talk" to each other.

Standardized documents speed up the transit of goods, or identify sensitive or dangerous cargoes that may be handled by people speaking different languages.

Standardization of connections and interfaces of all types ensures the compatibility of equipment of diverse origins and the interoperability of different technologies.

Agreement on test methods allows meaningful comparisons of products, or plays an important part in controlling pollution—whether by noise, vibration or emissions.

Safety standards for machinery protect people at work, at play, at sea... and at the dentist's.

Without the international agreement contained in ISO standards on metric quantities and units, shopping and trade would be haphazard, science would be unscientific, and technological development would be handicapped.

Source: This text is reproduced from the ISO Web site of the International Organization for Standardization, ISO. More information on ISO can be obtained from any ISO members and from the Web site of ISO Central Secretariat at the following address: *http://www.iso.org.* Copyright remains with ISO.

Looking at competition from this perspective helps you focus on the mind of your Target Customer. The name of the competitive game is *change*. It is the constant process of positioning and repositioning your product or service to meet the changing needs of customers, markets, and the economy. You will use your positioning strategy to distinguish yourself from your competitors and to create promotions that communicate that position to your Target Customers.

Another way to look at your competitors and situations is with a SWOT analysis that focuses on your strengths and weaknesses, as well as those of your competitors, in light of external opportunities and threats. By focusing on each of these areas, you will be able to develop a competitor matrix. You need to complete an internal analysis to discover the strengths and weaknesses of your own idea or firm. In addition, complete an external analysis of the threats and opportunities of the environment and your competitors. As you complete your analysis, you will be building your competitive advantages and positioning.

Key Points provides an excellent example of how four good friends evaluated the prescription eyeglass market and found a niche after evaluating the

Positioning strategy The placement of a product in the customer's eye through pricing, promotion, product, and distribution

SWOT An abbreviation that refers to an analysis of internal strengths and weaknesses, and external opportunities and threats industry from the inside and outside. They envisioned a step on their Target Customer's ladder for "a new concept formed with a rebellious spirit and a lofty objective: to create boutique-quality, classically crafted eyewear at a revolutionary price point."

■ COMPETITION AND THE PRODUCT LIFE CYCLE

Like everything else in life and business, competition has a four-stage life cycle: embryo, growth, maturity, and decline. Examine these stages and look at ways you can utilize them to meet and beat your competition. Briefly, the four stages of the competition life cycle are as follows:

1. In the *embryonic* stage, the arena is empty. The vision is only yours—your idea for a product or service, and a tiny core market. Although, being the first mover in a market does not ensure success, following the lessons outlined here will add to the possible growth and prosperity of your idea.

2. As your industry *grows,* competitors smell money and attempt to penetrate the arena—to take up positions they hope will lead to profit. Curious Target Customers come from all directions. You have visions of great success.

3. As the industry *matures,* competition is fierce, and you are forced to steal customers to survive. You have the option of designing an entirely new business model, which is not a guarantee for succeeding but provides a chance to start something new. Shelf velocity slows, production runs get longer, and prices begin to slide.

4. As the industry goes into *decline,* competition becomes desperate. Many businesses fail; weary competitors leave the arena.

> **Penetrate the arena** Calculated thrust into the marketplace to secure market share

As discussed previously, competitive life cycles have been greatly compressed over the past few years due to global growth, rapid prototyping, technology, and marketing speed. For example, a few years ago, the embryonic stage for a cell phone might have lasted as long as one year. Today that stage is shortened to a month or two, if that. Today movement from one phase to another can occur at blinding speeds and competition enters much quicker into the fray. Thus, becoming profitable is much more of a challenge and the time to do so is shortened immensely

It is not unheard of for a product to go through one of these four cycles in a matter of months. In fact, some products will transition through the entire four cycles in one or two months.

In high-tech businesses, for example, a common rule of thumb is two to three months—that is, there are two to three months from the birth of an idea to product penetration. Beyond that, competitors have already entered the market, and the product begins to enter the growth and in some cases maturity phase.

> **Rapid prototyping** Creation of working models using computer aided design (CAD)

What all this means is that to survive, you must constantly be in touch with the market through CI, and you must always compete vigorously. Keep in mind that you will have no control over how fast the cycle moves, but you will have control over how you plan and react to changes. Figure 5.3 will help you understand the general cyclical changes more clearly.

Where is your selected industry and segment on the competition life cycle? What does this mean to you if you are a start-up venture? What are the implications for your survival? When your industry enters maturity and decline, will you be ready with Plan B? Are you going to be a one-product wonder? The following information will help you gain a further understanding of each stage.

figure **5.3**

Product Life Cycle and Strategies

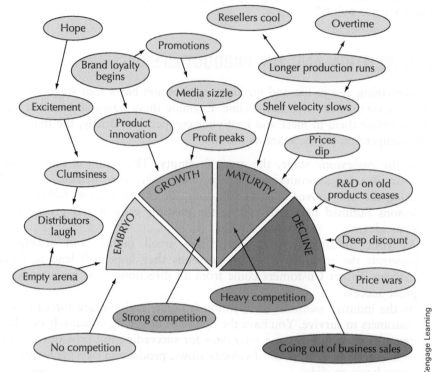

Different competitive strategies are needed at each stage of the product life cycle.

© Cengage Learning

Competition Life Cycle

The Embryonic Stage

Excitement, naïve euphoria, thrust, clumsiness, a high failure rate, and much brainstorming mark the embryonic stage. Pricing is high and experimental. Sales volume is low because the market is very small, and production and marketing costs are high.

You need to locate your core customer base and stress the benefits of your product. Educating the customer may be necessary and costly. Competition has not yet appeared. It is difficult to find distributors, and resellers demand huge gross margins. Profit is chancy and speculative. Shrewd entrepreneurs, however, can close their eyes and divine the presence of a core market. Keep trying! The writers of *Chicken Soup for the Soul* went to more than 30 publishers before they found the one that launched their multimillion-dollar empire. Tenacity is now and should be forever a part of your entrepreneurial vocabulary and actions.

The Growth Stage

Product innovation, strong product acceptance, the beginnings of brand loyalty, promotion by media sizzle, and ballpark pricing mark the growth stage. Distribution becomes increasingly important. Resellers who laughed during the embryonic stage now clamor to distribute the product. Strong competitors, excited by the smell of money, enter the arena, as do new Target Customer groups. Profit percentages show signs of peaking.

The Mature Stage

Peak customer numbers mark the mature stage. Design concentrates on product differentiation instead of product improvement. Production runs get longer, so firms can take full advantage of capital equipment and experienced management. Resellers aren't as excited anymore. Advertising investments increase in step with competition. Some firms go out of business. Prices are on a swift slide down, and competition is very heavy. At this stage, you should only enter the market if you have a unique twist on the product or truly provide a better product. But first ask yourself, "Can I realistically convey this message to my Target Customer?" See how DLC Resources highlighted in the Passion feature operates in a mature market by focusing on technology, communication, and environmental awareness.

The Decline Stage

The decline stage is marked by extreme depression and desperation in the marketplace. A few firms still hang on. Research and development cease, promotion vanishes, and price wars continue. Opportunities may emerge for entrepreneurs in service and repair. Diehards fight for what remains of the core market. Resellers cannot be found; they have moved on to new products.

■ COMPETITION AND POSITIONING IN A MATURE MARKET

Sometimes it becomes clear to a lone entrepreneur or a big business think tank that making a change in the arena can spell opportunity in a mature market. Although we have encouraged you to aim for growth markets and growth industries, that is not always possible or desirable. But competing in a mature market takes even more creativity.

Change in the arena Transform a product or service by adding a benefit that has immediate customer appeal

The change may be very small—a slight change in one aspect of the product or service (such as the proverbial "new mouse trap")—but the effect on the market can be very great indeed. Consider how Redbox cornered the market in what many first believed was a dying market, that of DVD rentals. The world of business—large and small—is filled with stories of such breakthroughs, and the common thread of these stories is the discovery of an area of vulnerability in the existing product or service.

Area of vulnerability Competitor's soft underbelly or Achilles' heel–a weakness ready for you to exploit

Entrepreneurs love to hear these stories, and it is no wonder: such stories contain lessons and inspiration. That is why we include several here, as well as Warby Parker highlighted in the Key Points.

If you are in a mature industry, you will have to win customers away from competitors to survive. The name of the game is dictated first and foremost by your customers and second by your competitors. Continually learn from your competitors and customers to adjust your product or service to meet the needs and wants of the market. Guide your business back into growth segments, and thus create your own niche by using three major thrusts:

1. Beat the competition with superior service.
2. Create a new arena.
3. Create uniqueness by continually changing your product or service.

Beat 'em with Superior Service

Tire Pro

James Grenchik's father had died a year earlier, and James was left with the opportunity to carry on the family tire business. Because tires were lasting longer, he became quite concerned with the viability of his business. James tried price promotions and distress sales in an attempt to drive his competitors out of business, but these old techniques did not seem to work anymore, and profits declined.

In fact, every time James looked around, there seemed to be a new competitor setting up shop in his market. Costco became a major competitor as well. Discouraged, James finally decided that this was no way to do business or, for that matter, to live. He had two choices—get out of business or change. Before he went any further, he needed to analyze his competitors. He sat down with his employees and a few customers and developed a

ACTION STEP 30

Construct a Competitor Matrix (Figure 5.4)

The purpose of Action Step 30 is to rank your competitors and to visualize the positioning of each in the marketplace. Whenever you unearth some hard data, compare it with industry averages. Keep looking for those areas of vulnerability.

Now that you have a good picture of your major competitors and your Target Customers' desired benefits, you are ready to complete a competitor matrix. Pull out Action Steps 27, 28, and 29.

1. List all of your major competitors on the vertical axis; list all of the important benefits to your Target Customers and vital elements for the operational success of your business in rank order on the horizontal axis.
2. Rank each competitor on a scale of 1 to 10 for each category, 10 being the best. Determine the total for each competitor. Next, place and rank your new venture on the matrix and rate yourself. Note that the competitive marketplace is imperfect. Sometimes a few miles or a few hundred miles can make a significant difference in how competitive a business must be. If a mature marketplace is saturated, keep exploring other areas.

You may find an underserved market that will welcome you instantly with healthy profit margins. By the time you have finished the Action Steps in this chapter, you will have an excellent overview of your competitors, and opportunities will be in your hands.

competitor matrix (see Figure 5.4). Action Step 30 will guide you in completing a competitive matrix for your business.

After months of soul searching, family discussions, networking, brainstorming, and reviewing his matrix, James finally decided to change. Here's what James did:

1. He created a partnership with two key groups. First, he sold 25 percent of his business to a major tire manufacturer and retailer that he knew was the best in the market. His major competitor would now be his partner.
2. James sold 24 percent of his business to his key employees. They had been with him a long time, and he knew they were hungry to own a piece of his pie. Now his best employees were also his partners.
3. He created uniqueness by changing his product through service add-ons. These new services were the result of cooperative brainstorming by everyone in the firm after completing a thorough analysis of competitors' offerings. In addition, for three weeks each employee was to question each customer about additional services they might like to see Tire Pro offer. Tire Pro's implementation of customer suggestions and competitor intelligence follow :
   a. Tire Pro now offers an installment plan for farmers who need tires early in the growing season when they experience cash flow problems. This action also created a new profitable arena—finance. With the financial clout of its new manufacturing partner, Tire Pro entered the finance business.
   b. All customers are given free tire rotations every four months on their cars and trucks. At the same time, they get a free report card on potential

figure 5.4

Tire Pro's Competitor Matrix

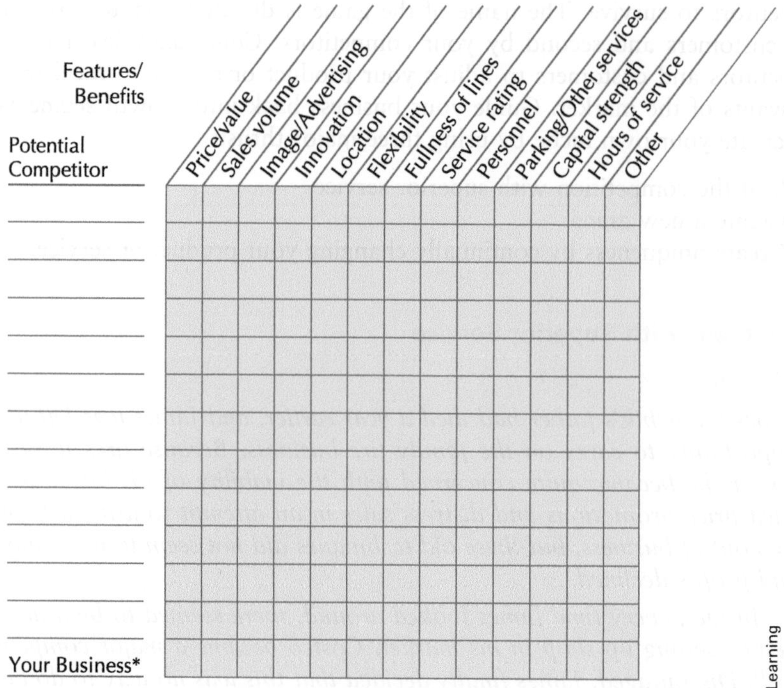

The competitive test matrix can help you evaluate your potential competitors. Use the features/benefits list as a guideline or checklist. Select or add those features/benefits that make sense for your particular business, industry, or competitive situation.

© Cengage Learning

trouble spots. This new service strategy has changed their product from just tires to "tires with a free rotation and inspection." Reminder post-cards and emails are sent to each customer every two months, which keeps Tire Pro's name in front of their customers while providing a welcome service.

c. *Customers who want a tire repaired can also pick up coffee and doughnuts, and have access to free Wi-Fi to check the commodities and weather reports. Puzzles and coloring books were also added for the children. The new Tire Pro Facebook page has become quite popular as customers are posting wanted and for sale requests for used farm equipment. (One Newport Beach Lexus dealer now offers a putting green for its customers along with a boutique carrying Tommy Bahama clothing and Oakley sunglasses. These may not be the best marketing tools for South Dakota farmers, but they are just right for the Lexus-driving entrepreneurs of Orange County, California.)*

d. *Everyone at Tire Pro now answers the phone with their first name and a pleasant hello, which is much easier now that they are making money again! Efforts have been made to reduce noise and increase safety in the tire bays providing a much calmer and better experience for both employees and customers.*

James and his new partners are now making money by providing the best products and services. But be aware that most of the adjustments they made involved labor or marketing expenses, which must be recouped through increased profit and sales. His core product is tires, but James is now also in the financing business. Tire Pro is now ready to open a second outlet. Changes in financing, personnel, service, and competitive techniques rescued Tire Pro from a declining sector.

Core product Item possessing perceived benefits that best fit customers' needs

Even if you start out in a growth market, one thing is certain: One day your market will enter a mature stage and eventually a declining one. You must adjust your product or service regularly. Be ready for changes, which may occur overnight.

Create a New Arena

Let us see how Jackson George, owner of Media Room Havens, successfully changed the arena by developing a niche for himself in a very mature construction market.

Media Room Havens

Positioning Your Business

Jackson George's family had been in the new-home construction business for 20 years. After a falling out with his family, Jackson knew he wanted to remain in the same type of business but wanted to specialize and find a niche for himself.

Many of his friends were looking for media rooms. At parties, Jackson's friends complained that their family rooms were no longer ideal for their flat screen TVs and surround sound systems. There were never enough electrical outlets, family members complained of sound coming through the walls, and they wanted more privacy. In addition, they wanted custom-designed spaces and lighting to fit their individual needs.

Jackson kept listening and started scouting the area to see if anyone specialized in media rooms. He found firms specializing in bathrooms, closets, kitchens, family rooms, and home offices, but no one was in the media room market.

He sat down with five of his friends and brainstormed about media rooms. After about five hours, the information indicated to Jackson that his

friends were willing to spend about $40,000 to $60,000 each for a customized media room. Jackson went into high gear, reading every magazine, researching small home-based businesses on WorkingSolo, searching sites for high end sound and video equipment, movie theater seating, sound absorbent flooring and wall coverings, block-out window coverings, and specialized lighting systems. Jackson's best friend's sister, Susan Pollack, became his first customer. Susan agreed to show her media room to prospective customers for three months in exchange for additional lighting.

To keep the competition at bay for a short time, Jackson limited his advertising and built his first three media room projects through word of mouth. Once he was established, Jackson developed his advertising and marketing with a professionally photographed portfolio of his projects. Because few competitors had developed expertise in working within the media room niche, Jackson was a tough competitor. Knowing the benefits his customers desired gave him the edge when competitors came knocking and bidding.

■ CREATE UNIQUENESS THROUGH CHANGE

Change is the most predictable element of competition. Thus, the entrepreneur needs to keep one eye on the market and the other eye on Plan B.

For three years, Tom Burns has sucessfully operated his Internet business, which allows him considerable freedom to be creative and many hours of free time to spend with his family. Before going into business for himself, Burns trained as an electrical engineer and spent 20 years in the aerospace industry.

Always Ready with Plan B

eBay Entrepreneur Tom Burns

Tom Burns has marketed and sold over 100 products during the past three years on eBay. He started out selling his own artwork and his friend's album cover collection. Feeling good about his success with these ventures, he opened up a store on eBay for his artwork.

Although he was finding success, financially he knew he could make additional money on eBay, so he decided to sell products he found at his local Costco just to see what would happen. Well, what happened was he hit an unexpected goldmine!

After buying products directly from Costco, he decided to contact several manufacturers and found a few would happily drop-ship the products for him, which allowed him to have no capital tied up in inventory. Basically, he could just process eBay orders, which he did as he traveled the world, ducking into Internet cafes for an hour or two each day to answer e-mails and conduct business.

Plan B came whenever his products from Costco gained competition and were thus no longer profitable to sell. He needed to be able to cut those products immediately and find new ones. Always knowing this was the game he would need to play made him continually search for new items. Finding items was not difficult, but finding those without heavy competition was hard. Tom persevered. He shopped frequently, and whenever he found potential products, he would research them on the Internet; and then before investing in any inventory, he would try out several products on eBay.

The key for Tom was to never fall in love with his products; he was willing to change whenever the need arose.

You Can Do It!

We have provided you with a number of stories about entrepreneurs who worked with and learned from competitors; they brought about significant changes in the marketplace. It is altogether possible that some day, we may be telling such a story about you. Yes, you can do it, too—but to start, you must do these things:

- Know what business you are in.
- Know your Target Customers.
- Know your competition.
- Know the benefits of your product or service.
- Develop strategies to capture and maintain your position.
- Give free rein to your creativity and your entrepreneurial spirit.

Surprise us! Surprise your Target Customers! Surprise yourself!

PASSION

A "Green" Landscape Company Focused on Strong Relationships

Landscape companies, according to John Holbert, vice president of DLC Resources, Inc., are considered relatively unsophisticated, blue-collar enterprises.

"Usually, we're not recognized as being especially innovative in approach, or in use of advanced technology," he said. That's partly why the entire company is "extremely proud to be associated with the Spirit of Enterprise Award. It's a huge honor for us." DLC Resources, Inc. received the *Edward Jones Spirit of Enterprise Award*.

A commercial landscape company, DLC Resources currently works with 29 master-planned communities throughout the Phoenix metro area. The company works at establishing close ties with each homeowner's association and its residents.

"Other companies may have 300 contracts," Holbert said. But, he observed, "that often turns into a kind of revolving door. We believe that each community needs to be a good fit for us."

The company's founders, he said, began building a culture of communication from the very beginning, in 1989. "We know we need to have good relationships with our clients, our vendors, and our employees and each is equally important to nurture."

The company takes a proactive approach to building solid relationships with their clients. "It's part of our culture. We want to be experts in the various kinds of landscaping in our communities—how we can best work together to maintain landscaping that works for them and our region—and that takes time."

"There are hundreds of [different] trees, thousands of plants," he explained. "It takes an innovative approach with technology and creativity to manage the landscapes well, and it requires a partnership with the communities."

DLC Resources maps and tracks every critical tree, bush and planting for every client landscape, using a database system linked to GIS technology.

This allows the company to quantify each client's landscape assets, calculate the value, design care programs attached to annual budgets, and track and record results. Practices can be tailored to specific needs within each landscape.

In striving to be environmentally responsible, the company works to develop water management programs that allow for sufficient water to keep landscapes healthy, while economizing on usage. They program watering, and rigorously track usage so that water is kept at "just right" levels for various plant varieties.

The company also replaces all two-cycle power equipment annually, thereby gaining additional efficiencies in fuel and emission reduction. They've recently downsized the company car fleet to Hondas, and now own three hybrids. They'll add more as other cars need to be replaced, Holbert said.

"We intend to be industry leaders in environmental awareness," he added.

Holbert said that it's critical for small businesses to "know what you're best at, stay focused, and remember your employees are your most important asset. You need to support them, mentor them, and provide good leadership. It pays huge dividends."

Source: "Entrepreneurs Pursue Passions and Profits," August 29, 2007, from *www.knowwp-carey.com/article.cfm?aid=588* (Accessed November 8, 2012). Reprinted with permission.

■ SUMMARY

Now that you have identified your Target Customers and have evaluated your competition, it is time to ask yourself the questions we began the chapter with: Is this a plus for your customer? Is this something your competitors will find difficult to copy? And a new question, if your business idea is copied will you be prepared with Plan B?

Customers do not change their habits easily, and businesses do not switch suppliers without extensive analysis. Unless you offer something the others do not, your customer will not take a chance on purchasing your product or service, and you will struggle.

Competing on price alone is a very tough road. The big guys can almost always hold out longer than you and put you under more quickly than you could ever expect or believe. Review your touchpoints, your competitive research, and the interviews you have done with your prospective customers to determine how you will appear unique in their eyes during their experience with you and your product or service.

Conducting competitor research and competitive intelligence, while essential for a start-up, should be an ongoing process for every business to ensure success. Learning the process at the beginning and reinforcing it throughout your business operations will help you stay on top of your competitors. Your customer will tell you what he or she wants—*if* you will only *listen* and observe.

After completing the Actions Steps in Chapter 6 (Location) and Chapter 7 (Marketing/Promotion), return to Chapter 5's Action Steps and revise in light of what you have discovered. Add to your competitor touchpoints and revamp the competitor matrix.

Today, products and services go through the four life-cycle stages rapidly. Being on top of your customers' needs and the competitive changes in the marketplace is more important than ever. Use research, constant evaluation of your competitors, and close contacts with customers, suppliers, and salespeople to stay on top of the curve. Learn from your customers and competitors, and let that knowledge help guide your business into a growth market, where the action is.

Last thoughts from Harvard professor Dr. Michael Porter, leading authority on competitive strategy, and Joan Magretta:

"Compete to be unique. Focus on innovating to create superior value for your chosen customers, not on imitating and matching rivals. Give customers real choice and price becomes one competitive variable. But understand that doing this profitably means accepting limits and making tradeoffs-you can't meet every need of every customer. Nothing is more absurd-and yet more widespread-than the belief that somehow you can do exactly what everyone else is doing and yet end up with superior results."

From *http://blog.hbr.org*

■ THINK POINTS FOR SUCCESS

- Do it smarter.
- Do it faster.
- Do it with more style.
- Provide more features.
- Adjust your hours.
- Provide more service.
- Treat your Target Customers like family; consider their needs.
- Be unique.
- Change the arena through innovation.

- Know your niche.
- Disarm the competition by being superior, safer, or more user friendly.
- Remember that a new firm seldom can win a price war.
- Know that old habits are hard to break; provide your Target Customer a compelling reason to switch.
- Develop your own monopoly.
- Talk to your Target Customer constantly and truly listen.
- Thrive, don't just survive!

■ KEY POINTS FROM ANOTHER VIEW

Hip Eyewear: Warby Parker's New Spectacles

On a warm afternoon in downtown Manhattan, Dave Gilboa is trying on glasses, and it isn't going well. At one shop, none of the frames the saleswoman suggests look remotely good on him. "Every time I go into an optical shop, I think: When are these places going to go out of business? It's a terrible shopping experience," says Gilboa.

Gilboa and his shopping companion that day, Neil Blumenthal, aren't disinterested observers: They are co-chief executives and co-founders of Warby Parker, a 17-month-old company that sells eyewear online. Customers test the start-up's retro-style glasses, which go for $95, including prescription lenses, through a mail-order, try-it-at-home program. The frames, and the business model, have attracted a devoted following among young, trendy professionals. "Sometimes if something's cheap, it's dumb," says entrepreneur and designer Andy Spade. "Warby Parker has done it intelligently." The start-up's success—Warby Parker has sold more than 50,000 pairs of glasses, says it's profitable, and raised $1.5 million from investors in May—is inspiring competition from more established retailers.

Hip though its frames may be, Warby Parker was started at a bastion of business conservatism, the University of Pennsylvania's Wharton School. In the fall of 2008, Blumenthal and Gilboa, both then 28, were in the first year of its MBA program, kicking around ideas with classmates Andrew Hunt and Jeffrey Raider. They wondered why glasses—uncomplicated, easily broken, and mass-produced—often cost as much as an iPhone. Blumenthal, who before business school, worked at a nonprofit that gives glasses to people in developing countries, believed he knew why: "The optical industry is an oligopoly. A few companies are making outrageous margins and screwing you and me."

A quick primer, then, on the $16 billion optical industry: Luxottica (LUX), based in Milan, is one of the heavyweights in question. It owns LensCrafters, Pearle Vision, Sunglass Hut, and the optical shops in Target (TGT) and Sears (SHLD); it owns Ray-Ban, Oakley, and Oliver Peoples; it manufactures, under license, eyewear for more than 20 top brands, including Chanel, Burberry, Prada, and Stella McCartney. "They've created the illusion of choice," says Gilboa. And inadvertently they've created an opening for an indie anti-brand brand such as Warby Parker. Luxottica declined to comment.

By early spring of 2009 the four founders had a look in mind. They call it modern vintage, a bold, often boxy style that was already popular in hipster neighborhoods. It took them months to christen the new business, however. They found the names Warby and Parker in some unpublished writings of Jack Kerouac that the New York Public Library discovered that summer. Meanwhile, they'd started designing and testing frames on fellow students. They eventually came up with 27 styles and now have 50. "It's great to start a business in business school," says Gilboa. "We had 820 classmates who were our target consumer category, who came from all over the world."

Warby Parker uses the same materials and the same Chinese factories as Luxottica. It can sell its glasses for less because it doesn't have to pay licensing fees, which can be as much as 15 percent of the $100 wholesale cost of a pair of glasses. Warby Parker doesn't have to deal with retailers, either, whose markups can double or triple prices, it says. And at least for now, the founders are content with lower margins.

Since graduating in 2010, Gilboa and Blumenthal have been running the company from a Manhattan office so small that many staffers squeeze around a single conference table. The other two founders sit on Warby's board of directors. Over the past several months the company's staff has nearly tripled in size, to 40 employees, and they are about to move to a more comfortable setup in SoHo. Blumenthal, cheery and earnest, doesn't need glasses but wears Warby's Huxley frames on occasion. He's in charge of design, communications, and customer service. Gilboa used to sport $500 frames from Prada; now he wears the Japhy, a design described on the site as being for the "contemporary intellectual." He oversees operations.

As they were putting together their company, the founders came up with a business model they figured would appeal to the habits and ethics of their hipster customers. Warby's free home try-on program lets people test five frames at a time. On its website, Warby Parker offers a way to upload photos and "try on" frames virtually. Creating such individualized shopping experiences on a large scale is the next big thing online, says Gene Munster, a senior research analyst at Piper Jaffray (PJC): "It's e-commerce 2.0." Warby also has a social mission. For every pair of glasses it sells, it helps someone in need buy a pair—though not one of Warby's creations. "The glasses are stylish here, but in most parts of the world people would be ridiculed for wearing them," Gilboa says.

At Wharton, the founders began a "brand ambassador" program to get the attention of Penn's undergraduate population. It continues in Warby's post-collegiate life. The company's 75 unpaid promoters now include a buyer at Macy's (M), the maitre d' at Eleven Madison Park, and the chef behind the Dante Fried Chicken food truck in Los Angeles. They get a free pair of glasses and a discount code to share with friends. Blumenthal says he's looking for "people who don't take themselves too seriously but take world issues seriously." In choosing ambassadors, he finds the answer to one question, in particular, telling: What was the last costume you wore? (For Blumenthal, it was as *Jersey Shore*'s Snooki, for a Halloween office party.)

Competitors have begun eyeing Warby Parker's corner of the market. In June the discount fashion site Bluefly (BFLY) introduced Eyefly, which sells custom, vintage-looking glasses for $99. Says Blumenthal: "They blatantly stole our business model, our aesthetic, our checkout process, even one of our photographs." He says Warby is preparing to sue for copyright infringement regarding the photograph. Melissa Payner, the CEO of Bluefly, told *Bloomberg Businessweek* the photo was intended only as a placeholder, put there by a vendor helping to build the site, and was quickly taken down. "We are in the company of great competition and see significant opportunity for more players," she says.

Warby Parker is already moving in a new direction. Recently, the founders decided that Warby Parker needs a place for people to browse and mingle in the real world. They currently have a small, appointment-only showroom, but will soon open a 2,500-square-foot store in SoHo. "We want to be the first fashion brand that got its start online," says Blumenthal.

Source: Berfield, Susan, Hip Eyewear: Warby Parker's New Spectacles," June 30, 2011. From *http://www.businessweek.com/magazine/hip-eyewear-warby-parkers-new-spectacles-07012011.html*, (Accessed May 30, 2012). Used with permission of Bloomberg L.P. Copyright © 2012. All rights reserved.

■ ACTION STEPS

■ KEY TERMS

Image_Source/iStockphoto.com

Location and Distribution
Evaluating Alternatives

Learning Objectives

- Explore channels of distribution.
- Increase awareness of the role location plays in your strategic Business Plan.
- Consider location alternatives.
- Explore running your business from home.
- Investigate co-working spaces, enterprise zones, and incubators.
- Understand the importance of the right location for retail bricks-and-mortar success.

- Use primary and secondary research to refine customer profiles and select a location.
- Consult commercial real estate brokers in your search for a location.
- Review major points in leasing agreements.
- Investigate commercial and manufacturing location issues.
- Review Internet options.
- Learn the importance of multichannel distribution.

Channels of distribution Chain of intermediaries who move product from producer to consumer or industrial customer

Multichannel distribution Use of more than one channel of distribution to reach customers

Multichannel promotion Reaching customers at many different points with various promotional techniques

Two of the most important decisions an entrepreneur has to make are how to distribute products and where to locate the business. Previously, these two decisions were easy, as most entrepreneurs selected one location and one **channel of distribution**. In today's business world, **multichannel distribution** and **multichannel promotion** alternatives are the norm.

Today, with the vast range of options in distribution, location, promotion, and pricing these four variables are melding together and need to be looked at together more closely than ever. With multichannel distribution, we are also confronted with the issue of multichannel promotion and assuring that both are integrated to meet the needs and eyes of your Target Customers. Since we are now reaching customers at various distribution points and through various promotion activities it is imperative that sellers work to reduce channel confusion and conflict for both distributors and customers. Look to Janie McQueen's profile in Key Points as she reaches out to multiple channels.

As we suggested previously, target market selection and competition need to be addressed together. We now suggest you read both Chapter 6 and 7 on promotion before beginning the Action Steps in this chapter. New avenues, which meld promotion, location, and distribution—such as eBay, Amazon, and Shopify—continually emerge, with new opportunities appearing each day; technology is unstoppable and unlimited. Keep your eyes open to all changes as competition can rear itself so quickly today and your response time will determine your overall success.

As we look down the road—which is a superhighway—we ponder how promotion, distribution, pricing, and location issues will evolve as the mobile phone is becoming our "remote control for life," as predicted by Rohit Talwar, founder of Fast Future. The idea of reaching people and offering products and services anytime, anyplace, or anywhere, is happening today. Incredible opportunities await the entrepreneur who is ahead of the technological curve and fearless in his approach to change.

■ CHANNELS OF DISTRIBUTION

Figure 6.1 highlights the common distribution channels used for consumer goods and services, business goods and services, and electronic distribution. Today, one firm may offer products through multiple channels such as retail stores, online retailing, and private branding through wholesalers. Your goal is to determine which channels offer you the most profitable and sustainable business opportunities. Once your initial distribution channels have been established be open to constant channel changes and new possibilities.

Intermediaries (wholesalers, agents, brokers) perform many functions: sorting, grading of products, transportation, risk taking, and possibly even financing. But one of the most important roles intermediaries perform is providing access to markets and customers through their extensive contacts and experience. Knowledge is power, and listening to the suggestions intermediaries provide is essential for your success.

Buyers at Nature's Best, with years of experience and knowledge of customers as well as competitive products, work closely with their suppliers in

figure **6.1**

Distribution Channels & Ecommerce Business Models

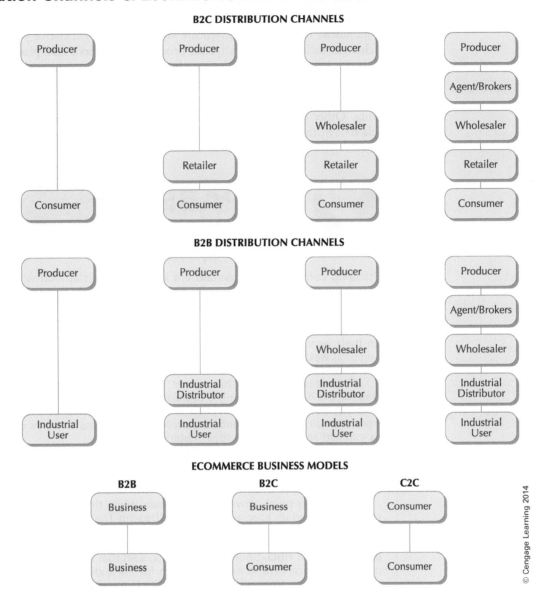

perfecting packaging, sizing, and taste. Consider store buyers one of the best sources of market research information you have.

One hot sauce seller looked at the market and said, "Wow, I can offer twice the hot sauce for not much more than the others." This attempt failed when he realized people are used to buying hot sauce in small bottles. That is what they want, and what they will buy! A good wholesaler would have guided him in the right direction initially.

The physical location you choose will be largely dependent on your distribution strategy and whether you are a B2B or B2C business. If your business will be distributing consumer goods, a cell phone, home office, or garage may work; while B2B businesses may require a large warehouse and a bricks-and-mortar location to meet with customers.

Following in the footsteps of many businesses, such as Victoria's Secret, you might start with a catalog and end up with a bricks-and-mortar store. Or you may be like successful Internet retailer Warby Parker, highlighted in Chapter 5, who also chose to distribute their trendy eyeglasses through displays inside bricks and mortar established "hipster" stores. So as you explore channels, understand that technology and the market may lead you down a different path than you first intended. Your sense of adventure and new skills will enable you to adapt to the changes melding the 4 Ps (price, product, promotion, and place). Chapter 7 and comic, Louis C. K.'s profile provides further insight to the melding process.

Louis C. K. was one of the first mainstream comedians to pursue a new distribution channel for comedy: a direct producer to consumer model via personal website. Other comedians have followed his lead and as you can see from the article below, they see it as one channel amongst many.

PASSION

Comics Are Now Selling Laughs by the Download
By Dave Itzkoff

Stand-up comedians of a certain era knew they had arrived when Johnny Carson invited them to a desk-side seat on *The Tonight Show*. A generation later, the gold standard was getting a solo comedy special on HBO. But in the Internet era, the yardstick for success has been redefined.

A handful of top-tier performers have begun producing stand-up specials on their own, posting them online and selling them directly through their personal websites, eliminating the editorial control of broadcasters and the perceived taint of corporate endorsements.

While this straight-to-the-Internet strategy is far from ubiquitous in stand-up, it is already having a profound impact on the comedy landscape, enabling online content providers and individual artists to take more turf from television networks and empowering comedians to be as candid (and as explicit) as they want in their material.

"It's a very rare thing, where you answer to no one at all as a comedian," said Aziz Ansari, a stand-up comic and actor who released his first online performance special on Tuesday. "Now you can even put it out the way you want."

The turning point arrived in December, when the comedian Louis C. K. released a stand-up special, "Live at the Beacon Theater," that was sold only as a $5 download, without electronic copy protection, from his website.

Louis C. K., who stars in the FX series *Louie* and has performed in comedy specials on HBO, Showtime and Epix, said that he was seeking minimal outside interference and maximum ease for his audience.

"I don't have to go, 'Here's this product,' to whatever company," Louis C. K. said, "and then cringe and shrug and apologize to my fans for whatever words are being removed, whatever ads they're having to watch, whatever marketing is being lobbed on."

The experiment worked: produced at a cost of $250,000, "Live at the Beacon Theater" sold more than 220,000 downloads and grossed over $1.1 million — enough for Louis C. K. to give $250,000 in bonuses to his crew and donate a further $280,000 to charities.

Other comedians following Louis C. K.'s online trail say that they have been contemplating Internet-only projects for several months.

Jim Gaffigan, an actor and stand-up comedian, said he began seeking new platforms for his material after a routine he performed about McDonald's was partly edited out of a 2010 Comedy Central benefit special.

Mr. Gaffigan said he considered many commercial routes, including licensing; selling a new stand-up performance to an online content provider like Netflix, Amazon, or YouTube; or making it available free to viewers who watched a block of commercials first.

But Mr. Gaffigan said he was able to turn down unfavorable deals and corporate ties after Louis C. K. upended "the perception of selling something on your website as being kind of icky."

He added: "My manager was like, 'You're not going to sell it on your website like that.' And I'm like, 'Why wouldn't I?' "

(continued)

(continued)

Instead, Mr. Gaffigan will release his next special — with his McDonald's routine intact — on April 11 for a $5 fee, with $1 from each sale going to charity.

For the comedians taking their material directly to the Internet, the decision is as much a reflection of a desire to serve online-savvy audiences, as it is a lack of other options.

Pay-cable channels like HBO and Showtime, comedians say, are too focused on scripted programming, while on basic cable, Comedy Central offers specials to nearly everyone, with little quality control and licensing deals that are not lucrative.

"I don't get any money from the specials that air on Comedy Central," said Mr. Ansari, who also stars on the NBC comedy *Parks and Recreation*. "I haven't seen any checks from the DVDs, CDs. If I just put it out in a traditional way, I wouldn't have made any money, so why don't I do it this way?" Comedy Central said Mr. Ansari had been paid a six-figure advance and continues to receive residuals on his last televised special.

Kent Alterman, Comedy Central's head of original programming and production, said that the number of stand-up specials it shows was "in service to our audience and our business," and that only "a very rarefied community of comedians" commanded followings large enough to make Internet-only programs viable. Many performers —even those with a large fan base — would still go to Comedy Central for "the marketing muscle that we have and the enormous exposure they get," he said.

(One case in point is Louis C. K., who released his Grammy Award-winning comedy album, "Hilarious," on Comedy Central Records.)

HBO says it still seeks top-tier performers for specials but is mindful of a glut of comedy on television, while Showtime's entertainment president, David Nevins, said, "It's fair to say Showtime needs to renew our focus on it."

The Internet has been happy to capitalize on content that television has neglected. Last month Yahoo! offered a free live performance by the HBO host Bill Maher (one that ended with Mr. Maher's donating $1 million to the pro-Obama SuperPAC Priorities USA). Yahoo! said this special has generated more than 2 million streams and that it hopes to add more such shows, seeing stand-ups as an inexpensive but powerful way to build brand identification with viewers.

"Musicians can have personas," said Erin McPherson, who is Yahoo's head of video programming and originals, "but comics are themselves, and their fans relate to them almost as friends. They have that intimate, one-on-one connection."

Mark Greenberg, a former Showtime and HBO executive who is now the president and chief executive of Epix, a cable and online network that focuses on movies and live events, said that programmers' interest in stand-up was partly demographic: comedians bring more male viewers and especially desirable younger viewers, whom programmers can't afford to ignore "unless your attitude is that you're going to be retired in 10 years and you don't care," he said.

Still, Mr. Greenberg was skeptical that other comedians would be able to duplicate the online sales results that Louis C. K. enjoyed.

"There's no bigger report card than pay-per-view," Mr. Greenberg said. "The first person that does 30,000 buys instead of 200,000, that person's going to sit there and say, 'Why did I fail?' And it's going to affect them as an asset."

Not every comedian sees the Internet as the salvation of the stand-up special. Patton Oswalt, a comic who often appears in film and television roles, said that by being transparent about their production budgets, Louis C. K. and other web pioneers had taught him a lesson he could apply to future televised specials.

But Mr. Oswalt, whose last special was jointly paid for by Showtime and Comedy Central, said that if he did an online-only special it would be "when I'm ready — I'm not going to do that model because it's the fashion right now."

Louis C. K. said his next special might not follow the Internet model. "I think there's huge potential," he said, "but potential means there might be nothing."

(continued)

ACTION STEP 31

Fantasize Your Perfect Location

Sit down where you will not be disturbed and brainstorm the ideal location for your business. With pencil and paper or fingers on the keyboard, let yourself dream. Draw a mind map or use a list format.

If your location is retail, start with your Target Customer. For example, if opening a candy or coffee shop, you might want to locate in the center of New York's Grand Central Station, where tens of thousands of people pass by every hour. Or if you were opening an extremely upscale clothing boutique, you might visualize a location on Rodeo Drive in Beverly Hills.

Once you have the general idea of the state, region, city, and neighborhood you want, using the information in this chapter and in Chapter 7, write down what other items would be important to you and your Target Customer. Writing down everything you dream will give you a starting point as you move out to explore the possibilities.

1. If you are going to be an Internet-only business, you need to begin researching your options immediately. Review your options via Internet distribution channels from Figure 6.1. Start to investigate your options, various websites, costs, and methods used by each channel. Remember, many businesses will be looking at multiple channels. How will you integrate these channels to build synergy?
2. If you will need a manufacturing or distribution site, see the second half of the chapter.
3. If you are going to be home based, read the section on the home office option and go directly to Action Step 32.

Cottage industry Home-based business conducted by family members with their own equipment and skills

Virtual business Firm without walls

(continued)

And Mr. Gaffigan said he was not staking his entire career on his web experiment, predicting he could still license his new performance to Comedy Central if it flopped online.

"It's a gamble with the crops," he said. "This is one harvest. You're going to use some piece of equipment that could make it twice as productive."

That said, Mr. Gaffigan would still prefer success to failure. "Just to be clear," he said, "I have four children, and they're very young, and I have a woman who gets pregnant looking at babies."

Source: DAVE ITZKOFF, "Comics Are Now Selling Laughs by the Download." From The New York Times, 20 Mar 2012 © 2012 The New York Times. All rights reserved. Used by permission and protected by the Copyright Laws of the United States. The printing, copying, redistribution, or retransmission of this Content without express written permission is prohibited.

The perfect location and distribution strategy differs for every enterprise and industry. If you are in the house-cleaning business, you can work from a van with a cell phone. If you are in the mail-order business, you can work from a "cocoon" or a post office box. But if you are selling high-end furniture, a specific retail or Internet location may be best. If you are manufacturing products, you might want to be where the best qualified and skilled workers are located. If you are shipping goods overseas, you may need to locate near shipping lanes.

Action Step 31 asks you to brainstorm the perfect location for your business, review the Action Step now and complete. As you continue your research throughout the next two chapters, continue to add your ideas to this Action Step. Since 50 percent of small businesses are home-based businesses we will begin exploring that as the first location option.

■ HOME OFFICE OPTION

What happens if you want to operate your business from your home, car, or iPhone? First, congratulations! You may be on the right track. In this updated version of the cottage industry, more and more of us will be working out of our homes and operating virtual businesses. In fact over 50 percent of all businesses today are home-based businesses according to the SBA.

Chris Guillebeau, author of *The $100 Startup*, encourages people to become "roaming entrepreneurs" plying their trade wherever they roam. With today's technology and communication tools this is not only possible but also probable. Businesses highlighted in his text include weekend retreats for crafters, media production, bloggers, group triathlon trainers, and many more.

All types of services and products are now provided by home-based businesses. Principal Technical Services, a supplemental staffing firm, operated out of a home, with the president and her son sharing his old room, and three other full-time employees working out of their homes—and it was number 143 on *Inc.* magazine's top 500 companies. Staff meetings were held at the kitchen table.

We are all too familiar with the Dells, Apples, Facebooks, etc., which have begun in dorm rooms or garages. In California during the 90s, many people just thought if they had a garage they could get rich. Although if you have read this far, you know it takes much more!

Technology allows people to work within the home today in ways that were impossible even a few short years ago. With the growth in service- and knowledge-based industries, chances are good that one day, you will be operating some sort of business out of your home either full-time or part-time. In planning to set up your business at home, however, your location analysis is still important.

There are a number of critical location questions you are going to have to consider: Do local zoning laws and my homeowner's association allow me to operate a home-based business? How do I balance my family and work life?

How do I best set up an office within my home? Will I be able to maintain a professional appearance to my clients?

If you have a business that requires employees or customers to come to your site, your alternatives will be limited by parking spaces, neighbor issues, zoning laws, and physical space. Also, find out if delivery services will deliver and pick up at your home. They may be willing to deliver, but only to the door and not inside your home. This may pose a problem if you have large, heavy deliveries, or you cannot leave packages outside.

Home offices are an excellent place to start your business, and you will be joining 18 to 32 million (depending on who is counting!) fellow home-based entrepreneurs. Many entrepreneurial ventures have been able to grow to multimillion-dollar businesses while based at home. However, staying in your home still requires planning and discipline. Recommendations include hiring babysitters, arranging for back-up equipment, designing office space with comfortable furniture and adequate computer equipment and telephone lines, and planning your daily work schedule with breaks, so you do not become a hermit.

Dorothy Ling, a professional writer, drives for coffee each morning to signify that her workday has begun. Casey Trout, a financial planner, has a routine of officially closing the office for the day at 5:00 p.m. by walking out his back door and walking in his front door.

You need to learn to manage your work time so that not *all* of your time becomes work time. The lure of the computer and work continue to pull, and it is sometimes 14 hours later when you realize you have not seen the light of day. It is imperative that you take a break from sitting if you are working at your computer. Go on short walks for a drink or snack, walk the dog, or step out into the sun to keep your circulation moving. Also, make sure your office and desk areas are set up ergonomically correct. Try not to have your office in the center of family activity. At the end of the end of the day, close the door and join the world.

Basements, garages, spare bedrooms, and even closets have become home offices. In fact, today there is a booming business in prefab office sheds, studios, and gazebos from companies like Summerwood Products to meet the needs of home-based entrepreneurs.

If you can start in your home and stay as long as possible, it will be cost efficient. Also, the longer you keep costs low, the less likely you are to require outside money. Thus, you will be able to maintain control and ownership of your business. You must remember, however, that you *are* running a business that just happens to be run from your home. Work hard to make sure you control the business and the business does not control you.

Corporate downsizing, early retirement, high unemployment, families and single parents needing additional income, are just a few of the factors fueling the growth of home-based businesses. Never before has technology been available to make the dreams of so many a reality as the cost of entry into the entrepreneurial world has fallen greatly encouraging many to strike out on their own.. Although starting a business in your home is easy, it does not mean that you should not consider other alternatives in your decision.

If your business requires storage, business deliveries, meeting food health and safety standards, hazardous materials, employees, and constant privacy, you will need to look to other locations or rectify these issues before starting. Also, consider how long you will be able to stay in your home if your business grows.

If you need to meet with clients, consider coffee shops and restaurants. Breakfast meetings work well and they are the most economical to host. Professional conference and meeting spaces rented by the hour or day can be located online at Desk Wanted.

Review your homeowner's coverage with your insurance agent. If you have customers coming to your home, your present insurance may not be adequate. Additional insurance requirements for home-based businesses are available in Chapter 12. With your accountant, review the pros and cons of home office tax

Coworking space Flexible workspace for flexible people

ACTION STEP 32

Is a Home Business in Your Future?

Before starting a business in your home, answer the following questions: What are the benefits? What are the negatives? What is my distribution strategy? How will I reach my customers?

1. **List reasons to work at home.** Start with the obvious: low overhead, close to snacks, an easy commute, and familiar surroundings. If you have children and want to be near them, working at home is one solution. Keep listing.

2. **List the problems of working at home.** How do you handle interruptions? How do you show that you are serious? How do you focus amidst clutter? If you have clients, where do you see them? What is the zoning situation in your neighborhood? Keep listing.

3. **List solutions to the problems raised in number 2.** If you are being interrupted, you need to get tough. Set up a schedule, and post a notice: "Dad's working from 9 to 11. Lunch will be served at noon. If Dad does not work, there is no lunch!"

4. **Go technical. What will it cost you?** Consider expenses such as computers, scanners, printers, servers, and so on.

5. **Where will your workspace be?** Garage? Basement? Bedroom? Den? How can you keep it yours? What will it cost to make the space usable, private, and productive?

6. **Check out your home insurance.** (See Chapter 12) What does it cover? What additional coverage do you need, and what will it cost?

7. **Check out health insurance if needed.** If you did not do this earlier, now is the time! Can you qualify for insurance? If so, what will be the cost? (See Chapter 1 and Chapter 12) Please note the issues surrounding health insurance are in flux.

8. **Seek advice.** Talk with your family and friends who own home-based businesses. What are their concerns? What are your concerns?

deductions and consequences. The following Internet sites will provide the answers to many of your questions about working at home:

SOHO
Working Solo
The $100 Startup

Home-based businesses employing others operate with IM, Skype, Intranets with calendars, online scheduling, and document sharing. All combine to provide the necessary technology. Some companies have hundreds of consultants working throughout the world, meeting at a central location once a month or less. Other businesses offer an office but expect only a certain percentage of employees to be in at any one time. Again, you are building a business for *you*, so decide what will work best for you and your employees.

One unique virtual venture, Future Work Institute, has a "core group of 20 consultants, but also maintains relationships with 80 on-call diversity experts." Founder Margaret Regan's four-story townhouse has become the headquarters; she lives on the second and third floor, devotes the fourth floor to a twice-monthly meeting space, and the ground floor office is used to accommodate out-of-town consultants. If you have always dreamed of working at home, complete Action Step 32. A coworking space may prove another location alternative.

■ COWORKING SPACE

For the entrepreneur who wants to leave his own house and likes working surrounded by others, one alternative is to locate a coworking space. You basically rent desk time in a facility, which provides any or all of the following: conference rooms, massages, desk space, coffee, computers, computer experts, presentation equipment, storage lockers, free WIFI, Tuesday taco nights, and most importantly, a sense of community. Space is available by the hour, day, or month. Coworking provides space for solo entrepreneurs, as well as facilities large enough to hold several companies with more than 25 employees.

Use of coworking spaces has doubled each year over the past six years and there are now over 1,100 coworking spaces throughout the world. If you are doing business anywhere in the world, log on to Deskmag or DeskWanted to locate a desk or meeting space! For those seeking an office outside of the home on a daily basis, you may find a chance to build contacts and grow with others. Even the lone wolf wants the companionship of others occasionally who are dreaming the same entrepreneurial dream and thus can use coworking spaces on a drop in basis.

Entrepreneurs who choose to grow their businesses within these coworking spaces are not forced into long-term commercial leases in buildings, which may become inadequate if their firm scales up quickly.

Larger coworking spaces have movable walls, and as a firm grows or shrinks the spaces are adjusted accordingly. Coworking spaces run anywhere from $300 to $1,000 per month per employee. Spotify and Zappos are examples of just two firms that ignited in San Francisco's RocketSpace coworking offering.

The spaces come in all shapes and sizes, and form to fit the needs of the local entrepreneurs primarily. Two listings follow:

Seattle: The Branch Coworking Office 8503 Roosevelt Way NE Seattle, WA 98115 *http://www.mapleleafbranch.org/* A mixed-use coworking space near Maple Leaf Park in the heart of North Seattle, The Branch promotes itself as a place where anyone can work comfortably. The space is equipped with 18 desks, Wi-Fi, a laser printer, flat-screen monitors for use, a conference room for use, presentation equipment, free coffee and tea, and a kitchen. In true west coast fashion, the office is dog friendly and offers bike storage.

Hours: 8 a.m. - 5 p.m. Mon-Fri Daily rate: $20

Source: "10 Great Co-working Spaces Across the U.S." by Kirsten Cluthe, PC Magazine, July 6, 2011. Retrieved from http://www.pcmag.com/slideshow/story/266509/10-great-co-working-spaces-across-the-u-s/ 9. Reprinted with permission of Ziff Davis, Inc.

San Francisco: Next Space   28 2nd Street San Francisco, CA 94105 http:// nextspace.us/ NextSpace aims to reinvent the way people work. The space is designed to foster human interaction. It's a nice concept and a good reason to check the space out the next time you're looking for a place to work in San Francisco. For $20 per day, you get Wi-Fi, phone, mail services, storage lockers, a conference room, and access to presentation equipment. Oh, and there's free coffee.

Hours: 8:30 a.m. - 5:30 p.m. Mon-Fri, with 24-hour access available Daily rate: $20

Source: "10 Great Co-working Spaces Across the U.S." by Kirsten Cluthe, PC Magazine, July 6, 2011. Retrieved from http://www.pcmag.com/slideshow/story/266509/10-great-co-working-spaces-across-the-u-s/ 9. Reprinted with permission of Ziff Davis, Inc.

The next time you are in your home office finding it hard to focus, wishing you could have coffee with someone, or just wanting to pitch your ideas with others, log on and find a coworking space. You never know what synergy will spring from meeting other entrepreneurs. If you desire more support, look into joining an incubator— some of which are very easy to get into and others that are incredibly competitive.

■ INCUBATORS

Business Incubators

Business incubator Home for emerging business

Incubators nurture young firms by helping them survive and thrive during the challenging start-up period. More than 950 incubators provide trained, professional assistance in marketing, financing, and technical support. You will usually share office space, access to equipment, and storage or production areas.

Generally, your firm will remain in an incubator for one to three years. Academic institutions, economic development organizations, and for-profit entities sponsor incubators. Two of National Business Incubation Association's (NBIA) 2012 outstanding clients and incubators are highlighted below.

> Incubators—Survive and Thrive!

NBIA 2012 Outstanding Incubator Client: Nontechnology Category
Hometown Health TV Leesburg, Fla. Marc Robertz-Schwartz, founder
Incubator: University of Central Florida Business Incubation Program
Employees: 1 full-time employee and 14 local contractors
www.yourhometownhealth.com

Hometown Health TV produces "Good Things for Those Who Wait." Recognizing that patients sometimes spend significant amounts of time in medical waiting rooms, media and marketing professional Marc Robertz-Schwartz set out in 2009 to create an educational product to help make the waiting room experience more enjoyable. With the support of several central Florida physicians, the company launched "Hometown Health," a monthly hour-long video program that provides health and wellness information through a network of medical office waiting rooms, county health departments, local cable networks and the Internet. The show also provides a way for area healthcare professionals to share their expertise on health issues with both existing and new patients watching the videos. As market demand for its media and marketing services expanded, Hometown Health TV, a client of the University of Central Florida Business Incubation Program in Leesburg, Fla., created a sister company, Apple Seed Marketing, in 2011 to expand its production expertise to clients outside the healthcare field.

Incubator's role: It hasn't been easy to launch, build, and grow a new business and a spin-off company during the worst economy in over a century, but Robertz-Schwartz says the company's affiliation with the Leesburg incubation program has contributed greatly to its early success. "UCFBIP/Leesburg has been an invaluable resource for guidance, information and networking," he says. "Just being in an environment with like-minded individuals provides an unquantifiable opportunity to tap into others' experiences, knowledge and unbiased opinions – something rarely available for most in-home start-ups." In addition to receiving business guidance by participating in the incubation program, the company has even signed two new clients based on introductions made by UCFBIP/Leesburg Site Manager James Spencer.

Source: *http://www.nbia.org*, The National Business Incubation Association (Accessed June 5, 2012). Reprinted with permission.

NBIA's 2012 Dinah Adkins Incubator of the Year, General and Special Focus
South Side Innovation Center, Syracuse, NY, Bob Herz, Director
Incubator size: 13,500 square feet
Incubator clients: 27 resident and approximately 330 affiliate
Incubator graduates: 29
www.southsideinnovation.org, Project of the Whitman School at Syracuse University

Achievements: Since 2006, the South Side Innovation Center has played an important role in helping to create an entrepreneurial community in one of the poorest neighborhoods in Central New York. Through its Inclusive Entrepreneurship program, SSIC provides a seamless approach to entrepreneurial training and services for clients, from initial assessments of personal and professional skills through help with business plan development, access to its community business partners program, aid in entity creation, access to micro-credit loans and help in opening markets.

SSIC provides services to all interested entrepreneurs, but it also has targeted programs for traditionally underserved entrepreneurial groups including low-income individuals, people with disabilities, women and minorities. "The expansion of Inclusive Entrepreneurship has led to our ability to provide services even to typically hard-to-reach populations, including a contract with the State Commission on the Blind and Visually Handicapped, under which we provide services to blind and visually impaired individuals, and a grant to provide entrepreneurial services to survivors of domestic violence, among many others," says Bob Herz, SSIC director.

In addition to traditional incubation services, SSIC houses a WISE Women's Business Center (funded by the U.S. Small Business Administration); Start-Up NY, an entrepreneurial training program for persons with disabilities; SBA PRIME (Program for Investment in MicroEntrepreneurs), assisting low-income entrepreneurs; a community test kitchen; and an Entrepreneurial Assistance Program (funded by New York state), focusing on business counseling, business plan development and training. Since inception, SSIC has provided more than 1,500 entrepreneurs with hands-on business counseling, training and mentoring and has helped create over 130 new businesses.

Source: *http://www.nbia.org*, The National Business Incubation Association (Accessed June 5, 2012). Reprinted with permission.

Incubators provide a "home" to grow your business at a time when the support and expertise of others is essential to the launching of your business. Usually in the start-up phase, funds are not available to pay for expertise, nor is there background enough to know what services and professionals are available. Being surrounded by like-minded entrepreneurs is an incalculable benefit for budding entrepreneurs; without this support entrepreneurship can be a very lonely endeavor.

In addition, an incubator often allows one to pay less than market rent, receive discounted professional services, and gain access to administrative support. Review the incubator information highlighted in the Entrepreneurial Resource, and conduct research to determine if an incubator could be the right "home" for your venture.

Some incubators focus on very specific industries such as software, medical services, biotechnology, or sustainable products. Many of the incubators focus on preparing their clients for fundraising and some take a "small piece of equity in exchange for a small amount of cash and entry into the program." Who knows— you could be the next successful incubator client, like Dropbox, Airbnb, or Reddit.

■ BRICKS-AND-MORTAR LOCATION FOR RETAIL AND SERVICE VENTURES

According to the old axiom, "location, location, location" is the key reason for retail business success. To some extent, and especially in bricks-and-mortar retail, this philosophy has a great deal of merit. Although in essence, if you will be selling on the Internet, "location, location, location" basically refers to

Entrepreneur's Resource

Incubate Your Baby for Success

To determine which incubators in your area might help drive your business to success, contact the National Business Incubation Association (NBIA), *http://www.nbia.org* for a list. When analyzing which incubator might best serve your entrepreneurial needs, follow NBIA's tips below.

Tips for Evaluating Incubators

Tips for Entrepreneurs

Just as incubators screen prospective clients, so too should entrepreneurs screen prospective incubators. Here are some questions to ask when considering entering an incubation program.

Finding a Quality Program

Track record

- How well is the program performing?
- How long has the program been operating?
- Does it have any successful graduate companies and if so, how long have they been in business independent from the incubator?
- What do other clients and graduates think of the program?

Graduation policy

- What is the program's graduation policy, i.e. what are the incubator's exit criteria?
- How flexible is the policy?
- How long, on average, have clients remained in the program? (Incubators typically graduate companies within three years.)

Qualifications of manager and staff

- How long has the current staff been with the program?
- How much time does staff spend on site?
- Have they had any entrepreneurial successes of their own?
- Do they actively engage in professional development activities or are they a member of a professional/trade association to keep them up to date on the latest in incubation best practices?

Finding the Right Match

Does the incubation program offer the services and contacts you need?

What services do you need to make your venture successful? Business plan development, legal and accounting advice, marketing, Internet access, or specialized manufacturing facilities? Is access to a particular market critical? Then consider finding an incubator that specializes in that market. Special focus incubators are programs that work with companies within a particular niche, such as gourmet foods, biotechnology, the arts and software. Be sure the program offers what you need or can connect you to service providers who can meet those needs.

Do you meet the incubator's criteria?

Find out the incubator's qualifications for accepting clients before applying. For example, some incubators expect prospective clients to have fully developed business plans, whereas others require a less developed idea and offer business plan development assistance.

Is the program's fee structure right for you?

Most for-profit incubators exchange space and services for an equity share in their client companies, whereas most nonprofits charge fees for space

(continued)

(continued)

and services. If a large cash infusion and speed to market are essential for your business success, then giving up equity in your company in order to secure quick cash may be right for you. But if you believe you have the skills to raise your own funding (with some assistance), don't want to give up any equity in your venture and are willing to build your company more slowly, then paying fees for services and space may be a better choice.

Source: The National Business Incubation Association (NBIA).

appearing in the top five of a Google search. Many ventures will find themselves both selling on the Net and opening a bricks-and-mortar store. It is interesting to note that where many forecasted the demise of bricks-and-mortar retailing 15 years ago, only 8 to 10 percent of retail sales occur online today.

Retailing has remade itself many times over and is doing so again today. The reality is, you must make a compelling reason for a customer to come to your store. Think about how Apple packs them in each and every day when almost all of the stores' products can be bought online.

One of the biggest challengers for retailers today is capturing the customer who comes in looking for a product but leaves after checking his iPhone for a cheaper price online or a nearby store. This trend, known as "showrooming" is made even harder as online firms may be offering free shipping and no sales tax. While only 8-10 percent of retail sales currently completed online, experts estimate 50 percent or more of in-store sales are influenced by digital information. Also, keep an eye out for legal changes regarding sales tax parity, which may offer local retailers a more even footing to compete with the 13th largest retailer—Amazon—and others. Also, Amazon's push to offer same day delivery may have a very large impact on local retailers.

In light of showrooming and trying to buck the Amazon trend, Anne Pachett, a bestselling novelist, and her business partner opened up Parnassus Books in Nashville. Recognizing that bookstores are a tough business in light of eReaders and Amazon, they are endeavoring to build a community of readers within their store. Fortunately, they have captured their readers' energy and the activity in their store today reminds one of an Apple store.

A good physical retail location, such as Parnassus Books found, can make everything easier for a new retail business. A highly visible building that is easy for your customers to reach may save you advertising dollars. Although, once you have been discovered and your customer base is well established, location may be less important. Nonetheless, for most retail firms, a prime location is desirable, but often comes at a hefty cost; and it is expensive to relocate.

If purchasing a franchise (Chapter 14), most experienced and successful franchisors will provide you with excellent site location expertise and assistance. In fact, such expertise is one *reason* to purchase a franchise so make sure you have it. If purchasing an ongoing business, you most likely will be inheriting a location. Reading through this chapter and completing the Action Steps will help you decide if the location is worth the cost imbedded in the purchase price or if a new location will increase profitability.

If you are planning to rent a location for a number of years or purchase a building, site selection is critical, and most retail leases reflect this importance in their duration—usually 5 to 10 years—and complexity: 50 to 75 page leases are not unusual. In this chapter, we ask you to define the perfect location, then we lead you through the process of finding such a place for your business using primary and secondary research and, if necessary, negotiating a lease that will serve you well.

A cautionary note is in order, however: What you believe will be a good location is certainly relevant, but *more* important is what your Target Customer

Showrooming Viewing products at bricks and mortar stores and them buying online for less

Lease A legal contract for occupancy

believes is a good location. You have to be able to climb inside your customer's mind to answer the question, "What is the best location?"

■ RETAIL LOCATION FILTER

When the search for possible locations for your business begins, you need to decide what you really want from your location. The following list will help you zero in on your ideal business location. Use a scale of 1 to 10, 10 being the most important, to rate the relative importance of each item on this list. When you finish scoring, go back and note any factor above 5—and focus the rest of your research on these factors. Questions below focus on bricks-and-mortar retail and service businesses. Although, many of the questions also apply to commercial and manufacturing location decisions with some adaption needed. You will need to adjust the questions for online businesses too.

Target Customers

How far will the Target Customers you profiled in Chapter 4 be willing to travel? How much traffic will they put up with? What hours will you need to be open to serve them? If your business is located in Manhattan, your target-market radius may be a three-block radius; if you are located in a rural area, your customers may come from within a 120-mile radius. Will you need to travel to your clients or deliver products to your customers (flowers, dry cleaning, plumbing, pizza, etc.)? If so, how far can you travel and still make a profit? Will phone, e-mail, IM, and Skype suffice to keep you in touch with clients?

Consider highway access, construction, and other potential obstacles that could make coming to your place of business inconvenient or unpleasant. Check out plans for potential road construction and closings. Visit your city hall and attend city and county planning meetings. Read past meeting minutes as well. If you are a bricks-and-mortar retailer, make sure you review the same for cities within your area that you compete with as large retailers or centers may be moving in.

Neighbor Mix

Who is next door? Who is down the street? Which nearby businesses target your customers? If you are considering a shopping center, who is the anchor tenant (the big department store or supermarket that acts as a magnet for the center) and are they drawing your Target Customer?

Neighbor mix The industrial/commercial makeup of nearby businesses

Anchor tenant A business firm in a commercial area that attracts customers

Competition

Do you want competitors miles away or right next door? Think about this one: If you are in the restaurant or automobile business, it can help to be on "restaurant row" or on the "mile of cars." Competitors concentrated in one area cuts down customer driving time and allows for easy comparison shopping. Does your competition have a strong hold on the market? Is there room for additional competitors?

Security, Safety, and Parking

How safe is the neighborhood? Is it as safe as a nursery at noon but an urban nightmare at midnight? Is there anything you can do to increase security? Are you willing to be the first in an area to try to turn it around? What can you do to mitigate any problems? Is adequate safe parking available? Is the area safe for your employees if they have to work and close late in the evening?

Labor Pool and Education

Who is working for you, and how far will they have to commute? Does your business require more help at certain peak periods of the year? How easy will it be to hire and retain employees? Will you need skilled or technical laborers? If so, where are the nearest sources? Is the site near a bus, train, carpool, or subway stop? Is there a labor pool of trained engineers and scientists? Can you draw from the potential pool of part-timers, teens, students, and seniors? Is affordable housing available for your employees? Are educational facilities nearby to provide employee training and also to provide research capabilities and experts in your field? How are the local schools rated? Do local colleges and universities offer entrepreneurial assistance?

Labor pool Qualified people who are available for employment near one's business location

Restrictions and Opportunities

What laws and regulations (federal, state, county, city, and merchants' association) will affect your location? For example, what are the restrictions on signs, hours of business, wages, parking, deeds, waste management, zoning, covenants, and employee parking?

Restrictions City/county laws governing business locations

Services

What is included in the rent (security, trash pickup, sewage, maintenance) and who pays for those services that are not included? Are adequate fire and police protection available?

Costs

Costs include the purchase price, closing, rehab, and furnishings if you are buying; otherwise, they are the rent or lease costs. We generally advise against buying property and starting a business at the same time, because it diverts precious energy and capital that you need. Also keep in mind taxes, insurance, utilities, improvements, and routine maintenance costs—you need to know who pays for what. Can you negotiate any of these expenses?

Ownership

If you are still planning to buy property, who will advise you on real estate matters? Consider a lease with an option to buy. Hire an experienced real estate attorney in your area to review any leasing or sales contract before signing.

Present and Past Tenants

What happened to the past tenants? What mistakes did they make, and how can you avoid those mistakes? If three restaurants have failed in a location, don't make the assumption you know something the others didn't. If at all possible, contact present and past tenants and listen to what they have to say. Benefit from their experience.

Space

If you need to expand, can you do it there, or will you have to move to a new site? Moving is very expensive, so consider potential growth while evaluating your location decision. If you anticipate fast growth, do not sign a long-term lease.

History of the Property

How long has the landlord owned this property? What is the lease status of the other tenants? Is it likely the property will be sold while you are a tenant? If the property is sold, what will happen to your business? If the property goes on the market, do you want the first right to meet an offer? What improvements have been made and which need to be made?

Taxes

Check property and sales taxes. Also, try to find out if there are any plans for property reassessments or increased state or local sales taxes.

Approvals

Have you considered necessary approvals, such as those required from health officials, the fire marshal, the city planning office, and the liquor licensing board?

Physical Visibility

Does your business need to be seen? If so, is this location easily visible? If not, can you make alterations to increase visibility? Make sure current or future landscaping will not block signage and if it does, will the owners trim? Will possible roadwork affect ability to see signs or affect traffic flow?

Life-Cycle Stage of the Area

Is the site in an area that is embryonic (vacant lots, open space, emptiness), growing (high-rises, new schools, lots of construction), mature (building conversions, cracked streets, sluggish traffic), or declining (decrepit buildings, emptiness)? What will the area be like in five years? What do the municipal planners have in mind for the area? What is the quality of life? If the property is in a declining area, subsidies may be available for employee training or building rehabilitation. Can you take advantage of these? Are you ready to be a pioneer and risk taker?

Community Support

Is a strong entrepreneurial support community available? What local and state economic-development incentives exist for your location? Read the many articles published by *Inc.* and *Fast Company* that rate entrepreneur friendly communities. For independent retailers and restaurants, San Luis Obispo, California; Gainesville, Florida; Durham, North Carolina; and Boulder, Colorado are four examples of cities that truly support their own. Look for towns where residents will go out of their way to buy local from nonfranchise operations.

Image

Is the location consistent with your firm's image? How will nearby businesses affect your image? Is this an area where your customers would expect to find a business like yours? Look for a place that you can develop to reinforce a positive perception of your business for the customer.

As you look toward a bricks-and-mortar location for your retail or service business, you will have many options that include the following retail centers: local neighborhood, downtown business district, neighborhood or strip centers, community shopping centers, regional malls, and outlet and retail/entertainment centers.

■ RETAIL AND SERVICE BUSINESS LOCATION INFORMATION

Retailers and service providers tend to stay in a location for a while, because it is expensive to pack up, move, and reestablish a business. This is why location selection is a very important decision. You need to make sure you are in the heart of your target market or are able to reach your target market from your site. Where do you go for that information?

We discussed using the Census Bureau, city and county data, and independent research firms such as Claritas and EASI Demographics in Chapters 4 and 5. Most of the information covered in those chapters is also applicable to the location decision, and it should be reviewed and researched in more depth, for the location portion of your Business Plan. We highlight several additional sources throughout the chapter to show how secondary information can assist you.

If you are selling primarily through e-mail, direct mail or catalogs, review the information from Chapter 7 on advertising sources and mailing list procurement and from Chapter 4 on geographic, demographic, and psychographic information to clearly focus on your Target Customer.

The geodemographic databases will be helpful for locating business-to-business customers and for manufacturing or research site selection. Providers of the data assist clients in accessing the most relevant information required for location decision making. To explore site selection further, read *GeoWorld*, a magazine that focuses on the use of geographical information systems (GIS) and location intelligence (LI). You can also visit their website at *http://www.geoplace.com* to review many of the online services available. Visit Steve Blank's Startup Tools and Marcy Phelp's Research on Main Street sites for links to further in-depth geodemographic tools.

For retail establishments, site-location ring studies are frequently conducted to evaluate one-, three-, and five-mile rings around your potential site. Comparing sites using ring studies allows you to see which site would be best for your business. One location might cost twice as much in rent, but if it pulls in three times the Target Customers, the rent becomes a less important factor. Visit EASI Demographics for further information. The spending pattern reports from Claritas, GeoVALS, and Roper's LifeMatrix (introduced in Chapter 4), will help to define your customer as well.

In Chapter 4 we presented the Claritas Prism NE customer groups for Susan's Healthy Gourmet customers. Following are the top three lifestyle groups for zip code 46323, Hessville, an area of Hammond, Indiana, outside of Chicago. From the description of the groups below, it is obvious they would not be a part of Susan's target market for healthy prepared meals; consider what types of retail and services the following groups are most likely to purchase and what type of stores they would desire to shop in:

Domestic Duos: Domestic Duos represent a middle-class mix of mainly over-55 singles and married couples living in older suburban homes. With their high school educations and fixed incomes, segment residents maintain an easygoing lifestyle. Residents like to socialize by going bowling, seeing a play, meeting at the local fraternal order, or going out to eat.

Source: Mybestsegments.com, *http://www.yawyl.claritas.com* (Accessed May 22, 2008).

Blue-Chip Blues: Blue-Chip Blues is known as a comfortable lifestyle for ethnically diverse, young, sprawling families with well-paying blue-collar jobs. The segment's aging neighborhoods feature compact, modestly priced homes surrounded by commercial centers that cater to child-filled households.

Source: Mybestsegments.com, *http://www.yawyl.claritas.com* (Accessed May 22, 2008).

New Beginnings: Filled with young, single adults, New Beginnings is a magnet for adults in transition. Many of its residents are 20-something singles and couples just starting out on their career paths—or starting over after recent divorces or company transfers. Ethnically diverse—with nearly half its residents Hispanic, Asian, or African

American—New Beginnings households tend to have the modest living standards typical of transient apartment dwellers.

Source: Mybestsegments.com, *http://www.yawyl.claritas.com* (Accessed May 22, 2008).

Once you are in business, continually monitor customer information and use that data to refine your Target Customer description. As you narrow your focus through careful profiling you will be able to better determine pricing, merchandise mix, and new site selections.

Josie Rietkerk, owner of Caterina's, found when owning gift and candy stores in six airport locations, the merchandise mix needed to be different in each store; the customer profile varied from airport to airport, although they were all within a 60-mile radius. The merchandise mix was also dependent on whether the store was located in a terminal which served international customers, business travelers on short-hop flights, or travelers on cross-country hauls.

Site location experts and associations develop various worksheets and analyses of locations and demographics. Many associations will approximate the customer population you need within a certain radius to support a store location, including looking at where the nearest competitors may lie.

If you are opening a business that is highly dependent on foot or car traffic, we suggest you hire an expert to assist you, as secondary data alone cannot provide you with all the information you need. An example would be if you were located in a place where most of your potential customers were accustomed to driving north to access retail establishments. You would need to recognize that your customer base would be highly limited unless your location was easily accessible to northbound drivers and you offered a compelling reason to drive to your location. Changing customer-buying and driving habits is difficult. Attempt only if you have a lot of excess cash with which to entice people into your store with advertising and promotions and if you have the funds to hold on till you establish a strong customer base.

Develop a location worksheet for your business based on the material at the beginning of the chapter, demographic and psychographic information of your customers, and additional expertise from site consultants. Before you begin though, you might want to check first with associations that represent your industry for their site location information as well. Once you have selected a physical area for your business you will need to work with a real estate broker to help you procure a building or lease.

■ ROLE OF AGENTS AND BROKERS

There is so much to know and analyze when making location decisions and an *experienced* commercial real estate broker can save you time and money. He or she can guide you through the maze of what is available and advise you on leases, rents, taxes, terms, financing, zoning, and transportation options.

Selecting the right broker may be as simple as asking for recommendations from friends or businesspeople in your networking groups. Brokers tend to specialize in retail, manufacturing, warehousing, or office space. When you call to request information about a particular property, you will be connected to the listing agent. If you like what you hear about the property but do not feel comfortable with that particular agent, do not be concerned. Usually, any agent or broker can show you any listed property; he or she does not have to be the listing agent. Keep in mind, however, if an agent shows you property and then you choose not to use that agent to complete the transaction, there may be problems.

Commercial brokers are paid primarily by the landlord or seller and earn their commissions only when a deal is final and money changes hands. Do not let yourself be rushed. Falling in love with a property before you know what is involved in the lease or purchase will definitely give the seller the edge in negotiations. Brokers

ACTION STEP 33

Seek Professional Help for Site Selection

After reading the chapter, visit a commercial real estate office or online broker's site to gain further information. Commercial real estate firms have access to planning reports and demographic information that will tell you a lot about growth in the community. If they are doing their job, they will also have information about major road plans and additional developments. Make an appointment to visit with a broker, prepare your questions, dress professionally, and explore your options.

Leave your checkbook at home!

affiliated with large commercial firms have extensive research departments at their disposal and should be able to help you with demographic data collection in addition to the material you have gathered on your own.

You can save an agent a lot of time if you have already defined your present and future needs. If you compare each site against your ideal location, you will probably have several workable alternatives.

On-site leasing agents are usually employees of the developer and thus are responsible for filling the building. You can choose to deal directly with the on-site agents. However, most will cooperate with any independent commercial broker you have engaged.

To begin your location search, start at Loopnet (see Figure 6.2) for retail and commercial listings. If you spend time on Loopnet, you will gain basic knowledge of what is available in your community and the going lease rates before meeting with a broker. If you live in a smaller community, driving through the town may work better as you seek leads to properties for lease.

Also, as we have said many times, checking actual costs before completing your final Business Plan is essential. Don't make assumptions. Gather real data and real numbers as you do not want to find out too late that your plans are not financial feasible. Also, you will want to compare the cost of leasing your own facility against the options of remaining in your home or using a coworking space. If your business requires leasing or purchasing a site, complete Action Step 33.

Anticipate the Unexpected

Bette Lindsay always had a soft spot for books and she finally chose to open a new bookstore in a shopping center. She researched everything—trends, census data, newspapers, reports from real estate firms, suppliers—but she failed to anticipate an important potential pitfall, dependency on an anchor tenant.

My husband and I researched small-business opportunities for almost two years, and my heart kept bringing me back to books. I've read voraciously since I was seven years old, and I love a well-written story. So when a new shopping center was opening a mile from our home, I told my husband, "This is it."

Everything looked perfect. They had a great anchor tenant coming in—an upscale food market that would draw lots of traffic. The broker we'd been working with during most of our search showed us the demographics of the area, which documented that we were smack in the middle of a highly-educated upper income market. According to statistics put out by the federal government, a bookstore needs a population of 27,000 people to support it. Our area had 62,000 people, and the closest bookstore was more than 20 miles away.

Everything else looked good, too. We had lots of parking. The neighboring entrepreneurs—three hardy pioneers like us—were serious about their businesses and excited about the center's growth and opportunities.

We wanted to be in for the holiday season, because November and December are the peak months for bookstores, so we set a target date of mid-September. Construction work was still being done on the anchor tenant's building when we moved in, which concerned us.

We started off with an autograph party, and we ran some bestseller specials. Even though construction work from our anchor tenant blocked our access, we had a very good Christmas that year. We started the New Year feeling very optimistic.

One day in mid-January, construction work stopped on our anchor tenant's new building. Two weeks later we read in the paper that the company had gone bankrupt.

Well, the first thing I did was call the landlord. He was out of town, and his answering service referred me to a property management company. They said they knew nothing about what was happening and that all they did was collect the rent. January was slow. So were February and March. In April, two businesses in the center were forced to close down. The construction debris continued blocking customer access. It was a mess. In May I finally reached the owner and tried to renegotiate the lease, but his story was sadder than mine.

Fourteen months after we moved in, a new anchor tenant finally opened! We hung in there, but we lost about $100,000 in sales—and it will take a long time to recoup.

Renegotiate a lease Obtaining a new or modified contract for occupancy

■ BEFORE YOU SIGN A LEASE

When you decide to rent a commercial location, the property owner's lawyer will draw up a lease document. Although its language is very specific, the terms spelled out are provisional; that is, the terms are proposed as a starting point for negotiation. Nothing you see in the contract is set in stone—unless you agree to it. Obviously, the terms proposed will favor the property owner.

Assume nothing when it comes to leases. Review the proposed lease seriously with your own real estate attorney, with others who have experience with leases, and possibly with some of the tenants if the property is located in a center or multiuse building.

How to Rewrite a Lease with Your Lawyer's Assistance

You live with a lease, and a landlord, for a long time. If you are successful in a retail business, your landlord may want a percentage of your gross sales receipts. If you are not successful, or if problems develop, you are going to need several Plan Bs and an escape hatch. For example, your lease should protect your interests:

Escape hatch A provision to cancel or modify a lease if the landlord fails to meet the specified terms

- If the furnace or air-conditioning system breaks down
- If the anchor tenant goes under
- If the building is sold
- If half the other tenants move out

The possibility of these and other negative circumstances needs to be dealt with in precise words and precise numbers in the lease.

Always try to negotiate reduced rent until the anchor tenant opens for business, and make the lease itself contingent on the anchor's leasing and opening. Also, you will want an escape clause stating that if and when the anchor tenant leaves, you may leave also. You also want to ensure that you are protected if the building is sold and that other tenants cannot disturb your business operations.

Read the lease slowly and carefully. When you see something you do not understand or do not like, draw a line through it. After discussing these issues with your attorney, she may be able to rewrite the lease or at least the parts which are imperative to you. Make sure that the owner, or the leasing agent, indicates his or her agreement with your changes by initialing each one. Remember this is your lease as well as the owners. Here is a checklist to start you on your rewrite:

Rewrite a lease Alter the wording of a lease to protect your interests

1. Escape clause: If the building does not shape up, or the area goes into eclipse, you will want to get out fast. Be specific. Write something like "If three or more vacancies occur in the center, tenant may terminate lease."
2. Option to renew: Common leases today are for 5 years unless you are a major player, such as Pier 1, in which case the lease might be for 10 years. Options to renew are usually for 2 to 5 years. You should be planning for at least a 5-year run for retail. If you are afraid to sign for 5 years, rethink your commitment to your retail business.
3. Right to transfer: Circumstances might force you to sublet. In the real estate trade this is called "assigning your lease" Usually assigning requires landlord approval of the new tenant. Be sure the lease allows you to transfer your lease hassle-free if such circumstances arise.
4. Cost-of-living cap: Most leases allow the property owner to increase rents in step with inflation based on the Consumer Price Index (CPI). To protect yourself, insist on a cost-of-living cap so that your base rate does not increase faster than your landlord's costs. Try for half of the amount of the CPI increase; if the CPI rises 4 percent, your rate will go up only 2 percent. Such an agreement is fair because the owner's costs will not change much. Major tenants in your center will insist on a cap, so you should be able to negotiate one also. Proceed with confidence.

Option to renew A guaranteed opportunity at the end of a lease to extend for another specific period of time

Cost-of-living cap An agreement that the rent from one year to another cannot be increased by more than the CPI (Consumer Price Index) for that period

5. Percentage lease: Percentage leases are common in larger retail centers. They specify that the tenant is to pay a base rate plus a percentage of the gross sales; for example, $3 per square foot per month plus 5 percent of gross sales over $500,000 per year. It is important that you make realistic sales projections, because the natural break-even point—the maximum amount of gross sales before percentage rent kicks in—is negotiable. The percentage rate itself is also negotiable.

6. Floating rent scale: If you are a pioneer tenant of a shopping center, negotiate a payment scale based on occupancy. For example, you may specify that you will pay 50 percent of your lease payment when the center is 50 percent occupied, 70 percent when it is 70 percent occupied, and 100 percent when it is full. You cannot build traffic to the center all by yourself, and motivation is healthy for everyone, including landlords.

7. Start-up buffer: There is a good chance you will be on location fixing up, remodeling, and so on long before you open your doors and make your first sale. Make your landlord aware of this problem, and try to negotiate a long period of free rent. The argument: If your business is successful, the landlord who is taking a percentage will make more money in the long run. If your business does not do well or if it fails, the landlord will have to find a new tenant. You need breathing space. You have signed on for the long haul. By not squeezing you to death for cash, the landlord allows you to put more money into inventory, equipment, service, and atmosphere—the things that make a business successful.

8. Improvements: Unless you are extremely handy, you do not want to lease a space with nothing more than a cement floor and a capped-off cold-water pipe. With most retail sites, however, a plain vanilla shell with very few tenant improvements is the norm. If the economy is slowing down or in a recession, tenant improvements will be easier to negotiate. Find space that does not require extensive and expensive remodeling if cash is tight. Do not go under before you get going.

9. Use clauses: Caterina's, an ice cream and candy store, had included the word *beverages* in the use clause, which the landlord approved. The landlord came back later to Caterina's owner and told her she could not sell smoothies or coffees. Fortunately, the owner showed the lease to the landlord and pointed out the word *beverages*, and no more was said. Additionally, the storeowner had inserted into the lease that she would not sell "soft-serve yogurt." When she began to sell hard-packed yogurt, the landlord came calling. Again, she pulled out the lease. Wording your lease properly can mean the difference between success and failure.

Common area maintenance (CAM) Direct and indirect costs of maintaining property charged to leasee

10. Common Area Maintenance (CAM): Leases contain clauses that cover the cost of gardeners, building repairs, trash, and so on. Understand the CAM charges before leasing; they can vary greatly. Make sure your CAM charges are based on your square footage. If a portion of the center is empty, be sure the landlord—not you—pays the CAM charges for the empty square footage.

11. Parking and storage: Determine before signing the lease how many parking spots for employees and customers you are assigned, or share in common with other tenants. Also, ask if any spots are reserved or have time constraints. Investigate the usable amount of storage space available.

12. Option to purchase: Consider requesting that an option or right of first refusal to purchase the building be included, in case you want to purchase the building as your business grows.

13. Option for expansion: Include an option for right of first refusal for additional space that may become available, thus securing space for your business without requiring a costly move.

Triple net or NNN lease Tenant responsible for part or all of the insurance, taxes, and maintenance

14. Triple net or NNN lease: The landlord will bill each tenant for insurance, taxes, and operating expenses.

15. Relocation clause: Allows landlord to move you to "comparable space." Strike this clause as you do not want to hassle with moving your startup.

Depending on the current economic situation, adjusting the lease may be easy or it may be almost impossible. In a tenant's market request free rent, rather than reduced rent. Consider negotiating a shorter lease term for a little higher monthly lease rate. Another option, ask for the shortest lease term and one year options without automatic rent increases. Try to preserve your flexibility, as most entrepreneurs will benefit from knowing they have options.

Tenant's market Leasee has advantage due to slow economy

■ ADDITIONAL LOCATION DECISION FOR MANUFACTURERS

If you are involved in manufacturing, your search for a good location will be focused on labor supply and energy availability and cost, taxes, zoning restrictions, access to transportation corridors, and proximity to suppliers and customers. You will focus on the economy of the state, county, region, and city where you want to locate. Talk with state and local government officials and local Chambers of Commerce and economic development groups. Many of these groups will work with you to locate and develop a site. In addition, they may have knowledge of sites that you can rehab and thus reduce costs and possibly receive government incentives.

In fact, every state and local economic development office throughout the United States will be more than happy to send you vast amounts of data on their area. Tax incentives, job training, reduced-cost utilities, and infrastructure such as roads and utilities are just a few of the jewels states and cities will dangle in front of you. Many low-income areas—including inner city and rural locations—are anxious to lure new enterprises and offer incentives to employers willing to hire and train as few as five people.

■ ALTERNATIVE RETAIL LOCATIONS

Many interesting alternative retail locations exist today. These include a circuit for retailers who travel to colleges on a monthly basis, hawking their wares to college students. Another entrepreneur we highlight in the text owned six stores inside airports.

One local photographer not only talked with his customers during street art fairs, but more importantly he listened to them. When over 40 people in town had requested professional photography lessons, he knew he had another venue for his business. Thus, he now offers classes but only in the winter, when his fair business is closed down due to bad weather. These classes keep cash flowing all year long.

Swap Meets and Fairs

In many parts of the country, incredibly lucrative opportunities for retailing are found at local or regional weekly or weekend swap meets. For example, Thursday night's street fair VillageFest in Palm Springs draws retailers from Arizona and New Mexico; San Luis Obispo, California, draws jewelry, food, and clothing dealers for weekly Farmer's Markets attended by thousands.

In Southern California, many retailers and craftspeople net more than $100,000 a year working only two 12-hour days a week at the Orange County Marketplace swap meet (although additional hours are spent off-site ordering and preparing for the weekend). For many small retailers, starting at a swap meet provides an excellent way to test the market and pricing levels. In addition, swap meets and fairs offer incredible opportunities for seasonal businesses. One family runs a summer fair food kiosk business, and all of the family members, including the parents and young adults, attend college full-time during the rest of the year.

Kiosks

An age-old form of retailing has made a comeback—the pushcart is now the "kiosk." Locating your retail business in a kiosk will make you part of an over $10 billion retailing venue, according to *Specialty Retail Report*, an industry-publication based in Boston (*http://www.specialtyretail.com*). Kiosks provide a low-risk environment in which to launch a specialty retail operation, with malls throughout the United States currently generating up to 10 percent of their income from kiosks.

With a low cost of infrastructure, the ability to change product quickly, and the mall owners' desire to have unique and diverse products, a kiosk may be a retailing venue for you to explore. Testing the water for your products can be done inexpensively, and since you are mostly one-on-one with your customer, extensive market research can be conducted during the selling process. Some large mall owners work directly with their kiosk tenants, advising and training in hopes the entrepreneurs will build successful businesses and add additional kiosks in other malls.

QVC

With 15,000 average orders per hour, QVC provides an incredible opportunity as an alternative channel of distribution. Many large firms use it as one of their channels as well as small upstart firms who can make it through the rigor of the QVC vetting process. Kathy Dahl Crifasi, a San Clemente, CA entrepreneur distributes her Hipzbag, a small handbag that is worn on the hip and holds essentials including a cell phone, through the following channels: 1) online on her company website 2) through wholesalers and 3) QVC. Her Hipzbag was recently named a QVC Bestseller and Customer Favorite. For additional QVC information see below:

Selling on QVC: Nice Work if You Can Get It

by Anne Fisher

So you think you have a pretty hot product. What if you could show it directly to people via a television channel that reaches 166 million homes worldwide, as well as the 6 million monthly visitors to the channel's website? What if most of those shoppers were loyal repeat customers, credit cards at the ready? And wouldn't it be fun to hear them boost your sales while you're on the air as they call in to say how much they love your stuff?

It's not too good to be true; it's QVC. Launched in 1986, the West Chester, Pa.-based channel broadcasts live 24 hours a day, every day except Christmas, offering about 60,000 products annually. Viewers call in an average of 15,000 orders per hour. Since its inception, $7.5 billion-a-year QVC (the letters stand for quality, value, and convenience) has shipped more than 1 billion packages in the U.S. alone.

QVC is even more tight-lipped than most private companies. No one there will say how much of a cut QVC gets on sales of each product, for instance, and vendors are prohibited from revealing any numbers if they want to stay on the air. But it's fairly clear that a hit product on QVC is akin to a license to print money.

There's just one catch: Getting on is tough. Very tough.

First, QVC's 170 buyers look for a unique product (ideally, a patented one) that isn't widely available elsewhere. It has to be made of top-quality materials. If you're trying to get your foot in the door on QVC, don't be surprised if an inspector drops by to examine your manufacturing process. Next, whether the product is a piece of jewelry, a small appliance, or an item that falls into one of the other dozens of categories of goods that QVC sells, it can't just sit there looking ordinary. It needs what Teddy Marcus calls "a 'wow' factor."

Mr. Marcus started a company called Arcs & Angles that has been selling shower curtains on QVC for 12 years. The patented curtains have holes that enable them to slip directly onto curtain rods, so they can be hung without hooks. When he unfurls them on the air, QVC's phones start ringing.

"It's been great for business, but [this route] isn't for everyone," he says. "You have to be a talented salesperson, first to sell to QVC and then to impress its viewers."

You also have to be willing to submit to exhaustive vetting. Dr. Irwin Smigel, whose dental practice on Madison Avenue at East 59th Street maintains the pearly whites of George Clooney, Johnny Depp, Jennifer Lopez, and many other celebs, invented and patented a line of products–toothpaste, floss, rinse–called Supersmile. Six years ago, QVC approached Dr. Smigel and his wife and business partner, Lucia, about putting the brand on the air. They agreed. QVC then spent a year and a half poring over independent scientific analyses to make sure that Supersmile really whitens teeth.

"It's been fantastic for us," says Dr. Smigel. "There's no other way we could compete with companies like Procter & Gamble that can spend $90 million to market a single brand of toothpaste.

"But the scrutiny they put us through was extraordinary," he continues. "If you have a product that is mostly hype, it just won't fly."

Want to give QVC a whirl? Go to *www.qvc.com* and click on "Vendor Relations" to get started. Good luck.

Source: Anne Fisher, "Selling on QVC: nice work if you can get it." Reprinted with permission, Crain's New York Business March 12, 2010. © Crain Communications Inc.

■ INTERNET

We believe you must use the Internet as a channel of distribution and/or as a way to market your business or service. Changes on the Net happen at warp speed, so instead of providing you with information that will soon be outdated, we are providing only the basics here in the text and suggest that you seek e-commerce and e-marketing information online to make sure you are utilizing the most up-to-date information.

Operating on the Net requires all of the major functions that are part of any business. However, the medium and channel used to achieve are different. Creating a strong loyal customer who will pay a fair price for your goods is still the goal of any entrepreneur. The three major e-commerce business models operating are business to business (B2B), business to consumer (B2C), and consumer to consumer (C2C). (See Figure 6.1.)

Today, many firms are using the Net to not only sell products, but services as well. Many firms start online businesses sometimes unsure how they will monetize their business in the future with the belief that they will be able to as the environment changes so rapidly. Instagram did it! Pinterest did it too!

Monetize To turn into money

Many bloggers have found gold by following their passions. Antique toys, traveling with grandchildren, edible gardens, retirement investing, and chocolate desserts make for interesting blogs, which over time draw enough daily views to enable bloggers to reap rewards through advertising revenue. Also, many bloggers promote themselves right into paid speaking gigs. According to CBS News, "There are almost as many people making a living as bloggers as there are lawyers." If you have something interesting to share, creating a blog is easy and takes only minutes with Word Press. However, promoting the blog takes time, effort, talent, and a little luck just like any business.

The B2B model offers incredible opportunity for substantial sales as the orders are much larger in size and the number of customers is usually fewer, allowing you to take time to build relationships. The efficiency, 24/7 availability, and instant collection of payment, all allow reduced transaction time and help with cash flow for companies. Also, due to the openness of the Net, you can track your competitors very easily. However, this is both a blessing and a curse as price and product comparisons are so easy for customers to make. Thus, you must offer something else of value to ensure repeat business.

The melding of stores, online, catalogs, etc. is becoming the norm and many firms are following to compete and capture the customer who is always tied to her smartphone. This model will continue its meteoric rise as smartphones allow billions access to a computer in their pockets. A recent *Technology Review* piece provides the following:

- Right now the world has 1.4 billion PCs in use. "Mobile phones, on the other hand, are already selling more than 1.4 billion units every single year."
- Today there are seven billion people in the world and six billion mobile cellular phone subscriptions.

To capitalize on the B2C market easily, consider setting up shop on one of the "storefront" options who also offer support services like Yahoo!, eBay, Amazon, and Shopify. Within just an hour or two your store could be up and running! These platforms provide easy design setups, sometimes shipping, and easy payment collection. Online platforms use web analytics, allowing firms to be incredibly responsive to their changing customers' needs and sensitivity to pricing and advertising.

If you produce artwork or handcrafts, check out Etsy or the myriad of other sites allowing artists and crafters an outlet. Many crafters who are true artisans have found customers who are able and willing to pay for the quality workmanship and time involved in producing art. Websites allow artists to tell their compelling stories, which draw the customer not only into the art but also the artist.

Many companies use YouTube as one of their many advertising/distribution channels. Depending on your product this is certainly an avenue to explore as it can be done at very low cost and you can experiment very easily. Read Chapter 7 to see how the founder of Orabrush succeeded using YouTube.

We have seen many entrepreneurs use eBay and Craigslist as venues as well, either to ply their entire business or to use as one channel. Tom Galat became very entrepreneurial when he needed to pay his rent. "Couch Man" saw a free couch on the sidewalk one day, threw it in his truck, took it home, cleaned it thoroughly, took beautiful pictures of the "new" couch, posted them on Craigslist, and within 24 hours the couch sold for $250. He was hooked. For two hours of work, he thought, $100 an hour was not too bad!

"Couch Man" is an example of consumer to consumer (C2C) e-commerce, which is growing rapidly along with the shared economy discussed in Chapter 2. As classified newspaper ads have gone by the wayside, they have been replaced with Craigslist and many people today are making an excellent living by selling or reselling goods on it.

The Internet continues to evolve and entrepreneurs are discovering new ways to capture the power of the net and the smartphone customer. The possibilities are endless and ever changing. If you are not flexible, you will not survive.

■ SUMMARY

Before making location decisions, reconsider your personal preferences and dreams, Target Customers, taxes, technology, available resources, and the future.

Channel decisions are among the most challenging you will make in establishing your business. In today's world, one needs to recognize that you will not make this decision once, but many times, as new channel opportunities continue to develop. As discussed earlier, the melding of location, distribution, pricing, and promotion for the marketing of products and services changes constantly.

In completing your research, use the information and resources in Chapters 4 through 7 to determine the best channels for your business. You will also need to access the current research information on Net metrics. Most of the Action Steps in this chapter can be applied and adjusted for Internet businesses. Hard and projected data not only will be appreciated by your lenders as they read and consider your Business Plan, but such data will also help you learn about employee costs, housing patterns, retail sales, and the stability of the community.

Explore the opportunities of virtual businesses, various Internet locations, and incubators. Staying in your office or garage may help you conserve cash for many years, or possibly forever.

Some short journeys will help you recognize how extremely important the location decision is for bricks-and-mortar retail businesses. First, walk up and down the main business street of your town. Walk it on different days (weekends, weekdays), and at different times of the day (midmorning, noon, afternoon, and evening rush hour). Take notes on what you see happening. What stores are closing? What new stores are opening? Where is service good?

Now that you have walked the town, it is time to roam the Net in the same way and assess: Which sites are growing? Which sites are slowing down? What opportunities are there for you to capitalize on? The physical location decision is very important for bricks-and-mortar retailers, and for Internet entrepreneurs their placement on a Google search is equally important to success.

We have focused this chapter primarily on retail businesses, but the process of site selection for manufacturing is fraught with more issues and complications. For a manufacturing business, the labor market, land costs, rent, ability to expand, taxes, and employee and legal issues play a major role in the location decision. Consider hiring experts to guide you in your decision making if the location decision will be costly to change.

After viewing and analyzing all of the data available, you may choose to locate your business based primarily on personal factors or passions, such as a desire to remain near your family, to be close to fly-fishing in the river near your home, to stay near your community and church or your children's schools, or to live near the beach or out in the middle of nowhere. Or you may have altruistic motives, such as wanting to create jobs in the inner city.

Remember, you are trying to not only grow a business, but also to build a life based on your dreams. Do them both with passion.

Change is inevitable. Embrace it!

■ THINK POINTS FOR SUCCESS

- The irony of the search for a retail or business start-up location is that you may need the best retail site when you can least afford it.
- Take your time selecting a location. If you lose out on a hot site, keep looking. Do not give up; there are always more places. However, compromising may be an extremely costly decision, and waiting for the right location may be worth it.
- Begin with a regional analysis that will allow you to compare neighborhoods or areas.
- A site analysis should include everything that is unique to a specific building or space. Even many successful centers have some dead traffic areas. Hire a retail specialist for insight and recommendations.
- Who are your neighbors? Are they attracting your type of customers or clients? What will happen if they move or go out of business?
- Know the terms and buzz words and be aware that they may mean slightly different things in each contract or lease agreement.
- Everything is negotiable: rent, signage, improvement allowances, rates, maintenance. Do not be afraid to ask.
- Talk to former tenants; you may be amazed at what you learn.
- Never sign a lease without consulting an attorney who is experienced in lease negotiations.
- Be willing to seek out and pay for the advice of trained professionals.

- Coordinate your various distribution channels and make sure your image is consistent throughout the channels. When choosing several channels, you want to build synergy.

- Capitalize on the low cost entry to Internet commerce.
- Take Risks!

■ KEY POINTS FROM ANOTHER VIEW

Getting Goods on Store Shelves

By Sarah E. Needleman

In mid-2009, Janie McQueen asked retailers in her native Beaufort, S.C., if they would carry a line of baby apparel hand-sewn by her mother. But even though she knew many of the shopkeepers by name, none would bite.

Experts say the best strategy is to research venues that are a strong fit and prepare a compelling and succinct sales pitch.

So she turned to the Internet, listing the bonnets and bucket hats on Etsy.com, an online crafts market, as well as on a website she created for her business. Still, only a handful of buyers placed orders through either platform.

Finally, a networking connection introduced Ms. McQueen to a sales representative specializing in children's attire. The result, she says, was a contract that landed her mother's craftwork in 48 clothing boutiques nationwide by the end of her first year in business, in exchange for a small percentage of the wholesale price of the items they sold.

"It helps to have a rep," says Ms. McQueen, because such a person gives an unknown entrepreneur "more credibility." She counts her mother, Mary Patrick, as her business partner, and says their start-up, Susu & John, ended 2010 with $25,000 in gross sales. The company is now profitable, she adds.

For entrepreneurs with products to sell, a wide range of sales channels abound—from boutiques to big-box stores to online marketplaces. But identifying appropriate retailers—and striking deals with them—can be a challenging first-time endeavor. Experts say the best strategy is to research venues that are a strong fit and prepare a compelling and succinct sales pitch.

"You want to look at outlets that sell similar kinds of products. You try lots of different things and see what works," says Bruce I. Newman, a professor of marketing at DePaul University in Chicago.

For some entrepreneurs, cold-calling retailers does work. Sisters Kim Mack and Staci Douglas did this when launching Out of the Box, a Clayton, N.C., wholesaler of key chains and ID tags. The duo targeted dozens of shops that sold similar or complementary products. "Sometimes we were fortunate, and sometimes we weren't," says Ms. Mack, adding that for every client they signed, they requested referrals to other potential buyers.

They also paid for booths at consumer-product trade shows, spending as much as $3,500 for a five-day event. They snagged 12 retail clients at the first one alone. And they met industry professionals, who later introduced them to merchants who became clients. Networking is "a way of opening doors," says Ms. Mack, a stay-at-home mom who took up entrepreneurship after her husband became unemployed in late 2008.

Today, Out of the Box's products are for sale in some 200 gift boutiques nationwide. The company's revenues more than tripled last year from 2009, yielding a net profit, says Ms. Mack. The duo is now ramping up production for a deal in the works with a major department store.

Betsy Hauser also secured her first retail customers through a trade show. Her start-up, Mutt Huttz, a Cramerton, N.C., maker of customized dog-crate covers, charges brick-and-mortar clients $20 for a floor sample, fabric swatches and a catalog to showcase in their stores. The shops' customers can then place orders that Ms. Hauser fills and sends back to the retailers.

Ms. Hauser started Mutt Huttz in 2007 because she was struggling to make ends meet in a low-paying job at a nonprofit. To secure more clients, she next launched a direct-mail campaign, sending promotional postcards to 150 pet boutiques and doggie daycare centers around the country. Twenty-five placed orders.

Separately, Ms. Hauser spent $2,500 to build a website that could process orders direct from consumers. To draw traffic, she spent $150 a month on Google AdWords to get her website high on search results for terms such as "dog crate covers" and "luxury pet kennels." Later, she hired a search-engine optimization firm to boost her website's rankings, for a one-time $1,200 fee.

Ms. Hauser says the online exposure led to deals with 15 e-commerce vendors, who take orders for her crates on their sites in return for a small percentage of the wholesale price of each order they process.

Mutt Huttz posted $100,000 in revenues last year and is now profitable, Ms. Hauser says.

Source: Sarah E. Needleman, "Getting Goods on Store Shelves." Reprinted by permission of WSJ.com, Copyright © 2011 Dow Jones & Company, Inc. All Rights Reserved Worldwide. License numbers 3042101284810 and 3042120488742.

■ ACTION STEPS

■ KEY TERMS

Image_Source/iStockphoto.com

Connecting with and Engaging Customers
Marketing and Promotions

CHAPTER 7

Learning Objectives

- Learn how to communicate with Target Customers using a wide range of promotional methods.

- View exceptional customer service as the key to promotion.

- Determine the dollar value of your customer and the importance of all employees acting as salespeople.

- Promote your business through free ink and free air.

- Learn how to use newswire services.

- Appreciate the importance of networking.

- Understand the value of personal selling.

- Learn how to use sales reps effectively.

- Explore the vast array of web offerings.

- Develop the best **promotional mix** for your business.

- Attach price tags to promotion ideas.

Promotional mix All the elements that blend to maximize communication with your Target Customers

174

Promotion is the art and science of moving the image of your business to the forefront of a prospect's mind. The word *promotion* comes from the Latin verb *movere,* which means, "to advance, or to move forward." *Promotion* is an aggressive word, so learn to say it with passion!

Moving your product into your customer's mind through multiple promotional channels is imperative today and your message must be consistent throughout the platforms. Thus, in the past your newspaper and TV advertising had to be consistent. Now add to those your website, tweets, YouTube channel, advertisements on tablets and smartphones, and so on. By engaging customers at each step in the search and buying process, you have the opportunity to retain them as customers and build trust and loyalty, which are the foundation of any venture. Thus, you must promote on multiple platforms with a consistent and integrated marketing plan.

Coordinate online and offline marketing efforts seamlessly so customers will not be confused. The use of multiple promotion channels combined with multiple distribution channels, can be synergistic. As these two areas are melding due to technology, and changes are occurring on a daily basis, we have presented marketing and promotion basics in this chapter. However, you must be responsible for keeping up on the latest technology to take full advantage of changing opportunities. The Entrepreneurial Resources that follow will give you a head start.

Wrap the 4 Ps of price, product, promotion, and place around the needs of your Target Customers, and continue to rewrap them when the needs, technology, or the environment shifts. However, do not get so

Entrepreneur's Resource

Marketing and Entrepreneurial
Blogs/Twitter Feeds to Follow

The following blogs and their Twitter feeds will keep you up to date with changing technology as well as highlight successful entrepreneurs using evolving technology to grow their ventures.

Seth Godin	Church of the Customer
Steve Blank	Young Entrepreneur
Guy Kawasaki (How to Change	Quick Sprout
the World)	Under30CEO
Guerilla Marketing	Mashable
Duct Tape Marketing	Social Media Examiner
Small Business Trends	Kikolani
Small Business Brief	The Social Media Marketing Blog
Entrepreneur Daily Dose	

figure **7.1**

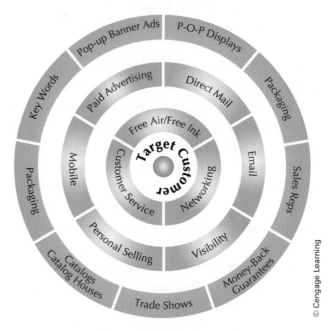

Connecting with Your Target Customer

© Cengage Learning

caught up in using technology that you forget the basics of marketing. As the head of measurement at Facebook, Sean Bruich, reminds, "With any new medium, we focus on the difference. But some of those core aspects of being successful in marketing—how to clearly communicate your value proposition and how to communicate new information to the consumer—those are not changing."

In this chapter we ask you to first survey a wide variety of promotional avenues before you decide on your promotional strategy while encouraging you to remain open to all options. Figure 7.1 highlights the promotional mix variables, which you will be drawing from to gain your customers attention, interest, desire and actions. The rapid changes in the Internet will provide new and challenging options which can occur overnight. To break through to your customers today you will need to be flexible and think out of the box to grab the attention of your customers while meeting their needs. Creativity! Creativity! Creativity!

■ MARKETING OVERVIEW

Promotional campaign Set of tactics designed to sell a specific product or service or to establish an image or benefit.

As you brainstorm for an optimum marketing strategy, take time first to examine successful promotional campaigns within your industry and others. Look at the unique ways firms have approached their target markets with specific attention to your target market. Hopefully, with this information in hand, you will forge a more creative promotional strategy to connect with your customer in a meaningful and memorable way.

Marketing has changed dramatically over the past few years and we anticipate the changes to be even greater in the next few years. However, marketing

PASSION

Passionate Entrepreneurs Meet at Startup Weekends

Startup Weekends are weekend-long, hands-on experiences where entrepreneurs and aspiring entrepreneurs can find out if startup ideas are viable. On average, half of Startup Weekend's attendees have technical or design backgrounds, the other half have business backgrounds.

Beginning with open mic pitches on Friday, attendees bring their best ideas and inspire others to join their team. Over Saturday and Sunday teams focus on customer development, validating their ideas, practicing LEAN Startup Methodologies and building a minimal viable product. On Sunday evening teams demo their prototypes and receive valuable feedback from a panel of experts.

The top eight reasons to attend:

Education:

Startup Weekends are all about learning through the act of creating. Don't just listen to theory, build your own strategy and test it as you go.

Build your network:

This isn't just a happy-hour. Startup Weekend attracts your community's best makers and do-ers. By spending a weekend working to build scalable companies that solve real-world problems, you will build long-lasting relationships and possibly walk away with a job or even an investor.

Co-Founder Dating:

We all know it's not just about the idea – it's about the team. Startup Weekend is hands down the best way to find someone you can actually launch a startup with.

Learn a new skill:

Step outside of your comfort zone. With a whole weekend dedicated to letting your creative juices flow, Startup Weekends are perfect opportunities to work on a new platform, learn a new programming language, or just try something different.

Actually launch a business:

Over 36 percent of Startup Weekend startups are still going strong after three months. Roughly 80 percent of participants plan on continuing working with their team or startup after the weekend.

Get face time with thought leaders:

Local tech and startup leaders participate in Startup Weekends as coaches and judges. Get some one-on-one time with the movers and shakers in your community.

Save money and get stuff:

Startup Weekends cost between $75 and $99 (less for students). Your ticket covers seven meals, snacks, access to exclusive resources from our global sponsors, a book from O'Reilly Media and all the coffee you can drink.

Join a global community:

Join over 45,000 Startup Weekend alumni, all on a mission to change the world.

Source: Startup Weekend, *http://startupweekend.org/about/* (Accessed July 2, 2012). Reprinted with permission.
Author Note: Startup Weekend is an Affiliate of the Kauffman Foundation.

success is still measured the same, by increased sales and loyalty of customers. Businesses today are built upon relationships you forge. Technological changes open many new avenues to offer products, reach customers, and increase customer loyalty and participation.

Buzz, also known as *word-of-mouth,* has always been considered the most effective of all marketing techniques. Facebook "likes" and Pinterest pins are really nothing more than word of mouth on a double espresso. And if you have developed a product or service that engages and pleases your customers, you will have raving fans that become your "sales force" through powerful social media and traditional "word-of-mouth." This buzz can come from customers, media, or the community so we will focus first on customer service, free ink or air, and networking, which are the first three elements surrounding your Target Customer in Figure 7.1. Participation has been coined as the fifth P in marketing, so engage and inspire others early on to take an active role in promoting your business.

Reaching customers, promoting products, analyzing buying habits, pricing products, tracking sales, and using web analytics all are improved by technology. However, the goal remains the same: Know and serve your customer.

Coremetrics, a "leading provider of on-demand analytics and precision marketing solutions" shares this:

> The one constant is that technology will evolve, consumers will become more sophisticated and more empowered, and it will become increasingly important to know your visitors and customers at an individual level, and to build long-term, deep relationships with them. Personalization and relationship marketing are becoming more of a reality. To be successful, marketers need a robust behavioral analytics solution and a complete record of all visitor behavior—not a sampling of data, and certainly not simple statistics about click-through and page hits. Only with a customer-centric data assets will marketers be able to harness the power of the Internet and provide their visitors with a truly personal experience that optimizes their business goals.

Source: *http://www.coremetrics.com/downloads/Coremetrics_web2.0_white_paper.pdf* (Accessed May 24, 2008).

The following questions are critical and need to be answered: What is your message? What is appropriate for your Target Customer? What can you afford to spend? What are your own and others' prior experiences? What are your immediate goals? What are your long-term strategies? What benefits will your customer receive? How can you be unique? And what will give you the biggest bang for your buck over the long haul not just in sales but in creating "buzz" as well?

Advertising dollars are shifting, as shown in Figure 7.2. The growth of advertising on mobile devices is predicted to sky rocket over the next few years. Reaching individuals on multiple media sources with consistency, repetition, and creativity will be the key to success.

Much of your marketing and promotion should be partially developed at this point through the past Action Steps, especially your customer touchpoints. You know the areas in which you must shine. The next step is to begin the promotion process that will highlight your strengths and uniqueness. Note that when you begin your marketing efforts there will be a trial and error phase and a tremendous learning curve to determine which efforts are most effective. You need to talk to your customers, track sales figures and profits, and make adjustments along the way. Be ready and willing to respond to change.

Now that you have visualized your customer with your collage (Chapter 4) and researched your competition and market niches (Chapter 5), it is time to plan a promotional strategy that is tailored to your customer and your distribution (Chapter 6) and pricing (Chapter 8) strategies.

Avoid wasting your dollars on, promotional schemes that will not work. For example, if your Target Customer is a college-educated, suburban female age 45 to

figure **7.2**

Shifting Advertising Dollars

US Print vs. Online Ad Spending, 2011–2016 (billions)

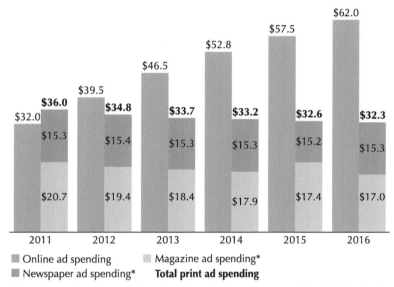

■ Online ad spending ■ Magazine ad spending*
■ Newspaper ad spending* **Total print ad spending**

Note: eMarketer benchmarks its Us online ad spending projections against the IAB/PWC data, for which the last full year measured was 2010;
eMarketer benchmarks its US newspaper ad spending projections against the NAA data, for which the last full year measured was 2010; *print only
Source: US Print vs. Online Ad Spending 2011-2016, eMarketer, Jan 2012. Retrieved from http://www.emarkerter.com/Article/Print.aspx?R=1008788 (Accessed July 13, 2012).
Reprinted with permission.

US TV vs. Online Ad Spending, 2011–2016 (billions)

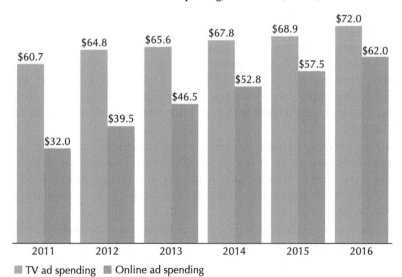

■ TV ad spending ■ Online ad spending

Note: eMarketer benchmarks its Us online ad spending projections against the IAB/PWC data, for which the last full year measured was 2010
Source: US TV vs. Online Ad Spending, 2011-2016, eMarketer, Jan 2012. Retrieved from http://www.emarkerter.com/Article/Print.aspx?R=1008788 (Accessed July 13, 2012).
Reprinted with permission.

(continued)

55 who earns more than $250,000, owns three cars, rides daily for two hours, and reads *Dressage Today* and *Equus,* your best chance of reaching her is with direct mail, which offers pinpoint marketing. If, on the other hand, your Target Customers are male, age 18 to 25, with high-school educations and incomes under $30,000, you will achieve better results with a YouTube or Facebook promotion.

Direct mail An advertisement directed toward specific Target Customers through mail

figure **7.2**

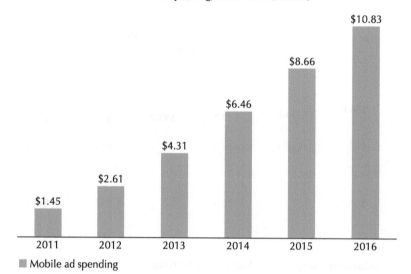

Shifting Advertising Dollars *(continued)*

US Mobile Ad Spending, 2011–2016 (billions)

- $10.83 (2016)
- $8.66 (2015)
- $6.46 (2014)
- $4.31 (2013)
- $2.61 (2012)
- $1.45 (2011)

■ Mobile ad spending

Note: Includes display (banner, rich media and video), search and SMS/MMS/P2P messaging
Source: eMarketer, Jan 2012

■ PROMOTIONAL STRATEGIES

The key to connecting with customers is to consider a wide variety of promotional mix variables (Figure 7.1), select several, and work diligently to integrate them to put forth a consistent message to your Target Customer as part of your marketing strategy. A closer look at many of these promotional mix variables follows throughout the chapter.

As you review the variables, please keep in mind the touchpoints from Chapter 5 and the gaps in the marketplace that you are trying to capitalize on. Remember, for each touchpoint, you have the opportunity to connect with your customer; many times, this will not be through traditional advertising but through building a relationship with your customer, which is the key to entrepreneurial success.

Of all the promotional mix elements, we believe exceptional customer service and engagement need to be at the center of your promotional strategy. Satisfied customers have *always* driven business success and the growth of social media makes it even more important to engage customers at your business and on your website.

Once customers have found your place of business or website, you must offer compelling reasons for them to stay, purchase, and return. Positive contact with your business and products drives further buzz. For most new businesses, advertising funds are limited so connecting and engaging early on with your first customers is essential in driving positive word of mouth both online and offline.

■ EXCEPTIONAL CUSTOMER SERVICE AS PROMOTION

Exceptional customer service provides your firm with three vital ingredients for growth: *relationships, reputation,* and *references.* Take the time and effort early on to learn everything you can about your Target Customers. The closer you are to your customers, the more likely you will be able to meet their needs. If you are passionate about your customers, you may be lucky enough to breed passionate customers who care about your success.

Customers who enjoy doing business with you will tell you how to improve, and they will provide constant feedback if they know you are listening and responding. Orobrush (see Key Points) provides an excellent example of a firm who spent a great deal of time successfully listening to their company's word of mouth chatter.

We challenge you to listen and encourage your customers' participation in your business. Out in the community or in your selected industry, satisfied customers will be your unpaid—and possibly your strongest—salespeople. This is a sales force no amount of money can buy! And customers who are referred to you by customers are usually half sold. Thus, capitalize on referrals.

Gaining a new customer costs five times more than retaining a customer. Thus, do all you can to retain your customers and practice continuous customer service improvement.

In addition to customer service, always focus on the realization that customers are buying a solution to a problem and want an exceptional and memorable experience. Make the benefits of your product real and offer customers more than they expect. In doing so, the experience with your firm will be one they will want to share with friends and colleagues.

You have studied your competitors and target markets extensively and you know the benefits and service levels not only desired but also expected. Exceptional customer service and building a memorable experience increase the bottom line, usually with relatively limited out of pocket costs. Any additional costs incurred should be considered part of your marketing costs. Complete Action Step 34 by returning to Action Step 28 on touchpoints to determine how you can make each touchpoint an exceptional experience.

Never forget little things mean a lot! A smile, a handwritten thank you, or a phone call from the company owner all cost nothing but a little time. It is surprising how little it takes to make a good impression today as personal touch is so absent in our lives. You want customers to shout your company name from the rooftops and spread it widely through Instagram, Pinterest, Twitter, Facebook, and so on.

Zappos, Nordstrom, and Southwest Airlines provide premiere customer service—learn their philosophies and follow their examples. Constantly read up on how firms are being responsive to their bricks-and mortar customers as well as their Internet ones. Your service levels should be the same -both online and offline. If feasible, adopt and implement the best service strategies into your business.

According to Guy Kawasaki, author of *Enchantment: The Art of Changing Hearts, Minds, and Actions*, "The three pillars of enchantment are likability, trustworthiness, and a great product or service. If you have these down pat, you could rub two sticks together and enchant people. If you don't have these three, you could spend thousands of hours and dollars on a 'shock and awe' social media campaign and still bomb."

To be effective, *everyone* in the organization must practice exceptional customer service in order to gain the trust of customers. It must be a way of doing business at all times, part of the company culture, and rewarded. Also, employees must know their responsibilities and have the freedom and authority to solve problems using the following techniques:

- Proactively serve the customer. ("How may I help you?")
- Display the power to act. ("How can I solve the problem?")

ACTION STEP 34

Exceptional Service through Touchpoints

Pull out Action Step 28 on customer touchpoints. With list in hand, brainstorm away and develop a way to make each touchpoint memorable for your Target Customer. In building exceptional customer service, you cannot just meet your customers' service needs—you must exceed them.

- If you are sending a package, what could you include to brighten someone's day?
- If you are serving them a fast-food meal, what could you do to make it quicker and more personal?
- If you are sending architectural drawings for review, how could you help them to better understand the drawings?
- If you own a candy store, what extra could you give each time a customer came in the door to promote return business?

Some tactics you come up with will not be possible due to time or money constraints. However, those you can incorporate will be greatly appreciated by your customers, and you will be on your way to enjoying an exceptional business. Keep refining your touchpoints. If you have an online and offline presence, complete the assignment for each. Consider also how these touchpoints might vary over the various platforms, PC, tablets, and mobile.

Remember everything matters, even your email tagline! One of our favorites is travel agent Ellen McDannel's, "The clock is running. Make the most of today. Time waits for no man. Yesterday is history. Tomorrow is a mystery. Today is a gift. That is why it is called the present", which she borrowed from Alice Morse Earle.

ACTION STEP 35

What Are Your Customers Worth? How Can You Make Their Dollar Value Memorable?

1. Review the chapter's dentist example.
2. Now determine the dollar value of *your* customer. Determine approximately how much your customer will spend in one year with your business. Multiply that number by the number of years you hope to keep them as a customer. For a retail store that figure might be 5 years, or for a fast food restaurant it could be 10 years. However, in the B2B world, business relationships often last 50 to 75 years!
3. Next, consider the number of future clients you can reasonably expect to gain through their word of mouth. In some industries that might be three or four. If you have a retail store, you easily could gain 8 to 10 customers through one raving fan passing a good word on. Take your estimated number of future customers and add one for the original customer, then multiply that figure by the figure in Step 2.
4. Next, design a creative and memorable way for you and your employees to remember the original dollar value of a customer and the dollar value of all those they may bring forth.

Your firm is in business to make a profit. You need your employees to understand that the only reason they receive a paycheck is because customers return! When customers are treated well, they return and bring additional customers. Everyone benefits from this scenario.

Free ink/free air Information about a business that is published or broadcast free of charge

Press release A news item written and sent to the media in an attempt to get cost-free promotion (free ink)

- Provide information. Educate and communicate with customers. ("No, we no longer sell Item B. However, let me show you Item C, which we now carry, and how it compares favorably.")
- Be sociable and willing to help your customer at all times with good eye contact and a smile.

When developing your customer-service credo for your firm, consider what is most important to your customers, and honor that first. However, remember that you cannot be everything to everyone, and be careful not to give away the store by offering more than you can provide profitably. Before moving on to other forms of promotion, we ask you to understand the dollar value of your customers.

What Is Your Customer Worth?

Take a moment to determine how much your customer is worth (without inflation). If you are a dentist, and your average client spends $200 twice a year in your office, your patient is worth a minimum of $400 ($200 × 2$) annually. If you plan to keep the patient over the next 20 years, he or she now becomes an $8,000 patient (ignoring inflations).

Would you and your employees treat customers differently if you envisioned the figure $8,000 emblazoned on their t-shirts? The answer for most is a resounding yes! Taking it further, what if that $8,000 customer brought in, on average, two family members and three friends into the dental practice? That customer is now at least a $48,000 customer, and we can even envision a much higher number as some will need fillings and crowns, which lead to added expenses for patients.

The trick here is for everyone in your firm to realize the dollar value of each potential customer they serve. How can you get everyone to remember the $400, $8,000, and $48,000 figures? How about associating the first number with a yearly Disneyland pass worth $400? Or if you are a bigger business, how about providing an $8,000 one-year lease on a $48,000 Mercedes?

Action Step 35 asks you to determine the dollar value of your customer and to think of creative ways to make those figures memorable to you and your employees. Build relationships one touchpoint at a time with great service and you will gain lifetime customers. Another inexpensive way to promote your firm is through the media using press releases and media contacts.

■ FREE INK AND FREE AIR

If you have a good story to tell, self-promotion may be the best way for you to spread the word. No one can sell your story better than you! You want your company name in reviews, features articles, interview shows, podcasts, YouTube interviews, and newspaper columns. However, to make that happen takes work on your part to craft your story to intrigue bloggers, magazine writers, and media mavens.

Free ink and free air establish your company in a believable way; your Target Customers will attach more credence to words that are not in the form of paid advertising and from third-party experts.

The traditional way to spread the word is through a formal press release, and today several organizations such as PRWeb make that possible. They "distribute to over 250,000 RSS subscribers, 20,000 web publishers and 35,000 journalists who have subscribed and receive news from PRWeb."

News release services will assist you in selecting the best channels to distribute your press release based on your target market and the purpose of each release. In addition, the firms will use SEO to measure the success and tracking of your press release. The data will assist you in refining future releases.

If not using a firm such as PRWeb, PRLOG, or FreePressRelease, you will need to determine yourself which specific media reaches your Target Customer, and contact the writers and reporters who cover your type of business. Often, publications, radio, and TV stations are seeking out new businesses and clever ideas. Every business is newsworthy in some way: Dig until you find something—new products, charity, controversy, photo opportunities, or humor.

Call, write, or e-mail with your entrepreneurial dream story. If you can demonstrate your product to the writers, even better! While you may want to be published in the most popular media or blog first, take time to seek out smaller publications and bloggers as well as those who focus on your niche. Oftentimes, the larger publications will pick up from the smaller media outlets. Never be afraid to pick up the phone. However, always be respectful of an individual's time and need for an excellent story not a mediocre one!

Another way to spread the word is Help A Reporter Out (HARO), which connects individuals and firms with reporters who are seeking stories and experts for their blogs, articles, or newscasts.

Make your press kit information clean, concise, and pleasant to the eye—send accompanying photographs and videos that present your 1) story 2) facility 3) product or service in use and 4) bios. Also, highlight your press kit and any press coverage on you site. Testimonials are very important as well.

When crafting your press release, review the list of PRWeb's dos and don'ts in Figure 7.3. Make sure you include the who, what, when, where, why, and how of your business. Also, follow the News Release Template instructions in Figure 7.4.

Another excellent source to spread the word are bloggers. To find the most influential bloggers in your industry, take time to research their sites, target markets, and stories and issues they cover. Technorati tracks over 1.3 million bloggers and rates the most influential. While on Technorati, review their blogging resources as you might want to consider a blog of your own at some point.

So far we have stressed relationship building with your customers and gaining free ink or air by enticing writers and bloggers with your interesting and unique story. Both of these have relatively low cost and are based on developing word of mouth promotion or "buzz." The next step we encourage you to take, again with very low cost involved and high impact, is networking.

■ NETWORKING

Another source of promotional power is networking groups, which carry the image of your business to a support group. Orange County networking consultant Susan Linn defines the term broadly: "Networking is using your contacts to get what you want. Commonly, networking is used to refer to group situations in which business people can interact. It's a current buzzword for the age-old principle: 'It's not what you know but who you know.'"

Networking gives you confidence and allows you to pass on helpful information to people who oftentimes are not directly competing with you—and to receive feedback and support. Being around others dreaming the same dream provides a place where you can ask for advice in a nonthreatening environment.

Why You Should Network

You have probably been networking all your life. In school you networked for information about teachers, courses, and clubs. When you moved into a new

figure **7.3**

Before You Write Your Release—A List of Do's and Don'ts

The Do's

Start Strong: You only have a matter of seconds to grab your readers' attention, so you want to capture it with a strong opening. Your headline, summary and first paragraph should clarify your news. The rest of your release should provide the detail.

Identify Yourself: If your release does not identify the source of the information within the first few paragraphs, you may lose the promotional value your release can provide.

Write Professionally: If your release contains hype, slang, excessive exclamation points or some other common mistakes chances are it will be viewed as an advertisement rather than a news release, which may hurt credibility. Or worse, a media outlet may pick up your release and publish without modification, opening any sloppy writing to a larger audience.

Limit Jargon: The best way to communicate is to speak plainly using ordinary language. Using an abundance of technical language and jargon limits your reading audience.

Make sure your Information is Informational and Timely: Think about your audience. Will someone else find your story interesting? Answer the question, "Why should anyone care?" Make sure your announcement contains information that is timely, unique, highlights something new or unusual, and provides useful information to your audience. In other words, don't make it an advertisement for your business.

Use Active Voice: Verbs in the active voice bring your press release to life. Rather than writing "entered into a partnership," use "partnered" instead. Do not be afraid to use strong verbs. For example, "The committee exhibited severe hostility over the incident" reads better if changed to "The committee was enraged over the incident."

Economize Your Words: Be concise. News search engines sometimes reject news releases with overly long headlines, excessive lists and high overall word counts. Eliminate unnecessary adjectives, flowery language or redundant expressions such as "added bonus" or "first time ever."

Proofread: Write your press release in a Word or other text document instead of writing it directly on the online submit page, so you can print it, proofread, rewrite and proofread again. The more time you take to do it right, the better your company's impression to the world.

The Don'ts

We have seen some of the best press releases on the Web. We've also seen some of the worst. Since your release is competing with hundreds, sometimes thousands, of other companies and organizations that are all vying for a reader's attention, it's best to make sure that your release is strong and free of mistakes. Remember, you won't get a second chance to fix a negative impression.

Here are a few things that should not be in any press release:

- All capital letters to emphasize anything.
- Grammatical errors.
- Lack of content and substance.
- Advertisements or promotional/fluffy language.
- Hype.
- The words "you", "I" or "we" outside of a quoted statement.

Avoid Clichés: You don't listen to clichés. Neither will your audience. Avoid phrases like "customers save money" or "great customer service" to announce or describe. Focus on the aspects of your announcement that truly set you apart from everyone else.

Pick an Angle: Make sure that your release has a good hook. Tying your information to current events, recent studies, trends and social issues brings relevance, urgency and importance to your message.

Use Anchor Text and Features: PRWeb news releases can accommodate multimedia files like images, video, links and other features that will capture the attention of your readers and highlight your news. Attach logos, head shots, product shots, photographs, audio files, video files, PDF documents or any other supplemental materials that build up your release. Use anchor text and hyperlinks to point readers back to your site ensures both your Website and your important keywords receive simultaneous promotion in your press release.

Illustrate the Solution: Use real life examples to illustrate how your company or organization solved a problem. Identify the problem and why your solution is the right solution. Give examples.

Don't Be Afraid to Toot Your Own Horn: Online news or press release distribution is a successful way to create expert status. If your company has reached a milestone, celebrated an anniversary, hired a new president, experienced significant growth or received an award, tell the world what you did right. Or, write a release that offers readers "tips" or help in your field of expertise.

Don't Give Away All the Secrets: If you're running a new promotion this season, tell readers where they can go to learn more. Provide links in your press release directly to the page on your Website where readers can learn the specifics about your news and then act upon it. If you give your readers no reason to click through to your site, they're not necessarily going to.

Stick to the Facts: Tell the truth. Avoid fluff, embellishments, hype and exaggerations. If you feel that your press release seems sensational, there's a good chance your readers will think so too.

Source: PRWeb. Online Visibility from Vocus. From "Writing Great Online News Releases" at *http://clubs.apha.com/Files/Writing-GreatOnlineNewsReleases.pdf*. Reprinted with permission.

figure **7.4**

News Release Template

Online Visibility from Vocus

What is a News Release?

A news release (also called a press release) is a document issued to the media, financial community, trade and industry analysts and consumers to announce a product, partnership, to drive traffic to your Web site, an acquisition, event, personnel announcement, or other newsworthy item. A news release can be used to announce a variety of information.

Consider the following topic examples: A new business; new product; announce an event; new partner; significant new customer; milestones; round of funding; or a joint venture.

Below is a basic template to follow for putting a basic news release together.

HEADLINE: Your headline should include keywords and must grab the Media's attention. Your headline should succinctly describe the advisory – some media members search only by headlines.

SUBHEAD: Not all releases need one, but if you're going to use one, make sure it's descriptive and builds on the headline?

DATELINE: Includes the city of origin, and the date of the release. When you issue the release over a newswire, the newswire's 'bug' will appear in the dateline to alert readers of its origin.

LEAD PARAGRAPH: This is the single most important paragraph in the whole release. If you don't draw your reader in here, you've lost them forever. This is your chance to set up your story in a single sentence or two.

SECOND PARAGRAPH: This is where you dive into more detail and set up story for the reader, giving some more background or context.

BODY: This is where you give all the relevant information for your reader, facts, stats, customer testimonials and other third-party information. Write with your audience in mind.

BOILERPLATE: This is the platform to tell your audience about your organization. Keep it brief; just who you are and what you do.

CONTACT INFORMATION: Make sure to include contact name, phone number, and email address for your readers to use if they require more information. This can go either at the top or the bottom of the press release. If you distribute the release over the wire, the contact information will appear at the end per standard formatting requirements.

{THINGS TO INCORPORATE INTO YOUR RELEASE}

KEY WORDS: Using strategically placed keywords throughout the release makes it easier for your audience to find the release when searching the web for information.

QUOTES: Having quotable quotes is a highly effective way of getting key messages out; keep them easy for readers to understand.

Source: PRWeb. Online Visibility from Vocus. From *http://www.prweb.com* (accessed Jun 19, 2012). Reprinted with permission.

community, you networked for information about doctors, dentists, car services, babysitters, and bargains—all the details that make up daily life.

On the job, you networked your way to sales leads, brainstormed your way to better design, or huddled with fellow managers or co-workers to solve problems. Many also network everyday online with Facebook and LinkedIn, gaining incredible access to potential customers, employees, partners, and affiliate businesses. Although, fellow entrepreneurs say nothing beats face to face contact.

As an entrepreneur, you can network your way to a surprising number of new customer connections, which can lead to success. Develop your networks and build core groups of people within them. Some networks grow naturally from the loose association of people you already know, and because you are at the center, you will benefit from the relationships, camaraderie, and support.

Core groups Clusters of influential, key individuals who share a common area of interest

Networking Organizations

The bottom line is people do business with people they know and are most comfortable with. Do not hesitate getting out into the world to meet people who can help develop your business and move your dream forward. When others spread the word about you, it is like having your own private, unpaid sales force working for you! This does not just happen. It takes work, time, and trust to develop solid relationships.

Joining a networking organization is not enough. You must become an active member of the organization. Take a position of leadership. Meet and spend time with everyone you can. Do things for others in the organization. Attending meetings is not enough, it is only when you make a name for yourself within these groups that you receive the benefits of networking. Make networking a way of life!

Be sure you have your elevator speech from Action Step 23 down pat, because you will have many chances to present it. But before you join an organization, ask yourself:

- What is the purpose of this organization?
- What type of people do I enjoy being with, and are they part of this group?
- Do I want to make a political or social statement with this involvement?
- Am I participating solely for business purposes?
- How can my involvement in this network help promote my business?

Most organizations will allow you to attend at least one meeting free with no obligation to join. We suggest you attend various organizational meetings to determine which groups best fit your personal and business needs, as well as determine which organizations' members are most likely to be in contact with your target market.

What type of networking groups are out there?

Trade organizations focus on a particular industry and provide an opportunity to share primarily with your peers. They are an excellent place to make contacts; to find suppliers, attorneys, accountants, and so on. Involvement at the local level may lead to positions at the national level, which will widen your exposure.

Sales-leads clubs generally meet weekly for breakfast, lunch, or dinner to share leads. BNI and Leads Club are two of the larger organizations. Log on to their sites to locate your nearest group. Only one member from each type of business is allowed and the members are encouraged to bring sales leads for other members and to become part of your unpaid sales force. These groups work very well for insurance, accountants, medical and dental professionals. Anyone providing a service such as remodeling, architecture, or auto repair will also benefit. Remember though no amount of networking will make up for a poor product or poor service. So if you want others to spread the word, have a great product with excellent service and back it up! Offer a little extra as well!

Political clubs provide excellent opportunities to expose your business widely; but if you are a local retail or service business, tread lightly as politics and business don't always mesh.

Women's organizations such as the American Association of University Women (AAUW), Women in Communications (WICI), and the National Association of Women Business Owners (NAWBO) focus on social issues, trade, or business efforts. Many also offer professional support and entrepreneurial training.

Chambers of Commerce are excellent sources of local business contacts and provide social events for their members as well as training, directories, and in some cases access to legal services and insurance.

Local social, community, and charity groups such as Kiwanis, Lions, and Rotary, Susan G. Komen (Race for the Cure), or the Alzheimer's Association offer the power of community participation to reach local customers. Many mortgage brokers and real estate agents have found participation in a local PTA have paid off handsomely by increasing their client pool. Serving on a charity board may also expose you and your business to fellow board members who are "the movers and shakers" in a community or at a national level in the United States. While working together, board members gain respect and rapport for each other over time, which often leads to future business relationships.

Visit many groups, join several, and participate heavily in a few. Grow your contact base and hopefully your business.

During a recession, one small business marketing consultant continued to network heavily in six organizations. At one point, she was donating 20 to 30 hours of her time weekly just to keep busy. As the recession wound down and the good times started to roll, her business skyrocketed. Her contacts were back in business, and so was she! She has *never* advertised and has relied totally on word-of-mouth and community contacts for customers. Networking does not cost anything but time, and it can yield incredible results for those willing to develop relationships.

Due to social media's impact on promotion today, we have focused the first three promotion techniques to draw buzz for your business from your customers, media, and your community. If these three become your "raving fans," your need for paid promotional advertising will be greatly reduced and allow you to use funds saved to grow your business. Let others blog, Twitter, Facebook, and more for you!

■ ADDITIONAL PROMOTIONAL ELEMENTS

Paid Media Advertising

A surefire way to advertise is via radio, television, newspapers, magazines, the Internet, and trade journals. With a good ad and the right medium, you can reach right into your Target Customer's mind and create the desire to buy. If you are targeting female consumers between the ages of 13 and 16, Internet and mobile advertising are two of the best mediums. For any paid advertising, you will need to be incredibly creative to cut through the clutter as the average person is exposed to over 5,000 ad impressions per day.

Grabbing your potential customers' attention is the first step; developing their interest, which is generally done with the words used in a print ad or music in radio or video, is the second. Creating a desire is the third step, and the final step is when the customer takes action, and the cash register starts ringing or you swipe a credit card with Square. Profit, though, comes when customers come back and purchase again and again.

For advertising costs, you will need to access the rate cards and media kits, which are available online for most media (see Chapter 4 for further information). Most entrepreneurs do not realize the enormous expense of paid advertisements. The advertising rates for print and online newspapers and yellow pages are surprisingly high, but for many businesses, these are the most effective marketing tools to reach their local target markets.

Traditional media also play a key role in the social marketplace, as paid advertising stimulates both online and offline word of mouth. According to Ed Keller and Brad Fay, authors of *The Face-to-Face Book: Why Real Relationships Rule in a Digital Marketplace*, "Fully one-quarter of conversations about brands include an explicit reference to ads. In fact, television advertising is far and away the single driver of consumer conversation."

Paid advertising has some obvious drawbacks: 1) it can be very expensive to create an effective ad 2) preferred placements are reserved for the big spenders 3) costly repetition is usually essential for success and 4) continuity amongst all platforms you use is essential.

Preferred placements The best locations within a publication, a store, or a website, or the best time slots on TV or radio

Be sure that a large percentage of the listeners, viewers, or readers are in one of your Target Customer groups; otherwise, your message will be ineffective. Your practice with profiling in previous chapters should make you much wiser in selecting the proper media than the average entrepreneur.

Many local publications have excellent in-house advertising managers who may help you develop ads and work on placement and timing. Some local cable stations have interns who will develop commercials for free or at a minimal cost. It is wise to access the wealth of creative and experienced individuals who will develop focused advertising directed to your target audience. Many will also compete for your business and using their professional services can be very cost effective.

Internet advertising requires constant diligence, as your options change rapidly. One of the best parts of web advertising comes from the tremendous tracking of sites and clicks through web analytics. Also, the ability to change regarding what is and what is not working allows you to make your web advertising very responsive to the Target Customer, in a "real time" manner.

One option for Internet advertising is purchasing banner and pop-up ads often through an affiliate program, which exchanges a commission for sales generated through the sponsoring website. Another is to buy ads on Facebook or other sites, where you will pay a click through rate (CTR). However, note only 1/2000 Facebook ads are clicked on! If using the Internet for any advertising, it is imperative to use SEO to determine the effectiveness of your advertising.

If you are developing your own advertising, stock photographs, illustrations, music, and video are available through large agencies such as iStockphotos and Getty Images as well as through smaller specialized agencies such as Southwest Florida Stock Photos. You describe what you want—for example, two clean-cut, in love, Midwestern 18-year-olds on a movie date. The photo provider finds the photograph, and for a royalty payment, you are allowed to use it. Professional photographers supply the providers with hundreds of thousands of photographs, which they then categorize.

For a small fee or perhaps even free, you may be able to select an incredible photo to catch your client's attention in a print ad or a mailing piece. Selecting unique but appropriate video and music as well can set your advertising apart and both are available in a similar manner as stock photos. Use visuals as often as you can to tell your story.

Stock television and radio commercials are also available through firms that lease previously produced and successful local television commercials. For a fee, you lease the commercials for introduction into your local market—for example, a successful furniture commercial produced and aired in Spokane would have the firm's name replaced with your own and be shown in Topeka. Be sure the commercial you select is aimed at the Target Customers that you wish to reach.

Of course you can always create your own videos and if you're lucky, become a YouTube sensation like Orobrush, highlighted in the Key Points. Demonstrating your product creatively has certainly paid off for many entrepreneurs. Everyone dreams of creating a "viral video." Although, what makes a video go viral remains elusive.

Another option is to look toward your local cable stations not only for advertising but also to evaluate the video production services they may offer. Oftentimes, if you have a product that requires a lengthy demonstration to interest your customer, purchasing a 10- to 60-minute cable time slot may be an option. You could also consider developing a full-blown infomercial. If you decide to go this route, please watch and study the techniques used in the successful infomercials as there is definitely a formula for producing an effective message.

Today many students have excellent video production equipment and years of video experience, and they might provide an option for inexpensive ad production for TV, Facebook or YouTube ads.

Consider asking for help, advice, and information from marketing departments of newspapers and radio and television stations. Be sure to check out circulation figures, and when analyzing the costs remember that for paid advertising to work repetition is essential. Newspapers often offer targeted advertising in special supplements at reduced cost and are often appropriate for seasonal businesses, such as summer camps. The offers often include free editorial copy. All advertising or promotions you undertake should follow governing and ever changing laws.

Craigslist is the new gorilla in the classified ad world supplanting newspaper classifieds in many areas. One Orange County small retail furniture store owner saved $2,000 a month when he dropped all advertising after discovering almost all of his new customers found his store from his one line Craigslist listing. That $2,000 went straight to his bottom line and helped him survive the recession.

Point-of-Purchase Displays

A point-of-purchase (P-O-P) display encourages impulse purchases of last-minute items like nail polish, vitamin packs, beef jerky, and small toys. A sharp P-O-P must perform all of the selling tasks for you, serving as a tireless silent salesperson, always on duty. If your product is difficult to use, or the benefits are unclear to the Target Customer, the P-O-P will have to work hard to deliver your message.

P-O-P "Point-of-Purchase"—a display that acts as a silent salesperson for a specific product

There are, however, problems with these displays: 1) you cannot use them to sell large items, because they crowd customers at the cash register 2) merchants have limited floor, counter, and wall space available and do not always want to use it for P-O-Ps and 3) the display must sell itself and the product. A tacky P-O-P turns prospective customers off instead of on. Do weekly evaluations of all P-O-Ps. If this is your only distribution venue, consider hiring professionals to design your P-O-P's.

Packaging

For P-O-P displays, packaging may be the only other method of marketing and sales; but do not forget how important the packaging of any product is to your customer and potential sales. Review your competitors' packaging by purchasing their products and checking out the cost and effectiveness of their packaging. What can you do better? What can you do more efficiently? What can you do more cost effectively? How could the packaging be made more attractive or perhaps "greener"?

Professionals in the packaging and distribution fields will be able to work with you on the proper sizing of packages and provide you with the benefits of their years of experience. By adding "her story" to the product's label and a ribbon to the jar, one entrepreneur tripled her sales after acting on wholesalers' suggestions. Consider the following packaging points:

1. Spend time up front to design a package with a defining unique look.
2. Consider environmental issues.
3. Less is more in most cases.
4. Use your list of product benefits when designing labels.
5. Make sure package demonstrates clearly how product works and should be used.
6. Keep your visuals clean and clear as they will be used through all advertising mediums for consistency.
7. Encourage feedback from distributors and customers early on in the design process.
8. Refine, refine, refine, until you have achieved the best design mix of colors, text, and pictures.
9. Package design is both an art and a science and professional advice may be advisable.
10. Be sure packaging meets all legal requirements, protects the product, and provides ease of use for the customer.
11. Shelf space and shipping costs also should be addressed early on.

Catalogs

Catalogs are useful for homebound people, busy parents, and busy shoppers. Because we are pressed for time as a culture, more and more goods are now being purchased via catalogs oftentimes in conjunction with a website.

Customers shop at their convenience and do not worry about store hours, parking, or traffic. When thinking about most online shopping sites, they are basically online catalogs or product listings.

The National Mail Order Association reports over 20 billion catalogs were mailed in 2011. According to *Deliver* in 2009, "Online shoppers who receive print catalogs shop online more often and spend more meaningful time at retail sites." Thus, catalogs remain a strong force in multi-channel marketing.

If you attempt to print your own catalogs, be aware that several problems may occur: 1) the costs associated with design, artwork, photography, and mailing can be very expensive—especially if you attempt a four-color catalog 2) your product may not show well in print 3) the reader may not easily grasp the product's benefits and 4) it takes time and extensive resources to develop a successful mail-order catalog business.

If you are developing an Internet site to complement your catalog, make sure they are consistent. Clear visuals and online help sell your product in the same way as a printed catalog. Take time to review competing catalogs to assess how the type of models, product descriptions and depth of product offerings, fonts, and colors point to their target markets. On the web you can include chats, product reviews, recommendations, and videos to demonstrate products thus expanding customer engagement and interactivity. Many websites encourage Facebook "likes" but in reality, only "less than 1 percent of brand fans on Facebook have any type of active involvement".

Consider offering free shipping as Internet Retailer reports, "Unconditional free shipping serves as the most important online marketing technique." During the Christmas season over two-thirds of purchases involved free shipping and according to COMSCORE, 47 percent of all online orders include free shipping.

One DVD catalog retailer shared that each customer costs him $300 in marketing expenses before he turns a profit. Thus, long term repeat business is essential for financial success for both print and online catalogs. For further information on online retailing, log on to Internet Retailer.

Catalog Houses

Catalog houses such as Lillian Vernon do not usually manufacture what they sell, so they are always looking for good products. Log on to Catalogs.com for an extensive listing of catalogs and spend a good deal of time determining which catalogs sell directly to your target market. Products in catalogs are marked up (retailed) three to seven times what the catalog houses pay wholesale for them. Before contacting each catalog house, determine first if you can make a profit in dealing with these houses based on the products and prices in their current catalogs. If you can, contact the most promising catalogs for their submission process. The process should be followed exactly, as they receive thousands of product submissions and have developed a process which works for them.

Let major catalog houses do your promotion and distribution but make sure you can deliver in a timely manner if your product takes off. Ask for feedback from each catalog house regarding your product description. If your product does not fit their needs, they may help you locate a better catalog fit. The feedback will be invaluable, so *listen*. Such insight comes backed by years of experience and expertise.

Also, consider looking into QVC-type programs as well (see Chapter 6). Television shopping network teams search for items that can be sold in the tens of thousands. Their research is extensive, and they know what will move.

Direct Mail

This promotional tool lets you effectively focus your brochures and flyers directly at your target market. Direct mail is very important for small business,

Product description A list of features and benefits

because it can go to the heart of your target market; it is also used extensively in the B2B marketplace.

Direct mail advertising is both an art and a science as the industry has been tracking response and sales results for decades. Thus, they have accumulated what today is known as "big data," which can be manipulated to increase return on investment and used as "predictive knowledge."

If you are writing the content for your direct mail pieces, read the Direct Marketing Association's (DMA) material at *http://www.the-dma.org* before making the effort. Per customer, direct mail is very expensive and doing it ineffectively will do nothing but waste your money and time. If, after reading the DMA's material, you want to hire a professional direct mail expert—which we suggest—consider asking him or her to write your piece for a percentage of sales. A terrific, experienced writer may achieve excellent results if he or she believes strongly in your product *and* knows they will be sharing in the gold mine!

The success of direct mail depends on your ability to narrowly define the target market and develop an appropriate direct mail campaign. If the market is too fragmented for you to do this, direct mail is not for you.

Stay up nights if you have to. Refine, refine, and refine again until your Target Customer becomes the blueberry seed discussed previously in Chapter 4. If your aim is off, you have wasted all of your money on your mailings. Expensive direct mailings should not be undertaken early in your business, as at the beginning you do not usually have a good handle on your market. Once you are in business and know your market it will be easier to develop more accurate customer prospect lists and conduct targeted direct mail campaigns to your current customer base.

Check out mail list vendors online who will offer you (for a fee) the right to mail information one time to a selected list of your choice. Mail-list vendors work with you to select the proper mailing list, usually by combining many lists covering hundreds of variables to arrive at your "blueberry."

The success of many direct mail campaigns is based on working in conjunction with other media channels and again consistency is essential. *Deliver* highlights many innovative and successful direct mail campaigns.

Money-Back Guarantees

If you have not considered offering a guarantee as a form of promotion, consider it now. To reach security-minded customers you need to emphasize the no-risk features of your product or service and back up your guarantee with time and money.

One Orange County, CA entrepreneur upon purchasing a kitchen/bath remodeling business discovered the former owners had treated several customers horrendously. She decided to make good on their contracts winning not only their loyalty but also the respect of everyone they told. It was an expensive and risky initial move, but it was money well spent. If you do not provide money-back guarantees *and back them up*, you will have a very difficult time operating a business today especially online as negative reviews can be disastrous.

In retailing, figure 3 to 5 percent into your pricing to cover returned goods. If the product is fragile or easily misused—and people have been known to misuse just about everything—build in a higher figure to cover repairs or replacement costs. Be sure all employees understand the importance of honoring guarantees. Just one employee not abiding by your policy may have long-term adverse consequences. Negative word-of-mouth always travels like wildfire and with the net it can sometimes feel like the wildfire has been spiked with jet fuel!

Trade Shows

Trade shows display your product or service in a high-intensity environment to attendees who have a keen interest in your business area. Your appearance at the show asserts your position in the industry.

Research potential trade shows and attend several of them to determine which would be best for your firm. The costs can be very expensive as they add up quickly especially if you have to travel to shows. Booth rental space, displays, and setup costs usually surprise most novice trade show exhibitors. Furthermore, unless you are careful and study the floor layout, you could rent a space that is thin on traffic. Also, if you have not participated in previous shows, you may not be offered a choice location.

Share booth space with another entrepreneur or with a complementary business. Conduct market research while you are promoting, and listen carefully to everyone as this is one of the major reasons to present at a trade show. Have a plan and most importantly set aside time for customer follow-up after the show. Make a few calls to the most promising clients as soon as the show ends.

Traffic The number of potential buyers who pass by, view, or stop at a booth in a trade show; vehicles or pedestrians that move past a business site in the course of a normal day

Other Sales and Marketing Material

Become a source of information by producing brochures, white papers (authoritative reports), videos, newsletters, handbooks, product documentation, annual reports, newspaper columns for the layperson, or even the "bible" for your industry. Become a recognized expert in your field.

These are very effective and reasonably inexpensive promotional tools. If you are not handy with words, writing these materials may be an obstacle, but it is not an insurmountable one. Many writers can be hired online to work hourly or by the project. If you place any of these materials online, update frequently as you must again offer a compelling reason for customers to visit and revisit your website.

Blogs

If you have something to share and know how to write, a blog may be in your future. Word Press is an excellent starting point and advice is everywhere on the net to help you write, build, and promote your blog. Within hours you can be up and running!

Creating your first blog may be easy. However, promoting and maintaining your blog will take effort and time and without doing both you will not succeed. Readers who see that a blogger hasn't posted for weeks won't be back anytime soon and may even seek out your competitors.

Chet Frolich, an architectural and commercial photographer and owner of CMFPhoto and OC Stock Photo, explains, "Keeping my blog takes way more time than I ever thought. Think about your blog's purpose and who your audience is when posting. My potential clients and competitors visit my site to view upcoming building projects around the U.S. and also to determine the quality of my work." Frolich found his search engine rankings are positively affected by his blogging and makes sure his name is placed on each week's blog.

Another way to share you expertise is to take the time to post on influential sites in your industry and sites such as Quora to build your reputation. However, be sure you are providing up to date accurate information. Study the sites to familiarize yourself with the readers' needs and moods before posting.

Working Visibility

Develop and maintain a strong presence. Make yourself stand out from your competitors. One owner of a pool cleaning business wanted to set his firm apart and required all his pool cleaners to wear spotless white laboratory coats on their routes. In addition, the business paid for the cleaners' trucks to be washed each week. Because of the employees' professional appearance, people felt safer with the firm's cleaners in their yards and sales subsequently sky-rocketed. In addition, many of the neighbors asked, "Who are those guys in the white coats?"

Many service firms display their presence as they work—they put signs on everything: their business, their trucks, and their work sites. Wherever they are busy, they let people know it. Glen Frohlich of Glen's Landscaping was recently hired by a woman who said, "I called your company because for the last few months I've been watching all the landscapers in my neighborhood and you always send the same workers and they always come at the same time each week. None of the others do that." Remember your potential customers are watching you.

The drawback to visibility is similar to one of the drawbacks with P-O-P displays: If the presence you maintain does not sell itself—if it is unattractive, or if it calls attention to an unappealing part of your business—you will lose rather than gain potential customers. This is true online as well.

Be aware that one Instagram photo on Facebook or a YouTube video can send your business soaring or level it quickly. Everyone has a camera these days and they love to use them. According to the American Express Global Customers Service Barometer, if a customer has a good customer service experience she will share with 9 people and if it is a bad one the customer will share with 16 people. Take those figures onto Facebook, explode them out and see the devastating effect of negative comments or the wonder of positive comments.

Make good use of your public activities with signage that tells people who you are. Review your displays frequently. Make sure your clothing and signs tie into your overall promotional campaign in color, design, attitude, and so on; consistency is vital. Name recognition is the goal.

Personal Selling

It does not matter if you have never sold before; no one is a better salesperson than you. You *are* the business. It is your baby, and you will sell with more passion than anybody. Work hard to get *your* story out and sell, sell, sell! See the Passion Box in the chapter and attend a Startup Weekend to learn how to sell your story.

If you listen carefully, your Target Customers will tell you how to sell your product or service to them. That is why a good salesperson is an attentive listener, not a fast talker. Most customers love to talk with the owner of the business. Use that to your advantage. If you have a choice of spending time talking to prospective customers or doing something else, talk!

Unfortunately, personal selling is expensive, especially if you have to pay others to do it or if you are using too much of your own time. A sales force will boost your overhead unless you pay your salespeople on a commission-only basis. However, if you try to do it all yourself, you may not have the time and energy for other things that only you can do.

Personal selling Client service calls made by an individual salesperson or business owner

In the beginning, some entrepreneurs do not have many options. One inventor worked all night in his shop designing, took a nap, and then changed clothes for eight hours of selling on the road, only to return to his shop again at 5:00 p.m. to start over. Even when his firm was valued at over $40 million, he met with customers in the field. Building and maintaining relationships are essential for any small business.

Make everyone in your business a salesperson, including delivery and ware-house people, software programmers, accountants, and clerical workers. Never underestimate the importance of the people you hire to be the face of your company. Reinforce a positive attitude in all employees by reminding them that if nothing sells, the company will suffer. Your valuable Target Customers need a lot of tender loving care from everyone in your firm. Another alternative for reaching your customers is hiring professional sales reps-trained in the details and advantages of your business.

■ SALES REPS AS CONNECTORS

Sales reps Independent salespeople who sell a number of noncompeting but complementary products and services in a specific geographic area on a commission-only basis

Suppose you have a new product that has immediate sales potential across the country. How do you connect with the whole United States? Should you hire your younger brother to take care of it for you, or employ a sales force at a very large expense, or should you seek out a professional sales rep to act as a commissioned salesperson? The last option may be the quickest and most effective way into the market. When cash is king as in a startup, hiring employees is sometimes hard to justify.

An army of trained professional sales reps awaits your call. However, all sales reps are not equal; select carefully. Exercise caution, because the reputation of your sales reps will become your reputation. Accountability from your reps is vital.

Interview potential buyers of your goods and ask them to recommend reps that they consider the very best in their field and with whom they enjoy working with. When the same names surface several times, you will know whom to call. Reps usually represent several complementary product lines. Discuss with the rep how much time and energy she can devote to your product line.

Trade associations, shows, and journals also provide information on rep associations for additional sourcing. Often, reps attend trade shows to discover new products to carry; so if you have a booth, try to reach reps at your show. Aggressive reps will contact you if you have a hot product.

To determine the prevailing practices of commissions, territories, and termination agreements for your selected industry, contact national associations. Hire reps based on their knowledge of the industry, established customer base, and ability to sell to your customers effectively and efficiently.

You are in essence paying the reps for immediate access to the market and their expertise. Ask yourself how long it would take and how much it would cost to set up a sales force to have similar characteristics to the independent sales rep organizations. Another option might be to use your own sales force for certain markets and independent sales reps for other market niches.

Because reps work solely on commission, you are assured of a fairly aggressive sales team to promote your product or service. Reps allow you risk-free exploration of new markets as well.

Ask the reps:

- How many salespeople are in your firm?
- What is your sales background and specific experience in the industry?
- What geographic territories do you cover?
- What complementary lines do you represent?
- What ideas do you have for trade show presentations?
- Would you work with us on a regional rollout while we prepare for national coverage?
- May I participate in sales meetings and help train the reps on my product line?
- What sales call reports can I expect?
- What performance guarantees do you offer?
- What results have you achieved for similar companies?

Provide all the encouragement and support to your reps that you can; never stop being a cheerleader. Insist on frequent sales reports. Keep informed on what is going on in the field; pack your bags, and make calls with the reps. Encourage feedback from both your reps and their customers to help you evaluate your product line and your reps. Be available to trouble shoot for those in the field.

Provide your reps with good materials such as brochures, testimonials, and samples. In addition, conduct any training necessary for your product. Also, be willing to share information you gather on recent sales and the competition. For successful relationships and profitable sales, communication is key. Also, remember your rep is an independent sales person relying on commissions so pay them on time.

Sales Rep Resources

Manufacturer Representative Associations
    Manufacturers Agents National Association
        http://www.MANAonline.org
    Electronics Representatives Association International
        http://www.era.org
To locate sales representatives in foreign countries, contact the embassy or consulate for each country and speak to a trade expert. The Department of Commerce and resources cited throughout the chapters also provide trade information and contacts.

Specialty Advertising/Promotional Products

Lesley Ronson Brown, a specialty advertising specialist for over 15 years, shares that specialty advertising, now known as *promotional products,* is a targeted, cost-efficient means of promoting a company's products or services. For some small businesses, this can be a very effective use of marketing dollars.

Promotional products break through communications clutter and leave a lasting impression. In addition to client marketing, many companies use promotional products for internal marketing to their employees via recognition and employee motivation programs.

Promotional products keep a company's name or message in the front of a customer's mind. They can be used as a thank-you gift, a trade-show traffic builder, a goodwill builder, a customer or employee loyalty reward, or a new product or service introduction tool.

The cost of promotional products ranges from pennies to several hundred dollars. When selecting an item, key considerations are budget, quantity needed, time frame, the audience receiving it, and, of course, the goal. What are you trying to achieve? If you want the person to remember the business, try to make the promotional item creative, useful, and relevant to your business.

Preshow mailings also can be used to build traffic and name recognition. An eyeglass case can be mailed with an invitation to stop by and pick up a free pair of sunglasses. Or a restaurant gift card can be mailed but activated only if the recipient brings it to the booth and perhaps fills out a short marketing questionnaire. When used to build trade-show traffic, an item that involves the recipient can be effective at keeping a prospect at the booth, which allows time to qualify the prospect and generate interest in your products. Drawings for prizes and gifts can also be used to develop a mailing list or to ask market research questions of prospective customers.

Continuity advertising programs can be developed in which several gifts are sent over time, often with a theme. A baseball theme campaign could include a stadium-seat cushion, baseball, cap, pennant, ticket-shaped key chain, bat-shaped pen, cap-shaped paperclip dispenser, sound-chip card that plays "Take Me Out to the Ball Game," and a package of peanuts.

■ SMALL BUSINESS WEBSITE

Can your customers find you on the web quickly and when they find you does your site offer them the information they need? As many people use the web or their iPhone to replace maps, phonebooks, catalogs, address books, newspapers,

ACTION STEP 36

Brainstorm a Winning Promotional Campaign

Disregard all budgetary restraints. Pretend that money is no object. Close your eyes, sit back, and develop the ideal campaign for connecting with your Target Customers. It is okay to "get crazy" with this, because excellent, workable solutions often develop out of unrestrained thought.

- If your product or service needs a multimillion-dollar advertising promotion with endorsements by your favorite movie star, imagine that it is happening now. (And it could happen, if you purchased a tweet from one of the famous stars represented by Sponsored Tweets, some with almost 3 million followers.)
- If you need a customer list created in marketing heaven, specify exactly what you need, and it is yours.
- If you are looking for the services of a first-class catalog house, just whisper the name three times and you are in business.
- If your business at its peak could use a thousand delivery trucks with smiling drivers who make your Target Customers feel terrific, write down "1,000 smiling delivery people."
- If your product is small, brainstorm the perfect point-of-purchase device, perhaps one with slot machines whose money tubes are connected to your private bank vault. Watch the money roll in.

This chance to ignore costs will not come around again. (Reality is right around the corner.) But for now, have fun! Do not be afraid to put your passion for your business into your promotional ideas and campaigns. Creativity and passion can go a long way to promote your business. Remember to sell your story.

magazines, word-of-mouth recommendations and much more, a website and active involvement in web marketing are vital.

Throughout the text we have referred to your small business website, however, the specifics of website creation and development are beyond the scope of this text. The scope and development cost of your website will depend on whether the web is your primary promotion and/or distribution channel or whether it is one of the many channels you use.

Hopefully, at this point you realize that one of the reasons we are ending the chapter with website development is because it is only one tool in your marketing chest. The quality of your product and the relationships you build both offline and online are the real propellers of your business.

The web provides your firm visibility and a reach far beyond the borders of your town or state. If done right, your website will give you credibility and an opportunity to engage your customer.

Promoting and locating on the web are much easier than many believe. The openness of the platform, the willingness of others to share information, and the competition between the major websites combine to offer excellent free advice everywhere and very low cost of entry. Also, many platforms for webstores are available online such as Big Commerce, Shopify, and Magento and are incredibly easy to use.

As we all know the Internet changes at warp speed. Thus, we have provided just the website basics and encourage you to keep abreast of changes and offerings that will help you better reach your target market and promotional goals. One of the most important elements in web marketing is search engine optimization (SEO), which basically is the strategy to achieve the best ranking possible in the various search engines based on keywords and key phrases.

As the major players keep changing the rules, we suggest you log on and find the most up to date information on SEO. Many firms offer online tutorials and workshops to keep you abreast of the changes. Be prepared to be on top of SEO at all times. Hiring outside help is recommended, although with caution, as many people call themselves "SEO experts" and few truly are.

Company websites, Facebook, Pinterest, Instagram, Google, LinkedIn, YouTube, eBay, and others offer ever-evolving platforms for businesses in the web 2.0 world, which, according to Coremetrics, "encompasses multiple trends and many different technologies. The technologies enable consumers to interact with your company and other consumers, participate in and influence discussions, and control their experience."

Promote your website offline, as offline promotion can account for a major portion of first-time buyers. Try to make your website name easy to remember, and include the site on all advertising and any correspondence. Consider hiring professionals to design your website. Use stock photos and stock videos to enhance the professional appearance of your site. Design, of course, varies as to the target market; and if you have very different target markets, you should consider multiple sites but make sure they do not confuse your customers. Webpages should be designed so that your customer has a compelling reason to return frequently. Never stop learning about building and promoting your website as the rules and opportunities change on a daily basis!

Earlier we said that if you fail to plan, you are planning to fail. When it comes to promotion, if you fail to plan, you are planning to keep your business a secret. One way to avoid keeping your business a secret is to brainstorm an ideal promotional campaign with no holds barred and no worries about costs. Action Step 36 helps you consider all of your creative ideas before discarding any as unrealistic. Save the ideas you come up with in Action Step 36, because you will use them later.

As you have seen throughout this chapter, the entrepreneurs who succeed are the ones who have the best fix on their Target Customers and know how to wrangle all of their promotion options into a cohesive and consistent message. They are also the ones who understand the importance of market research, tracking, and evaluating their advertising expenses.

ATTACH PRICE TAGS TO YOUR PROMOTIONAL STRATEGIES

Developing a promotional plan requires five steps:

1. Determine your sales and marketing goals (e.g., sales of $750,000 for the year).
2. Develop strategies to achieve a goal (e.g., increase sales order size by 10 percent).
3. Create a specific promotional method for carrying out one or several of the strategies and have measurable objectives (e.g., mailer for special Christmas-shopping night with a goal of selling $20,000 worth of merchandise during the evening).
4. Detail and enact a program involving the specific promotion chosen following a predetermined budget (e.g., gold-embossed mailer sent to 300 best customers in November for special Christmas-shopping night with pastries, specialty coffees, and gift-wrapping at a cost of $1,750).
5. Evaluate the effectiveness of your promotional vehicles (e.g., expected return of $20 in increased sales for every $1 spent on advertising and promotion) and adjust as needed.

You have reviewed the importance of networking, customer service, advertising both offline and online, and a host of other promotional activities. Now you need to develop an integrated promotional campaign using the best elements to reach your Target Customer.

Remember, you can hire an ad agency to create great advertisements that bring in customers. However, only excellent customer service and products will bring them back and make your business profitable over time.

Time now to make decisions about your promotional mix. Look at the ideal promotional strategies you came up with in Action Step 36, pick the top four or five elements you can realistically carry out and integrate into a cohesive promotional campaign, and then determine the cost of each. Action Step 37 walks you through this process. Continue to focus your promotions on the Target Customer from your collage.

Do not be discouraged if high costs knock out part of your ideal promotional mix. That is why we filled Chapter 7 with so many inexpensive promotional ideas.

When bankers review business plans, they will definitely want to know how and at what cost you are going to reach your customers. A well-thought-out marketing and promotion plan will demonstrate to your reader that you have done your homework and recognize the costs involved in promoting your product or service.

SUMMARY

Positioning your business in the prospect's mind and keeping it there takes a concerted, constant effort. Anything that will advance the positive image of your business is worth considering. Survey the whole range of promotional strategies available, and then choose the promotional mix that best targets your customer with the funds you have available.

ACTION STEP 37

Attach a Price Tag to Each Item of Your Promotional Package

What will your customer connection cost? To get some idea, go back to Action Step 36, list the top four or five connections you want with your customers, and then research the cost of each. If the connections have no cost, outline how you will implement them. Imagine that you have chosen the following promotional mix:

Website: Determine the cost to develop, promote and maintain a website.

Direct mail: Find mail-list brokers online and contact them. Discuss your business and the markets you want to reach. Ask for recommendations on appropriate mailing lists and strategy tips. Discuss costs.

Personal selling: Budget time and money for sales staff, sales reps, or yourself to reach customers personally. If you plan on being the main salesperson for your firm, find networking opportunities and start building contacts. Allocate part of your salary and expenses as a promotional cost. If you are going to use sales reps, locate and determine their cost.

Determine the cost of any other promotional ideas you have developed including adwords, banner ads, and websites. Once you know the cost of each item of your promotional package, decide which you can afford. Which are best to deliver your message? How you can make each touch-point moment memorable?

Potential strategies include paid media advertising, free ink and free air, personal selling, trade shows, industry literature, networking, and exceptional customer service. Present a consistent message and keep the message simple and clear for the clients. Synergies will develop if you plan your promotional campaigns effectively.

With technology, new and innovative promotion and distribution opportunities will occur frequently. Be aware of these changes, experiment, measure their effectiveness, and determine how the new opportunities can help your company.

Focusing on the touchpoints will show you areas and niches where you can beat your competitors and where you should focus your promotions. Small companies have the advantage of being able to respond to their customers' needs immediately, which gives them great strength. Take advantage of your speed.

Make every member of your organization understand the importance of their job in the relationship between the customer and the company. If all your employees act as salespeople, you will have dramatically increased the size of your sales force, and your clients will notice the difference.

We also recommend that you seek creative solutions to the problem of small-business promoting. Take creative license and stretch the limits early on while launching your venture. If you are not creative, hire people who are to help you stand out from the crowd. A coordinated marketing plan focused on Target Customers is essential for long-term success.

■ THINK POINTS FOR SUCCESS

- Stand in your Target Customers' shoes. Refer back to your Target Customer collage and keep the customer in the center as you aim your promotions.
- Maintain your presence.
- Be unique with your promotions. Instead of Christmas cards, send Groundhog's Day or St. Patrick's Day cards.
- A world in transition means opportunities for entrepreneurs.
- To launch your mailing lists, give away something. In return, potential customers will give you their names and addresses.
- Create excitement—excitement sells. Rent a Santa, a dancing robot, or a hot-air balloon.
- Remember to promote the benefits of your product or service. People buy solutions. How will your service or product make their lives better? How will it make them happier? How will it save them time?
- People buy experiences. Make them memorable! Make them want to come back for more. Make them want to send their friends and family.

- Keeping a customer is far cheaper than finding a new one. Make the customer happy. When problems occur, ask the customer how you can solve them.
- Make customer service a passion.
- Passionate customers become walking billboards. Their desire for you to succeed will make you better. Strive for "raving fans."
- When you think you have it made, do not let your guard down—keep connecting with your customer. You will never be so big that you can afford to disconnect.
- Take the time to connect with customers who do not return. Be brave, and give them a call and find out why they are no longer your customers.
- *Listen* to your customers.
- Tell your story.
- Build relationships.
- Be creative.

■ KEY POINTS FROM ANOTHER VIEW

YouTube Sensation
Orabrush: Tongue cleaner and tongue foam!
2012 Webby Award Official Honoree, Orabrush, created an extremely successful social media campaign with a product few would imagine would become a YouTube sensation! We share below insights from the founders as well as the media sources that have highlighted Orabrush's hard work, planning and creativity.

The 75-year-old founder of Orabrush, Dr. Bob Wagstaff, after hawking his tongue cleaner for eight years with very little success approached a marketing research class at Brigham Young University to conduct a study. After completing their research, they declared that 92% of people would not purchase his brush online. Another student, Jeffrey Harmon, (not part of the team and today Cofounder and Chief Marketing Officer) suggested however that 8% of the Internet population *were* willing to purchase. Dr. Bob gave the student $500 to produce a video and the rest is social media history!

Orabrush's video's have gone viral, a one in 1,000 chance! Their YouTube channel with over 100 videos and 49 million channel views is number three in viewership and their app, "Bad Breath Detector" has had over 400,000 downloads. A product with almost no sales in 2009 now is sold in over 15 countries and in over 30,000 stores including Wal-Mart, Walgreens, and CVS chains.

Recently, David Kelley, founder and chairman of the global innovation and design firm IDEO joined Orabrush's advisory board. Their story, videos, and a 6 foot tongue all led to Orabrush's success and ability to engage such a high level design guru.

Jeffrey Harmon, shared that he reads every comment which comes in on Facebook and his team reads and responds to all the comments on Facebook, YouTube and Twitter as he believes that what is being said online is one's reputation. The comments also provide your "focus group". Product improvement has even come through buyer input. The original white bristle pad was revamped into a vibrantly colored pad thus allowing the "tongue gunk to take center stage and seem more effective".

Orabrush is launching a new product category through crowdfunding site Indiegogo in an effort to capitalize on the need for oral care for dogs. Jeff Davis, CEO of Orabrush said, "Just as YouTube leveled the playing field and allowed a small start-up like us to compete with major brands, crowdfunding will play a similar role with the Orapup."

Certainly, Orabrush has taken an unorthodox approach and it has definitely paid off. Jeff Harmon shared, "YouTube has helped normal people like Dr. Bob and a couple of college kids to take an idea, put it in front of people and get an honest response. We can now play on the same terms as huge companies—and be successful."

■ ACTION STEPS

■ KEY TERMS

Image_Source/iStockphoto.com

Start-Up Concerns and Financial Projections
Researching and Preparing Numbers

Learning Objectives

- Recognize the importance of numbers and how to keep score with them.

- Understand *your* responsibility in keeping track of numbers.

- Determine start-up costs.

- Discover ways to bootstrap your business.

- Focus on pricing as part of overall strategy.

- Determine seasonality scenarios.

- Deal with recessionary pressures.

- Develop sales projections and what-if scenarios.

- Prepare projected income statements.

- Learn cash flow is king!

- Understand importance of the balance sheet: assets − liabilities = net worth/owner's equity.

- Determine feasibility and profitability through break-even analysis.

- Explore financial software options.

- Learn how to use industry financial ratios and benchmarks.

We urge you in Chapter 8 to move beyond your product and marketing start-up plans and venture out into the uncertain financial future. Throughout the past chapters, you have been gathering information on marketing and location costs, target markets, and competition; and if you have not already run numbers, as suggested earlier, it is now time to change your focus from the creative side of entrepreneurship to the financial side—the side that keeps you afloat.

This chapter will help you to avoid running out of money, estimate your start-up costs, and prepare you for capital searching by developing the financial projections required by lenders and investors. Numbers work is time consuming and frustrating, but without it you are sure to fail. Do not make the mistake of many other entrepreneurs, who believed the numbers would work themselves out.

Key Points introduces you to open book management, which focuses on teaching employees what the numbers in a business really represent. When starting up, it is so hard for entrepreneurs and employees to see that when cash is flowing in it does not mean spend, spend, spend. What it should mean is reinvest, reinvest, reinvest! Grow, grow, grow!

Many entrepreneurs put all of their passion into selecting a site or developing a marketing plan, but unless you watch your finances passionately, all your other plans may never come to fruition. Use the measuring devices we present, and continue to revise projections as you acquire additional information. While in business, your numbers will constantly be revised each month as revenue, the economy, costs, and competitors fluctuate. Keep your eyes on the numbers and strive for positive cash flow and profitability.

■ CHART YOUR BUSINESS FUTURE WITH NUMBERS

Your first step is to ask questions about the financial state of your business. What will your start-up costs run? Which months will be strong? Which will be weak? What are your projected gross sales estimates for the first year? The second? The third? What is the potential profit? Can you project cash flow? What bank loans and lines of credit will be needed? Availability of vendor credit? How many employees will you need? How much will they cost? How will freight costs affect your bottom line? Will shipping revenue increase your profit? Can you add people to the team who will bring in cash infusions? What will your cash picture look like when your start-up dollars are spread over a full year? What is your burn rate and how long can you survive?

Burn rate Measure at which your cash balance is going down while waiting for profitability

How fast can your business grow? How will rapid growth affect your cash picture? Have any of your life or educational experiences prepared you for handling money in business? If not, what steps should you take to prepare yourself for handling your business's finances?

Generally, there are five areas you need to consider as you plunge into the numbers of financial management: start-up costs, pricing, seasonality scenarios, sales projections, and what-if scenarios with income, expenses, cash flow, and financial ratios. To conduct your research in these areas, there are many online and secondary resources to help you. One of the best is BizStats.com. Although no amount of research will eliminate the risk of starting your own business, it will make you more realistic and minimize the risk.

In conducting your research, access the financial ratio studies (Annual Statement Studies) published by the Risk Management Association. Every lending officer has a current copy, as do most business libraries. This publication, considered the bible for statement analysis, covers more than 190,000 businesses in 680 industries using NAICS codes and is also available via the Web at eStatement Studies.

Dun & Bradstreet Business Information Systems provides key ratios on more than 100 industries. Also, the U.S. Small Business Administration has key ratio reports by industry.

In addition, trade associations often provide the most comprehensive work on financial ratios and expected revenue and expenses. Contact them as early as possible for access to their information. No one set of figures will give you the financial numbers you need. However, delving through the secondary data combined with your primary research data should give you a fairly good idea on what the real numbers will look like. Recognize for many startup ventures in high tech hard numbers for comparison will be hard to come by thus increasing the risk and quite possibly increasing the rewards.

Start-Up Costs

It is important to determine your costs before proceeding. For some businesses, start-up costs will be minor; for others, major expenses are involved. A service business or Internet site may be up and going with only $100, whereas a retail store may incur more than $300,000 in start-up expenses. Manufacturing firms can incur start-up costs of more than $30 million.

Technology today allows entrepreneurs to launch and compete in record time at very low costs. With Skype for phone, Mint.com to keep track of accounts, Square Card Reader to accept credit cards, MailChimp, and a myriad of apps to track your business, you can be up and running with little out of pocket expenses. You can even sponsor a logo contest online for a low cost design!

Bootstrap Using one own's resources to support business

If you can bootstrap using your own funds, you will also be able to maintain control and ownership of your business. Any money saved during start-up will help cash flow later, so begin asking the following questions: What can you buy used? What are the advantages of leasing versus buying? How can you conserve cash?

Pricing

Freemium pricing Offering initial product or service free and then charging for premium ones

Dynamic pricing Fluid strategy adjusting prices to changes in demand level and type of customer

As for pricing, you will need to determine if your firm is going to attract clients or customers with low-cost pricing, if you will try to be in the middle of the road, or if you will try to attract the top tier of clients by offering premium services or products at premium pricing. Or will you use freemium pricing? What about dynamic pricing? Auction or bid pricing? The hardest part of pricing is making sure you have included *all* the costs involved in providing a product or service to customers. Volatility in pricing for commodities and changes in the economy also present major challenges for most entrepreneurs.

Seasonality Scenarios

Most businesses experience peaks and valleys. What will be your best and worst months? How will you manage cash flow? How will you deal with employee hiring, training, and scheduling through the year?

Entrepreneur's Resource

Facts and Resources for Women Entrepreneurs

The American Express "Open State of Women Owned Businesses Report" shares the following key statistics:

- In 2011, there were an estimated 8.1 million women-owned businesses in the United States, which accounts for 29 percent of all enterprises in the country.
- Nationally, the number of women-owned businesses has increased by 50 percent since 1997.
- Women-owned businesses generate $1.3 trillion in revenues and employ 7.7 million people in the United States.
- Between 1997 and 2011, the total number of businesses in the United States increased by 34 percent, while the number of women-owned firms increased by 50 percent and men-owned firms grew by only 25 percent.
- Women-owned firms employ 6 percent of the country's workforce and contribute 4 percent of business revenues.
- The fastest growing sectors of women-owned firms include educational services (up 54 percent), administrative and waste services (up 47 percent) and construction (up 41 percent).
- The industries with the highest concentration of women-owned firms are health care and social assistance (52 percent overall) and educational services (46 percent).

We have included a few helpful organizations and websites that will provide support, training, resources, assistance, and possibly even lead to financing sources. Many of these organizations have local chapters and centers to help you directly in your own community. Reach out and find other women dreaming the same dream as well as look for successful mentors within these organizations.

- National Association of Women Business Owners (NAWBO), *http://www.nawbo.org*
- Center for Women's Business Research, *http://www.womensbusinessresearch.org*
- Organization of Women in International Trade (OWIT), *http://www.owit.org*
- Association of Women's Business Centers, *http://www.awbc.biz*
- Count Me In, *http://www.countmein.org*
- eWomennetwork, *http://www.ewomennetwork.com*
- Ladies Who Launch, *http://www.ladieswholaunch.com*

Sales Projections and What-If Scenarios

Before you jump into a business, you need to determine how much income and profit it will generate in a given period of time to determine if you should proceed. By conducting extensive research and completing the Action Steps throughout this text, you should be able to make reasonable projections.

However, some entrepreneurs will be leaping into new technologies with new business and revenue models, thus hard numbers will be hard to come by. You may be entering a business where it is a leap of faith. Just make sure you have enough money behind you to support you until the money rolls in. During the dot.com boom, many business ideas were developed on the back of a napkin and funded based on little else. Unfortunately, great ideas don't always make great—or in some cases any—money!

In projecting your what-if scenarios, you need to project the very worst-case scenario, a realistic one, as well as the one you dream of. When using a spreadsheet, you should look at various elements such as sales, cost of goods sold, rent, salaries, and so on, and complete a first-year forecast. Lenders will request monthly projections for the first year and yearly projections for the next three to five years. If you are not willing to project your business out three to five years, you should rethink whether you should be in business.

Projected Income and Cash Flow Statements

Your research to date should help you develop projected profit and loss statements, also known as *income statements*. An income statement is unique to each individual company, and expenses are dependent on the area, clients, salaries, and so on. Costs vary greatly throughout the country, so when doing comparisons with others, make sure you are in the same geographical area. All expenses should be justified and supported through notes to your income and cash-flow statements. These notes will be the focus of your potential lenders, as each figure needs to be supported.

For many businesses, there is no time lag between delivering goods and receipt of payment. For others, a time lag of 15 to 60 days may exist. And some businesses, such as bed and breakfasts, collect cash up front. Find out what your selected industry standard is, and develop your projected cash flow accordingly. You will need to expend cash for labor, taxes, rent, utilities, inventory, and other expenses. If your business is to stay afloat in the interim, you have to know where every dollar is going. You must make arrangements for financial infusions long before additional funds are required.

Balance Sheet

A balance sheet shows a scale with assets on the left side and liabilities and owner's equity on the right side. For many start-ups, the balance sheet will contain few assets, but as the business grows, the balance sheet becomes an important tool to gauge the financial health of your organization.

Break-Even Analysis

In simple terms, a break-even analysis shows you the point where you will pay your bills; after that point, you will begin to realize a profit from additional sales. If you complete a break-even analysis that clearly shows that you will need to reach sales of $500,000 in the second year of business, you can then use what-if scenarios, spreadsheets, and other information to determine if that sales figure is realistic in light of the competition, location, product, and economy.

Financial Ratios

Published ratios from your associations and others will guide you in developing your projected statements. Lenders will evaluate and compare your financial ratios to others in your selected industry and regional area and their lending decisions will be based on how you stack up.

■ START-UP COSTS AND CONCERNS

When successful entrepreneurs are interviewed and asked what surprises they had not anticipated, in almost every case, they respond that it cost more and took longer than they had anticipated. Start the planning process, do the required research, and make the best realistic estimates you can so that you are not caught off guard.

figure **8.1**

Start-Up Concerns and Costs Worksheet

I. Taxi Squad (people who can assist you)
   - A. Lawyer
   - B. Banker
   - C. Accountant/bookkeeper
   - D. Insurance agent
   - E. Commercial real estate agent
   - F. Mentor
   - G. Consultants
   - H. Suppliers
   - I. Chamber of Commerce
   - J. SBA, SCORE
   - K. Partners, board members
   - L. Software developers

II. Organization
   - A. Federal ID number
   - B. DBA ("doing business as," fictitious business name)
   - C. Partnership agreement
   - D. Corporate bylaws
   - E. Employees
   - F. State ID number

III. Licenses, Permits
   - A. Business license
   - B. Resale permit
   - C. Department of Health
   - D. Beer, wine, liquor
   - E. Fire inspection permit
   - F. Environmental permits

IV. Location
   - A. Lease review (lawyer)
   - B. First and last month's rent (rent payments during improvements may be negotiable)
   - C. Security deposit
   - D. Leasehold improvements (negotiate with landlord)
     1. Signage
     2. Lighting
     3. Electrical/plumbing
     4. Flooring
     5. Construction
   - E. Insurance (see Chapter 12)
   - F. Security system
   - G. Utilities, deposits, estimated monthly costs
     1. Electric
     2. Gas
     3. Water
     4. Phone installation
     5. Internet services
   - H. Other

V. Auto
   - A. Auto/Truck(s)
     1. New/used
     2. Lease/purchase
   - B. Insurance
   - C. Maintenance, repairs

VI. Equipment
   - A. Office
   - B. Retail space
     1. Storage Cabinets
     2. Display cases
     3. Refrigeration
     4. Shelving/storage
     5. Other
   - C. Warehouse
   - D. Manufacturing area
   - E. Kitchen/Dining area
   - F. Computer hardware and software
   - G. Cable/phone

VII. Insurance
   - A. Liability
   - B. Workers compensation
   - C. Key person
   - D. Health
   - E. Business
   - F. Auto
   - G. Fire
   - H. Other

VIII. Setup
   - A. Business cards/Letterhead
   - B. Website
   - C. Accounting setup
   - D. Customer tracking/point of sale
   - E. Other

IX. Inventory (What are the minimum/maximum and average inventory requirements needed on hand to do business on your first day?)

X. Advertising and Promotion
   - A. Fliers/brochures
   - B. Displays
   - C. Ad layouts
   - D. Media costs (newspaper, radio, other)
   - E. Web site development
   - F. Other

XI. Banking
   - A. Checking account
   - B. Savings/money market account
   - C. Credit
     1. Credit cards
     2. Personal lines of credit
     3. Loans
     4. Credit from suppliers/vendors
     5. Merchant services

XII. Employees
   - A. Application/employment forms completed
   - B. Training program
   - C. Tax forms
   - D. Payroll services

© Cengage Learning

To begin, we have provided a Start-Up Concerns and Cost Worksheet, Figure 8.1, which is a generic worksheet. You will need to add and subtract items from the worksheet to fit your business operation. As you complete your Business Plan in Chapter 15, you should return to this list to make sure you have dealt with all of the concerns on your final list. In fact, as you work through the remainder of the chapters, keep Figure 8.1 and Figure 8.2, the

Start-Up Requirements Worksheet, nearby and add to them as concerns and costs arise. Many of the items on the list are discussed in detail in later chapters.

Action Steps 38 and 39 will help you anticipate potential surprises and costs, such as those that befell Ginny Henshaw.

Unexpected Costs

The reason I decided to start a day-care center was because I really loved children, and my experience as a preschool teacher and camp administrator led me to believe I could do it. I talked it over with my family, and they said they would help out if I got in over my head. If only they had known!

I think we planned things pretty well. We found a good location—smack in the middle of a neighborhood of young families with an average of 2.3 children. We worked hard, but it was fun, and it made us feel a part of something important. We spent many hours making sure we complied with myriad of laws and regulations required of day-care centers.

About three weeks before our opening, we called the light and power people to ask them to turn on the lights. "Sure thing," they said. "Just send us a check for $3,000, and the lights will be on."

"What?" I asked. "Did you say $3,000?" We had around $10,000 in the kitty, but that was earmarked for emergencies.

"That's right. You're a new commercial customer with a good credit rating. That's the reason the figure's so low for your tonnage," they said, "it's right on the money."

"Tonnage? What tonnage?"

"Your air conditioner," they said. "You have a 5-ton unit on your roof. Figure you run it for a month, that's $1,100. The other $400 is for lights and gas."

"But we're not planning to run the A/C!" I said. "The ocean breeze here is terrific. We don't need the air conditioner."

"Sorry, ma'am. Our policy is pretty clear. As I said, sometimes we get three months' deposit, but for your business, we'll only require the two. Is there anything else I can help you with today?"

"No," I said. "Nothing."

If you exceed your budgeted start-up costs and have limited reserves as Ginny and most do, your first year may be very difficult. Think of every way you can save: buy used, borrow, barter, or beg. Many businesses fail in the first year as they do not have enough working capital to get them through. Conserve cash at all times!

Worth more than $5 million, one successful oil entrepreneur demands his staff check the local library before purchasing any book. *Cash is king!* Especially at the beginning, do not squander cash.

■ BOOTSTRAPPING

It is no secret that start-ups are expensive, and those first few months can be a make-it-or-break-it time for the entrepreneur. When you are out of money, you are out of business! This is definitely the time to care passionately about each and every dollar that comes in and goes out of your business. Guard each dollar jealously so you can make your dollars work efficiently. If you work to conserve the dollars you do have, you will not have to shake the money tree so hard to find additional dollars.

Tips to Conserve

1. Get paid up front if you can.
2. Persuade vendors to give you more **trade credit or dating** and more time to pay.

Trade credit or Dating A vendor's extension of the payment term into the near future

———————————————————— figure **8.2**

Financial Start-Up Requirements Worksheet*

Initial Expenses

Down Payment if Buying Business/Franchise _____

Franchisee Fee _____

Legal and Professional Fees _____

Office supplies _____

Office equipment _____

Brochures/design/letterhead, business cards, etc. _____

Web site development _____

Utility deposits and installation _____

Rent/lease deposits _____

Licenses/Permits _____

Banking/credit card set-up fees _____

Computer _____

Software _____

Insurance _____

Construction costs/Signage/Fixtures/Equipment _____

Fixtures and equipment installation _____

Phone, Internet, servers/routers, etc. _____

Grand Opening promotional costs _____

Operating Cash _____

Other _____

Total Initial Expenses

Total Monthly Expenses

Salary of owner-manager _____

All other salaries and wages _____

Taxes and social security _____

Rent _____

Advertising/promotion _____

Freight/postage _____

Utilities _____

Operating supplies _____

Telephone/cell phones _____

Internet/web hosting _____

Insurance (health/business/vehicle) _____

Car/truck payments _____

Interest on loans _____

Maintenance and repairs _____

Taxes _____

Travel/equipment _____

Banking/credit card fees _____

Legal and professional fees _____

Monthly royalties/fees _____

Other _____

Other _____

Total Monthly Expenses x (3-6 estimate) _____

Start-up Inventory x (3-6 months estimate) _____

Other Expenses

Personal living expenses (3-6 months estimate) _____

Other _____

Cushion _____

Total Other Expenses _____

Total Start-Up Costs _____

(Total Initial Expenses + [Total Monthly Expenses × (3 to 6 months)] + [Start-up Inventory × (3–6 months)] + Total Other Expenses)

* Please adjust worksheet to fit your particular business.

© Cengage Learning

3. Lease your equipment. Investigate purchasing used equipment but have it looked at thoroughly before paying for it. (Check out Craigslist and eBay, ask industry insiders for leads)
4. Run a lean operation; do not waste anything.
5. Work out of your home if you can for as long as you can.
6. Ask your landlord to make on-site improvements and finance the cost over the term of the lease.
7. Keep track of everything. Try to resell whatever waste or byproducts you have in your business.
8. Take markdowns quickly on dead goods. If they do not sell at markdown, dump or donate them. Turn merchandise.
9. Use as little commercial space as you can. Be creative!
10. If your customers do not visit your business facility, it does not have to be highly visible or attractive. Doors for desktops work!
11. When you have to borrow money, shop around. The most expensive cash is the cash you never planned for.
12. Make sure your liquid cash is earning interest.
13. Add employees slowly and carefully.
14. Open a line of credit and establish a credit card for the business if at all possible.
15. Make "conserve cash" your firm's mantra and make sure you ingrain this mantra in your employees.
16. Always check for deals on free shipping, coupons, etc.

We agree with Norm Brodsky leading *Inc.* writer who encourages entrepreneurs to, "Forget about making a splash. Forget about everything except getting your capital to last until you do not need it anymore. You do not have to give up on your dreams. Dreams are important. Just wait until you can afford them."

(*Inc.*, December 1995, p. 27, *http://www.inc.com/magazine/19951201/2505.html* (Accessed July 21, 2004)).

Seeking Financial Advice and Support

There is a boatload of surprises awaiting every entrepreneur who enters the marketplace. We talked about Plan B, formulating your strategy, checking and double-checking your market, and peering into the future to see what lies ahead. There is another angle to planning; it is called *seeking advice*.

Think for a moment about where you are right now on your road to the marketplace. You are halfway through this book. You have analyzed your skills and needs and have probed your past and surveyed your friends. You have discovered what success means to you, and you have plotted trends and found your industry segment. You have profiled your Target Customer, studied the demographics, and developed a promotional campaign. You have examined the competition and used your new eyes to find a dynamite location. If you have not yet found several entrepreneurial gurus to help you with financial advice, it is now time!

Where might you find a entrepreneurial financial business guru? What about your accountant? What about the real estate broker who helped you with your search for a location? What about your business insurance specialist, your lawyer, your distributors, your potential customers or your competitors? What about your SCORE counselor?

Use your network to help locate financial advisors to help you look realistically at potential surprises as well as projected sales and financials. Their advice will save you time, money, and frustrations and will help you avoid costly errors at the beginning.

On-site improvements Modifications to real estate to accommodate the special needs of the business

Dead goods Merchandise no longer in demand

Liquid cash Funds that are immediately available, usually held in checking or other accounts

Entrepreneurial guru A wise person on the sidelines who can help you with advice and counsel

ACTION STEP 38

Attach Price Tags to Starting Your Business

Sit down at your desk and look around with new eyes.

1. List the items on your desk and those you use on a daily basis.
2. List your expenditures for things you cannot see, some of which you might take for granted. These include such things as insurance, rent, utilities, taxes, legal and accounting services, and so on. (Chapter 12 covers insurance in depth.)
3. Beside each tangible item and each intangible expense, write down how much it will cost.
4. Use the Start-Up Worksheets (Figure 8.1 and Figure 8.2) to serve as guides as you develop your start-up costs. If you have located more specific worksheets for your particular business; you should use those to complete this Action Step.

As you gather more information, you will be able to refine the numbers on the worksheets. By the time you reach Chapter 15, you will be able to produce an accurate representation of start-up requirements for your Business Plan.

■ PRICING YOUR PRODUCT OR SERVICE

In principle, the price you charge for your product or service must be acceptable to you and to your customer. From your customers' perspective, an acceptable price depends on competitive alternatives for your product or service in addition to the perceived value. As for you, your price can be based on any number of pricing considerations. But it is fairly safe to say that ultimately, you will be trying to maximize sales revenue and profits.

New businesses often make the mistake of charging either too little or too much for their product or service. To help you avoid making one of these mistakes, we outline four pricing methods. But use caution: The process of setting a price can become quite complicated and technical, and in many industries, changes occur rapidly, and profits fluctuate as well. You may need to seek professional help in setting prices.

Keep in mind your customer is not buying a product or service but a solution to a problem. You need to make that solution a benefit to them and include that value in your pricing model. As you look at your competitors, be totally honest as you evaluate their offerings. View the product in the way your customer views the product, not how *you*, personally, view the product. Also, once your business

ACTION STEP 39

Preparing for Surprises

Take time to brainstorm a list of surprises that could cost you money or time and thus threaten the survival of your business. Use our checklists to help you get started.

1. Ask business owners in your industry what surprises they encountered and how they handled them. Also, once you select a site, ask your fellow business neighbors about their experiences and the surprises you may face in your location.
2. Talk to vendors, suppliers, customers, and insurance brokers. Ask. Probe.
3. When you finish your list, put a checkmark beside each item that may incur additional costs, and then try to estimate what those potential costs may be.
4. How will you cover unforeseen expenses? What amount of money should you put aside for unexpected events?

Continue to revise these lists as you gather information. When you reach Chapter 15, the information will help you in writing your final Business Plan.

PASSION

Bootstrapping a Business with A Fun Idea

Knit Wits: Don We Now Our Ugly Christmas Sweaters

Everyone I know has favorite holiday traditions. They range from rituals handed down through generations to quirky accidents that seem to work their way into seasonal celebrations. Lately, I've noticed a new tradition taking hold among friends and colleagues: the ugly Christmas sweater party.

The origin of these parties is up for debate, but Costco member Adam Paulson, one-third of Team Ugly—a group of friends who started *www.ugly christmassweaterparty.com*—writes that Vancouver, British Columbia, has been holding an ugly-sweater charity event since 2001. Cities such as Toronto; Kansas City, Kansas; and Indianapolis have been hosting similar charity events for the past six or seven years.

Paulson has worked on the website with college friends Brian Miller and Kevin Wool since its inception in 2006. The trio, who all live in northern Indiana, had attended a few ugly-sweater parties, and Miller purchased the domain in anticipation of the themed shindigs taking off.

The site operated primarily as a blog until 2009, when, explains Paulson, people started "emailing the blog, letting Brian know that they were having a real tough time finding ugly Christmas sweaters. So we saw an opportunity to monetize the URL as well as start one of the most unique companies on the World Wide Web. We had all been to a couple ugly Christmas sweater parties before we started the company and saw how much fun people were having."

Paulson says that on November 14, 2009, he went to Goodwill and bought nearly 60 sweaters. The guys photographed all of them and put the pictures online at the website. They sold out in a day.

"From there we went from Goodwill to Goodwill to Goodwill, picking them up," Paulson tells *The Connection*. After storing more sweaters than a person could wear in one holiday season, the friends found a storage facility and now have a scout who helps with finding ugly sweaters.

Eventually an agent approached Team Ugly and asked them to put together a book proposal. Once the proposal was approved, the trio set out to write the *Ugly Christmas Sweater Party Book* (Abrams, 2011).

Source: The Costco Connection, December 2011, Stephanie E. Ponder. Reprinted with permission.

Markup A percentage of your cost of sales that is added to the cost to determine selling price

is established, realize you will constantly need to re-evaluate your pricing and profitability.

Retail stores have traditional **markups** that might range from two to four times the cost of the product. Direct mail and catalogs may have markups of four to seven times the product cost. Or infomercials may offer products at a loss and make up for the loss with very high handling and delivery charges.

To price your products correctly so that you are able to realize a profit, you need to recognize *all* of the costs involved in delivering your product or service. Figure 8.3, Pricing Considerations, provides information on the elements involved in pricing electrical services. Talking to others in your industry will provide you with the true costs involved for *your* particular product or service. Again leading edge businesses will find few numbers to support their dreams.

In some industries, such as automotive and collision, the manufacturer or insurance company sets the price paid based on the labor and material costs. You need to decide if these numbers are numbers you can work with and still profit. Sometimes you will need to forego certain customers, who cannot leave you with a fair profit.

Supply, demand, competition, your business and revenue models, and your target market will determine the pricing of your products. Be careful not to price your product too low; customers may think it is cheap and will not buy. There are two fools in regard to pricing: one prices too high, and one prices too low. Recognize that some items are price-sensitive and some are not. You will be

figure 8.3

Pricing Considerations for an Electrical Contractor (sample from the back of a local contractor's bill)

Insurance (workers compensation, health, liability, theft, property, etc.)

Training and Retraining

Licensing

Trucks (maintenance, gas, repairs, insurance, licensing)

Electrical Equipment and Supplies

Taxes (income, property, social security, etc.)

Advertising

Tools and Supplies

Rent and Utilities

Administrative Costs (scheduling and billing, ordering, stocking supplies)

Salaries and Benefits

Business Expenses (accountant, legal, computers)

© Cengage Learning

able to increase your margins on those products and services that have little price sensitivity.

The Internet allows customers to have instant price comparison information and thus is putting many local retailers in price competition with Internet offerings. When asked to meet Internet pricing, retailers oftentimes have to choose to lose a customer or lose money.

Couponing with Groupon and its clones have thrown an additional wrench into pricing today. Many customers today demand discounts and are less loyal to businesses; often times, just chasing the next good deal.

Pricing several years ago was a relatively easy part of running a business but technology has now made it much more difficult and challenging. However, for others, the success of their business will come from the use of technology in developing new business and revenue models to capitalize on the changes.

Market research and analysis of your competitors' pricing and offerings should provide you with a starting point. In addition to the competition your product or service faces, you should also assess the customer service demanded by consumers. Both of these areas were covered in the Action Steps in Chapter 5.

As mentioned previously, price is one of the most difficult elements to compete on and still realize a profit. No matter how well you plan your pricing, you need to be flexible and make adjustments quickly if necessary. If your product is sold only on the Internet, the ability to test and adjust product pricing rapidly is one of your biggest advantages.

As you price your products or services, include a percentage for bad debts. Also, if you are in retailing, price in 3 to 5 percent for employee and customer theft—a fact of life. In many businesses, theft from insiders is the larger issue.

Professional thieves have targeted high-tech manufacturers that produce commodity products. After stealing the products, they are relabeled and dumped into the marketplace, where prices fall rapidly. Thus, we suggest you stay vigilant on any theft activities within your industry. Also, contact associations for estimated loss percentages, and heed their advice on loss prevention.

Common Pricing Methods

1. Competitor-Based Pricing

In Chapter 5, we asked you to review your competitor touchpoint analysis and state the prices of your products or services relative to your customers' perception of the competition. In fact, we were asking you to calculate your price relative to the market. We wanted you to find out what prices were acceptable to your potential customers given their possible choices and competitive options. Many new business owners begin their pricing strategy by first determining what prices or price range the target market will accept relative to the competition. This is often referred to as competitor-based pricing and is sometimes referred to as market-based pricing.

Competitor-based pricing or **Market-based pricing** Setting a price range whose main focus is competitor pricing

The price of your product or service depends on your competitors' prices, but you will also have to figure out your costs. If the market price cannot cover your costs, then your business is going to lose money. And naturally, you want to make sure that the price you charge is enough to yield a profit. This leads us to a second approach, called cost-plus pricing or profit-based pricing.

Cost-plus pricing or **Profit-based pricing** Setting a price that covers all costs plus a profit

2. Cost-Plus Pricing

One of the most common errors novice business owners make is pricing based solely on the costs to produce the product or service and leave out many other costs. Thus, Figure 8.3 lists out all the costs involved in offering electrical contract services and Action Step 40 will ask you to do the same for your business. If you set your price based solely on cost, your business will not make any profit. The price you charge must also take into consideration your profit expectations. There are different methods for calculating a price which will take profit into account. A simple and common formula for estimating price per unit follows:

$$\text{Selling price} = \text{total cost per unit} + \text{estimated dollar profit per unit}$$

Your costs for producing a particular product or supplying a particular service will include three broad costing groups: 1) direct material costs, or your cost of supplies; 2) direct cost of labor for producing your product or service; and 3) overhead, or fixed expenses, which are indirect costs such as rent and advertising.

Your estimated profit will depend on a number of factors: the type of product or service, the market demand, the economy, competitors, and so on. If available, rely on your primary and secondary research, such as industry averages for your type of business, as a guide when setting a profit target.

3. Industry Norm or Keystone Pricing

Some types of businesses charge prices according to certain generally accepted or industry standards. This is called keystone pricing or industry-norm pricing. Two examples of this approach might be setting the price at triple the cost of goods sold or two times the labor costs.

The concept of markups might also help you determine your price. A markup is a percentage of your cost of sales that you add to the cost to determine your selling price. Note that you do not include overhead costs in your mark-up calculation; include only your costs for materials and supplies. For example, if the selling price is $3 and the cost is $2, the markup is calculated as follows:

$$\begin{aligned}
\text{Markup} &= (\text{price} - \text{cost})/\text{cost} \\
&= (\$3 - \$2)/\$2 \\
&= 1/2 \\
&= .50, \text{ or } 50 \text{ percent}
\end{aligned}$$

Markups are calculated in some cases as a percentage of costs and in others as a percentage of the selling price. In the above example, the 50 percent markup was calculated as a percentage of cost. If we had calculated the markup as a percentage of selling price, then the markup would be 33 percent, or ($3 − $2)/$3.

If you know what the standard or industry markup is for your product or service, then you can estimate a selling price. For example, if you are selling greeting cards, and you know that the industry markup on the selling price is 50 percent, then you can determine an estimated selling price. Although, your final price will ultimately depend on direct and indirect costs, the competition and the market demand for your unique product or service. The reality is some unique cards may have markups of 300% but they are probably aimed at a very different market than those with a 50% markup. You must know your market and what price it will bear.

4. Premium Pricing

Premium pricing means setting the highest price target consumers will pay for a product or service given their needs, values and the competitive options. Your ultimate goal or strategy is to try to focus on a specific market segment, then create uniqueness and differentiate your product or service in the eyes of the customer. Some pricing analysts refer to premium pricing as the highest price the market will bear. If your product or service is inelastic, it means that your customers, on average, will be willing to buy your product or service even if your prices are on the high side relative to those of your competitors—because

Keystone pricing or Industry-norm pricing Setting a price that depends on generally accepted industry standards

Premium pricing Setting the highest price target consumers will pay for a product or service given their needs, values, and the competitive options your customer values the fact that your product is different. For example, Coach purses and Lamborghinis are premium priced. Premium pricing is also often used in the introductory phase of products and services, which are unique, and thus buyers are willing to pay extra for early acquisition.

Other Pricing Methods

These four broad methods are not the only options available. For example, two additional common pricing strategies used mainly by larger firms include:

- Penetration pricing—pricing new products or services artificially low to quickly gain sales and market share discouraging others from entering the market. Usually firms lose money in the short term in hopes of long term gain.
- Price skimming—setting prices high initially to appeal to consumers who are not price sensitive and striving for maximum return, then lowering prices as competitors enter the market. Strategy usually used in the introduction phase of a product with "early adopters" and "innovators" as the primary target markets.

Penetration pricing Setting initial or introductory price artificially low to attract customer attention and build market share quickly

Price skimming Pricing high to attract customers who buy the newest items and want to be trend setters

Pricing Strategies

Depending on your business idea, you might need additional information and guidance than that provided above. Also, many businesses operate in highly volatile pricing environments, where you must be constantly aware of the major price fluctuations caused by commodity price changes and shifts in supply and demand. Those who are selling on the Internet will find a myriad of pricing strategies, because competitors' prices are clearly evident and can be researched by both you and your customers. Some online vendors change their prices daily or in real time to reflect competitors' prices and or their own inventory; such pricing is also known as *dynamic pricing*.

The price you charge for your product or service will depend on a number of factors, including costs of production, market considerations, competitive forces, geography, size of business, product, service distribution channel, and economy. We suggest that you begin your pricing analysis by first considering the premium price strategy, then follow up by making sure that this price will cover your costs and lead to a profit.

Many small business owners think they should start out with low prices to attract customers, but in most cases, this is a mistake. In general, small businesses should not aim to sell products or services at the lowest market price. Penetration pricing should be reserved for large firms, such as Coca-Cola and Wal-Mart, who want to increase their market share and dominate the market.

In developing a pricing strategy, be flexible and expect changes to occur frequently and often rapidly. Pat Watt of Ikebana Designs shared how difficult it was to price her unique flower arrangements, as wholesale market prices fluctuated daily depending on the weather, season, and supply.

Complete Action Step 40 now and consider how you will deal with recessionary and inflationary pressures. Remember pricing is both a science and an art and for most entrepreneurs a great deal of trial and error.

■ SEASONALITY SCENARIOS

For some businesses, sales will remain fairly steady from month to month. However, most businesses, especially those in retail, experience seasonal variations. From your discussions with others, you should be able to gain a handle on

ACTION STEP 40

Discovering Costs and Developing a Fair Price

1. Review Action Steps 28, 29, and 30 from Chapter 5. If you have learned further information, revise your answers and utilize them in developing your pricing strategy.
2. Read trade magazines, talk with business owners, association representatives, distributors, competitors, and possibly even other owners in similar lines of business to make a list—such as the one in Figure 8.3—to encompass all of the many costs you will incur to get the product or service to your client. Most entrepreneurs will not recognize all of the costs involved and will therefore price their products or services below cost. As a result, they will not make a profit.
3. Once you have made the list of the costs and activities, take the time and energy to determine the actual expenses involved with each. BizStats.com (see Entrepreneurial Resource) may be of benefit in your research.
4. Begin by pricing your product using the primary pricing method utilized in your industry.
5. How do you want your product or service to be seen from the customer's viewpoint compared to your competitors? Business Plan readers will be interested in how you developed your pricing strategy from a numbers and a research standpoint. Justify your reasoning with facts and figures.
6. Discuss any of the major pricing issues your firm will need to deal with.
7. Continue to add relevant pricing information to this Action Step as you work through the rest of the chapters.
8. Complete a break-even analysis once you have completed the chapter (see Figure 8.9).

possible variations and work the numbers into your sales and cash-flow projections. Also, do not make an assumption that if you purchase a business located in a vacation area that you and your business will be able to buck the nature of a seasonal business. You may be able to offer reduced pricing, which brings a few additional customers to help with cash flow during low periods, but they may not add much to your profitability.

For the bookstore Know It All, it was fairly easy to determine inventory requirements based on the information provided by the American Booksellers Association. But to determine seasonal adjustments in sales, the owners sought out several bookstore owners in nearby towns to help determine monthly profit and loss and cash-flow projections based on monthly sales variations. One local bookstore owner shared the following sales breakdown.

Monthly Sales Breakdown for Retail Bookstore

January (6.5 percent)

"January is an anticlimax to Christmas, but it is still busy because of gift certificates and exchanges. I run some good specials at the end of January, prior to taking yearly inventory. Even though sales are slowing down, I have to order new titles because publishers (our suppliers) provide advance notice of their spring lists."

February (4.5 percent) and March (5 percent)

"Very quiet. I take inventory, weed out stuff that didn't sell, send it back, and usually feel bad when I see the restocking fees. I meet publishers' reps who are out on the road pushing new titles. On February 13, I have a red-and-pink sale for Valentine's Day and on March 15, an Ides-of-March sale. Next year, I'm planning a St. Patrick's Day tie-in."

April (5 percent)

"Still slow. We get a slight jump in sales after April 10, mostly because spring vacations give people time to read."

May (8 percent) and June (8 percent)

"Two holidays—Mother's Day and Father's Day—plus weddings and graduations give us our second-busiest season. Art books and gift editions do well during this time."

July (6 percent) and August (7 percent)

"We're not in a tourist area, and summers for us are slow. We sell mostly easy-to-read paperbacks and lots of landscaping books. Our minds, though, are on ordering books for Christmas."

September (9 percent)

"Back-to-school purchases. We're interviewing people for Christmas jobs and making last-minute purchases of gift items."

October (10 percent) and November (12 percent)

"The start of the busy season. Customers sense it, and we can feel the momentum. The rush is just around the corner. We usually hire more sales help at this time."

December (19 percent)

"The crush. Our computer does a great job of tracking sales. It is different every year, but with two years of great data gathering behind me, I have a feel for what really happens. And that helps us plan ahead for the next year."

© Cengage Learning

Entrepreneur's **Resource**

BizStats.com

Your business needs to present reasonable sales and financial projections. If you have the back-up data to support each of your numbers, lenders will feel more comfortable that you have done your homework. But more importantly you need to be comfortable going forth with a business that can support your projections and become profitable.

Locating financial statistics and ratios to benchmark your projections can sometimes prove difficult, but one site for free data, *http://BizStats.com*, may lead you directly to the numbers you are seeking. If you need more up to date figures, for a small additional fee, seek out data on BizMiner.

If you want to find sales per square foot, retail sales per store, safest and riskiest small businesses, sizes of various industries and markets, financial benchmarks and ratios, and much more, log on to BizStats and BizMiner. Examples of BizStats free online statistics follow:

BizStats Free Data for Food-Beverage Stores with $750K Revenue

Income-Expense Statement

Food-Beverage stores	2008	Your Inputs
Sole Prop Annual Average Sales, Income & Expense		
Sales	100.00%	$750,000.00
Inventory (% of Sales)	6.41%	$48,064.25
Cost of Sales	71.65%	$537,382.06
COS-Labor Portion	0.84%	$6,336.07
Gross Profit	28.35%	$212,617.94
Salary-Wages	5.09%	$38,189.94
Contract Labor-Commisions	0.36%	$2,700.83
Rent	3.20%	$24,015.80
Taxes	1.46%	$10,955.66
Interest paid	0.55%	$4,101.04
Amort. & Dep.	0.85%	$6,401.74
Advertising	0.38%	$2,857.34
Benefits-Pension	0.08%	$562.60
Insurance (non-health)	0.66%	$4,971.49
Home Office Expense	0.02%	$122.66
Other SG&A Exp.	9.31%	$69,795.54
Total Expenses	21.96%	$164,674.61
Net Profit	6.39%	$47,943.33
Total Direct Labor & NP	12.33%	$92,469.34

BizStats.com

SG&A Detail

Food-Beverage stores	2008	Your Inputs
Sole Prop SG&A Detail		
Sales	100.00%	$750,000.00
Car and truck expenses	0.78%	$5,817.19
Legal and professional services	0.27%	$1,990.79
Meals and entertainment deducted	0.02%	$148.89
Office expenses	0.16%	$1,226.31
Repairs	0.64%	$4,815.87
Supplies	1.32%	$9,924.66
Travel	0.10%	$737.37
Utilities	2.32%	$17,413.06
Other business deductions	3.70%	$27,721.42
Total SG&A	9.31%	$69,795.54

BizStats.com

(continued)

(continued)

Ratios

Food-Beverage stores	2008
Sole Prop Average Average Financial Ratios	
Return on Sales	6.39%
Return on Gross Profit	22.55%
Net Cash Turnover	13.77
COS:Inventory	11.18

BizStats.com

Source: www.bizstats.com/sole-proprietorship-business-financials/retail-7.0000/food-beverage-stores-7.0500/show (Accessed April 23, 2012).

ACTION STEP 41

Complete Seasonality Scenario and a Projected Profit and Loss (Income) Statement

1. Write a seasonality scenario for a typical year in your business. Look around at obvious forces such as weather, holidays, buying patterns, etc.—and relate these to the life-cycle stage of your product, location, and competition. You will also need to gather information from business owners and from trade associations.

2. Now answer the following: When does your selected industry collect money? Before the sale? During? After? Long after? When will you have to pay for your inventory? What is the shortest time lag you can see between the time you pay for inventory and the time you receive money (payment, hard dollars) for the sale of that inventory? What is the longest time lag? When will you declare a lag a bad debt? If you are in manufacturing and have to alter, re-shape, or rebuild raw materials into a product, what kind of time lag will there be?

3. Generate monthly numbers for the year:
   a. Using data from trade associations and small-business owners, forecast your sales for the year.
   b. Figure your cost of goods sold and subtract that figure from sales. This gives you your gross profit.

(continued)

After the first year of business, seasonal sales forecasting will become easier. Keep very careful records the first year so that you will know how your own peaks and valleys correlate with the seasonality of your selected industry. Most businesses are seasonal, and you will need to develop strong control systems to manage your financial resources. Begin to identify alternative sources of credit, and find ways to collect cash from customers so that you will be able to handle cash flow changes.

One dentist found his business could vary as much as 30 percent per month. People bring their children in during the summer months for checkups, and many insurance companies' dental allowances need to be utilized by the end of June or December, thus causing a large increase in business during those two months and the rest of the summer. Contact your association and competitors to determine how your firm's sales may be subject to monthly changes; complete a seasonality scenario now, and use it as you complete your projected income statement in Action Step 41.

■ ECONOMIC CYCLES

If you are in business for more than a few years, you will begin to recognize the economic cycles of not only your specific business but those of the broader economic conditions. When a slowdown hit in 2008, many firms were caught by the severe downdraft in sales and subsequent profits. Many new firms that had not saved for that proverbial "rainy day" were caught scrambling and many did not survive.

Cash is king in a recession so try to conserve as much as possible. Cut expense to the bone and trim all the fat. Track your expenses religiously, train employees to perform multiple functions. Focus on quality and customer service. Fight hard to retain your customer base and if possible partner with them to help each other. Drop unprofitable and draining customers who drain time and energy from your business. Do not rely on only a few customers, as if one sinks, you may sink also. Make sure your salespeople do not accept orders from firm's in arrears just to pad their commissions.

Ed Horton, Matt Kuchinsky, and Kevin Ryan, CPAs and partners in the accounting firm Citrin Cooperman & Company, offer additional accounting tips in case of a downturn:

Keep an even closer eye on your budget and receivables. "Review expenses, sales, margins, cash flow, and other indicators so that you can make informed decisions in an economy that can be shifting relatively quickly," Horton says. Also watch receivables: "They can be an indicator of how hard your clients are being hit with a downturn," Kuchinsky says.

Get tough on collecting payments. Part of watching receivables is ensuring you have a healthy cash flow. "This includes reviewing and revising your processes for collecting payment and getting more aggressive with reminders, phone calls, and offering payment by credit card," Kuchinsky says. That last item, he says, is worth the 1.5 percent processing fee to keep the cash flowing into your business.

Negotiate with vendors. "Many vendors will provide a discount for payment up front," Ryan says. "Others will provide discounts to loyal and longtime customers. Request an extension of credit with them so that your business can pay invoices in 60 days, and not 30."

Source: Laura Tiffany, "Surviving a Slow Economy," Entrepreneur Magazine, 27 March 2008. Copyright © 2012 Entrepreneur Media, Inc. 1212:SH

(continued)

c. Add up all expenses and subtract them from gross profit. Note in your income statement how you arrived at each figure. This gives you the net profit before taxes.

d. Subtract taxes. (Uncle Sam uses what we might call "old eyes." You will be taxed on paper profit, so you have to build in this figure.) The figure you arrive at is your net profit after taxes for the year.

If you do not have Excel, go online to the many calculators and complete your income statements, start-up costs, and cash-flow projections. Also, as you continue your research, constantly refine your numbers and add specific notes to back up any figures or projections in your Business Plan. Remember that the notes section of your financial plans will be analyzed in depth by bankers and investors.

Recessionary periods can bring even the most successful businesses to their knees when customers do not pay. Reliance on only a few customers can make this happen even quicker. One Southern California electronics distributor's accountant flagged a customer for being 90 days in arrears. However, an eager sales manager processed and delivered to an order for over $100,000 to that same customer with full knowledge of the situation. His "commission" greed overrode the company's profit goal. If you are a small firm, keeo tight control between your accounts reveivables and sales.

Many well-run businesses fail in recessionary times, and we again remind entrepreneurs not to take such failures personally. A very successful retail entrepreneur for over 30 years paid cash for his Rolls Royce and just two years later would have been happy and lucky to own a nice sedan.

During tough times we have seen people be very creative. Calling back on clients for leads, calling past clients and offering to do smaller projects than they were willing to do before, teaming up with others to offer services and share office space and employees, moving to areas of the country or world where they could operate more efficiently, and a myriad of other actions can be taken just to stay afloat.

The owner of a southern California furniture design center with a 10,000-square foot furniture showroom shared, "It was like the lights went out one day and the phones never rang again!" Shocked and disheartened, she was forced to liquidate her beautiful showroom with a no minimum bid auction. Watching her furniture go for pennies on the dollar had to be excruciating, but through it all she was gracious to those who purchased—and they and others have not forgotten. She regrouped, took her design business back into her home and recently reopened an office for her again growing interior design business. She is standing tall with the respect of many in her community who no doubt will reward her for her talent and grace!

A designer of model home interiors, Linda Sherman of Studio Hill Design, suffered a severe downturn in her business when home building ceased. To keep busy, she took on small projects and never stopped contacting builders throughout the entire time. She worked every day in her office, honing her skills and keeping track of the design market, so when the turn came she would have contacts in place and current ideas ready. Recently, she took on one major condominium project and several smaller model home projects. She is definitely on the way back up. Also, many of her former competitors are out of the market, which should make it easier as she moves forward with her contacts, experience, talents, and confidence.

GLOBAL**VILLAGE**

Start-Up Chile's Global Footprint
Are you adventurous? Looking for startup capital?

Start-Up Chile, an almost two-year old initiative, has rapidly gained traction around the world. However, while it carries a similar name to other national initiatives around the globe, it has a very different approach.

Unlike the Startup America or StartUp Britain movement, Start-Up Chile works more like a focused incubation program than a platform for initiatives or public relations. Startups from any part of the world can apply for the program and those selected receive a U.S. $40,000 government grant as seed capital, a one-year work visa, office space, and unlimited access to its extensive network of local and global contacts. The selected businesses must come to Chile for a minimum of six months, after which they are free to take whatever steps necessary to grow.

The success of Start-Up Chile has expanded beyond attracting talent. It is creating an increasingly fertile entrepreneurship ecosystem by fulfilling the mission spelled out in one of the program's promotional videos: "They arrive. They work. They connect. They leave—and Chile stays connected."

The program now has an annual budget of about $15 million per year and a pile of more than 1,600 applications from 70 countries, nearly 500 participants, and now 220 foreign start-ups in Chile that employ 180 locals and 143 abroad. In fact, Horacio Melo, executive director of Start-Up Chile, recently told *The Santiago Times* that he had been visiting Silicon Valley to advise others on the Start-Up Chile model.

According to Melo, of the 84 teams that were in Start-up Chile's first generation of companies, only about 15 to 20 percent stayed—the rest couldn't find investors there. Now starting with its third generation of companies, the program's leaders report much growth in terms of local and foreign investment.

For example, the Harvard Business School graduates behind SaferTaxi, which was part of the second round of selected companies, received U.S. $1 million from a U.S. investor, and have since extended their company's operations from Chile to Brazil, Argentina, and the U.K. The first batches of foreign startups have raised so far a total $8 million in venture capital financing from firms in Argentina, Brazil, France, the U.S. and Uruguay.

Source: Adapted from the "Policy Dialogue on Entrepreneurship." Retrieved from *http://www.entrepreneurship.org/en/Blogs/Policy-Forum-Blog/2012/April/Start-Up-Chiles-Global-Footprint.aspx* (Accessed April 23, 2012). Reprinted with permission.

■ SALES PROJECTIONS AND WHAT-IF SCENARIOS

The financial community wants to make sure that you spend time researching your projections, because sales drive everything else. You also want to minimize surprises—even "good surprises" can wreak havoc with a well-thought-out plan if, for example, you receive ten times the orders you expected and simply do not yet have the resources to deal with them.

You have already conducted an industry overview. You may have identified total sales internationally, nationally, statewide, and in your service area. After factoring industry and local growth, determine which part of the market you can reasonably expect to penetrate in the first, second, and third years.

For your Business Plan, attach any appropriate printed data to your market research section in the appendix to prove and support your sales numbers. Fine-tune these numbers by showing your own research and including notes from industry experts that support your assumptions on projected sales. Every number you present in your Business Plan should have back-up support and be justified. When you list your competitors, estimate their market share and the part of their market that you have targeted. Projections are well-documented estimates. A third party's estimate will hold a great deal of weight for your reader, so quote as many sources as you can to support your numbers.

Lucy's projections in Figure 8.4 are based on past retail experience and research. Advertising and marketing expenses in this example are low due to the unique airport location. Rent is 22 percent of gross sales—with minimal marketing costs and a captive market, this expense is understandable. Salaries and payroll expenses are included. The owner, who will take a salary, will manage the store. If she did not take a salary, she would be putting in "sweat equity." Pay attention to the way notes have been added to Lucy's projections to explain the numbers. Be sure you do the same on your projections, and be able to support and defend the notes to lenders and investors.

When projecting sales, you may want to consider doing high, low, and medium sales projections. This will allow you to make plans for your expenses and revenues based on various scenarios. With Lucy's' sales projections in hand, the owner could now begin to look at what-if scenarios. What if salaries increased by 10 percent? What if rent could be reduced by 2 percent? What if workers' compensation and other insurances increased by 3 percent? What if cost of goods sold increased by 5 percent due to increased freight charges?

During your research, you have discovered many potential financial surprises, and playing these out on paper may give you some idea of the financial impact changes and surprises could have on your bottom line.

■ INCOME STATEMENT AND CASH-FLOW PROJECTIONS

An income statement (Figure 8.5) demonstrates on paper when you are going to make a profit. Figure 8.6 graphically represents a cash-flow diagram and shows infusions of capital, sales, and the outflows of cash as well.

A cash-flow projection (Figure 8.7) shows whether you can pay bills and when you will need cash infusions to keep going. Both of these projections are essential to the survival of your business. Some worksheets include both on one statement. For your Business Plan, you will be required to present monthly income statements for the first year and yearly statements for the next three to four years. Cash-flow statements should also be projected on the same basis.

Income statements (see Figure 8.5) track revenue and expenses but do not tell the whole story. Even a documentary movie can only be shot from one angle at a time. Action Step 41 leads you through a monthly projected income statement. In addition, be sure to include projected cash-flow scenarios in your Business Plan. It is nice to watch paper profits, but be alert to what is happening to your real cash. Figure 8.6 shows the typical pattern of cash flows.

Projections involve more than just sales. You also need to project the turnaround time for collections and other time lags so you can have a feel for the way cash will flow through your business. You need to discover all expense categories involved with your business to be able to make proper projections. Forecasting your income and cash flow is like projecting a moving picture of your business. If you are careful in how you prepare your numbers, that movie will be reasonably accurate.

© Cengage Learning

figure 8.4 — Lucy's Income and Expense Projections for Various Sales Levels

Upscale Specialty Women's Boutique

Category	$50,000/mo Amount	% of Gross	$60,000/mo Amount	% of Gross	$70,000/mo Amount	% of Gross	$80,000/mo Amount	% of Gross	$90,000/mo Amount	% of Gross
Gross Sales	$600,000.00		$720,000.00		$840,000.00		$960,000.00		$1,080,000.00	
Cost of Goods	$240,000.00	40%	$288,000.00	40%	$336,000.00	40%	$384,000.00	40%	$388,800.00	36%
Gross Profit	$360,000.00	60%	$432,000.00	60%	$504,000.00	60%	$576,000.00	60%	$691,200.00	64%
Operating Expenses:										
*Salaries/Benefits/Payroll Taxes	$108,000.00	18.0%	$129,600.00	18.0%	$151,200.00	18.0%	$172,800.00	18.0%	$194,400.00	18.0%
Telephone/Pagers	$900.00		$900.00		$900.00		$900.00		$900.00	
Maintenance/Cleaning/Supplies	$600.00	0.1%	$720.00	0.1%	$840.00	0.1%	$960.00	0.1%	$1,080.00	0.1%
Insurance including Worker's Comp	$24,000.00	4.0%	$24,480.00	3.4%	$25,200.00	3.0%	$26,880.00	2.8%	$29,160.00	2.7%
**Advertising	$3,200.00	0.5%	$3,440.00	0.5%	$3,680.00	0.4%	$3,920.00	0.4%	$4,160.00	0.4%
Internet/Computer Services	$900.00		$900.00		$900.00		$900.00		$900.00	
***Rent	$132,000.00	22.0%	$158,400.00	22.0%	$184,800.00	22.0%	$211,200.00	22.0%	$237,600.00	22.0%
General and Administration	$60,000.00	10.0%	$72,000.00	10.0%	$84,000.00	10.0%	$96,000.00	10.0%	$108,000.00	10.0%
Operating Supplies	$4,200.00	0.7%	$5,040.00	0.7%	$5,880.00	0.7%	$6,720.00	0.7%	$7,560.00	0.7%
Banking/Merchant Services	$7,200.00	1.2%	$8,640.00	1.2%	$10,080.00	1.2%	$11,520.00	1.2%	$12,960.00	1.2%
Store Displays	$1,800.00		$1,800.00		$1,800.00		$1,800.00		$1,800.00	
Other Misc. Expenses	$1,800.00	0.3%	$2,160.00	0.3%	$2,520.00	0.3%	$2,880.00	0.3%	$3,240.00	0.3%
Total Expenses	$344,600.00	56.8%	$408,080.00	56.7%	$471,800.00	55.7%	$536,480.00	55.5%	$601,760.00	55.7%
Net Income Before Taxes	$15,400.00	2.6%	$23,920.00	3.3%	$32,200.00	3.8%	$39,520.00	4.1%	$89,440.00	8.3%

*Salaries include owner salary.
**Advertising minimal due to airport location.
***Rent based on 22% of gross sales.

figure **8.5**

Casey's Auto Restoration Monthly Income Statement

Profit and Loss YTD Comparison

	July	% of Income	August	% of Income	September	% of Income	October	% of Income	November	% of Income	December	% of Income	Jan.-Dec.	% of Income
Ordinary Income/Expense														
Income														
EPA Fees	37.54	0.2%	29.50	0.1%	41.50	0.1%	26.46	0.1%	27.70	0.1%	32.50	0.1%	358.82	0.1%
Labor	12,952.70	51.9%	13,474.10	42.9%	19,135.60	51.8%	11,543.70	50.2%	10,817.10	57.9%	20,062.41	39.6%	164,322.43	46.0%
Paint and Materials	2,312.00	9.3%	2,871.20	9.2%	3,820.80	10.3%	2,710.20	11.8%	2,451.50	13.1%	3,847.35	7.6%	35,018.95	9.8%
Parts	8,405.35	33.7%	12,729.12	40.6%	12,259.07	33.2%	7,589.52	33.0%	5,102.55	27.3%	23,705.18	46.8%	141,726.85	39.7%
Storage and Towing Fees	386.00	1.5%	558.00	1.8%	0.00	0.0%	283.00	1.1%	0.00	0.0%	252.00	0.5%	2,490.00	0.7%
Sublet Labor	842.00	3.4%	1,717.00	5.5%	1,669.60	4.5%	879.00	3.8%	273.00	1.5%	2,781.78	5.5%	13,170.12	3.7%
Total Income Expense	24,935.59	100.0%	31,378.92	100.0%	36,926.57	100.0%	23,011.88	100.0%	18,671.85	100.0%	0,681.22	100.0%	357,087.17	100.0%
Advertising	231.00	0.9%	20.00	0.1%	125.00	0.3%	0.00	0.0%	60.00	0.3%	0.00	0.0%	496.00	0.1%
Automobile Expense	88.74	0.4%	141.45	0.5%	88.92	0.2%	125.90	0.5%	166.27	0.9%	174.72	0.3%	910.46	0.3%
Bad Debts	0.00	0.0%	0.00	0.0%	199.16	0.5%	0.00	0.0%	0.00	0.0%	757.68	1.5%	984.84	0.3%
Bank Service Charges	73.85	0.3%	82.68	0.3%	82.28	0.2%	119.81	0.5%	119.92	0.6%	77.15	0.2%	1,466.37	0.4%
Cost of Sales														
Paint	1,826.36	7.3%	1,731.68	5.5%	1,317.84	3.6%	1,067.88	4.6%	1,881.73	10.1%	2,016.98	4.0%	21,094.92	5.9%
Parts	9,248.52	37.1%	10,133.31	32.3%	4,557.14	12.3%	5,052.40	22.0%	8,428.09	45.1%	9,096.16	17.9%	107,068.30	30.0%
Sublet	3,743.69	15.0%	4,949.78	15.8%	5,280.50	14.3%	3,387.50	14.7%	6,504.95	34.8%	6,461.69	12.7%	58,992.54	16.5%
Towing	361.00	1.4%	30.00	0.1%	376.00	1.0%	252.00	1.1%	252.00	0.5%	271.00	0.5%	1,718.00	0.5%
Total Cost of Sales	15,179.57	60.9%	16,844.77	53.7%	11,531.48	31.2%	9,759.78	42.4%	16,814.77	90.1%	17,845.83	35.2%	188,873.76	52.9%
DMV Renewal	0.00	0.0%	0.00	0.0%	0.00	0.0%	0.00	0.0%	0.00	0.0%	0.00	0.0%	49.00	0.0%
Dues and Subscriptions	0.00	0.0%	0.00	0.0%	88.70	0.2%	0.00	0.0%	80.00	0.4%	0.00	0.0%	257.40	0.1%
Equipment Lease	0.00	0.0%	700.00	2.2%	420.00	1.1%	0.00	0.0%	0.00	0.0%	0.00	0.0%	6,020.00	1.7%
Insurance														
Fire	130.00	0.5%	130.00	0.4%	0.00	0.0%	0.00	0.0%	0.00	0.0%	0.00	0.0%	260.00	0.1%
Health	0.00	0.0%	0.00	0.0%	0.00	0.0%	0.00	0.0%	69.00	0.4%	0.00	0.0%	256.00	0.1%
Liability Insurance	210.00	0.8%	0.00	0.0%	0.00	0.0%	0.00	0.0%	253.00	1.4%	0.00	0.0%	673.00	0.2%
Other	0.00	0.0%	130.00	0.4%	0.00	0.0%	0.00	0.0%	0.00	0.0%	0.00	0.0%	130.00	0.0%
Total Insurance	340.00	1.4%	260.00	0.8%	0.00	0.0%	0.00	0.0%	322.00	1.7%	0.00	0.0%	1,319.00	0.4%
Interest Expense														
Finance Charge	0.00	0.0%	0.00	0.0%	0.00	0.0%	0.00	0.0%	325.12	1.7%	110.46	0.2%	1,015.59	0.3%
Other	0.00	0.0%	717.81	2.3%	125.00	0.3%	125.00	0.3%	0.00	0.0%	0.00	0.0%	842.81	0.2%
Total Interest Expense	0.00	0.0%	717.81	2.3%	125.00	0.3%	125.00	0.3%	325.12	1.7%	110.46	0.2%	1,858.40	0.5%
Licenses and Permits	0.00	0.0%	0.00	0.0%	290.00	0.8%	0.00	0.0%	0.00	0.0%	478.54	0.9%	1,584.25	0.4%
Miscellaneous	0.00	0.0%	0.00	0.0%	0.00	0.0%	0.00	0.0%	0.00	0.0%	1,000.00	2.0%	1,000.00	0.3%
Office Supplies	293.83	1.2%	123.86	0.4%	238.72	0.6%	41.20	0.2%	152.33	0.8%	37.00	0.1%	2,932.67	0.8%
Payroll Expenses	3,056.88	12.3%	2,971.14	9.5%	2,712.78	7.3%	2,841.96	12.3%	3,200.20	17.1%	2,712.78	5.4%	33,332.39	9.3%

(continued)

figure 8.5

Casey's Auto Restoration Monthly Income Statement (continued)

Profit and Loss YTD Comparison

	July	% of Income	August	% of Income	September	% of Income	October	% of Income	November	% of Income	December	% of Income	Jan.-Dec.	% of Income
Professional Fees														
Accounting	0.00	0.0%	0.00	0.0%	0.00	0.0%	0.00	0.0%	0.00	0.0%	0.00	0.0%	350.00	0.1%
Environmental	0.00	0.0%	0.00	0.0%	0.00	0.0%	0.00	0.0%	0.00	0.0%	0.00	0.0%	204.01	0.1%
Total Professional Fees	0.00	0.0%	0.00	0.0%	0.00	0.0%	0.00	0.0%	0.00	0.0%	0.00	0.0%	554.01	0.2%
Rent	2,625.00	10.5%	3,245.00	10.3%	5,260.00	14.2%	0.00	0.0%	2,755.00	14.8%	5,384.50	10.6%	33,811.15	9.5%
Repairs														
Equipment Repairs	0.00	0.0%	0.00	0.0%	0.00	0.0%	0.00	0.0%	0.00	0.0%	0.00	0.0%	340.00	0.1%
Total Repairs	0.00	0.0%	0.00	0.0%	0.00	0.0%	0.00	0.0%	0.00	0.0%	0.00	0.0%	340.00	0.1%
Supplies														
Office	42.52	0.2%	45.40	0.1%	59.00	0.2%	718.20	3.1%	502.11	2.7%	268.26	0.5%	7,139.15	2.0%
Shop	484.56	1.9%	500.57	1.6%	550.02	1.5%	0.00	0.0%	73.80	0.4%	152.97	0.3%	531.73	0.1%
Tools	0.00	0.0%	0.00	0.0%	0.00	0.0%	718.20	3.1%	428.31	2.3%	115.29	0.2%	6,555.32	1.8%
Total Supplies	527.08	2.1%	545.97	1.7%	609.02	1.6%	0.00	0.0%	0.00	0.0%	0.00	0.0%	52.10	0.0%
Taxes														
Property	1,048.30	4.2%	32.14	0.1%	877.20	2.4%	0.00	0.0%	0.00	0.0%	0.00	0.0%	1,957.64	0.5%
Total Taxes	1,048.30	4.2%	32.14	0.1%	877.20	2.4%	0.00	0.0%	0.00	0.0	0.00	0.0%	1,957.64	0.5%
Telephone	0.00	0.0%	549.43	1.8%	118.02	0.3%	282.78	1.2%	272.34	1.5%	359.32	0.7%	3,669.02	1.0%
Utilities														
Cable	43.19	0.2%	43.19	0.1%	43.19	0.1%	43.19	0.2%	43.19	0.2%	43.19	0.1%	414.38	0.1%
Gas and Electric	343.99	1.4%	310.70	1.0%	312.19	0.8%	100.11	0.4%	297.42	1.6%	292.97	0.6%	3,215.74	0.9%
Trash	140.53	0.6%	101.62	0.3%	0.00	0.0%	203.24	0.9%	101.62	0.5%	101.62	0.2%	1,273.41	0.4%
Water	53.95	0.2%	51.39	0.2%	54.19	0.1%	57.27	0.2%	0.00	0.0%	112.26	0.2%	462.90	0.1%
Total Utilities	581.66	2.3%	506.90	1.6%	409.57	1.1%	403.81	1.8%	442.23	2.4%	550.04	1.1%	5,366.43	1.5%
Total Expense	24,045.91	96.4%	26,741.15	85.2%	23,175.85	62.8%	14,293.44	62.1%	25,212.29	135.0%	29,756.28	58.7%	293,921.94	82.3%
Net Ordinary Income	889.68	3.6%	4,637.77	14.8%	13,750.72	37.2%	8,718.44	37.9%	-6,540.44	-35.0%	20,924.94	41.3%	63,165.23	17.7%
Other Income/Expense														
Other Income														
Interest Income	0.82	0.0%	1.40	0.0%	0.91	0.0%	0.33	0.0%	0.66	0.0%	1.40	0.0%	9.94	0.0%
Total Other Income	0.82	0.0%	1.40	0.0%	0.91	0.0%	0.33	0.0%	0.66	0.0%	1.40	0.0%	9.94	0.0%
Net Other Income	0.82	0.0%	1.40	0.0%	0.91	0.0%	0.33	0.0%	0.66	0.0%	1.40	0.0%	9.94	0.0%
Net Income Before Taxes	890.50	3.6%	4,639.17	14.8%	13,751.63	37.2%	8,718.77	37.9%	-6,539.78	-35.0%	20,926.34	41.3%	63,175.17	17.7%

© Cengage Learning

figure **8.6**

Cash Flow

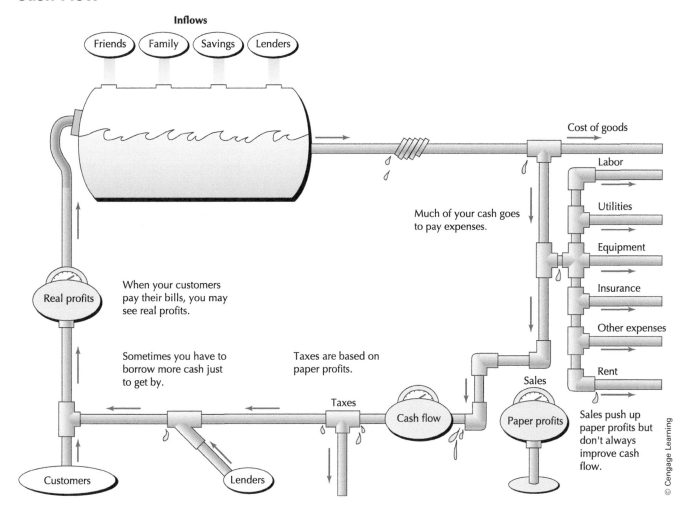

Cash-flow projections are a tool used to help you control money. The life-blood of any business is cash flow, and many businesses are profitable but fail because of cash-flow problems. Without completing pro forma cash flows, entrepreneurs can easily underestimate their cash needs and fail early on. Tim Berry, President of Palo Alto Software, provides the following hard and fast cash-flow rules:

10 Critical Cash Flow Rules

Protect your business from a common cause of failure by following these cash management tips.

Cash flow problems can kill businesses that might otherwise survive. According to a U.S. Bank study, 82 percent of business failures are due to poor cash management. To prevent this from happening to your business, here are my 10 cash flow rules to remember.

1. **Profits aren't cash; they're accounting.** And accounting is a lot more creative than you think. You can't pay bills with profits. Actually profits can lull you to sleep. If you pay your bills and your customers don't, it's suddenly business hell. You can make profits without making any money.

2. **Cash flow isn't intuitive.** Don't try to do it in your head. Making the sales doesn't necessarily mean you have the money. Incurring the expense doesn't necessarily

figure **8.7**

R & J Enterprises' Statement of Cash Flow

For the Years Ended December 31, 2012, 2013, 2014

	2012	2013	2014
Cash Flows from Operating Activities:			
Cash Received from Customers	$1,665,361	$1,260,814	$782,750
Cash Paid to Suppliers and Employees	(1,374,758)	(1,059,580)	(659,112)
Interest Received	1,213	1,620	0
Income Taxes Paid	(6,050)	(1,500)	(800)
Interest Paid	(41,867)	(21,122)	(10,898)
Net Cash Provided by Operating Activities	243,899	180,232	111,940
Cash Flows from Investing Activities:			
Purchases of Property, Plant, and Equipment	(102,341)	(323,899)	(41,492)
Vehicle Lease Deposit	0	473	0
Purchase of South River Location	(21,400)	0	0
Small Business Administration Loan Costs	0	(5,577)	0
Net Cash Provided Used in Investing Activities	(123,741)	(329,003)	(41,492)
Cash Flows from Financing Activities:			
Bank of America Line of Credit	0	51,928	0
Payments on Bank of America Line of Credit	(569)	0	(3,523)
Loans from Members	0	100,000	0
Payments on Loans from Members	(20,032)	(14,595)	0
Loan for South River Location	10,000	0	0
Payments on Loan for South River Location	(4,350)	0	0
Small Business Administration Loans	0	100,000	0
Payments on Small Business Administration Loans	(34,399)	(19,666)	(17,470)
Equipment Lease Financing	42,518	40,516	15,741
Payments on Equipment Leases	(15,863)	(13,565)	(2,328)
Contributions by Members	31,400	69,100	37,023
Distributions to Members	(113,566)	(159,331)	(115,137)
Net Cash Provided by Financing Activities	(104,861)	154,387	(85,694)
Net Increase (Decrease) in Cash and Cash Equivalent	15,297	5,616	(15,246)
Cash and Cash Equivalents at Beginning of Year	31,317	25,701	40,947
Cash and Cash Equivalents at End of Year	**$46,614**	**$31,317**	**$25,701**
Reconciliation of Net Income to Net Cash Provided by Operating Activities:			
Net Income	$139,565	$95,362	$75,882
Adjustments to Reconcile Net Income to Net Cash Provided by Operating Activities:			
Depreciation and Amortization	79,282	54,682	33,535
(Increase) Decrease in Inventory	5,688	(48,863)	(2,096)
Decrease in Interest Receivable	0	0	1,698
(Increase) in Deposits	(9,990)	(650)	(3,789)
(Increase) in Prepaid Interest	(4,563)	(11,891)	(2,298)
Increase in Accounts Payable	28,375	79,263	6,903
Increase in Wages Payable	2,979	6,404	497
Increase in Accrued Taxes Payable	2,563	5,925	1,608
Net Cash Provided by Operating Activities	**$243,899**	**$180,232**	**$111,940**

© Cengage Learning

mean you paid for it already. Inventory is usually bought and paid for and then stored until it becomes cost of sales.

3. **Growth sucks up cash.** It's paradoxical. The best of times can be hiding the worst of times. One of the toughest years my company had was when we doubled sales and almost went broke. We were building things two months in advance and getting the money from sales six months late. Add growth to that and it can be like a Trojan horse, hiding a problem inside a solution. Yes, of course you want to grow; we all want to grow our businesses. But be careful because growth costs cash. It's a matter of working capital. The faster you grow, the more financing you need.

4. **Business-to-business sales suck up your cash.** The simple view is that sales mean money, but when you're a business selling to another business, it's rarely that simple. You deliver the goods or services along with an invoice, and they pay the invoice

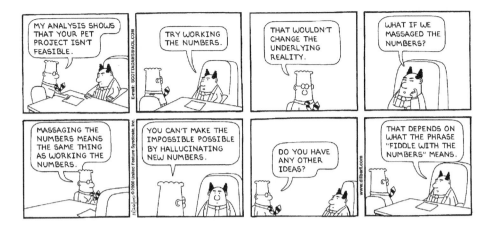

Source: Dilbert © Scott Adams/UNIVERSAL UCLICK.

later. Usually that's months later. And businesses are good customers, so you can't just throw them into collections because then they'll never buy from you again. So you wait. When you sell something to a distributor that sells it to a retailer, you typically get the money four or five months later if you're lucky.

5. **Inventory sucks up cash.** You have to buy your product or build it before you can sell it. Even if you put the product on your shelves and wait to sell it, your suppliers expect to get paid. Here's a simple rule of thumb: Every dollar you have in inventory is a dollar you don't have in cash.

6. **Working capital is your best survival skill.** Technically, working capital is an accounting term for what's left over when you subtract current liabilities from current assets. Practically, it's money in the bank that you use to pay your running costs and expenses and buy inventory while waiting to get paid by your business customers.

7. **"Receivables" is a four-letter word.** (See rule 4.) The money your customers owe you is called "accounts receivable." Here's a shortcut to cash planning: Every dollar in accounts receivable is a dollar less cash.

8. **Bankers hate surprises.** Plan ahead. You get no extra points for spontaneity when dealing with banks. If you see a growth spurt coming, a new product opportunity or a problem with customers paying, the sooner you get to the bank armed with charts and a realistic plan, the better off you'll be.

9. **Watch these three vital metrics:** "Collection days" is a measure of how long you wait to get paid. "Inventory turnover" is a measure of how long your inventory sits on your working capital and clogs your cash flow. "Payment days" is how long you wait to pay your vendors. Always monitor these three vital signs of cash flow. Project them 12 months ahead and compare your plan to what actually happens.

10. **If you're the exception rather than the rule, hooray for you.** If all your customers pay you immediately when they buy from you, and you don't buy things before you sell them, then relax. But if you sell to businesses, keep in mind that they usually don't pay immediately.

By: Tim Berry the president of Palo Alto Software Inc., based in Eugene, Ore., which produces business planning software. He is also the author of *3 Weeks to Startup* and *The Plan-As-You-Go Business Plan*, published by Entrepreneur Press.

Source: Tim Berry, "10 Critical Cash Flow Rules," Entrepreneur Media, 30 November 2007. Copyright © 2012 Entrepreneur Media, Inc. 1212:SH

Review Lucy's (Figure 8,4), Casey's (Figure 8.5), and R&J Enterprises' (Figure 8.7) projections. What would you recommend to these entrepreneurs? Could the owners increase sales dramatically to improve cash flow and income? Reduce expenses? If so, which expenses? To increase cash flow, look beyond the initial product or service and possibly extend your facilities and products. Signal Physical Therapy leases space at lunch time to a Pilates instructor thus bringing in additional revenue in an otherwise down time to increase cash flow. If needed, she could also lease space on the weekends to a yoga instructor for workshops. Be creative.

Are you willing to put in sweat equity? Are your projections realistic? Will you be able to forgo taking a salary for a few months if serious cash-flow problems occur? When you have completed your projections, show the results to an expert, and ask if they look accurate. It is better to know the truth now, while you are working on paper; paper truth is a lot easier than reality on the wallet.

■ BALANCE SHEET

Balance sheet Financial snapshot of assets, liabilities, and equity

A balance sheet is a picture of what your business owns and owes. Three categories make up a balance sheet: *assets* (anything of monetary value your business owns) minus *liabilities* (money owed to creditors) equals *net worth* (owner's equity).

Figure 8.8, Casey's Auto Restoration's Balance Sheet, shows his current financial picture. As your business continues to prosper, the net worth should increase substantially. Any of these numbers that are not in sync with industry standards should be addressed in footnotes on the balance sheet. Thus if a business has high accounts receivables, but the owner knows the major account will be paid within 20 days, and payment is late due to flooding and loss of records, it should be noted.

Account receivable Money owed to a firm

Comparing your own balance sheet over time and also comparing it with others in your industry will provide you with a fairly good thermometer reading. In addition, check the relevant financial ratios discussed later in the chapter regularly to assess your firm's financial standing and solvency.

figure 8.8

Casey's Auto Restoration's Balance Sheet

As of December 31, 2012

Assets	
Current Assets	
Cash	5,000
Accounts Receivable	$10,000
Less: Allowance for bad debts of	$300
Net Accounts Receivable	9,700
Inventory	40,000
Prepaid Expenses	1,000
Total Current Assets	55,700
Fixed Assets	
Land	50,000
Buildings and Equipment	$600,000 (at cost)
Less Accumulated Depreciation of $300,000	(300,000)
Notes Receivable	1,000
Other Assets	4,000
Total Fixed Assets	355,000
Total Assets	$410,700
Liabilities	
Current Liabilities	
Accounts Payable	5,000
Accrued Expenses	2,000
Note Payable—Equipment	30,000
Total Current Liabilities	$37,000
Long-Term Liabilities	
Building Loan	270,000
Total Long-Term Liabilities	270,000
Total Liabilities	$307,000
Equity	
Owner's Equity	$103,700
Total Liabilities and Equity	$410,700

© Cengage Learning

■ BREAK-EVEN ANALYSIS

Knowing a few key numbers will help you avoid painful surprises. If you know your estimated costs (variable and fixed) and gross sales, use a break-even formula that will tell when you will start making money. A break-even analysis is particularly useful at 1) start-up time, 2) when you have completed your income and expense projections, and 3) when you are considering launching a new product or service (Figure 8.9). As your costs change throughout production, reworking these numbers at all times is essential.

Notole Figures Surprise Owners

A small manufacturing company was completing a plan for its second year of operation. Its first-year sales were $177,000, and a sales breakdown for the last 3 months of their first year looked like this:

── figure **8.9**

Notole Break-Even Analysis

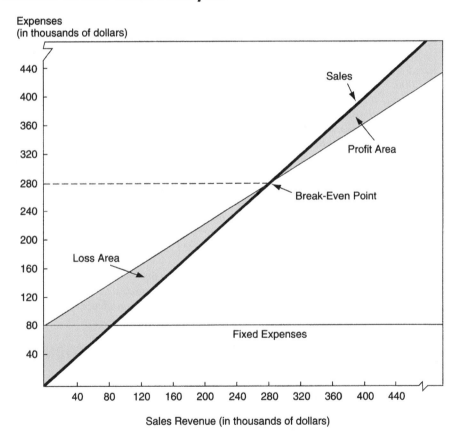

Projected sales:	$562,000
Projected fixed expenses:	$82,750
Projected variable expenses:	$392,000

$$\text{Total sales needed to break even:} \quad \frac{\text{Fixed}}{\text{Expenses}} \div \left(1 - \frac{\text{Variable expenses}}{\text{Sales}}\right)$$

$$\$83,000 \div \left(1 - \frac{\$392,000}{\$562,000}\right)$$

$$\$83,000 \div (1 - .6975)$$

$$\$83,000 \div .3025$$

$$\$274,380$$

Break-even range: $270,000 to $280,000

© Cengage Learning

October	$15,000
November	24,000
December	29,000
Total	$68,000

The owners took a look at the numbers and called in a consultant to help. The consultant gathered information from sales reps, owners, and customers, and then projected that sales for the second year would be a whopping $562,000. The owners reacted with disbelief.

"You're crazy," they said. "That is more than three times what we did last year."

The consultant smiled. "Didn't you tell me you were going to add three new products, and new reps in March, June, and September?"

"Yes, but—"

"And what about those big promotions you've got planned?"

"Well, sure, we've planned some promotions, but that doesn't get us anywhere near three times last year."

"All right," the consultant said. "Can you do $275,000?"

The owners got into a huddle. Based on the fourth quarter, they were sure they could stay even, and four times $68,000 (the fourth-quarter sales) was $272,000. They knew they had to do better than last year.

"Sure, no problem. We can do $275,000."

"All right," said the consultant, rolling out his break-even chart. "I've just projected $562,000 in sales for the year. To break even, you only need about $ 275,000."

"Hey," the owners said, "we're projecting $90,000 the first quarter."

"I'm glad you're thinking my way," the consultant said. "Because if you do not believe you can reach a goal, you will never get there."

"Just tell us what to do," the owners said.

Based on a careful cash-flow analysis, the consultant determined that the company would need to borrow money. The owners knew their business—industry trends, product line, competitors, sales, and promotion plans—but what banker would believe such growth? The key to getting the loan would be to convince the banker that the company could do better than break even. The consultant prepared a break-even chart on the $562,000 sales figure (see Figure 8.9). Note in the chart that after $275,000 in sales, the firm will have passed its break-even point and will be earning a profit.

Their banker granted the loan, realizing the company could pass the break-even point with room to spare. The key, as is usual in business, was a combination of numbers and facts to support them along with the owner's confidence.

■ LEAVING A PAPER TRAIL AND SOFTWARE APPLICATIONS

If you are a typical entrepreneur, you are not real big on details, and you are very busy; nonetheless, you know it is important to keep good records. A good starting point is to download *Starting a Business and Keeping Records*, IRS Publication 583. Your records need to be thorough and complete so that your accountant can take full advantage of all tax deductions and complete your tax records and financial statements.

Many beginning entrepreneurs commingle their business accounts with their personal accounts. This is bad business practice and is frowned upon by the IRS. An accounting software package, separate checking accounts, and your own efforts will alleviate this problem.

Be sure to track expenses thoroughly, and keep all receipts for as long as your accountant tells you to. Limit any petty cash expenditures so that you know where the money is flowing.

At the very start of the process of opening your business, purchase a computer and track your financial activity using one of the major accounting programs provided by QuickBooks, Peachtree, or Microsoft Money. In addition to these, many programs are now available online with tracking for free or at a very low monthly cost.

These programs will 1) track your expenses and income 2) help you reconcile your bank accounts 3) help you manage payroll and invoices 4) help you manage inventory 5) help you manage customer reports and 6) help you develop proposals. In addition, all financial statements required by lenders will be at your fingertips at all times. If you decide to have an open book management philosophy such as IRMCO, highlighted in Key Points, your numbers will be easy to share as well. Also, with good up-to-date records at hand, you will also be able to substantiate your asking price if someday you decide to sell.

When preparing cash-flow and income statements, software allows you to play with what-if scenarios easily. With several scenarios in hand, meet with your accountant and financial advisor to gather feedback. In addition, costing out your products and services and determining pricing will be much easier with software that allows you to see alternatives side by side for easy comparison. Also, if you are in a volatile commodity-pricing situation, having ready access to software for pricing scenarios is a must.

Your software should include word processing, spreadsheet, database management, accounting and bookkeeping, and website development programs. Many of these programs can be purchased as an integrated office suite. In addition, you may want to purchase software recommended by your association that is already adapted to your particular industry needs. Or, you can choose to hire a software consultant to customize an off-the-shelf package to meet your needs. If you operate your business solely on the Internet, additional specialized and custom software is available for managing and tracking. As your firm grows, additional productivity software may be required.

Even with accounting software, consider hiring a bookkeeper familiar with your software to assist you. Expect to hire a bookkeeper for 8 to 20 hours a month for a small business with revenue of less than $750,000. Please note that even if bookkeepers and accountants manage your firm's accounts, *you* remain responsible for the money flowing through your firm. If you have little knowledge of numbers, enroll in a basic accounting class so that you can follow the cash flow and understand the financial statements.

You need to track your finances daily and be aware of your daily cash balances. One accountant shared, "My client consistently overdrew his account at the cost of $300 a day, which was actually his projected daily profit!" Obviously doing this for just a few days a month would severely affect your cash flow and profitability.

Timely monthly closings allow your bookkeeper or yourself to easily prepare quarterly tax payments. Thus, keeping you compliant with tax regulations and escaping any late fees.

Always remember, cash is king and you are the one responsible for the numbers! Read and heed the advice in Karen Berman and Joe Knight's, *Financial Intelligence for Entrepreneurs*, so you can be the king of your numbers!

■ FINANCIAL RATIOS

Calculating a few simple ratios will help you analyze how your venture compares with other businesses in your selected industry. Lenders use ratios as measuring devices to determine the risks associated with lending. Again, use BizStats and other secondary sources to determine industry ratios. To the entrepreneur, ratios are control tools for maintaining financial efficiency and hopefully staying afloat.

Current Ratio

Does the business have enough money to meet current debt? Have you anticipated a safety margin for losses resulting from uncollectible funds owed to the business? Most start-up ventures are undercapitalized. The current ratio is computed from the balance sheet. Divide current assets by current liabilities. If current assets are $200,000 and current liabilities are $100,000, you have a current ratio of two. Many lenders see this as a minimum, and they like to see that you have at least twice as much invested as you owe. The current ratio is the most widely used method to determine the financial health of a business.

Quick (Liquidity) Ratio

The quick ratio tells you if you have cash on hand or assets that can be converted into cash quickly to pay your debts. The more liquidity, the better. An untapped credit line will help beef up your liquidity.

Return on Investment

Return on investment (ROI) is the favorite tool of investors and venture capitalists. This ratio shows the return expressed as a percentage of their financial investment. Investors and entrepreneurs want the highest return, or profit, for the least amount of money invested. Additional financial ratios are shown in Figure 8.10.

■ SUMMARY

Not surprisingly, many entrepreneurs find it difficult to project numbers for their businesses. There are several explanations for this:

- They are action people who are in a hurry; they do not think they have time to sit down and make projections.
- They are creative; their strengths are greater in the innovation area than in the justification area.
- They tend to think in visual terms rather than in numbers.
- They believe they cannot fail.

Business is a numbers game, and despite an entrepreneur's feelings about numbers and projections, survival in the marketplace depends on having the right numbers in the right color of ink. This chapter, and your past and future research, should smooth the way for you to work with the numbers you need to move forward.

The point behind projecting numbers is to make the numbers as realistic as possible. You need to relate each projection to your specific business and to industry standards and then to *document* them in your Business Plan. The case studies and examples in this chapter demonstrate how to make your projections believable to your banker and to yourself. Your numbers may seem reasonable to you, but you must make them seem reasonable to others as well. Make them believable by keeping them realistic and by documenting them properly.

What you do not need during the start-up phase is expensive surprises that knock you and your business for a loop. Before opening your doors, anticipate as many potential unpleasant surprises as possible, and have a plan of action for each one of them. For example, what will you do if:

- Your anchor tenant leaves?
- Your website is ineffective?
- The customer who accounts for 75 percent of your business declares bankruptcy?

figure **8.10**

Financial Ratios

Ratio Name	How to Calculate	What It Means in Dollars and Cents
Balance Sheet Ratios		
Current	$$\frac{\text{Current Assets}}{\text{Current Liabilities}}$$	Measures solvency: the number of dollars in current assets for every $1 in current liabilities *Example:* A current ratio of 1.76 means that for every $1 of current liabilities, the firm has $1.76 in current assets with which to pay it.
Quick	$$\frac{\text{Cash + Accounts Receivable}}{\text{Current Liabilities}}$$	Measures liquidity: the number of dollars in cash and accounts receivable for each $1 in current liabilities *Example:* A quick ratio of 1.14 means that for every $1 of current liabilities, the firm has $1.14 in cash and accounts receivable with which to pay it.
Cash	$$\frac{\text{Cash}}{\text{Current Liabilities}}$$	Measures liquidity more strictly: the number of dollars in cash for every $1 in current liabilities *Example:* A cash ratio of 0.17 means that for every $1 of current liabilities, the firm has $0.17 in cash with which to pay it.
Debt-to-worth	$$\frac{\text{Total Liabilities}}{\text{Net Worth}}$$	Measures financial risk: the number of dollars of debt owed for every $1 in net worth *Example:* A debt-to-worth ratio of 1.05 means that for every $1 of net worth the owners have invested, the firms owes $1.05 of debt to its creditors.
Income Statement Ratios		
Gross margin	$$\frac{\text{Gross Margin}}{\text{Sales}}$$	Measures profitability at the gross profit level: the number of dollars of gross margin produced for every $1 of sales *Example:* A gross margin ratio of 34.4% means that for every $1 of sales, the firm produces 34.4 cents of gross margin
Net margin	$$\frac{\text{Net Profit before Tax}}{\text{Sales}}$$	Measures profitability at the net profit level: the number of dollars of net profit produced for every $1 of sales *Example:* A net margin ratio of 2.9% means that for very $1 of sales, the firm produces 2.9 cents of net margin.
Overall Efficiency Ratios		
Sales-to-assets	$$\frac{\text{Sales}}{\text{Total Assests}}$$	Measures the efficiency of total assets in generating sales: the number of dollars in sales produced for every $1 invested in total assets *Example:* A sales-to-assets ratio of 2.35 means that for every $1 dollar invested in total assets, the firm generates $2.35 in sales.
Return on assets	$$\frac{\text{Net Profit before Tax}}{\text{Total Assests}}$$	Measures the efficiency of total assets in generating net profit: the number of dollars in net profit produced for every $1 invested in total assets *Example:* A return on assets ratio of 7.1% means that for every $1 invested in assets, the firm is generating 7.1 cents in net profit before tax.
Return on investment	$$\frac{\text{Net Profit before Tax}}{\text{Net Worth}}$$	Measures the efficiency of net worth in generating net profit: the number of dollars in net profit produced for every $1 invested in net worth *Example:* A return on investment ratio of 16.1% means that for very $1 invested in net worth, the firm is generating 16.1 cents in net profit before tax.
Specific Efficiency Ratios		
Inventory turnover	$$\frac{\text{Cost of Goods sold}}{\text{Inventory}}$$	Measures the rate at which inventory is being used on an annual basis *Example:* An inventory turnover ratio of 9.81 means that the average dollar volume of inventory is used up almost ten times during the fiscal year.
Inventory turn-days	$$\frac{360}{\text{Inventory Turnover}}$$	Converts the inventory turnover ratio into an average "days inventory on hand" figure *Example:* An inventory turn-days ratio of 37 means that the firm keeps an average of 37 days of inventory on hand throughout the year.

(continued)

figure **8.10**

Financial Ratios (continued)

Ratio Name	How to Calculate	What It Means in Dollars and Cents
Accounts receivable turnover	$$\frac{Sales}{Accounts\ Receivable}$$	Measures the rate at which accounts receivable are being collected on an annual basis *Example:* An accounts receivable turnover ratio of 8.00 means that the average dollar volume of accounts receivable are collected eight times during the year.
Average collection period	$$\frac{360}{Accounts\ Receivable\ Turnover}$$	Converts the accounts receivable turnover ratio into the average number of days the firm must wait for its accounts receivable to be paid *Example:* An average collection period ratio of 45 means that it takes the firm 45 days on average to collect its receivables.
Accounts payable turnover	$$\frac{Cost\ of\ Goods\ Sold}{Accounts\ Payable}$$	Measure the rate at which accounts payable are being paid on an annual basis. *Example:* An accounts payable turnover ratio of 12.04 means that the average dollar volume of accounts payable are paid about 123 a year.
Average payment period	$$\frac{360}{Accounts\ Payable\ Turnover}$$	Converts the accounts payable turnover ratio into the average number of days a firm takes to pay its accounts payable. *Example:* An accounts payable turnover ratio of 30 means that it takes the firm 30 days on average to pay its bills.

Source: From KURATKO, ENTREPRENEURSHIP 4E, 4E. © 1998 Cengage Learning.

Expecting and *planning for* the unknown may make the difference between the success and failure of your business. Looking at the future will help you eliminate some surprises, and it may even cause you to question whether you are truly ready to take the plunge. Remember: no one can anticipate everything, and your start-up will cost more than you expected and take longer than you planned.

■ THINK POINTS FOR SUCCESS

- It is cheaper and easier to make mistakes on a spreadsheet before you go into business.
- When you visit your banker to ask for money, make sure you know how much you are going to need for the long run.
- Projecting your numbers will help you gain understanding and control over the variables of your business—numbers, employees, promotion mix, product mix, and the peaks and valleys of seasonality.

- Purchase accounting software on day one.
- Cash flow is king.
- Remember marketing guru Seth Godin's advice, "The goal, no matter what you sell, is to be seen as *irreplaceable, essential,* and *priceless.* If you are all three, then you have pricing power."
- Walk away if the business is not going to work financially. There will always be other opportunities.

■ KEY POINTS FROM ANOTHER VIEW

Open-Book Management

The path to a winning workplace can begin in an unusual way. For an Evanston, Illinois-based manufacturing company, IRMCO, it started in the mid-1980s, when owner and CEO William O. Jeffery III was suffering from terminal cancer. Jeffery committed his final years to making IRMCO a better place for his employees and its products better for his industrial customers. He replaced the oil and animal-fat–based lubricants IRMCO had made for decades with more environmentally friendly, water-based products.

As Jeffery overhauled his company's product line, he also reshaped the way management dealt with employees. "He got extra focused on people," recalls his son and IRMCO's current CEO, William C. "Jeff" Jeffery, who runs the 22-employee company with his brother, Bradley. A key first step was to put in place what is now commonly referred to as "open book" management, in which all financial details, except payroll, are shared with employees on a regular basis.

Opening the books, especially with an employee profit-sharing plan in place, clears away any workers' feelings that the company is a piggybank for the owners. "Employees can see what is available for my brother and me to take out," says Jeff, who represents the fourth generation of family owners. "When they see during tough times that we aren't taking money out, they understand that we are all in this together. It helps create goodwill." General manager Jennifer Kalas, who worked at two other industrial companies before IRMCO, also notices something different. "People are aware of what's going on, the budget, where the money is being spent," she says. "People take ownership."

The culture of openness, trust, and cooperation has evolved under the Jeffery brothers through other programs. The brothers use the metaphor of the wolf pack—"the only perfect team in nature," says Jeff—to build teamwork and information sharing. Monthly "wolf pack" meetings with all employees provide a forum for business updates, question answering, and nominations for the "lone wolf" award for exceptional work. At the end of each quarter, the winner is drawn from a hat and presented with $250 of "wolf dough" that must be spent on some kind of celebration.

The teamwork idea extends to intradepartmental cross training, where a red book of job tasks and responsibilities is provided to—and is expected to be understood by—all employees. This flexibility has been an important asset in allowing IRMCO to operate through the good times and bad. As general manager, Kalas points out, "In the good times, we don't have to add more people, so that in the bad times, we don't have to lay them off."

In fact, times have been rough at IRMCO for more than a year, as the company is heavily dependent upon auto industry suppliers, which have been hit hard by the economy. IRMCO has adapted, however, supported by the undercurrent of employee–management goodwill.

The company has even managed to make money without having to resort to layoffs or the elimination of core programs. However, there is always a give and take. A salary freeze is in effect, and an open-ended tuition reimbursement program, which employees took advantage of to further their education and leave, has since been replaced. Now, IRMCO applies for state job-training grants to fund half of the tuition costs and is targeting specific skill improvements. Thus, the company is aligning itself more closely with the interests of its employees. Other programs have remained intact, such as a $250 wellness bonus for demonstrated improvement of mind or body.

While many of his customers are "getting crushed," Jeff leaves no doubt that there is a clear line connecting his company's relative success and its legacy of trust and support. "We are nimble and creative, with smart people communicating and working together." Sounds like a howl from a wolf pack.

Source: © 2006 Winning Workplaces, *http://www.winningworkplaces.org* (Accessed March 3, 2008).

■ ACTION STEPS

Action Step 38   Attach Price Tags to Starting Your Business *208*

Action Step 39   Preparing for Surprises *209*

Action Step 40   Discovering Costs and Developing a Fair Price *214*

Action Step 41   Complete Seasonality Scenario and a Projected Profit and Loss (Income) Statement *216*

■ KEY TERMS

burn rate *201*

bootstrap *202*

freemium pricing *202*

dynamic pricing *202*

trade credit or dating *206*

on-site improvements *208*

dead goods *208*

liquid cash *208*

entrepreneurial gurus *208*

markups *210*

competitor-based pricing or market-based pricing *211*

cost-plus pricing or profit-based pricing *211*

keystone pricing *212*

Premium pricing *212*

Penetration pricing *213*

Price skimming *213*

balance sheet *226*

accounts receivables *226*

Image_Source/iStockphoto.com

Shaking the Money Tree
Locating Hard Cash

Learning Objectives

- Discover your risk tolerance.

- Determine your credit situation.

- Explore credit card usage and risks for your business.

- Understand inherent risks in borrowing from friends and family.

- Scour the lending arena for money to fund your new business.

- Introduce strategies for approaching bankers.

- Become familiar with the programs and services of Small Business Administration (SBA) and Small Business Development Centers (SBDCs).

- Explore vendor financing.

- Understand the dynamics of crowdfunding.

- Learn how to access angel financing.

- Explore the venture capital market and the changes occurring within.

Would it sound too easy if we told you to go out and simply shake a money tree to secure financing for your business? Yes! You know it will *not* be that easy. First you must become familiar with the world of money. Then you need to discover the financial resources you personally have. Finally, you must discover the pros and cons of each money branch (see Figure 9.1). Once you have accomplished these things, you might be surprised at how money

figure **9.1**

Shaking the Money Tree

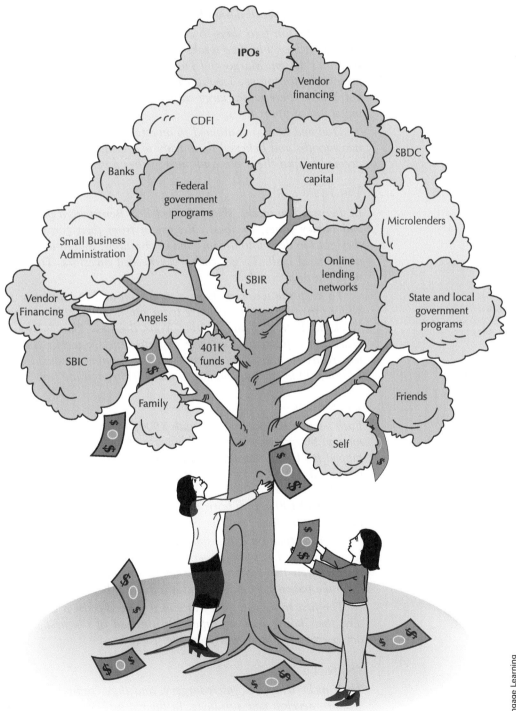

© Cengage Learning

turns up when you have a good Business Plan *and* you shake the right branches.

Looking for Money: Hawkins Case Study—Surgery Shunt

The Prototype

Don Hawkins started his career as a model maker in a large medical manufacturing firm. Don had talent and was envied and admired because he usually got the models routinely right the first time.

Margo Mckay, a product manager at Don's firm, often sought out Don when she needed help on a glitch that slowed production. One day, over a cup of coffee, Margo confided to Don that she had a micro surgeon friend looking for a special design for a wound drainage device.

It took Don four days to comb through the medical literature on microsurgery. It took him five weeks to develop the prototype based on the micro surgeon's design. Margo and Don went to the president of their company to present the prototype. Two weeks later the president shared that the firm did not believe there was a large enough market for the product for the firm to invest and support it.

Don and Margo continued to investigate the market further over the next two months and believed there truly was a market for such a product. They decided to quit their jobs and put together a venture team.

The Team

In the next few weeks, they recruited Bob Bernstein, a production supervisor, and Nancy Jones, the best salesperson from their former employer. Before they got too deep into dreams and celebrations, Margo warned the group they would need cash. To get cash, they needed investors. To get investors, they needed a Business Plan.

To keep the weak spots to a minimum and to maximize their strengths, all four members of the venture team enrolled in a college course titled "The Weekend Entrepreneur: Writing Your Business Plan." By organizing their ideas and capitalizing on their expertise, in six weeks their Business Plan was ready to present to investors. Their numbers showed they would need $2,000,000 in start-up capital to make it through the first 18 months.

The Money

Each partner had to come up with $500,000, a quarter of the first-year's seed money. Margo refinanced her houses with a home equity line of credit. Don tapped his Uncle Marvin, who was worth several million, for $400,000 and borrowed $100K from his 401k. Nancy found two investors, a couple of go-getter doctors, with $200,000 each and sold her rental condo to raise an additional $100K. Bob borrowed from his credit union and cashed in two life insurance policies.

Their destination was a small warehouse where the rent was cheap and the security great. The microsurgery trade show was 62 days away. For a piece of the corporate pie, a shrewd attorney waived his fee for doing the patent work. With the patent pending in hand, production began on Don's prototype.

The first trade show they attended proved to be a goldmine. On opening day, their booth was swamped. By the end of the first day, orders for the device exceeded their first-year sales forecast.

The Niche

Their niche truly was microsurgery, and they continued over the next three years to develop new products. In their third year, Don discovered the solution to a problem that had confounded two generations of optical surgeons.

Line of credit Bank agrees to loan up to a set amount and borrower draws on that amount as needed, either secured with property or unsecured

To obtain approval would take two to three years and with such a long lag time between production and sales, developmental costs would hurt the firm, maybe even take it under.

Then their CPA introduced them to Dream Funds, a venture capital group in Minneapolis. This was Dream Funds' deal: In return for 60 percent of the company's stock, Dream Funds would deposit $20 million in the company's bank account. Although they didn't want to lose control of the company, the financial opportunity for all was too good to pass up.

■ BEFORE COMMITTING MONEY

Don and his colleagues put up their *own money first*. Committing your own nickel is essential for *all* entrepreneurs. Lenders and investors will make sure you have committed your own resources before they will commit theirs. You have already completed Action Step 3 from Chapter 1, which asked you to complete a budget and a personal financial statement, and the Action Steps in Chapter 8, which asked you to determine your start-up costs, cash-flow requirements, and break-even point. So you now know the amount of capital you need to begin your business and the amount you have available. Now, it is time to reconcile and determine how to fund the difference.

The vast majority of ventures are self-financed in the start-up stage. Thus, you first must consider your own risk tolerance, your credit history, and the availability of your own cash. As you move forward from self-financing, you will need to determine the amount of risk you want to take and if you want to dilute your ownership in the firm by taking on investors.

If you plan to purchase an ongoing business, owner financing may be available to you and is discussed in Chapter 13. Some franchises have developed special financing agreements with banks for new franchisees. So, if you are opening the franchise door, check Chapter 14 for further information.

Determine Your Risk Tolerance

How much are you willing to risk? $10,000? $20,000? $200,000? $2,000,000? Are you willing to go deeply in debt for your venture? Are you willing to work as hard as one sushi vendor, who worked for more than seven years—and spent millions of dollars—before he hit on a successful way to flash-freeze his product?

Are you willing to give up a successful career with benefits for the unknown? If you lose your house, will you be devastated, or will you pick yourself back up and start again like a true entrepreneur? One Hilton Head Island building contractor was a millionaire at age 22 and lost it, a millionaire again at age 28 and lost it and a millionaire again at 35. Is this a roller coaster you are willing to ride?

Remember, you must also consider the risk tolerance of the members of your family and any persons you partner with. If additional capital is needed down the road, will you and your partners be able to provide equal shares? If not, how will this affect your partnership?

■ CREDIT REPORTING AGENCIES: WHAT DO THEY KNOW ABOUT YOU?

Loan officers, crowd source lenders, and sometimes, even family members will look first at your credit report before even talking with you about a loan. If the credit report does not pass, you are sunk! Take action to determine your credit history before ever searching for money. Approximately 25 to 40 percent of all credit reports have one or more problems, and it is your responsibility to clear these problems up before searching for capital. Oftentimes these are errors and omissions and not your fault. These problems can be very time consuming to clear up. If you have late payments or mortgage deficiencies, your credit report will reflect these issues.

Credit reporting agencies keep track of your financial moves—the good, the bad, and the ugly—including bill paying, credit (requested and denied), loans, liens, and legal judgments. Information is retained for 7 years, and bankruptcies stay on the records for 10 years.

Credit inquiries from potential lenders will show up on a credit report. Unfortunately, often times lenders request credit information without your authority, and only by obtaining a copy of your credit report will you discover these requests have been made. Lenders do not want to see that you have been requesting credit at a lot of places in a short period of time.

Be warned: What might appear minor to you, such as one missed or late payment, may not appear minor to potential lenders. *Never* miss a house payment! Making a house payment 30 days late will drop your credit score dramatically. If you have unpaid medical bills, try to avoid letting them go to collections. A lower credit score may cost you thousands of dollars due to higher interest rates. No outside agency can guarantee that incorrect items can be removed from your credit reports. Thus, tread carefully with firms who make such guarantees.

Many young people today have a tough time building a credit rating as they use their debit cards and not credit cards for purchases. It may be a smart way to control your expenditures; however, it is not helpful for building credit. Start to use your credit cards and pay off the balance each month in order to build credit. Also, if you rent, make sure all rental checks are delivered on time and a record is kept, as this is another excellent way to build credit.

Most entrepreneurs will depend on their own credit histories as they reach out for money. Mistakes are very common and other people's credit records can show up on your record, especially if you have a common name. Thus, check with each of the three separate credit bureaus three to six months before you anticipate needing money; if there is a problem, you will have time to take the necessary steps to correct it. The trend for using Fair Issue Credit Organization (FICO) scores to determine small-business loan eligibility continues to grow, so you need to make every effort to see to it that your score is as high as possible. Review the following key factors from BankRate in Figure 9.2 and pull your credit score to determine what steps you need to take immediately to improve your credit score.

According to Fair Isaac, a credit scoring developer, the average FICO score in the United States in 2012 was 692. However, a score of over 760 will usually qualify for the very best rates. The Fair and Accurate Credit Transactions Act provides consumers the right to request one free credit report through the website *www.annualcreditreport.com*, which contains reports from each of the following three major credit report agencies:

- Equifax—*http://www.equifax.com*
- Experian—*http://www.experian.com*
- Trans Union Corporation—*http://www.transunion.com*

Credit Karma is another excellent site for keeping track of your credit score and services are free. For a more detailed credit report, access FreeCreditReport .com or myFico.com. However, beware there are associated fees for many of their offerings.

Cautionary Steps

Gather your personal financial statement from Action Step 3 in Chapter 1, your credit score, and the start-up costs from Chapter 8. It is now time to ask how much money you are willing and able to personally commit.

figure 9.2

Credit Scores Made Simple

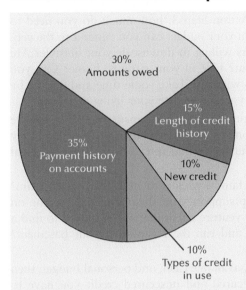

1. Payment history on accounts
2. Amounts owed
3. Length of credit history
4. New credit
5. Types of credit in use

FICO score pie chart used with permission from Fair Isaac Corp.

1. Payment history on account (35 percent)

Paying your bills on time is the most important thing you can do for your FICO score. Mind the due date, and make sure your payments have made it to the lender by then. Allow for 7 to 10 business days for your payments to arrive, or if you're paying online, adequate processing time.

2. Amounts owed (30 percent)

The second biggest factor, amounts owed, translates to how close to the credit limits you are on your cards. "If you're trying to max out your score, you want to charge less than 10 percent of the card's limit," says Ulzheimer, adding that he's frustrated that 50 percent is sometimes advised because nothing "magical" happens with your credit score if you're charging 50 percent of your credit limit. "At least realize that a higher percentage won't win you as many points," he says.

3. Length of your credit history (15 percent)

The third factor is the length of your credit history. Only time can help you there, but one mistake people can avoid here involves closing old credit cards. Closing an old credit card shortens the length of your credit history and lowers the total credit you have available from all your accounts. With a lower total credit limit, you end up looking more maxed out than you really are. You actually benefit from the unused card, he says, because it helps your utilization ratio—how much you owe compared to your available credit.

But suppose you have an old, unused retail card that has a high interest rate. Ulzheimer, who formerly worked for Fair Isaac, says that first off, interest rates are not factored into the FICO score. To keep the card open, he advises using it periodically to buy small items and then pay off the balance. The benefit of keeping unused cards comes when you do need to charge a large balance. Because your credit limits are so high, the large balance will affect your credit score less. There is a component for having too many credit cards, he says, but it's worth fewer points than charging too much on fewer cards.

4. New credit (10 percent)

The fourth category, new credit, refers to applications you've put in recently for new credit. It includes recent inquiries, how many recently opened accounts you have, how old each account is, and how old each inquiry is. Every time you apply for in-store credit, for example, you're giving permission to pull your credit report and that counts against your score. Not every inquiry will count against your score, however. According to myFICO.com, the FICO scoring model ignores mortgage and auto inquiries generated in the 30 days before scoring and counts older mortgage and auto inquiries made within a short period of time—a 14—or 45-day window, depending on the version of the FICO scoring model—as one inquiry.

5. Types of credit in use (10 percent)

The fifth category looks at the different types of credit you have. You'll likely have a better score with a mix of revolving credit, and installment credit, such as mortgages and car loans. That said; don't take on more debt than you can handle simply to improve your score. Paying your bills on time earns you more points than having a pleasant potpourri of credit accounts.

Source: *Bankrate.com*, N. Palm Beach, FL, 2012. "Credit scores made simple," Financial Literacy 2007, written by *Bankrate.com* with quotes used by John Ulzheimer, (accessed April 28, 2012).

Are you able to sell any of your assets for cash? Take a second or a third mortgage on your house to raise capital? Refinance your car or house at a lower rate? Sell your baseball card collection? Take a loan from your 401(K)?

As you review your budget from Action Step 3, how much do you need to live on each month? How much extra in your budget can you commit to the venture? Are you and your family members willing to downscale your lifestyle? Are you willing to rent? Share an apartment? Live in your parents' home? Can you dine out less? Buy a cheaper car or go without? Take some time and go line by line on your budget to determine how you can reduce your living expenses.

Are you willing to go without health and disability insurance? If you have answered yes, stop and reconsider as one trip to the emergency room can easily run up a $12,000 bill. Note that two-thirds of bankruptcies occur due to medical expenses.

What sacrifices are you and your family willing to make for your dream? Can you obtain a part-time job to help support your dream? Can you hang on to your present job and start your new venture part-time? Do you need to find a partner who has cash? Can you start and run the business in your basement? Bedroom? Living room? Garage?

Once you know your start-up costs, available cash, and personal budget, then you must determine the amount of secured and unsecured credit you have to draw upon. This will provide a general picture of how the financial world rates you at this time. Taking this step will determine if there are any untapped sources of funds available for your business or personal expenses.

Utilize Table 9.1 and your last credit card statements to determine your available credit. If your credit cards have very low limits, now may be the time to call the bankcard issuer and ask them to raise your limit before you open your business or quit your job. You may also want to note on Table 9.1 the due dates of each credit card. In the past, late payments were not costly but today they can double your interest rates!

When you have filled in the amounts for each of your credit accounts, add them up. Surprised? Few people are aware of how much credit they really have. There are a few additional concerns you might want to address. For example:

1. Check out the costs and possibility of continuing your present health insurance or purchasing new insurance. If you are unable to qualify for a private insurance plan, a group plan might be available through a business trade association or possibly through a state program. Look into high deductible plans. Many entrepreneurs find they need one member of their family to continue working for a company that provides family coverage. (see Chapter 12 and keep abreast of the changing laws regarding health insurance).

2. Apply for additional credit cards or increased limits. Check with BankRate.com for cards with the best terms and highest limits. Use specific cards only for business expenses. Pay bills (as they are due) with company checks or use a company reserved debit card. Banks do not care who pays, as long as they are paid. However, paying with your company debit or credit card will provide you excellent documentation for your bookkeeper. It will also help at tax time as you will have good records for the IRS.

3. Consider applying for a personal line of credit. Usually, depending on the Four Cs of credit (your capital, character, capacity, and collateral), you can obtain anywhere from $5,000 to $50,000 of unsecured credit at very attractive rates. If you have a personal line of credit it may give you some breathing room as you begin your new venture. If you need it to finance the new business, credit is available. If not, it will be the security blanket there for you if unexpected expenses should pop up—and they will.

4. Explore the possibility of a home-equity loan or home-equity line of credit.

Four Cs Capacity, collateral, character, and capital

Home equity loan Set amount of money borrowed at one time backed by the property usually with fixed interest rate

Home equity line of credit Set amount of money to draw on over time as needed secured by the property usually with variable interest rate

—table **9.1**

Your Current Untapped Financial Sources

Source	Due date	Limit	Available
Retail Stores			
Macy's			
Target			
Others			
Oil Companies			
Exxon			
Others			
Bank Credit Cards			
American Express			
Visa			
MasterCard			
Discover Card			
Others			
Personal Lines of Credit			
Bank			
Savings and Loan			
Credit Union			
Others			
Home Equity			
Total Credit			

© Cengage Learning

5. Check into borrowing from your 401(K) plan, although CPA David Wasserstrum, partner in charge of executive compensation and employee benefits at Weiser LLC, refers to 401(K) plans as "the lender of last resort." The maximum you can borrow is $50,000 or 50 percent of the vested balance, whichever is less. If you default on your 401(K) loan payments, the money borrowed will be treated as a distribution and taxed as ordinary income. Rollovers for Business Startups (ROBS) are another way to use your own retirement resources for startup funds. If you select this method, tread carefully as the IRS watches these types of investments closely and accessing all or a substantial part of your retirement funds can put your family's future at risk.

With regard to points 2, 3 and 4, bankers are much more relaxed about extending credit to a "steady citizen"—a person with steady employment income. In addition, you would be making arrangements for the money when you did not need it, and bankers tend to like lending money to those who have no real need for it.

Do not quit your job until you have finished your Business Plan, researched your finances, and have funds in place. You need to have enough money to withstand setbacks. If you do not have a reserve fund for setbacks, your dream may die early. Do not be surprised when your business does not support you right away in the manner to which you have become accustomed or would like to be.

Your Bottom Line

You are not risking your own capital and providing sweat equity for *just* an immediate paycheck or return. You are building your business's potential. If you only consider the income from the first year or two, you will not be able to justify risking your capital or working 12- to 14-hour days. You must look ahead three to five years. Money is a strong motivating factor; just thinking about it should keep your business on the success track. Additional thoughts to consider as you explore the bottom line for starting and building your business follow:

- **Income stream** What can you count on from your business? Salary? Profit? Benefits? Company car? Insurance? Travel? Retirement fund? What can you count on in the first year? The second year? Subsequent years?
- **Profit from sale of business:** What is the potential profit if the business is sold? Acquired? Or taken public? What will you leave to your children?
- **Profit life cycle:** How long will it take for your business to move from start-up to a profit position? Many businesses take two to three years to show a profit. What happens to your cash flow and investment if you project profit-making status to be three to five years down the road? Can you wait? Do you want to wait? What if you are not profitable, but your idea is scalable for others with large investment capital and your firm is purchased? (You are lucky and probably in a fast moving high-tech venture!)
- **The rule:** *Your business should provide you with two sources of financial return: an income stream and growing equity. If you have income without equity, you are just replacing your former income. If you have equity without income, you will not have the money you need to live on.*

■ SHAKING THE MOST FRUITFUL BRANCHES FIRST

Shaking the money tree takes effort for most entrepreneurs. Although many outside financial resources are available, they *all* come with strings attached. Control of the business, family and friends' emotions, your risk tolerance, your dreams, and taxes are all issues that should play a part in determining which branches of the money tree you can and should shake.

Sitting down with a knowledgeable small-business accountant or attorney will provide insight into the financial world. Although there are many funding opportunities available to entrepreneurs, more than 90 percent of start-up capital comes from self-financing, friends, and family—which means banks and other sources provide less than 10 percent of start-up capital. The headline making firms, like Instagram, bought by Facebook for $1 billion with only 13 employees, are *very* rare!

After self-financing, according to the Angel Resource Institute, start-up financing breaks down as follows: friends and family, $60 billion; angel investors, $20 billion; state funds, $0.5 billion; and venture capital, $0.3 billion. Be realistic!

Bootstrap Relying on one's self to start business with own resources

Most new ventures are begun by entrepreneurs who bootstrap. As you move from the initial startup phase friends and family may be willing to make loans or invest. Banks usually fund established businesses; although SBA guaranteed loans and micro lending institutions can benefit new ventures. If you can prove your business has some legs, angel investors may be willing to look at your business. Crowdfunding may come into play early on for you as well. With the passage of the Jumpstart Our Business Startups Act (JOBS) the crowdfunding platforms are growing and create increased new funding options. Venture capital will come usually once you have a proven product in a highflying market.

Crowdfunding Individuals who network together to pool smaller sums of money to fund growing ventures

If you bootstrap your business from the beginning, you may find yourself on *Inc.*'s annual listing of the 500 fastest-growing businesses in the country. Almost half of the businesses on the list started in the home, and a recent overall list had an average start-up cost of only $20,000! It does not always take large amounts of capital to launch your business. With today's technology, ventures can be launched with $100! However, it *will* take enormous amounts of risk taking, time, energy, and passion.

■ SELF-FINANCING

Your Money and Your Credit

We have discussed several ways to tap into your financial resources. Many individuals are unable to tap into home equity, retirement, stock, or bond funds; therefore credit cards may come to the rescue. For many entrepreneurs, credit cards become the standard way of accessing capital to keep the doors open and the fires burning.

More than 30 percent of entrepreneurs use credit cards routinely in their businesses to help with cash flow. However, it is *always* safer to use cold hard cash to start and support your business, if possible, before depending on credit cards.

Many of the larger credit card companies, such as American Express, court small-business owners. Unfortunately, many of the small-business credit cards, which provide excellent recordkeeping and benefits, are available only to businesses with a two-year track record. When selecting cards, consider the following:

- **Payment dates:** If you have several cards with varying closing and payment dates, you may be able to manage your cash flow creatively by using the cards in tandem.
- Annual Percentage Rate (APR): Check Bank Rate (*http://www.bankrate.com*) for the lowest current credit card rates. If you have a card and are paying too high of an APR, call the credit card company and request that they lower the rate. Yes, this can work!
- **Annual fees.** Beware of changing and higher fees.
- **Maximum credit limits:** Call your current credit card issuers and request an increase in your credit line. Many times all it takes is a phone call.
- **Additional fees:** Make sure any "extras" you receive with the card are worth paying for.
- **Grace periods:** This is extremely important if you are using the card to manage cash flow.
- **Mileage points or other incentives:** Determine if these are worth the potential annual fees.
- **Late fees:** *Never* incur late fees. They can be exorbitant and can negatively impact your credit report and interest rate.

Annual Percentage Rate (APR)
Yearly interest rate cost over the term of the loan including fees and additional costs involved with transaction

Judicious use of credit cards can be a lifesaver for many entrepreneurs. They help track expenses and build a financial history. But unless you realize that the credit card bills need to be paid on time, and that there are spending limits, you may find yourself in over your head—and your business underwater. Be sure to read all inserts with your credit card statements, because extra fees and changes in the credit terms may occur. It is your responsibility to be aware of these changes. In addition, make sure to include repayment of credit card debt, along with interest charges, in your Business Plan. Note that your consumer cardholder agreement may not allow for funding your business. However, use is standard practice in the entrepreneurial community. Keep the cards you use for personal business separate from the cards you use for your business if possible.

■ FAMILY AND FRIENDS

For many entrepreneurs, heading to Mom and Pop and their friends is the second branch they shake. If you plan on making it your next stop, think again. According to many experts, parents may be one of the largest single sources of start-up capital in the United States, but having a banking relationship with your parents is fraught with potential problems.

Before continuing further, ask yourself, "Is this venture worth damaging or losing my relationship with my parents or my friends?" At the moment, you may just be thinking about speeding ahead with your venture, and all you can see is success; the reality is, however, you could fail. If you do, you might not be able to pay your parents back in a timely fashion—or ever.

Consider their emotional ties to money. Especially if your parents or grandparents lived through tough financial times, for those individuals money equals security. If you borrow from them, they may never truly feel secure until you have completely paid the funds all back.

Also, if you take a trip to Paris while you still owe them money, will you feel guilty? Will you feel guilty if you purchase a new car? Will you truly be secure in expanding your business if you are not secure in your lending relationships? If you are borrowing money from friends or family, be absolutely sure that the loss of that money will not affect the lender's future or lifestyle. Your dream is not their responsibility. Borrowing Grandma's last $50,000 is not fair to Grandma.

In addition to borrowing money directly from family and friends, you may consider asking them to cosign loans as another way to help you. By cosigning they are legally obligated for the *entire* debt. Also, their personal borrowing capacity and credit score will be impacted and now limited by cosigning for you.

Friends and family may be more willing to loan you money if you put up your house, car, or jewelry as collateral. One firm, National Family Mortgage, will help you arrange a home mortgage agreement between relatives, thus allowing you to tap home equity with family members holding the deed to your home and providing capital to you. Remember in tough economic times, friends and family must limit their obligations to others. One "Bank of Mom and Dad" decided to use their capital to help their children start their businesses. But, it was made clear to all members that *the parents*—not the children--would decide what loan amount, interest rate, and payment plan were acceptable in light of the possible risks and returns of each investment. Everyone in the family knew different terms were based on the "idea" or "product" and the current interest rate environment when the loan was undertaken.

Rather than risking the capital of those you love, consider remaining at your job and save for another year before striking out on your own. Mixing money and personal relationships is never easy, and with family and friends it tends to be even more emotional and volatile. Long-running family issues come into play, and sibling relationships may also be harmed. There are unseen and unknown issues for both parties. How will you deal with them? If your folks get sick, will you be able to pay back the loan? If your dad and mom want to be part of the business to oversee their investment, how will you feel?

If you are still willing to borrow from friends and family after honestly reviewing potential issues and problems, here are a few things you can do to alleviate some of the difficulties and make it work best for all parties:

- Put everything in writing.
- Make it a business loan, not a personal loan. Have loan papers drawn up. State the amount, payments, duration of loan, interest rate, payment date,

collateral, and late-payment penalties. Search online for firms who will handle the paperwork and collections for you.

- Include a loan provision for repayment, in part or in full, in case of emergencies. This will alleviate much of the stress and concern for both parties.
- Discuss thoroughly with your family and friends the company's goals. Make sure they understand that the funds will be needed for a certain length of time. If the business starts to be profitable, the money will still be needed for working capital.
- Make clear to relatives and friends the difference between a loan and equity in the firm. Many who lend funds may also expect ownership in the company or want to participate in its financial success beyond the return of the funds they have loaned. Clearly state terms at time of funding.
- Discuss your fears for potential problems, and encourage lenders to discuss their issues as well. Putting feelings and concerns out on the table early may stem future problems.

Borrowing from friends and family can be successful, but it is hard work and takes exceptional people with good relationships who have no axes to grind. *Tread lightly and carefully. Friends and family cannot be replaced.*

■ BANKS

Although most ventures begin with an entrepreneur's own capital and the capital of friends and family, a small number of entrepreneurs are able to tap into traditional bank financing. If you have other sources of income and collateral—such as home equity, stocks, or bonds—you may be able to borrow against your assets for funding.

Although banks are in the business of lending money, they also have a responsibility to their depositors. Therefore bankers tend to choose the safest deals. They want to help businesses expand, but they have to be picky. Banks can help you in many areas, but they are neither investors nor venture capitalists, so do not expect them to take risks.

Your chances to receive a bank loan increase substantially after being in business several years, when you can demonstrate to the bank that yours is a viable business by providing them with past sales records and tax returns. They also usually focus their loans on providing access to working capital, real estate, or equipment.

A small, local community bank, where the chief loan officer may be a part owner, may be an excellent choice for small business banking. You are hunting for a permanent relationship, not merely a place to park your money, and you are more likely to find it in a small community bank. Contact the Independent Community Bankers of America (ICBA) for access to more than 5,000 members.

Also, network with your attorney, accountant, suppliers, and customers to locate a loan officer who deals with businesses in your industry and of your size. However, bear in mind that your business could eventually outgrow a small bank and that some firms need support services, such as import–export assistance, that only a large bank can offer.

Microlending programs, which generally refer to business loans of less than $35,000, are available through various banks and economic development programs including the Small Business Administration (SBA). These small loans give new hope to fledgling entrepreneurs. According to SBA research, more than 500 banks and organizations participate in microlending programs, providing billions of dollars in start-up and working capital funds for entrepreneurs.

Microlending Very small, often short-term loans, for those who lack collateral

Entrepreneur's **Resource**

ACCION: Capital Available for Struggling Entrepreneurs

ACCION USA's mission is to "give people the financial tools they need to improve their lives". By providing microloans to men and women who have traditionally been shut of the credit market and banking sector, ACCION opens up credit for low and moderate-income small business owners in selected areas of the U.S. and around the world.

In the U.S., ACCION offers business loans from $500 to $50,000 with repayment terms of 1 to 60 months along with financial education to micro-entrepreneurs. Many of these loans are offered through an agreement with the SBA. The program offers competitive fixed interest rates and closing costs of 3–5% of the loan.

Several different programs are offered, including transition loans available for purchasing an existing business, startup business loans up to $50,000, Brewing the American Dream Loan up to $25,000 for businesses in food, beverage and hospitality. In addition, they offer green loans and access to credit card processing.

Check out ACCION's website to view their many client success stories and to learn more about their programs and loans.

For further information, see the Entrepreneurial Resource highlighting one microlender, ACCION. In addition, check out Kiva and the Opportunity Fund for further microlending sources.

Several large banks, such as Chase and Bank of America, provide assistance to fledgling businesses with big plans. Also, creative leasing programs may be available through these larger banks. Both community and large banks work directly with the SBA in funding guaranteed loans. Check which of the lenders in your area are the major funders of SBA loans. If you are purchasing a franchise, many of the larger established franchises have agreements with banking institutions, thus making the loan process smoother and quicker.

BOTTOM LINERS

"One last question: Have you begged for a loan before?"

Source: © Tribune Media Services, Inc. All rights reserved.

Lenders' Expectations

In general, traditional bankers tend not to make start-up loans other than microloans without home equity or stocks to secure the loan. Even when they do, they expect:

1. A very solid Business Plan with good projections and supporting data— numbers are king. Bankers use the RMA's *Statement Studies: Annual Financial Ratio Benchmarks* and *Industry Default Probabilities and Cash-Flow Measures*, previously discussed in Chapter 8. Make sure your numbers are in line with the firms in these annual statement studies and provide support data for any that deviate. Bankers live and breathe numbers, and so must you when you present your Business Plan.
2. Experience in managing a business, preferably in the same industry.
3. Background in the industry—the longer and broader the better.
4. Enough other assets for the borrower to live on while the business is growing—typically 6 to 12 months.
5. Your personal financial commitment to be a major part of the financing.
6. Possibly a cosigner who guarantees your loan.
7. A second salary in the family.
8. Generally at least two to three years of successful operation. Once again, unsecured bank lending is rare for start-ups without collateral.
9. Projected income statements that demonstrate you are willing to take a reasonable salary, or no salary, in the beginning.
10. A detailed explanation of exactly how the funds will be used.
11. A compelling product or service with strong marketing.
12. Capacity to repay the loan in a timely fashion.
13. A solid business or social relationship with the potential borrower.

Unsecured bank loans or lines of credit may not be available to an entrepreneur even after three to five years of successful business operations. Realistically, your personal assets and your business assets are therefore intertwined for a long time, whether you like it or not.

Strategies for Working with Your Banker

Bankers may lead you to money sources you may have not considered, and they may provide a gateway to the world of money. Seek your banker's advice on pulling your Business Plan together. If you ask for your banker's input, he or she may have a harder time refusing financial assistance later on.

In the SBA section that follows, a paperwork checklist is provided for SBA-guaranteed loans. A similar checklist will be required by most lending institutions.

Bring your banker into your information loop, and involve him or her in your business idea. Stop thinking about a banker as someone who will lend you an umbrella only on a sunny day; that may be true today, but it may not be true in the long run. You would not lend money to a stranger, so make sure your banker knows exactly what you are up to.

Lure a banker to your turf if you have a retail or manufacturing operation. Say, "It's difficult to explain to you exactly what my shop is like. Why not come out for a look? We could have lunch. How's Thursday around noon?" On your own turf, you will be at ease and in a stronger position.

Comparison shop for money just as you would shop for any major purchase. The deals could surprise you. However, like any major purchase, price is *only* one factor to consider. You are most likely looking for a long term banking relationship and should consider your local community banks as well as the major banks. The following questions will guide you in your search.

SBA-guaranteed loans Loans insured by the federal government for up to 90% of the loan.

Information loop A network of people who need to be kept informed about your business

Your turf One's place of business or the place one feels most comfortable

Equipment lease Long-term arrangement with a bank or leasing company for the use of capital equipment for a certain period of time

What are your lending limits?

What is the loan approval process and who makes the final lending decisions?

What experience does your bank have working with businesses in my industry?

Could you recommend a highly qualified lawyer? Bookkeeper? Accountant? Computer consultant? Advertising consultant? Patent attorney?

Are you interested in writing equipment leases?

What terms do you offer on accounts receivable financing?

Does your bank offer businesses Visa and MasterCard accounts? If so, what credit limit would be available?

What handling charge would I have to pay on credit card receipts?

What interest can I earn on my business checking account?

Do you have a merchants' or commercial window?

Do you have a night depository?

If you cannot lend me money, can you direct me to people who might be interested in doing so?

Do you make SBA-guaranteed loans?

If I open up a business checking account here, what other services will be available?

What specifically will you be looking for in my Business Plan?

Make Your Banker a Member of Your Team

A helpful banker can be an entrepreneur's best friend and a member of his or her auxiliary management team. Business growth demands money from external sources, and the more successful you become, the more likely you will need a close banking relationship to help you finance prosperity.

Manufacturers often fall into financial trouble very fast; they have to wait for their customers to make payments, which might take months to receive. Bankers are more willing to help if they understand your needs and know you are trying to anticipate them.

Entrepreneur's **Resource**

Small Business Development Centers (SBDCs)

Federal funds are awarded to state universities and economic development agencies to establish Small Business Development Centers (SBDCs) at universities, chambers of commerce, and community colleges. With over 60 centers and 1,000 service locations, the SBDCs provide assistance in marketing, finance, technology transfer, and management to entrepreneurs. SBDC programs will not usually fund your venture, but will help prepare you to seek funding.

Specialty programs exist within each state to meet the changing needs of the state's economy and to exploit the assets of each area. For example, the AZSBDC network offers the Veterans' Assistance, Clean Technology, and the Government and Contracting Procurement programs to their members. Key Points highlights Indiana's 2012 SBDC Emerging Business Edge Award-winning firms, including technology, retail, and entertainment ventures. Following are additional programs offered in several different states:

North Carolina SBDC Boating Industry Services

Supporting existing marine businesses

The SBTDC's Boating Industry Services (BIS) provides a range of business services and one-on-one counseling, including management and operations, marketing and sales, business expansion, personnel, and regulatory.

Creating new jobs and new businesses

BIS, working in conjunction with statewide economic development agencies, serves as a confidential resource for potential new-to-the-state boating

(continued)

(continued)

industry business owners. This effort is promoted through trade shows, media ads and articles, monthly newsletters, and its website.

Focusing on boating industry resources and marketing

The *www.NCwaterways.com* website serves as the program's internal and external database of North Carolina businesses, identifying over 3,500 companies by service and/or products provided in the marine sector. It offers business users access to information on education and training, business and regulatory services, and the boating industry job market.

Source: "Boating Industry Services," Copyright © 2014 NC SBTDC. From *http://www.sbtdc.org/ programs/boating_industry/*, (Accessed October 17, 2012). Reprinted with permission from NC SBTDC.

Nebraska SBDC's Lean Enterprise Manufacturing Solutions

NBDC is the exclusive NIST/MEP-CERTIFIED LEAN manufacturing service provider in the state. NBDC/MEP **lean manufacturing** consultants have years of industrial experience in lean enterprise manufacturing operations using Kaizen Events, Set-up Reduction, Total Productive Maintenance, Value Stream Mapping, and Pull/Kanban.

NBDC/MEP DOES NOT JUST TRAIN PEOPLE in lean enterprise manufacturing. We lead organizations in making necessary change. In our workshops, your employees and managers not only learn to talk the talk, but walk the walk. Assisted by **experienced lean consultants**, they will apply lean enterprise techniques and information to address an immediate identified goal of your company at your company site. We don't just teach. We enable companies, just like yours, to initiate and implement risk-free continuous improvement culture.

Source: "Manufacturing Growth and Improvement," Nebraska Business Development Center, University of Omaha. From *http://nbdc.unomaha.edu/lean/*. Reprinted with permission.

Check out your state's SDBC programs. If you have specific needs that are not met by a program in your state, search the Internet for other state programs that could meet your needs. Relocation might be good for your business if services are available in another area.

Free SBDC counseling may prove to be more helpful than you could ever imagine for your new or growing venture. One of the best reasons to use these centers is to access the contacts they have developed through the years with government agencies, bankers, higher education, suppliers, and possibly even your potential customers.

Lean manufacturing Eliminating "waste" both in time and costs

ACTION STEP 42

Befriend a Banker

Money creates its own world. There are several doorways into that world, and your banker sits at the threshold of one of them.

Start with a familiar place, the bank where you have your checking account. Make an appointment to talk to the chief officer (president, vice president, or branch manager). Use Questions for Your Banker in this chapter as a guide. If you are happy with your banker's answers, talk over the possibility of opening a business account for your business. If you have money tucked in a money-market fund somewhere, ask about the bank's money-market accounts. Check out business checking and bank fees, and compare them to other banks. We know this can all be accomplished online. However, when your business faces an emergency you'll be glad you know your banker personally.

If you have specific lending needs such as exporting or leasing, seek out lenders who offer such services.

Initiate a banking relationship by completing Action Step 42, Befriend a Banker. If you have tapped out your own resources, investigated borrowing from friends and family, made a few bank inquiries, and there is still not enough in the money pot, it is time to shake a few other branches.

■ SBA PROGRAMS

Many people find out about SBA loan programs through local bank referrals, Small Business Development Centers (SBDCs) (see Entrepreneurial Resource), and the Service Core of Retired Executives (SCORE) offices. In 2012, SBDCs served over 1 million clients and SCORE provided over 330,000 clients with mentoring and workshops.

In 2011, the SBA "gross loan approvals reached $19.6 billion in the agency's general business, or 7(a), loan program and $4.8 billion in capital investment loans issued in the 504 program." The SBA is primarily a guarantor of loans made by commercial and nonbank lenders who serve as intermediaries, such as ACCION.

The guarantee is between the SBA and the lending institution. If the business goes under, the government repays a major portion of the loan. Real estate loans are a major component of the SBA loan portfolio, because they are collateralized and more secure than other loans.

Banks, lending in cooperation with the SBA, want to see at least a 20 to 30 percent commitment of personal funds before they loan money (current lending is temporarily allowing for lower commitments). Your local SBA office will provide you with a list of major SBA-guaranteed lenders in your area. Use the most experienced and successful ones as they will cut through government red tape most efficiently.

Several major SBA programs, their functions, and customer information provided by the SBA are highlighted below. If you plan to export, the information highlighted in the Global Village will lead you to a vast array of additional resources for financing international trade ventures. For further details and for the latest information on SBA programs, visit the SBA website.

SBA Program Snapshots

The SBA offers numerous loan guarantee programs to assist small businesses.

PROGRAM: Basic 7(a) Loan Guaranty
FUNCTION: SBA's primary and most flexible loan guarantee program, guaranteeing 70 to 90 percent of the financing from commercial lending institutions for a variety of general business purposes. If the borrower does not repay the loan, the government will reimburse the lender for its loss, up to the percentage of the guarantee. Loan funds of up to $5 million can be used for real estate, furniture, fixtures, and equipment. Loans extend to 25 years for fixed assets and 10 years for working capital.

PROGRAM: Microloan, 7(m) Loan Program
FUNCTION: Working capital, inventory, supplies, furniture, fixtures, machinery, and/or equipment loans are provided for a maximum loan amount of $50,000 with the average being $13,000 for up to six years. Intermediaries such as ACCION, highlighted in the chapter, provide training and support as well as funds.

PROGRAM: 7 (a) Express & Pilot Programs
FUNCTION: Express loan programs offer streamlined and expedited loan procedures to borrowers with turnaround in as little as 36 hours. Lower interest rates may also be available through the Express programs. Program primarily aimed at active duty military personnel, veterans, and borrowers from distressed communities.

PROGRAM: Certified Development Company (CDC), a 504 Loan Program
FUNCTION: The 504 loan program provides long-term fixed-rate financing to acquire fixed assets (such as real estate or equipment) for expansion or modernization.

Source: *www.sba.gov*, (Accessed November 20, 2012).

In addition to the programs already discussed, other major avenues of government assistance may be of value to you, especially if you need equity capital, research funding, or are trying to start, expand, or purchase a business in a low income area.

- Small Business Investment Companies (SBICs) are private lenders licensed by the SBA to provide equity capital to small businesses. The recipients may give up some ownership, but not necessarily control, in exchange for the funds. Offering both debt and equity financing, the SBICs expect to recoup their investment in five to seven years. In addition, according to New Markets Venture Capital (NMVC), the program has been developed to "promote economic development and the creation of wealth and job opportunities in low-income geographic areas and among individuals living in such areas."
- The Small Business Innovation Research (SBIR) program provides direct funding for development efforts oftentimes through university research and is one of the largest sources of early stage financing with over $2 billion invested annually. The program offers an opportunity for entrepreneurs to work on innovative research ideas whose potential products can meet the research needs of the federal government and lead to future commercialization. For

"feasibility" development, $150,000 is available; and $1 million is available to take a product from "development to prototype." See the Entrepreneurial Resource in Chapter 3 for more information and a profile of Touch Graphics, a successful recipient of SBIR funding.

- STTR program's mission is "to support scientific excellence and technological innovation through the investment of federal research funds in critical American priorities to build a strong national economy." Funds are available for businesses working with nonprofit research institutions. The STTR program requires that a small business collaborate with the institution early on and incorporate basic science research into products.

- Over 1,000 Community Development Financial Institutions (CDFI) serve economically distressed communities by providing credit, capital, and financial services that are often unavailable from mainstream financial institutions. CDFIs provide funding for individuals and communities outside the mainstream—financially, socially, and geographically. Their goal is to promote job creation, affordable housing, and financial literacy. CDFIs are affiliated with community development banks, credit unions, loan funds, and venture funds.

  CDFIs are willing to loan to borrowers with less than pristine credit who are willing to accept advice and support from the institutions. In areas where good jobs are scarce, such as depressed or rural areas, funding may be available for $2,000 to $300,000.

Additional state programs and local development authorities can be extremely flexible in their financing programs and are very helpful and interested in securing financing for growing and existing businesses. Flexible loans with low down payments are often available. Throughout the text we have highlighted many additional funding programs, in the Entrepreneurial Resource boxes and Key Points.

SBA/Bank Financing Checklist

The following SBA loan application checklist gives a fair idea of the *major* paperwork required for applying for any business loan whether with the SBA or other source. The SBA's Application for a Business Loan, Form SBA-4, is included in Appendix C. Additional forms are available on the Web and at local SBA offices. For further information, contact the SBA Answer Desk at (800) UASK-SBA (827-5722) or visit *http://www.sba.gov.*

Use the checklist below to ensure you have everything the lender will ask for to complete your application. Once your loan package is complete, your lender will submit it to the SBA.

SBA Loan Application Checklist

1. **SBA Loan Application**: SBA-4.
2. **Personal background and financial statement**: To assess your eligibility complete the following forms:
   - Statement of Personal History - SBA Form 912
   - Personal Financial Statement - SBA Form 413
3. **Business financial statements**: To support your application and demonstrate your ability to repay the loan, prepare and include the following financial statements:
   - *Profit and loss (P&L) statement*: This must be current within 90 days of your application. Also include supplementary schedules from the last three fiscal years.
   - *Projected financial statements*: Include a detailed, one-year projection of income and finances and attach a written explanation as to how you expect to achieve this projection.

4. **Ownership and affiliations**: Include a list of names and addresses of any subsidiaries and affiliates, including concerns in which you hold a controlling interest and other concerns that may be affiliated by stock ownership, franchise, proposed merger, or otherwise with you.

5. **Business certificate/License**: Your original business license or certificate of doing business. If your business is a corporation, stamp your corporate seal on the SBA loan application form.

6. **Loan application history**: Include records of any loans you may have applied for in the past.

7. **Income tax returns**: Include signed personal and business federal income tax returns of your business' principals for previous three years.

8. **Résumés**: Include personal résumés for each principal.

9. **Business overview and history**: Provide a brief history of the business and its challenges. Include an explanation of why the SBA loan is needed and how it will help the business.

10. **Business lease**: Include a copy of your business lease, or note from your landlord, giving terms of proposed lease.

11. **If you are purchasing an existing business**: The following information is needed for purchasing an existing business:
    - Current balance sheet and P&L statement of business to be purchased
    - Previous two years federal income tax returns of the business
    - Proposed Bill of Sale including Terms of Sale
    - Asking price with schedule of inventory, machinery and equipment, furniture and fixtures

Source: Adapted from *http://www.sba.gov/content/sba-loan-application-checklist*, (Accessed April 28, 2012).

■ VENDOR FINANCING

An often-overlooked technique for reducing your capital requirements is to probe your vendors and suppliers for the best prices and terms available. When opening a business you most likely are looking for extended payment periods from 30 to 90 days out. Basically if granted, you are receiving a 30 to 90 day interest free loan. Only suppliers who view you as a good financial risk and a potential large customer will consider offering you these extended terms. But with a strong Business Plan in hand and a good sales pitch, you may impress and be offered generous terms if you are lucky. The status of the economy and the competitive nature of the business will also come into play.

Vendor statement A personally designed form that allows you to negotiate with each vendor from a position of informed strength

A small business must buy professionally, and a vendor statement will help you do just that. With this form, your vendors' verbal promises become written promises. How well you buy is as important as how well you sell, because every dollar you save by buying right drops directly to the bottom line. The vendor statement will help you negotiate the best terms and prices available. The following list provides the basics for a vendor statement:

1. Vendor's contact information
2. Sales rep's contact information
3. Amount of minimum purchase
4. Existence of quantity discounts (how much and what the requirements are to earn them)
5. Availability of dating or extended payment terms
6. Advertising/promotion allowances
7. Policies on returns for defective goods, including who pays the freight
8. Delivery times

9. Assistance (technical, sales, training, etc.)
10. Warranties and guarantees
11. Product literature, point-of-purchase material, and website provided
12. Support for grand opening, such as if the supplier will donate products or provide other support
13. Special services the sales rep can provide
14. Website, online purchasing, drop shipping, credit card purchases
15. Vendor's signature, the date, and the agreement that you will be notified of any changes to the above immediately

Remember, the information the vendor provides is the starting point for negotiations. You should be able to negotiate more favorable terms with some vendors because they want your business. Revise your application form as you learn from experience how vendors can help you. If you are a new business, you will most likely be required to *personally* guarantee payment of your purchases in writing or only receive COD shipments. Thus, as a new account, you need to convince vendors and suppliers that you will be around, successful, and become a very important customer soon.

When purchasing major equipment for your business, look into finance or capital leasing firms who offer extended payment terms and where the equipment serves as collateral. Unfortunately, one needs to be careful in the lease financing arena as scam artists are known to prey on start-ups. Complete due diligence research on potential firms and only deal with reputable ones.

Now it is time to prepare your own vendor statement form with Action Step 43.

ACTION STEP 43

Designing a Vendor Statement Form

One of the best ways to save money is to ask for help from your vendors or suppliers. To do that, you will need to create your own special form that specifies the terms to be negotiated.

Be firm. Be pleasant. Be tough. Prepare your list of necessary information using the list of 15 suggestions provided. The vendor form provides talking points. Most vendors hold something back; design your form to help you learn what those things are, and get the best deal for your business.

Before negotiating, determine the standard terms offered in the industry. During negotiations, use a lot of open-ended questions like, "What else can you do for me?" Remember, vendors will also ask you for detailed information. Dating and credit may be very limited for new accounts.

COD Paid in full upon delivery

ANGELS WITH MONEY

Another source of funding can come from "angels", people who are willing to invest in your startup as individuals or part of an angel investment group. While Janice was sharing her concept and Business Plan for a firm focusing on home health care for the chronically ill and disabled with her best friend Sally, Carol, Sally' mother, popped in and said, "That sounds like a great idea. Tell me more." After a few hours, the "Angel Carol" chose to invest $100,000 for a 30 percent share of the business. In addition, Carol offered to have dinner meetings once a week and provide business counseling. Her 30 years in various health care management positions made her a great mentor for Janice's home health care agency.

Angels may just appear, but such appearances should not be counted on. Thus, you will need to search out potential investors. The first step is to tell all your friends and family about your business idea and ask them if they have any possible contacts for you. Your research and their contacts may unearth potential investors. Always follow up with *anyone* who expresses an interest. Research shows that a business angel interested in your venture very often lives within 10 miles of you.

Angels come in many different sizes and types—from the small investor who just came into money to the professional investor who wants to help others follow their passion. Most angels like to invest in companies where they have knowledge and experience in the industry. Ideally, your angel will not only support the financial part of your business but will also offer contacts and experience; in the end, such assistance may be far more important to your success than investment capital.

Individual angel financing is appropriate for entrepreneurs seeking $20,000 to $2,000,000 in capital who have a product or service, which will entail rapid

Seed stage Firm in early development

growth in sales and company value. Angels are primarily investing their own personal capital and come in primarily in the seed stage of financing. The reality TV show, *Shark Tank*, provides an example of companies reaching out to angels in a unique way for seed funding.

Specific industries and some communities offer angel networks, some of which offer a matchmaking process for professional investors and entrepreneurs whose capital limits may far exceed $2,000,000. Private or college-sponsored investors' forums are offered where individuals are given 3 to 15 minutes to present their idea to potential investors. Such forums are an excellent place to sell your idea, receive feedback, and possibly secure financing. SBA research reports that 250,000 angels provide more than $20 billion annually to 300,000 new and expanding businesses each year. Your chance of finding an angel may be better than you thought!

Many individual angel investors have joined forces to form investor groups throughout the country that focus investments on a local or regional basis, as well as choosing to select specific industries on which to focus. In addition, the Internet is chock-full of angel/entrepreneur matching sites.

The Kaufman Foundation has formed the Angel Resource Institute (ARI) to increase the number of individual angels and provide training in mentoring entrepreneurs. To reach out to angels and angel groups, visit the ARI and the Angel Capital Association (ACA) websites. Presented below is Tech Coast Angels general introduction:

Tech Coast Angels

Who we are?
- Largest angel investment organization in the U.S. founded in 1997.
- Approximately 300 members in 5 regional networks cover all of Southern California.
- Our members have diverse backgrounds in almost every industry (not just tech).
- Many of our members are entrepreneurs and have experience in running start-ups.

What have we done?
- We have invested in over 200 companies.
- Our members have invested over $120 million in these companies.
- Our portfolio companies have gone on to attract over $1 billion in additional investment capital.
- Last year over 600 companies applied to TCA for funding. We funded 17 of them.

What do we provide to entrepreneurs?
- Critical business connections.
- Provide hands-on practical mentoring.
- Provide help in building out the management team.
- Help raising additional venture capital funding.

Tech Coast Angels is actively seeking great start-ups to fund. TCA brings connections, knowledge, mentoring, and operational assistance to bold early-stage entrepreneurs with game-changing ideas. Let us help you to turn your vision into a sustainable and successful business.

Tech Coast Angels is ever-mindful that some of the world's greatest companies began with angel investments and we take our commitment to that tradition seriously. The nearly 300 members of TCA collaborate with each other on due diligence and then make individual decisions regarding potential investments. Not limited to the technology industry, our members invest in exciting companies in a wide range of industries including biotech, consumer products, Internet, IT, life sciences, media, software, and environmental, among others. TCA is a not-for-profit organization.

Tech Coast Angels is a catalyst in helping build Southern California's economy into a thriving center of technology and entrepreneurship. Our members are very active in the entrepreneurial community, attending and participating in conferences, networking events, entrepreneurial competitions, and other venture capital events. Our relationships with the major colleges and universities in Southern California provide us both access to potential commercialization opportunities and expertise that is invaluable as we analyze potential investments.

Additionally, we receive numerous investment opportunities for review from angel groups across the United States. Our relationship with the venture capital community often gives us early looks at deals from them that fit our investment criteria. TCA also has an excellent relationship with the major economic development agencies in Southern California, which are often a referral source of entrepreneurial /investment ideas. All of these sources keep our deal pipeline full which is critical in creating a high quality diversified pool of investments for our members.

Source: Tech Coast Angels, "About Us," from *http://www.techcoastangels.com/about-us*, (Accessed May 2, 2012). Reprinted with permission.

Locate your local angel investor groups and see what they have to offer. Attend their workshops, participate in their mixers, listen to their podcasts, and become active in the organization. As you develop your business, you may be able to make a presentation to the angels in one of their "pitch" contests. Review the information in your elevator pitch from Chapter 3, and continue to refine it with your marketing ideas and financial data—your pitch will need to be very persuasive as you try to entice angel investors or venture capitalists. In Chapter 7 angels and venture capitalists, who are involved with accelerator and incubator programs, are discussed. These programs and investors offer incredible resources for those involved primarily in tech related industries.

■ VENTURE CAPITAL FIRMS

With venture capital firms, we enter the world of high rollers and high flyers. Unlike banks, which lend money that is secured, usually by real estate, venture capitalists do not lend money; they buy a piece of the business. They gamble on the business's rapid growth, hoping to reap a 300 to 500 percent return on their investment within three to eight years. See Figure 2.7 to view the industries venture capital is funding today.

Venture capitalists usually do not invest in start-ups. They look for firms that have a proven business model and/or product, whose revenue can be ramped up quickly and whose potential profit market is very large. In 2011, venture capitalists had over $29 billion invested in firms. (See Figure 9.3).

The big payoff for most venture-capital investment firms occurs when enough investors want in on the action through an initial public offering (IPO) of common stock. Although most often, the venture is acquired by another firm before an IPO takes place. Thus, when the business goes public or is sold, the venture capitalists take out their original investment and, it is hoped, reap a substantial profit. Venture capitalists generally enter into many deals spreading their risk among them. They hope to hit a home run; but understand, many of the firms will be foul balls, walks, or strikes. Thus, they spread their risk capital over many ventures.

Venture capitalists vary, but most prefer to enter the financial picture at the second stage of a firm's development—when the business has proven its potential and needs a large infusion of cash to support rapid growth. Currently, they tend to prefer high-tech concepts in embryonic industries with high growth potential. The funders look for compelling ideas backed by a strong, experienced team. Credibility of your financial projections and a validation of your research and sales results are essential to gain credibility with venture capitalists.

Initial Public Offering (IPO) Selling stock to the public for the first time

figure 9.3

Venture Capital Disbursements and Commitments

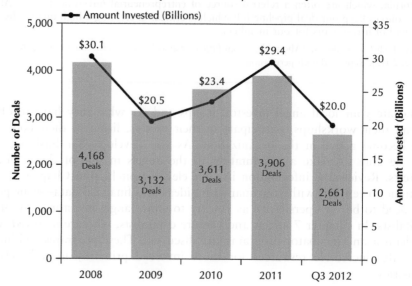

Total Venture Capital Investment by Year 2008–Q3 2012

Source: PricewaterhouseCoopers/National Venture Capital Association MoneyTree™ Report, Data: Thomson Reuters

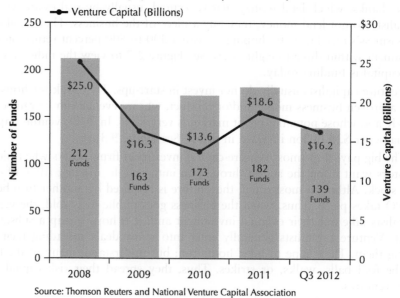

Fundraising by Venture Funds by Year 2008–Q3 2012

Source: Thomson Reuters and National Venture Capital Association

(continued)

Venture capitalists come in many forms. For example, there are family firms (Rockefeller), industrial firms (GE), banks, and others such as large insurance and finance companies. Most venture-capitalist firms target specific industries such as health care, biotechnology, the Internet, software, or telecommunications.

—figure **9.3**

Venture Capital Disbursements and Commitments *(continued)*

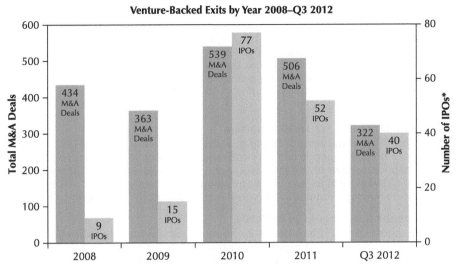

Venture-Backed Exits by Year 2008–Q3 2012

M & A Deals, Mergers and Acquisitions IPO's - Initial Public Offerings

Source: Thomson Reuters and National Venture Capital Association

*Includes all companies with at least one U.S. VC investor that trade on U.S. exchanges, regardless of domicile.

Source: National Venture Capital Association - NVCA.

One example is SAIL Venture Partners, headquartered in Costa Mesa, California, which specializes in finding firms in the energy/clean-tech sector that are "doing good while doing well." Managing partner Alan Sellers shares, "In our case, we look for global, multibillion-dollar markets. You have to be able to grow the product throughout the world profitably. Those kinds of markets aren't entirely easy to find, but you don't need a huge percentage of the market to succeed. If we get 5 percent of it, we're doing really well." An overview of one company in SAIL's portfolio follows:

ACTIVEION

Activeion is the developer of the ActiveionPro, a hand-held device that has the proven ability by ionization to turn ordinary tap water into a powerful cleansing and disinfectant agent that returns back to tap water after the job is done. This technology replaces traditional cleaning products containing dangerous chemicals in home, office, and schools. Converting to just one ActiveionPro for general-purpose cleaning in commercial applications is equivalent to saving 93 gallons of gasoline and two barrels of oil; and for every two units deployed for cleaning; one metric ton of coal is offset.

Source: Sail Capital Parters, *www.sailcapital.com*, (Accessed May 2, 2012). Reprinted with permission.

The *Directory of Venture Capital & Private Equity Firms*, available in most large public libraries, provides names, addresses, and desired investments of over 2,300 venture-capital firms. Also, local business magazines frequently profile regional venture capitalists. Use these sources and others online to determine which firms are interested in your selected industry and to determine the firms' minimum and maximum investment levels. You might discover venture funds, such as those unearthed by Evergreen Lodge's social entrepreneurs, highlighted in the Passion feature.

GLOBAL**VILLAGE**

Export Loan Programs

The SBA has placed a priority on helping small business exporters by providing a number of loan programs specifically designed to help them develop or expand their export activities. If you own or wish to start a small export business, the following loans may be available to you:

Export Express Program

Fast and easy loans for small exporters
Small business exporters are taking advantage of the world market and selling billions of dollars of goods and services overseas every year. In fact, 70 percent of all exporters have fewer than 20 employees. If you are one of these businesses, or would like to join in this growing trend, and you think you are too small to receive government sponsored export financing, think again!

Streamlined financing up to $500,000
SBA Export Express offers flexibility and ease of use to both borrowers and lenders. It is the simplest export loan product offered by the SBA and allows participating lenders to use their own forms, procedures, and analyses. The SBA provides an answer in 36 hours or less.

Who is eligible to receive Export Express financing?
Any business that has been in operation, although not necessarily in exporting, for at least 12 full months and can demonstrate that the loan proceeds will support its export activity is eligible for Export Express.

What can the loan funds be used for?
Loan proceeds may be used for business purposes that will enhance a company's export development. Export Express can take the form of a term loan or a revolving line of credit. As an example, proceeds can be used to fund participation in a foreign trade show, finance standby letters of credit, translate product literature for use in foreign markets, finance specific export orders, as well as to finance expansions, equipment purchases, and inventory or real estate acquisitions, etc.

How do I apply?
Interested businesses should contact their existing lender to determine if they are an SBA Express lender. Lenders that participate in SBA's Express program are also able to make Export Express loans. Application is made directly to the lender. The lenders use their own application material in addition to SBA's Borrower Information Form. Lenders approve the request and then submit a limited amount of eligibility information to SBA's National Loan Processing Center.

Export Working Capital Program (EWCP)

SBA's Role in Export Financing
Many banks in the U.S. do not provide working capital advances on export orders, export receivables or letters of credit. Because of that, some small businesses may lack necessary export working capital to support their export sales. That is where an SBA program can make the difference. SBA provides lenders with up to a 90 percent guarantee on export loans up to $5 million as a credit enhancement, so that the lenders will make the necessary export working capital available.

The SBA delivers its export loan program through a network of SBA Senior International Credit Officers located in U.S. Export Assistance Centers throughout the country. These specialists understand trade finance and are available to explain SBA's export lending programs, the application process, and forms and to guide exporters in selecting appropriate payment methods. They can also link companies to specialists for increasing export sales and managing foreign payment risk.

(continued)

(continued)

Exporters can apply for EWCP loans in advance of finalizing an export sale or contract. With an approved EWCP loan in place, exporters have greater flexibility in negotiating export payment terms—secure in the assurance that adequate financing will be in place when the export order is won.

Benefits of the EWCP
- Financing for suppliers, inventory or production of export goods
- Export working capital during long payment cycles
- Financing for stand-by letters of credit used as bid or performance bonds or down payment guarantees
- Reserves domestic working capital for the company's sales within the United States
- Permits increased global competitiveness by allowing the exporter to extend more liberal sales terms
- Increases sales prospects in under-developed markets which have high capital costs for importers
- Contributes to the growth of export sales
- Low fees and quick processing times

International Trade Loan Program

The International Trade Loan Program offers term loans for fixed assets and working capital to businesses that plan to start or continue exporting, or that have been adversely affected by competition from imports and need to retool to become more competitive. The proceeds of the loan must enable the borrower to be in a better position to compete. The program provides the lender with a 90 percent guarantee on loans up to $5 million.

How Funds May Be Used
Funds may be used for the following purposes for long term fixed assets:

- Acquisition
- Construction
- Renovation
- Modernization
- Improvement
- Expansion

Funds may also be used for the refinancing of an existing loan.

Who is Eligible for an International Trade Loan?
International Trade loans are available to small businesses that are in a position to expand existing export markets or develop new export markets, or small businesses that have been adversely affected by international trade and can demonstrate that the loan proceeds will improve their competitive position.

For More Information
SBA staff can help you by weighing financing options and risk mitigation as well as providing you with advice and more details about SBA loan products and application procedures. Contact your local U.S. Export Assistance Center to learn more about the programs and whether your business might qualify.

Source: *http://www.sba.gov/content/export-loan-programs* (Accessed April 30, 2012).

vFinance provides a questionnaire shown in Figure 9.4 for people who would like to know if they are ready for venture-capital funding. Take time to review the questions to determine if venture capital is in your future and take the quiz online at *www.vfinance.com* to discover how investors will assess your business idea.

Throughout the chapter we have presented many financing options, but the truth is the funding market changes on a daily basis, with government funding

figure **9.4**

Are You Ready for Venture Capital?

1. **What is the current development stage of your business venture? Choose only one.**
   - **Idea**: Conceptual product without revenues/customers/employees
   - **Start-up**: Prototype product with preliminary sales
   - **Growth**: New product—minimum revenues
   - **Expansion**: Established product with customers—close to break even
   - **Mature**: Established—operating at a profit

2. **What is the value added by your product or service? Please compare to direct and indirect competitors in your industry.**
   - Similar product to others
   - Product offers new features not available elsewhere
   - Radically new product and service with overwhelming advantages
   - Product with 20% to 50% cost–benefit advantage
   - Product with greater than 50% cost–benefit advantage

3. **How developed is your relationship with customers? Pick the best one.**
   - None yet
   - Some identified
   - Signed letters of intent
   - Current test customers
   - Paying customers
   - Established repeat customers

4. **What are your "trailing revenues"? (i.e., sales for the past 12 months)?**
   - None
   - Less than $100,000
   - Between $100,000 to $1M
   - Over $1M
   - Over $5M

5. **What are your expected revenues four years from now?**
   - Less than $1M per year
   - Over $1M but less than $10M per year
   - Over $10M but less than $100M per year
   - Over $100M but less than $500M per year
   - Over $500M

6. **What is your expected market share in your industry in 4 years?**
   - Do not know
   - Less than 20%
   - Between 20% and 40%
   - Between 40% and 70%
   - Over 70%

7. **How large are your target market and industry? Note that you should be very specific. (For example, selling peanuts at the circus puts you in a very small market, not in the multibillion-dollar food or entertainment industry). Base your answers on the preceding two questions, or revise your answers from above.**
   - Less than $10 M per year
   - Over $10M but less than $100M per year
   - Over $100M but less than $500M per year
   - Over $500M but less than $1B per year
   - Over $1B

8. **What is the current state of competition in your industry?**
   - Unidentified competitors
   - Many small competitors
   - Several large competitors dominate the industry
   - One or two large competitors dominate the industry

9. **What is your relative size versus your competitors?**
   - Similar size/advantage over others
   - One of the first movers into the industry
   - Best network and alliances with exclusive contracts
   - First Place: Currently larger by 10% to 49% over next competitor
   - First Place: Currently the largest by 50% over next competitor

10. **What intellectual property does your venture currently have?**
    - None
    - Trademarks and copyrights
    - Process patents
    - Patent-pending technology
    - Patented technology (granted)
    - Patented technology implemented in product
    - Patented technology with royalty stream

11. **Is your key executive team (CEO/CFO/Marketing/CIO/Ops) on board?**
    - Founders only—top spots pending funding
    - CEO and others currently on a part-time basis
    - CEO and others have full-time commitment
    - CEO and others have worked on venture for over 1 year full-time

12. **Has top management had previous successes?**
    - None … yet!
    - With previous employers
    - Small-business success
    - IPO or company sold for > $10M but < $100M
    - Company sold for >$100M
    - IPO taken to market for > $100M

13. **How much money has management committed to the venture so far. This is pure capital, without any in-kind or labor costs.**
    - None
    - Less than $10,000
    - Between $10,000 and $100,000
    - Between $100,000 and $500,000
    - Over $500,000

14. **What are the most likely exit scenarios for your investors, i.e., how will they get their money back in 5 years?**
    - Have not thought about it
    - Interest payment
    - Dividends
    - Sale to management
    - Sale to strategic buyers
    - IPO

15. **What detail exists for your financial statements?**
    - None written yet
    - Basic income statement only
    - Detailed income statement, balance sheet, and cash flows
    - Complete set of statements reviewed by accountant
    - Complete set of statements audited by accountant

16. **How developed is your marketing plan?**
    - None written yet
    - Promotion, pricing, and distribution addressed
    - The above, plus branding and image
    - Test-marketed branding and marketing

17. **How much market research have you done for new or follow-on products?**
    - None
    - Industry literature

(continued)

figure **9.4**

Are You Ready for Venture Capital? *(continued)*

- o Surveys
- o Focus groups
- o Market tests with selected customers
- o Functioning product with multiple customers
18. **How does your Business Plan address inherent risks?**
    - o Best-case scenario is realistic
    - o Worst-case scenarios are outlined
    - o Multiple scenarios are considered and planned
    - o Measures to counter risk are identified
    - o Measures to counter risk are implemented
19. **How detailed is your Business Plan document?**

- o None written yet
- o Executive summary of about four pages
- o Business Plan written by CEO, about 20 pages
- o Total business and operational plan, ready to implement
- o Professionally written and edited plan
20. **How much venture capital are you seeking right now?**
    - o Less than $200,000
    - o Between $200,000 and $1M
    - o Between $1M and $5M
    - o Over $5M

Source: vFinance, Inc. From *http://www.vfinance.com* (Accessed May 2, 2012). Reprinted with permission.

changes and new technology offering new ways for entrepreneurs and investors to meet and commit to each other. Thus, we present in Figure 9.5 an article discussing seven major forces affecting raising money for both startup and venture capital. The article focuses on the software industry primarily but the disruptive technologies are affecting most funding today. As an entrepreneur, your job will be to keep abreast of these changes. Access Stanford Professor Steve Blank's excellent website for the most up to date funding information especially for high-tech companies. Amazing financing options exist today and more are just around the corner!

After thoroughly reviewing all your financing options, it is time to test the waters with Action Step 44.

figure **9.5**

The Seven Forces Disrupting Venture Capital

SEMIL SHAH

Saturday, April 28th, 2012

For the past few years, I have read over what seems like hundreds of blogs and thousands of tweets that either directly claim or indirectly hint at a disruption of traditional venture capital. For some, the factors relate to the economy, that limited partners and institutional investors were reviewing their investment approaches. For others, it seemed as if there was too much money in the asset class, that there was too much money chasing too few real opportunities. There seemed to be a long laundry list of why venture capital was undergoing this shift, but never any thread that could lay out all the factors and synthesize just how each factor contributed to shift, until now...

(Note: 1. *Since "venture capital" is applied to many different industries with vastly different economic structures; this post will focus on software startups. 2. I am not going to list examples below because there are too many and I don't want to exclude any particular companies.)*

First, we have Amazon: It's cheap to build, host, test, and optimize software. Amazon Web Services, for instance, **reduce** operational costs for young companies, directly impacting a startups' burn rate. Whereas in the past a not insignificant part of an investment may be allocated to hosting, Amazon's innovation has helped entrepreneurs better manage costs and dampened the need for venture capital investors to help out early with operational expenses.

(continued)

ACTION STEP 44

Prepare to Meet Your Lenders

Know who your potential lenders or investors are and why they should want to help you.

Part A. List potential lenders and investors. Begin with family and friends and move on to business acquaintances and colleagues. Do not forget to include institutional lenders.

Part B. Now list reasons why lenders or investors should risk their money on your venture. What inducements are you offering potential investors? Creative inducements are certainly part of crowdfunding. The following chapters will discuss the legal form of your business and you will need to ask yourself if incorporation would encourage additional investment.

Part C. Check out the popular crowdfunding sites.

Part D. Test your proposed pitch with your colleagues. Explain that this is just a test, and that you would like their honest feedback on your presentation and the business itself. Watch their reactions, and listen carefully to all their questions and objections. Take the time to write down thorough answers to each of their questions and objections. Send an email to your colleagues with your responses. Ask them to review your responses and ask if they have any additional questions or thoughts. Are there any questions or objections still remaining? If so, take time now to find the answers, as your investors may ask the same questions. Be prepared.

Part E. Time to go out and meet with potential lenders and investors and shake additional branches of the money tree. Good luck!

figure 9.5

The Seven Forces Disrupting Venture Capital *(continued)*

Secondly, Angel Investors: Once a product gets to some proof of concept, an entrepreneur can raise seed funding from an incredibly wide range of sources. Those that are either connected or lucky can solicit checks from family, friends, former bosses and colleagues, or they join incubators (more on this below), or reach out to relatively obscure or more well-known angel investors, all the way up to small institutional funds, what some people refer to as "Super Angels" or "MicroVCs," or websites dedicated to pairing investors with investment opportunities (more on this below). The flood of early-stage capital has triggered some venture capital firms to also invest in the seed stage, where they have to compete directly with smaller funds or vehicles, though a small handful of firms have resisted and focused on Series A-style investments.

Third, we have AngelList: Simply one of the most disruptive forces to the venture industry, the folks behind **AngelList** have created extremely useful social software that pairs investors with investment opportunities. For angel investors, AngelList provides an asynchronous way to scout, monitor, track, and communicate with potential investment; for startups, the system provides an opportunity for them to network, build reputation and good signals, and connects them to a wider range of potential funders. The disruption AngelList provides to venture capital is that the system could theoretically be used for larger Series A and B fundings, and in some cases, probably has. It remains to be seen if it can scale across to this level, but given how much it has accomplished in a few years, it's not out of the question.

Fourth, we have Kickstarter and crowdfunding: For some particular startups that aren't able to secure seed funds, either from angels, super angels, angel-focused software, or venture capitalists that make seed investments, they can leverage crowdfunding platforms like **Kickstarter** to tap into an even wider pool of available funds. And now with the JOBS Act, which will **allow** for crowdfunding of certain startups in certain situations, new companies can now raise small amounts of money from many different people, just as a political candidate may use small online donations from a large base to raise funds.

Fifth, there's Y Combinator: While there seems to be an incubator popping up weekly nowadays, the system, network, and brand built by the partners at **Y Combinator** has, in a relatively short period of time, captured significant power in the early-stage ecosystem by attracting, vetting, and training technical entrepreneurs on the ins and outs of how to start technology companies. Each class in Y Combinator prepares for their Demo Day, and each company has the option to **accept** $150,000 in convertible debt — and not just from anyone (more on this below). Having this cash on hand affords these companies a bit more time and runway should they need it, and gives them some negotiating leverage when talking to larger investors who are keen to invest, sometimes resulting in higher valuations that venture capitalists have to compete against.

Sixth, is "New" Venture Capital: The money given to these YC companies isn't just normal money — it's in part from a new style of venture capital pioneered by firms like Andreessen Horowitz (**A16Z**) and **DST**. While DST has made big bets and partnered with YC, A16Z has also raised large funds with a relatively small partnership, choosing instead to challenge the traditional venture capital personnel structure by operationalizing services across functional areas such as business development, recruiting, public relations, and sales. For a founder, the services offered in this model are attractive, and this has motivated some other venture capital firms to change their own structures in an effort to provide more services to their companies. Additionally, the A16Z investment thesis, which seems to be designed around a belief that this is a particularly unique period of opportunity for transformation both on the web and in mobile and that a small share of winners in these categories will produce outsized returns. As a result, they seem to be willing to pay higher prices, which either forces traditional venture to compete or wait for the next thing.

And, finally, seventh are secondary markets: Now that early-stage shareholders (investors, founders, employees) of certain companies can sell their shares on these secondary markets, such as **SecondMarket** or **SharesPost**, they are able to access liquidity much earlier in the past. On the flip side, larger venture capital funds that may have **missed out** on the next big thing because the new company was incubated, or crowdfunded, or funded via a social network or small or large angel investors may have a chance to own a piece of the entity through these markets. In some cases, venture capital firms have been quite opportunistic to buy and sell shares of larger web companies in a short period of time, making a quick flip and marketing to the world that they, too, have invested in a particular company. While these markets provide venture capital with access, they also have to compete with a larger number of firms for these deals, a factor that could drive up prices and thereby affect returns.

(continued)

─────────────────────────────── figure **9.5**

The Seven Forces Disrupting Venture
Capital *(continued)*

All of these forces combined, and each individually in their own way, have altered the landscape for traditional venture capital in software. It is on average significantly more difficult for traditional firms to find early-stage opportunities because there is more competition for those investments, and once a company does breakout and require more institutional funding, the prices for those rounds may not look like they have in the past. Some of this is reflective of the competitive forces that set market prices for private companies, or, depending on where you sit, is simply the new price to pay in order to own a piece of these coveted assets.

And while we're able to analyze what has happened so far, I have no clue what the next few years will hold. Will the next big breakout originate from an incubator, will it be funded by software platforms, or will it be discovered by a small set of angels and venture capitalists, as it has for so many years to date? In the great race to find incredible talent before others, and the great race to own shares in private companies, there are more questions here than answers, but there's no denying that it will be fascinating to see unfold.

By: TechCrunch *columnist **Semil Shah** currently works at **Votizen** and is based in Palo Alto. You can follow him on Twitter **@semil***

Source: From TechCrunch, "The Seven Forces Disrupting Capital." Content © 2012 AOL Inc. TechCrunch is a trademark of AOL Inc. Used with permission.

PASSION

The Resort that Serves its Staff

Evergreen Lodge Founders Turn Around Yosemite lodge and Employees Around 2001, the founders of Evergreen Lodge began renovation on a lodge and added 50 new cabins after raising an initial $10 million through loans and obtaining equity investment from both public and private sources outside Yosemite in Groveland, California. The lodge currently has 90 cabins spread throughout a beautiful forest, dining facilities, and a full service guided recreation department.

But what makes Evergreen Lodge unique is the owners' passion for "creating a supportive environment and rewarding work experience for their staff". One passion the owners have is for an employment internship program for urban low-income young-adults, which they now self-fund. Offering career-oriented training, work experience and access to vast recreational experiences available at Yosemite, the Lodge hopes to train individuals to gain entry into full-time positions at the Lodge and in their communities. Evergreen aims to give back to society as it grows its business.

Evergreen Lodge works with Juma Ventures, which supports and brings their expertise to the internship program. In addition, the Lodge works with Pacific Community Ventures, a non-profit working to invest and develop California businesses, which can bring economic gains to low-income communities.

Companies, like Evergreen Lodge, who "use the power of business to solve social and environmental problems" can be certified as B Corporations today. The lodge joined Method, Dansko, and Seventh Generation, amongst others as founding members. Over 600 companies are now certified and you can find out more about B Corporations at *http://www.bcorporation.net*.

■ SOCIAL ENTREPRENEURSHIP FUNDING

Social entrepreneurs need to seek various funding sources that specialize in providing capital to those wishing to affect social change. Ashoka, Acumen Fund, Skoll Foundation, and the Kauffman Fund are excellent starting points as well as the Foundation Directory Online.

In addition to direct funding, try crowdfunding and discover the many social entrepreneur organizations that sponsor awards and offer incentives to solve problems. One such source is InnoCentive, "the global innovation marketplace where creative minds solve some of the world's most important problems for cash awards up to $1 million. Commercial, governmental, and humanitarian organizations engage with InnoCentive to solve problems that can impact humankind in areas ranging from the environment to medical advancements." Reach out!

Source: *https://www.innocentive.com/ar/challenge/10300000016.*

■ SUMMARY

Few start-up firms have access to venture-capital markets, bank financing, vendor credit, or angels at the beginning. The majority of ventures start from the bottom up—with self-financing and capital from friends and family.

Be prepared to put in sweat equity for at least the first few years. Learn how to conserve capital and manage debt and accounts receivables. By bootstrapping early on, you will be able to maintain ownership. If you are fulfilling your customers' needs and keeping your nose to the grindstone, your day will come.

Money creates its own world. It has its own customs, rituals, and rules. Before you start asking people for money for your business, research the world of money. Read constantly, because in the field of entrepreneurial financing, changes come on a daily basis. Find someone who knows more about money than you do. Ask questions. Listen. As you continue to work on your Business Plan, remember what lenders are looking for:

- Capacity and time frame of repayment
- Character and commitment of borrower
- Strong idea with identifiable target market in a growing market
- Collateral
- Background and experience of management team

Keep excellent financial records. When investors come calling; you will be prepared with the documents they want to see. How many customers do you have? What repeat business do you have? What is your average sale? How do you make money?

■ THINK POINTS FOR SUCCESS

- Your banker may be a doorway to the world of money. Use that door.
- Conserving capital is essential in the beginning and prudent at all times.
- Take as little capital out of your business as possible.

- In dealing with bankers and vendors, use lots of open-ended questions, such as "What other steps do you think I need to take to improve my Business Plan?"
- Become operational as fast as you can.
- Aim for your break-even point and strong cash flow as soon as possible.

■ KEY POINTS FROM ANOTHER VIEW

2012 Indiana SBDC Emerging Businesses Edge Awards Winners

The ISBDC EDGE Awards celebrate Economic Development & Growth through Entrepreneurship. EDGE Award recipients fall into one of two categories: Emerging or eEstablished businesses. Eligibility is limited to clients of the ISBDC who in the past year have received one-on-one confidential counseling with a trained ISBDC Business Advisor, participated in ISBDC programs, or used ISBDC tools and business resources. EDGE Award recipients have been selected locally by the regional ISBDC staff who work directly with the business.

Btown Delivers
Bloomington, IN

Franc Perrelle first came to the ISBDC in November of 2010 seeking help with starting-up a food delivery business in Bloomington. The WC ISBDC initially assisted Franc with a business feasibility analysis and help with the legal and governmental aspects of starting up. After the first meeting, Franc decided to use the Business Plan Pro software package to write his business plan. In four counseling sessions over the next three months, Franc completed his plan and received assistance and feedback on topics ranging from market analysis to financial projections. During this time, the ISBDC provided First Research reports, ESRI demographic reports, and ProfitCents reports in conjunction with counseling to strengthen Franc's plan.

He utilized his own assets to fund the startup of Btown Delivers, which opened in February 2011. Btown Delivers provides delivery services for restaurants that typically do not have their own delivery service via online orders at www.btowndelivers.com and phone orders. Since the company's startup, the WC ISBDC has assisted in operations, marketing and future strategic growth planning. Btown Delivers has steadily grown from the initial startup one-person operation to five drivers as of November 2011. The company utilized its own resources and strengths to expand into a new market niche providing delivery and logistics services for medical offices in several cities in Southern Indiana in the second half of 2011. They are currently planning on expanding both their restaurant and medical delivery business to other cities in Indiana in 2012.

CPR – Cell Phone Repair
Evansville, IN

Scott Hutslar came to the Southwest ISBDC for assistance in reviewing his business plan, which included his financial projections, and to discuss financing options for the purchase of a franchise, Cell Phone Repair. The SW ISBDC helped review the financials of the business plan, provided him with some answers on local licenses, and passed on some names for his facility remodeling. Scott was able to open the business on January 2011 with three full time employees and is looking to expand into Jasper.

Echo Karaoke
West Lafayette, IN

Jim and Brian first came to the Hoosier Heartland ISBDC through the Entrepreneur Certificate Program at Purdue in May of 2009. They were primarily looking for assistance with their business plan.

Their business idea was Echo Karaoke, Purdue's Premier Karaoke & Lounge, with the target market being Asian Purdue students. Their advantage is the karaoke machines that have been imported from Hong Kong that provide family-style entertainment with over 70,000 songs.

The HH ISBDC provided assistance in developing a business plan, financials, legal structure, obtaining proper licensing, and general operations of the business.

Jim and Brian held a "soft opening" for Echo Karaoke in June 2011, which had a great turnout. They never expected such a huge crowd that evening, or the abrupt end to the night when the power went out! Over the past five months Echo Karaoke added 10 staff, secured around $300,000 in financing, and has had over 700 singers pass through their doors.

Fish Face Photo Booths
Indianapolis, IN

Fish Face Photo Booths started November 2010 and makes/markets photo booths for clients wanting to rent them for events and for vending applications. Fish Face was started by Beth Johnson, who wanted to create higher quality and more reliable photo booths than what were currently on the market. Fish Face was recently featured in the international trade magazine *Fun World Magazine*, highlighting Fish Face's social media capabilities.

Fish Face has sold photo booths to clients all over the United States and the world, including Spain, Poland, Mexico, Saudi Arabia, Australia, and Morocco. The SBDC assisted Beth on her business plan and encouraged her to enter the Entrepreneurship Advancement Center's business plan competition, which they won and received a prize package valued at $25,000 in January 2011. As production and sales ramped up in 2011, and with the addition of three employees, the SBDC has provided ongoing counseling on business strategy and technical assistance on exporting regulations and procedures.

Respiratory Medical Solutions
Lawrenceburg, IN

Josh Veid and Lou Grove first visited the Southeast ISBDC in October of 2010 for assistance in developing a business plan after reading about the ISBDC in the local paper. The primary focus of the business is offering durable medical equipment to be used in the home.

During the start-up phase, Josh and Lou received guidance in the areas of business planning, financial projections, assessing market potential, and determining appropriate levels of start-up inventory and industry assessments. With their personal investment of $17,000 as well as $10,000 from silent investors, Respiratory Medical Solutions opened in Lawrenceburg in November of 2011. RMS, Inc. carries an inventory of medical supplies including sleep disorder therapy products, mobility products, diabetic shoes, aids to daily living and scrubs and medical accessories.

Throughout the last year, the SBDC has offered additional assistance in financial decision-making, resulting in a $10,000 line of credit, assisted RMS with updating their business plan to secure grant funding, and has offered ongoing support for both branding and marketing opportunities as well as sales staff training.

Although it took nearly a year to complete, RMS has recently been accepted by two prominent insurance companies. The first several months of operations were challenging, but RMS has expanded their product offerings in the second quarter of 2011, resulting in a substantial revenue increase.

SWAT – Severe Weather Alert Team
Muncie, IN

In the summer of 2011, Brad Maushart, Brandon Redmond, Chris Bergin, and Joe Krupa approached the EC ISBDC for help with multiple aspects of running their business. The four are "storm chasers" and wanted to turn their fascination with weather into a tourism business.

After an initial assessment, the business advisor determined that the clients needed to produce a business plan, understand how their corporate structure needed to operate, and understand proper handling of the finances and marketing. Since their goal was to enable the principals to leave their current occupations and concentrate fully on their new business, the counselor set up a program to cover all of their concerns.

SWAT (Severe Weather Alert Team) chases storms for a deeper understanding of what is going on in the skies above. They chase storms in 13 different states. SWAT not only chases severe and inclement weather, but provides real time updates to media outlets, the National Weather Service, and to the general public. SWAT recently signed a partnership with WXIN Fox 59.

Voice To Print Captioning, LLC
Crown Point, IN

When her daughter developed some hearing loss, Kathy Cortopassi decided that she wanted to expand her court reporting business to include services for the disabled. Kathy came to the Northwest ISBDC in early 2009 for this expansion assistance. Because she was looking for peer advice on running a business, the NW ISBDC introduced her to the local BPW-Business & Professional Women. Kathy received strategic planning assistance, which resulted in her opening her first office at the Entech Innovation Center in Valparaiso. She has recently moved to a new office at the Purdue Technology Center in Crown Point.

Kathy plans to grow her business significantly in 2012 by adding four new products. As a result, she will need additional capital and the NW ISBDC is now working with Kathy to help her revise and update a business plan in order to secure the financing she will need. Kathy has rewritten the marketing strategy part of her plan using market research provided by the ISBDC. She hopes to reach a new market with the provided information on hearing loss among veterans returning from Iraq and Afghanistan. She estimates an increase of sales of over 100% and adding at least one employee a quarter.

Source: "2012 Emerging Businesses EDGE Awards Winners," ISBDC, from *www.isbdc.org/2012-emerging-businesses-edge-awards-winners/*, (Accessed April 28, 2012). Reprinted with permission.

■ ACTION STEPS

Action Step 42 Befriend a Banker   249
Action Step 43 Designing a Vendor Statement Form 253

Action Step 44 Prepare to Meet Your Lenders 262

■ KEY TERMS

line of credit 236
Four Cs *240*
home-equity loan *240*
home-equity line of credit *240*
bootstrap *242*
Crowdfunding *242*

Annual Percentage Rate (APR) *243*
microlending *245*
SBA-guaranteed loans *247*
information loop *247*
your turf *247*
equipment leases *248*

Lean manufacturing *249*
vendor statement *252*
COD *253*
seed stage *254*
initial public offering (IPO) *255*

Image_Source/iStockphoto.com

Legal Concerns
Staying Out of Court

Learning Objectives

- Understand the importance and necessity of professional legal advice from the start.

- Decide which legal form is best for your business and you.

- Explore the good, the bad, and the ugly of partnerships.

- Review the advantages and disadvantages of forming a Limited Liability Company, S Corporation, and a C Corporation.

- Explore nonprofit opportunities.

- Understand legal escape routes.

- Explore family business issues.

- Review patent protection.

- Understand copyright laws.

- Take action to protect your trademark or service mark.

- Investigate and explore licensing your invention.

In your interviews of successful entrepreneurs, you have probably run across the four main legal forms for small business: sole proprietorship, partnership, corporation, and Limited Liability Company. Which is the right organizational form for you?

Incorporate Form an artificial, immortal business entity

It is common, although not always advisable, for an entrepreneur to start out as a sole proprietorship or a partnership and then to **incorporate** later. But after you explore the options throughout the chapter, you may decide to incorporate sooner than later. Many social entrepreneurs are entering the market under new organizational structures, which we will explore later as well.

No doubt you have also interviewed many entrepreneurs who are part of a family business. Since such a large portion of businesses today are operated by family members, we will explore the benefits and issues surrounding their operation.

Lastly, the chapter will take a turn and look at protecting your newly formed business with the proper use of patents, trademarks, and copyrights. And also look at licensing your product as another way to enter the entrepreneurial world.

■ IT PAYS TO LOOK AHEAD

Where is your business headed? Who will be a part of your business? If you enter a partnership, how will you exit? What liabilities could occur? Are your personal assets sheltered? Is insurance in place? Are you aware of various tax structures and potential changes?

Imagine that you are in a great business with a partner you trust and respect. When should you incorporate or sign a partnership agreement? Perhaps sooner than you think. That's what Phil Johnson would tell you now.

Sail Away

The Power Sailor, Sunbiz, was my idea. My partner, Steve, said it would break us, and I should have listened to him. We'd been friends for at least a dozen years and we'd been partners for the past three. This year we were each going to clear more than $200,000.

I had this idea that we could buy a boat for the partnership; write off the down payment as an expense, and do our company image a world of good.

"Image, Steve," I said. "Image."

"Uh-oh," Steve said. "Here we go with the immeasurable intangibles."

"It's not intangible when you think about those prospects coming from Chicago next week," I said. "A cruise to Captiva Island should soften them up, don't you think?"

Write-offs Legitimate business deductions accepted by the IRS

The first payment wasn't due for a month, and when Steve and I took the boat out with our wives, I felt like a prince of the sea. We'd pulled off a smooth deal, and I patted myself on the back every time I thought about the write-offs.

Our boat, Sunbiz, boosted business, just like I'd thought it would. We closed the Chicago deal and were busy on a couple of other deals that looked promising. We made the first payment with no trouble, and when Steve countersigned the check, he admitted he was beginning to like the boat.

Countersigning A situation in which two or more signatures are required before action can occur

For a couple of weeks, Steve took his laptop and slept on the Sunbiz. I didn't recognize this early sign. We took the Sunbiz out one weekend with four prospects from St. Louis, and Steve seemed preoccupied. I closed the deal late on Sunday, 15 minutes before putting them on the plane for home. But when I called Steve's house to tell him the good news, his wife, Mary, told me he was still at the boat.

Monday, Steve didn't come to work until almost noon. He looked tired, but he handed me his projections and we got on with planning our strategy for the next couple of months.

"Anything wrong, partner?" I asked. "You seem a little far-off today."

"Sorry," Steve said. He was never one to admit to having problems. "My mind wandered a bit there. Where were we?"

On Thursday, Steve still didn't make it to work after missing Wednesday. I called his house in the morning. No answer. I thought of driving down to the dock to check the boat, but didn't. When I arrived at the dock with clients later that day, there was no Sunbiz. A dock worker said Steve had taken off early that morning.

I was in shock. There I stood, with two clients in deck shoes and shorts.

Then Joey, the guy who pumps gas, came up waving a gas bill for $800—one I'd thought Steve had paid. And the bad news didn't end there. The next day, a fellow who sells radar equipment called me with a $2,000 bill.

My cell phone rang. It was Mary, Steve's wife. She read me Steve's goodbye letter—he was off to explore the world.

Now my stomach was really hurting. My partner Steve was gone and I was going to have to cover all his business debts, including the payment on the Sunbiz. Terrific!

The problem was that Steve and I had never seen the need for having anything in writing. We were both men of good faith. We had each pulled our weight in the business, and we had balanced each other's skills.

Now that Steve was gone, I felt lost, angry, and betrayed. For the first time in 22 years of business, I made an appointment to talk to a lawyer. He shook his head and said, "Let's try to solve this problem!"

Last week, when I was closing the business down and preparing to return to work for my old boss, I received a postcard from Steve, from Tahiti. "Sorry, Phil," it read. "Didn't mean to run out on you. It was the only way I could handle it. These things happen. Your partner, Steve."

■ HIRE AN EXPERIENCED ATTORNEY AT THE BEGINNING

If you do not want to end up left high and dry like Phil, start your search for a good, experienced small-business attorney now. Whether you are opening a business as a sole proprietor, a partnership, or a corporation, attorneys will help you:

- Create the right business structure for the venture—a structure that gives the protection, tax treatment, and flexibility you will need.
- Review advertising and marketing materials to ensure no state or federal laws are violated.
- Organize your human resources department to keep you outside the courtroom; hiring and firing employees is problematic to say the least—improper handling of even one employee can cost you your business.
- Research and protect you in regards to product liability.
- Review all contracts and agreements before you sign.
- Protect intellectual property through proper use and development of trademarks, service marks, copyrights, and patents.
- License your product.
- Handle collections and bankruptcy problems.
- Plan your exit strategy.
- Write partnership agreements and buy–sell agreements.

Network with your contacts to secure a lawyer with experience in your industry. Many laws are state specific, so you also need someone well versed in your state's laws. This is not the time to save money by using your niece who just passed the bar examination.

Large law firms may prove very advantageous for rapidly growing biotechnology, environmental, and manufacturing firms, all of which often

Product liability Legal exposure if a customer becomes ill or sustains injury or property damage because of a faulty product

Trademark A word, phrase, logo, design, or anything used to identify goods or services and differentiate them from competitors

Service mark Used to protect services offered

Copyright Protects the expression of an idea

Patent Right to make, sell, offer for sale or use an invention

Bankruptcy Legal and financial process if a debtor's financial obligations are greater than his or her assets

Exit strategy A plan to disengage from business at a future point in time

Buy–sell agreement An advance contractual agreement that determines how a business is to be valued if one or more partners buys out another

ACTION STEP 45

Interview Lawyers

1. Network your business contacts for the names of three to five attorneys with experience in forming small business corporations and partnerships. Concentrate on those with experience in your industry.
2. Contact the state bar association and review information on each attorney.
3. Review the most promising candidates' websites thoroughly and access any online reviews. Contact three or four of the most promising candidates and set up appointments to interview prospective lawyers. The first thing to look for is someone you can get along with. Then look for experience in the world of small business. A hot trial lawyer may have a lot of charisma, but you want a nuts-and-bolts, experienced, small-business or entrepreneurial specialist who can save you time, pain, and money.
4. During your meeting, discuss fees and costs for such things as drawing up a complex partnership agreement or a buy-sell agreement. In addition, discuss the legal cost of setting up a corporation. Ask what steps you can take to keep legal fees in check. Note: However, legal fees are not an area you want to scrimp on.
5. A good lawyer will offer perspectives that will be helpful in the formation of your business. You may have to search for a while, and it will cost you, but there is no substitute for good legal help. After your interviews, review your impressions of each attorney, and determine which one you could work well with over the long run. Who are you most compatible with? Who do you believe you could have the best rapport with? Who do you trust? Who can introduce you to the most valuable players in your industry? Select your lawyer and move forward in a good strong working relationship.

Attorney-client privilege Confidentiality of communications

Retainer fee An agreement to secure attorney services for a fixed fee within a given period of time or for a specific legal problem

have specific legal and technical issues. Expertise is vital for initial and continued success in these types of businesses, and thus they require the resources of a large firm. Also, the laws and interpretation of the laws are constantly in flux and only those who deal daily with them will be able to guide you properly.

If you are dealing with intellectual property and/or international customers and manufacturers, access and utilize the sources in the chapter's Entrepreneurial Resources and Global Village. Complex issues require experienced legal professional advice.

Another important role an attorney plays is to provide you entrée into his or her "circle" of contacts throughout an industry and to bankers, investors, advertising agencies, and accountants. No amount of money can buy you such ready access.

Business litigators are attorneys who primarily handle lawsuits. Initially, you are more likely to be looking for a transactional attorney whose specialty is handling corporate and contract matters. If you are dealing in an industry or an area known for litigation, then having a firm that covers both litigation and transactions would be preferable. Before hiring an attorney, contact your state bar to make sure the person is in good standing.

Along with a strong attorney, you need to have an experienced accountant, financial planner, banker, and insurance agent on your team. Their support and expertise will keep you on track, out of jail, and protected from unforeseen circumstances. Develop an attorney–client relationship before an employee or customer sues you or your partner leaves for Tahiti. Preventive legal fees are far less costly than clean-up fees if you are sued.

After you have networked to find several lawyers, contact each of them to set up a half-hour consultation. Prepare for your meetings by listing several questions you have about your business as well as questions about financial issues. You are looking for someone you are comfortable with and someone who understands the needs of your business. The attorney–client privilege covers your meetings, so be honest and share relevant information. If you are prepared and organized, you will be able to gather a great deal of information in a short time. Select someone with a reputation for integrity and experience in your industry. Complete Action Step 45.

Understanding How Lawyers Operate and Reducing Your Legal Costs

Lawyers either charge by the hour for services they render or they work on a retainer fee based on prepaid hours. Or you may have access to a prepaid legal plan in which you receive a variety of services for a flat annual fee. In addition, in the high-tech sector, lawyers may be willing to work for stock options or other alternative forms of payment. Legal fees range from $150 to more than $500 an hour. Specialized attorneys, such as patent or copyright experts, have hourly charges that may top $800.

To benefit from each appointment with your lawyer, arm yourself first with basic legal research you conduct using the library or Internet. This will cut down the time you spend with the lawyer and may reduce your fees.

As suggested throughout the text, using online legal resources and books does *not* eliminate the need for—and should *never* be used as a substitute for—professional legal advice from your attorney. However, legal online sources *do* provide an excellent starting point for gathering information. In addition, many of the sites provide guidelines on selecting legal counsel, which may be of great service—especially if you need to locate a specialized attorney, such as a trademark specialist.

The following sites, in addition to many others provided throughout the text, offer excellent preliminary information:

- **American Law Source Online** is a compilation of links to U.S. legal information as well as links to Mexican and Canadian resources.
- **Findlaw** includes basic legal information concerning contracts, employment, and patents.
- **Internet Legal Resource Group** links to over 4,000 websites and is an excellent source of legal forms.
- **American Patent and Trademark Law Center** provides access to basic patent and trademark information.
- **Legal Information Institute** provides access to constitutions, codes, court opinions, statutes, enterprise law, etc.
- **Nolo**'s vast legal workbooks, manuals and website will assist you.
- **More Business** offers access to articles with advice covering legal, marketing, and technology issues.

Again, these and other sites provide excellent information and advice, but *always* use experienced legal counsel when conducting business transactions.

■ WHICH ORGANIZTIONAL STRUCTURE IS BEST FOR YOU?

Only you, your lawyer, business and tax advisors together can decide what form your business should take based on your present situation, the litigation and dynamics within your industry, and the future you desire. Discuss the following with your advisors before making the determination:

- International exposure
- Tax implications
- Liability issues
- Litigiousness of customers, employees, and businesses in your state
- Plans for business growth
- Family structure and family member involvement in the business
- Relationship with potential partners
- Capital requirements
- Exit strategy
- Employment issues
- Possible tax losses which can be carried forward
- Taking your firm to a public offering (if you are so inclined and in an industry which warrants this question)

Spend time and money consulting with your financial team to determine what organizational structure is best for you early on. There are many pitfalls along the way and change can be costly. Let your team provide guidance and help you avoid major errors.

The legal form of your business is just that-a form, a shape. To your customers, the particular form you choose may not be obvious; but to you, the right shape is absolutely essential. You want your business to be rock-solid, stable, and protected, and you want to be able to change its form if the first choice does not work.

Beyond the mental images we have of these forms of ownership, there are business realities—and various amounts of paperwork. Table 10.1 summarizes the differences among the various forms.

table **10.1**——————————————————————————————————

Comparison of Business Entities

Applicable Factor	Sole Proprietor	Partnership	Limited Liability Company*	S Corporation	C Corporation
Formation	None	Partnership agreement	Articles of Organization filed in state recognizing LLCs	Articles of Incorporation Must meet criteria to file as S Corp	Articles of Incorporation
Owner Eligibility Number of Owners	One	Two or more for limited partnership; one or more general and one or more limited for general partnership	No limit	Max 100 Shareholders	No limit
Type of Owners	Individual	No limitation	No limitation	Individuals and certain trusts	No limitation
Capital Structure	No stock	No limitations (multiple classes)	No limitation	Only one class of stock	No limitations (multiple classes permitted)
Liability	Unlimited	General partners jointly and severally liable. Limited partners are generally limited to capital contributions.	Limited to member's capital contribution	Limited to shareholders' contributions	Limited to shareholder's capital contributions
Operational Phase					
Tax Year	Calendar year	Generally calendar year	Generally calendar year	Generally calendar year	Generally any year permitted (limit for personal service corporation)
Tax on Income	Individual level	Owner level	Member level	Owner level	Corporate level
Allocation of Income/ Deductions	N/A	Permitted if substantial economic effect	Permitted if substantial economic effect	Not permitted (except through debt/equity structure)	Not permitted (except through multiple equity structure)
Character of Income/ Deductions	Flow-through to individual	Flow-through to partners	Flow-through to members	Flow-through to shareholders	No flow-through to shareholders

*Some states (New York, for example) use the term LLP—Limited Liability Partnership.

© Cengage Learning 2014

■ EVALUATING BUSINESS STRUCTURES

Fictitious business name statement An accurate and easy-to-find record of the responsible party who is conducting business

To open a sole proprietorship, you might need only a city license, a resale license, and to file a Fictitious business name statement (also called a Doing Business As or DBA) in your local newspaper. If you plan to have employees, you will need to obtain an employer's identification number (EIN) from the federal government (see Appendix C).

The legal paperwork for a partnership is sometimes as simple as that for a sole proprietorship, if all parties agree on basic concepts. You can form a partnership with just a handshake and if you are *very* lucky it might work. But, we strongly urge you to hire a lawyer to prepare a partnership agreement that will protect you from trouble. Do not be left high and dry. The 10 percent or less of small businesses in the United States who are in partnerships know the importance of selecting partners wisely and carefully.

Subchapter S corporation Legal entity that may provide positive tax treatment for small business

A limited liability company (LLC) may be ideal for closely held firms. It offers limited personal liability protection to all owners, termed members, and is treated like a partnership or Subchapter S corporation on members' individual tax returns. This avoids the double taxation of income (tax on business profits and individual income) and is usually less costly to form than a corporation. An LLC operating agreement must be filed with the state (see Figure 10.1).

Forming a corporation takes the most paperwork but gives you more flexibility and a shield that may protect you in case your products or services harm someone. Table 10.1 briefly summarizes the major business entities.

Sole Proprietorships

Most small businesses begin as sole proprietorships. If you start a business on your own without partners, you are a sole proprietor *unless* you form an LLC or corporation. If this form is your choice, the paperwork will be relatively easy. Check with your local city offices to determine which licenses will be needed to operate in your city or refer online to business.gov.

If you are a service business, you may be required to purchase a license to conduct business in *each* city in which you operate. In some cities, inspectors visit work sites to ensure that all businesses are in compliance.

Recently, one contractor was surprised to find a neighboring city was using air surveillance to locate remodeling projects. One of which was his and he had not procured a license to operate in the city. The fine was stiff. With new technology comes many additional ways that your business can and will be tracked both online and offline. Thus, procure required licenses—fines are considerably more expensive than licenses.

Discuss tax requirements with your accountant, insurance matters with an insurance representative, and legal issues with an attorney before you open your doors. If you are conducting a business in a name other than your own, the Uniform Commercial Code (UCC) requires that you publish notice in your community newspaper to notify customers and creditors of who owns the business. Corporations may be exempt. Contact your newspaper for the DBA forms, fill out the forms, and send a check—usually for less than $100—to the newspaper to complete the process. Normally, this must be done prior to opening your bank account.

For a moment, list all the advantages of a sole proprietor in one column and then take a few minutes to see how each of those advantages can oftentimes turn into disadvantages. For example, being your own boss is wonderful--until you want to take a vacation, get sick, or need another viewpoint or additional capital.

Also, you can make your own hours. Unfortunately, many entrepreneurs find they work 60 to 80 hours a week. However, it may be possible to come in early and stay late!

You are the final and oftentimes only decision maker. However, many entrepreneurs express that they feel very lonely at times and overwhelmed with the pressure.

Seek out support amongst other entrepreneurs who understand "living and working the dream," both the advantages and the disadvantages. Throughout the text we have highlighted many organizations who provide local as well as national and international support. Many entrepreneurs also join local Meet-up or start-up groups and others form their own support groups.

Partnerships

A partnership, as many like Phil find out too late, is only an accounting entity. It does not shield you from legal trouble. It will not make your business immortal or continuous, and it is taxed in the same way as a sole proprietorship. The main advantages of a partnership are that it hopefully offers financial and moral support.

A partnership is made up of at least two parties. There can be more, but the more partners a business has, the trickier decision making becomes. Think of a ship with a dozen captains—who will chart the ship's course?

Limited partnership Two or more partners, where one partner is liable only for the amount of her investment

In a limited partnership composed of two or more limited partners and one general partner, the general partner assumes both the managerial duties and the downside risk. A limited partner's liability is restricted to the amount of his or her original investment, as long as he or she has had no role in management decisions. *Do not enter into such a partnership without legal advice.*

You can form a partnership with a handshake and dissolve it without one; however, it is not advisable to proceed with any partnership, *including* those with family members or friends, without the benefit of legal counsel.

Dissolution of partnership The separation of partners, an eventuality that needs to be prepared for with intricate planning and much thought

When forming your partnership, one of the major contingencies to consider is the dissolution of the partnership. Partnerships can end as a result of death, illness, divorce, lack of interest, financial or philosophical differences, or desire for a change in lifestyle. Protect your business, yourself, and your loved ones.

Key person life or disability insurance Financial protection for the firm in case of death or disability of key employees or owners

In case of death, these agreements are often funded by "key person" life insurance policies on the owners so that if one dies, the other owners can collect the life insurance policy's proceeds and use those funds to buy out the deceased's interest in the business. "Key person" disability insurance policies can also be purchased.

For dissolving the partnership under other circumstances, your buy-sell agreement should indicate who will evaluate the business, how payment will be made by the remaining partners, and over what time period. As your business grows and changes, you will want to reevaluate your agreement. When partners split up, and most eventually do, a buy-sell agreement may keep the dissolution out of court and emotions to a minimum. Think of it as a prenuptial agreement.

A partnership is somewhat of a paradox. In a legal sense, the partnership does not do much for you; but as many partners admit, there are sound psychological and financial reasons for going into business with someone else

What are some of those reasons? Say you have analyzed your personal skills, and realize you need balance in a couple of critical areas. For example, you may be an engineer who can come up with 20 original ideas a day, but you could not sell ice in Florida in the summer. Or perhaps you do not have much money, so you need a partner who can supply your new business with capital. Many successful business owners could never have started or succeeded in business without a partner.

Before committing to a partnership, realize that friendship alone will not resolve business problems. All involved partners need to assess what each brings to the table and then decide if what is brought is worth the complications of a partnership. There will be many unspoken fears and needs for all involved parties in the begining and along the way. Thus, keeping the lines of communication open is essential for survival.

Business counselors and lawyers run lucrative practices trying to work out the problems of warring partners. To reduce problems, do your research before starting a partnership, and talk continually to keep the partnership successful. You must trust your partners.

Remember you most likely will spend more time each week with your business partner than your marriage partner. A partnership is oftentimes like a marriage but without love. During tough times in a marriage, factors such as duty, commitment, and children may hold the partnership together. What will hold your business together during the rocky times?

Concerns to discuss with potential partners follow:

Questions for Partner Discussion

- **Management and control:** Who will make the final decisions on both small and large issues? Who will have control and responsibility for each area of the business? One advertising agency partnership solved the final decision maker status by trading off the presidency each year.
- **Dispute resolution:** How will disputes between the partners be resolved? Will you use mediation or arbitration if you reach a stalemate? Or flip a coin?
- **Financial contributions:** How much will each partner contribute? It is necessary to look at not only initial contributions but also possible future financial injections. An initial 50–50 partnership may turn into a 75–25 partnership if capital needs arise and only one partner has additional funds available. How will each of you deal with this change? If one partner supplies the risk capital and another the sweat capital, how will profits be divided? How will profits and responsibilities change if the financial contributions, time commitments, or responsibilities change?
- **Time and contributions:** How much time will each partner commit? And are these contributions considered equal, if one is a design engineer and the other is doing administrative work only? Will profit distributions reflect variances in time, effort, and experience?
- **Demise of the partnership:** If the partnership is to be dissolved, how will the ending be dealt with? What plans are in place for a buy-out procedure? How will the valuation of the business be determined in the event of a partner's death or disability or the sale of the business? What steps should you take to protect the business and its transfer?
- **New partners:** Can new partners be added? If so, what will be the process for accepting additional partners? How many partners are you willing to take on? Do current partners have veto power over the addition of a new partner?
- **Communication styles:** You don't have to have the same style but you *do* have to understand and work with each other's styles. Check out some of the resources in Chapter 12 on "Rounding Out the Personalities of Your Team" to help you uncover your communication styles and open up discussions.
- **Participation of family members as employees and their input into the business:** See Key Points for additional practical information.
- **Ethics:** Review the ethics material in Chapter 12. Answer the ethics questionnaires separately, and then sit down with your partners and discuss your answers. Better to discover ethical differences now rather than in the courtroom later.

In addition, discuss values, work ethic, dreams, and work-life balance issues. Check your partner's financial and work history thoroughly. Remember you will be liable for your partner's actions. Work only with a partner, who you respect and who brings credibility and integrity in to the partnership.

On the surface, partnerships make a lot of sense. Two or more entrepreneurs face the unknown together and pool their skills and money raising more capital than one person alone. However, forming a successful partnership will be challenging and sometimes difficult. It also should be fun and stimulating.

Partners need to have each other's backs and each should believe they are supported. Remember, you will rise or fall together.

After the previous questions and topics are discussed, you may be ready to review sample partnership agreements online for further discussions with your partners. These should serve as a starting point and are *not* meant to become your partnership agreement, as each state's statutes vary. Your lawyers will be happy to work with you to help you develop a good solid legal partnership agreement.

Reviewing the issues in this chapter, the ethical issues in Chapter 12, and the sample agreements with your potential partners should help you evalvate the potential of the partnership. If all looks good, it will be time for you to take the information you have gained and discuss final agreements with your attorneys.

But before meeting with your attorney, return to the Action Steps in Chapter 1 first to make sure you and your partners are dreaming the same dream.

Limited Liability Companies

Most states have recently allowed LLCs as an acceptable form of business. This entity limits liability but does not limit the number of investors; it also allows profits to be distributed in a manner other than in proportion to investors' capital contribution as a "pass-through" tax entity. It is expected that LLCs will be the entity of choice for closely held businesses in the near future, because they are designed to provide the tax flexibility and ownership of partnerships with the limited liability features of corporations.

The operating agreement sets out the company's membership and operational rules. In addition, the agreement states how members' profits and losses are shared. LLCs provide the pass-through tax treatment that has been available to partnerships and Subchapter S corporations. However, talk with your tax advisor as you may also choose your LLC to be treated as a C or S corporation for federal taxes. The best tax treatment option for your LLC will be based on your business needs, future of the LLC, and your particular circumstances.

The required documentation, known as *articles of organization*, is less detailed than articles of incorporation and usually less costly. See Figure 10.1 for a sample state registration application for articles of organization.

The articles of organization contain an "operating agreement" that resembles a partnership agreement. LLC members may manage the business themselves or delegate such authority to active managers. If a member decides to leave the LLC, they will be compensated for their equity and a new member can be written into the business with an amendment to the operating agreement.

Most state statutes require that identifying information such as "limited liability company" or "LLC" appear in the name of the company to notify others of the limited liability enjoyed by the organization. Be careful: if an LLC is not properly structured, it will be taxed as a corporation.

LLCs generally will not be appropriate for existing corporations or businesses that raise, or want to raise, capital through the public or venture-capital markets. If you are considering converting to an LLC, be aware there may be tax consequences. Thus, it is vital that you consult competent tax, legal, and accounting advisors. A few states allow LLPs (Limited Liability Partnerships), which contain liability exceptions for certain professional service firms such as doctors, architects, engineers, and so on. Consult the laws in your state.

Corporations

In general, we think most owners of small businesses fail to incorporate because they do not see the signals their businesses are giving them. Ask yourself if there is any chance that your employees, customers, or suppliers might sue you. The truth is that for almost all firms, a great deal of risk for lawsuits exists; therefore incorporating as a Subchapter S corporation, which allows for a pass-through of the profits and losses to the shareholders, or a standard C corporation should be seriously considered.

Employees driving your vehicles, customers being harmed in some way by a product or service—in ways you would never believe or consider—and customers or employees slipping and falling are just a few of the potential litigious situations that may occur. Consider the following reasons for incorporation:

1. **You limit your liability:** A corporation acts as a shield between you and the world. If your business fails, your creditors cannot come after your house, your condo, your car, or your hard-won collectibles—provided you have

followed the rules. And that is the key. To keep your corporate shield up, make sure you: 1) hold scheduled board of directors' meetings 2) keep up the minutes' book and 3) act as if you are an employee of the corporation. However, the fact is almost all entrepreneurs use most of their personal assets as collateral for their business loans, so the limited liability provided by a corporation may not limit your risk of some personal financial loss. Ask your attorney and industry associations how to reduce liability issues within your firm's operations. Safety precautions, disclaimers on products, having your employees covered by very high liability policies on their own cars, and proper hiring and firing methods are just a few ways to reduce financial risk. Chapter 12 covers many others.

2. **To change your tax picture:** Discuss with your CPA how passive and active income will be handled, as well as retained earnings for each type of corporation.

3. **To upgrade your image:** What does the word *corporation* mean to you? Apple? Intel? Wal-Mart? Google? It comes from the Latin *corpus*, which means "body." To *incorporate* means to make, form, or shape into a body. Looking at it from that angle, *incorporating* starts to sound creative. As a corporation, you may enjoy more prestige, attract better employees, and have more clout in the world.

4. **To have the opportunity to channel some heavy expenses:** Medical and insurance premiums and FICA payments become business expenses.

5. **To guarantee continuity:** If one owner jump ships and high tails it to Australia, dies, or becomes ill, the corporation keeps on chugging because you have gone through the red tape and planning to set it up that way.

6. **To offer internal incentives:** When you want to reward special employees or retain your best ones, you may offer stock or a promotion—for example, a vice presidency—in addition to, or in place of, pay raises. Becoming a corporate officer carries its own special excitement, and this gives your firm increased flexibility.

7. **To raise additional capital:** You can sell stock to potential stockholders who will become shareholders in the firm.

According to *NOLO.COM*, a C corporation may be advised over an LLC if the following factors exist:

1. "You expect to have multiple investors in your business, or you plan to raise money from the public.

2. You want to set up a single-member LLC, but you live in a state that requires two or more members.

3. You would like to provide extensive fringe benefits to owner–employees.

4. You want to entice or keep key employees by offering stock options and stock bonus incentives.

5. Your accountant has reviewed the issue of self-employment taxes and weighs in on the decision."

Subchapter S Corporations

In addition to LLCs and the standard C corporations, there are Subchapter S corporations, which are semi-corporate bodies that limit an owner's liability while still allowing a pass-through of business losses to the personal income statements of the owners, founders, and others. Subchapter S refers to the section of the IRS code that describes the way the corporation will be taxed.

The number of stockholders is limited to 100. The IRS has specific time requirements for filing, and some states do not recognize the tax aspects of the Subchapter S category, so verify your state laws. In a Subchapter S corporation, you cannot have any corporate stockholders, partnership stockholders, or trusts as investors. For this reason, most S corporations lose their S status when venture-capital firms invest.

figure **10.1**

Illinois Limited Liability Company Act

Form **LLC-5.5** October 2010 **Secretary of State** Department of Business Services Limited Liability Division 501 S. Second St., Rm. 351 Springfield, IL 62756 217-524-8008 www.cyberdriveillinois.com	Illinois Limited Liability Company Act **Articles of Organization**	**FILE #** This space for use by Secretary of State.
Payment must be made by certified check, cashier's check, Illinois attorney's check, C.P.A.'s check or money order payable to Secretary of State.	**SUBMIT IN DUPLICATE** Type or print clearly. This space for use by Secretary of State. **Date:** **Filing Fee:** $500 **Approved:**	

1. Limited Liability Company Name: _____
    The LLC name must contain the words Limited Liability Company, L.L.C. or LLC and cannot contain the terms Corporation, Corp., Incorporated, Inc., Ltd., Co., Limited Partnership or L.P.

2. Address of Principal Place of Business where records of the company will be kept: (P.O. Box alone or c/o is unacceptable.)

    _____

    _____

3. Articles of Organization effective on: (check one)

    ☐ the filing date

    ☐ a later date (not to exceed 60 days after the filing date): _____
                                                 Month, Day, Year

4. Registered Agent's Name and Registered Office Address:

    Registered Agent: _____
                    First Name   Middle Initial   Last Name

    Registered Office: _____
    (P.O. Box alone or c/o   Number   Street   Suite #
    is unacceptable.)

                                         IL
                    City   ZIP Code

5. Purpose(s) for which the Limited Liability Company is organized:
    The transaction of any or all lawful business for which Limited Liability Companies may be organized under this Act.
    (LLCs organized to provide professional services must list the address(es) from which those services will be rendered if different from item 2. If more space is needed, use additional sheets of this size.)

    _____

    _____

    _____

    _____

    _____

6. Latest date, if any, upon which the company is to dissolve: _____
    (Leave blank if duration is perpetual.)   Month, Day, Year

♻ Printed on recycled paper. Printed by authority of the State of Illinois. December 2011 — 2M — LLC 4.15

(continued)

figure **10.1**

Illinois Limited Liability Company Act *(continued)*

LLC-5.5

7. **(Optional)** Other provisions for the regulation of the internal affairs of the Company: (If more space is needed, attach additional sheets of this size.) _____

_____

_____

_____

8. The Limited Liability Company: (Check either a or b below.)

    a. ☐ is managed by the **manager(s)** (List names and addresses.)

    _____

    _____

    _____

    _____

    b. ☐ has management vested in the **member(s)** (List names and addresses.)

    _____

    _____

    _____

    _____

9. Name and Address of Organizer(s):

    I affirm, under penalties of perjury, having authority to sign hereto, that these Articles of Organization are to the best of my knowledge and belief, true, correct and complete.

    Dated _____, _____
    Month & Day   Year

    1. _____   1. _____
       Signature   Number   Street

    _____   _____
    Name (type or print)   City/Town

    _____   _____
    Name if a Corporation or other Entity, and Title of Signer   State   ZIP Code

    2. _____   2. _____
       Signature   Number   Street

    _____   _____
    Name (type or print)   City/Town

    _____   _____
    Name if a Corporation or other Entity, and Title of Signer   State   ZIP Code

Signatures must be in black ink on an original document. Carbon copy, photocopy or rubber stamp signatures may only be used on conformed copies.

♻ Printed on recycled paper. Printed by authority of the State of Illinois. December 2011 — 2M — LLC 4.15

Source: Illinois Limited Liability Company Act. Retrieved from *http://www.cyberdriveillinois.com/publications/pdf_publications/llc55.pdf*. Reprinted with permission of the Illinois Secretary of State's Office.

Subchapter S corporations are required to supply stockholders with a "K-1" tax report by April 15 of each year and you must follow a calendar tax year with few exceptions. S corporation status may be dropped if you find there are tax advantages to being a regular corporation, but timing as always is important. Consult your tax attorney.

Nonprofit Corporations

Many social entrepreneurs today are interested in reaching out to solve social, health, and environmental problems through profit and nonprofit organizations. Formed much in the same way as profit making firms, nonprofits have limited liability for the trustees, officers, and members and possess unlimited life. You must apply to the state for nonprofit status and to the IRS for approval of your tax-exempt status by completing IRS Form 1023 or IRS Form 1024 and follow the sometimes lengthy and time consuming process.

Use an an attorney to help you complete your paperwork; each state requires different forms and agency approvals. Thus, log on to GuideStar to link to your state's resources, which you should access early on in the process. Your state may even have a separate state office designed to help nonprofit organizations. Also, access a wealth of information at the Council of Nonprofits and The Foundation Center. Help is just a phone call, tutorial, or workshop away.

Two additional excellent resources to learn more about nonprofits and social entrepreneurship are Idealist and Ashoka. Idealist links you to helpful federal and state resources and Ashoka highlights many social entrepreneurs and their fellows such as Elizabeth Hausler (see Passion). Throughout the text, we have highlighted many sources to assist you in fulfilling your dream of making the world a better place, as well as highlighting many social entrepreneurs operating as profit, nonprofit and hybrid ventures.

Technically your nonprofit organization will be defined as a 501(c)(3) public charity or 501(c)(4) social welfare organization. Your nonprofit organizations should follow through with most of the text's Action Steps, adjusting them to fit the nonprofit's situation.

Many nonprofits need to raise substantial financial resources and frequently sell products to support their nonprofits by developing a profit making arm to support their nonprofit activities. As this is quite complicated from a tax standpoint, do not attempt this without legal and accounting counsel. With the many different forms nonprofits are taking today, it is oftentimes hard to distinguish them from profit making firms.

■ FAMILY BUSINESSES

Mother-son, brother-sister, cousins, married couples, and entire families all are part of a growing trend in business today. The statistics in Figure 10.2 (see page 283) highlight the immense impact family businesses play in our economy and in job creation. Many of the issues discussed in the partnership section of this text can also be applied to family businesses and thus you should review those steps and address them with any family members who you go into business with.

One size doesn't fit all when designing a family business as no two family structures or relationships are the same. Thus, there is no cookie-cutter formula, but respect and communication are key to any family business.

Some family businesses require all members work outside of the business for a minimum of five years with the hope they will gain experience and insight and be ready to commit to the family business. Others, not sure if needed you can decide believe kids should start sweeping the floors early on and not work outside but devote themselves to the family business learning early on what it really takes. In some families being part of the family business is a birthright and in others, members must work hard proving themselves before they are brought into the family fold.

PASSION

Passionate Engineer Designs Sustainable Safe Housing

Elizabeth Hausler Awarded $100,000 2011 Lemelson-MIT Award for Sustainability

Cambridge, Mass. (February 2012)–Lemelson-MIT Award for Sustainability. As a child, Elizabeth Hausler loved playing with Lincoln Logs™, connecting each piece to create one solid structure. The daughter of a mason, Hausler's interest in building and engineering was reinforced throughout her adolescence when she would spend summers working for her father, learning the ins-and-outs of sturdy bricklaying. As an adult, Hausler observed the devastating effects of homes not being built with the same diligence she had been taught – especially in natural disaster-prone regions of the developing world. She saw an opportunity to provide a man-made solution to this man-made problem. For her ability to create sustainable, safe housing solutions in developing countries through an innovative implementation model, Hausler is the recipient of the 2011 $100,000 Lemelson-MIT Award for Sustainability.

With her innate enthusiasm for construction, Hausler enrolled in a general engineering program at the University of Illinois at Urbana-Champaign and later a doctoral program in civil engineering at the University of California Berkeley. Halfway through her doctoral program, after learning of the destruction and loss of life caused by poorly-built homes during the 2001 earthquake in Gujarat, India, Hausler was inspired to use her engineering skills to benefit humanity. She won a Fulbright fellowship to India to study and assist with post-earthquake reconstruction. Following her work there, she continued to pursue her passion and skill at socially-engineered home construction in China, Haiti, and Indonesia.

During her fellowship, Hausler witnessed challenges with costly, unsustainable, donor-driven reconstruction models. She believed a new model – one that did not reinvent the wheel but made small, culturally-accepted, and affordable changes to the current construction methods – was needed for sustainable adoption and impact.

In 2004, Hausler's approach to building earthquake-resistant homes became the basis of the business model for Build Change, her nonprofit group with the mission of greatly reducing deaths, injuries and economic losses caused by housing collapses in developing countries.

Along with technological design improvements, the core of the organization is its implementation model for natural disaster reconstruction. By promoting homeowner-driven construction, where builders are trained to construct low-cost homes with locally-available materials and improved techniques, Build Change empowers homeowners to manage their own building process. Currently, Hausler and Build Change crews are working in Morne Lazarre, Haiti, an area still suffering from the after effects of the 2010 earthquake.

Hausler has received significant recognition for her work to date in developing countries, most recently being chosen as a 2009 Ashoka-Lemelson Fellow and a 2008 Tech Awards Laureate. In 2006, Hausler was featured as an ABC News World News Tonight "Person of the Week" for her work in Indonesia following the 2004 tsunami, and in 2004 she was selected as an Echoing Green Fellow.

Hausler is an inspiring role model for budding engineers, demonstrating that engineering and research skills, combined with creativity and innovation, can make lasting, positive changes in the world for those in need.

Source: Adapted from "Elizabeth Hausler: 2011 Lemelson-MIT Award for Sustainability," MIT Copyright © Massachusetts Institute of Technology. Retrieved from *http://web.mit.edu/invent/a-winners/a-hausler.html* (Accessed April 10, 2012). Reprinted with permission.

As in any business, families will have to deal with differing goals, ethics and commitment. In addition, the desire for family-work balance will vary among the members and may be a major issue. Generational issues will also occur as in many businesses two, three, or even four generations are involved.

Entrepreneur's Resource

Family Businesses—Who Can Help?

A wealth of information and assistance is available in your community for your family business venture through family business centers and consultants, which can be found through the Family Firm Institute's site, *http://www.ffi.org*. The Institute provides listings internationally and nationally by country and state and includes private business counselors, accounting firms, lawyers, and therapists who deal with entrepreneurs in family businesses. In addition, listings of most of the family business centers available at colleges throughout the nation are included.

Consulting, coaching, seminars, research, legal advice, and roundtables for family entrepreneurs are available at many family business centers for reasonable fees. Following are two of the best centers in the country according to *Fortune Small Business* magazine:

Cox Family Enterprise Center

Coles College of Business, Kennesaw State University
Editorial office of the *Journal of Family Business Strategy*

The Center provides research, newsletters, consultations, and sponsorship of the Georgia Family Business of the Year Award Banquet. In addition, Kennesaw offers an Executive MBA for Families in Business. The Center offers a forum that provides knowledge and experience on topics most crucial to family business success and survival. It focuses on the strategies used by real family firms to take advantage of opportunities and overcome challenges. Additionally, the forum provides efficient access to leading expertise in accounting, banking, insurance, law, financial management, business strategy, human resources, succession planning, and family dynamics. Moreover, the forum provides a relaxed environment where important family business issues can be openly addressed, and it encourages the exchange of ideas and information among family business owners and leading experts.

Source: *http://coles.kennesaw.edu/centers/cox-family-enterprise/index* (Accessed March 30, 2012).

Loyola University of Chicago Family Business Center

For fourteen years, the Family Business Center (FBC) has served over 100 family businesses of varying sizes, industries, and complexity. Today, the needs of FBC members continue to push the frontier of family enterprise research to new levels. Our innovative programs provide the opportunity for our members to share knowledge and cultivate synergies with one another. After a decade of nurturing family enterprises, FBC endeavors to become the premier research and learning center for family-owned businesses in the United States.

Source: *http://www.luc.edu/fbc* (Accessed March 30, 2012).

Family Business Review (quarterly) follows the issues surrounding family businesses, which present their own set of relationship and business challenges. We suggest you seek out other family businesses that have trod the same path for their expertise, experience, and support. Participate in monthly forums with others, and seek out professionals experienced in dealing with family enterprises. Key Points provides additional information on how to keep your family business healthy.

Although many entrepreneurs do not see the need for formal, written legal agreements between family members—be they spouses, children, or siblings—we cannot emphasize enough the need for such documents. There are those rare partnerships between family members that never experience a problem, but rare is not common. Protect yourself, your business, and your relationships both within and outside the business.

—————————————————————— figure **10.2**

8 Facts About Family Owned Businesses*

- 80% of the world's businesses are family owned.
- Family-run businesses account for more than half of the nation's gross domestic product.
- Nearly 35% of family-owned businesses are Fortune 500 and other large companies including Ford, Koch Industries, Cargill, Wal-Mart, Weyerhaeuser, Loews, and Ikea.
- Approximately 60% of all public companies in the US are family controlled.
- Family-owned businesses account for 60% of total US employment, 78% of all new jobs, and 65% of all wages paid.
- Many family businesses were started after WWII.
- More than 25% of family firms expect the next CEO to be a woman.
- More than 30% of all family owned businesses survive into the second generation.

Based on research we have conducted every year since 1985. See our RESEARCH page for more specifics.

Source: Cox Family Enterprise Center, Coles College of Business, Kennesaw State University. Reprinted with permission.

You may want to meet with family business consultants (see Entrepreneurial Resources), legal advisors, and accountants to develop and plan your personal, business, tax, and financial affairs. As your business grows, relationships will change. Family members will join or leave the organization. As the business develops, you will also need to develop a succession plan. Return to your advisors as your business grows and changes to make sure you affairs are in order.

> **Succession plan** Method to assure continuation of firm by selecting and developing individuals to lead firm if owner leaves

If you are forming a business with your spouse, make sure you understand each other's work style and personalities. Oftentimes, spouses join forces as they have complementary skills. However, to be successful you both now need to honor those skills and not question each other's decisions continually. A new term for husband-wife partnerships has been coined "copreneur."

It is very difficult for married couples to turn the business off when in essence their business is the financial center of their personal lives as well. Married couples need to work very hard to maintain their marriage, personal and professional lives.

■ TRADEMARKS, COPYRIGHTS, AND PATENTS

Trademarks, copyrights, and patents are important elements of your business. Without protecting them, you may lose your business, your ideas may be stolen, or your products may be copied.

THE FOLLOWING 2012 MATERIAL ON PATENTS, TRADEMARKS, AND COPYRIGHTS IS PUBLISHED BY PERMISSION FROM THE COPYRIGHT HOLDER: KNOBBE, MARTENS, OLSON, AND BEAR, LLP. BECAUSE INTELLECTUAL PROPERTY LAWS ARE SUBJECT TO CHANGE, CONSULT WITH YOUR INTELLECTUAL PROPERTY COUNSEL RATHER THAN RELYING ON THIS MATERIAL ALONE FOR LEGAL ADVICE.

Trademarks: Ten Things You Should Know to Protect Your Product and Business Names

1. **What Is a Trademark?**

   A trademark is a brand name for a product. It can be a word, phrase, logo, design, or virtually anything that is used to identify the source of the product and distinguish it from competitors' products. More than one trademark may be used in connection with a product, for example, COCA-COLA® and DIET COKE® are both trademarks for beverages. A trademark represents the goodwill and reputation of a product and its source. Its owner has the right to prevent others from trading on that goodwill by using the same or a similar trademark on the same or similar products in a way that is likely to cause confusion as to the source, origin, or sponsorship of the products.

   A service mark is like a trademark, except it is used to identify and distinguish services rather than products. For example, the "golden arches" mark shown below is a service mark for restaurant services. The terms "trademark" or "mark" are often used interchangeably to refer to either a trademark or service mark.

2. **How Should a Mark Be Used?**

   Trademarks must be used properly to maintain their value. Marks should be used as adjectives, and not as nouns or verbs. For example, when referring to utilizing the FACEBOOK® website, do not say that you "Facebooked" or that you were "Facebooking." To prevent loss of trademark or service mark rights, the generic name for the product should appear after the mark, and the mark should appear visually different from the surrounding text. Use a different type size, type style, color, or quotation marks for the trademark or service mark, as in OAKLEY® sunglasses, KATE SPADE® handbags, or STARBUCKS® coffee. You may also use an asterisk (*) after a mark, where the asterisk refers to a footnote explaining the ownership of a mark.

   If a mark is not used correctly, the exclusive right to use it may be lost. For example, trademark rights can be lost if the mark becomes the generic name for the product. Kerosene, escalator, and nylon were once trademarks, but are now generic names. Because competitors need to be able to describe their products, no one can own the exclusive right to use generic terms.

   If a mark is registered with the U.S. Patent and Trademark Office, the federal registration symbol ® should be used next to the mark. If the mark is not federally registered, the letters TM may be used to indicate a trademark, or SM to indicate a service mark.

3. **What Is a Trade Name?**

   A trade name is the name of a business. Unlike trademarks, a trade name can be used as a noun. It need not be followed by generic terms.

   It is permissible to use all or a portion of a trade name as a trademark or service mark. "Jelly Belly Candy Company" is a trade name. JELLY BELLY® is a trademark when used on candy, and may be a service mark when properly used with Jelly Belly Cycling Team events.

4. **Does My Incorporation or Fictitious Business Name Statement Give Me the Right to Use My Business Name?**

   Most businesses form a corporation or file a fictitious business name statement. Neither the certificate of incorporation nor the fictitious business name statement gives a business the right to use a trade name that is likely to cause confusion with a trade name, trademark, or service mark that was previously used by someone else in the same area of trade.

   The state or county agencies that issue the certificates of incorporation and fictitious business name statements do not perform searches sufficient to ensure that one's use would not infringe another's prior rights.

A court's determination of trademark infringement will override any fictitious business name statement or any certificate of incorporation. Further, the legal test that the courts apply to determine the right to use trade names, trademarks, or service marks does not require that the names or marks be identical; it requires only enough similarity to cause a likelihood of confusion. Thus, neither of these filings means that you have the right to use your name in the advertising, promotion, or sale of goods or services.

5. **Must Trademarks Be Registered?**

There is no requirement to register your mark, but there are many advantages to doing so. A federally registered mark is presumed to be a valid mark and the registrant is presumed to have the exclusive right to use the trademark throughout the United States on the goods or services listed in the registration. A registered mark will also be revealed in searches conducted by other businesses in their effort to avoid selecting marks that may conflict with those of others. In addition, only federally registered trademarks or service marks may use the ® symbol.

After five years, the registration may become incontestable, which significantly limits the grounds on which competitors can attack the registration. An application for a federal registration may be filed before a mark is used in commerce, assuming the applicant has a good-faith intent to use the mark. Actual use must begin, however, prior to the issuance of a registration.

Marks may also be registered in each of the 50 states. The advantages of a state registration vary according to the laws of each state. Most states require that you use a mark on goods or services before applying for the registration. A California trademark registration, for example, is usually faster, less expensive, and less difficult to obtain than a federal registration. It also allows its owner to sue infringers under several California statutes that offer advantages not available under federal law. A California trademark registration, however, has no force or effect outside of the state.

6. **What Is a Trademark Search?**

There are a number of professional search services that may be used to help ensure that your mark or trade name does not conflict with the rights of another business. The goal of such searches is to avoid spending time, effort, and money promoting a product name or business name, only to find out that it conflicts with someone else's rights.

These searches are typically performed through trademark lawyers who evaluate the search report to determine if there is an actual or potential conflict with another name or mark. This evaluation depends upon the consideration of numerous legal factors and case law decisions.

7. **Is My Product's Shape or Packaging Protectable?**

The non-functional features of a product's shape or packaging (its "trade dress") may be protectable if they are sufficiently distinctive to identify the owner of the trade dress. Product shapes are being protected with ever-increasing frequency. For example, the appearance of a "C" clamp, a RUGER® 22-caliber pistol, a fingernail polish bottle, and the red border and format of TIME® magazine have all been protected against look-alike competitive products.

To help achieve this type of protection, non-functional and distinctive product features or packaging should be selected. These features should then be promoted through "image" advertising or "look for" advertising so that customers recognize the product shape or packaging and associate it with a single source.

8. **Can I Register My Trade Dress?**

If your trade dress is non-functional and is either inherently distinctive or has acquired customer recognition from sufficient promotion of the protectable features, it may be registered as a trademark. For example, the progressive orange color effect of LE CREUSET® enameled cast-iron cookware and the shape of a HERSHEY KISS® chocolate have been registered with the U.S. Patent and Trademark Office.

9. **What About Protection in Foreign Countries?**

Trademark owners who have not registered their marks in foreign countries may find that the mark has been appropriated by a third party who was the first to register in that country. Many foreign countries regard the first to register in that country as the owner of the mark, even if it is a pirate who saw the mark in the United States and appropriated it. This pirate may even be a trusted foreign distributor of the U.S. trademark owner.

Foreign pirates may be able to prevent the original U.S. trademark owner from using or registering the mark in one or more foreign countries. In some cases it may be possible to recover the mark, but the U.S. owner may face expensive litigation or exorbitant demands from the pirate.

If a U.S. product is sold overseas, care must be taken to ensure that the U.S. federal registration symbol ® is not used unless the mark is registered in the foreign country where the product is being sold. Some countries have both civil and criminal penalties for using the ® symbol with a mark not registered in that country. Improper use of the ® symbol may also make the mark unenforceable in some countries.

10. **Where Can I Get Information on Protecting Productand Business Names?**

Information on trademarks may be obtained from the Trademark Unit of your Secretary of State's Office. Information on federal registrations may be obtained from the U.S. Patent and Trademark Office at *www.uspto.gov*.

The assistance of a lawyer experienced in trademark matters can help avoid problems before they arise. To contact a trademark lawyer or learn more about Knobbe Martens, visit *www.knobbe.com*.

Copyrights: Ten Things You Should Know to Protect Your Artwork, Ads, Writings, and Software

1. **What Is a Copyright?**

Copyright protection exists in any original "expression" of an idea that is fixed in any physical medium, such as paper, digital media, or film. Copyrights cover such diverse things as art, music, technical and architectural drawings, books, computer programs, and advertisements. Copyrights protect only the expression of an idea, not the idea itself; they do not protect facts, short phrases, or slogans.

Because copyright protection requires originality, it bars others from copying copyrighted work to create substantially similar works. It is possible, however, for two very similar works to be independently created, with each author owning a separate copyright. For example, if two strangers stand next to each other and each take a photograph of the same scene, each would own a copyright on his or her respective photograph.

2. **What Protection Does a Copyright Give?**

Copyright protection encompasses a bundle of exclusive rights that include the right to: (1) reproduce the work; (2) make derivative works; (3) distribute copies by sale, lease, or rental; (4) publicly perform certain works such as plays or audiovisual works; and (5) publicly display certain works such as pictorial or sculptural works.

Compilations of actual data, like names or part numbers, may be copyrightable, but the protection is limited to such things as the selection and arrangement of the information. Facts by themselves cannot be protected by copyright, even if considerable time and expense went into compiling the facts. In appropriate cases, trade secret protection may be available for the factual information.

Copyrights may be licensed or transferred together or separately. For example, an author may grant a book company the rights to reproduce a book, may grant a movie studio the rights to make a movie derived from the book, and may grant foreign distribution rights to other companies.

3. **Are Websites Copyrightable?**
A website may embody numerous works protectable by copyrights. For example, protected works may include individual graphic images within web pages, textual content of web pages, or the visual appearance of entire web pages. Copyrights may also protect certain selections or arrangements of data or images embodied in a website, such as a library of thumbnail graphic images of Caribbean fish, or a database of recipes to prepare an authentic Southwestern dish.

Other copyrightable subject matter includes original sequences of computer instructions that: (1) format web page content; (2) hyperlink to other web pages; (3) prompt users for input; (4) respond to user input; and/or (5) carry out other related processes. Examples may include sequences of markup language (e.g., HTML) instructions, CGI scripts, or JAVA modules.

Authors who create copyrighted works available for downloading via the Internet should be careful to use appropriate notice. If they do not, an implied license to do more than simply download the work for viewing may be granted. To limit the scope of an implied license, a copyright owner should include an express limitation in addition to a standard copyright notice. For example, if the copyright owner intends that the work be viewed only, then the owner may wish to include the following notice: "The recipient may only view this work. No other right or license is granted."

As with any other copyrightable subject matter, website-related works can only receive copyright protection if they are original works of authorship, embodying, or fixing the independent expression of the author or authors. Generally, copyright protection arises automatically upon fixing such expression in a tangible medium such as computer memory. While copyright protection is automatic and does not require copyright notice, the owner of copyrights related to a website may further discourage copying by including a copyright notice on protected features.

4. **How Long Does a Copyright Last?**
U.S. copyright protection for works created after January 1, 1978, will last for the life of the author plus 70 years after his or her death. If the work was created for an employer by an employee within the scope of his or her employment, the copyright protection will last for 95 years from the date of first publication or 120 years from the date of creation, whichever is shorter.

If a U.S. work was created before January 1, 1978, the copyright can last for a total of 95 years, assuming that the owner has not inadvertently forfeited his or her work to the public domain by not using appropriate notice or filing the necessary renewals in a timely manner. Determining precisely when the term of the copyright ends and who owns any renewal rights are complex matters for which legal advice should be sought.

5. **If I Use Only 10%, Can I Use Copyrighted Works?**
If the portion taken is the heart of the copyrighted work or from a widely recognized portion of the work, then infringement can exist even though less than 10% of the copyrighted work is taken. The test for copyright infringement is whether the accused work is copied from and "substantially similar"

to the copyrighted work. While the copyright statute provides "fair use" guidelines, these are evaluated case by case. Thus, there is no single "rule" or fixed amount regarding the portion of a work that one must change in order to avoid infringement. If you have concerns about specific situations, you should consult with an experienced copyright lawyer.

6. **Must Copyrights Be Registered?**

Under current law, a copyright need not be registered until a U.S. citizen wants to file a copyright infringement lawsuit. Early registration, however, offers the copyright holder some significant advantages. For example, if a work is registered before an infringement commences, the infringer may be liable for statutory damages of up to $150,000 for each copyright that is infringed, and may also have to pay the attorney's fees incurred by the copyright owner in the lawsuit. It is advisable to register within three months of publication in order to claim the maximum remedies under the Copyright Act.

7. **Do I Need a Copyright Notice?**

For U.S. works first published after March 1,1989, a copyright notice is not necessary to maintain copyright protection. Using a copyright notice, however, makes it difficult for other people to claim that they are "innocent" infringers who were misled by the absence of a copyright notice. For U.S. works first published between 1978 and 1989, the omission of a copyright notice from published works could result in the loss of copyright protection unless certain steps were taken in a timely manner. For U.S. works first published before 1978, omission of a copyright notice from published works usually resulted in the loss of any copyright protection.

A copyright notice consists of the copyright symbol, ©; the year a work is first published; and the name of the copyright owner (e.g., © 2012 Knobbe Martens Olson & Bear LLP). If a sound recording is copyrighted, use P with the first publication date and owner. If the copyrighted material is revised, add the year of the revision to the copyright notice. It is also advisable to add "All rights reserved."

8. **Do I Own the Copyrights I Pay Others to Create?**

You probably do not own the copyright material you pay independent contractors to prepare, unless you have a written agreement transferring the ownership of any copyrights.

While a business usually owns the copyrights in works created by full-time employees within the scope of their employment, the business has only limited rights to use copyrightable works created by independent contractors. Ownership of works created by employees, but not in their normal course of employment, varies with the facts of each case. Also, certain types of copyrightable works are entitled to "moral rights" protection, which must be considered at the time of any transfer of copyrights.

Ownership issues are often complex. An experienced copyright lawyer should be consulted on such issues.

9. **Do Foreign Countries Protect Copyrights?**

The United States has long been a member of the Universal Copyright Convention, through which copyright protection may be obtained in many foreign countries. In 1988, the United States joined the Berne Convention, through which copyright protection may be obtained in the vast majority of foreign countries.

Obtaining and enforcing copyrights in foreign countries require compliance with the laws and treaties of each individual country. A lawyer knowledgeable in copyright law should be consulted about any specific needs.

10. **Where Can I Get More Information on Copyrights?**

Information on copyright registrations may be obtained from the Register of Copyrights, Library of Congress, in Washington, DC, at *www.copyright.gov*.

The Copyright Office Catalog contains approximately 20 million records for works registered and documents recorded with the Copyright Office since 1978.

The assistance of a lawyer experienced in copyright matters can help avoid problems before they arise. To contact a copyright lawyer or learn more about Knobbe Martens, visit *www.knobbe.com*.

Patents: Ten Things You Should Know to Protect Your Business

1. **What Is a Patent?**

   A patent is a right granted to inventors by the government to exclude others from making, selling, offering for sale, using, or importing an invention. The U.S. Government has issued over eight million patents during the past 200 years. These patents cover many types of inventions and discoveries, including machines, compositions of matter, methods, computer software, plants, microorganisms, and designs. Three types of patents are available in the United States.

   The first, called a "utility patent," covers useful inventions and discoveries, which are defined in the claims of the patent. Generally, a utility patent expires 20 years from the day a regular patent application is filed for the invention. In addition to the claims, a utility patent includes a written description of the invention and also often includes drawings. A second type of patent, called a "design patent," covers non-functional, ornamental designs shown in the drawings of the design patent. This type of patent expires 14 years from the date it issues. The third type of patent gives the owner the right to exclude others from asexually reproducing a patented plant, or from selling or using an asexually reproduced patented plant. Plants that are sexually reproduced (i.e., through seeds) or tuber propagated can be protected under the Plant Variety Protection Act.

2. **How Do I Obtain a Patent?**

   To obtain a utility patent, the invention defined in the patent claims must be new and nonobvious to a person of ordinary skill in the field of the invention. Many patents are combinations of previously existing parts combined in a new, nonobvious way to achieve improved results. A design patent requires a new, non-functional, ornamental design that is nonobvious to an ordinary designer in the field of the invention. In all cases, the initial evaluation and patentability decision will be made by an examiner at the U.S. Patent and Trademark Office. Only the first and original inventor(s) may obtain a valid patent. Thus, you cannot obtain a patent in the United States for an invention you saw overseas, because you are not the first or the original inventor. Similarly, someone who sees your invention cannot obtain a valid patent on it because that person is not the first or original inventor. Someone else could, however, improve your invention and then patent the improvement. It typically takes a year or more after filing the U.S. application before the examiner sends the initial evaluation of patentability.

3. **What Is a Patentability Search?**

   When a U.S. patent application is filed, the Patent Office will conduct a search of prior patents from both the United States and foreign countries, and may also search for prior nonpatent references. Inventors can have a similar patentability search conducted in order to better evaluate the cost and probability of obtaining patent protection for their invention. Evaluation of patentability search results is complex, requiring not only an understanding of the pertinent technology, but also of patent law. The U.S. Patent Office tests and authorizes persons with appropriate technical backgrounds to file and prosecute patent matters before the Patent Office. You should consider contacting a registered patent attorney authorized to practice before the U.S. Patent and Trademark Office to assist with your evaluation.

4. **What Is a Patent Notice?**

A product or accompanying literature can be marked with a patent notice such as "Patent," "Pat." or "Pat. No.," together with the patent number or a website address that associates the product with the patent number when the product, or the method used to produce the product, is patented. Marking the patented products with a patent notice can enhance the ability to collect damages from an infringer. The term "Patent Pending" means a patent has been applied for, but has not yet issued.

5. **When Must I Apply For a Patent?**

If two different inventors were to apply for a patent for the same invention, every country except the United States would award a patent to the first inventor to file. Conversely, the United States would award a patent to the party who invented first. However, on March 16,2013, the law in the United States will change to be consistent with the "first to file" system prevalent outside the United States. In any event, an application for a patent must be filed in the United States within one year of the first date that the invention is: (1) disclosed in a printed publication; (2) publicly used; or (3) offered for sale. A patent in the United States is valid only in this country. In most foreign countries, a patent application must be filed before any public disclosure is made anywhere in the world. The rules for determining when an invention is publicly disclosed, used, or offered for sale are complex, and you should seek the advice of a patent lawyer if you have a question in this regard. By treaty with most, but not all, foreign countries, if a U.S. application is filed before any public disclosure is made, a foreign patent application may be filed up to one year after the U.S. filing date. Thus, if a U.S. patent application is filed before any public disclosure of the invention, the option to pursue foreign patent rights in many foreign countries is preserved for one year. Filing a U.S. patent application after a public disclosure, however, usually prevents filing in most foreign countries.

U.S. patent laws also provide for an informal and less expensive filing, called a "provisional patent application," to preserve patent rights for 12 months. It also extends the term of the patent for one year. The provisional application is not examined and lapses after 12 months. Accordingly, a regular patent application must be filed within those 12 months in order to claim the benefit of the provisional application's filing date. Likewise, foreign applications generally must be filed within those 12 months.

6. **Is There a Worldwide Patent?**

There is no single, worldwide patent. Each country has different patent laws and, therefore, rights provided by a patent are enforceable only in the country or countries issuing the patent. For example, a U.S. patent can prevent an infringing product that is made overseas from being sold in the United States, but will not generally prevent the product from being sold in a foreign country. There are several international treaties that enable most of the initial steps in the patenting process to be consolidated for many countries, provided there was no public disclosure before the U.S. application was filed. Ultimately, however, the patent application must be filed in each country where a patent is sought and translated into an official language of each such country. The Patent Cooperation Treaty allows the additional cost of translating and filing in each foreign country to be delayed for up to 30 months from the U.S. filing date. During this 30-month period, it is often possible to test the market for the product and better judge the potential benefits of pursuing foreign patent protection.

7. **Does a Patent Guarantee My Right to Sell My Product?**

   A U.S. patent gives its owner the right to exclude others from practicing the patented invention for the duration of the patent. However, it does not actually give the owner the right to make, use, or sell the patented invention. It is thus possible to have an improved and patented product that infringes a prior patent. For example, one person obtains a patent for a chair. Later, a second person obtains a patent for a rocking chair. The first person may be able to stop the second person from selling the rocking chair if the rocking chair incorporates claimed subject matter of the original chair. In such a case, the second person's rocking chair infringes the first person's patent.

8. **What Is an Infringement Study?**

   An infringement study determines whether an unexpired patent has claims that might encompass a product or method that is being made, used, offered for sale, or sold without authorization by the patent owner. If it is determined that a product or method may infringe someone else's patent, the design may be altered to avoid infringement, or a license may be negotiated with the patent owner. Infringement studies require an in-depth understanding of both the applicable patent law and the pertinent technology. Accordingly, you should consider contacting an experienced patent lawyer for such infringement studies.

   If a defendant is found guilty of willfully infringing another's U.S. patent, the court can triple the damage award and require the payment of the patent owner's attorneys' fees. Thus, questions of patent infringement should not be taken lightly. A written opinion from a competent patent counsel that provides a well-reasoned basis showing that the patent is either invalid or not infringed can be helpful in defending against a charge of willful infringement, even if a court ultimately does not agree with the arguments in the opinion.

9. **Are Patents Worth the Cost?**

   Although recent judicial decisions, pending legislation, and proposed Patent Office rule changes may make it more difficult to obtain and enforce patents in the United States, patents remain extremely valuable to most technology companies. A well-crafted patent portfolio can attract investment dollars and provide a substantial competitive advantage. Patents can be used to exclude competitors from a company's core technology, block competitors from improving their own technologies or innovating within the company's commercial market, and discourage competitors from asserting their patents against the company. Patents car also provide substantial value through licensing revenue and through enhanced negotiation leverage. For example, Texas Instruments, Inc., is reported to have received $600 million in patent income. Polaroid's lawsuit against Eastman Kodak shut down Kodak's entire instant-camera facility, and the damages awarded totaled nearly a billion dollars. Thus, patents can be worth the investment to their patent owners. On the other hand, those accused of patent infringement should take prompt steps to minimize their exposure.

10. **Where Can I Get More Information on Patents?**

    Additional information on patents may be obtained from the U.S. Patent and Trademark Office in Washington, DC. Copies of patents are accessible over the Internet from the U.S. Patent Office and other private companies. The U.S. Patent and Trademark Office website (*www.uspto.gov*) contains information on more than eight million issued U.S. patents.

    The assistance of a lawyer experienced in patent matters can help avoid problems before they arise. To contact a patent lawyer or learn more about Knobbe Martens, visit *www.knobbe.com*.

Source: Knobbe, Martens, Olson, and Bear, LLP. Use of company names and trademarks is soley for the purpose of examples, and does not imply sponsorship, affiliation, or endorsement by respective trademark owners. © 2012, Knobbe, Martens, Olson & Bear, LLP. All rights reserved. The full version of this publication can be found at: *http://www.knobbe.com/news/2012/06/ip-101-trademarks-copyrights-and-patents-brochure*.

The above information provided by one of the leading intellectual property firms in the United States offers an introduction and hopefully stresses the importance of having trained professionals in your corner. The Global Village provides sources for international intellectual property laws and the following sites are excellent sources recommended by *Entrepreneur* for U.S. firms.

U.S. Patent and Trademark Office (USPTO.GOV)
The site offers a wealth of information about patents, trademarks, and IP law and policy.

INVENTNOW (INVENTNOW.ORG)
Tied to nonprofit innovation site Invent.org, this youth-oriented microsite does an excellent job of boiling down the complexities of managing an IP portfolio into easy-to-manage steps. This is the place to dip you toe in the IP waters.

GOOGLE PATENTS (GOOGLE.COM/PATENTS)
Equal parts helpful and entertaining. Google Patents delivers information on more than 7 million existing patents, from mouse traps to a hydraulic system for serving sushi and beyond.

PAT2PDF (PAT2PDF.ORG)
A very handy web-based tool that finds patents and downloads them as PDFs. It's a critical tool for those taking the DIY path.

INVENTORS DIGEST (INVENTORSDIGEST.COM)
An online hub loaded with inventor and IP developer news, as well as IP trends and tips.

PATENTWIZARD (PATENTWIZARD.COM)
Designed by a patent attorney, the site helps you take the critical first steps toward filling an early provisional patent.

PATENT PRO (PATENTPRO.US)
This full-featured (and incredibly complex) PC-based patent filing software takes work to learn, but can help entrepreneurs create a working patent.

Steve Blank's Startup Tools is an excellent site which will lead inventors and website and software developers to an incredible host of additional resources. Also, please note when researching in this area, The America Invents Act, instituting patent law reform and enacted in 2011, will take full hold in 2013. Thus, make sure when accessing information online that it is up to date with current laws.

■ LICENSING YOUR PRODUCT

Those inventors who choose not to produce and manufacture their products may elect to sign a product licensing deal with a firm that has the financial, production, and marketing resources to bring the product to market. Many times inventors do not have the time or desire to take their product to market, or the time is ripe for the product, but it will take too much time to arrange for financing and manufacturing if they undertake the manufacturing themselves. Also, many engineers and scientists are more interested in inventing products than running a business.

A very thorough online Inventor's Handbook produced by the famous Lemelson-MIT program addresses product licensing in depth. Securing a license for your product takes a great deal of work and most likely will entail hiring others, including legal counsel, who can assist you in your efforts; less than 10 percent of entrepreneurs seeking licensing are successful. Research, work hard, and be one of them!

GLOBAL**VILLAGE**

International Intellectual Property Laws

International laws are a major concern to a growing number of U.S. exporters and importers due to the increased technological and informational content of products and services. Before conducting business abroad, familiarize yourself with the appropriate patent, trademark, copyright, and trade secret laws of the country in question. According to The American Society of International Law, "Other areas of intellectual property law include rights of publicity, moral rights, misappropriation, unfair competition, geographic indications of origin, database protection, licensing, trade dress, plant variety protection, integrated circuit protection, and paracopyright (including laws that prohibit circumventing anti-piracy technology)."

Use the Internet resources below for your initial research, and then work directly with international intellectual property attorneys. Laws, both in interpretation and enforcement vary from country to country. However, there are a number of ways of protecting your firm in a foreign market, and each has its own merits according to circumstance and the country.

Lawyers well versed in the acceptable practices as well as developing laws will be able to keep you in compliance and help with future legal issues. You do not want to lose your business over a legal technicality.

To track down information on international intellectual property laws, use the following resources:

The **American Society of International Law's e-RG (Electronic Resource Guide)** is an excellent guide which includes research strategies, primary and secondary sources, recommended websites, blogs, organizations, electronic newsletters, and discussion lists.

The **World Intellectual Property Organization (WIPO)** tracks worldwide changes and development of intellectual property and also provides access to various databases of international intellectual property laws, registrations, and treaties.

The **Cornell University Law School Legal Information Institute** offers a comprehensive collection of international materials.

The **Global Legal Information Network (GLIN)** through the Library of Congress provides a searchable database of laws, regulations, and other complementary legal sources.

The **National University of Singapore's A Select Guide to Patent and Trademark Information** and **WIPO Gold** both online resources focus on patent, trademark, and other filing databases.

© Cengage Learning

The Sloan brothers of Startup Nation share that before taking on a new product and paying a licensing fee, "Companies will evaluate such criteria as customer feedback, retail price points, unit costs to manufacture, competitive landscape, manufacturing feasibility, and market opportunity." Their licensing tips follow.

Ten Tips for Landing a Product-Licensing Deal

By the Sloan Brothers

Here are some things we learned along the way about trying to land a product licensing deal.

1. **Know Your Stuff.** First and foremost, to have any chance of licensing your invention, you must *know your stuff*. You have to become an expert in the field in which your invention applies. You should be able to rattle off who the competition is, what the potential market size is, what the projected demand for your product is, and why your product is the best to meet and satisfy that market demand.

2. **Know the Downside.** While it is important to be passionate about your idea, it's also important to be sober. Your credibility will be assessed by potential licensees partly based on whether you present a realistic analysis of the risks the licensee will have to deal with—things like product failure, the potential for slower-than-expected customer adoption, etc.

3. **Present like a Pro.** Information you present to potential licensees should be provided in written form and in a PowerPoint presentation. The information should include market research data, competitive analysis information, patent status, and extent of coverage. It helps to provide a letter from your patent attorney summarizing the initial search results and any other pertinent opinions relating to the extent and value of the patent coverage awarded to you. Also include your product specifications, drawings, prototypes—even if they demonstrate only what the product looks like without the actual functionality. Add to this presentation your production cost estimates, testimonials you've collected, and any and all other materials that help demonstrate the potential your invention has in the marketplace.

4. **Get It Protected.** Big corporations usually have intellectual property or licensing departments specifically set up to handle and manage the inflow of product licensing opportunities. Most of these offices will not accept any submission of a licensing opportunity for which a patent has not yet been issued. And many will not sign a confidentiality agreement, while many others will require that only their own agreement be signed. In some cases, companies might be willing to sign your confidentiality agreement, but only rarely.

5. **Submit Smart!** Work closely with your intellectual property attorney when submitting an idea to a potential licensee to ensure that your idea is adequately protected. Never sign a confidentiality agreement without first having an attorney review it. And never turn over materials to a company without your attorney giving you the green light. It may be dangerous unless you have adequate patent protection in place or a confidentiality agreement that your attorney deems sufficient to protect your intellectual property.

6. **Analyze Your Targeted Licensee.** Always do research on the company you're targeting prior to pitching to them. Check to see if the potential licensee has the manufacturing and distribution capability you need already in place. If they do, their risk is mitigated to a substantial degree, and they will be much more likely to seriously consider the opportunity. Believe it or not, though, you may have to educate them on how your product can fit into their existing lines of business.

7. **Don't Reinvent Procedures.** It's important to follow the established protocol of a licensee when submitting your idea for consideration. If you attempt to bend the rules, your submission can be stopped dead in its tracks before ever being given consideration. If a targeted licensee has a licensing office, always start there to get a case file started at the company's licensing office, and attend to their confidentiality procedures.

8. **Find a Champion.** Once you have clearance from the company to present your idea, always try to find a champion from within the company who gets excited about your idea and works to "pull" the idea into the company rather than you simply attempting to "push" the idea onto the company.

9. **"No" Is an Opportunity.** Remember, it's always safer for the company to say *no* to an idea than it is to say *yes*. The key is to be able to overcome the likely onslaught of negative responses the company will undoubtedly throw your way. It's imperative— even in the midst of a *no*—that instead of hanging up or walking out in defeat, you ask to understand specifically *why*. If someone says *no* to you, that's a perfect opportunity to learn. Immediately ask *why*. What are the concerns? Are they insurmountable? What could be done to address the concerns? You'll use what you learn to create a *yes* next time around.

10. **Multiple Baskets.** As the old saying goes, don't put all your eggs in one basket. Relying on a single potential licensee just adds more risk to a challenge that already has plenty of inherent risk. It's smart to approach more than one potential licensee to increase your odds for success. Further, playing multiple bidders off of each other can actually put some well-needed leverage on your side of the negotiating table by bringing out the competitive nature of the potential licensees. Ultimately, if you generate serious interest—and your aim is to license your invention to just one licensee—be sure you know when to stop playing competitors against each other. The moment you select your licensee, you'll have to begin building good faith with them, and you don't want bad blood to tarnish how they perceive you, and work with you, in the long run.

Bottom Line

While obtaining a license from a third party to produce and sell your product is very challenging, it can be done. And if you properly prepare and equip yourself for the challenge, you have a shot at the dream of landing that product-licensing deal and collecting royalties while the licensee does all the work and takes all of the risk.

Source: Adapted from The Sloan Brothers, "10 Tips for Landing a Product Licensing Deal." Copyright © 2012 StartupNation, LLC. All rights reserved. (*http://www.StartupNation.com*). Reprinted with permission.

■ SUMMARY

Determining your legal form of business should be undertaken with the advice of your attorney, accountant, and business advisors. As your firm grows and changes reassess your decision with your legal and financial team, but be aware that changes to the business form can be difficult and costly.

Partnerships can be a rocky road so evaluate your need for a partners and your choice of partners thoroughly. Do *not* enter into *any* business partnership without legal assistance.

Family businesses can provide extreme satisfaction for many and for others it can be a struggle. Evaluate carefully, communicate fully, and successfully profit together. And don't forget to have a sense of humor

Protecting yourself through copyrights, trademarks, patents, and licensing requires the assistance of intellectual property counsel. Legal issues are significant and have many nuances and complications. Thus, never skimp on finding the best legal advice available. As for the information gleaned from the Internet, user beware.

■ THINK POINTS FOR SUCCESS

- We only remember what we want to. Get *everything* in writing.
- If your business is small and you like it that way, keep it simple. But still take steps to protect yourself.
- Most growth businesses need outside infusions of cash. Your business structure may hinder or enhance your ability to reach out for money.
- Do not pay Uncle Sam more than you have to, but make sure you pay what is due. Have your accountant and lawyer structure your business according to your needs and the laws.

- Even if you incorporate, a banker may still want a personal guarantee for loans, and this guarantee may be in place for years to come.
- The increasing incidence of lawsuits should encourage most businesses to consider incorporating.
- Protect your business through proper adherence to the laws regarding intellectual property.
- Success of your family business is dependent on communication.
- Whatever business structure you choose, work hard, persevere, and hope for a little bit of luck!

■ KEY POINTS FROM ANOTHER VIEW

12 Keys to Family Business Success

By the Sloan Brothers

Family members start a major portion of new businesses launched in the United States every year. Brothers come to mind, of course.

Whatever the family ties, however, starting a business with a spouse, parents, siblings, children, or other family members presents unique challenges over and above the usual problems a start-up faces. That's why **only one in three family businesses survives to the next generation.**

In the start-up stage, the dangers can be especially acute. Family members sometimes join the excitement of a business start-up without a clear idea of their role once the business is underway. If family is involved in your start-up venture, you should be clear up front about compensation, exit plans, and other details before they become a problem.

We've given this a great deal of personal reflection and come up with 12 essentials for striking the right balance when starting a family business.

12 Essentials for Striking the Right Balance in a Family Business

Set some boundaries. It's easy for family members involved in a business to talk shop 24/7. But mixing business, personal, and home life will eventually produce a volatile brew. Limit business discussions outside of the office. That's not always possible, but at least save them for an appropriate time—not at a family wedding or funeral, for example.

Establish clear and regular methods of communication. Problems and differences of opinion are inevitable. Maybe you see them already. Consider weekly meetings to assess progress, air any differences, and resolve disputes.

Divide roles and responsibilities. While various family members may be qualified for similar tasks, duties should be divvied up to avoid conflicts. Big decisions can be made together, but a debate over each little move will bog the family business down.

Treat it like a business. A common pitfall in a family business is placing too much emphasis on "family" and not enough on "business." The characteristics of a healthy business may not always be compatible with family harmony, so be ready to face those situations when they arise.

Recognize the advantages of family ownership. Family-owned businesses offer unique benefits. One is access to human capital in the form of other family members. This can be a key to survival, as family members can provide low-cost or no-cost labor or emergency loans. Firms run by trusted family members can also avoid special accounting systems, policy manuals, and legal documents.

Treat family members fairly. While some experts advise against hiring family members at all, that sacrifices one of the great benefits of a family business. Countless small companies would never have survived without the hard work and energy of dedicated family members. Qualified family members can be a great asset to your business. But avoid favoritism. Pay scales, promotions, work schedules, criticism, and praise should be evenhanded between family and nonfamily employees. Don't set standards higher or lower for family members than for others.

Put business relationships in writing. It's easy for family members to be drawn into a business start-up without a plan for what they will get out of the business relationship. To avoid hard feelings or miscommunication, put something in writing that defines compensation, ownership shares, duties, and other matters.

Don't provide "sympathy" jobs for family members. Avoid becoming the employer of last resort for your kids, cousins, or other family members. Employment should be based on what skills or knowledge they can bring to the business.

Draw clear management lines. Family members who often have a present or presumed future ownership stake in the business have a tendency to reprimand employees who don't report to them. This leads to resentment by employees.

Seek outside advice. The decision-making process for growing a family business can sometimes be too closed. Fresh ideas and creative thinking can get lost in the tangled web of family relationships. Seeking guidance from outside advisors who are not affiliated with any family members can be a good way to give the business a reality check.

Develop a succession plan. A family business without a formal succession plan is asking for trouble. The plan should spell out the details of how and when the torch will be passed to a younger generation. It needs to be a financially sound plan for the business, as well as for retiring family members. Outside professional advice to draw up a plan is essential.

Require outside experience first. If your children will be joining the business, make sure they get at least 3-5 years business experience elsewhere first, preferably in an unrelated industry. This will give them valuable perspective on how the business world works outside of a family setting.

Our Bottom Line

It's hard enough launching a company without the added pitfalls and potential baggage of family relationships. But family businesses have some great advantages over others—mainly a dedicated pool of people ready to stand behind your effort. If your start-up is a family business, you'll need to take extra steps to avoid burnout, ensure on-the-job harmony, and attract advice from business experts outside the family circle.

Copyright © 2008 StartupNation. All rights reserved.

Source: The Sloan Brothers, "12 Keys to Family Business Success." Copyright © 2008 StartupNation. All rights reserved. (*http://www.StartupNation.com*). Reprinted with permission.

■ ACTION STEP

■ KEY TERMS

Image_Source/iStockphoto.com

Build, Maintain, and Thrive with a Winning Team

Teaming with Passion and Following the Law

Learning Objectives

- Accept that you cannot do everything well.

- Understand the importance of balance to the survival of your business.

- Explore new ways of putting together a team, including a virtual organization.

- Look back and see if you have found others who can join with your venture.

- Investigate using independent contractors.

- Explore employee leasing.

- Recognize the legal pitfalls in interviewing, hiring, and terminating employees.

- Understand the true cost of an employee.

- Learn the importance of labor law compliance.

- Avoid sexual harassment lawsuits.

- Determine the importance and cost of workers' compensation insurance.

- Learn how to round out your team.

- Locate mentors to guide you.

Building a winning team can be one of the most enjoyable and challenging tasks you will face as you grow your business. However, now is the time for *you* to build the team of *your* dreams. You are taking a huge risk in starting a business, so surround yourself with those who you will enjoy being around for many hours each and every week. This is your opportunity to build a team of people who will support your dream. To do so, first look at yourself objectively, and then build a team that will fulfill your business, psychological, and financial needs to be a successful entrepreneur. Chapter 11 will show you various ways to build a winning and strong team.

Create a team of people who have a common purpose and specific goals. In a small venture, it is important to share the rewards of success with your team players. Remember, each employee in a small business plays a significant role in its success. As the leader of your company, you must represent and live by the mission you have set forth for your firm. One of your primary responsibilities will be to inspire your employees with your passionate behavior. Strive to consistently communicate your vision to all members of your team. Key Points delineates specific traits to look for in entrepreneurial employees who will help you build a successful venture.

It is fun being an entrepreneur. You are on your own, doing your own thing, running your own show. And one of the toughest things you have to admit is that you cannot perform all business tasks with the same success, nor should you. Once you acknowledge and accept where you need help, today's options for finding assistance are vast.

Balance, proportion, the right people, and the right personalities are equally important in building a winning team. You want a team that brings experience, expertise, knowledge, and passion to the table. Figure 11.1 provides ten keys to help you build a thriving entrepreneurial organization that will lead to success and profitability.

figure **11.1**

Keys to Hiring and Shaping an Entrepreneurial Team

Entrepreneurial teams grow and thrive when the founders and employees believe in the business and are willing to take risks to grow the venture. Look to the following steps as you build your team.

1. Communicate belief in growth and need for team players.
2. Hire highly committed people.
3. Look for attitude not just aptitude.
4. Seek individuals who are willing and able to think outside the box.
5. Hire "entrepreneurial" employees.
6. Look for tenacity and persistence.
7. Search out self-motivated individuals.
8. Delegate responsibilities.
9. Reward employees.
10. Celebrate individual and team successes.

© Cengage Learning

■ THE FOUNDING TEAM

Anyone reading your Business Plan will be most impressed by a founding team with industry-related experience, complementary skills, and a record of achievement. Investors want you to learn on *your* dime and time, not theirs. They will be evaluating the team's background in depth. Prove to investors that your team members have the experience, ability, and pedigree to ensure success. Information about the founding team is the most-read and often the first-read section of any Business Plan.

The following management team examples are not full-blown résumés but brief biographies that demonstrate that the founders understand what they are doing. Vendors, bankers, and investors believe past success is the greatest indication of future success.

Manufacturing Team

Bill Jones and Lee Gray spent more than 11 years in the fitness business, Bill as a product designer and Lee as a sales representative. Bill developed and patented the FastBike, an exercise bicycle that burns energy faster than a stair climber, and he has sold more than 10,000 units. Lee has been in the top 10 percent of Acme Exercise Equipment's sales force for the past 4 years and has been personally responsible for more than $8 million in sales.

Bill has hired Lee to be vice president of sales. A recently retired manufacturing manager of Sport Tech, Ed Riggs, has been hired to serve as vice president of manufacturing. Ed has an operations management degree from Purdue University and managed a light assembly manufacturing plant for more than 20 years. He also teaches quality control management classes part-time at two universities. Jan Wilkes, a retired CPA with manufacturing experience, has agreed to serve as CFO on a part-time basis.

Restaurant Team

Dorothy Lennon won many prestigious awards as executive chef of the Daniel Gray Hotel, and she is well known in the community. As one of the founders of Éclair, she will work full-time and serve as president. Ms. Lennon is certified as a master pastry chef and trained in Paris at the Culinary Institute. She will supervise the kitchen and own a majority interest in the limited liability company. Leslie Perk was, until December, a training manager for the French Connection restaurant chain. Ms. Perk will act as general manager under the direction of Ms. Foltz. Pat Watter is a minority investor, who intends to retain her position as food and beverage manager of Crooked Creek Country Club but will be available as needed to monitor inventory and accounting activities.

Virtual Team

Nancy Hipp, a graphic artist from Indianapolis, will develop the Internet site for a children's online bookstore, Annie Gale's. Cindy Barn, who recently retired from a New York management position in publishing, will serve as the fulfillment manager for all Internet orders. She will continue living in New York. Three teachers—Pat Tran in Arizona, Peggy Galt in Florida, and Troy Ball in Iowa—will answer all customer inquiries and review all new books. Jennifer Shue and Amy Peters, both children's librarians, will pen book descriptions and review books from their homes in the Northwest.

No matter how you begin your business, at some point you will find yourself needing the assistance of others. The previous examples illustrate solutions found to round out a team. As you look to fulfill your business needs, remember to search for people who will balance your skills and personality.

In one firm, the owner had poor customer-relation skills; he scared off all but the hardiest customers and employees. His brother realized that the business was headed for disaster. Taking a chance, he approached his brother, the owner. They agreed that the front office and customers should be off limits for him. Several months later, the business was back on track, and the employees and customers were relieved and happier.

Find what you do best and hire or sub out the rest!

First, we will discuss various ways to acquire the help you need to grow your business without hiring full or part-time employees.

■ THE VIRTUAL ORGANIZATION AND OUTSOURCING

Virtual organizations and outsourcing have not only become buzzwords, they are a reality for millions of small businesses today. The advancements in technology and the ease of communication allow entrepreneurs to compete with larger firms without sacrificing scale, speed, or agility. However, when it comes to forming the team, legal issues are rampant, costly, and difficult; thus, many turn to virtual organizations and outsourcing to produce their products and services.

Let us examine how the old motion picture studios used to work. They owned real estate, studios, and equipment; they had performers under contract; and they owned many other fixed assets with which they cranked out movies, both good and bad. Most of the old movie studio giants have gone the way of the dinosaurs.

In their place today are project teams of highly creative people, hired just in time to make a great picture, who will disband after the project until the next opportunity presents itself. They rent everything they need, and each aspect of the film is outsourced to specialists. Virtual organizations are like forming an all-star team to exploit a market opportunity.

An advertising agency may consist of a solo entrepreneur who presents his client with a promotion solution. Once the solution is approved, the entrepreneur assembles freelance graphic designers, copywriters, photographers, models, performers, and media experts to produce the promotion package. The virtual advertising agency has little overhead and can bring together the best talent quickly and efficiently, which will provide the client with a high-quality campaign at a lower cost. Today's technology allows even solo entrepreneurs to compete with the big guys quite often.

Suppose you have an idea for a new widget. You develop a prototype, demonstrate it at a trade show, and take orders. Do you build a factory and hire workers? Or may outsourcing be your answer? By using NAISC codes and industry sources, you can locate assemblers, packagers, box makers, food mixers, toolmakers, public warehouses, sales agents, and whatever else when the need arises.

Bobby Chade of Scotty B's Hot Sauces found after buying a small firm that he needed to find new suppliers and his search ensued. One question he faced, "Would the company sales quickly outgrow the small packers or would he need to look for a packer who would be able to meet his needs if sales took off?" He choose a larger packer in hopes that as sales grew they would accommodate the growth.

One printer discovered that her sales ability far exceeded her desire to produce printed materials, so she redefined herself as a "printer's broker" and used her knowledge to select from a wide variety of printers available for the most appropriate product. She sold her own small shop to an employee and increased her income several times over by providing assistance to customers who knew little about printing. Her virtual organization had just-in-time access to more than 50 experienced and specialized printers.

With continued corporate downsizing come mushrooming opportunities for alert virtual entrepreneurs. The benefits include:

- Having access to the skills and experience of proven experts in their field
- People competing to perform work for you through crowdsourcing
- Paying only for services needed
- Obtaining variable production quantities
- Gaining higher reliability
- Achieving better quality and consistency
- Having lower internal developmental costs

GLOBAL**VILLAGE**

www.export911.com
Portal to the World of Exporting and Importing

To learn more about exporting and importing, one free resource is Export 911 (*http://www.export911.com*). The site directs you to specific information on the business of exporting, covering such topics as letters of credit, bar codes, export labeling, product inspections, export cargo insurance, and so on.

The site's thousands of links are broken down into the following areas:

Gateways to Global Markets
Export Department
Purchasing Department
Shipping Department
Production Department
Administration Department
Product Coding

© Cengage Learning

Consider a Virtual Organization and Consider Outsourcing

1. Make a list of people or firms who might assist your efforts on an as-needed basis either as employees, independent contractors, or consultants. To keep your overhead to an absolute minimum, ask and shop around; look for those people and businesses who share your vision. Make adjustments to your list as you continue to explore.
2. If you will be outsourcing design, graphics, accounting, human resources, manufacturing, or order fulfillment, it is now time to research prospective sources and also to explore costs. Chapter 8 asked you to look at your start-up and operating costs, and you may have conducted your outsourcing research at that time. If not, now is the time! Explore crowdsourcing.
3. Explore joint ventures.
4. Explore strategic alliances.

- Maintaining flexibility to instantly address new market opportunities
- Lower benefit and worker compensation costs
- Lower recruiting and training costs

With the above benefits in mind, the virtual organization needs to be extremely customer-driven and opportunity-focused. Performance standards are critical and there must be agreement and a shared vision among all the participants.

The virtual organization might exist for weeks or years—and then, when the opportunity has been fully exploited, it might disband quickly. Develop an exit plan when you develop a virtual organization, so you know where you are headed. Action Step 46 will help you explore the virtual organization alternative. In high-tech environments virtual organizations are commonplace as the technology moves so rapidly, firms need to respond with lightning speed and precision.

■ PARTNERSHIPS WITH OTHER FIRMS

Consider as partners those firms with special capabilities that will share the risk in bringing a product or service to market. For example, if you have a new product, a team that includes retailers or end users could solve a lot of your distribution issues. Businesses usually form partnerships or associations in two fundamental ways: one as a joint venture and the other being a strategic alliance.

A joint venture is usually a goal-oriented cooperation among two or more businesses. It involves the creation of a separate organization owned and controlled jointly by the parties. The joint venture usually has its own management, employees, production systems, and so on. Cooperation is limited to defined areas and often to a predetermined time frame. Sample joint venture contracts can be found online at Public Legal and Inc.

A strategic alliance is a goal-oriented cooperative effort among two or more businesses based on formal agreements and a Business Plan. In contrast to a joint venture, however, it usually does not involve the establishment of a separate new organization. The objective of a strategic alliance is to improve the competitiveness and capabilities of the individual members by using the strengths of the team. Depending on the need, the network may be organized in a variety of forms with regard to function, structure, and organization.

Joint Venture Partnership formed for a specific undertaking resulting in the formation of a new legal entity

Strategic alliance Partnership formed between companies to create a competitive advantage

■ INDEPENDENT CONTRACTORS

independent contractors Works on tasks, sets own schedule, paid on freelance basis

Using independent contractors on an hourly or project basis can an excellent way for you to start your business. It will keep your overhead low at startup. Although, many people misunderstand the rules for independent contractors. If you tell a worker when to start and stop work, and if you supply tools or office equipment, you *may* have an employee. On the other hand, if the work assignment is task-driven, if the worker sets his or her own hours, if you pay by the job and not by the hour, and if most of the work takes place away from your office using the worker's resources, then you *may* have an independent contractor relationship.

You *may* save money if your workers are independent contractors—no Social Security, Medicare, workers' compensation insurance, health insurance, retirement benefits, paid holidays, vacations, sick days, and so on. Most employers can locate workers who will work without mandated benefits—but sooner or later a contractor will get hurt, apply for unemployment, or attempt to collect Social Security benefits. When they do, the government may come back to the employer with high fines and penalties as they may view the contractors as employees.

Review independent contractor rules with a CPA and your attorney, because the rules are rigid and the fines can be high. In addition, independent contractor status receives a high level of state and IRS scrutiny. An abbreviated version of IRS Publication 15-A (Figure 11.2) provides further information.

Be aware that state employment laws may be even more stringent than federal rules. According to California Attorney Robert Wood, "California's Labor and Workforce Development Agency can fine you for 'willfully misclassifying' an employee from $5,000 to $15,00 per violation. Also the penalty goes up to $25,000 per violation if you commit a 'pattern and practice' of 'willfully

figure **11.2**

Employee or Independent Contractor?

(Excerpted from IRS Publication 15-A)

An employer must generally withhold federal income taxes, withhold and pay social security and Medicare taxes, and pay unemployment tax on wages paid to an employee. An employer does not generally have to withhold or pay any taxes on payments to independent contractors.

Common-Law Rules

To determine whether an individual is an employee or an independent contractor under the common law, the relationship of the worker and the business must be examined. In any employee–independent contractor determination, all information that provides evidence of the degree of control and the degree of independence must be considered.

Facts that provide evidence of the degree of control and independence fall into three categories: behavioral control, financial control, and the type of relationship of the parties. These facts are discussed below.

Behavioral control. Facts that show whether the business has a right to direct and control how the worker does the task for which the worker is hired include the type and degree of:

Instructions that the business gives to the worker. An employee is generally subject to the business' instructions about when, where, and how to work. All of the following are examples of types of instructions about how to do work.

- When and where to do the work
- What tools or equipment to use
- What workers to hire or to assist with the work
- Where to purchase supplies and services
- What work must be performed by a specified individual
- What order or sequence to follow

The amount of instruction needed varies among different jobs. Even if no instructions are given, sufficient behavioral control may exist if the employer has the right to control how the work results are achieved. A business may lack the knowledge to instruct some highly specialized professionals; in other cases, the task may require little or no instruction. The key consideration is whether the business has retained the right to control the details of a worker's performance or instead has given up that right.

Training that the business gives to the worker. An employee may be trained to perform services in a particular manner. Independent contractors ordinarily use their own methods.

(continued)

— figure **11.2**

Employee or Independent Contractor? *(continued)*

Financial control. Facts that show whether the business has a right to control the business aspects of the worker's job include:

The extent to which the worker has unreimbursed business expenses. Independent contractors are more likely to have unreimbursed expenses than are employees. Fixed ongoing costs that are incurred regardless of whether work is currently being performed are especially important. However, employees may also incur unreimbursed expenses in connection with the services that they perform for their employer.

The extent of the worker's investment. An independent contractor often has a significant investment in the facilities or tools he or she uses in performing services for someone else. However, a significant investment is not necessary for independent contractor status.

The extent to which the worker makes his or her services available to the relevant market. An independent contractor is generally free to seek out business opportunities. Independent contractors often advertise, maintain a visible business location, and are available to work in the relevant market.

How the business pays the worker. An employee is generally guaranteed a regular wage amount for an hourly, weekly, or other period of time. This usually indicates that a worker is an employee, even when the wage or salary is supplemented by a commission. An independent contractor is usually paid by a flat fee or on a time and materials basis for the job. However, it is common in some professions, such as law, to pay independent contractors hourly.

The extent to which the worker can realize a profit or loss. An independent contractor can make a profit or loss.

Type of relationship. Facts that show the parties' type of relationship include:

- *Written contracts describing the relationship the parties intended to create.*
- *Whether or not the business provides the worker with employee-type benefits, such as insurance, a pension plan, vacation pay, or sick pay.*
- *The permanency of the relationship.* If you engage a worker with the expectation that the relationship will continue indefinitely, rather than for a specific project or period, this is generally considered evidence that your intent was to create an employer–employee relationship.
- *The extent to which services performed by the worker are a key aspect of the regular business of the company.* If a worker provides services that are a key aspect of your regular business activity, it is more likely that you will have the right to direct and control his or her activities. For example, if a law firm hires an attorney, it is likely that it will present the attorney's work as its own and would have the right to control or direct that work. This would indicate an employer–employee relationship.

IRS help. If you want the IRS to determine whether or not a worker is an employee, file Form SS-8, Determination of Worker Status for Purposes of Federal Employment Taxes and Income Tax Withholding, with the IRS.

Misclassification of Employees

Consequences of treating an employee as an independent contractor. If you classify an employee as an independent contractor and you have no reasonable basis for doing so, you may be held liable for employment taxes for that worker (the relief provisions, discussed below, will not apply). See Internal Revenue Code section 3509 for more information.

Relief provisions. If you have a reasonable basis for not treating a worker as an employee, you may be relieved from having to pay employment taxes for that worker. To get this relief, you must file all required federal information returns on a basis consistent with your treatment of the worker. You (or your predecessor) must not have treated any worker holding a substantially similar position as an employee for any periods beginning after 1977.

Misclassified Workers Can File Social Security Tax Form. Workers who believe they have been improperly classified as independent contractors by an employer can use Form 8919, (Uncollected Social Security and Medicare Tax on Wages), to figure and report the employee's share of uncollected Social Security and Medicare taxes due on their compensation.

Source: *http://www.irs.gov* (Accessed March 3, 2012).

classifying' workers. These penalties are in addition to existing penalties, interest, and taxes for misclassifying contractors."

If you choose to pay a person as an independent contractor, understand that if the person becomes disgruntled and you have not followed the IRS rules, they may blow the whistle on you. Also, if your competitors feel you have an unfair advantage by treating those working for you as independent contractors, they may also turn you in to the IRS and you may find you firm under investigation.

■ EMPLOYEE LEASING

Consider employee leasing as a way to reduce administrative costs, paperwork hassles, legal issues, and costly benefits. Not unlike leasing physical property, in this instance you will be leasing people—employees—whose leasing organization handles payroll and most, if not all, of the human resource functions. The human resource services they offer can be bundled together or offered a la carte.

A leasing firm will help you stay in compliance with the myriad of federal, state, and local employment laws. California and federal labor codes run more than 460 pages, so keeping in compliance is a full-time job. According to the Hiring Checklist provided by HRCalifornia, affiliated with the California Chamber of Commerce and an excellent fountain of information and support, there are more than 25 steps you need to take for EACH new hire. One can easily see why many small business owners claim that over 25 percent of their time personally is spent on employee paperwork. Each entrepreneur needs to value his or her own time and use it most productively, and paperwork does not bring in sales or lead to profits.

HRCalifornia stated the following California employment laws would be changing in 2012: "credit check, pregnancy disability leave, willful misclassification of independent contractors, written commission agreement, notice of pay details, organ and bone marrow donor leave, genetic information, gender expression, e-Verify, interference with rights under leave laws, administrative penalties, wage penalties, farm labor contractors-wage notices, agricultural labor relations, insurance non-discrimination act, state contracts-gender or sexual orientation discrimination, apprentice programs, safe lifting-hospitals, workers' compensation, and DFEH procedural regulations."

If you are operating in more than one state, each state will have their own changes, such as California, which you will be required to institute in your company. If you hire through an employee-leasing firm, you will be able to transfer the majority of the responsibility for compliance to them.

In addition to the legal issues, one excellent advantage of large PEO's is their ability to offer employees health insurance benefits and retirement programs that are not usually available to smaller ventures. Oftentimes, new firms lose out on top employees or cannot keep their best employees because they cannot offer these benefits. Due to economies of scale, large leasing firms are able to provide these benefits to your leased employees at an affordable cost. For your protection, we suggest you only use a leasing organization that possesses a strong track record and a sound financial background. The National Association of Professional Employer Organizations provides further information on employee leasing.

Employee leasing may appear to cost more initially, (approximately 2 to 6 percent of payroll) but allows for additional benefits. For example:

- Background screening checks are completed by the leasing organization.
- Termination issues are eliminated. If the person does not fit the position, you can send him or her back to the leasing organization.
- Turnover is reduced.
- They cover workers' compensation.
- They are responsible for training and development.
- They adhere to best practices and policies.
- Hiring costs such as advertising, interviewing time, reference checks, and so on are reduced.

■ THE FIRST EMPLOYEES

When to hire your first full-time employee is a question often asked. You may require full-time employees immediately, but many small firms do well using part-timers, temporary workers, or independent contractors until the owners have a strong feel for what needs to be done and who is best suited to do the job. Some firms never hire full-time employees and always choose to use part-timers, as illustrated in the example of Charlene Webb.

A Team of Part-Timers

Charlene Webb built a winning team with part-time employees. After she sold her gourmet cookware shop, she opened a women's specialty clothing store. The shop is small—about 2,000 square feet—and located in a small shopping center in an upscale community of about 60,000 people.

Charlene discovered her ideal employees were local women who were active in community life and who preferred to work only one day a week. Monday's saleswoman is a golfer whose country-club friends come in to visit and buy from her on her day at the store. Tuesday the tennis player is on duty, and her friends have followed her. Wednesday, a sailing instructor and officer of the largest sailing club in the area; Thursday, a leader of hospital volunteers; Friday, a well-known PTA member takes over; and Saturday, an attorney's wife. All of the highly energetic women know fashion, and their customers' lifestyles and needs. In addition to being employees, they also serve as unpaid market researchers. They never tire from the routine, and they are excellent customers and employees. Also, they serve as walking store models at all times due to receiving a 50% discount on everything in the store.

Charlene demonstrates in her stores how a well-connected group of part-time employees can surpass full-timers. But for most businesses, that will not be the case; for them, full-time commitment and loyalty will be part of their hiring goals and future growth.

If you require someone with a high level of technical skills, or a person who will take your organization to the next level, you may need to provide an extra carrot, depending on the economy and industry. Talented workers may prefer the entrepreneurial adventure to big business bureaucracy, and they may work for less if they share your vision and passion for entrepreneurship and foresee a future financial payoff. Many firms, especially in high-tech, are able to hire employees who receive a percentage of the business in return for accepting a lower salary.

As you continue to add people, you must understand that competence is not the only criterion to consider. You are assembling a venture team that wants to see growth and prosperity as much as you do. It is impossible to grow and expand until you have people who are not only capable but also motivated to ensure success. Key Points provides an additional excellent discussion of desirable characteristics for entrepreneurial employees.

The quest for new employees begins with a written job description, which should be relatively short--one to one and half pages. A simple list of bullet points describing major activities and responsibilities that apply to the work environment and physical requirements, is needed. For example, "An air conditioned office environment requiring repeated moving and lifting of boxes weighing up to 50 pounds each

- using a computer for 4-6 hours per day
- traveling required twice a month to Chicago
- annual meeting required once a year in Florida
- driving company van and making deliveries throughout city"

You may not find a perfect fit, so do not fence yourself in with too many specifications. However, a small business cannot afford a misfit or an unproductive person. Also, beware of negative individuals who can make everyone unhappy.

If past experience is not critical when hiring, look into hiring graduating students from vocational, trade, and professional schools. Local colleges and high schools also have placement offices. Also, inexperienced employees can sometimes be found through programs offered through social agencies that might subsidize the training of workers, as Evergreen Lodge highlighted in Chapter 9 found.

Also, consider public and private employment agencies. In addition, temporary agencies may be able to locate short-term help. Hiring through a temporary agency allows you to check out the person before actually hiring him or her for full-time employment. Many business owners hire from agencies to reduce the paperwork and liability of hiring workers directly. Or as suggested previously, hire through a PEO.

Monster.com, LinkedIn.com, and Craigslist.com may also be recruiting sources for you. If you require someone highly educated and skilled in a very specific area, you may also need to use a professional recruiter. Also, many job posting sites on the Internet target specific markets and may also prove helpful. National associations often allow job postings and listings on their Internet sites as well. In many industries, a tweet or Facebook posting will bring in potential employees.

If you are just starting out, you may want to network your way through your contacts. E-mail job descriptions to your friends and associates, and see if any of them will act as recruiters for you. Keep in mind, though, that terminating someone recommended by a friend or family member might prove difficult, and one of the most important requirements of a small business is the ability to let go of an employee as soon as possible if he or she is not working out. Networking also possesses the risk that you may hire a relative or an executive of a customer or competitor's firm, which could potentially be a problem.

What *is* critical in hiring is your effort to make sure you have investigated the applicants to the best of your ability within legal parameters. Unfortunately, terminating employees can trigger lawsuits—and justified or not, they can cost you an incredible sum of money and time. Be sure you have a qualified and experienced attorney on call at all times to assist you with employment law issues.

Be prepared: You *will* have employee turnover in the beginning. Either they will quit or you will decide to terminate their employment. Restaurants and retail stores should over hire for the opening months.

Develop personnel policies to cover hiring, terminating, and managing your employees. Human resource associations and state Chamber of Commerce agencies have excellent tools to help you develop materials and policies. If you provide an offer letter to an employee, list compensation based on a weekly or monthly basis so as not to imply a long-term commitment. Although, it might be best not to provide an offer letter at all; in some instances, it may imply a contract. You want to maintain that the relationship is "at will," meaning that you can terminate the employee whenever you want. Your policies need to be reviewed so that they do not compromise the "at will" status. Check your state laws to determine if you are an "at will" state. And even if you are in such a state, there is still significant risk in any employment termination decision. Always consult with your attorney before terminating an employee.

Additionally, if you are a firm with competition and privacy concerns, contact your lawyer to discuss drafting noncompete and confidentiality agreements for your employees. In high-tech industries, these agreements are commonplace.

One source that allows you to develop policies using online software is located at *http://www.hrtools.com*. Remember, any form you take from the Internet should be reviewed by your attorney for compliance with individual, state, and federal laws.

Due to potential problems inherent in the hiring and employment process, we recommend firms such as Integrity, ADP, or Paychex to assist you in managing required legal paperwork and payroll. Such firms also provide you with legal updates and will make sure you are in compliance with the vast state and federal laws. Upon reading only one of ADP's newsletters, you will know

— figure **11.3**

Top Tips for Avoiding Legal Trouble with Employees

By Attorneys Amy DelPo and Lisa Guerin.
You can't afford to ignore or mishandle employment problems. A botched employment situation can cost you millions of dollars if it turns into a lawsuit. Protect yourself using these commonsense tips:

1. Treat your workers with respect. Workers who are deprived of dignity, who are humiliated, or who are treated in ways that are just plain mean are more likely to look for some revenge through the legal system—and juries are more likely to sympathize with them. For example, if you march fired workers off the premises under armed guard, publicize an employee's personal problems, or shame a worker in public for poor performance, you can expect trouble.

2. Communicate with your workers. Adopt an open-door policy and put it into practice. This will help you find out about workplace problems early on, when you can nip them in the bud. And it will show your employees that you value their opinions, an important component of positive employee relations.

3. Be consistent. Apply the same standards of performance and conduct to all of your employees. Workers quickly sour on a boss who plays favorites or punishes scapegoats. Successful discrimination lawsuits start when you treat workers in the same situation differently.

4. Give regular evaluations. Performance evaluations are your early warning system regarding employment problems—and your proof that you acted reasonably, in case you end up in court. In the worst cases, evaluations can be valuable proof in a lawsuit, illustrating that you put a poor performer on notice and gave him a chance to improve. In the best situations, they can turn a poor performer into a valued worker. You can find detailed information about giving performance evaluations in *The Performance Appraisal Handbook* by Amy DelPo (Nolo).

5. Make job-related decisions. Every workplace decision made should be guided by job-related criteria—not by a worker's race or gender and not by a worker's personal life or your personal biases. Making business-related personnel decisions makes economic sense and will keep you out of lawsuits for discrimination, violation of privacy, and wrongful termination.

6. Don't punish the messenger. Employers get in trouble when they discipline whistleblowers or workers who complain of harassment, discrimination, or unsafe working conditions. Take action to deal with the problem itself, not with the employee who brought the problem to your attention.

7. Adopt sound policies and follow them. An employee handbook is an indispensable workplace tool that can help you communicate with your employees, manage your workforce, and protect your business from lawsuits. But once you adopt policies, you have to follow them. If you bend the rules, your workers won't take them seriously. Some courts have found that employers who don't follow the policies set out in their employee handbook or personnel manual might be on the hook for breach of contract. You can find detailed information about giving performance evaluations in *Create Your Own Employee Handbook: A Legal & Practical Guide*, by Amy DelPo and Lisa Guerin (Nolo).

8. Keep good records. If a worker sues you, you'll have to not only remember and explain what happened, but also prove that your version of the story is accurate. To make your best case, keep careful records of every major employment decision or event for each worker—including evaluations, disciplinary warnings, and reasons for firing.

9. Take action when necessary. Once an employment problem comes to your attention, resist the temptation to hide your head in the sand. Take action quickly, before it turns into a real mess.

10. Be discreet. Loose lips about employee problems are a surefire way to bring the law down upon your head. An employee could sue you for defamation or could haul you into court for causing her emotional distress, for creating a work environment that is hostile or poisoning the well with prospective employers. The stakes are high, so protect yourself by giving information on a need-to-know basis only. You can find more information on employee privacy rights and other workplace issues in *The Manager's Legal Handbook, The Basics*, by Amy DelPo and Lisa Guerin (Nolo).

Source: Reprinted with permission from the publisher, Nolo, Copyright 2004, *http://www.nolo.com* (Accessed March 7, 2012).

immediately that it would be impossible for you to be able to keep up with the legal changes affecting the employer–employee relationship. Employment law has become a very difficult road for most employers to travel, and we advise that you *never* travel it alone. Avoid penalties for missed filing dates and potential filing errors by hiring a payroll services firm.

Adhering to the law, acting with good intentions, and using payroll services may enable you to reduce employment issues. Please review Figure 11.3 for additional tips for avoiding legal troubles.

■ INTERVIEW AND STAY OUT OF COURT

Interviewing can be considered an art, but the questions you ask must not only be insightful—they must also be worded to keep you out of court. Consider the questions discussed in the following section before conducting your first interviews.

Ask the Right Questions

Use open-ended questions to start the applicant talking, but avoid too much small talk; you may inadvertently ask an illegal question, such as, "Grenchik—that's an interesting last name. What nationality is it?" A question of this type might be construed by the applicant as national-origin discrimination.

Develop a list of questions appropriate to the position you want to fill based on the job description and responsibilities you have defined. To avoid any charges of discrimination, ask each applicant for the same job the same questions. Any written application form also needs to be reviewed by your attorney to make sure it is also not discriminatory. The following sample questions will help you begin to prepare your own list of interview questions:

1. How did you prepare for this meeting?
2. What are some of the obstacles you have overcome on previous jobs?
3. How have you worked independently on the job in the past?
4. What gives you satisfaction in a job?
5. What have been your most memorable work experiences?
6. What do you expect from an employer?
7. Have you ever organized an event? Explain.
8. What did you like and dislike about your last job?
9. How do you handle change and uncertainty?
10. Give an example of when you were a team player in your last position.
11. What do you do best at work?
12. When I call your last two employers, what are they going to tell me?
13. What type of challenges do you like best?
14. Describe a problem in your last job and how you resolved it.
15. How best can a boss support you?

For jobs requiring specific experience, remember that past behavior is the best predictor of future behavior. To learn the past behavior of the interviewee, formulate questions that ask for very specific examples germane to your business. Through the questions, you are trying to assess the person's behavior, relevant skills and abilities, knowledge, and experiences. If you are hiring an office manager you might want to ask, "How did you juggle the various staff personalities and job tasks in your last job?"

Try to determine how fast people think on their feet and how creative and innovative they are as well. Ask a few questions like, "If you bought an office chair from Ikea, how would you begin to assemble it?" "How would you use social media to promote our product?" "In you last job, what would you have done to increase employee morale?" In a new venture each employee may wear many hats, and you want to assess the flexibility of your new hires.

Hiring entrepreneurial employees is challenging. However, looking for employees who possess integrity, willingness to learn and grow, as well as possess good common sense and a high level of energy and enthusiasm can be a good start. In addition, look for employees who have a strong sense of responsibility and drive.

During your interviews, make sure you have uninterrupted time to put the applicant at ease, to listen thoroughly to comments, and answer questions the applicant may have. Take notes throughout the process, and encourage the applicant to ask questions. Make your purpose for the interview clear, and explain the interview and hiring process, including time frames, checking references, and completing background checks.

At the end of the interview, review your notes and your thoughts. Ask yourself the following questions: 1) Is this person able and willing to do the job? 2) Is this person someone I can manage? 3) Will I and the other team members enjoy working with this individual? 4) How will my customers view this prospect?

Action Step 47 asks you to determine additional questions you would add to those above to fit your particular job specifications, industry, and work situation. To determine how responsible applicants are, and how well they take instructions, one retailer requires all applicants to bring their picture ID and Social Security card to the first interview. She explains to the applicants that unless they bring these two items, she will not interview them when they arrive. Approximately 40 percent of the applicants forget one or both items and thus do not receive an interview or a job.

At the end of the interview, and after you have selected several potential employees, investigate their past with reference checks through their previous employers. Depending on the area of the country you live in, this may be easy—or it may prove *very* difficult.

Checking References

If you have any doubts about the importance of checking references, review ADP's 2010 Screening Index report covering over 6.5 million job applicants (Figure 11.4).

Again, professional payroll service firms and PEOs will also perform reference checks, which can save you time, money, and paperwork and also ensure your compliance with the law. The following points, as well as Figure 11.4, underscore the importance of reference checks:

1. Employee theft is the leading reason for merchandise losses according to the National Retail Federation's Security Survey.
2. Hiring an illegal alien can result in fines of up to $10,000, according to the Immigration and Naturalization Services.
3. Cost of employee turnover is very high as you must now recruit, hire, and train a new employee; and you can expect lower productivity until the new employee is up to speed.

ACTION STEP 47

Interview Questions

1. Remember the guiding principle: *All inquiries should be directly job-related.*
2. Review the list of interview questions in the text and the Key Points article in this chapter. Next, determine how you can legally adjust these questions to fit job specifications, your industry, and the work situations of your future employees.
3. Make a list of the questions based on the above and all the additional information throughout the chapter.
4. Prepare a short, three- to five-minute introduction to your firm, the specific job, and the job's requirements to present to prospective employees.
5. What steps will you take to share your passion for the business with employees?

---

figure **11.4**

Latest Benchmark Screening and Selection Statistics

ADP's Screening Index charts hiring risks in the workplace and helps employers assess the value of their own background screening programs.

The 2010 Screening Index, based on more than **6.5 million individual background checks** completed by ADP® in the 2010 calendar year – nearly a million more than in 2009 – revealed:

A review of background checks across eight industries – automotive, business services, construction, healthcare, hospitality, manufacturing, retail, and transportation – provides a number of significant vertical observations.

- Business Services industry screened records had the lowest number of previous workers' compensation claims (2%) and negative reference responses (1%).
- Automotive dealers continued to have the highest percentage of driver records showing one or more violations (44%) and four or more violations (9%), year over year.

- Hospitality (65%) and Automotive dealer (64%) records had the highest percentage of reference checks reflecting variances between what an applicant provided and what a source reported.
- Transportation industry records continued to reflect the most accurate reference data.
- Construction, Hospitality, and Retail had the highest percentage of records that reflected a criminal record in the last seven years (each 9%, respectively), while the Healthcare industry had the lowest rate at 4%, and Business Services and Transportation records, each 5%, respectively. All of these were unchanged from the 2009 Index.
- Overall, 46% of employment, education and/or reference check showed discrepancy.
- Forty five percent of credit records showed judgments, liens, bankruptcies, on referrals to collections.
- Six percent of checks revealed previous worker's compensation claims.

Source: *http://www.screeningandselection.adp.com/resources/screeningIndex.html* (Accessed March 7, 2012).

4. Workplace violence is a serious safety and health issue today. Violence can be directed to fellow employees and managers as well as customers.
5. The use of drugs and alcohol in the workplace adds risk for the employee, fellow employees and customers.

Negligence in hiring or in terminating bad hires in a timely fashion may result in lawsuits from potential employees, employees, and family members of employees who are harmed by an employee. With average settlements of over $500,000 and jury awards of up to $3 million for negligence, once again you see the financial as well as the personal cost. Thus, careful hiring and monitoring of employees at all times is essential for any small business to assure a safe working environment.

Because of potential libel lawsuits, employers are very reluctant to provide information about past employees, thus making it necessary to investigate the backgrounds of potential employees in other ways. However, when doing so the laws are very strict, vary by state and industry, and also are in constant flux. Thus, we strongly suggest firms hire outside third party vendors to conduct background checks.

Inconsistency in following any of the rules, security of the background data information, and difficulty of accessing national, state, and county records are additional reasons to use third party vendors. One of the newest twists to background searching is the use of Facebook, Twitter, and LinkedIn. While using these and other online sources may prove advantageous in recruiting and hiring, they may also prove very disadvantageous if used improperly. Thus, use the sites with extreme caution and legal advisement.

For employment screening services, review the services of *http://www.hireright.com* and *http://www.adp.com*, along with others. HireRight's services include searching DMV records, professional license and credential verifications, social security validation, sex offender databases, and civil court records, as well as many others, for around $100 per screening with a two-day turnaround. Before conducting employment screening or using any screening services, we suggest you consult with your attorney.

If the driving record of a prospective employee shows four moving violations in the last year, would you reconsider? What if the person has relocated 10 times in the past 7 years? Or if he or she has lied about a degree? Not considering these factors can cost you a great deal, so spend the money to hire correctly, and terminating will be less frequent and less costly.

Please note that you are required by law to inform candidates of their rights, and in many cases there are disclosure and authorization forms required. The Federal Credit Reporting Act states that if you are denying employment based in whole or in part on the content of a background credit report, the candidate must be notified of such action, and they must receive a copy of the credit report and the consumer agency's name and contact information. Pre-employment credit checks are banned in 5 states for most jobs and over 14 other states are considering doing so as well.

Many employers may also want to perform drug and blood tests. However, the laws regarding testing are complicated and sometimes confusing. If you are considering testing, contact your attorney for legal advice; making a mistake in this area could prove *very* expensive. Industry associations provide additional information on hiring and screening practices.

■ WHAT DO EMPLOYEES REALLY COST?

If you plan on hiring employees, consider *all* the costs associated with hiring, training, and retaining employees. Only when one understands the total employee cost can one begin to determine pricing and profitability of products and/or services to be offered. Also, recognizing the total employee cost will help you communicate more effectively with your employees in terms of the value of their compensation package. Factors to consider include:

- Recruiting and hiring
- Salary
- Employment taxes—Social Security, unemployment, and Medicare
- Worker's compensation insurance
- Benefits—health, retirement, dental, vacation, sick leave
- Space, furniture, equipment
- Additional management time
- Any additional perks you might offer—child care, car allowance, and so on
- Training

Each employee will cost you 130 to 200 percent of his or her salary due to the above costs. Employees in an entrepreneurial venture need to pull *more* than their own weight, so choose wisely. To keep abreast of salaries and wages, use salary comparison information from the following Internet sites: Salary.com, Monster, JobStar, Glassdoor, and PayScale. Several of these sites will provide you with custom salary reports at very reasonable fees in addition to their free online data.

To gain accurate information on actual wage and salary rates, contact similar employers in your area and review area online listings. Salaries and wages during the past few years have been affected greatly by the economy and being aware of these changes will help you stay abreast and thus set your wages appropriately. Local unions and trade associations are valuable sources of compensation data. In volatile employment markets, wages can fluctuate greatly and you must stay on top of the changing wages in your marketplace.

■ LABOR LAW COMPLIANCE

Ignorance is not an acceptable defense if you are charged with breaking the labor laws shown in Figure 11.5. Check with government agencies to be sure that you do not overlook any legal requirements. The penalties for failure to comply are stiff, and firms have lost their businesses due to noncompliance. Again, do not enter this realm without professional assistance. Contact the following federal organizations to learn about your legal responsibilities:

- Occupational Safety and Health Administration (OSHA)
- Equal Employment Opportunity Commission (EEOC)
- Department of Labor (DOL)
- Internal Revenue Service (IRS)
- U.S. Department of Justice, Americans with Disabilities
- U.S. Citizenship and Immigration Service (USCIS)

In addition to the federal offices, you will need to contact your state offices for further employment law information. In addition, some cities have additional laws that affect employment and wages. State laws supersede federal laws if they are stricter than the federal laws. You will need to obtain a federal employment identification number by filing IRS Form SS-4 (see Appendix C), and then register with your state's employment department for payment of unemployment taxes. In addition, you or your accountant must file IRS Form 940-EZ or IRS Form 940 to report your federal unemployment tax each year.

Another issue to consider is the eligibility of employees to work in the U.S. According to the Department of Homeland Security, "E-Verify is an Internet-based system that allows an employer, using information from Form I-9, Employment Eligibility Verification, to determine the eligibility of that employee to work in the United States." According to the USCIS site, "While participation

figure **11.5**

Major Laws of the Department of Labor

The Department of Labor (DOL) administers and enforces more than 180 federal laws. This brief summary is intended to acquaint you with the major labor laws and not to offer a detailed exposition. For authoritative information and references to fuller descriptions on these laws, you should consult the statutes and regulations themselves.

Wages and Hours

The **Fair Labor Standards Act** (FLSA) prescribes standards for wages and overtime pay, which affect most private and public employment. The Wage and Hour Division administer the act. It requires employers to pay covered employees who are not otherwise exempt at least the federal minimum wage and overtime pay at one-and-one-half times the regular rate of pay. For nonagricultural operations, it restricts the hours that children under age 16 can work and forbids the employment of children under age 18 in certain jobs deemed too dangerous. For agricultural operations, it prohibits the employment of children under age 16 during school hours and in certain jobs deemed too dangerous.

The Wage and Hour Division also enforces the labor standards provisions of the Immigration and Nationality Act (INA) that apply to aliens authorized to work in the U.S. under certain nonimmigrant visa programs (H-1B, H-1B1, H-1C, H2A).

Workplace Safety and Health

The **Occupational Safety and Health** (OSH) **Act** is administered by the Occupational Safety and Health Administration (OSHA). Safety and health conditions in most private industries are regulated by OSHA or OSHA-approved state programs, which also cover public-sector employers. Employers covered by the OSH Act must comply with the regulations and the safety and health standards promulgated by OSHA. Employers also have a general duty under the OSH Act to provide their employees with work and a workplace free from recognized, serious hazards. OSHA

enforces the act through workplace inspections and investigations. Compliance assistance and other cooperative programs are also available.

Employee Benefit Security

The **Employee Retirement Income Security Act** (ERISA) regulates employers who offer pension or welfare benefit plans for their employees. Title I of ERISA is administered by the Employee Benefits Security Administration (EBSA), formerly the Pension and Welfare Benefits Administration, and imposes a wide range of fiduciary, disclosure, and reporting requirements on fiduciaries of pension and welfare benefit plans and on others having dealings with these plans. These provisions preempt many similar state laws. Under Title IV, certain employers and plan administrators must fund an insurance system to protect certain kinds of retirement benefits, with premiums paid to the federal government's Pension Benefit Guaranty Corporation (PBGC). EBSA also administers reporting requirements for continuation of health care provisions required under the Comprehensive Omnibus Budget Reconciliation Act of 1985 (COBRA) and the health care portability requirements on group plans under the Health Insurance Portability and Accountability Act (HIPAA).

Unions and Their Members

The **Labor-Management Reporting and Disclosure Act** of 1959 (also known as the Landrum–Griffin Act) deals with the relationship between a union and its members. It protects union funds and promotes union democracy by requiring labor organizations to file annual financial reports; by requiring union officials, employers, and labor consultants to file reports regarding certain labor relations practices; and by establishing standards for the election of union officers. The act is administered by the Office of Labor-Management Standards (OLMS).

Source: U.S. Dept. of Labor, *http://www.dol.gov/opa/aboutdol/lawsprog.htm* (Accessed March 8, 2012).

in E-Verify is voluntary for most businesses, some companies may be required by state law or federal regulation to use E-Verify. For example, most employers in Arizona and Mississippi are required to use E-Verify. E-Verify is also mandatory for employers with federal contracts or subcontracts that contain the Federal Acquisition Regulation E-Verify clause."

Source: *http://www.uscis.gov/portal/site/uscis/menuitem.eb1d4c2a3e5b9ac89243c6a7543f6d1a/?vgnextoid=e94888e60a405110VgnVCM1000004718190aRCRD&vgnextchannel=e94888e60a405110VgnVCM1000004718190aRCRD*

The situation with E-Verify is constantly changing and we suggest you keep in contact with your state Chamber of Commerce, third-party human resource provider, and your employment lawyer so that you remain compliant. A sample I-9, Employment Eligibility Verification form can be found in Appendix C.

Review the requirements for complying with the Americans with Disabilities Act (ADA) before undertaking your tenant improvements and before conducting any interviews or hiring. If you are not clear on the legal requirements, remember: Ignorance is not bliss—you are still required to adhere to all the laws. Again a third party vendor will keep you abreast of the laws in this area.

Be aware of overtime and employment laws, particularly those laws pertaining to employment of anyone under 18. Post a copy of the labor laws conspicuously, where everyone can read them. If you have even *one* non–English-speaking employee, also post the laws in that employee's language. Go to DOL site to locate the federal posters that you must by law display in your workplace. Also, adhere to your state's poster requirements as well.

In addition to complying with state and federal labor laws, you must also comply with all federal, state, and sometimes local tax laws. See Chapter 12 for a brief review of employee taxes. *Hire a payroll services company to prepare payroll and to ensure compliance with all employment and tax laws.* As stated previously, the cost of these services is a fraction of the cost of the time it would take you to become an expert on labor law or the cost of fines for non-compliance. An approximate cost for monthly services would be about $200 for a firm with five employees.

In addition to complying with the above laws and regulations, two additional major issues face most employers today: sexual harassment lawsuits and increasing workers compensation costs.

Sexual Harassment

Small businesses are not immune from sexual harassment issues and lawsuits. Federal, state, and local laws and ordinances may apply to your growing firm. To limit your firm's exposure, communicate and educate your workforce about what constitutes sexual harassment. See the EEOC site for further information. In addition, your firm must make clear to all employees that sexual harassment will not be accepted or tolerated at any time amongst the employees or in their interactions with customers and suppliers. It is imperative that sexual harassment issues are dealt with consistently and fairly within your firm.

According to the EEOC, "sexual harassment can occur in a variety of circumstances, including but not limited to the following:

- The victim as well as the harasser may be a woman or a man. The victim does not have to be of the opposite sex.
- The harasser can be the victim's supervisor, an agent of the employer, a supervisor in another area, a co-worker, or a nonemployee.
- The victim does not have to be the person harassed but could be anyone affected by the offensive conduct.
- Unlawful sexual harassment may occur without economic injury to or discharge of the victim.
- The harasser's conduct must be unwelcome."

Prevention is the best tool to eliminate sexual harassment in the workplace. Provide sexual harassment training to employees and establish an effective complaint or grievance process which includes taking immediate and appropriate action when an employee complains.

It is also unlawful to retaliate against an individual for opposing employment practices that discriminate based on sex or for filing a discrimination charge, testifying, or participating in any way in an investigation, proceeding, or litigation under Title VII.

Source: U.S. Equal Employment Opportunity Commission, *http://www.eeoc.gov/eeoc/publications/fs-sex.cfm* (Accessed March 8, 2012).

To help guard against sexual harassment liability, outline a written policy with the help of an employment attorney to include 1) the reporting process 2) the investigation process and 3) potential outcomes based on the investigative findings. In addition, disseminate your firm's sexual-harassment policy to all employees, and document that they have received the policy. Hire third-party presenters so employees will feel more comfortable and misinterpretations will be reduced during training.

Take all complaints seriously. If you need to investigate a sexual-harassment complaint, hire an experienced third party. The cost of sexual-harassment lawsuits can sink any entrepreneur, so beware and prepare.

Set a zero tolerance policy for sexual or other forms of harassment. Such actions will set a tone of professionalism for your employees in their dealings both inside and outside of the company.

Workers' Compensation Laws

Depending on your state's statutes, workers' comp insurance may cover medical care, temporary and permanent disability, vocational rehabilitation services, and death benefits for on-the-job injuries or occupational illnesses. The insurance is provided as basically no fault insurance.

Each state develops its own worker compensation requirements and statutes and thus if you are employing people in different states you must be aware of each states' constantly changing statutes. Thus, another reason why we suggest hiring a third party is to keep you in compliance with all laws.

To access your state's workers' comp laws go directly to the state's department of labor site. You will need to determine if the people working for you are independent contractors or employees. Depending on your state laws, their required coverage will vary. Also, the legal definition of an independent contractor can vary from state to state.

You will also need to classify your employees properly into one of the more than 700 worker classification codes used. If you classify workers improperly, you may face penalties if an employee is injured on the job.

Workers' comp insurance is primarily obtained through commercial insurance carriers, although this varies by state. Some states allow self-insured coverage or provide state worker compensation programs.

Insurance rates are based on previous claims adjusting for both the frequency and the severity of injury and costs involved. When doing expense projections, one of the largest costs some businesses face is workers comp insurance. If you are in the construction field, these costs will be extremely high.

Also, in some states, mental and emotional stress workers' comp claims are growing rapidly increasing overall premiums. States may also provide benefits for victims of workplace violence. If you hire minors, make sure they are legally allowed to perform the job because if they are injured on the job you will be subject to additional fines under workers' comp.

To reduce workers' comp claims and insurance increases, keep your employees safe on the job. Insurance rates are calculated as a percentage of each $100 in payroll. If one pays their employees partly under the table, be aware the employee will request their workers' comp based on their total pay not just what appears on their paychecks. If this is the case with one of your employees, the workers' comp department may audit your firm and the financial and legal penalties can be high. Being honest is costly but being dishonest can be even more costly!

■ TEAM MEMBERS

Action Step 48 uses the idea of balance to scout potential team members. If you are able to imagine how each candidate will work in your new venture, you are well on your way to building a winning team.

ACTION STEP 48

Brainstorm Your Ideal Team

What do you need to win at the entrepreneurial game? Money, of course, and energy—tremendous energy. (You have that, or you would not have read this far.) You also need hardwork, a terrific idea, intensity, the ability to concentrate, a sense of industry and thrift, curiosity and tenacity, and the ability to be organized.

And you need people: people to support your effort, people to balance your skills, people to take up the slack, people to help you with tasks you find distasteful or do not understand. People will help your passion become reality.

1. Analyze yourself first. What do you like to do? What are you good at? What do you hate to do? What does your business need that you cannot provide yourself? Who can fill those needs? Start building your ideal team.

2. After you have taken the time to do some research into your own personality, especially your strengths and weaknesses (refer back to the Action Steps you have already completed), you will begin to get a feel for what kind of help you need in your venture. Is there anyone out there who can balance your skills? Now that you have the idea of balance firmly in mind, network your vendors and your competitors for potential team members. Whenever you meet someone new, ask yourself: "How could this person fit into my new business?"

3. Keep looking for your future team with new eyes. Make a list of all potential team members, the role they could play, and their strengths and weaknesses. What will it take to have them join your team?

Working 60 to 80 hours a week and spending more time together with your venture team than with your family—may be the reality of your new business. So, how do you keep the employer–employee relationship strong and healthy? It is one of the toughest parts of the job for many an entrepreneur. To understand the potential pitfalls, and to explore ways to avoid problems, review the following advice.

Boss vs. Buddy

It is human nature to want people to like you, but separating the roles of boss and buddy can help head off management headaches. That does not mean you need to chuck compassion when you become a manager. Warmth and openness are valuable elements of an effective working relationship. Nor do you need to adopt an aloof attitude that says, "I'm above all the grunt work that I hired you to do." Workshop contributor Karen Bankston points out that new companies especially are finding those nonhierarchical structures in which managers and employees work together can be productive and morale boosting.

"Those issues are separate from treating people differently based on how well you get along with them," contends Susan Stites, a human resources consultant with Management Allegories in Madison, Wisconsin.

The two foremost risks of befriending employees are the potential conflict of interest and discomfort level in giving friends job performance feedback, and the perception of unfairness.

The latter pitfall surfaces regularly when a work group plans after-hours outings or social gatherings around activities, and some employees are not interested in or cannot join in. For instance, some employees may have family commitments that limit their spare time.

"A common lament is, 'I have kids to go home to. I can't go out and party,'" Stites notes. "Those people always feel left out the day after everyone else goes out on the town. It can be very demoralizing."

Stites recalls a management retreat she attended several years ago that included a morning on the golf course. "I was the only one there who didn't golf, and I felt really closed out the next day from all the in-jokes that came out of that golf game."

Thus a good rule of thumb is to plan social activities that everyone enjoys at a time when everyone can attend.

Another issue is the interplay of personalities in the workplace. Effective managers need to get along with people with varied approaches to life and work. Stites cites the example of companies that suffer when the presidents "hire themselves." They end up with a staff that supports their strengths—and magnifies their weaknesses.

"A manager needs to be a role model in accepting diversity in work and thinking styles and in capitalizing on that diversity," she suggests. Building on everyone's strengths is a foolproof recipe for success and for turning personality differences into complementary assets.

To learn more about personalities in the workplace, Stites suggests that managers look into seminars on personality profiling by Myers-Briggs, Social Styles, and DISC. They can be expensive, but they are well worth the money, even for managers in small companies.

"Coach" and "mentor" may be better titles than "friend" to strive for when you become a boss. "There's been a lot of recent emphasis on those terms," Stites adds, "but I think good business leaders—even back in the twenties when everything was autocratic—have always been good mentors."

Source: Adapted from Karen Bankston, published on NFIB online, *http://www.nfib.com/object/ 1583908.html* (Accessed March 17, 2008).

Rounding Out the Personalities of Your Team

If you are an entrepreneur, you like to move fast. You want quick answers and quick action. You have studied the marketplace and found your market niche. You did not think you would need much of a team, but now you are growing so quickly that you have to do some team building. You want to move fast, so you need a key to human behavior. You want people who can help you, not harm you, because every person counts in small business. A test—called an *assessment instrument* in the training field—might help you locate the key that unlocks the door behind which your team awaits.

We would like to point out that the search for the key to human behavior is not a recent phenomenon. In the earliest civilizations, astrologers and stargazers tried to explain human behavior based on the four elements: earth, air, fire, and water. In the fourth century BCE, Hippocrates, who gave us the Hippocratic Oath, kept the four-part framework developed by the astrologers but changed the labels to choleric, phlegmatic, sanguine, and melancholic.

Today, we find behaviorists renaming the quadrants again, some calling them driver, expressive, amiable, and analytical; and others using controller, organizer, analyzer, and persuader. If you are an entrepreneur, there is a good chance you are either a dominant driver–controller or an expressive inducer–persuader. In either case, you are busy leading and charging, so you need help with details and organization. Find a simple test, take it yourself, and use it to help build your team. However, before using *any* test with job applicants or employees, check with your attorney to determine if the test is legal as a screening, evaluation, or training device. Access these sources for help:

1. The counseling–testing center of your local community college or university
2. The Internet under "human resource training"
3. Myers-Briggs Inventory Test
4. DISC personality testing
5. StrengthFinder testing

The above will lead you to free and low-cost personality testing which may help you understand yourself better and discern the areas in which you need balance in building your team.

According to Winning Workplaces, a nonprofit dedicated to helping small and mid-sized companies build strong teams, believes a Winning Workplace is one that:

- "Gives employees ownership over their work and empowers them to make a difference.
- Creates and communicates a compelling vision for their people, providing employees with a sense of meaning and purpose in their jobs.
- Recognizes and celebrates workers' accomplishments.
- Openly and honestly shares business information and challenges with employees, and engages them in the decision-making process.
- Understands and addresses employees as whole individuals with lives outside of work.
- Creates an environment of esprit de corps that boosts morale and an acceptance of change."

One Winning Workplace, Headsets.com, highlighted in the Passion feature adheres to their "six core Building Blocks of a Winning Workplace:

- Trust, Respect & Fairness
- Open Communications
- Rewards & Recognition
- Teamwork & Involvement
- Learning & Development
- Work/Life Balance"

Source: "What is a Winning Workplace?" from *http://www.winningworkplaces.org/ aboutus/faqs.php*, (Accessed November 21, 2012).

Entrepreneur's Resource

Global Entrepreneurship Week (GEW)

What is Global Entrepreneurship Week?

Global Entrepreneurship Week is the world's largest celebration of the innovators and job creators who launch start-ups that bring ideas to life, drive economic growth, and expand human welfare. During one week each year, GEW inspires people everywhere through local, national, and global activities designed to help them explore their potential as self-starters and innovators. These activities, from large-scale competitions and events to intimate networking gatherings, connect participants to potential collaborators, mentors, and even investors—introducing them to new possibilities and exciting opportunities. More than 24,000 partner organizations hold events during GEW that directly engage more than 7 million people each year.

How big is Global Entrepreneurship Week?

- 123 countries have active national GEW campaigns.
- 25,000 partner organizations plan and conduct activities to occur during GEW.
- 40,000 events, activities, and competitions occur during GEW.
- 10 million people around the world participate in GEW events, activities and competitions.

Where is Global Entrepreneurship Week happening?

Everywhere. Last year, 37,561 activities took place in 104 countries during Global Entrepreneurship Week. This year, 123 countries are celebrating GEW, so it should be even easier to find an event to participate in—check our global database of activities for one near you (*www.unleashingideas.org*). If there isn't something close, you can always plan your own.

Who can get involved in Global Entrepreneurship Week? And how?

Anybody. Anywhere. Anytime. Organizations can get involved in a variety of capacities—planning events and activities as a local partner, promoting the initiative as a Global Partner, or even coordinating the initiative for an entire country as a Host. Individuals interested in exploring their entrepreneurial potential can find a broad array of activities—from local events to global competitions. Entrepreneurs and investors can share their ideas and experiences—face-to-face or online. How you get involved is up to you. If you want a little guidance, connect with the Host for your country (*www.unleashingideas.org/hosts*).

How can I connect with others participating in Global Entrepreneurship Week?

In addition to connecting face-to-face during GEW events and activities, participants can continue their conversations year-round through a handful of official GEW social media channels: Twitter, @unleashingideas and @gewusa; Facebook, *www.facebook.com/unleashingideas*; LinkedIn; YouTube, *www.youtube.com/unleashingideas*; and Flickr, *www.flickr.com/unleashingideas*.

Source: Global Entrepreneurship Week. Retrieved from *http://www.unleashingideas.org/* (accessed March 8, 2012). Reprinted with permission.

ACTION STEP 49

Who's in Charge? Time to Impress Your Business Plan Reader

Investors and vendors are often more interested in the founders than in the Business Plan itself. Experience in the same type of business, and former business experience or ownership, are powerful positive components of the plan. You will need to focus on past responsibility and authority. Present the balance and diversity of your founding team.

Several paragraphs in the Business Plan may be sufficient for each key founder. If experience is lacking, discuss consultants or committed strategic partners who will bring balance to the management team and contribute experience and special skills. You may also want to include an organizational chart in your Business Plan's appendix.

If at this time you do not have your team in place, write bios and résumés of your dream team and supporters.

1. Write short, strong bios for each member of your team to include in your Business Plan.
2. Write complete résumés for each major member of your team. These will later be added to the appendix of your Business Plan.
3. If you are rounding out your team with major support from consultants or strategic partners, write up several paragraphs explaining their roles.

Now it is time to begin to formulate your own impressive and winning team by completing Action Steps 48 and 49. Remember to build your team with passion and to demonstrate that passion in your Business Plan.

Find Mentors

In addition to being a mentor and coach to your employees, if you are starting-up a business for the first time, there is a good chance *you* may need mentors—fellow entrepreneurs who provide advice and encouragement. Perhaps you have mentors already. If not, how can you find such help? First, network with your friends, co-workers, and business associates. Tell them that you are looking for successful business owners with good track records. The perfect mentor would be one with experience in your particular market segment. Second, join your local chamber of commerce and one or more civic clubs if appropriate. Consider joining professional associations to make further contacts.

Keep your eyes peeled for a mentor appearing on the horizon. If your community has a chapter of Service Corps of Retired Executives (SCORE), contact them to see if you can find a match. If not, use their email services. Both services are highlighted in the Entrepreneurial Resource feature. Many successful long-term mentorships take place via email and Skype.

In addition to the traditional routes for finding mentors, the Internet has opened up more avenues for you to find like-minded individuals who share your dreams, as well as possible mentors. LinkedIn, Twitter, Facebook, as well as Google and Meetup may lead you to mentors and entrepreneur groups.

Entrepreneur's Resource

SCORE Mentoring

SCORE, (Service Corps of Retired Executives) sponsored by the SBA, provides face-to-face and email mentors to over 180,000 entrepreneurs a year. For forty years and with over 13,000 mentors, SCORE has been encouraging those with just an idea, those who are ready to launch, and those who want to grow their current business. Many of the mentors come with 30–40 years of extensive and wide-ranging backgrounds. Their expertise and encouragement may be just what you need.

Your local SBA office will match you with the best mentor to meet your needs if you want to have a face-to-face mentor. If for some reason your match does not work out, ask for another mentor.

To locate an email mentor, search online the mentoring skills database for experts in business operations, technology and IT services, sales, finance or business strategy. In addition, you may also access mentors with industry experience in international trade, hospitality, retailing and wholesaling. If you are planning to sell to the government, you will be able to communicate with a mentor who has years of experience and insight into what may be a foreign world to you. Mentors oftentimes are able to open doors for new ventures to wholesalers, suppliers, and possibly even customers.

When one is wrapped up in starting a business, it can be very helpful to have another perspective from a seasoned entrepreneur. SCORE mentors are a sounding board to try out new ideas with someone who does not have a personal or financial stake in your business. SCORE mentoring is free for the asking, so logon to Score's website and find a mentor who can help you grow your venture.

Many entrepreneurs have become bloggers, and you may find a community of fellow entrepreneurs as well as mentors, at various sites such as IdeaCrossing and Business Owners' IdeaCafé. New mentoring opportunities continue to develop online, so stay abreast of new sites.

Once you have located several candidates, develop a set of questions and arrange a meeting or send an e-mail; you want to pick the brains of all the candidates. Here are some things to consider when selecting a mentor:

- Do you feel comfortable with this person?
- Can you trust him or her?
- Is he or she easy to communicate with?
- Does he or she have experience and contacts that can help your new business?
- Will he or she consider mentoring you for at least 6 months?

Keep in close contact with your mentors as you develop and grow your business. Maintain contact by keeping in touch at least once a month. Your mentors may be able to help you establish banking connections and vendor–supplier relationships. A good mentor can be invaluable for checking your leases, contracts, and marketing materials. Providing encouragement, passion, and moral support however may prove to be more important to you.

PASSION

Passion for Listening to Employee Needs

Headsets.com

Mike Faith started Headsets.com 10 years ago, and the retailer has quickly grown to become one of the major players in the nearly $2 billion U.S headsets industry. A large portion of the staff of the San Francisco, CA-based business comprises a customer service call center that processes headset orders.

Call centers, it should be noted, have a reputation for high turnover. And, unfortunately, the reputation is not unfounded. A new study by Cornell University finds that U.S. call center turnover rates range from 25 to 50 percent. That means a lot of people coming through the door to take the seat of outgoing call center employees.

At Headsets.com, that revolving door has a jam in it. Mike Faith, the president, CEO and founder of the company, instituted a system where prospective candidates—for the call center, shipping department or any area—are interviewed at least seven or eight times before they're hired. What's more, some of these interviews are with the company's voice coach and psychologist.

"Each employee is really a key hire for us," Faith says. He isn't kidding. Many employees have started their tenure with the company in the call center and explored growth opportunities that have arisen as the business has grown. Two such employees are Rick Mills, who was a customer service phone rep in 2002 and is now CFO; and Courtney Wight, who also started as a phone rep a year and a half ago and is now customer service manager.

"The interview process is long—I remember when I went through it—but then once you work here you can see that everyone wants to work here and everyone likes it here," Wight says.

Connecting the interviews to the current culture, for those employees Headsets.com brings on, is the previously mentioned voice coach involved in the interview process, Ken Welsh. Hailing from Australia, Welsh handles coaching and team building for some big name clients in addition to Headsets.com, including BMW, Coca-Cola, and IBM. Wight says her staff is reinvigorated whenever Welsh shows up, and that has led to improved morale, service and, consequently, sales.

(continued)

(continued)

Welsh is one of four global business coaches to which all Headsets.com employees have access. Besides the voice coach and the psychologist, who's based in San Diego, there's a management and organization consultant from the U.K. and a U.S.-based NLP (neuro-linguistic programming) practitioner.

"There's a huge payoff with the coaches," says Mills, who has used a few of them himself. "Sometimes it's tough to go to your supervisor with issues you're having—you don't know how it affects their impression of you as an employee. But if you have this outside person who's trained to help you, it goes a long way toward feeling like you have an open avenue not only to advance, but to work through challenges at work and ways to improve."

Of course, when the coaches aren't around, the leadership continues to work to identify opportunities to help employees succeed in their roles and to grow. Faith says that new employees who have been with the organization for 90 days receive a $600 "training allowance"; after a year the amount increases to $1,500 (the same amount is awarded annually thereafter). The allowance can be applied to work-related or personal growth pursuits. "They can even spend it on something connected to their *next* job, if they decide they don't want to work here," Faith says.

Helping this focus is the fact that Headsets.com's leadership tries to take the inverse approach to one of Corporate America's major worker gripes: managers who love to look for things done wrong and exploit these acts.

"We try to catch somebody doing something right, instead of doing something wrong," says Tiffany Rawson, who started with the company about two and a half years ago as a shipper and is now manager of the shipping department. "If someone is doing something wrong, I'll point it out, but I try to balance it by making sure I still find those things that they're doing right—the kinds of things that tend to go unnoticed day to day."

This kind of active, positively focused management has not gone unnoticed by the company's employees. They respond in kind not only by working harder, but by pitching their ideas, in which Faith readily places stock to help grow the business. Wight made note of two internal e-mail addresses where she encourages her staff to send ideas about anything having to do with the company. "They could be large or small, and they go right to Mike," she says. Many of the ideas are acted upon, and employees are rewarded financially for their extra contribution.

As with many businesses, especially smaller enterprises, at Headsets.com their product is their passion. One need look no further for evidence of this than the Staff Recommendations page on their website, where many of the customer service reps have posted short descriptions of their headset of choice and why they love it. It's clear by seeing their pictures, showing them in their favorite headset, that they're some of the people keeping the revolving call center door from swinging on needlessly.

Company: Headsets.com, Inc.
Website: *www.headsets.com*
Industry: Headsets retailer
Location: San Francisco, CA
Number of employees: 52
Sales: $31 million.

Source: "Success Stories: Listening to Employee Needs" Copyright © 2001–2011 Winning Workplaces. All Rights Reserved. From *http://www.winningworkplaces.org/library/success/listen_to_empl_needs.php* (Accessed March 8, 2012). Reprinted with permission.

■ SUMMARY

An entrepreneur's venture team often goes beyond bankers, lawyers, and accountants. A single-person entrepreneur today may never need to hire an employee to prosper, as many of today's successful firms use strategic partners, outsourcing, and strategic alliances for almost everything.

But if you grow beyond your own capacity and need to hire employees, hire wisely, train carefully, and encourage always. Remember, very few employees will ever have the "fire in the belly" for your business as you do. If you expect them to believe in your dream as much as you do, you will be disappointed. Remember, this is "your baby," and unless you are willing to share the financial successes, your employees are not likely to share the same passion for your dream.

Review your options for hiring part-time employees, independent contractors, leased employees, as well as full-time employees. Build the best team you can under current constraints.

With employment laws expanding and litigation out of control, we highly recommend hiring outside third-party vendors to keep your paperwork in line and your firm compliant with the multitude of rapidly changing federal and state laws.

You have the right, responsibility, and opportunity to build a culture for your firm and employees. What kind of environment do you want to provide for your employees? Strict and by the book? Easy going and free flowing? Open door? Jeans and T-shirts? Three-piece suits? Employees who can rise from inside the firm? Hiring from outside? Offering the best benefits around? Child-friendly policies?

You wanted your own business. Now you must passionately design and grow the environment you want to work in with the type of people you enjoy working with.

■ THINK POINTS FOR SUCCESS

- People tend to "hire themselves." How many more like you can your business take?
- A winning team may lurk in your network.
- Look to your competitors and vendors for team members.
- Your company is *people*.
- Balance the members on your team.
- Have each employee write objectives for his or her responsibilities within the business.
- You cannot grow until you have the right people.
- When you hire the wrong person, terminate them thoughtfully with legal counsel and in a kindly fashion as soon as you realize the error. Start over learning from your mistake.
- How much of your team can be part-timers and moonlighters?
- Weigh the pros and cons of a virtual organization.
- Understand legal ramifications of hiring independent contractors.
- Consider the pros and cons of employee leasing.
- Find a mentor.
- Control workers' compensation costs.
- Follow all federal and state employment laws, and consult with professionals to keep you in compliance.
- Educate and train employees to recognize and eliminate sexual harassment and discrimination from the workplace.
- Build your team with passionate employees
- Create the company culture you desire.

■ KEY POINTS FROM ANOTHER VIEW

Seven Characteristics of Highly Effective Entrepreneurial Employees

Writing on the MIT Entreprise Forun website, Joe Hadzima and George Pilla suggest a short list of the characteristics needed by employees in fast-growing entrepreneurial organizations. Keep these in mind when interviewing. Can you think of other, similar characteristics?

Ability to Deal with Risk

An effective entrepreneur and his employees have to operate effectively in an environment filled with risk and make decisions when lacking critical resources or data.

Results Oriented

An effective entrepreneurial employee is able to cut through and resolve problems that divert others and possess common sense.

Energy

An entrepreneurial employee consistently generates output that is higher than could be reasonably expected. He or she is self-motivating and sets his or her priorities with minimal guidance.

Growth Potential

An effective entrepreneurial employee willing accepts much higher levels of responsibility than is usual for the position, title, experience level, or salary. She or he acts as a strong role model, trains and coaches others, and is a good candidate to move on to a supervisory role.

Team Player

A successful entrepreneurial employee accepts accountability and ownership for his or her area of responsibility and expects others on the team to do the same.

Multitasking Ability

Not only must an entrepreneurial employee accept new duties, assignments, and responsibilities, but in today's business environment he or she must be able to do this while continuing to perform prior assignments and tasks.

Improvement Oriented

The Right Stuff employee is willing to suggest changes and improvements frequently and encourages others to do so also.

So when you interview each new employee or manager, look beyond the mere facts of the résumé. Does what you see suggest that this candidate has what it takes to make a real contribution to your fast-growing entrepreneurial organization?

■ ACTION STEPS

Action Step 46   Consider a Virtual Organization and Consider Outsourcing *301*
Action Step 47   Interview Questions *309*

Action Step 48   Brainstorm Your Ideal Team *314*
Action Step 49   Who's in Charge? Time to Impress Your Business Plan Reader *318*

■ KEY TERMS

joint venture *301*

strategic alliance *301*

independent contractors *302*

Image_Source/iStockphoto.com

Protect Your "Baby" and Yourself

Insurance, Crime, Taxes, Exit Strategy, and Ethics

Learning Objectives

- Understand the importance of protecting your assets through insurance.

- Explore insurance needs for your specific business.

- Investigate and initiate loss-prevention strategies for both internal and external crimes.

- Build awareness of cyber-crime issues.

- Recognize the need to file all tax forms in a timely manner.

- Understand the importance of tax planning—not just tax filing.

- Prepare for your exit from the start.

- Recognize that ethical behavior is required of the owner before ethical behavior can be expected of the employees.

- Understand the daily ethical dilemmas entrepreneurs face.

- Learn seven steps to better decision making.

You will work incredibly hard to start and grow your business, but you also must work equally as hard to *protect* the business that has become your "baby." Using insurance wisely, paying taxes as required, negotiating effectively, protecting your firm from computer security breaches, and following ethical principles will keep your business on track for success.

The Internal Revenue Service (IRS), lawyers, and computer hackers are formidable foes. Be prepared!

In addition, you need to plan for the future by planning for the finish. In other words, when you begin your business, you need to plan for how you will exit your business. When reviewing your exit strategy, we will ask you to return to the questions in Chapter 1, which asked you to assess your reasons for starting a business.

Protecting your business also includes short- and long-term tax planning, and we cannot emphasize enough the need for a team composed of insurance advisors, legal counsel, and accountants. In the Action Steps, we ask you to take steps to protect your "baby" and yourself.

■ INSURANCE AND MANAGING RISK

What risks does my business face? Product liability? Employment liability? Customer Injury? Shoplifting? Floods? Technology breaches? Disability? Loss of partner? The list could continue for a very long time. Work with your insurance broker to decide which risks you need to insure for, which of these you need to assume the risk for, and which you need to share the risk and responsibility.

A trained experienced business insurance broker will work with you to assess your firm's potential risks and recommend specific coverage. In addition, you need to discuss and determine the amount of risk you are willing to assume in accordance with the level of deductible you can afford.

Contact others within your industry for insurance broker recommendations. In addition to the broker's advice, we recommend you work with your trade or business associations to determine if they offer assistance or insurance for their members. Group policies, due to volume purchasing, may be available to members at a reduced cost.

In addition to assessing your needs, both brokers and associations may have recommendations on how to reduce and prevent losses. In many circumstances, they offer online and/or onsite training programs to assist clients. As you grow, your associations' knowledge of state/federal/international insurance issues will be of great importance to you and help secure your business.

First and foremost, protect your business by providing safe equipment and working conditions, hiring competent employees, training employees, and warning employees of any existing dangers. In addition, make sure you follow all state and federal laws.

As you meet with your advisors, they will consider the following with you:

- Probability of a loss
- Size of any potential loss
- Your financial resources available to meet a loss if one occurs
- The probability of lawsuits (some industries and areas are heavily targeted)

Can you eliminate all risks and losses? That is doubtful. Can you reduce risk? Yes, but you also *must* assume risk.

How do you decide whether a particular risk should be transferred to an insurance company or assumed? Calculate the maximum potential loss that might result. If the loss would force your company into bankruptcy or cause serious financial damage, *recognize the risk and purchase insurance to help protect your assets.*

Losses that occur with predictable frequency, such as shoplifting and bad debts, are usually absorbed by the business and are often budgeted as part of the normal costs of doing business. Thus, the cost of the loss is incorporated into the price of the product or service.

Where probability of loss is high, a more effective method of controlling the cost of the loss is to both adopt appropriate precautionary measures and purchase better than adequate insurance. The key to purchasing insurance, and all risk management, is: *Do not risk more than you can tolerate losing.*

Insurance Planning

In general, the following are a few of the risks, which are covered by insurance if you have followed the law:

- Personal injury to employees and the general public. Retail stores and fast food restaurants have become targets for slip-and-fall claims.
- Legal action stemming from hiring, firing, sexual discrimination, libel, slander, and so on.
- Loss to the business caused by the death or disability of key employees or the owner—an essential coverage needed to protect your firm's future.
- Loss or damage of property—including merchandise, supplies, fixtures, and buildings. A standard fire insurance policy pays the policyholder only for those losses directly caused by fire. Make sure when dealing with your insurance agent that you understand your policy and coverage thoroughly.
- Loss of income resulting from interruption of business caused by damage to the firm's operating assets (storms, natural disasters, electrical blackouts).

Other indirect losses, known as *consequential losses*, may be even more harmful to your company's welfare. Protect yourself against these losses by obtaining business-interruption insurance. Consequential losses include the following:

- Extra expenses of obtaining temporary quarters
- Loss of rental income on buildings damaged or destroyed by fire, if you are a landlord
- Loss of facility use
- Continuing expenses after a fire—salaries, rents paid in advance, interest payments, and so on
- Loss of customer base

Also, in every state an employer must insure against potential workers' compensation claims. However, employee coverage and the extent of the employer's liability vary from state to state. Workers' compensation cost differs greatly by occupation and the risk involved and can cost up to 42 cents on every dollar you pay your employees.

Ask your insurance company if they have any loss-prevention services for training employees, and use them to the fullest extent. If your employees speak several different languages, you are responsible for making sure *everyone* thoroughly understands the safety rules. (See Chapter 11 for further information on workers' compensation.)

General liability covers most kinds of nonemployee bodily injury, except that caused by automobiles and professional malpractice. In some cases, coverage may even extend to trespassers. As a business owner, you may also be liable for bodily injuries to customers, pedestrians, delivery people, and other outsiders—even in instances in which you have exercised "reasonable care."

PASSION

Passion for Silence and Helping People with Disabilities
How an Earplug Company Supports Jobs for 200 People with Disabilities

Posted by Gwen Moran | March 22, 2011

Thanks to the ambient noise of his University of Southern California college campus and the surrounding urban chorus of screeching tires, police sirens, and the occasional gunshot, Douglas Pick needed some sleep. Many nights, while a student at USC's Lloyd Greif Center for Entrepreneurial Studies, earplugs delivered the silence he craved.

After leaving a job at A&M Records in 1992, Pick put the lessons from his USC days to work to research earplugs. His nights on the L.A. university campus had made him a strong believer in the benefits of the tiny foam noise blockers. He saw opportunity in the sector and, later that year, launched DAP World from his apartment in Studio City, California.

Early on, Pick woke at about 4 a.m. to work on marketing, sales, and operations. On afternoons, with the help of family and friends, he assembled products on his dining room table. Within five years, Pick's Hearos earplugs were distributed nationwide, and he needed to expand his operations. His home-based manufacturing system was no longer sufficient to meet demand, he says.

Pick was reluctant to take on the overhead necessary to house and run his own manufacturing facility and "all of the baby-sitting aspects of having employees," he says. But in October 1997, one of his suppliers suggested he meet with New Horizons, a North Hills, CA-based nonprofit organization that assists and employs developmentally disabled adults. New Horizons' facility was equipped to take on DAP World's manufacturing process and could also handle fulfillment and shipping.

"I had looked at other options, but I didn't like to take the business outside of U.S. borders. They were incredibly cost-competitive because the State of California, along with private contributions, helps subsidize them," Pick says.

Today DAP World, now based in Aliso Viejo, CA, sells more than 36 million pairs of its Hearos and Pretty in Pink earplugs each year to retailers like Walgreens, Walmart, Rite Aid, and CVS, generating roughly $5 million in annual gross revenue. Those numbers support jobs for more than 200 people at New Horizons. Pick calls the operations there "essentially flawless," with 99.8 percent of all shipments arriving on time at key retailers. The 0.2 percent that go astray? Carriers are usually to blame, not New Horizons, Pick says.

Pick also lauds the commitment of the people working for him through New Horizons. In 2010, he created a fund called Hearos Help to support New Horizons programs and to provide perks to all employees. Last year, part of his $10,000 donation was used to fund a picnic to thank employees for their dedication.

As DAP World expands its product lines, Pick says New Horizons will continue to be the manufacturing and logistics partner of choice.

"They are my trusted partner," he says, "so I can focus on the growth opportunities of the business."

Source: Gwen Moran, "How an Earplug Company Supports Jobs for 200 People with Disabilities," 22 March 2011, Entrepreneur Magazine. Copyright © 2012 Entrepreneur Media, Inc. 1212:SH

In highly litigious states, you may need substantially higher liability coverage to protect your business. As your business grows, ensure you have adequate coverage to meet the laws and potential problems in the various states and countries your firm is operating within.

Vehicle use is a major source of liability claims. Under the "doctrine of agency," a business may be liable for injuries and property damage caused by employees operating their own or someone else's vehicle while on company business. The company may have some protection under the employee's liability policy, but the limits are probably inadequate. If it is customary or convenient for employees to use their own vehicles while on company business (e.g., salespeople on the road or covering a route), purchase non-ownership liability insurance.

The best form of general liability insurance for a small business consists of a comprehensive general liability policy, combined with a comprehensive auto liability policy and a standard workers' compensation policy.

Finding an insurance broker who is familiar with your line of business is very important; such experience and knowledge may help to insure you are covered properly. Review various scenarios with your broker.

Types of Coverage

Insurance can be purchased to cover almost any risk. However, most business owners commonly protect themselves with the types of property and liability coverage listed below. Additional insurance needs are listed in Figure 12.1. Some entrepreneurs, such as diamond jewelry designers who often transport over $1 million in diamonds to show their clients, may require specialized types of insurance which will not be available through standard insurance brokers.

Standard Coverage

1. **Fire and general property insurance:** protects against fire loss, vandalism, hail, and wind damage.
2. **Consequential loss insurance:** covers loss of earnings or extra expenses when business is interrupted because of fire or other catastrophe (see item 4).
3. **Public liability insurance:** covers injury to the public, such as customer or pedestrian injury claims.
4. **Business-interruption insurance:** coverage in case the business is unable to continue as before.
5. **Crime insurance:** protects against losses resulting from burglary, robbery, and so forth. Fidelity bonds provide coverage from employee theft.
6. **Malpractice insurance:** covers against claims from clients who suffer damages as a result of services that you perform.
7. **Errors and omissions insurance:** covers against claims from customers who suffer injury or loss because of errors you made, things you should have done but failed to do, or warnings you failed to supply.
8. **Employment practices liability insurance (EPLI):** covers against claims from employees for employment practices related to sexual harassment, wrongful discharge, discrimination, breach of contract, libel, and so on.
9. **Key-person insurance:** covers the death, dismemberment, or physical disability of owners or key employees. Discuss tax treatment of premiums paid and that of the potential proceeds (in case of death) with your tax specialist.
10. **Product liability insurance:** covers injury to the public resulting from customer use or misuse of a product.
11. **Disability insurance:** covers owners and employees against disability and usually allows for payments to continue during rehabilitation. Disability for an owner is a *far* greater risk than death, but few owners insure themselves adequately against such risk. Do not make this mistake.
12. **Health insurance for employees:** check with state and federal laws to determine the coverage required. Laws and regulations in this area are changing rapidly and we suggest you hire professionals or outside firms who will make sure you are compliant.
13. **Workers' compensation insurance:** protects employees if they are injured on the job (see Chapter 11 for further information).

figure **12.1**

Insurance Information Institute Checklist

LIABILITY

- [ ] Comprehensive General
  - [ ] Premises/Operations
  - [ ] Products/Completed Operations
  - [ ] Owners & Contractors Protective
  - [ ] Contractual – Blanket
  - [ ] Contractual – Schedule
  - [ ] Personal Injury
  - [ ] Advertising Injury
  - [ ] Medical Payments
  - [ ] Broad Form Property Damage
  - [ ] Watercraft
  - [ ] Liquor Liability
  - [ ] Incidental Medical Malpractice
  - [ ] Fire Legal Liability
  - [ ] Employees as Insured
  - [ ] Extended Bodily Injury
  - [ ] New Organizations Insured
  - [ ] Pollution and Clean-Up
  - [ ] Limited Worldwide Products
- [ ] Workers Compensation
- [ ] Aircraft
- [ ] Owned Automobiles
- [ ] Leases or Hired Automobiles
- [ ] Drive Other Car
- [ ] Auto Medical
- [ ] Bailee Liability
- [ ] Directors & Officers' Liability
- [ ] Employment Practices Liability
- [ ] Professional Liability
- [ ] Railroad Protective Liability
- [ ] Signs
  - [ ] Pavements/Underground Property
- [ ] Glass
- [ ] Contamination/Pollution Clean-up and Removal
- [ ] Debris Removal
- [ ] Functional Replacement Cost
- [ ] Vacancy Permit
- [ ] Satellite Dishes

BUILDINGS

- [ ] Basic Causes of Loss
- [ ] Broad Causes of Loss
- [ ] Special Causes of Loss
- [ ] Coinsurance
- [ ] Earthquake
- [ ] Flood
- [ ] All Risk D`IC (Difference in Conditions or Gap Filter Coverage)
- [ ] Replacement Cost
- [ ] Inflation Guard
- [ ] Agreed Value
- [ ] Building Ordinance
- [ ] Outdoor Property
- [ ] Signs/Glass
- [ ] Pavements/Underground Property
- [ ] Contamination/Pollution Clean-Up and Removal
- [ ] Debris Removal
- [ ] Functional Replacement Cost
- [ ] Vacancy Permit
- [ ] Satellite Dishes

BUSINESS INCOME

- [ ] Business Income
  - [ ] Loss of Earnings
  - [ ] Continuing Expenses
- [ ] Extra Expenses
- [ ] Dependent Properties
- [ ] Extended Property of Indemnity
- [ ] Payroll Limitation/Exclusion
- [ ] Tuition and Fees
- [ ] Building Ordinances

BOILER AND MACHINERY

- [ ] Boiler Machinery
- [ ] Business Income
- [ ] Outage

BUSINESS PERSONAL PROPERTY

- [ ] Basic Causes of Loss
- [ ] Broad Causes of Loss
- [ ] Special Causes of Loss
- [ ] Earthquake
- [ ] Flood
- [ ] Value Reporting Form
- [ ] Replacement Cost
- [ ] Peak Seasonal Form
- [ ] Improvements and Betterments
- [ ] Manufacturer's Selling Price
- [ ] Valuable Papers/Records
- [ ] Accounts Receivable
- [ ] Crops
- [ ] Animals
- [ ] Auto Physical Damage
- [ ] Aircraft Physical Damage
- [ ] Marine Hull Damage
- [ ] Transported Property
- [ ] Equipment Floater
- [ ] Salesperson's Floater
- [ ] Installation Floater
- [ ] Processing Floater
- [ ] Parcel Post
- [ ] Computers
- [ ] Other High Value Property
- [ ] Coinsurance

MANAGEMENT PROTECTION

- [ ] Life
  - [ ] Key Person
  - [ ] Proprietor
  - [ ] Partnership
  - [ ] Corporation
- [ ] Business Continuation
- [ ] Retirement Continuation
- [ ] Retirement Benefits
- [ ] Personal Auto Liability
- [ ] Offers' and Directors' E&O
- [ ] Split Dollar
- [ ] Deferred Compensation
- [ ] Disability Buyouts
- [ ] Overhead Insurance

HUMAN FAILURE

- [ ] Employee Dishonesty
  - [ ] Blanket
  - [ ] Schedule
- [ ] Money and Securities
- [ ] Other Property
- [ ] Forgery and Alteration
- [ ] Computer Fraud
- [ ] Extortion
- [ ] Innkeepers
- [ ] Lessees of Safe Deposit Boxes
  - [ ] Safe Depository
- [ ] Securities Deposited with Others
- [ ] Public Employees Fund
- [ ] Financial Institutions Bond

EMPLOYEE PROTECTION

- [ ] Group Life
- [ ] Group Disability
- [ ] Major Medical
- [ ] Accidental Death and Dismemberment
- [ ] Hospitalization—Surgical
- [ ] Pension
- [ ] Profit Sharing
- [ ] Keogh
- [ ] ESOP
- [ ] Dental
- [ ] Vision Care
- [ ] Legal Expenses
- [ ] SEPPs (Substantially Equal Periodic Payments)

Source: Insurance Information Institute, *www.iii.org*. Reprinted with permission.

14. **Extra equipment insurance:** covers specialized equipment not covered in standard policies.
15. **Directors' and officers' liability insurance:** if company stock is held by outside investors, directors and officers, they should be protected from liability claims.
16. **Cyber crime insurance;** protects company against data loss and liability
17. **Other:** see checklist (Figure 12.1).

According to the Insurance Information Institute, *http://www.iii.org*, about 40 percent of small-business owners carry no insurance at all because of cash concerns. If you cannot afford minimal insurance coverage, rethink your Business Plan and delay starting your business until you *can* afford adequate coverage. One mishap or incident can destroy everything you have worked for; and for most entrepreneurs, personal fortunes are on the line as well as their businesses. Do not let this happen to you.

Obtaining reasonably priced health insurance is a challenge for small businesses, and associations may be able to assist with this crucial element of insurance planning. As of the writing of this text, the health insurance industry and laws are in flux so we highly suggest you keep abreast of the changes and act accordingly.

Home-based and e-commerce businesses should not overlook the need for insurance and should meet with an insurance broker. Depending on the type and size of business, you may be able to add an endorsement onto your current homeowner's policy or may purchase an In-Home Business Policy.

With the Insurance Checklist for Business Owners (Figure 12.1) in hand and with the knowledge you have gained from your insurance research and this chapter, it is time to sit down with your insurance broker or association representative to determine your specific insurance needs and costs while completing Action Step 50. If your needs are standard and your sales are less than $3 million, you may be able to purchase an off-the-shelf Business Owner's Policy (BOP), which will save you money. BOP packaged policies offer basic liability and property coverage, to generally "low risk" businesses where serious accidents or disaster are unlikely. As your business grows, additional insurance may be required.

■ EMPLOYEE CRIME: BE PREPARED—TAKE PREVENTATIVE STEPS

According to the U.S. Chamber of Commerce, 30 percent of small-business failures can be attributed to employee theft—a sobering statistic, no doubt, for any entrepreneur. Prepare and take preventative steps not to be in this 30 percent. Seeing your hard work and money go down a rat hole because of employee theft is enough to crush even the hardiest entrepreneur.

You must be prepared to prevent both internal crime and external crime. Your trade organization may be helpful in providing you with loss-prevention information pertinent to your industry. In addition, large insurers offer specialists to work with industry-specific issues such as the following:

- Credit card fraud (See Figure 12.2)
- Check deception
- Shoplifting
- Cyber crime (See Figures 12.3 and 12.4)
- Cash mishandling
- Bookkeeping theft
- Fraudulent refunds
- Counterfeit money
- Fitting room theft
- Burglary
- Robbery
- Bomb threats
- Theft of items from stockroom, layaway, and displays
- Computer fraud
- Sabotage
- Theft of private information
- Manipulation of time card data
- Illegal use of company time
- Fraudulent expense reports

ACTION STEP 50

Protect Your Venture

1. Network your way to a business insurance broker and/or your trade association.
2. Read information online from your association and from various insurance websites that focus on your industry. Make a list of questions.
3. Review your insurance needs with your broker.
4. Discover the cost of insuring your business for the first year. Also, discuss how your insurance needs and costs may change as your firm grows.

figure 12.2

Credit Card Fraud: 5 Steps to Protect Your Business

From the National Federation of Independent Business (NFIB) Legal Center

To defend your business against credit card fraud, consider the following:

1. Get all the information related to the credit card.
Have the caller read the cardholder's name—exactly how it appears on the card—along with all 16 account digits, the card verification number, and the card's expiration date, as well as the complete address and phone number associated with the account holder. Do not immediately ship goods to customers who are unable to or refuse to provide a full name or offer a possibly bogus name or address, such as Joe Smith or 123 Main Street. Make sure you get the card verification number in this case because three- or four-digit codes do not appear on credit card receipts. Since many fraudulent transactions result from a stolen number rather than a stolen card, a customer who is able to supply this number is less likely to be in possession of a stolen card.

With this information, you will be able to use the address verification service. This service works by comparing the billing address supplied by the customer with the bank's database. You can also call the card-issuing bank and ask them to make a courtesy call to the customer to verify the charge. Visa claims that the use of the card verification method can reduce chargebacks by as much as 26 percent.

2. Be wary of orders that use different "bill to" and "ship to" addresses.
This can be a sign of fraudulent credit card use. Request telephone numbers for both addresses if the customer wishes to ship the order to a different "ship to" location. With the information you collected, you can use a website like *www.anywho.com*, which integrates telephone numbers, maps, and e-mail addresses to check for bogus billing addresses.

3. Watch out for unusually large next-day delivery orders.
Orders larger than the typical size of orders at your business should raise a red flag, as should orders requesting next-day delivery. Fraudulent users need to have their orders approved and delivered before the fraud is discovered, and the order is canceled. And fraudulent users are not concerned with cost, since they do not plan to pay. Also, watch out for to international orders. While of course not all overseas orders are fraudulent, some countries, especially developing nations, have a bad reputation for fraud. Experts advise against shipping international orders that have different "bill to" and "ship to" addresses.

4. Do everything possible to validate the order before it is shipped.
When orders are not placed in person, it may be beneficial to have the customer fax copies of both sides of the credit card. It may also be helpful to request a copy of his or her state-issued identification card, which provides additional proof that the customer is the true credit card holder. If the customer does not know all the information you are asking for or have it in his or her possession, he or she may give up.

5. Take immediate steps to reduce damage if fraud is discovered.
First, call the police to report the crime, then call the cardholder's issuing bank and ask someone to place a courtesy call to the cardholder. Have the person at the bank mention that you have the address where the charged product is being shipped. When the cardholder returns your call, convince him or her to report the crime to the police in the city where the product was shipped. You may be able to recover the stolen merchandise.

Most importantly, trust your instincts. If the caller does not seem completely confident about the information he or she is supplying, or you do not feel comfortable sending merchandise, don't do it. It may be better to lose an order than to risk giving away your merchandise for free.

Source: NFIB, "Credit Card Fraud: 5 Steps to Protect Your Business." From *http://www.nfib.com/business-resources/business-resources-item?cmsid=29075*, (accessed March 20, 2012). Reprinted with permission.

Sweethearting Unauthorized discount to customers

- Sweethearting (discounts for family and friends)
- Theft of trade secrets
- Theft of intellectual property

We seldom meet an entrepreneur who has not experienced one or more of these problems. Take action promptly when any of these take place in your firm and make it known that none of these actions will be tolerated. Do not look the other way or believe crime cannot occur in your organization. Keep your eyes and ears wide open. Explain to your employees the financial consequences of shoplifting and employee theft. One retail storeowner recently wrote the following letter to her employees regarding merchandise theft:

"Theft in our store is a serious problem. For each $2 candy bar we sell, we pay 10 percent of our gross sales (20 cents) to our landlord. The cost of the candy bar is 86 cents, and we have a 10 percent (20 cents) additional overhead on gross sales. Thus our costs are $1.26. This means that we need to sell three $2 candy bars (with a net profit at 74 cents each) to cover the loss of just one candy bar. Please keep your eyes on our customers. In addition, please understand that the employee policies regarding free food and sweethearting are there to protect our business and your job."

As that owner has discovered, theft cannot and should not be tolerated. It must be guarded against constantly and dealt with immediately. Talk with others who run similar businesses to find out ways employees have stolen from them and what tactics they used to reduce theft within their own firms.

If in retailing, watch your employees carefully; if an employee rapidly switches to another display screen or appears to hide the screen as you come by, this may serve as a warning to you. Also, look for employees who claim computer issues are causing them to lose track of transactions.

Watch for cashiers who seem to have excessively long lines or lingering customers. Also, keep an eye on customers who always insist on a certain cashier or wait around until their chosen cashier is available. If employees are responsible for closing at night alone, make sure a closing routine is written down and followed by each employee. Be vigilant; your survival and success depend on it.

One restaurant manager always insisted on closing out the register every night, never took a vacation, and never missed closing. Everyone was thrilled, including the owners, to have such a conscientious employee; that is, until they realized he did these things because he was stealing. In fact, the owner of the restaurant shared, "We think he stole more than $110,000 in two years. We trusted him like he was our own son and thought he loved the restaurant as much as my wife and I. But we found out what he really loved was the cash drawer!"

Pre-employment testing, background checks, drug testing, mystery shoppers, awareness training, and employee hotline programs can reduce, but not eliminate, retail theft. Surveillance technology and well-designed point-of-sale software will limit theft and may discover the culprits. Shifting managers around to different stores and to different shifts may also serve as a deterrent.

Establish your firm's code of conduct and have new employees sign and review. According to O'Brien and Associates, loss prevention consultants based in Ontario, Canada, "The code of conduct should clearly state that the taking of merchandise or cash without payment or management authorization—or helping others to do so—are violations that may result in disciplinary action up to and including termination of employment and possibly criminal charges."

■ CYBER CONCERNS

Be vigilant in your protection of employee, customer, and company data. To ensure that all data within your firm is kept private and secure, hire professionals to help protect your business by installing and maintaining appropriate software and to provide training to your employees. Costs to secure data are minimal compared to the losses that occur if customer data is comprised, money transferred illegally, trade secrets emailed, or information on individual drug testing of job applicants is posted on Facebook.

Cyber crooks aim for unsuspecting and unprotected small businesses, and they change their tactics frequently. Thus, your firm requires an expert not only to set up a secure system, but also to constantly review and make changes to thwart the crooks that come from within your company and those who hack into your system from the outside.

Review 5 Reasons Cyber Security Matters to Small Business (Figure 12.3), 10 Cyber Security Tips for Small Businesses (Figure 12.4), and explore the online FCC Small Biz Cyber Planner. In addition, credit card fraud (see Figure 12.2) via cyberspace also poses a serious threat to your organization.

figure **12.3**

5 Reasons Cyber Security Matters to Small Businesses

By Heather Clancy | December 28, 2011

Smaller businesses often think they are "too small" to be worth hackers' notice, but that assumption could be devastating. Security is absolutely positively the most important infrastructure that small companies need to make. Here are five reasons why:

1. Smaller companies are more likely to be attacked than bigger ones. Don't believe me? Symantec.com, which keeps statistics on this sort of thing, suggests that 40 percent of attacks are against organizations with fewer than 500 employees, versus 28 percent against bigger companies. Remember, there are lots of people who could make trouble this way. Not just big groups with something to provide, like cyber hacktivist Anonymous, but disgruntled former employees or business partners.

2. Breaches are potentially business-ending events. Depending on the statistics you believe, the average cost of a breach or cyber security incident is about $190,000. Do you have that sort of money to lose? Even more serious: about half of small businesses still don't back up their data, so what is lost is lost forever. Which means your business might be lost forever. The Federal Communications Commission has published a useful cyber security guide you might want to consult.

3. Can you be sure you are properly controlling the access of your employees and business partners? This will only be a bigger factor, as personal tablets and smartphones become more commonly used as business tools. Improperly managed client-side software is one of the biggest known cyber security threats, allowing people to see information that they really shouldn't be able to see AND allowing rogue malware to enter your infrastructure. I am dealing with a problem like this right now. Even though certain files I post to my non-profit's website are "gated," for some reason, they can be accessed publicly if the right link shows up in a Google search.

4. Attacks could ruin your company's reputation. I know that they say all publicity is good publicity, but think about how embarrassed Stratfor must be this week. After all, this is a security consulting company. According to the reports about the incident, the reason that the hackers were able to steal so much data—up to 200 gigabytes—and make use of it was because certain information was not encrypted. Stratfor should have known better, and so should your company.

5. Your company could be putting its best customers at risk. In assessing the security risks for their business, some owners and managers fail to consider that it isn't just your own data you need to worry about; it is that of your customers. Anyone involved in health care already has this mantra beaten into their brain, but any company that engages in business-to-business activity with much larger businesses needs to consider their needs as the driver for their own security plans.

Source: Heather Clancy, "5 Reasons Cyber Ssecurity Matters to Small Businesses," December 28, 2011. Used with permission of ZDNET Copyright © 2012. All rights reserved.

Never stop reading about security issues affecting your industry. Build a "culture of security" amongst your employees spreading that sense of security to your customers as well. "Business owners are legally required to protect customer and employee personal information and can face significant state and/or federal fines if they're found to be noncompliant and privacy is compromised," according to Oliver Brew, the vice president of technology media and telecommunications underwriting for Hiscox, a specialty insurer offering privacy protection policies.

With YouTube, Facebook Twitter, and the plethora of other sites, firms today face another major risk-that of "reputational risk" according to Jonathan Copulsky, author of *Resilience: Managing Risk and Recovery in a High-Speed World*. Protecting your reputation isn't new, but it is just so much harder to rein in and track all the digital risks. Attacks can come from customers, competitors, employees and suppliers and can affect any entrepreneurial venture. Recognize that what others are saying about you on YouTube, Twitter, and Facebook oftentimes become more important than what you are saying about yourself.

Protect your business and your reputation or you will not have a business! Hire carefully, as data theft and other actions by dishonest or disgruntled employees pose a huge threat today. One disgruntled employee with a cell phone camera and a YouTube video or Instagram photo can destroy you.

Phishers, smishers, employees, and competitors want your data and will do anything to access it. Staying ahead of thieves and changing technology is tough, but necessary. To reduce your financial exposure to the risks involved you may want to consider purchasing cyber-crime liability insurance.

─── figure **12.4**

10 Cyber Security Tips for Small Businesses

Broadband and information technology are powerful tools for small businesses to reach new markets and increase sales and productivity. However, cybersecurity threats are real and businesses must implement the best tools and tactics to protect themselves, their customers, and their data. Visit **www.fcc.gov/cyberplanner** to create a free customized Cyber Security Planning guide for your small business and visit **www.dhs.gov/stopthinkconnect** to download resources on cyber security awareness for your business. Here are ten key cybersecurity tips to protect your small business:

1. Train employees in security principles. Establish basic security practices and policies for employees, such as requiring strong passwords and establish appropriate Internet use guidelines, that detail penalties for violating company cybersecurity policies. Establish rules of behavior describing how to handle and protect customer information and other vital data.

2. Protect information, computers, and networks from cyber attacks. Keep clean machines: having the latest security software, web browser, and operating system are the best defenses against viruses, malware, and other online threats. Set antivirus software to run a scan after each update. Install other key software updates as soon as they are available.

3. Provide firewall security for your Internet connection. A firewall is a set of related programs that prevent outsiders from accessing data on a private network. Make sure the operating system's firewall is enabled or install free firewall software available online. If employees work from home, ensure that their home system(s) are protected by a firewall.

4. Create a mobile device action plan. Mobile devices can create significant security and management challenges, especially if they hold confidential information or can access the corporate network. Require users to password protect their devices, encrypt their data, and install security apps to prevent criminals from stealing information while the phone is on public networks. Be sure to set reporting procedures for lost or stolen equipment.

5. Make backup copies of important business data and information. Regularly backup the data on all computers. Critical data includes word processing documents, electronic spreadsheets, databases, financial files, human resources files, and accounts receivable/payable files. Backup data automatically if possible, or at least weekly and store the copies either offsite or in the cloud.

6. Control physical access to your computers and create user accounts for each employee. Prevent access or use of business computers by unauthorized individuals. Laptops can be particularly easy targets for theft or can be lost, so lock them up when unattended. Make sure a separate user account is created for each employee and require strong passwords. Administrative privileges should only be given to trusted IT staff and key personnel.

7. Secure your Wi-Fi networks. If you have a Wi-Fi network for your workplace, make sure it is secure, encrypted, and hidden. To hide your Wi-Fi network, set up your wireless access point or router so it does not broadcast the network name, known as the Service Set Identifier (SSID). Password protect access to the router.

8. Employ best practices on payment cards. Work with banks or processors to ensure the most trusted and validated tools and anti-fraud services are being used. You may also have additional security obligations pursuant to agreements with your bank or processor. Isolate payment systems from other, less secure programs and don't use the same computer to process payments and surf the Internet.

9. Limit employee access to data and information, and limit authority to install software. Do not provide any one employee with access to all data systems. Employees should only be given access to the specific data systems that they need for their jobs, and should not be able to install any software without permission.

10. Passwords and authentication. Require employees to use unique passwords and change passwords every three months. Consider implementing multifactor authentication that requires additional information beyond a password to gain entry. Check with your vendors that handle sensitive data, especially financial institutions, to see if they offer multifactor authentication for your account.

The FCC's Cybersecurity Hub at http://www.fcc.gov/cyberforsmallbiz has more information, including links to free and low-cost security tools. Create your free small business cyber security planning guide at www.fcc.gov/cyberplanner.

To learn more about the Stop.Think.Connect. Campaign, visit www.dhs.gov/stopthinkconnect.

Source: "Ten Cybersecurity Tips for Small Businesses" from *http://transition.fcc.gov/Daily_Releases/Daily_Business/2012/db1018/DOC-306595A1.pdf*, (Accessed date 11/20/2012).

■ THE TAX MAN COMETH

What are the laws when it comes to taxes? What forms do I have to fill out? If I am audited, how can I protect myself? These are just a few of the questions answered in IRS Publications 334 and 583, "Tax Guide for Small Business" and "Starting a Business and Keeping Records." Table 12.1 lists the most common tax forms businesses are required by law to file. Schedule C (Profit or Loss from Business) and Schedule C-EZ (Net Profit from Business) for sole proprietors are provided in Appendix C.

For those conducting commerce throughout the world, use the excellent *International Tax and Business Guides* for over 65 jurisdictions produced by Deloitte, one of the leading international accounting firms. In addition, access Deloitte's International Tax Source (DITS) website for their global insights and perspective.

In the United States, you will at least be responsible for corporate or personal income taxes, employment taxes, sales taxes, and property taxes. If you have employees, you need to file an Application for Employer Identification Number, Form SS-4 (found in Appendix C).

Some taxes apply only to the employer, some are levied on employees, and some apply to both employer and employees. Federal employment taxes include federal income tax withholding, Social Security and Medicare taxes, and Federal Unemployment (FUTA) Tax. Many employees do not realize the significant financial impact taxes play in operating a business. Thus some firms, such as IRMCO (see Key Points from Another View in Chapter 8), allow employees access to financial information through an open-book management system.

In addition to federal taxes, you will also be responsible for state, county, and local taxes. State and federal rules do not always mesh, so be sure you understand both systems. An *experienced* CPA who specializes in your selected industry will be able to keep you on track of acceptable IRS practice. The IRS offers additional help for business owners on their website, providing specialized tax information by industry through their Audit Technique Guides.

The best thing you can do for your business is to keep excellent records of *all* transactions. A retailer was recently audited, and the audit took one day instead of the usual three—the result of excellent record keeping and no problems! The IRS and your accountant will tell you exactly what is required and expected.

While tax preparation is essential, your CPA can be of greatest assistance to you in *tax planning*. As tax laws are constantly in flux, your accountant's advice should include guidance on when best to defer or when best to accelerate income and deductions to take advantage of tax timing. Your account also stays abreast of future tax changes and can advise accordingly.

In addition, owning a business offers many entrepreneurs the opportunity to shield income with excellent retirement planning options; if undertaken legally and properly, these can be of great financial advantage both in the short term and in the long term. With your accountant's expertise, you may be able to build a substantial retirement program and prepare for your exit strategy in the most profitable manner.

Taxes are not your expertise (and nor should they be), so hire those whose expertise it is and follow their advice. Keep your accountant abreast of any major business changes or future plans and *make sure your accountant is an active partner on your financial planning team*.

Income Taxes

If you owe less than $1,000 in federal tax for the year, or if you paid no income taxes last year, you *may* not need to pay estimated taxes. But the majority of

—table **12.1**

Which IRS Forms Must I File?

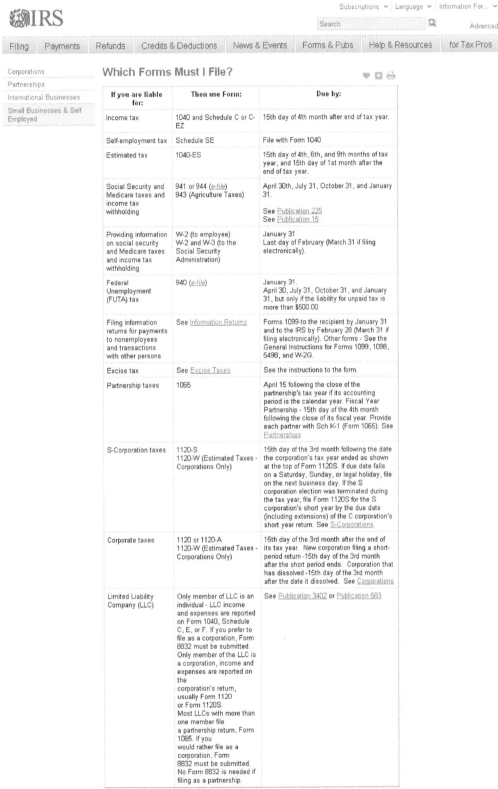

IRS

Search 🔍 Advanced

| Filing | Payments | Refunds | Credits & Deductions | News & Events | Forms & Pubs | Help & Resources | for Tax Pros |

Corporations
Partnerships
International Businesses
Small Businesses & Self Employed

Which Forms Must I File?

♥ ⊞ 🖶

If you are liable for:	Then use Form:	Due by:
Income tax	1040 and Schedule C or C-EZ	15th day of 4th month after end of tax year.
Self-employment tax	Schedule SE	File with Form 1040
Estimated tax	1040-ES	15th day of 4th, 6th, and 9th months of tax year, and 15th day of 1st month after the end of tax year.
Social Security and Medicare taxes and income tax withholding	941 or 944 (*e-file*) 943 (Agriculture Taxes)	April 30th, July 31, October 31, and January 31. See Publication 225 See Publication 15
Providing information on social security and Medicare taxes and income tax withholding	W-2 (to employee) W-2 and W-3 (to the Social Security Administration)	January 31 Last day of February (March 31 if filing electronically).
Federal Unemployment (FUTA) tax	940 (*e-file*)	January 31. April 30, July 31, October 31, and January 31, but only if the liability for unpaid tax is more than $500.00
Filing information returns for payments to nonemployees and transactions with other persons	See Information Returns	Forms 1099-to the recipient by January 31 and to the IRS by February 28 (March 31 if filing electronically). Other forms - See the General Instructions for Forms 1099, 1098, 5498, and W-2G.
Excise tax	See Excise Taxes	See the instructions to the form.
Partnership taxes	1065	April 15 following the close of the partnership's tax year if its accounting period is the calendar year. Fiscal Year Partnership - 15th day of the 4th month following the close of its fiscal year. Provide each partner with Sch K-1 (Form 1065). See Partnerships
S-Corporation taxes	1120-S 1120-W (Estimated Taxes - Corporations Only)	15th day of the 3rd month following the date the corporation's tax year ended as shown at the top of Form 1120S. If due date falls on a Saturday, Sunday, or legal holiday, file on the next business day. If the S corporation election was terminated during the tax year, file Form 1120S for the S corporation's short year by the due date (including extensions) of the C corporation's short year return. See S-Corporations
Corporate taxes	1120 or 1120-A 1120-W (Estimated Taxes - Corporations Only)	15th day of the 3rd month after the end of its tax year. New corporation filing a short-period return -15th day of the 3rd month after the short period ends. Corporation that has dissolved -15th day of the 3rd month after the date it dissolved. See Corporations
Limited Liability Company (LLC)	Only member of LLC is an individual - LLC income and expenses are reported on Form 1040, Schedule C, E, or F. If you prefer to file as a corporation, Form 8832 must be submitted. Only member of the LLC is a corporation, income and expenses are reported on the corporation's return, usually Form 1120 or Form 1120S. Most LLCs with more than one member file a partnership return, Form 1065. If you would rather file as a corporation, Form 8832 must be submitted. No Form 8832 is needed if filing as a partnership.	See Publication 3402 or Publication 583

References/Related Topics:

- Filing and Paying Your Business Taxes

Page Last Reviewed or Updated: 2012-08-02

Source: IRS/USA.gov.

small business owners will be required to pay estimated income and self-employment taxes on April 15, June 15, September 15, and January 15 of the following year. In most states, you will also be required to send estimated payments to the state. See the IRS website and your state's website for help calculating your tax payments. If calculations are not done properly, and you pay too little, you will be responsible for penalties.

Excellent additional tax information can be found online at TurboTax, H&R Block, and TOOLKIT websites amongst others. In addition, please visit the IRS Video Portal for Small Business (Entrepreneurial Resource) site, which will walk you through many of the tax issues discussed in this chapter.

Self-Employment Taxes

A tough tax for many sole proprietors to absorb is the self-employment tax. As of 2012, the self-employment tax rate on net income was 15.3 percent. This includes 12.4 percent for Social Security (old-age, survivors, and disability insurance) and 2.9 percent for Medicare (hospital insurance). The 2012 rate of 15.3 percent applies to the first $110,100 of net income and the 2.9 percent applies to all income earned above that amount. To calculate your tax, use Schedule SE in Appendix C or the most updated Schedule SE online at *http://www.irs.gov*. For some relief, one-half of the self-employment tax is deductible from your gross income.

Employment Taxes

Keeping up with employee taxes and laws is a headache for most employers. As recommended in Chapter 11, use a payroll service and an excellent accountant. Some employers pay their employees cash in an illegal attempt to save on taxes and worker's compensation. If an employee is injured, the deception will be discovered. Fines are heavy. In addition, if an angry and disgruntled employee calls the IRS to report you, the IRS *will call* and come after you! Another possibility is that a competitor might report you to the IRS for suspected tax evasion. Tax laws and regulations are a burden, but they are *not* to be avoided or taken lightly at any time.

If you have employees, be sure to order Form 940-Employer's Annual Federal Unemployment Tax Return and Publication 15, Circular E-the Employer's Tax Guide. As an employer, you must remit half of your employees' Social Security and Medicare taxes, unemployment taxes (which are only the responsibility of the employer), and possible state disability taxes.

Sales Taxes

For sales tax and resale numbers, contact your State Board of Equalization. Some states tax both products and services, others tax certain products only. Each state's list of products that are exempt varies, and also when and how you submit your taxes vary as well. Check with state offices where your business operates to determine requirements. Laws regarding internet sales tax are in flux and your tax accountant and attorney should keep you informed and in compliance.

Many owners attempt to avoid reporting cash sales transactions to avoid taxes. This is not a wise idea; the IRS has many ways to determine your true sales figures. For example, they might look at the number of disposable cups you purchased and thereby determine how much coffee you sold; or they may review your water and electric bills to estimate how many loads your laundromat washed and dried. Do not forget to remit the proper collected sales tax as audits are not fun!

If you are starting up, try to make realistic quarterly sales tax estimates. If projections are too high, you will be required to post a higher bond to get a

Bond Guarantee of payment

Entrepreneur's Resource

IRS Video Small Business Portal for Taxpayer Information

Source: IRS.gov.

resale number and permit. Use the numbers you found in your research for Chapters 8 and 9 for your estimates.

Final Tax Thoughts

Fines for violations of tax laws are considerable. Once you have been audited, your chances of being audited again increase. Although, realize most everyone is audited at some time or another. So be prepared with excellent record keeping, a payroll service firm to support you, and a good accountant to represent you. In addition, excellent records from the start will provide a paper trail for potential lenders, partners, suppliers, and potential buyers or investors of your business. Complete Part 1 and 2 of Action Step 51 after reviewing tax information from this chapter, IRS publications and videos, and past chapters.

■ EXIT STRATEGY

How do you plan to exit your business and receive the return on your personal and financial investment? Some entrepreneurs pursue a small business to create long-term capital appreciation. Others dream of leaving a successful, viable business to their children or employees (either slowly or at once). Some entrepreneurs hope to work 30 hours a week, pull as much cash out of the business as possible, and close it down in 10 years to retire. Working even less is the dream of those reading Timothy Ferris' book, *The 4-Hour Work Week Blueprints*.

Building a business and positioning it to be acquired by another firm is another alternative, which many serial and software/internet entrepreneurs pursue. Franchising your business may also be a goal. Lastly, many dream of an IPO. A dream, which in 2010 came to fruition for only 157 entrepreneurial firms!

In reality, your exit options may also change over the years due to the economy, technology, employees, and possibly even legal changes which affect the viability of your business. In addition, personal issues may come into play such as divorce, new marriage, children, illness, death of a partner, any of which may change your path. Or you may decide to pursue another dream earlier than expected. Thus your exit plans need to be somewhat flexible.

To insure that the transfer of your business is as profitable as possible, you will need to work with your lawyers and accountants. The legal form of your business may have a significant impact on tax consequences in the immediate term, as well as for the potential sale or transfer.

If your exit strategy changes at any time, you need to contact your legal and tax-planning team to review your options. Do not assume you know what steps are necessary for a smooth transition, as they are in constant flux. Your team is paid to keep abreast of those changes. Focus on the business cycle, your firm's management needs, and the market you are serving.

One alternative exit strategy, an **Employee Stock Ownership Plan** (ESOP), is available for owners who would like to share their business with their employees. An ESOP makes the employees of a company now owners of the company through stock ownership. ESOP's provide tax advantages to employees and the business owner. In addition, an ESOP may provide an excellent corporate finance and retirement strategy. If you follow this option, locate an experienced ESOP specialist through the ESOP Association for further information.

If you are seeking investment capital, your investors need to know your personal financial goals and anticipated time frames. Venture capitalists and angel investors are looking at investing for usually three to five years.

One entrepreneur, when faced with developing his exit strategy, recognized after assessing his personal time, investment capital, and length of time to capture an acceptable return, decided that not getting in was preferable to getting out later! Forcing yourself to look down the line may open your eyes to the reality of owning your own business. For entrepreneurs who are involved in fast-paced business, which require limited resources to begin and where energy, effort, and an idea lead to quick success or failure, a formal exit strategy may be less important.

As you progress through the chapters, take note of Chapter 13 on Buying a Business. From the start of your business, keep in mind how others will evaluate yours when it is for sale. Hopefully, this will spur you to build an ethical and strong business which others will want to purchase, enabling your exit to be profitable!

In answering the exit strategy questions, you are brought back to your original goals for opening a business. Always work to maintain control of your entrepreneurial dreams along with your financial and personal goals. After reviewing your early Action Steps, complete Parts 3 and 4 of Action Step 51.

IPO Initial public offering first-time sale of stock

ESOP formal plan where employees become owners

ACTION STEP 51

Tax and Exit Strategy Planning

1. Review the tax material provided in this and past chapters. Make a list of all tax forms you will need and print them out. Read through the IRS's *Small Business Tax Guide*. Make a list of any questions you might have.
2. Contact the IRS or your accountant to find the answers to the questions discovered in point 1 above.
3. Review Action Steps 1 through 5 in Chapter 1 and make the appropriate changes to your original plans based on what you have learned in this chapter and changes you have made on your journey.
4. Begin to develop your formal exit strategy, which will be included in your final Business Plan.

GLOBAL**VILLAGE**

Business Ethics in a Global Marketplace

When it comes to business, the world is shrinking – the global marketplace is becoming more accessible with each day and every transaction. Although business has brought people together, culture has kept us different.

When dealing in business with people of other cultures, it is important to keep differences, whatever they may be, in mind. It's important to understand that the global marketplace is a diverse one, and that your potential clients may have different perspectives on ethics and proper behavior than those to which you are accustomed.

Find Common Ground

Remember that the second you step into the global marketplace, you need to be in a global state of mind. Leave behind American jargon and opt for general, direct and courteous ways of communicating thoughts, feelings and ideas.

Don't speak the language? Find someone who does. When it comes to translating, take no short cuts. It is important that you and your client have a clear understanding of what you are discussing.

Also, research the country and the culture of those with whom you will be working. It is important that you know the boundaries when it comes to asking personal questions. What you think is polite chitchat could actually be an offensive question to someone else.

Be Accommodating

Broadening your marketplace broadens your workday. If you're working with someone who is halfway around the globe, a nine-to-five workday won't always cut it. Be prepared to put in the occasional late and odd hours to make sure that everything is running smoothly 24/7.

Not only should you be available when someone needs you, but also so should any company information. Be sure that your employees and partners around the world have access to the information they need in the language they need. Also, make sure there is someone they can contact, should they need additional support. Remember, toll-free numbers don't work outside of North America, so your co-workers in other countries will need a direct-dial number.

Keep it Legal

When dealing in business on a global level, some of the basic rules still apply: Play it straight. Under the Foreign Corrupt Practices Act, it is illegal for any individual, firm or anyone in connection with the firm to pay, offer to pay or bribe in any fashion foreign government officials to obtain or retain business. One exception to this act is "grease payments," where firms will pay lower level government officials to secure routine government actions.

Getting into the global marketplace is challenging, but it's an extremely rewarding endeavor if you do it right. Just be sure that you're informed and ready to take on the responsibilities involved, and you'll find the global marketplace is a great place for your business to be.

Source: NFIB, "Business Ethics in a Global Marketplace." From *http://www.nfib.com/business-resources/business-resources-item?cmsid=22753*, (accessed March 20, 2012). Reprinted with permission.

ACTION STEP 52

Assess Ethical Positions and Design Your Venture's Code of Conduct

1. Respond to questions in Ethical Issues for Entrepreneurs (Figure 12.5).
2. Next, have potential partners—including family members—complete the questionnaire as well. Then sit together over a cup of coffee and discuss your answers.
3. Do you see any potential problems? If so, how will you work the problems out?
4. Are your potential partners people you want to be in business with?
5. Discuss the Ethical Principles for Entrepreneurs in Figure 12.6. Which areas do you and your potential partners agree and disagree on?
6. How will you solve your differences with your partners when you disagree on an issue from an ethical standpoint?
7. Review Figure 12.7. How would your ethical decision making change if you followed these steps?
8. Develop your firm's code of conduct. Use the Center for the Study of Ethics in the Professions at the Illinois Institute of Technology's website to help you complete this Action Step. Excellent resources and sample codes are available through the Center's website to assist you. Remember, you have the chance to design the business and workplace of your dreams; setting ethical standards is one step on the ladder to success.

■ ETHICS

You will be confronted with many ethical issues in running your business. How you react will set the tone for your employees and the future of your company. When you began this venture, you took great risks. Now protect and honor your business through your actions. You are the leader of the band and your employees *will* follow your lead. Make a decision how *you* want to lead.

Recognize your decisions will affect the following stakeholders: employees, partners, customers, suppliers, the community, and the environment. Building trust between the stakeholders and your firm through ethical behavior should be your goal.

Figure 12.5 lists some potential ethical issues and dilemmas entrepreneurs face, many of which have been discussed in the text. Review these issues on your own to determine where you stand. If you have partners, ask them to review the issues and then meet to discuss all of your individual thoughts. Knowing what your partners truly believe and where they stand ethically can prevent potential problems for your business. Completing Action Step 52 will help you determine where possible conflicts may lie regarding ethical issues amongst your partners.

Navigating the ethical differences among various countries proves challanging. One entrepreneur pulled out of Latvia when he discovered to continue operating there would compromise the ethical standards he had set forth for his corporation. Review the Global Village feature for further information concerning operating ethically internationally.

We have included a list of Ethical Principles for Entrepreneurs (Figure 12.6), to serve as a guide as you encounter the many ethical dilemmas facing you. Knowing where you stand and what you believe can make the hard decisions much easier. Oftentimes today's technology is moving so quickly that knowing what to do ethically can sometimes be difficult; but without any standards or codes it becomes impossible. Guidelines such as those presented in Figure 12.6, Key Points from Another View, and the Josephson Institute's Seven-Step Path to Better Decisions (Figure 12.7) assist individuals to act in the best interest of others even in uncertain times or circumstances.

An old saying, "What goes around, comes around" has certainly rung true for Douglas Pick, founder of DAP featured in the Passion box. He has found an incredible way to give back to society by providing jobs for 200 people with disabilities. And these employees have given back to him by providing an "essentially flawless" operation.

Online sites provide sample codes of ethics as guidelines for you to use as you develop your own company code of ethics. Your code sets the tone for your business and becomes part of the culture of how you treat your employees, customers, competitors, and suppliers. When your employees wonder whether something is right or wrong, they will have a guide to help them decide and hopefully a good example set from the top.

One of the easiest guidelines to follow is the Golden Rule, "Treat others as you want to be treated." Another is the Rotary International Test, Four-Way Test, which asks four simple questions:

- Is it the TRUTH?
- Is it FAIR to all concerned?
- Will it build GOODWILL and BETTER FRIENDSHIPS?
- Will it be BENEFICIAL to all concerned?

Being ethical requires hard work! Expecting and demanding it of your employees will require your lead without compromising. In regards to tough issues, ask your employees, "Would you want this posted on Facebook or our company's website?"

figure 12.5

Ethical Issues for Entrepreneurs

How important is each of the following to you?
4 = Very important, 3 = Important, 2 = Not very important,
1 = Not important

1. _____ Expecting a "full day's work for a full day's pay" work ethic.
2. _____ Not allowing petty theft (i.e., supplies, telephone, photocopying, etc.)
3. _____ Not cheating on expense accounts.
4. _____ Not allowing employee acceptance of gifts or favors from vendors.
5. _____ Not distorting or falsifying internal reports.
6. _____ Not allowing cheating or overreaching on benefits (sick days, insurance, etc.)
7. _____ Sexual or racial non-discrimination in hiring, promotion, or pay.
8. _____ Invasion of employee privacy.
9. _____ Providing safe and healthy working conditions.
10. _____ Providing honest, fair, and timely work appraisals.
11. _____ Not recruiting for employee's replacement without telling employee being replaced.
12. _____ Not allowing strategies or technical justifications to deny employees' earned benefits.
13. _____ Dealing fairly with employee complaints.
14. _____ Having fair expectation of paid staff.
15. _____ Providing adequate compensation.
16. _____ Providing adequate recognition, appreciation, or other psychic rewards to staff.
17. _____ Promoting "healthy" competition among employees.
18. _____ Promoting "good" communication.
19. _____ Promoting mutual support and teamsmanship.
20. _____ Fair product pricing.
21. _____ Commitment to honest and truthful marketing and advertising.
22. _____ Providing and ensuring safe and healthy products.
23. _____ Fair handling of customer complaints.
24. _____ Providing truthful tax reports and financial statements.
25. _____ Protecting the environment.
26. _____ Avoidance of bribes, payoffs, or "grease" to union or public officials.
27. _____ Doing business in countries with inhumane or anti-American policies.
28. _____ Community involvement and philanthropy.

Source: Josephson Institute of Ethics, Los Angeles, CA.

figure 12.6

Ethical Principles for Entrepreneurs

Ethical values, translated into active language, establish standards or rules describing the kinds of behavior an ethical entrepreneur should and should not engage in. The following list of principles incorporates the characteristics and values that most people associate with ethical behavior. Ethical decision-making systematically considers these principles.

1. **HONESTY.** Ethical entrepreneurs are honest and truthful in all their dealings and they do not deliberately mislead or deceive others by misrepresentations, overstatements, partial truths, selective omissions, or any other means.

2. **INTEGRITY.** Ethical entrepreneurs demonstrate personal integrity and the courage of their convictions by doing what they think is right even when there is great pressure to do otherwise; they are principled, honorable, and upright; they will fight for their beliefs. They will not sacrifice principle for expediency or be hypocritical or unscrupulous.

3. **PROMISE-KEEPING AND TRUSTWORTHINESS.** Ethical entrepreneurs are worthy of trust, they are candid and forthcoming in supplying relevant information and correcting misapprehensions of fact, and they make every reasonable effort to fulfill the letter and spirit of their promises and commitments. They do not interpret agreements in an unreasonably technical or legalistic manner in order to rationalize noncompliance or create justifications for escaping their commitments.

4. **LOYALTY.** Ethical entrepreneurs are worthy of trust, demonstrate fidelity and loyalty to persons and institutions by friendship in adversity, and display support and devotion to duty; they do not use or disclose information learned in confidence for personal advantage. They safeguard the ability to make independent professional judgments by scrupulously avoiding undue influences and conflicts of interest. They are loyal to their employees and colleagues. They respect the proprietary information of their former employer, and refuse to engage in any activities that take undue advantage of their previous position.

5. **FAIRNESS.** Ethical entrepreneurs are fair and just in all dealings; they do not exercise power arbitrarily, and do not use overreaching nor indecent means to gain or maintain any advantage nor take undue advantage of another's mistakes or difficulties. Fair persons manifest a commitment to justice, the equal treatment of individuals, and tolerance for and acceptance of diversity and are open-minded; they are willing to admit they are wrong and, where appropriate, change their positions and beliefs.

6. **CONCERN FOR OTHERS.** Ethical entrepreneurs are caring, compassionate, benevolent, and kind; they live the Golden Rule, help those in need, and seek to accomplish their business objectives in a manner that causes the least harm and the greatest positive good.

7. **RESPECT FOR OTHERS.** Ethical entrepreneurs demonstrate respect for the human dignity, autonomy, privacy, rights, and interests of all those who have a stake in their decisions; they are courteous and treat all people with equal respect and dignity regardless of sex, race, or national origin.

8. **LAW ABIDING.** Ethical entrepreneurs abide by laws, rules, and regulations relating to their business activities.

(continued)

figure 12.6

Ethical Principles for Entrepreneurs (continued)

9. **COMMITMENT TO EXCELLENCE.** Ethical entrepreneurs pursue excellence in performing their duties, are well informed and prepared, and constantly endeavor to increase their proficiency in all areas of responsibility.

10. **LEADERSHIP.** Ethical entrepreneurs are conscious of the responsibilities and opportunities of their position of leadership and seek to be positive ethical role models by their own conduct and by helping to create an environment in which principled reasoning and ethical decision making are highly prized.

11. **REPUTATION AND MORALE.** Ethical entrepreneurs seek to protect and build the company's good reputation and the morale of its employees by engaging in no conduct that might undermine respect and by taking whatever actions are necessary to correct or prevent inappropriate conduct of others.

12. **ACCOUNTABILITY.** Ethical entrepreneurs acknowledge and accept personal accountability for the ethical quality of their decisions and omissions to themselves, their colleagues, their companies, and their communities.

Source: *Ethical Obligations and Opportunities in Business: Ethical Decision Making in the Trenches*, Josephson Institute of Ethics, Los Angeles, CA.

With the Internet and privacy issues at the forefront today, companies need to be extremely diligent in protecting the privacy of their employee and customer data. When delving into these areas, we suggest contacting attorneys who are up to date on the latest laws covering privacy issues. In addition, one must be ever vigilant to managing a firm's online reputation, as discussed earlier.

Build your dream in an ethical fashion, provide constant and consistent messages to your employees, train employees to follow a strict code of ethics, treat customers as you would want to be treated, and you just may be on your way to providing a business where employees want to work and where customers want

figure 12.7

The Seven-Step Path to Better Decisions

1. **Stop and Think**

   One of the most important steps to better decisions is the oldest advice in the world: think ahead. To do so, it's necessary to first stop the momentum of events long enough to permit calm analysis. This may require discipline, but it is a powerful tonic against poor choices.

   The well-worn formula to count to 10 when angry and to 100 when very angry is a simple technique designed to prevent foolish and impulsive behavior. But we are just as apt to make foolish decisions when we are under the strain of powerful desires or fatigue, when we are in a hurry or under pressure, and when we are ignorant of important facts.

   Just as we teach our children to look both ways before they cross the street, we can and should instill the habit of looking ahead before they make any decision.

   Stopping to think provides several benefits. It prevents rash decisions. It prepares us for more thoughtful discernment. And it can allow us to mobilize our discipline.

2. **Clarify Goals**

   Before you choose, clarify your short- and long-term aims. Determine which of your many wants and don't-wants affected by the decision are the most important. The big danger is that decisions that fulfill immediate wants and needs can prevent the achievement of our more important life goals.

3. **Determine Facts**

   Be sure you have adequate information to support an intelligent choice. You can't make good decisions if you don't know the facts.

   To determine the facts, first resolve what you know and then what you need to know. Be prepared to get additional information and to verify assumptions and other uncertain information.

   Once we begin to be more careful about facts, we often find that there are different versions of them and disagreements about their meaning. In these situations, part of making sound decisions involves making good judgments as to who and what to believe. Here are some guidelines:

   - Consider the reliability and credibility of the people providing the facts.
   - Consider the basis of the supposed facts. If the person giving you the information says he or she personally heard or saw something, evaluate that person in terms of honesty, accuracy, and memory.
   - Remember that assumptions, gossip, and hearsay are not the same as facts.
   - Consider all perspectives, but be careful to consider whether the source of the information has values different than yours or has a personal interest that could affect perception of the facts.
   - Where possible seek out the opinions of people whose judgment and character you respect, but be careful to distinguish the well-grounded opinions of well-informed people from casual speculation, conjecture, and guesswork.
   - Finally, evaluate the information you have in terms of completeness and reliability, so you have a sense of the certainty and fallibility of your decisions.

(continued)

——————————————————————————————————— figure **12.7**

The Seven-Step Path to Better Decisions *(continued)*

4. **Develop Options**

   Now that you know what you want to achieve and have made your best judgment as to the relevant facts, make a list of options, a set of actions you can take to accomplish your goals. If it's an especially important decision, talk to someone you trust, so you can broaden your perspective and think of new choices. If you can think of only one or two choices, you're probably not thinking hard enough.

5. **Consider Consequences**

   Two techniques help reveal the potential consequences.

   - *Pillar-ize" your options.* Filter your choices through each of the Six Pillars of Character: trustworthiness, respect, responsibility, fairness, caring, and citizenship. Will the action violate any of the core ethical principles? For instance, does it involve lying or breaking a promise; is it disrespectful to anyone; is it irresponsible, unfair, or uncaring; or does it involve breaking laws or rules? Eliminate unethical options.
   - *Identify the stakeholders and how the decision is likely to affect them.* Consider your choices from the point of view of the major stakeholders. Identify whom the decision will help and hurt.

6. **Choose**

   It's time to make your decision. If the choice is not immediately clear, see if any of the following strategies help:

   - *Talk to people whose judgment you respect.* Seek out friends and mentors, but remember, once you've gathered opinions and advice, the ultimate responsibility is still yours.
   - *What would the most ethical person you know do?* Think of the person you know or know of (in real life or fiction) who has the strongest character and best ethical judgment. Then ask yourself: What would that person do in your situation? Think of that person as your decision-making role model, and try to behave the way he or she would. Many Christians wear a small bracelet with the letters WWJD standing for the question "What would Jesus do?" Whether you are Christian or not, the idea of referencing a role model can be a useful one. You could translate the question into: "What would God want me to do?" "What would Buddha or Mother Teresa do?" "What would Gandhi do?" "What would the most virtuous person in the world do?"
   - *What would you do if you were sure everyone would know?* If everyone found out about your decision, would you be proud and comfortable? Choices that only look good if no one knows are always bad choices. Good choices make us worthy of admiration and build good reputations. It's been said that character is *revealed* by how we behave when we think no one is looking and *strengthened* when we act as if everyone is looking.
   - *Golden Rule: Do unto others as you would have them do unto you.* The Golden Rule is one of the oldest and best guides to ethical decision making. If we treat people the way we want to be treated, we are likely to live up to the Six Pillars of Character. We don't want to be lied to or have promises broken, so we should be honest and keep our promises to others. We want others to treat us with respect, so we should treat others respectfully.

7. **Monitor and Modify**

   Since most hard decisions use imperfect information and "best effort" predictions, some of them will inevitably be wrong. Ethical decision makers monitor the effects of their choices. If they are not producing the intended results, or are causing additional unintended and undesirable results, they reassess the situation and make new decisions.

Source: Michael Josephson, *Making Ethical Decisions*, Josephson Institute of Ethics, *http://www.josephsoninstitute.org*, Los Angeles, CA, 2002.

to purchase products or services. If that is the case, you will be closer to your goal of turning a profit in a business you enjoy.

■ SUMMARY

Protect your business, your reputation, yourself, and your employees by insuring against losses, paying taxes on time, and acting ethically. It is not worth taking unnecessary or unethical risks after all the effort you have taken to create "your baby."

Determine your insurance needs early and pay to protect your business and personal investment. Work with an experienced agent in your selected industry who is qualified as a business insurance broker.

Work with your accountant (CPA) and a payroll service to be sure you are complying with *all* federal, state, and local tax laws. Tax planning is an important element in the financial success, longevity, and exit strategy of your business. Your accountant and financial advisors should help you stay in compliance with current laws and help you plan for the future. An experienced financial business advisor must be part of any entrepreneurial team.

Protect your business from internal and external crime. Take all financially feasible loss-prevention measures and insure as needed. Establish a code of conduct for your firm and discuss it openly and frequently with your employees.

Plan your exit strategy early on, because it will guide you throughout your venture. Your exit strategy may also well determine the form of business you should undertake at the beginning (corporation, LLC, or sole proprietorship).

Act ethically and responsibly; your actions will set the example for your employees and customers.

■ THINK POINTS FOR SUCCESS

- Protect your investment with insurance.
- Reduce the risk of employee theft and crime with loss-prevention strategies.
- Find and hire an expert accountant and financial advisor.
- Pay taxes on time.

- Keep impeccable, organized records. They will help you survive an audit and enhance your ability to sell your business.
- Plan your exit strategy.
- Follow the golden rule.

■ KEY POINTS FROM ANOTHER VIEW

A Good Start—New Ventures Can Make Ethics Part of Their Business Plan

By Kirk O. Hanson

The entrepreneur has so many things on his or her mind: the "value proposition," the features of the product or service, financing, technology, building the team, getting the phones installed, just surviving from month to month. What role can and do ethics play in the critical first months and years of a company's existence? What can the entrepreneurial team do to *give* ethics a role in the start-up?

The study of how ethics works in companies known as "organizational ethics" has unfortunately focused primarily on larger enterprises. Starting in the mid-1980s, many larger companies established ethics programs staffed by ethics officers. These officers have encouraged others to study how they operate and to measure the effects of their programs. Those who study organizational ethics, fortunately, have been just as interested in how other enterprises those without formal ethics programs succeed in making their companies ethical and value-centered. These insights help us examine how start-ups deal with ethics.

It is obvious the start-up company is unlikely to establish a formal ethics program or appoint an ethics officer, though some start-up CEOs proudly declare that they are the new ventures "ethics officer." Even without a formal program, however, start-ups can create and many have created a very effective commitment to ethical practice.

Examination of the best practices of these start-ups reveals several key steps new ventures can take to make ethics a distinguishing mark of the start-up's culture:

1. **Ethical start-ups recognize the ethical dilemmas that surround them in the first few months.** The pressures to cut ethical corners are great in a start-up.

How much puffery do you use in presenting your idea to venture capitalists? How do you divide stock ownership and options fairly among the founding team and later hires? How reliable does a product have to be before you ship it? How creative can you be in your accounting when the value of your stock is so sensitive to a stumble? When a deal falls through, how quickly do you tell your board and your funders? How generous can you afford to be in employee benefits in the early days?

2. **Ethical start-ups make ethics a core value of the enterprise.** Start-up founders have discovered that they must explicitly embrace doing business ethically to counter the temptations to fudge various standards. Ethics should appear in business plans, in company mission statements, and in all other company documents.

3. **The ethical entrepreneur finds early opportunities to make his or her ethical commitment real.** A Silicon Valley entrepreneur who took over a months-old company recently refused to send faulty financial data to the venture capitalists, over the objections of his new team. "You just don't do business that way," reflects the entrepreneur, who enjoys both financial success and a superb reputation today. He communicated clearly from that day the ethical standards he and the company would follow.

4. **The ethical entrepreneur anticipates the ethical tensions in day-to-day decisions.** As business plans are written and product capabilities are described, the ethical tension between the truthful and the "hopeful" is inevitable. As a start-up tries to attract top talent, there is an unavoidable ethical tension in determining how rosy a picture to draw for the prospect. The ethically thoughtful entrepreneur anticipates these tensions and talks about them with the team before the situations are confronted.

In later years of a company's life, this practice will become more formal "ethics training."

5. **The ethical entrepreneur welcomes ethical questions and debates.** Some situations cannot be anticipated, and the ethical entrepreneur must always keep an open door so that new ethical issues can be worked out. Even the willingness to take time to discuss and resolve tough ethical dilemmas gives the signal that ethics is important in the start-up.

6. **The ethical entrepreneur is watchful about conflicts of interest.** It is hard to single out one area of particular ethical concern in start-ups because there are so many of importance. However, the world of high-tech start-ups emphasizes partnerships, strategic alliances, and "virtual relationships." These arrangements are rife with opportunities for conflicts of interest where an entrepreneur or start-up employee can line his or her own pockets to the detriment of the organization. An early and consistent stand against questionable conflicts of interest is an important dimension of a start-up ethics effort.

7. **The ethical entrepreneur talks about the ethical values all the time.** The frantic pace of start-ups and their rapid growth create short memories and a staff that is often very new to the enterprise. Only by continually articulating the ethical commitment can the entrepreneur be sure the members of the organization particularly new hires understand the ethical commitment and know it is real.

8. **The ethical entrepreneur weeds out employees who do not embrace the ethical values of the company.** Hiring is among the most important strategic steps a start-up takes. Inevitably, the venture will hire some individuals who believe financial success, perhaps just personal financial success, is the only value. The ethical entrepreneur is on the lookout for "teammates" who do not share the company's values and weeds them out before they can do damage to the reputation or culture of the firm.

9. **The ethical entrepreneur looks for opportunities to engage the company in the community.** The start-ups preoccupation with meeting product and financial goals and with its own growth can lead to blindness about anything other than personal gain. Ethical entrepreneurs find ways to engage the team in community service and to emphasize the continuing importance of the team's family relationships.

10. **The ethical entrepreneur takes stock occasionally.** Just as the entrepreneur must keep an eye on the start-up's cash flow and produce a balance sheet periodically, so he or she must also take stock of the company's commitment to its ethics and other values.

11. **The ethical entrepreneur renews the commitment to ethical behavior.** Companies change as they grow. The most pressing ethical dilemmas of a $10 million or $100 million company differ from those of a fledgling start-up. Ethical values and the commitment to ethical behavior must be recast and re-communicated periodically, preparing the company and its employees to deal with the ethical dilemmas currently faced.

The rewards of being an ethical start-up are many. Personal and team satisfaction is the most prominent. Workers who feel free to act ethically and to deal with others ethically feel better about themselves. Greater personal satisfaction translates into higher productivity and to lower turnover.

For the individual entrepreneur, a reputation for ethical dealing can increase the opportunities for business partnerships and lower the "transaction costs" of managing an ongoing relationship. "The ability to trust the other party and to do business on a handshake speeds up the progress we can make," commented one entrepreneur. A reputation for ethical dealing can make it much easier to attract employees and financing to the current venture or the next.

Kirk O. Hanson has served as the Executive Director of the Markkula Center for Applied Ethics, at Santa Clara University since 2001.

The views expressed on this site are the author's. The Markkula Center for Applied Ethics does not advocate particular positions, but seeks to encourage dialogue on the ethical dimensions of current issues.

Source: Markkula Center for Applied Ethics.

■ ACTION STEPS

Action Step 50 Protect Your Venture *329*
Action Step 51 Tax and Exit Strategy Planning *338*

Action Step 52 Assess Ethical Positions and Design Your Venture's Code of Conduct *340*

■ KEY TERMS

Image_Source/iStockphoto.com

Buying a Business
Maneuvering Through the Pitfalls

Learning Objectives

- Evaluate advantages and disadvantages of buying a business.

- Explore avenues for locating businesses for sale.

- Examine an opportunity from the outside.

- Understand the role attorneys, appraisers, consultants, and accountants play in purchasing a business.

- Explore inside a business to determine if the numbers are accurate.

- Realize the importance of conducting due diligence and the steps necessary.

- Understand how business brokers operate.

- Learn how to protect yourself from dishonest sellers and brokers.

- Assess the market value of a business for sale.

- Explore online sources of business sales and transactional data.

- Evaluate good will and ill will.

- Learn steps to protect yourself.

- Prepare for negotiations.

- Learn the ins and outs of seller financing.

So far you have been exploring starting your own business from the ground up; but another doorway, purchasing a business, may offer you a better option. As you begin searching for a business or franchise to purchase, do not fall in love with a "deal"; but instead, fall in love with a business that will fulfill your financial needs and personal desires. Return to the beginning Action Steps in Chapter 1, where you explored your interests, strengths, weaknesses, and your "Inc. plan." Review your thoughts. As you will be expending a great deal of your time, money, energy, and emotion, choose wisely based on intuition and factual information. Knowing the amount of funds you have available is one of the first steps you must take before beginning your search for an established business for sale. Trust yourself and follow your passion.

In this chapter you will learn several ways to locate and evaluate businesses for sale. Although our focus in this chapter is on ongoing independent operations, many of the tactics can be applied to evaluating franchise opportunities as well. Chapter 14 focuses specifically on franchising and multilevel marketing.

Purchasing the right business or franchise requires careful effort and a tremendous amount of skepticism at all times. Read both chapters, as many of the concepts and evaluation tools apply to both doorways.

After exploring independent business and franchise offerings, you may discover through your research these doorways are not for you. If so, your time and effort spent were not fruitless, as what you have learned may have stopped you from making an unprofitable decision. Or, it may lead you to develop your own successful business based on what you have discovered.

When you buy an ongoing business, you are hopefully purchasing an income stream from a proven business. You may also be buying **inventory**, an excellent location, **good will**, and an agreement that the seller will not compete with you. When you buy a new franchise, you are primarily buying the right to use a name. You may also be buying a training program, a Business Plan, advertising assistance, lease negotiation assistance, and purchasing advantages. However, you may also be obtaining an established franchise location, which has been in operation for some time, and thus will be buying all of the above.

It cannot be emphasized enough that you must be aware of the traps that are inherent in purchasing a business. Informed and experienced advisors, who are familiar with your industry, are essential. No purchase should be undertaken without extreme due diligence and legal representation.

Investigate each deal thoroughly and completely. Focus on finding the right opportunity first and the right price and terms second. Spend time searching for an opportunity that fits you. Will this be something you will enjoy doing day in and day out? Can you see yourself at work each day, improving the business? Are the customers the type of people you want to interact with? Are the employees the type of individuals you want to

Inventory Items carried in stock

Good will An invisible commodity used by sellers to increase the asking price for a business; often it's worth the price.

supervise and work with? Does this look like fun? Are you passionate about the business? What is the long-term potential?

Make sure the business opportunity will be able to show a profit and a return on your investment. If you purchase an ongoing business, someone else has already taken the initial risk and high cost of starting a business from scratch. Your goal is not to pay too much for their risk taking.

We caution you to not buy a business and then completely revamp it within a short period of time. Eager and egotistical entrepreneurs oftentimes believe they can do much better than the previous owner. But you purchased the business because it was profitable, and it was profitable because of the systems and products in place at the time of purchase. Do not discount them.

By now you are far enough along on your quest to sense the atmosphere of the marketplace, and it is time to explore businesses for sale. Talking to sellers is just one more step toward expanding your entrepreneurship education. Have fun, but leave your checkbook at home.

■ WHY PURCHASE A BUSINESS?

The overwhelming reason for buying an established business is money, primarily the ongoing income stream. *If* you do your research and *if* you strike a good deal, you may start making money the day you take over an ongoing business. Because most start-ups plug along for months—on average two to three years—before showing a profit, it is smart to consider this doorway to business ownership. For those who must have an immediate positive income stream, this may be the very best doorway. Other items to consider when buying an existing business include the following:

1. If you find a "hungry seller," you may be able to negotiate good terms. You might be able to buy into a business for very little up-front cash and negotiate seller financing. See Key Points for seller financing specifics.
2. Fixtures and equipment will be negotiable. Be sure the equipment is in good working condition and that it has been well maintained. Ask to see all service records and have fixtures and equipment appraised. Never assume.
3. Training and support may be available through the seller and may be negotiated. If the seller is financing, he or she will have a stake in your success. Many banks prefer some seller financing, as they believe it secures the seller's interest and thus the bank's interest. You may request that the owner continue to work in the business for a short time to help you adjust and to serve as a bridge with the customers and suppliers.
4. An established customer base should be in place. You will need to determine how loyal the customers are and whether there is good will or ill will. If the customer base is not strong or loyal, figure this into your price negotiations. If business has recently been souring, good will may be difficult to quantify. Assess the cost and possibility of rebuilding customer loyalty. Also, make sure the business is not dependent on only a few customers or clients.
5. Relationships with suppliers and distributors are in place. Make sure you spend time talking with each to determine the status of the relationship. They may provide great insight into the owner's business. Also, attempt to ascertain if there are any special agreements between the owner and the suppliers and distributors that are based on friendships, which may not continue when you purchase the business.
6. The location may be excellent and not easily duplicated. Determine if the lease can be reassigned to you. Have your attorney review the lease and also

Ill will All the negative feelings about a business; the opposite of good will

GLOBAL**VILLAGE**

Throughout the chapter we have presented international stories and resources, hopefully which have opened your eyes to new opportunities. The following quick quiz should help you assess if you are ready and willing to take advantage of entering into the international marketplace.

Test Your Export Quotient

	YES	NO
1. Are you entrepreneurial?	☐	☐
2. Do you have a reliable, service-oriented character?	☐	☐
3. Are you a natural networker who builds and maintains relationships?	☐	☐
4. Do you see yourself as highly organized and research oriented?	☐	☐
5. Have you a sense of mission?	☐	☐
6. Do you possess good communication skills?	☐	☐
7. Is a sales, marketing, or distribution background featured in your résumé?	☐	☐
8. Do you excel in finance and business-related subjects?	☐	☐
9. Do you pride yourself on your strong negotiating skills?	☐	☐
10. Are you experienced in handling complex documentation?	☐	☐
11. Are you an avid follower of global politics?	☐	☐
12. Do you have the ability to speak and write more than one language?	☐	☐
13. Are you sensitive to different cultures?	☐	☐
14. Do you consider yourself able to adopt ideas easily, even under pressure?	☐	☐
15. Are you well-traveled or curious about other cultures:	☐	☐

Total (award 1 point for every "yes")

Evaluating Your Score

1–6: Although you have acquired some skills related to exporting, you need further assessment to find out if you are suited to this field.

7–10: You show a keen interest in the subject. However, you should consider increasing your knowledge, language, and technical trading skills training.

11–15: You have a high rating in the critical factors that make companies and individuals successful in the exciting field of global trade.

Source: Excerpt from Global Entrepreneurship, Module 1, p. 13. Copyright Forum for International Trade Training. Used with permission.

discover if the owner of the building has other goals for the location. If in a multiple unit building, take time to check out the other businesses. Make sure you conduct due diligence to determine if there are any planned changes for the shopping areas, community, environmental restrictions, roads, and so on that may affect the continued success of the current location.

7. Employees may possess specialized knowledge, which benefit the business immensely. In high-technology industries, purchasing businesses for brainpower is common practice. You will have no guarantee, though, that the employees and their expertise will remain—you must consider the possibility that key employees may leave and compete.

8. Existing licenses and permits may be difficult to replicate. Check with your attorney and licensing agencies to determine the availability and process of transferring licenses and permits before proceeding with any purchase. Also,

research if there are licenses and permits which the owners do not possess which they should. If so, you will need to determine the cost, availability, and time frames to acquire. Be sure to include these new costs and time frames in your financials and operational plan.

9. You will be able to see actual financial data and tax-reporting forms. Investigate! Assume they have two sets of books and ask to see both; some firms have three sets. Be skeptical of all reported numbers in any cash-only business.

10. An inside look into the business operation will determine if using additional technology could increase operational effectiveness and thus profits. Throughout the book we have asked you to explore all business functions where increased efficiency, technology, cost reduction, a change in marketing, or distribution strategies could increase sales and profit. Keep these potential opportunities in mind at all times as you examine businesses for sale.

11. Completing your due diligence will reduce but not eliminate uncertainties when purchasing a business.

■ HOW TO BUY AND HOW NOT TO BUY

Smart buyers scrutinize everything about a business with a microscope, computer analyses, and sage advice from business gurus. They do not plunge into a business for emotional reasons. For example, you may have eaten lunch around the corner at Millie's with your pals for years, and when the place goes up for sale, nostalgia may make you want to write out a check for it on the spot. That would be a *wrong* reason to buy.

In purchasing an ongoing business, you will need to use the expertise of experienced business brokers, accountants, small-business attorneys, and business appraisers. As when searching for all professionals, use your eyes and ears to search out the best. References are important for each part of your team and should be checked thoroughly. Not only do you need others who are trustworthy and experienced, you also need brokers who have experience in the particular industry and area where you are purchasing a business. Contact several references and inquire how the advisors aided their decision making. Also, ask what the advisors did poorly and what questions they wished they would have asked up front. *If* utilizing trained, experienced, and honest brokers, the advisors' fees and commissions should be considered minimal when compared to their invaluable expertise.

FranNet and VR Business Brokers are two of the largest franchised business brokerage firms in the United States. In addition, many independent brokers will serve your needs. Brokers can be very specialized, for example, one former dentist in Southern California serves as a broker only for dental practices.

Business brokers have assisted thousands of individuals in realizing their dreams and reaching their financial goals. Always remember, however, brokers work for the seller, and that is where their allegiance lies. Meet with several to find the right fit. Try not to sign exclusive agreements with brokers. If a broker talks about selling you a particular business without first spending a few hours getting to know you, your background, and your financials, walk away.

In addition, locate an attorney with expertise in business-sale transactions and an accountant who both thoroughly understand the tax implications involved in the transfer of a business. They may discover interesting legal and tax loopholes that will benefit both buyer and seller. Experienced *industry* accountants will also know where owners hide their problems and where there may be potential for additional profits and tax advantages.

Keep in mind; every business in the country is for sale at some time. Deals are like planes. If you miss one, another one will be along soon.

Good buys are always available to the informed and careful buyer, but they may be difficult to discover. Seeking the right business to buy is much like an

Business broker A real estate professional who specializes in representing people who want to sell their businesses and represents buyers as well employment search: the best are seldom advertised. In contrast, the worst business opportunities are advertised widely. When you see several advertisements for a particular type of business, you know where the unhappy businesspeople are.

Running your own advertisement may be a good idea. This was true for one man, who ran the following advertisement in the business section (not the classifieds) of a large-circulation Midwestern newspaper:

Tired of golfing and tennis. Ready to build and manage again. Sold successful business at 35. Desire to buy manufacturing business with more than $6 million in annual sales. Email H.G. at newbusinessfartooyoungtoretire@gmail.com.

H.G. received more than 20 replies and said reading the proposals was educational and entertaining. After he reviewed the proposals, he traveled throughout the country and visited with several sellers. In his search, he did not find one buyer or business he was comfortable dealing with. Honesty seemed to be in short supply. Thus, he joined the estimated 90 percent of people who seek to purchase an established business who never close on their dream. If you want to buy a business, you will need to be diligent in your efforts and patient.

Another lucky buyer did find her dream business when the owner of a craft store located in a Chicago suburb posted the following on her website:

I am the owner of Quilt Designs and I moved to California in January 2009 and have been overseeing the store from afar. I have decided that it is now time to pass the torch to someone who would love to own the store as much as I have. So Quilt Designs is for sale. I am in no hurry and I will continue to stock the shelves and bring in new merchandise while we find someone who wants to call Quilt Designs their own.

Quilt Designs has been a profitable business for 18 years, and I expect to see it continue for many more. I decided to make this announcement to my customers first, because I think there may be a customer out there who is looking for just this opportunity. A new owner can bring their own energy and personality to Quilt Designs, and it will thrive. Some owner financing may be available. Please contact me if you are interested and would like more information.

The owner received 10 inquiries to her posting, shared information with several, and finally sold to a buyer who refinanced her home, received support from a SBDC, and accepted a small amount of seller financing. Also, during negotiations, the buyer requested the seller reduce the store inventory to reduce the selling price and the owner agreed to do so.

Spread the Word

Once you are ready to look for a business to purchase, inform everyone you know that you are a potential buyer and leads may follow. But before spreading the word, set your parameters. Look at the industry desired, size of business, potential sales, profit potential, and time frame in which you will purchase the business as well as your funds available. Again, these should be based on the work you completed in Chapter 1 and your initial research of the industry you want to enter. A few tips:

1. Inform your friends, family members, club members, church friends, and anyone else you associate with.
2. Contact everyone you can in your chosen industry—manufacturers, resellers, agents, dealers, distributors, suppliers, trade associations, and so on; let them know you are looking.
3. Ask your network of bankers, attorneys, CPAs, and community leaders to help you in your search.
4. Advertise your desires in trade journals and answer ads that have been posted. In addition, trade associations may rent their member lists; use them to send query letters or emails to members or post online.

ACTION STEP 53

Spread the Word

1. If appropriate, email people, and post on Facebook or Twitter, expressing your desire to purchase a business. Lay out your parameters and ask the recipients to forward to anyone they think might be of service to you in your search.
2. From the list on this page, select three or four avenues to locate businesses for sale in your industry or area.
3. Locate three businesses and interview the owners.
4. Summarize your thoughts after each visit.

It is best to learn of businesses for sale by networking, but you may find the most eager sellers advertising in your local newspaper or through online listings such as Craigslist or eBay.

Leave your checkbook at home when you visit. This action step will cost you practically nothing, maybe just a few breakfasts or lunches. Your goal at this point is to explore opportunities not purchase a business.

5. Send letters or emails of inquiry to potential sellers you have identified (see Action Step 53).
6. Network your way to the best business brokers in your area or industry.
7. Talk with firms that deal in mergers and acquisitions.
8. Do not allow yourself to be rushed; time is your ally, and the deals will get better.
9. Check out businesses you would like to operate and buy. Ask the owners if they would consider selling.
10. Knock on doors. You may be surprised!
11. Look for owners who want to retire or sell due to partnership disagreements, illness, retirement, boredom, or divorce.
12. Look for businesses that are not doing well that you believe your expertise and energy could improve. Make sure the business is not in a shrinking marketplace. If you are an experienced business owner, taking this step may be worth it. If not, be wary.
13. Check out businesses with a great product but possibly poor marketing or a poor location. Would a new location or a great marketing campaign help the business take off? If it is a manufactured product, could reducing the costs of production by moving the facility reduce costs enough to make the business profitable? Would closing the retail location and selling only online be a more profitable business model? Remember, you are not just looking for increased sales, but increased profits.
14. Visit BizBuySell (see Figure 13.1), BizQuest, and national and local business broker sites.
15. Review ads in the *Wall Street Journal*, industry and local business journals.
16. Use Internet blogs and social networking sites judiciously to spread the word and look for opportunities.

Use Action Step 53 to spread the word and discover opportunities. Buyer beware!

■ BEGIN TO INVESTIGATE OPPORTUNITIES

After interviewing a few potential promising opportunities, it will be time to play marketplace detective. This section suggests some techniques that will make you feel like a super spy. After investigating each business from the outside, you will be ready to move inside, review the books, and talk to the owners in an attempt to learn the *real* reasons they are selling. Unfortunately, Ben and Sally Raymundo did not look deep enough and learned about fraud the hard way.

A Story from the Suburbs

Ben and Sally Raymundo bought a women's sportswear store, GeeGees, in a thriving suburban community about two miles from a regional shopping mall. They learned too late that the seller had a more profitable store in another part of the county whose store's records were used to misrepresent the store they bought. Here are the particulars:

1. *The seller moved the computerized register from the higher-volume store to the store she wanted to sell so that the store's sales were greatly inflated.*
2. *The sales price was fixed at inventory plus $40,000 for good will. This seemed a bargain for a store whose cash register records showed it was grossing $800,000 per year at a 50 percent average gross margin.*
3. *Ben and Sally paid full wholesale value ($100,000) for "dead goods", already shopworn and out of date. The owners probably combined the dead goods from both stores and brought them to the store Ben and Sally purchased without them being the wiser. The goods eventually had to be marked down to less than $20,000.*

4. *Ben and Sally assumed the remainder of an iron-clad lease at $6,000 per month, and the landlord made them sign a personal guarantee that pledged their home as security on the lease.*

5. *The location proved to be a dead foot-traffic location in a marginally successful center.*

Fortunately, Ben had kept his regular job. Sally worked at selling off the unwanted inventory and replaced it with more salable stock hoping to survive. They spent $36,000 for advertising during the 12 months they stayed in business. It was another year before the landlord found a new tenant and Ben and Sally could get out of the lease. GeeGee's was a tough and very expensive mistake for Ben and Sally.

Learn from Others' Mistakes and Keep Digging

What could Ben and Sally have done to avoid this fiasco? Many things. They could have asked the mall merchants how well the shopping center and the store were doing. They also should have observed the store and the shopping mall traffic themselves before they committed. Parking in front of the store and counting customers and packages would have been beneficial. Checking out the inventory in person would have also helped. They could have insisted that Sally be allowed to work in the store prior to or during the escrow period, with a clause that would have allowed them to bail out.

Ben and Sally were honest, hardworking people who took the seller at face value—a huge mistake! Talks with suppliers and others might have uncovered the seller's fraud. They are now suing. The CPA and attorney they have *now* hired could have really helped them *before* they purchased the business. Hiring experts after the fact usually proves expensive, because it puts them on the defense rather than on the offense. The chance of any financial recovery through legal means is slim for Ben and Sally.

Some sellers do not count the value of their own time and money as costs of doing business. This makes the firm show an inflated return on investment (ROI). Suppose a firm earns $100,000 per year and has an inventory of $250,000. This could be a poor investment if the seller, his spouse, and their two children work a total of 160 hours per week and if a $250,000 investment could earn 4 percent or more per year in high-yield tax free muni bonds.

If the business you are considering is a retail business, have friends visit the store at different hours throughout the day to assess how many people are actually working. For many families who run a business that has become their life, honestly assessing the time they devote to the business can be very difficult; your research may help provide you with more accurate data on which to base your purchasing decision.

Look at each deal from the viewpoint of what it would cost to hire a competent manager and employees at market wage rates. In this case, let us suppose you had to pay $50,000 a year for a manager, $30,000 a year for an assistant, and $40,000 a year for two hourly employees. You will have spent $120,000 plus benefits and lost the opportunity to earn another 4 percent on your investment. Yes, this would be a no-brainer, but a lot of businesses with even less going for them are bought every day.

It is time now to venture out and investigate a business on your own. Remember what you have learned from Ben and Sally's bad experience, and take along your new eyes and your camera. You will be surprised how much there is to see. Action Step 54 tells you how to do it.

Know When You Need Outside Help

We have already discussed the need for a team of small business gurus to help you realize your dream of small-business ownership. If you have any lingering doubts about the business you are researching, you may need the perspective of someone who is more objective than one of your team players. If you are not the

ACTION STEP 54

Study a Business from the Outside

Studying a business from the outside will tell you whether you should go inside and probe more deeply. Adjust the five steps below for manufacturing, wholesaling, service, or Internet businesses. If you are entering into a new industry, sit down with others with industry experience and pick their picks as to what you should be focusing on.

1. **Make sure the business fits into the framework of your industry overview.** You want a business that is in the sunrise phase, not the sunset phase, of the life cycle.

2. **Diagram the area.** What is the location, and how does the area fit into the city and county planning for the future? What is the life-cycle stage of the community? Where is the traffic flow? Is there good access? How far will your Target Customers have to travel to get there? Is parking adequate? Is the parking lot a drop-off point for carpoolers? What is the employee pool of the area?

3. **If the business is a retail business, take photographs of the exterior.** Analyze them carefully. Is the building in good repair? What are the customers wearing, driving, and buying? What can you deduce about their lifestyle? Take photographs on different days and at different times of day.

4. **Talk with and analyze neighbors.** What do the neighboring businesses know about the business for sale? Will their businesses help draw Target Customers to your business? Do you want to be close to competitors—Restaurant Row, Mile of Cars, and other such successful business areas—or do you want to be miles away? Could a competitor move in next door the day after you move in? Ask the tenants about their leases, but understand that each lease can vary.

5. **Interview customers.** What do they like about the store? Is the service good? What changes would they recommend? What services or products would they like to see added? Where else do they go for similar products or services?

6. **Check with local authorities.** What are the plans for this location? What is the local municipality planning to do with sewers, roads, and signage? Are there any new proposals for building permits?

Sherlock Holmes type yourself, hire someone who is. You may have to put your dream on hold as a result of this kind of investigation, but you will save money in the long run.

Georgia Webster had some doubts about the business she and her husband were considering. See what you can learn from the Websters' experiences.

Saved by a Bulldozer

Fred and I graduated from college in 2006. We both loved sports and were college athletes, so with our parents' financial backing we decided to look around for a sporting goods store to buy.

We found the perfect store to buy: The Sports Factory, located a block from a city swim complex, three blocks from a new Pilates and yoga studio, and a quarter mile from a park where volleyball, softball, and soccer tournaments are held every month.

A friend of ours, an accountant, checked over the books. He said they looked perfect. "Great profit and loss statement," he said, "and accounting ratios you wouldn't believe for this business. If you arrive at the right terms, you could clear $40K every quarter, and that's only the beginning. This guy doesn't even promote the store."

We learned from the owner that he wanted to sell the store because he was tired of it—the long hours, being tied down, and so on. He'd been at it for a dozen years and he wanted to start enjoying life. We contacted Harry Henkel, a local entrepreneurship professor, who offered to spend about two to three hours investigating for $600.

Two days later, Harry, our marketplace detective, called and said he had some news, "I talked to a bulldozer driver working across the street from the Sports Factory today and he told me the property is being developed into a seven-store retail complex, and one of the stores is going to be a discount sporting goods store."

I asked him if the owner knew, and if maybe that's why he's so "tired."

"Yes, I believe so," Harry said. "I double-checked at the city planning office, and the building permit was issued six weeks ago."

Georgia and Fred Webster came very close to buying the right business at the wrong time. The outsider's perspective and detective work helped them avoid making a terrible mistake. As valuable as these outside perspectives are, however, you have to have an inside look to truly get a feel for the business you are investigating.

■ EXPLORE BROKERS AND LISTINGS

Once you have learned all you can from the outside, it is time to cross the threshold for a look at the inside if the opportunity looks promising. Don't waste your time or the owners' time if you are just looking under the hood but not ready to buy. This is an important, time-consuming process, but it is an important milestone in your quest. Searching for a business and completing proper due diligence may take you anywhere from 2 to 12 months.

There are two ways to gain entry inside the business: either contact the owner yourself or receive assistance from a business broker. Professional brokers have access to many listings and may be the only way you will be allowed into some businesses for sale.

Meet with several brokers to find a good fit and hopefully be led to promising opportunities. Be prepared for disappointment as you explore businesses for sale. You will probably look at a great many businesses before you find anything close to your requirements. Nevertheless, you will learn and benefit from the journey.

Dealing with Brokers

Business brokers are active in most communities and industries, and they play an important role in matching up sellers with buyers. Their level of competency ranges from specialists who know as much about fast-food franchises as Taco Bell owners do, to part-timers who know so little about business that they will only waste your time.

A broker has a fiduciary responsibility to represent the seller and is not paid unless he or she sells something. Typically, the broker's commission is around 10 percent for businesses less than $1 million, but the percentage is much less on large deals, and everything is open to negotiation. You may prefer a buyer's broker; although they are rare, their first responsibility is to you—but the seller will still pay the commission.

Some sellers list with brokers because they do not want it generally known—to their customers, employees, or competitors—that they want to sell their business. Others who list with brokers, however, do so out of desperation because they have already tried to sell their business to everyone they know.

Spending time with a skilled broker can be a fascinating educational experience. If you want a particular type of business, and you are able to examine a half-dozen that are on the market, you may end up with a better grasp of the overall business situation than the current owners.

Network your business contacts to locate competent brokers. Then, Interview several brokers to determine which ones you are most comfortable with and which are the most trustworthy. Can they explain cash flow forecasting, advantages of earn-outs, and bulk sales law? Ask for referrals. And as we have said so many times before, leave your checkbook at home. Do not let anyone rush you. A good business broker will provide several services, and those that follow provide an idea of what to expect from your broker.

Matching Buyers and Sellers   If you are a buyer, a good business broker will interview you thoroughly to determine your needs, desires, personal and financial goals, and limitations. From your responses and your broker's knowledge of the market, opportunities will be presented to you that best suit your interests, desired lifestyle, abilities, and financial resources. Sharing your Chapter 1 Action Steps with your broker would be an excellent start and would save a lot of time, energy, and frustration as the broker prescreens businesses for you. Do not work with any broker who does not take the time and energy to understand you and your needs. You will be wasting your time.

Determining Fair Market Value   Professional business brokers develop strong working relationships with various business, land, commercial, and equipment appraisers who may assist in determining the fair market value of an ongoing business. Their contacts with attorneys and accountants are invaluable. Remember at all times you are paying for and benefiting from your broker's expertise and contacts and if they have neither, find another broker.

Facilitating the Negotiating Process   Buying a business is an emotionally charged process; you are making a lifestyle decision, as well as making a long-term major financial investment. You will therefore benefit greatly from an experienced third party serving as a go-between. Your broker, who will not receive a commission check from the seller until the sale closes, hopefully understands the motives behind each party and thus keeps the process moving forward

Untangling Red Tape   Assistance in acquiring necessary permits and licenses, as well as help with locating financing and reputable escrow companies, are all part of the responsibilities of a professional broker.

The BizBuySell website, affiliated with the *Wall Street Journal,* is a database of businesses for sale, which can be searched by state, county, business category and asking price. In addition, one can search for home-based and Internet businesses as well as those that are relocatable. Figure 13.1 highlights BizBuySell sample listings for manufacturing, Internet, and retail businesses. Please note the broker listings focus the businesses in the very best light. Thus, when you are reading the ads, keep in mind the ads are written so that each will sound like a "must buy today" investment!

Fiduciary Legal relationship between two or more parties with loyalty and trust

Earn-out The seller agrees to accept a portion of his payment for the business from the business's future earnings

Bulk sales law Uniform Commercial Code governs transfer of goods from seller to single buyer

figure 13.1

Samples of Business Brokers' Listings from BizBuySell

Commercial Casework & Millwork Business for Sale
Tennessee

Seller Financing Available

Asking Price: $379,900	Inventory: $50,000.00*
Gross Income: $700,000	Real Estate: N/A
Cash Flow: $175,000	Year Established: 1965
EPITDA: N/A	Employees: 7
FF&E: $283.000.00*	
Business Types: Furniture and Fixtures/Lumber and Wood Products	

*included in the asking price

Business Description

Due to owner wanting to retire, this casework and millwork business is being sold. Scope of past projects include: hospitals, doctor and dental offices, restaurants, assisted living facilities, churches, schools and colleges, historical renovations, etc. Business operating since the 1960s has proven itself as a recession-proof business, continuing operation through the recession of 1980s recession and again during this recession. Business has a proven record of producing net profits of over $100K in a year during the height of this past recession. Annual sales through the recession have consistently remained in the $575K to $750K range with pre-recession annual sales over of $1.2 million. Currently, the business is set up and operating out of a 12,000-sq. ft. leased facility near Nashville, TN. Equipment includes, but not limited to: 5 head Weinig molder, Weinig tooling grinder, molding profile knives, rips saw, 2 dust collectors, forklift, digital Holtzer panel saw, smaller panel saw, 20 planer, Brandt edge bander, many types of large saws, shaper, boring machines, hinge boring machine, 36 wide belt sander, air compressor, lg band saw, table saws, electric pallet jack, case clamp, plastic laminating shop for tops, etc., router tables, 2 spray systems, installation tools. All saws and machines have been well maintained replacement tooling for almost all machines. Four vehicles: including 24 international box truck, Chevy 14 box truck, Ford cargo van, and a Chevy pickup truck. All inventory. Office equipment, HP plotter, drafting tables, computers, software (including estimating software), website, etc. In the last few months alone we have bid close to $1 million in new projects, most of which are still open to be awarded. We continue to bid daily. Bids will be included in sale. We are still in operation with projects under contract. Included is entire customer base. We are pricing the business for a quick sale at $379,900. Serious inquiries.

Detailed Information

Facilities: Currently the business is set up and operating out of a 12,000-sq. ft. leased facility near Nashville, TN (month to month lease).

Competition: Nashville provides an excellent business location. Nashville has not been hit hard by the recession, as some other places, due to its central location and sound business environment. According to local news Nashville is poised for large growth in the immediate future with some of the top corporations in the country and world expanding into the middle Tennessee area.

Growth/Expansion: Expansion possibilities are endless. We have worked all over the U.S. with little to no advertising.

Financing: Some owner financing many be available with very large down payment.

Support/Training: Yes, if needed.

Reason Selling: Retirement

---

4 Year Old Drop Shipping Baby Gifts Business (Highly Automated)-Internet Retail
New York, New York (New York County) (Relocatable)

Asking Price: $330,000	Inventory: N/A
Gross Income: $656,000	Real Estate: N/A
Cash Flow: $163,000	Year Established: 2008
EBITDA: N/A	Employees: 1
FF&E: N/A	Consume Services (B2C)
Business Types: General Internet	

(continued)

figure **13.1**

Samples of Business Brokers' Listings from
BizBuySell (continued)

Business Description

As the world population grows, so too does the demand for exquisite baby gifts. This is a business that was founded in 2008 and has been growing year after year. This is a 100% drop-ship business that focuses on selling premium baby gifts and party favors all across the U.S. The owners are meticulous in all aspects of the business and strive to be the best possible. The business generated over $650K in gross sales in 2011 and had a gross profit margin of 32%. After all expenses, the total owner's benefit for 2011 was over $150K. The site is ranked extremely highly organically for key industry search terms and is one of the top players in the industry. Unlike many sites last year, this site increased their traffic and sales throughout the year rather than lose due to Google's Panda update. This speaks to the quality web business that they have built throughout the several years. Their products have been purchased by some of the largest corporations in the world including Dream-Works, Symantec, HP, Microsoft, Dell, Pepsi, and Coke. Just recently a gift was purchased from them that was sent to Ivanka Trump for Donald Trump's latest grandchild, Arabella. This again speaks to their great customer service and quality products as we all know the Trumps demand the BEST. The owners are looking to move on from this venture to focus on the offline consulting business. But they are more than willing to stay on board to help the new owner transition the business properly by showing them the ropes, introducing them to their suppliers, and making sure they understand all aspects of the business so there is no hiccup in service for clients.

Detailed Information

Support/Training: Seller is willing to train buyer in all aspects of the business.

Reason Selling: Seller has another offline business that needs more attention.

Busy Carpet and Flooring Store-Sharp!
Oklahoma City Metro Area, Oklahoma (Oklahoma County)

Seller Financing Available

Asking Price: $200,000	Inventory: $10,000**
Gross Income: $570,000	Real Estate: N/A
Cash Flow: $91,000	Year Established: N/A
FF&E: $62,000*	Employees: 1

*included in the asking price
**not included in the asking price

Business Description

This is not your ordinary carpet and flooring store! The owner has developed an efficient model that makes the business very profitable with low overhead and with low inventory requirements. And, the location is fantastic. This is a great business for anyone that wants to use their creative talents in helping customers improve their homes. If you are a husband-wife looking for a business to work in together, or want a business for family to work in, this is a perfect fit! Don't put this one off. This profitable business is a snap to run and the owner is there to help you along the way, including financing the right buyer!

Detailed Information

Facilities: Appealing store jam packed with product samples. Located in super busy commercial shopping area with lots of drive-by traffic.
Competition: There are a couple of flooring businesses considered competitors in their market area, but this business has some strategic advantages.

Growth/Expansion: The owner has a mix of residential and commercial customers, but feels the best avenue for growth and profitability is in the residential sector, which he has not had the time or motivation to do.
Financing: Seller will finance with $60,000 down.

Support/Training: Seller has 2 other unrelated businesses that he needs to manage.

Source: Samples of Business Brokers' Listings. Retrieved from *http://www.BizBuySell.com* (Accessed February 14, 2012). Reprinted with permission.

ACTION STEP 55

Study a Business from the Inside

Looking at a business from the inside enables you to determine its real worth and to see what it would be like to own it. In the chapter's past Action Steps you have been exploring, but now you ready to look at hard data.

Make an appointment—or have a business broker arrange it—to take a serious inside look at the business or businesses you think you might want to buy. Before you go, review all information in this chapter and make a list of detailed questions. Do not allow anyone to rush you.

Leave the checkbook at home; this initial fun is free.

Nondisclosure agreements Legal contract which restricts sharing of information

Non-piracy agreement Contract to prohibit use of proprietary company information

■ HOW TO LOOK AT THE INSIDE OF A BUSINESS

Once you have wedged your foot in the door and have established yourself as a qualified potential buyer, you will be able to study the inner workings of the business. Take full advantage of this opportunity, and do not stop until you have investigated the business thoroughly and *all* your questions are answered.

Does the thought of walking into someone's business for the purpose of snooping around, looking at the books, and asking the owner probing questions still fill you with anxiety and make you nervous? It should not. Sellers expect prospective buyers who are seriously looking for a business to buy to do those things. After reading this next section, you will be ready for Action Step 55, investigating a business close up.

Study the Financial History

What you need to learn from the financial history is: where the money comes from and where it goes. Ask to see all financial records, preferably audited ones, for at least the past three years, and take your time studying them. Hire an accountant with *industry experience* to review the records. Your aim in buying an ongoing business is to step into an income stream. The financial and sales records give a picture of how fast the stream is flowing and where there might be dams along the way.

Before allowing you to review financial documents, most sellers and brokers will screen and qualify you as a potential buyer. They only want to show company financial data to those buyers with the financial ability to purchase. You will be required to present your personal financial data to the seller or broker. In addition, signing a nondisclosure agreement assures the seller that you will not talk to employees, suppliers, or customers until an appropriate, agreed-upon time. You will also be prohibited from disclosing any information about the business to others except your advisors, who also must not disclose any information. You may also be requested to sign a non-piracy agreement, which prevents you from pirating the business's system, products, or ideas.

Review cash-flow statements, profit and loss statements, accounts receivables, and payables. If the seller has a stack of accounts receivable a foot high, remember that, in general:

- After 3 months, the value of a current account's dollar will have shrunk to 90 cents.
- After 6 months, it will be worth 50 cents.
- After a year, it will be worth 30 cents or less, depending on the industry.

Review every receipt you can find. If a fast-food owner tells you she sells 2,000 hamburgers per week, ask to see the receipts from the suppliers. If none are offered, ask permission to contact the suppliers for records of shipment. Make her prove to you what she has bought from suppliers so you can accurately measure sales. If the seller will not cooperate, run—do not walk—away; the seller is hiding something. You can use this technique with any firm that is buying and marking up material or merchandise.

Evaluate closely any personal expenses that are being charged to the business. This allows you to get a clearer picture of the firm's true profits. Your accountant will help you with this.

It is also a good idea to review canceled checks, income tax returns (preferably for the past three to five years), and the amount of salary the seller has been paying himself or herself. If your seller was stingy with his or her own salary, decide whether you could live on that amount. Also, look for items that the seller may have purchased for his home or personal life and run through the business thus offsetting the low salary.

Many cash businesses will be very difficult to evaluate. Owners many times skim cash off the top and do not report it to the IRS. Beware of cash-only businesses.

If the seller brags that she does not pay her taxes, ask yourself if you can trust her. If she is willing to lie to the IRS, which can land her in jail, she will more than likely be willing to lie to you.

Make sure the owner has not been paying his employees in cash. If he has, employee costs will be grossly underestimated, as operating a legal business requires paying social security, workers comp, and unemployment insurance. Explore whether family members or friends are working in the business and not getting paid or are being paid under the table. If so, projected employee costs will need to be revised. Many owners also underestimate the number of hours they personally work. If you will be hiring a manager to run the business, you may need to hire a full-time manager and an assistant manager to cover the number of hours the owner alone has been willing to devote to the business.

The following due diligence list points out items you need to review with the owner, your accountant, your attorney, business broker, and other professionals before you are able to determine the value of any business. Depending on the industry, additional items will need to be evaluated as suggested by your team of experts. Following the steps we have outlined in Chapter 13 may take you several weeks or months. Do not skip any steps in your haste to purchase a business and hopefully a positive and profitable income stream. Some of the following items can be completed at the start of your search for a business, but before finalizing any deal make sure you have completed the entire list as well as the Final Before-You-Buy List at the end of the chapter.

Due Diligence: Items for Review

Accounting services contract
Accounts payable records (if not being paid within 30 days, be on alert)
Accounts receivable records (aging?)
Advertising agreements with media companies (usually not assumable)
Agreements (franchise, other)
Appraisals (equipment, land, buildings)
Bank account statements including deposit receipts, checking-account statements with canceled checks
Building (physical condition, upgrades required for plumbing, electrical, safety, accessibility)
Community relationships and support
Contributions and dues records
Copyrights, trademarks, patents
Corporate minutes book
Credit-card company agreements
Creditworthiness of customers
Customer agreements (if wholesale business-be very wary if only a few exist)
Employment contracts (oral or written) and evaluation of each individual's roles and major responsibilities within the firm
Equipment service and lease agreements (check to see if assumable; if they are—which is rare—what will it take to assume)
Equipment suppliers list
Financial statements for past three to five years—income statements, cash flow, and balance sheets (hopefully audited)
Fixtures and furniture (condition and possible upgrade or replacement cost)
Industry relationships and reputation
Insurance policies, including property, product liability, medical, business interruption (beware of potential large increases)
Inventory (current or out of date?)
Labor union issues
Leasehold agreements and options to renew

Legislation or pending legislation that might affect the business (hire experts to delve into this area if needed)

Licenses and fees

Liens

Listing of any outstanding liabilities (including out of court settlements and employee benefit claims or potential claims)

Maintenance records, receipts, and agreements

Manufacturing agreements

Marketing (copies of marketing and sales literature)

Merchandise return information and statistics

Noncompete agreements

Number of customers and percentage of sales

Organizational structure and individual responsibilities

OSHA and any other legal requirements (sometimes these exist and owners are not abiding by the laws)

Payroll records

Personal and financial affairs of sellers (private investigators provide services)

Personnel policies including vacation, sick leave, maternity, commissions, deferred compensation, pensions, stock options, and profit sharing

Pricing review and compare to competition

Recipes/computer models/codes/etc.

Records of litigation and notice of litigation pending against the business or anyone associated with the business

Reputation of business, owner, products/service (both online and offline)

Roles and responsibilities of owners and top employees

Sales records

Supplier agreements and contracts

Taxes, including personal property, municipal, sales, and employment taxes, along with IRS returns (three to five years)

Travel and entertainment details

Utility bills, including telephone (consider possible utility changes that might adversely affect business—i.e., skyrocketing electric costs)

Warranties, invoices, titles, encumbrances, operating instructions, manuals

Websites and agreements with advertisers

Word of mouth (evaluating good will and ill will)

Zoning (potential changes)

© Cengage Learning

Evaluate Tangible and Intangible Assets

If the numbers initially look good, move on to assess the value of everything you can touch, specifically real estate, equipment and fixtures, and inventory. Pay advisors and consultants to guide you in assessing the assets.

1. **Real estate:** Order an outside professional appraisal of the building and the land. Review deeds, titles, liens, and title insurance, and have them reviewed by your attorney. Have property inspected.

2. **Equipment and fixtures:** Remember, these are used. You can arrive at a fair idea of current market values by asking equipment dealers and searching online for similar items. Scour your area for the best deals, because you do not want to tie up too much capital in equipment that is outmoded or about to come apart. Nor will you probably have the cash flow to repair or replace equipment in the short term. Suppliers and brokers have lots of leads on used equipment, so check with them. If you are not an expert in the equipment field, seek help from someone who is. Expensive used equipment will need to be appraised by an equipment specialist.

3. **Inventory:** Before you close, count the inventory yourself and make sure the boxes are packed with what you think they are. Make certain you specify the exact contents of shelves and cabinets in the purchase agreement. Do not be careless and write in something vague like: "All shelves are to be filled." Specify what goes on the shelves. Once you have made your count, contact suppliers to learn the current prices. If you find merchandise that is

damaged, out of date, out of style, soiled, worn, or not ready to sell as is, do not pay full or even half price for it. *Negotiate*. This is salvage merchandise, and it should have a salvage price tag.

4. **Lease/Location:** How important is location to success? Parking? Walk-in or drive-by traffic? Transportation? Signage? Storage space? Expansion capabilities? Are there deferred maintenance costs?

5. **Website:** Will you have access to all the coding and has it been done properly? Firm's use of Facebook, Twitter, and the company website? Webanalytics available?

Talk to Insiders   There is no substitute for inside information. Every detective takes it seriously.

1. **Suppliers:** Will they agree to keep supplying you? Are there past difficulties between seller and suppliers that you would inherit as the new owner? Are alternative suppliers available? Remember, you may initially be dependent on the suppliers and the relationships which currently exist.

2. **Employees:** Identify key employees early. In small business, success may rest on the shoulders of one or two people, and you do not want them to walk out the day you sign papers. One San Diego women's consignment store owner shared that one of her employees accounted for 50% of the sales in the store and without her the business would be worth substantially less. Usually though business owners will forbid you to talk with employees until the sale is finalized. Thus, discovering who the key players are may not always be easy. Oftentimes, the key players may not even be recognized or acknowledged by the owners. You must honor this request no matter how difficult it may make your decision. If and when you are able to talk with the employees, consider all they have to share with you. Providing incentives to keep key employees may be necessary. Thus, include those incentive costs when determining the final terms of the sale.

3. **Competitors:** Identify major competitors and interview them to learn what goes on from their perspective. Expect some bias, but watch for patterns to develop. Are there price wars? What sets apart each competitor? What sets this opportunity apart from the others? (Review Chapter 5 for competitor research clues.)

4. **Customers:** Who are the major customers? What percentage of sales is generated from the major players? Is their loyalty to the business, the owner, or even possibly salespeople?

Analyze the Seller's Motives

People have many reasons for selling their business. Some of these reasons favor the buyer, and others favor the seller. The following reasons may favor the buyer:

1. Retirement
2. Too busy to manage—seller has other investments
3. Divorce, family problems
4. Disgruntled partners
5. Expanded too fast—out of cash
6. Poor management
7. Burned out or lost interest
8. Ill health
9. Change in lifestyle
10. Wants new challenge
11. Owner incapable of embracing new technology

Beware of the following reasons for sellers wishing to exit their businesses:

1. National or local economy in a decline
2. Specific industry declining
3. Intense competition (from changing distribution, international, etc.)
4. High or rising insurance costs
5. Increasing litigation and costs
6. Skyrocketing rents
7. Technological obsolescence or costly new technology needed to compete
8. Problems with suppliers
9. High–crime-rate location
10. Lease not being renewed
11. Area in decline
12. Employment issues (potential lawsuits, changes in employment law, and attrition of best employees)
13. Proposed changes in international/federal/state/local issues and/or legislation affecting products/manufacturing/employees/distribution/marketing

■ EXAMINING THE ASKING PRICE

Many owners view selling their firm as they would view selling their homes; that is, they are emotionally attached to the business and therefore overvalue its worth. Pride also plays a role: They want to brag about how much they sold out for. If you run into irrational and emotional owners, walk away or turn to your professional team to intervene and develop a fair agreement. In addition to reviewing all past records, you need to assess the future financial outlook for the business, the economy, and the industry. Remember you are buying the future not the past. Take the time to write a complete Business Plan based on the Action Steps throughout the text before you purchase a business. These steps will force you to look toward the future where your new business will operate and where your profits will come from.

Now that you have looked inside and outside of the business, reviewed the firm's past history, and most importantly assessed future potential, you and the seller must agree on a price and terms that are beneficial to both of you. In this section, we provide you with several ways to value businesses, online information, and professionals to guide you. As noted earlier, price is only one element in the negotiations; we encourage you to look at all the issues.

The final sales price of any business is dependent on a multitude of factors. In addition to the actual financials the seller will present, the economy, competition, and motivation of both seller and buyer will play a large role in the final negotiations and pricing. While there are many valuation methodologies presented below, the final price and terms will be determined by what one willing seller will accept from one willing buyer. Your key is to find that spot. In your search for the "right deal" you will need to first look toward outside data for comparable sales information.

Online Sources of Sales and Transactional Data

Online private-firm resources provide financial information on businesses that have been sold and those currently for sale. Most of these databases can be searched by company size, location, sales, income, number of employees, NAICS and selling price. In addition, many of these databases provide information on individual transactions regarding terms. When using comps, please note that individual sales vary greatly as each sale is unique. Thus, it is very hard to compare apples to apples. In addition, sales comps may not be recent and pricing will be affected greatly by either a declining or improving economic climate and availability of financing. Sales comps thus can be used as only one of the benchmarks in your offering price.

Table 13.1 illustrates BizComp's compilation of data on restaurants sold throughout the United States in the $2 to $3.5 million range. To determine comparisons for your area and selected industry, BizComp reports can be purchased online. Please note when reviewing business that are for sale and that were sold, the average multipliers for the firms for sale are substantially higher than the multipliers for those firms that *have* sold. In other words, lots of dreaming on the part of sellers!

table **13.1**

BIZCOMPS® Advanced Search Results

Prepared: 10/28/201112:16:12 PM(PST)

Search Criteria

Total transactions found meeting criteria: 16
Your search results are based upon this criteria:

1. SIC Code ('5812')
2. Country (United States)
3. Annual Gross Revenues ($000s) (2000–3500)
4. Sale Date (mm/dd/yyyy) (1/1/2005–12/31/2006)

Transaction Summary

Statistic	Count	Range	Mean	Median	Harmonic Mean	Coefficient of Variation
Sale Date	16	3/31/2005 - 11/12/2006	N/A	N/A	N/A	N/A
Annual Gross	16	$2,000 - $3,400	$2,386	$2,283	N/A	N/A
SDE	16	87.000 - 550.000	343.25	350.00	N/A	N/A
Sale Price (Excludes Inventory)	16	$300 - $1,600	$792	$737	N/A	N/A
SDE To Annual Gross	16	0.037 - 0.216	0.143	0.158	N/A	N/A
Rent To Annual Gross	15	0.019 - 0.086	0.059	0.060	N/A	N/A
Sale Price To Annual Gross	16	0.13-0.62	0.34	0.35	0.27	0.43
Sale Price To SDE	16	1.26 - 5.23	2.53	2.65	2.20	0.40

Transactions

No	SIC Code	Business Description	Annual Gross	SDE	SDE To Annual Gross	Sale Date	Sale Price	Sale Price To Annual Gross	Sale Price To SDE
1	5812	Restr-Family	$3,000	$295	0.098	1/6/2006	$395	0.132	1.339
2	5812	Restr-Gourmet Foods	$2,100	$225	0.107	6/23/2005	$600	0.286	2.667
3	5812	Restr-Breakfast/Lunch	$2,000	$325	0.163	6/30/2005	$700	0.350	2.154
4	5812	Restr-Seafood	$3,000	$400	0.133	7/13/2005	$505	0.168	1.263
5	5812	Restr-W/Cocktails	$2,000	$275	0.138	7/13/2005	$750	0.375	2.727
6	5812	Restr-Family	$2,042	$87	0.043	7/29/2005	$455	0.223	5.230
7	5812	Bakery Restaurant	$2,366	$88	0.037	3/31/2005	$300	0.127	3.409
8	5812	Restr W/Cocktails	$3,400	$550	0.162	12/6/2005	$1,600	0.471	2.909
9	5812	Restr-Family	$2,000	$375	0.188	11/12/2006	$995	0.498	2.653
10	5812	Deli-Restaurant	$2,650	$504	0.190	2/3/2006	$935	0.353	1.855
11	5812	Fast Food	$2,200	$200	0.091	4/7/2006	$434	0.197	2.170
12	5812	Restr-Italian	$2,500	$541	0.216	4/24/2006	$930	0.372	1.719
13	5812	Restr-Seafood	$2,060	$318	0.154	6/26/2006	$860	0.417	2.704
14	5812	Restr-Family	$2,442	$522	0.214	10/2/2006	$724	0.296	1.387
15	5812	Fast Food-Teriyaki	$2,411	$412	0.171	10/31/2006	$1,500	0.622	3.641
16	5812	Restr-Family	$2,000	$375	0.188	11/12/2005	$995	0.498	2.653

Copyright © 2011 Pacific Services, Inc. All rights reserved.
(888) BUS-VALU [287-8258], (503) 291-7963

Source: Business Valuation Resources, *www.Bvmarket.com* (Accessed February 12, 2012). Reprinted with permission.

Additional sources for pricing reports and evaluation reports can be found at Pratt's Stats, BizBuySell, association websites, business appraisers, and brokers. An illustration of an individual transaction report from BizComp and a detailed transaction report from Pratt's Stats are shown in Tables 13.2a and 13.2b.

First Research offers excellent industry profiles and financials that cover the competitive landscape, products, operations, technology, sales, marketing, finance, regulation, regional and international issues, human resources, recent developments, business challenges, trends, opportunities, and potential questions for business owners. Even if you were considering purchasing a business, but you had little knowledge of the industry—something we would not recommend—such a report would be an excellent starting point for you. Even if you are familiar with the industry, you will be sure to learn additional information from the reports. Available online, the reports cover financial ratios, balance sheets, and income statements for over 200 industries.

Valuation Methodologies

How do buyers and sellers arrive at a fair selling price? They do so first by looking toward comparables; next, by looking at rule-of-thumb pricing (described below); then evaluating income; and looking at assets.

While sellers' initial pricing may be based on emotion, they soon realize that arriving at an acceptable selling price for both parties, will include further indepth financial analysis undertaken by accountants and/or business evaluation experts.

The Entrepreneurial Resource "Interactive Pricing Worksheet on BizBuySell.com" leads to excellent cash requirements' and pricing worksheets. After you have completed your initial financial research, you will be able to use the worksheets to guide you in your financial negotiations. If you are purchasing a specific type of business, more appropriate worksheets may be available; work with your accountants to determine which methods are most appropriate for your industry.

table 13.2a

BIZCOMPS Transaction Report

BIZCOMPS® Transaction Report Prepared: 1/16/2008 12:04:44 PM (PST)

Transaction Details

Business Description	Tour Operator
SIC	4725 Tour Operators
NAICS	56152 Tour Operators
Location	Missouri
Number Of Employees	4

Transaction Data

Sale Date	1/31/2006
Days On Market	252
Ask Price (000)	$650.0
Sale Price (000) (Excludes Inventory)	$550.0
Percent Down	15.0%
Terms on Outstanding Consideration	7 Yrs @ 8.5%

Income Data ($000's)		**Asset Data ($000's)**	
Annual Gross Sales	$1,040.0	Inventory Value	$0.0
Franchise Royalty	No	Furniture, Fixtures and Equipment	$10.0
SDE	$135.0	Value Of Real Estate	N/A

Operating Ratios		**Valuation Multiples**	
SDE/Annual Gross Sales	0.130	Sale Price/Annual Gross Sales	0.529
Rent/Annual Gross Sales	0.01	Sale Price/SDE	4.074

N/A = Not Available
Copyright © 2008 Pacific Services, Inc. All rights reserved.
(888) BUS-VALU [287-8258], (503) 291-7963

Source: Business Valuation Resources, *Bizcomps.com* (Accessed February 12, 2012). Reprinted with permission.

table 13.2b

Pratt's Stats Transaction Report

Pratt's Stats® Transaction Report Prepared: 1/18/2008 12:13:24 PM (PST)

Seller Details

Company Name:	Quality Care Solutions, Inc.
Business Description:	Software and Information Technology Solutions for the Healthcare Payer Industry
SIC:	7372 Prepackaged Software
NAICS:	511210 Software Publishers
Sale Location:	United States
Years in Business:	N/A Number Employees: N/A

Source Data

Public Buyer Name:	TRIZETTO GROUP INC
8-K Date:	1/16/2007
8-K/A Date:	3/27/2007
Other Filing Type:	N/A
Other Filing Date:	N/A
CIK Code:	0001092458

Income Data

Data is "Latest Full Year" Reported	Yes
Data is Restated (see Notes for any explanation)	No
Income Statement Date	12/31/2005
Net Sales	$48,100,000
COGS	$19,423,000
Gross Profit	$28,677,000
Yearly Rent	$1,037,000
Owner's Compensation	N/A
Other Operating Expenses	N/A
Noncash Charges	$1,779,000
Total Operating Expenses	$22,744,000
Operating Profit	$5,933,000
Interest Expenses	$152,000
EBT	$5,822,000
Taxes	$0
Net Income	$7,937,000

Asset Data

Data is Latest Reported	Yes
Data is "Purchase Price Allocation agreed upon by Buyer and Seller"	No
Balance Sheet Date	9/30/2006
Cash Equivalents	$11,372,000
Trade Receivables	$5,681,000
Inventory	$0
Other Current Assets	$3,823,000
Total Current Assets	$20,876,000
Fixed Assets	$2,714,000
Real Estate	$0
Intangibles	$1,605,000
Other Noncurrent Assets	$907,000
Total Assets	$26,102,000
Long-term Liabilities	$1,073,000
Total Liabilities	$21,243,000
Stockholder's Equity	$4,859,000

Transaction Data

Date Sale Initiated:	N/A
Date of Sale:	1/10/2007
Asking Price:	N/A
Market Value of Invested Capital*:	$148,200,000
Debt Assumed:	$1,000,000
Employment Agreement Value:	N/A
Noncompete Value:	N/A
Amount of Down Payment:	$147,200,000
Stock or Asset Sale:	Stock
Company Type:	C Corporation
Was there an Employment/Consulting Agreement?	No
Was there an Assumed Lease in the sale?	No
Was there a Renewal Option with the Lease?	No

*Includes noncompete value and interest-bearing debt; excludes real estate, employment/consulting agreement values, and all contingent payments.

Additional Transaction Information

Was there a Note in the consideration paid? No

Was there a personal guarantee on the Note? No

Terms:

Consideration: Cash in the amount of $147,200,000 and the assumption of the seller's debt in the amount of $1,000,000. In addition to the purchase price of $147,200,000, there was a $5,000,000 holdback (dependent on working capital) and a potential contingent payment of $7,000,000 based upon license and software maintenance revenues for the year of 2007. In addition, the Buyer incurred acquisition costs in the amount of $5,200,000.

Assumed Lease (Months): 55

Noncompete Length (Months): N/A

Employment/Consulting Agreement Description:

Terms of Lease: Future minimum lease payments total $4,617,000 through July 2010

Noncompete Description: N/A

Additional Notes:

EBT includes interest income of $41,000. Net Income includes a tax benefit of $2,115,000.

Allocation of the Purchase Price (allocates cash paid, holdback, and acquisition costs): Tangible assets $24,600,000, Goodwill $91,400,000, Customer relationships $39,900,000, Trade name $900,000, Core technology $9,500,000, Existing technology $6,700,000, Total assets acquired $173,000,000, Liabilities assumed ($15,600,000), Net assets acquired $157,400,000.

Quality Care Solutions, Inc. (QCSI) (the "Company") is a Nevada Corporation that develops, markets and licenses health insurance claims reimbursement, health insurance benefits administration, integrated care management and consumer-driven health care solutions throughout the United States primarily under term licenses. The Company's software products manage the interaction between payors (i.e., insurance companies, managed care organizations, government agencies, self-insured employers, third-party administrators, providers who maintain financial responsibility for healthcare claims and other enterprises that implement health plans and pay the majority of healthcare expenses), providers (i.e., physicians, dentists, medical and dental practice groups, laboratories, hospitals and other organizations that deliver care and services), and patients. This is performed by automating significant portions of the claims, benefit administration and enrollment processes such as analyzing a patient's healthcare plan and related coverage to determine patient eligibility for healthcare benefits, calculating the payor's and patient's responsibility for the claim, authorizing referrals to other providers, and providing products to assist with consumer directed health insurance enrollment and administration.

Valuation Multiples

MVIC/Net Sales	3.08
MVIC/Gross Profit	5.17
MVIC/EBITDA	19.22
MVIC/EBIT	24.98
MVIC/Discretionary Earnings	N/A
MVIC/Book Value of Invested Capital	24.98

Profitability Ratios

Net Profit Margin	0.17
Operating Profit Margin	0.17
Gross Profit Margin	0.60
Return on Assets	0.30
Return on Equity	1.63

Leverage Ratios

Fixed Charge Coverage	53.22
Long-Term Debt to Assets	0.04
Long-Term Debt to Equity	0.22

Earnings

EBITDA	$7,712,000
Discretionary Earnings	N/A

Liquidity Ratios

Current Ratio	1.04
Quick Ratio	1.04

Activity Ratios

Total Asset Turnover	1.84
Fixed Asset Turnover	17.72
Inventory Turnover	N/A

N/A = Not Available

Copyright © 2008 Business Valuation Resources, LLC. All rights reserved. www.BVResources.com^SM
(503) 291-7963

Source: *http://www.bvmarketdata* (Accessed February 6, 2008).

Entrepreneur's **Resource**

PRICING AND CASH REQUIREMENTS WORKSHEETS
from BizBuySell (interactive version online)

Overview of Business Pricing Method

The method used for BizBuySell's pricing calculations is a very basic model that is most appropriate for small privately held businesses. It is not a valuation method, but a simple way of calculating an approximate price for a small business. It is a good starting point in which to begin negotiations.

Calculate the earning power of the business to arrive at the goodwill factor of the business. This is then added to the fixed assets, the inventory and the furniture, fixtures, and equipment (FF&E). This total is the basic price of the business.

Remember, a seller may ask for more than this basic rule-of-thumb price, and the buyer may want to pay less.

Section 1: Adjusted Income and Expense Worksheet

Income (latest 12 months)

Sales	$ _____
Other Income	$ _____

Adjustments to Income. If there are any subtractions from the stated income such as a one-time income item, enter both a note describing the adjustment(s) as well as the dollar amount to be subtracted.

_____	($ _____)
Total Income	$ _____
Cost of Goods Sold	$ _____
Total Gross Profit (Total Income – Cost of Goods Sold)	$ _____
Expenses (latest 12 months)	
Owner's Salary	$ _____
Other Payroll	$ _____
Outside Labor	$ _____
Payroll Taxes	$ _____
Employee benefits (including medical and life insurance)	$ _____
Utilities	$ _____
Telephone	$ _____
Insurance (business only)	$ _____
Rent	$ _____
Travel and entertainment	$ _____
Auto (lease or loan payments)	$ _____
Auto expenses (gas, insurance, etc.)	$ _____
Legal and Accounting	$ _____
Depreciation	$ _____
Interest	$ _____
Advertising	$ _____
Dues and subscriptions	$ _____
Bad debt expense	$ _____
Supplies	$ _____
Miscellaneous expenses	$ _____
Total Expenses	$ _____
Net Profit Before Taxes (Total Gross Profit – Total Expenses)	$ _____

Adjustments to Expenses. Most methods used to arrive at a fair selling price are based on a reconstruction of the business's profit and loss statement. This process goes by several different names—normalizing the statements or adding back to the statements. What these adjustments do show is the true earning power or cash flow of the business. By adding all of the non-essential items not necessary to operate the business and the non-cash items plus the net profit, a more realistic cash flow for the

(continued)

(continued)

business can be depicted. If the business shows a loss, then the cash flow is the add-backs less the loss. Items to consider are:

Owner's salary	$ _____
Travel and entertainment	$ _____
Contributions to retirement and/or medical insurance programs	$ _____
Auto (lease or loan payments)	$ _____
Auto expenses (gas, insurance, etc.)	$ _____
Depreciation	$ _____
Interest expense	$ _____
Any other non-applicable expenses (note below)	
_____	$ _____
Total Adjustments	$ _____
Total Discretionary Cash Flow (Net Profit Before Taxes + Adjustments)	$ _____

Section 2: Assets Worksheet

1) Inventory The inventory is priced at seller's cost and included in the price you will calculate. This means that the seller must provide an estimate of the inventory for pricing purposes. It also means that that the full price will fluctuate as the inventory increases or decreases. It should be noted whether the suggested selling price includes the inventory and, if so, how much. The actual value of the inventory will be determined at the time of closing. If the inventory is of significant value it is recommended that an inventory service be used (consult your local yellow pages).

Inventory at Cost	$ _____

2) Furniture, Fixtures, and Equipment (FF&E) The value of the FF&E is also included in the price you will calculate. It is assumed that the value of the FF&E is the actual replacement value. If you need a rough "rule of thumb" for calculating the replacement value of the FF&E, take the FF&E depreciated value and multiply it by 150%.

Approximate Replacement Value of FF&E	$ _____
3) Discretionary Cash Flow (From Section 1)	$ _____
Basic Rule of Thumb Approximate Selling Price (Cash Flow + Asset Value)	$ _____

Section 3: Business Comparables

Use multipliers from your own analysis and research. (The online version will scan a large database of similar businesses for comparable multipliers.)

Last 12 Months Gross Income (From Section 1)	$ _____
Selling Price Gross Income Rule of Thumb	$ _____
(Gross Income Multiplier [0.00] × Gross Income)	
Discretionary Cash Flow (From Section 1)	$ _____
Selling Price Cash Flow Rule of Thumb	$ _____
(Cash Flow Multiplier [0.00] × Cash Flow)	

Summary: Basic Price Rules of Thumb

Based on all the factors contained in this Pricing Worksheet, the business under consideration has an estimated selling price within the range of the various "Rules of Thumb" developed above and summarized below:

Basic Rule of Thumb (Approximate Price)	$ _____
(Cash Flow + Asset Value)	
Gross Income Multiplier Rule of Thumb	$ _____
(Gross Income Multiplier [0.00] × Gross Income)	
Cash Flow Multiplier Rule of Thumb	$ _____
(Cash Flow Multiplier [0.00] × Cash Flow)	

(continued)

(continued)

Use all three of these figures to determine the approximate price range for the business. The multipliers used should be determined in conjunction with brokers and comps (both within similar industry, size, area, etc.).

CASH REQUIREMENTS WORKSHEET
from BizBuySell Buyer's Toolkit
Use this worksheet to calculate the cash necessary to purchase a business.

Section 1: INITIAL CASH

Total Cash Down Payment	$ _____
Inventory (if not included in purchase price)	$ _____
Other (explain)	$ _____
Total Initial Cash	$ _____

Section 2: EXISTING ENCUMBRANCES (Non-cash, to be assumed)

Existing Seller Loans	$ _____
Equipment Loan	$ _____
Other (explain)	$ _____
Total Amount to be Assumed	$ _____

Section 3: SELLER FINANCING

Non-cash, new loan created to be owed to seller	$ _____
Total New Loans	$ _____
Total Purchase Price (add sections 1 + 2 + 3)	$ _____

Section 4: CLOSING COSTS

Attorney or escrow fees	$ _____
Inventory service	$ _____
Insurance prorations	$ _____
Reimbursement of lease deposits	$ _____
Miscellaneous prorations	$ _____
Other	$ _____
Total Estimated Closing Costs	$ _____

Section 5: STARTUP COSTS

Utility deposits	$ _____
Liquor license fees	$ _____
Insurance costs	$ _____
Taxes, bonds, etc.	$ _____
Legal & accounting	$ _____
Workers compensation	$ _____
Prorations or other closing costs (not included in Section 4)	$ _____
Other (explain)	$ _____
Total Startup Costs	$ _____

Section 6: TOTAL CASH REQUIREMENTS

Total Cash Requirements (add sections 1 + 4 + 5)	$ _____

The above is furnished to assist the buyer in determining the amount of cash necessary to acquire a business.

Source: From BizBuySell.com. Reprinted with permission.

The pricing worksheet helps you to develop three rule-of-thumb pricing methods. These methods—in conjunction with the comparables, advice from your accountants, and knowledge of the seller's motives, the economy, and future of the business—should guide you in your offering price. As a buyer, the most important figures are not those from the past, but rather the future; specifically, what are the earnings and prospects of the economy in the short term and long term. This is why it is so important that you develop a Business Plan for any business you want to purchase. Looking only at past figures may not accurately reflect the potential of the business, which is what you are purchasing.

The cash requirement worksheet will allow you to work with different purchase scenarios to determine your cash requirements for the initial purchase and start-up phase of the business you are purchasing. You need to be careful to have enough cash on hand for day-to-day operations after initial cash and start-up needs are funded. Remember, as discussed previously, positive cash flow keeps you afloat. Do not neglect developing cash flow scenarios before any negotiation.

© Cengage Learning

General Rule-of-Thumb Pricing

The information below from BizBuySell serves as an illustration of rule of thumb pricing for bed and breakfasts and and fast food franchises.

INNS/BED AND BREAKFASTS

Rule of Thumb:

- $50,000–100,000 per guest room
- 3 times net operating income + $20,000–40,000 for aesthetics and task benefits plus value of real estate and furnishings

Pricing Tips and Information:

Income is usually $5,000 to $10,000 per guest room depending on location. Business evolved from stagecoach stops to about 20,000 B&Bs and inns today. Usually an antique house and furnishings, most have private baths now. Operating expense can range from $3,000 to $10,000 per room, depending on occupancy and size of building. What is the comparative value of the underlying real estate? What will the bottom-line return be?

Investment plus a lifestyle business. Cast a wide net when reviewing the rack rates of other lodging properties to establish pricing policies.

Debt service shouldn't exceed 40% of gross room income. Pay attention to building maintenance, marketing, and business records. The better these items are, the more positively you can value the property with business.

FRANCHISED FOODS

This category is dominated by McDonald's, Burger King, Wendy's, KFC, Dominos, Pizza Hut, Arby's, Diary Queen, Taco Bell, and Denny's—others are Subway, Blimpie's, Baskin-Robbins, and Schlotsky's.

Rule of Thumb:

- 1.7 to 2.3 adjusted earnings
- 5 to 6 times monthly gross sales

Asset value + 1 year's adjusted earnings
Expenses as a percentage of gross annual sales

Cost of goods	32–35%
Payroll/labor costs	18–20%
Occupancy Cost	6–7%

Considerations:

Stability of income, down payment & quality of franchisor

Labor costs typically represent 15–20% of gross food sales. Food costs generally run from 28% to a high 40% for red meat on the menu. Pizza shops run about 28–30%. Rent should not exceed 10%.

Check the franchise agreement. Who pays transfer and training fees? Does the franchisor have the first right to purchase the business?

Seller Financing:

5–7 years, however SBA loans up to 10 years can be obtained.

Rule-of-thumb pricing is more difficult to determine with rapidly expanding Internet and technology businesses. Although purchasing and evaluating online businesses is facilitated by the fact that all transactions are usually conducted via PayPal and credit cards. In addition, repeat sales, visits, and marketing efforts are usually tracked by the owner and are easily accessible. If you are purchasing an Internet business, utilize an appraiser and broker who are experienced in evaluating online businesses and who understand the intricacies of source codes, Webmasters, search engine optimization, programming, passwords, e-mail lists, webanalytics, and online security.

Business-Valuation Analysts

Additional evaluation specialists are available as Randall Lane shared in his *Inc.* magazine article, "What's Your Company Worth Now?": "There are two senior certifications for which you should look for when hiring an appraiser, although not every qualified firm will have them. The ASA (American Society of Appraisers) gives out an ASA (Accredited Senior Appraiser), which requires courses, exams, five years of experience, and peer review of reports. The IBA (Institute of Business Appraisers) certifies its CBA (Certified Business Appraiser) in much the same way. Strong recommendations from an expert's savvy, satisfied customers are better than any certificate."

Source: *http://www.inc.com/magazine/20030701/25661_pagen_4.html.(i.e)2%*.

Valuation professionals also may have experience as Certified Public Accountants (CPAs) and complete business evaluations for either the private or public sector. Their backgrounds will include accounting, tax law, auditing, finance, insurance, economics, and investments. Their coursework and experience may also include valuation theory, practical application, and litigation support that allows them to prepare a comprehensive analysis and competent valuation.

The analysts will determine which is the most appropriate methodology to value a specific business, taking into account the financials as well as industry comparisons and economic, business, and market risks. To find a qualified appraiser, contact either of the above associations and your contacts. A good appraiser's fee will be well earned, as the evaluation will be based on facts and figures rather than emotion, keeping you and the seller grounded.

■ PROTECT YOURSELF

Evaluate each business opportunity by the criteria we present in this chapter. When you find a business that is personally and financially a good fit for you, and have completed due diligence, pricing and terms will become the next issue. Your goal is the lowest possible price with the best possible terms. Start low; you can then negotiate up if necessary.

When asked to put down a deposit, place the money in an escrow account, and include a stipulation in your offer that says the contract is subject to your inspection and subject to approval of all financial records and all aspects of the business. Include an escape hatch so that you can get your deposit back—and back out of the deal—if things are not as represented.

One of the best things you can do to protect yourself is to work in the business for a few weeks before signing final papers, with the option to back out if you have a change of heart. One prospective entrepreneur, Sondra, fell in love with a retail photography business. Her business advisor suggested she work in the business for free for several weeks to explore the business further. She discussed the arrangement with the seller. While reluctant, the seller gave in.

After three weeks, Sondra knew that working with fussy children, crabby parents, and stressed teenagers brought her little joy. This was not the business for her. She continued on her search and recently purchased an established tutoring franchise after working there free for four weeks.

Entrepreneur's Resource

Federal Contract Opportunities

FED BIZ OPPS (Federal Business Opportunities)

Do you want to market your product or services to one of the biggest buyers in the world? If so, www.fbo.gov may be your entry into a $500 billion market of which over 20 percent is set aside for small businesses. The government pays its bills and buys literally anything you can think of!

Selling to the government takes persistence. However, if you are willing to learn how to sell to the government through FBO's own website, American Express' Open Forum Government Contracting Crash Course, or through workshops put on by various government agencies, you may find incredible customers. However, patience may be needed as one study found it took active small business contractors on average almost 20 months to land their first federal contract. Thus, once you are established, take time to explore this avenue if the business you are buying has not already. Buying an ongoing business may allow you more ready access into the government market as the firm already has a track record in place.

FBO.gov is the single government point-of-entry (GPE) for federal government procurement opportunities over $25,000. Government buyers are able to publicize their business opportunities by posting information directly to FedBizOpps. "Through one portal, commercial vendors seeking federal markets for their products and services can post, search, monitor, and retrieve opportunities solicited by the entire federal contracting community." The site allows over 600,000 registered small business owners access to a database which can be searched by agency, zip code, state, NAICS code, and set asides (special programs for example: Women Owned and Service Disabled Veteran-Owned Small Businesses).

Offices of Small and Disadvantaged Business Utilization, staffed within government agencies, and Procurement Technical Assistance Centers also offer services such as training seminars, matchmaking, information, and most important—expertise. Reach out!

Obtain a Noncompete Covenant

Once you buy a business, you do not want the seller to set up the same type of business across the street or elsewhere online. Customers are hard to come by, and you do not want to pay for them only to have them spirited away by a cagey seller. So secure an agreement, in writing, that the seller will not set up in competition with you—or work for a competitor, or help a friend or relative set up a competitive business—for the next three to five years. An attorney should make sure all loopholes are closed, with special reference to online competition.

Be sure to specify the exact amount you are paying for the noncompete covenant to assure the IRS will treat it properly.

Determine Whether Bulk Sales Escrow Is Required

You need to determine if creditors will tie up the inventory you are purchasing. If they will, the instrument you will use to cut those strings is a bulk sales transfer, a process that will transfer the goods from the seller to you through a qualified third party. In many states, bulk sales transfer is specified under a series of regulations known as the *Uniform Commercial Code (UCC)*.

If there are no claims by creditors, the transfer of inventory should go smoothly. If there are claims, you will want to be protected by law. Either consult an attorney who has experience in making bulk sales transfers, or arrange for an escrow company to act as the neutral party in the transfer. The quickest way to find an escrow company is to look in the Yellow Pages or online for "escrow". A better way is to ask your banker, broker, or CPA to recommend one. Try to find one who specializes in bulk sales escrows. If you do not transfer the company through a bulk sales transfer, protect yourself by holding funds to pay for unknown debts that might be lurking.

Escrow company A neutral third party who holds deposits and deeds until all agreed-upon conditions are met

Bulk sales escrow An examination process intended to protect buyers from unknown liabilities

Tax Issues

In structuring a business-purchase transaction, both the buyer and seller need to consider accounting and tax implications. As these can vary depending on the type of business and the specific tax issues faced by those businesses, an experienced business tax accountant should be at your side throughout the transaction. Also, an experienced accountant will discover how the business may have legally or illegally reported income in the past and thus help and protect you in the transaction. If lucky, your accountant may uncover possible value within the business that is not being realized due to improper accounting or tax planning.

During the purchase transaction, what may be best for one party may not be best for the other from an accounting and/or tax standpoint. Thus, negotiation and compromise will be necessary to arrive at a fair transaction for both parties. One goal for both parties should be to legally minimize the total taxes paid both during the transaction and in the future. Expertise and cooperation are necessary.

The timing of the transaction may impact the seller's tax situation, and you may need to compromise on that issue as well. In some cases, the seller's accountant may suggest structuring the transaction so payments are made over time to delay the taxable gain. The value added to any purchase transaction through the structuring of the tax implications for both sides may be substantial.

Negotiate the Value of Good Will

If the firm has a strong customer base with deeply ingrained purchasing habits, this has value. It takes time for any start-up to build a client base, and the wait for profitability can be costly.

Some firms have built up a great deal of ill will—customers who have vowed never to trade with them again and suppliers who won't sell to the business. A large proportion of the businesses on the market have this problem. If the amount of ill will is great, the business will have little value; it may be that *any* price would be too high. Ill will is very difficult, and sometimes impossible, to turn into good will. Do *not* assume you can change ill will to good will. It might not happen regardless of your efforts.

A smart seller will ask you to pay something for good will. Thus you will need to play detective and find out *how much* good will there is and *where* it is; and by the time you arrive at valuing the business this detective work should be completed. For example, consider the seller who has extended credit loosely. Customers are responding, but there is no cash in the bank. If you were to continue that policy and keep granting easy credit, you would be sacrificing your source of cash flow. Or maybe the seller is one of those very special people who is loved by everyone and will take that good will with him or her—like a halo—when he or she walks out the door.

You must negotiate the price of good will. Suppose the asking price for the business you would like to buy is $200,000 and that its tangible assets (equipment, inventory, and so on) are worth $125,000. In other words, the seller is trying to charge you $75,000 for good will. Before you negotiate, do the following:

1. Compare the good will you are being asked to buy to the good will of similar businesses recently sold.
2. Figure out how long it will take you to pay that amount. Remember, good will is intangible; you will be unhappy if it takes you years to pay for it. Even the most cheerful good will payments come out of profit.
3. Estimate how much you could make if you invested that $75,000 in T-bills.
4. Consider the time it would take you to attain the same profitability if you were to start a similar business from scratch.

This gives you a context in which to judge the seller's assessment of the value of good will, and you can use the hard data you have generated to negotiate a realistic—and no doubt, more favorable—price. But before you make an offer, discuss with your accountant the potential tax implications involved with good will. Action Step 56 will help you explore both good will and ill will.

■ THE DECISION TO PURCHASE

Too many people purchase businesses emotionally. They buy a business as if it were a home, a car, or a suit. They are drawn to businesses that they think will enhance their image and impress their friends and relatives. Physically attractive businesses are often the worst investments, because image-conscious buyers allow sellers to charge an unreasonable price. The "ugly" or "invisible" business may oftentimes provide the best return on time and investment.

Others view buying a business as buying a *job;* they look at the business as their new employer. Unfortunately, many buyers with this attitude lack the experience to make a good choice and often invest their personal savings or worse their 401(K)'s in ventures that demand 70 to 80 hours per week to operate and pay them less than their 40-hour-a-week jobs did.

If you think you are ready to make your decision, do not do it just yet. First, read the checklist that follows for important details you might have overlooked. Even if you *know* you have found your dream business, complete this checklist and the previous due diligence list before you sign the papers.

ACTION STEP 56

Probe the Depths of Good Will and Ill Will

1. How many products have you vowed never to use again? How many places of business have you vowed never to patronize again? Why?
2. Make a list of the products and services you will not buy or use again. Next to each item, write the reason. Did it make you sick? Did it offend your sensibilities? Was the service awful?
3. After you have completed your list, ask your friends what their positive and negative feelings are about the businesses they patronize. Take notes.
4. Study the two lists you made. What are the common components of ill will? How long does ill will last? Is there a remedy for it, or is a business plagued by ill will cursed forever?
5. Turn your attention to the business you want to buy. Learn as much as you can about the good will and ill will that exist toward the business. Spend as much time as you can with current and past customers, exploring their feelings toward the business. Have fun with this step, but take it seriously—and think about the nature of ill will when your seller starts asking you to pay for good will. Start putting dollars to the good will which truly exists.

The Final Before-You-Buy List

How long do you plan to own this business?
How do you plan to exit this business?
How old is this business? Can you sketch its history?
Is this business in the embryonic stage? The growth stage? The mature stage? The decline stage?
Has your accountant reviewed the books?
Have you estimated sales projections and discussed them with your accountant?
How long will it take for this business to show a *complete* recovery on your investment?
Have you investigated the business and owners thoroughly?
Have you calculated utility costs for the first three to five years? (With increasing rates, this can be a huge surprise. Looking at past years may not reflect future costs at all.)
What does a review of tax records tell you?
What is the compensation and benefits plan for employees?
What are the employees' expectations?

What is the expected employee retention?

Are there any unpaid employees?

Have you interviewed your prospective landlord?

Have you made spot checks on the currency of the customer list?

Who are the top 20 customers? The top 50?

Is the seller locked into fewer than four major customers who control the business?

Have you checked the value of the inventory you are purchasing with vendors and do you have the specific inventory and numbers in writing?

Have you checked the value of the equipment against the price of used equipment from another source?

Does your seller owe money to creditors? If so, who are they? Who is responsible for paying the creditors? (In an asset sale, you would not be responsible.)

Are you buying the receivables? If so, consider only buying those less than 90 days and value accordingly.

Has your attorney checked for liens on the seller's equipment and property?

Do maintenance contracts exist on the equipment you are buying? Has maintenance been conducted as recommended? Can you assume contracts?

Has your attorney reviewed all information and documents and answered all of your questions?

Have you determined how best to structure the purchase and business for tax purposes?

Are you able to obtain adequate insurance coverage at an affordable rate?

Are there any pending or potential product liability issues?

Have you checked to determine if there are any potential environmental issues with hazardous waste, the Clean Air Act, or new or pending legislation that might affect the business?

Is there any pending litigation?

Are you purchasing all brand names, patents, copyrights, logos, trademarks, and so on that you need?

Has the seller signed a noncompete covenant, and has your attorney reviewed it?

Will the key lines of supply stay intact when you take over?

Are you paying for good will but taking delivery of ill will?

Are you getting the best terms possible?

Have you treated your seller fairly?

Have you and your seller negotiated a transition period?

Are you buying an income stream and is it enough to pay your lenders and you?

Are you buying based on the future and not the past?

Do you have enough working capital to support the business for at least 1 year?

Are you passionate about the business and will it help meet your personal and financial goals?

■ PREPARE FOR NEGOTIATIONS

Let us say you know you are ready to buy. You have raised money, the numbers say you cannot lose, and you are ready to start negotiating. If you are an experienced entrepreneur, you already know how to negotiate. If not, read up on negotiating, and take an experienced business negotiator with you. Your appraisals, research, financials and broker's expertise should all be brought to the negotiating table.

First, when it comes time to talk meaningful numbers, the most important area to concentrate on is *terms*, not asking price. Favorable terms will give you the cash flow you need to survive the first years and then move from survival into success. Unfavorable terms may torpedo your chances for success, even when the total asking price is well below market value.

Second, when the seller brings up the subject of good will, be ready for it. Good will is a "slippery" commodity; it can make the asking price soar. It is only natural for the seller to attempt to get as much as possible for good will. Because you know this ahead of time, do your homework, and go in primed to deal. Action Step 56 will help you do this.

PASSION

Parents and Kids Want to Sell Goods
that Do Some Good

For decades, children have hawked candy and cookie dough to friends and family to help fund extracurricular activities and school playgrounds. Now a handful of entrepreneurs have set out to change that paradigm, offering ecologically friendly products for kids and parents to sell for school fund-raisers. From recycled wrapping paper to fair-trade coffee, the business owners are pitching the products as viable fund-raising alternatives for schools.

To date, Greenraising, a firm whose catalog features such products as recycled gift-wrap paper and reusable water bottles, has helped about 500 schools and nonprofits raise money, says Lisa Olson, who founded the Agoura Hills, CA, company last year. The company asks schools or nonprofits to distribute its catalog, from which customers then buy directly. For an item that costs, say, $20, Greenraising keeps $12 and returns $8 to the school or nonprofit.

Some eco-friendly fund-raisers have come to another realization as well: It's the parents who are taking on more of the fund-raising—largely because of fears about their kids' safety—and they'd rather buy and sell products that they want to use themselves.

Green Students Fundraising Ltd., a Toronto-based company, began by selling energy-efficient compact fluorescent light bulbs. But as more mainstream retailers began offering them, Mr. Berman says, the company wasn't able to compete on cost and knew it had to diversify. So, the company started selling stainless-steel water bottles, which got a lift from the recent outcry against bisphenol A, a chemical commonly found in plastic water bottles.

Lots of families also buy coffee, which is something that led eco-minded schools to contact Chris Treter, co-founder of Higher Grounds Trading Co., a fair-trade coffee roaster in Traverse City, MI. Fair-trade coffee is a concept begun a few years ago by small producers that wanted to show consumers their coffee is produced under conditions beneficial to workers and the environment. Schools looking to incorporate lessons about the environment and labor standards will call and ask if they can purchase the coffee for a fund-raiser, Mr. Treter says.

One challenge these companies face is coming up with products that parents and friends will purchase year after year. Both Greenraising and Green Students say they plan to periodically change the items in their catalogs to keep them fresh.

Source: Simona Covel, "Businesses Emerge to Help School Fund-Raisers Go Green." Reprinted by permission of WSJ.com, Copyright © 2008 Dow Jones & Company, Inc. All Rights Reserved Worldwide. License number 3042130539568 and 3042130639424.

In negotiating the purchase price, you will have worked with your accountant, attorney, and banker to determine what steps are best taken to insure the best tax breaks, continuity of the business, cash flow, and ability to continue to grow the business.

Chapter 9 covers financing—read it thoroughly and use it along with Chapter 8 to develop the numbers you will need to negotiate final pricing and terms. As we have stated before, each business is unique, and thus the numbers and financing structures will be unique for each seller and buyer.

When purchasing an established business most buyers are required to put about 30 to 50 percent down. Look to outside lenders or the seller themselves for a combination for the remaining financing. Sellers oftentimes will present several options, one being a full cash sale and the other one with some seller financing. In most cases, a full cash deal will come at a discount as the seller has no risk. For assuming financial risk, the seller will want to be rewarded and sometimes quite well. A thorough primer on seller financing can be found in the Key Points from Another View at the end of the chapter. Many small businesses cobble together financing from themselves, friends, family, seller financing, and bank financing, or any combination of these.

If you have done your background research well and present a thorough Business Plan for the firm you are acquiring to potential lenders and investors, you may find others who believe in you, the business and your vision. Chapter 9 will help you climb the money tree.

If you are short on cash, consider very carefully the additional following options. If another individual has shown interest in the business and is in the same financial position as you, you may consider a partnership. Another option, although one which should be taken very carefully, is to list the assets you are buying and refinance them. Or with the accounts receivables consider selling them to a factoring firm, which specializes in buying receivables at a discount.

Negotiating to purchase a business is an art and includes not only numbers but also the emotions and egos of both the buyers and sellers. You want to close on a deal in which you will be able to cover your expenses, pay your loans, and MAKE MONEY!

■ SUMMARY

There are two good reasons to explore businesses for sale: You will learn a lot by exploring the marketplace, and you may find a gem—a business that will make money right from the start. If you do purchase an ongoing business, remember the reasons you have purchased it: ongoing income stream, name, location, product selection, and so on. You have paid good money for an ongoing business—stick with the formula you have purchased until it proves you wrong. Many people who purchase a retail outlet or online store immediately change store design and product offerings only to fail miserably and wonder why. The customer base one has paid dearly for no longer wants to shop in the "new store"; they were happy with the old, and *that* is why they *were* loyal customers.

Trained and experienced attorneys, brokers, accountants, and bankers are necessary for you to complete a business purchase transaction. Sellers are tied emotionally to their business, and you are tied emotionally to your dream. You need impartial third parties to keep the sale on a rational basis. Accountants will be able to evaluate financial statements to determine where the owners are hiding money, bad debts, employee theft, and countless other problems and possibly even opportunities, which you might never discover on your own.

One of the most important formulas for you to consider in evaluating any business is the return on your effort (ROE):

$$\text{ROE} = \text{hours spent} \times \text{the value of your time per hour}$$

Be sure to purchase a business that meets your income needs. If you pay too much, there may not be enough left to pay yourself an adequate salary or to invest in new equipment, inventory, or marketing. If this happens, you will sour on the business early, and you may not be willing to put in the effort required for success. Be sure you factor in enough working capital for the first few years.

You should be willing to pay a much higher price for a firm with above-average growth potential, versus one that is declining. In fact, you should not buy a declining business unless you believe you can purchase it cheaply, turn it around quickly, or dispose of its assets at a profit.

Keep your checkbook at home as you initially explore and conduct your research. Make sure, once you have entered into any negotiations, that you do not sign *anything* without your attorney's review. If at all possible, work in the business before signing a final purchase agreement. Buy a business that fits your personal and financial needs and goals. Do not fall in love with a business—fall in love with the opportunity and profits the business will provide. Finally, follow your passions.

■ THINK POINTS FOR SUCCESS

- Stick to what you know.
- Do not buy a business you know nothing about. *However*, if you do not heed this warning, research the industry thoroughly and work in the industry or specific business before purchasing.
- Even if your seller looks absolutely honest, check him or her out anyway. Private detectives will run a thorough background check for very little money—a wise and excellent investment.
- Worry less about price; work harder on terms.
- Most good businesses are sold behind the scenes, before they reach the open market.
- Make sure you are there when the physical inventory takes place. Look in those boxes yourself.

- Get everything in writing. Be specific. Do not sign anything without understanding every word and your attorney's approval.
- Buying a corporation is tricky. Have an experienced corporate attorney assist you.
- Be ready to hold your own through the negotiation process, but do not nitpick. Look at the whole picture.
- Do not let a seller or broker rush you.
- Consider the cost involved in starting from scratch versus buying a business.
- Income stream is vital. Be sure it is there and that your loan payments will not take it all away from you.

■ KEY POINTS FROM ANOTHER VIEW

Seller Financing Basics: A Primer for Buyers and Sellers

By Glen Cooper, CBA

Most small business sales are financed, at least in part, by the sellers themselves. Offering seller financing puts the seller in a stronger position to get a better price and a faster sale.

Buyers nearly always need seller financing. Their advisors strongly recommend it. Seller financing acts like a bond for performance to assure that the seller will live up to the promises made to the buyer during the sales process. Seller financing is seen by most buyers as an indication that the seller has faith in the future of the business.

Buyers can expect, however, that sellers who offer seller financing must also act a lot like a bank! A buyer can expect to be asked to secure the loan and sign a personal guaranty.

What Is Seller Financing?

Sellers of small businesses usually allow the buyer to pay some of the purchase price of the business in the form of a promissory note. This is what is known as *seller financing*.

Seller financing is particularly common when the business is large enough to make a cash sale difficult for the buyer (over $100,000) but too small for the mid-market venture capitalists (under $5 million). Seller financing is also common when the business, for any number of reasons, does not appeal to traditional lenders.

A rule of thumb is that sellers will typically finance from one-third to two-thirds of the sale price. Many do more than that. It all depends on the situation; each transaction is unique. The interest rate of the seller note is typically at or below bank prime rates. The term of the seller note is usually similar to that of a bank.

For a service business that sells for $500,000, for example, the transaction might be structured as $150,000 down from the buyer and $350,000 in seller financing. The seller note might run for five to seven years and carry an interest rate of 8 to 10 percent. Monthly payments are the norm and usually start 30 days from the date of sale unless the payment schedule must be modified to allow for the seasonality of the business revenues. The seller note would also usually have a longer term if real estate were being financed.

When a seller offers seller financing, the price the buyer can afford to pay goes up as the amount of the down payment required by the seller goes down.

Why Would a Seller Offer Financing?

Sellers are nearly always reluctant to offer seller financing. Like all of us, they fear the unknown. Despite the advantages of playing bank, it is an uncomfortable role for them. They usually come around to seller financing only after some effort has been made to persuade them.

A seller's first encounter with this issue might be with the business broker. In many cases, but not all, the business broker will bring up the issue. Most business brokers agree that sellers need to offer seller financing, but not all are willing to discuss the issue at the beginning of the listing. When the buyer is unknown, the seller's fear of seller financing is greatest. Some brokers prefer to wait until the buyer prospect is known before suggesting the amount and terms of seller financing.

Offering seller financing up front, however, can attract buyers and speed up the business sale. This is the major issue that usually persuades a seller to offer some type of financing.

Seller financing is seen by buyer prospects as comforting proof that the seller is not afraid of the future of the business. Buyers are more likely to believe a seller's optimistic view of the business's future when seller financing is offered. Some buyers can't or won't look at businesses for sale unless seller financing is a possibility. The more buyer prospects that look at a business, the better the chance a seller has to get an acceptable offer. A seller can also get a better price for a business that has financing in place. As in nearly all buying situations, buyers are often focused on achieving a purchase on terms that allow them to buy with as little 'cash in' as possible, even if the long-run costs are higher.

Seller financing can also lead to a speedier sale. If the seller plays bank, then the deal gets done more quickly. Applying for a bank loan takes a long time for some buyers, and the rejection rate for new acquisition loans is very high—sometimes as much as 80 percent! Banks also move much slower than sellers, even when they do approve a loan. A seller is much more likely to grant a loan request, approve a transaction, and close it as fast as the attorney can get the agreements prepared. Banks take anywhere from 30 to 120 days to approve and close a loan. There is also the possibility that the bankers will give the buyer negative feedback about the business, so that the buyer backs out.

A seller may also see tax advantages and profitability in seller financing, but these alone are not usually compelling reasons to offer seller financing. Capital gains from a small business sale can be reported in installments if seller financing is in place. This stretches out the capital gains tax into future years. Charging interest is also profitable.

Sellers, however, are usually not as worried about tax liabilities as they should be until after the sale has taken place. They also usually believe they can get better interest rates from investments than from seller notes.

Why Should a Buyer Ask for Seller Financing?

Buying a business without seller financing is like buying a home without a homeowner's warranty. The seller note is a bond for performance. This is the major reason a buyer ought to ask for seller financing.

Beyond that, sellers have a strong motive to maintain the business good will if they have a remaining stake in its future ability to pay back the seller note. Without such an interest, sellers may choose to question the new owner's skills and integrity. After a sale takes place, the seller and buyer frequently disagree about the future of the business. This disagreement is a natural outgrowth of their different positions and can become serious. If a seller note is in place, the seller has a motive to temper any irritation caused by the buyer with forbearance.

Even with a noncompete agreement in place with the seller, the fact that the business owes the seller a major amount of money may change the nature of the seller's attitude. Instead of being indifferent or quarrelsome, a seller who is still owed money is more likely to be solicitous and genuinely helpful.

How Is Seller Financing Usually Secured?

Seller financing can be as creative as sellers and buyers want to make it. Most sellers, however, like to add security provisions in as many forms as possible. This can encompass personal guarantees as well as specific collateral, stock pledges, life and disability insurance policies, and even restrictions on how the business is run.

The most common requirement is for a personal guarantee by the buyer and the buyer's spouse. Sellers expect this. If a buyer objects, sellers immediately question their seriousness. A personal guarantee is not a specific lien on any particular buyer asset but is the guaranty that the buyer is placing all assets at risk as needed to satisfy the loan. If the seller note payments are not made, the seller has to proceed with the long process of formal foreclosure. But to satisfy the foreclosure, the seller will have access to all buyer assets. The spouse's signature is required to prevent the transfer of assets to the spouse's name to dilute the buyer's net worth.

Specific collateral is the other common source of security. If no bank financing is involved, the seller wants a first mortgage on any real estate and first security agreements on all personal property involved in the sale. Sometimes, the seller will require that the buyer offer additional security in the form of additional mortgages and security agreements on real and personal property that the buyer owns. If a bank is involved, the seller must usually settle for second place in the line of secured creditors behind the bank.

A third type of security is the "stock pledge." The buyer is required to form a corporation and give the seller the rights to "vote the stock" in case of seller note default. This allows the seller a speedier solution than foreclosure. If the terms of the seller note are not met, the seller can vote to require that payments be made and can even vote to replace management of the business. This threat is usually enough to guarantee seller note payments are not missed.

Life and disability insurance policies on key members of the buyer's new management team are less frequently used methods of adding security to a seller-financed transaction. Term life insurance is available at rates that are relatively low, so this is most common. Disability insurance is used less often because it is more expensive. The seller will typically want the business to pay for these policies up to the amount of the seller note. These policies stay in effect until the seller note is paid.

Restrictions on how the business is run are sometimes added. These restrictions can be in the form of requiring that the new owner preserve certain account or employment relationships, that certain operating ratios of the business are maintained, that the new owner's pay is limited, or that other important operating benchmarks are met until the seller note is paid. Most sellers won't use this form of adding to their own security as a creditor. They usually readily identify with buyer objections to any controls placed on the new business owner.

How Can Both Buyer and Seller Benefit?

If you are a buyer or seller and this all seems a bit intimidating to you, take heart! It's just as intimidating for the other party! Don't lose sight of the fact that this is just a normal transaction between two parties who must each benefit if a deal is to be struck.

Buyers are just looking for a fair chance to buy a job and a reasonable return on investment. They usually have modest goals about what they need to earn for the job they are buying. They are usually fair about how they define what they need to receive as a return on investment for the business risks they are assuming.

Sellers are mostly just ordinary people who once bought or started a business and now want to sell it. They want to get the most they can, but they have learned to be practical. They are usually persuaded by fairness and reasonableness. If not that, then they are at least eventually persuaded by the reality of what's possible.

If you are a buyer, seller financing can offer you better terms and a friendlier lender. You will be able to buy the business quicker because you won't have to wait a month for the bank's loan committee to meet. There are no loan processing or guarantee fees and, usually, no invasive lender controls or audits.

If you are a seller, I would advise an early commitment to seller financing. It will save you a lot of time. You'll get a better price because you'll see more buyer prospects. There are many more buyers who can afford to take a chance when the admission price is reasonable.

Seller financing, properly understood and employed, can really benefit both buyer and seller.

Source: *http://www.bizbuysell.com/seller_resources/seller_financing-basics/17/* (Accessed February 12, 2012).

■ ACTION STEPS

■ KEY TERMS

Image_Source/iStockphoto.com

Investigating Franchising
Reading Between the Lines and Listening

Learning Objectives

- Understand franchising's impact on the economy, employment, and our daily lives.

- Explore franchising as an alternative doorway into business ownership.

- Gain an overview of how the franchise system works.

- Evaluate the pros and cons of being a franchisee.

- Review what the franchisor and franchisee receives.

- Develop techniques for examining franchises and performing due diligence.

- Understand the purchasing process.

- Learn how to evaluate the franchise disclosure document.

- Understand risk–reward factors in buying into a "ground floor" opportunity or an established franchise for sale.

- Review and recognize why franchising may be the right doorway for some and absolutely the wrong doorway for others.

- Recognize the advantages of owning multiple locations and explore the opportunities to enter the franchise market with smaller locations.

- Realize why the true entrepreneur is always the franchisor.

- Explore multilevel marketing.

Your walk-through of opportunities in small business is almost finished. Decision time approaches. If you seriously considered franchising from the beginning, you may have begun your journey through the Action Steps with a franchise in mind, or you may be starting your journey with this chapter.

If you are beginning your search with this chapter, please make sure you also read Chapter 13. The information on buying a business, as described in that chapter, will dovetail with the information from this chapter. Once you have read Chapters 13 and 14, then go back and start through the text with Chapter 1. Writing a Business Plan for a franchise, while different, is equally as important as writing a Business Plan for a venture starting from scratch.

If you have been working through the text, you may now begin to apply those insights already gained through your search to franchising operations. You have spent months gathering data and talking to people with small businesses. You have spent time exploring opportunities that are up for sale and talking to sellers. If you want to write a Business Plan now, you could sit down and do it. But before you do that, however, there is one other doorway to explore: a franchised business.

■ FRANCHISING'S REACH

Did you scarf down an Egg McMuffin on your way to work? Did your kids lead you to YogurtLand or Baskin-Robbins for dessert last night? On your way from Tacoma to Taos, did you stop at an IHOP for pancakes? When you bought your home, did you happen to check out properties with a ReMax agent?

When was your last trip to a 7-Eleven store? When you needed a new transmission was AAMCO there for you? Did an ad by FASTSIGNS lead you to purchase a sign to promote your local concert?

If you want a business of your own but do not feel strong enough to strike out on your own without some support, check out a Play It Again Sports equipment franchise, a Sylvan educational franchise, or any other franchise of your choice.

Franchise Authorization granted by a manufacturer or distributor to sell its products or services for a fee

If you had money from an early retirement buyout package, a minimum of $80,000 in liquid assets and a minimum $250,000 net worth, would you purchase a Papa Murphys' franchise? Would you search the marketplace for an existing El Pollo Loco outlet that still had some legs? Or would you opt for a business offering home care to seniors, with a Home Instead or BrightStar franchise?

Whether or not you personally patronize franchises—although it is almost impossible not to, with the franchise market including burgers, real estate, construction, distributors, printing, tax preparation, equipment rental, travel agencies, childcare, education, cookies, and yogurt to name a few—the franchising game is big.

Franchisor A firm that sells the right to do business under its name to another for a fee but continues to control the business

Franchisee An individual who, for a fee, is licensed to operate a business under the franchisor's rules and directives

According to estimates from the International Franchising Association (IFA), there are more than 3,000 franchisors in the United States, with over 300 lines of businesses and 750,000 franchisees. Over 200 new firms offered franchises during the past year.

A study, prepared by IHS Global Insight on behalf of the International Franchise Association Educational Foundation, showed franchising provided over 8 million direct jobs and almost $800 billion of economic output in 2012. Almost 5 percent of GDP is generated through franchising. View information on specific business lines and their output and employment in Figure 14.1. Please note that 50 percent of franchise employment is concentrated in two areas—table/full service restaurants and quick services restaurants.

Franchising growth has slowed through the recession and Scott Shane, economics and entrepreneurship professor at Case Western Reserve University in Cleveland, issues words of caution for potential franchisees at any time: "Twenty years from their start, less than 20 percent of the franchisers will still be around," and "In fact, of the more than 200 new franchise systems established in the United

figure **14.1**

Franchising Output and Employment

Output Distribution by Sector: 2012

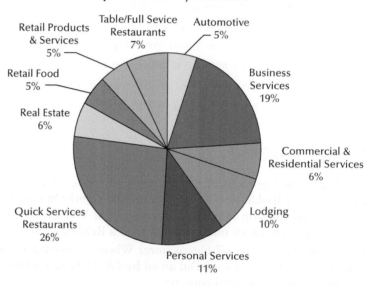

Employment Distribution by Sector: 2012

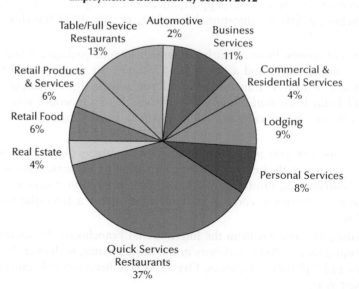

Source: IFA Educational Foundation. Reprinted with permission.

Entrepreneur's Resource

SBA Franchising Information and IFA Franchising Basics Course

Start your research with one of the unbiased sources, the SBA's "Consumer Guide to Buying a Franchise" for the basics. After reading this guide and information from the FTC site, it will be time to explore another franchising viewpoint.

The International Franchise Association (IFA) offers a free, online "Franchising Basics" course to encourage people to explore the franchise door from the franchisor's viewpoint. The course covers how franchising works, what questions you should ask when considering a franchise, what laws and regulations apply to franchising, companies and types of businesses available in franchises, pros and cons of franchising, the variety of franchising forms, and provides additional information resources. The IFA Franchise University's offerings also include $60 courses, such as Dynamic Demographics, Workplace Fundamentals, and Marketplace Fundamentals, which might be very useful as you develop a Business Plan for a potential franchise.

The American Association of Franchisees and Dealers (AAFD) also provides many resources, one being their online "Roadmap to Selecting a Franchise." As an organization, which represents the franchisee standpoint, you will be open to another viewpoint of franchising. Next, check out the blogs and resources in Figure 14.2, which primarily represent the franchisee standpoint.

For the latest updates on franchising from both viewpoints see, *Entrepreneur* magazine and the *Wall Street Journal*. Next, access the plethora of online franchising sites, which generally are sponsored sites, thus providing mostly the positive side of franchising.

Also, contact your local SBA/SCORE and SBDC offices to determine if they have formal workshops on franchising. Many of these are excellent, as they present both the franchisor and franchisee perspectives.

States each year, 25 percent don't even make it to their first anniversary." Franchises offer opportunity, but they should be evaluated as fully as any other business offering; and due to the nature of their long-term contracts, there can never be enough due diligence. Before you begin your search for a franchise we think it is important to first ask yourself if franchising is the right fit for you.

---

figure **14.2**

Online Franchising Communities and Blogs

The sites and blogs highlighted below provide excellent information, and many times very honest feedback, from franchisees and franchising experts. But when searching these sites, be forewarned: *buyer beware applies*. Many unhappy franchisees have axes to grind and attempt to do so through several sites. Also, brokers, who do not always represent both sides of the franchising coin, sponsor many online sites and blogs.

Blue MauMau

The Franchise King

The Franchise Chatter

Franchise Law Blog

The Franchise Pundit

Unhappy Franchisee

Franchise Business Review

If you do not find what you need with the resources above, Google the franchise of your choice and find additional franchisee blogs. Also, search Facebook, YouTube, and Twitter.

© Cengage Learning 2014

ACTION STEP 57

Explore Franchising on the Web

Take a couple of hours to check out the general franchising websites throughout this chapter and others you locate on your own.

1. Take an online franchising quiz at FranchiseHELP or at one of the many sites listed below and throughout the chapter. What are your results? Do you agree or disagree with the results?

2. Jump-start your search with these sources: AAFD, *Franchise Times*, About.com's franchise pages, *Franchise Update*, *Franchise World*, Franchise Business Review, Fran-Data, IFA, Inc., *Wall Street Journal* Small Business Franchising Section, and *Entrepreneur*. Which of these sites did you find most helpful? Why? What other sites did you locate?

3. Check out articles on the top 50 franchises, low-cost or international franchises, or whatever else interests you. What franchises are hot? What franchises are growing the fastest? Where are the happy franchisees? Where are the profitable franchisees? Do not get lost: Keep a list of the good ideas gleaned from your reading. This is your time to explore franchising.

4. After you have found a few franchises you are interested in, visit the resources in Figure 14.2 and read what the actual franchisees are reporting. What did you learn? What surprised you?

FDD (Franchise Disclosure Document) Instrument outlining 23 tightly defined areas required by the FTC to be revealed to prospective franchisees before any fees are paid or contracts signed

■ EXPLORING THE THIRD DOORWAY

Follow the steps throughout this chapter to discover if the third doorway is the right one for you. As the third doorway to business, franchising offers entrepreneurs ready access to an opportunity with business and marketing plans already in place. With personnel, advertising, and purchasing systems, the franchise entrepreneur needs primarily to execute the franchisor's plan and systems.

Before you begin your search for a franchise, you need to find out if you are franchisee material. One good starting point is the SBA's online workbook, "Is Franchising for Me?" If you search the net, you will find many more franchise quizzes online. However, many of the sites where you will find quizzes are sponsored by franchise brokers, who desperately want to sell you on the franchising concept. Keep your answers from Action Steps 2, 4, and 5, along with your answers to the online quizzes and your research from Action Step 57, in the forefront as you continue to explore franchising.

Remember, we have stressed throughout the text that you are not just buying a business but also a lifestyle. As you design your life, you want to know that your financial and personal needs will be met through your business.

If you do not like to follow systems, question everything, and always think your way is better, stop now. When purchasing a franchise you are buying into a system that must be followed exactly, or you may lose your franchise and your money!

Next, review your financial goals, balance sheet, and budget from Action Step 3. If you have decided you need to net $80,000 per year, then focus only on franchises where that is at least the average. Do not make the assumption that you will make a great deal more than the average franchisee. You will also need to determine your net worth and the amount of investment capital you have available before you begin your search, as many franchisors will prequalify you before sharing financial information.

Many franchisors will require a minimum of 30 percent of your own money invested into the business at the beginning. Without knowing how much you can invest and your financial situation, you will not know which franchises you can qualify for, so this must be done before your search begins. In addition, you and your family need to assess your maximum level of investment and the risk level you are comfortable with. In addition, consider the physical hours you are willing to work in your franchise. Also, ask yourself, "How much am I willing to lose?" Recommendations are for franchisees not to invest more than 25 to 50 percent of their net worth in a franchise.

Franchising Basics

The Internet has volumes of material on franchising, but *user beware:* Firms selling franchises develop most of the sites, thus their information and advice can be biased. Thus, utilize many of the sites and steps presented throughout the chapter to gain a broad perspective, along with those in Figure 14.2 and the Action Steps. All of these will help you assess if franchising is a doorway you want to explore further. If it is, the information and sites will guide you in developing the questions to ask as you explore the franchising doorway.

1. **FAQs:** Start with answers to frequently asked questions, which may include: What kind of franchises are available? Is financing available? Who provides the location and who negotiates the lease? How much money can I make?

2. **Terminology and getting started:** If you are new to franchising, you would be smart to acquire some of its specialized vocabulary. Check out the glossary of terms on one of the major sites. One of the key terms you will need to know is Franchise Disclosure Document (FDD), formerly

GLOBAL**VILLAGE**

A Franchise Overseas?

Suppose you like to travel, you speak several languages, and you want to explore business opportunities abroad; suppose you also want to determine if there might be an overseas franchisor looking for U.S. representation. If you latch onto a successful franchise that is already up and running, your chances for success are better. Attend one of the many international exhibitions throughout the world, as shown in the calendar below, or look at offerings at Franchise Direct and Franchise Seek International. If your dreams can stretch across the oceans, opportunities abound.

© Cengage Learning

known as a *Uniform Franchise Offering Circular (UFOC)*, a document provided by the franchisor to the prospective franchisee. Appendix C contains an FDD outline, which you should read through thoroughly early in your search. The FDD will give you a very good idea of how regulated the franchising industry is; it also will allow you to begin to formulate your questions about franchising in general, and for particular franchises as you continue your research. If you find a franchise you would like to know more about, you could ask the franchise to provide you an FDD or go online and purchase those available at several sites. You will need to delve through the FDD in great depth with your franchise attorney before signing any agreement.

3. **A click away, opportunities abound:** The FTC's website offers unbiased information and education with the following excellent primer, "Buying a Franchise: A Consumer Guide," FAQs for Buying a Franchise, and access to the "Franchise Rule Compliance Guide."

4. **Litigious Gloom:** The wonderful world of franchising is not all rosy sunsets and profits made easy. The FTC website leads you to case summaries involving franchisors and creative business developers who landed in court for attempting to sell opportunities that either did not exist or were misrepresented. Franchising is a very litigious business. Attorneys get rich over the problems associated with deceptive or irresponsible franchising. People who buy franchises have to do things *exactly* the way they are laid out in the franchise agreement; they cannot deviate from the system. When people *do* try to deviate from the system, they often end up in court. Franchise agreements are airtight and favor the franchisor.

After reading for several hours, using the websites noted in this chapter as a starting point, locate several franchises that interest you. Visit their webpages and explore their franchise opportunities. In addition, determine their major competitors, and explore their competitors' websites as well. In the past, you had to request a franchise information packet, but most of the franchisors' webpages include most of the information you will need to conduct preliminary research. A few states even have the FDD for franchises available online. Complete Action Steps 57 and 58 now.

Another good way to learn about franchising in a short time is to attend a franchise exposition. You can learn when and where they are to be held in your area by checking websites such as FranchiseHELP. If a franchise exposition is available in your area, complete Action Step 59. If you are adventurous, consider

ACTION STEP 58

Franchise Information Packet

After searching through potential franchise opportunities on the Internet, in magazines, and from the franchise directories, your next step is to request information from selected franchisors that you believe fit your needs.

At this point, you are the prospective buyer. You have the funds, the drive, and the will to succeed. The franchisor has a product to sell, which will be represented by the franchise information packet.

1. Although many franchise packets are available online, some franchisors choose to prequalify potential buyers before sending information packets. Take time to study your desired franchise and also several of their main competitors: Compare Subway to Blimpie's, Home Instead to Visiting Angels, and so on.

2. When you have examined the online packets, write a page or two summarizing what you have learned. Online you will be able to find several Franchise Comparison Worksheets. *Entrepreneur's* one may prove very useful. Focus on the need for the product or service, the uniqueness, and the advantages of the franchise format. Advantages should include economies of scale in advertising and bulk buying, the established goodwill of the name, the franchise track record, and the reputation of the franchisor. Since many franchises are based on fads, be sure to look forward 5 to 10 years.

3. Start to formulate questions for the franchisor and franchisees.

ACTION STEP **59**

Visit a Franchise Exposition

Most major cities have at least one franchise show a year.

1. Go to FrachiseHELP, Franchise Expo, Franchise Direct, or International Franchise Expo to determine if an expo will be in your area anytime soon. If one is available, attend the expo and talk with the exhibitors. Learn what you can from their sales presentations, and attend any free workshops.
2. Collect literature and select several franchises that seem worth a second look. When you come home, go online to see if there are any blogs, references, or success stories regarding your chosen franchise. Compose a brief summary of your findings, and present it to your colleagues. Have your colleagues evaluate the franchise along with you.

Remember, it is usually the small and new franchisors that exhibit at the shows, and their salespeople work on commission. Do not allow yourself to be persuaded; you are there to observe and evaluate, you are not yet ready to buy.

looking abroad for a franchise opportunity or bringing an international idea back to the states. One way to locate an overseas opportunity is to attend an international franchise expo locally or overseas as highlighted in the chapter's Global Village feature.

Keep your checkbook at home while you are exploring, because this is not the time to make any commitments. Up-front franchise fees are very profitable for franchisors, and an incredibly hungry and aggressive force of franchise salespeople can part you from your money quite easily. They know that many people looking for franchises are eagerly awaiting the lift-off of their dreams, and thus many people are vulnerable. Do not be one of them!

Another way to explore a particular franchisor would be to attend their annual convention. Contact the franchisor to determine the date of the next state, regional, or annual convention. If they will not allow you to attend because you are not an owner, consider planting yourself in the lobby of the convention hotel and asking questions of every franchisee you meet. You will no doubt learn a great deal in a very limited time.

■ BEWARE OF SCAMS AS YOU BEGIN YOUR SEARCH

Unfortunately, many scammers and schemers ply their wares to unsuspecting dreamers. We cannot emphasize enough the importance of conducting due diligence and using an experienced franchise attorney throughout the purchasing process. In addition, follow your gut. By reading, talking to franchisees, searching the net for stories, and consulting with your franchise attorney, you will be prepared. No one can eliminate the risk in purchasing a franchise, but you should do everything you can to reduce the risk.

The Top 10 Warning Signs of a Shady Franchise or Business Opportunity

If you're in the market to buy a business, protect yourself by being on the lookout for these ten warning signs of a franchise or business opportunity scam.

1. **The Rented Rolls-Royce Syndrome:** The overdressed, jewelry-laden sales representative works hard to impress you with the appearance of success. These people reek of money—and you hope, quite naturally, that it will rub off on you. (Motto: "Don't you want to be like me?") Antidote: Check the financial statements in the Franchise Disclosure Document; they're required to be audited.
2. **The Hustle:** Giveaway sales pitches: "Territories are going fast!" "Act now or you'll be shut out!" "I'm leaving town on Monday afternoon, so make your decision now." They make you feel that you'd be a worthless, indecisive dreamer not to take immediate action. (Motto: "Wimps need not apply.") Antidote: Take your time, and recognize "the hustle" for the crude closing technique that it is.
3. **The Cash-Only Transaction:** An obvious clue that companies are running their programs on the fly: They want cash so there's no way to trace them and so you can't stop payment if things crash and burn. (Motto: "In God we trust; all others pay cash.") Antidote: Insist on writing a check—made out to the company, not to an individual. Better yet, walk away.
4. **The Boast:** "Our dealers are pulling in six figures. We're not interested in small thinkers. If you think big, you can join the ranks of the really big money earners in our system. The sky's the limit." And this was in answer to your straightforward question about the names of purchasers in your area. (Motto: "We never met an exaggeration we didn't like.") Antidote: Write your Business Plan and make it realistic. Don't try to be a big thinker—just a smart one.
5. **The Big-Money Claim:** Most state authorities point to exaggerated profit claims as the biggest problem in business opportunity and franchise sales. "Earn $10,000 a month in your spare time" sounds great, doesn't it? (Motto: "We can sling the zeros with the best of 'em.") If it's a franchise, any statement about earnings—regarding others in the system or your potential earnings—must appear in the Franchise Disclosure Document. Antidote: Read the FDD and find five franchise owners who have attained the earnings claimed.

6. **The Couch Potato's Dream:** "Make money in your spare time … This business can be operated on the phone while you're at the beach … Two hours a week earns $10,000 a month." (Motto: "Why not be lazy and rich?") Understand this and understand it now: The only easy money in a deal like this one will be made by the seller. Antidote: Get off the couch, and roll up your sleeves for some honest and rewarding work.

7. **Location, Location, Location:** Buyers are frequently disappointed by promises of services from third-party location hunters. "We'll place these pistachio dispensers in prime locations in your town." (Motto: "I've got 10 sweet locations that are going to make you rich.") Turns out all the best locations are taken, and the bar owners will not insure the machines against damage by their inebriated patrons. Next thing you know, your dining room table is loaded with pistachio dispensers—and your kids don't even like pistachios. Antidote: Get in the car and check for available locations.

8. **The Disclosure Dance:** "Disclosure? Well, we're, uh, exempt from disclosure because we're, uh, not a public corporation. Yeah, that's it." (Motto: "Trust me, kid.") No business-format franchisor, with very rare exception, is exempt from delivering a disclosure document at your first serious sales meeting or at least 14 days before the sale takes place. Antidote: Disclosure: Don't let your money leave your pocket without it.

9. **The Registration Ruse:** You check out the franchisor with state authorities, and they respond, "Who?" (Motto: "Registration? We don't need no stinking registration!") Franchisors are required to register in 15 states; in Florida, Nebraska, and Texas, franchisors may file for exemption. Antidote: If you are in a franchise-registration state and the company is not registered, find out why. (Some companies are legitimately exempt.)

10. **The Thinly Capitalized Franchisor:** This franchisor dances lightly around the issue of its available capital. (Motto: "Don't you worry about all that bean-counter hocus pocus. We don't.") Antidote: Take the FDD to your accountant, and learn what resources the franchisor has to back up its contractual obligations. If its capitalization is too thin or it has a negative net worth, it's not necessarily a scam, but the investment is riskier.

Source: Adapted from Andrew A. Caffey, "How To Spot A Scam: The Top 10 Warning Signs of a Shady Franchise or Business Opportunity," *Entrepreneur Magazine*, 12 March 2001. Copyright © 2012 Entrepreneur Media, Inc. 1212:SH

Now that you know how to research the world of franchising, and protect yourself from scams, consider the three overwhelming reasons for buying a franchise: to benefit from name recognition, for brand loyalty, and for a strong business model. Consumers grow to trust brand-name products and services. Look at the items you purchase: Do you drink Coca-Cola? The Coca-Cola headquarters are in Atlanta, but the beverage is bottled by regional franchisees. Do you buy gas at Arco or ExxonMobil? They are franchises, too.

Franchised products and services are predictable and reliable. Many consumers go out of their way to do business with franchisors, and this customer loyalty may be worth paying for. Although, you need to assess whether paying the fees associated with a franchise will leave you with enough profit despite the customer loyalty. Also, consider the advertising fees required by the franchise agreement to keep that branding alive and well. Sales bring dollars, but profits keep you alive.

■ WHAT THE FRANCHISEE MAY RECEIVE

Let us examine what you can expect when you purchase a franchise from a franchisor—that is, when you become a franchisee. During your investigation of franchise opportunities, research each of these issues as part of your due diligence; the answers will vary greatly among franchisors.

Potential franchisees will be provided a Franchise Disclosure Document (FDD) that includes information on most issues. It includes contact information for present and past franchisees in the system. Many potential franchisees have found it difficult to contact past franchisees; with the revised FDD document, you will be able to contact at least 5 to 10 past franchisees to discuss their franchise experience. In addition, the new rules require franchisors to list independent organizations that have formed to represent franchisees. These groups may prove an invaluable resource for you. If there are franchise groups, contact them early on in your search.

New rules force franchisors to disclose litigation against franchisees relating to the franchise relationship within the past fiscal year. Disclosures must be updated within 120 days of the franchisor's fiscal year end. However, dig to make sure no new problems have occurred since the publication of the current FDD and that none are on the horizon.

Unfortunately, franchisors will not be required to disclose the names of their franchise sales brokers, though "gag clauses" signed by franchisees during the past three fiscal years *will* need to be disclosed. Earnings claims remain optional in the document. Only those financial claims that are stated in the FDD can be discussed by the franchisor with prospective franchisees. Finding real numbers is a challenge—but it is one that must be met, as your livelihood depends on those numbers.

If you purchase a franchise, each of the following areas should be explored fully with the franchisor, as well as current and past franchisees. Again, we stress that you also need to compare and contrast the offerings of competing franchisors. We recommend that you explore at least three franchises and their competitors.

Entrepreneur's Resource

Returning from War and Turning to Franchising with VetFran Program

By Olga Khazan

John Turner spent 12 years in telecommunications for the Army, and then a few more working in management positions for companies like NEC Global and Cisco. All along, he knew he wanted to eventually be in business for himself.

"I wanted to build my own company, and I knew the communications field the best," he said. "I realized I could leverage my years of service to get a leg up in the franchise world."

Turner wished to be part of a reputable company with less chance of failure than a standard start-up would have. So in November, he opened a Wireless Zone franchise near Capitol Hill.

"A good franchiser gives you all the tools you need to be successful, and you add your own hard work, determination and confidence," he said. "Anyone who has been successful in the military understands that type of system."

More than one million veterans of the wars in Iraq and Afghanistan will enter the workforce in the next five years. Rather than attempt to elbow

(continued)

(continued)

their way into the tight job market, some veterans are pursuing franchising because it mimics the rule-based system they grew accustomed to in the military.

"Veterans opening franchises is becoming a popular trend," said Joe Sharpe, economic director for the American Legion. "It seems like a good fit for them. It's like starting a business that's already been set up for you."

Several new programs aim to entice veterans to the world of franchising. The International Franchise Association runs one called **VetFran**, which requires that parent companies give veteran franchisees their "best deal" possible — often resulting in thousands of dollars off the initial franchising fee. There are more than 450 companies participating, and at least 2,100 veterans have opened franchises through the program so far.

Some companies go even further — the UPS Store recently announced it was giving away free franchises to 10 veterans who qualify. (Five have already been given out.) In February, CiCi's Pizza announced it will waive the franchise fee and offer a 50 percent cut on royalty fees to all qualified veterans who open CiCi's franchises and hire a veteran manager.

The financials differ, but opening a franchise generally involves paying an initial sum, ranging from thousands to hundreds of thousands, to the parent company, as well as an ongoing yearly royalty.

Some opt to cover the franchise fee by taking out a loan, and the **Small Business Administration's Patriot Express** loan program aims to reduce paperwork for veterans applying for business loans, including for franchises.

Wireless Zone gave Turner 10 percent off his franchise fee. Because of the **Patriot Express** program, he was able to get the rest of the money loaned to him within 60 days.

"Between the treatment that I got from Wireless Zone and the SBA, it made it that much easier," Turner said.

Several veterans emphasized that former servicemen like the structure and guidelines most franchisers provide. Ray Bramble, a former member of the U.S. Army's Presidential Escort Unit, opened an Aire Serv in Front Royal, VA. He previously owned a heating and air conditioning business, but he said he prefers the cut-and-dry franchising world. Aire Serv's head offices tell him the best equipment cost ratios, advise him on when to spend advertising dollars and train his technicians in customer service.

"In the military, if someone says, 'If you do this, this is the result you're going to get,' I see no reason to do it any different," he said. "I was successful with my own company, but not as stable as I am now."

Don't Skimp on Research

Franchising isn't always an easy path, however. Sharpe, from the American Legion, said veterans need to be careful which franchise organizations they buy into because not all companies are up-front about the returns a franchisee can expect.

Sean Kelly, a franchise consultant and publisher of the site UnhappyFranchisee.com, said franchising is a good path for veterans—as long as they find the right franchiser. Kelly has heard reports of high failure rates with some companies.

"They need to take a look at the franchise disclosure document that's provided to them — look at how many lawsuits have there been and call other franchisees," he said. "There are good franchises, bad franchises and really terrible franchises."

Sinclair also suggested veterans who want a franchise business start laying the groundwork early. "If you want to get out of the military, have a plan," he said.

Source: Olga Khazan, "Returning from war and turning to franchising," 2 March 2012. From The Washington Post, © 2012 The Washington Post All rights reserved. Used by permission and protected by the Copyright Laws of the United States. The printing, copying, redistribution, or retransmission of the Material without express written permission is prohibited.

Below you will find descriptions of the many benefits you may receive as a franchisee, as well as important areas to research in your quest for a franchise.

1. **Brand-name recognition:** If you ask the right questions and pick the right franchise, the marketing boost you receive from the name of your franchise will be worth the cost. This is truly a major portion of your up-front fees and you should be convinced you are getting what you pay for.

2. **Immediate, brand-loyal customers:** Determine if the franchisor has been operating in good faith and providing good products and services. Competition today is much stiffer and customers tend to be much less brand-loyal. Due to extensive discounting and couponing in the marketplace, one cannot count on the brand loyalty as in the past. Thus, you need to be realistic when completing your projections based on past sales. Also, with social media, a franchisor's reputation can be sullied very quickly; this can affect the customer brand loyalty and thus sales of all franchisees.

3. **Support:** Corporate support services may include site selection, employee training, inventory control, vendor connections, a corporate-produced Business Plan, and more. Never underestimate the importance of associating with other franchisees. They will often mentor and guide you, and you will have people to benchmark your numbers with. Many franchisees band together and form independent associations in addition to the formal franchisor networks that exist. You want to join a franchise where the franchisor is invested in the success of their franchises (and the people running them) and not strictly focused on selling them. We cannot stress enough the importance of talking to current and past franchisees to determine their experiences with the franchisor and the system.

4. **Training:** The franchisor will teach you the business, in anywhere from two days to six weeks, and may offer additional training as needed. Training may come at additional cost, so determine what is covered; be sure to inquire about training costs including materials, housing, airfare, and meals. Also, determine if there is ongoing training and if so, at what cost.

5. **Money:** The franchisor may also provide direct financing or assistance in locating and acquiring funds. Some franchises have relationships with large lenders, making financing readily available for qualified buyers. Even if the franchisor offers financing, review other financing alternatives to determine which option will be best for you. Some franchisors are also preapproved with specific lenders and the SBA. During the recession, franchisors have discovered the need to become heavily involved in assisting franchisees in obtaining reasonable financing.

6. **Planning:** You are buying a proven Business Plan, although if you are purchasing a franchise start-up, this may not be the case. You are buying a system, so make sure the system is in place and is profitable. We suggest you complete your own Business Plan for your specific site/area in conjunction with the franchisors. Adapt the Action Steps throughout the text to complete your plan.

7. **Bargains:** Collective buying power may bring economies of scale in purchasing goods, services, and promotion. One complaint of franchisees is that franchisors do not always pass these savings down. The franchisor thus may make a profit not only on the royalties but also on the goods sold to you.

8. **Psychological handholding and field visits from the franchisor:** Be sure to inquire, because support offered varies greatly among franchisors and even within areas. Spend time exploring these issues extensively with current and past franchisees. Too many visits can be overwhelming and make you feel like you are constantly under watch and too few visits provide scant assistance and support. Find out who actually conducts the visits and if they have any franchise experience themselves.

9. **Assistance in site selection and layout and design:** Large franchisors spend millions on research in these areas. Also, they may provide help in negotiating leases and purchases and their years of expertise and experience may prove invaluable. In addition, the clout they carry in the marketplace may allow you access into a mall or airport kiosk, which you might not be able to accomplish on your own.

10. **Standardized and pretested products:** Hopefully, your franchisor pretests all of the products and services they offer to you. In addition, you want to look for franchisors, which constantly are abreast of changes and react promptly by offering new services or products to a changing market. In such a dynamic business environment, we think this is key to purchasing any franchise. For the franchisor that cannot pivot and make changes quickly and within financial reason, the franchise and the franchisees will not survive. Discuss with franchisees how the franchise has dealt with the changing economy, new product developments, and target market needs.

11. **Promotional materials:** Websites, mailings, advertisements, flyers, store displays, and so on are often offered. Discuss with your franchisor the cost and requirements of purchasing such materials. Look into how social media is being handled by the franchisor. You want to know that they are monitoring and protecting the brand and have developed policies for their franchisees.

12. **Area or master franchises:** These offer you the opportunity to purchase an area and the responsibility to build the area with additional franchisees. Many entrepreneurs with strong sales and managerial skills have found riches with area franchises. Many franchisees own 20 to 100 franchise locations under one umbrella organization, and many successful franchisees own multiple franchise names as well. You may also want to investigate if current franchisees are offered new opportunities and resale franchises for sale first.

13. **Assistance of a store-opening specialist:** An experienced team of specialists may help effectively launch your business franchise with a grand opening event. Determine the costs involved and if any financial assistance is available?

14. **Operations manuals:** Ask to review these to see if they cover the material you will need. They can be minimal to extensive. If you are paying for expertise, the operations manuals should provide that expertise and hopefully help you operate an efficient business. You are purchasing a system—make sure it exists!

15. **Sales and marketing assistance:** If you are purchasing a service franchise, make sure the franchisor has developed a marketing system for prospecting for clients, sales presentations, and closing methods.

16. **National or regional advertising with single-message strategy:** Continuity of message is essential. Franchisors that flip-flop messages lose customers, and your success may depend on national advertising. Confused customers will fly the coop.

17. **Territory protection:** You will often be offered a certain territory or area in which to operate. Some franchisors do not offer protection and others provide only limited protection. Discuss this with the franchisees as well as the franchisor. Company owned stores sometimes compete with franchisees and this can pose a major problem.

18. **Software packages:** Integrated accounting, financial, personnel, marketing, and operating software may be available, free or for a fee. Check with the franchisor to determine who will update and service these packages and at what cost.

In addition to the areas you need to explore above, Figure 14.3 offers a very detailed list of questions to ask current and past franchisees, and you'll also find

Area or master franchise Business arrangement in which a franchisor sells the rights of an area or territory to a franchisee, who is normally required to sell or establish and service a specified number of franchises in its area within a specified time period

figure **14.3**

Talk to Franchisees Before You Join the Club!

By Jim Coen for http://franchisepundit.com

Being well informed at the start will improve your odds of success, of course, just as it does in any new job experience. The franchisees are the ones who can tell you the real deal: how well sales strategies hatched by the franchisor really work, what your day will be like, and when you might expect to break even, for example.

Before calling any franchisee you should have read the FDD, which will give you a wide range of information about the franchise. Some franchisees will have good experiences to report; others may preach doom and gloom.

Suggested Questions for Franchisees:

- How has the franchisor responded to your calls for support about business operations or any other general questions you may have had?
- Do you feel the franchisor cares about your success and is willing to help you as needed?
- How would you describe your overall franchisor/franchisee relationship?
- Did you receive assistance in site selection, lease negotiations, build-out and permit processes, or any other areas unique to the opening of the business?
- What happens in a typical day?
- What will go wrong?
- How long did it take for you to realize a return on investment?
- What are your approximate earnings, and are they in line with your expectations?
- Did the franchisor adequately estimate the amount of operating cash that you needed?
- Was the training the franchisor provided thorough, and did it sufficiently prepare you to run this business?
- Were there any hidden fees or unexpected costs?
- Is your territory big enough to hit your goals?
- Are there restrictions on the products you sell and use in your business?
- Are you required to use designated vendors?
- Does the franchisor advertise as much as it said it would?
- What type of business experience, education, and skills did you possess before buying this franchise?
- Why did you select this particular franchise system over others in the same type of business?
- Did the training only cover the operating system, or did the training prepare you to compete with other businesses providing similar products or services?
- Did you encounter any problems with the franchisor, the site, or establishing your business, and how did the franchisor respond to problems?
- What are your sales patterns like? Are they seasonal? If so, what do you do to make ends meet in the off-season?
- Are there expansion opportunities for additional franchise ownership in this system?
- Knowing what you know now, would you make this investment again?
- What are your thoughts on this industry, the products, and/or services available, and what trends do you see happening for the future?
- Do you have any issues or concerns with the franchise agreement? Were there any clauses that stuck out over others that may impact your relationship with the franchisor?
- Has the franchisor responded to any of your ideas about improving the franchise system?
- Are there any other franchisees or former franchisees you recommend I contact?

Questions to Ask Former Franchisees:

- Why did you leave the franchise system?
- Did the franchisor cooperate in helping you sell your franchise?
- If there was a termination or non-renewal, did the franchisor explain why and provide a reasonable opportunity for you to cure the problem?
- Would you consider buying a franchise from a different franchisor?

Remember, no one can predict how you will fare or whether you'll enjoy the business, but you need to know the mood and understand the mindset of the existing owners before you join their club.

Source: Jim Coen, "Talk to Franchisees Before You Join the Club!", 16 May 2007, from *http://franchisepundit.com/index. php/2007/05/16/talk-to-franchisees-before-you-join-the-club* (**Accessed February 1, 2012**).

additional questions in the Action Steps. Recognize that although the FDD of each franchisor spells out in detail what the franchisee receives and what is expected and legally required of the franchisee and franchisor, spending time with franchisees will tell you the reality and help you interpret the details of the FDD. By law, you must receive a copy of the FDD 14 days before you are asked to sign any contract or before any money changes hands. Please note that the contract you sign is a *long-term commitment* and should be addressed as such; do not sign a contract before extensive investigation and review by an experienced franchise attorney.

■ WHAT THE FRANCHISOR RECEIVES

Franchisors earn money in several ways:

1. Franchisors collect a one-time, up-front, nonrefundable initial franchise fee for the rights to use their name and system. This fee may range from $3,000 for a small service firm to well over $1.5 million for a well-established name, such as that of a hotel, auto dealership, or major restaurant. The franchise fee, paid upon signing the franchise agreement, usually covers 5 to 10 years, with some agreements up to 20 years. If any additional fee is due for subsequent renewal periods, it will be stated in the franchise agreement. Discuss with fellow franchisees past experience with renewals.

2. Royalty fees, which range from 2 to 15 percent of *gross* sales, are collected. Average royalty fees are 3 to 6 percent.

3. Additional advertising and promotion fees of 2 to 5 percent of annual gross sales will be directed primarily to national advertising, although a lesser amount may be allotted to local or regional advertising. Even if your franchise is not profitable, you *will* still be paying all of these fees.

4. Franchisors may profit on items they sell to franchisees. Delve into this area in depth.

5. Franchisors may make additional income through the sale of training materials, computer systems, and fees for training classes.

> **Franchise fee** One-time, up-front charge paid to franchisor

> **Royalty fee** Ongoing obligation to pay a franchisor a percentage of *gross* sales; may or may not include advertising fee

Read through Item 11 of the franchisor's FDD to understand what you are paying for, and talk to franchisees to make sure the franchisor is delivering on their promises. Franchisors may or may not pass on the volume rebates they receive from suppliers to their franchisees. Many independent franchisee organizations have negotiated with franchisors on this point over the years.

Some of the fees *may* be open to negotiation—especially with a new franchisor. For example, it might be possible to delay the royalty fee for six months or until the franchise is profitable. It is always a good idea to ask for concessions and for those concessions always to be made in writing. Advice from your attorney and accountant can provide back-up data to reinforce your negotiating points. Determining potential earnings when purchasing a franchise is challenging. Review Figure 14.4 and *dig as deep and as long as it takes to assure yourself that the franchise you want to purchase will support your financial goals.*

■ ADDITIONAL FRANCHISEE ISSUES AND CONCERNS

Note the following pitfalls that plague franchising in general, along with the concerns in Figure 14.5:

1. Intense competition with franchisors of fast-food outlets, quick-printing shops, and service businesses often oversaturate markets; this causes encroachment, which results in many failures. Talk with current and past franchisees concerning this extremely important point. Some very successful franchisees have found their sales and profits have plummeted when faced with competition from within their own organization, not only from new franchisees but also from company-owned stores. More and more organizations also are migrating sales to the Internet, and you need to understand how this will affect local stores.

2. Multilevel distributorships and pyramid sales schemes oftentimes only benefit the promoters.

> **Encroachment** Entry into another's territory

figure 14.4

Earnings Potential: Evaluate in Depth

You may want to know how much money you can make if you invest in a particular franchise system. Be careful. Earnings information can be misleading. Insist on written substantiation for any information you may receive that suggests your potential income or sales.

Franchisors are not required to disclose information about potential income or sales, but if they do, the law requires that they have a reasonable basis for their claims and that they make the substantiation for their claims available to you. When you review any earnings claims, consider:

Sample Size. Say a franchisor claims that franchisees in its system earned $50,000 last year. The claim may be deceptive if it doesn't represent the typical earnings of franchisees. The disclosure document should tell the sample size and the number and percentage of franchisees who reported earnings at the level claimed.

Average Incomes. A franchisor may claim that the franchisees in its system earn an average income of, say, $75,000 a year. Average figures tell very little about how individual franchisees perform. An average figure may make the overall franchise system look more successful than it is because just a few very successful franchisees can inflate the average.

Gross Sales. Some franchisors provide figures for the gross sales revenues of their franchisees. These figures don't really tell about the franchisees' actual costs or profits. An outlet with high gross sales revenue on paper may be losing money because of high overhead, rent, and other expenses.

Net Profits. Franchisors often do not have data on net profits of their franchisees. If you get net profit information, ask whether it includes information about company- owned outlets; they often have lower costs because they can buy equipment, inventory, and other items in larger quantities, or they may own, rather than lease, their property.

Geographic Relevance. Earnings may vary with geography. If it's reported that a franchisee earned a particular income, ask about the franchisee's location. The disclosure document should note geographic or other differences among the group of franchisees whose earnings are reported and your likely location.

Franchisees' Backgrounds. Keep in mind that franchisees have different skill sets and educational backgrounds. The success of some franchisees doesn't guarantee success for all.

Reliance on Earnings Claims. Franchisors may ask you to sign a statement— sometimes presented as a written interview or questionnaire—that asks whether you received any earnings or financial performance representations during the course of buying a franchise. If you heard or got any earnings representations, report it fully during an interview or on a questionnaire or other statement. If you don't, you may be waiving any right to contest the earnings representations that were made to you and that you used to make your decision to buy.

Financial History. The disclosure document gives important information about the company's financial status, including audited financial statements. You can find explanatory information about the franchisor's financial status in notes to the financial statements. Investing in a financially unstable franchisor is a significant risk; the company may go out of business or into bankruptcy after you have invested your money.

It's a good idea to hire a lawyer or an accountant to review the franchisor's financial statements, audit report, and notes. They can help you understand whether the franchisor:

- Has steady growth
- Has a growth plan
- Makes most of its income from the sale of franchises or from continuing royalties
- Devotes sufficient funds to support its franchise system

Source: FTC Consumer Guide to Buying a Franchise, *http://www.ftc.gov/bcp/edu/pubs/consumer/invest/inv05.shtm* (Accessed February 4, 2012).

3. Typically, current franchisees are offered new locations before they are offered to outsiders, meaning that the best opportunities are seldom offered to outsiders. Rarely is a new player offered a sure thing. New players may be offered those locations that have already been passed over or franchises that are being resold.

4. Termination clauses may be ambiguous. Thoroughly understand Item 17 in the FDD before proceeding. Failure is a possibility, so consider the financial consequences before signing. Termination and renewal clauses should be reviewed in depth with your attorney.

5. "Franchises that have closed or been sold back to the franchiser in the past five years of more than 5 to 10 percent in one year could mean many

figure **14.5**

Red Flags and Early Warning Signs

By W. Michael Garner, Attorney

The points listed below reflect factors that have arisen with respect to franchise sales that in many instances have proven to be troublesome. No one factor necessarily should stop you from buying a franchise, in and of itself, but if you find one or more of them, you should proceed with caution. These points do not constitute legal advice, which you can only get from a competent franchise lawyer.

1. Does the franchisor or its representatives or brokers talk about how much money you can make, or show you illustrations of how much money you can make? Those illustrations and statements, by law, should be only in the FDD. There are strict regulations on what a franchisor can say.

2. Does the franchisor suggest or point to particular franchisees that you should speak to in order to get an idea of how the franchisees are doing? Sometimes franchisors "cherry pick" franchisees that will only say good things. You should be wary if the franchisor has "cherry picked" the franchisees for you to talk to. The FDD should have a complete list of existing and former franchisees. You should be free to talk to any franchisee.

3. If the franchisor has not operated at least one company-owned store for at least three years, you should be cautious. It takes that long to work out kinks in the system.

4. Are you required to obtain product from only one source? Requirements that you purchase from a single source can drive prices up and quality down.

5. Does the franchisor have any history of bankruptcy or a recent and serious history of claims of fraud? You can find this information in the FDD. If so, you should investigate further.

6. Has the franchisor had experience in your particular geographic area, or is it on the other side of the country? Franchisors without experience in one area may not function well in another part of the country.

7. Has the franchisor had experience with franchisees or company-owned stores in the type of demographic that you are located in? If you are in a densely populated urban area and the franchisor's experience is in suburban locations the franchisor may not have the experience you need.

8. If you are planning to use retirement money—401(K) or IRA money—to purchase and finance the franchise, you should probably stop and re-evaluate. Even if the risk of failure is very small, the consequence of failure—losing your retirement—is disastrous. Don't do it unless you are extremely confident that it will work out.

9. New business, absentee owner. If you are planning to buy a franchise as an investment and to have it run by third-party managers, you should proceed with extreme caution. The model of an absentee owner who "supervises" the business is one that may work when the owner has come up through the ranks and actually done hands-on management in the business for a number of years. Especially if the franchise is new, or the franchisee is going to be the owner's first business venture, absentee ownership can be a recipe for disaster.

Source: "Red Flags and Early Warning Signs" retrieved from *http://franchisedealerlaw.com/resource-redflags.html* (Accessed February 3, 2012). Reprinted with permission.

franchisees have become disgruntled or unprofitable," according to Kelly Spors, small-business writer for the *Wall Street Journal.* Always interview several franchisees who have left the fold.

6. Litigation, which is contained in the FDD, should be a concern; look closely at this FDD element. It can be a warning signal or a flashing red light. Also, your research on the Internet may reveal potential litigation.

7. Brokers, with very little regulatory control, sell franchises, and buyers need to recognize that these brokers are compensated by the franchisor and thus may have the franchisor's best interest in the forefront, not the buyer's. See Key Points on for more information on this vital subject.

8. Legal recourse against the franchisor may be difficult due to FTC laws and airtight contracts.

9. Royalties are based on gross sales, not net profits; if franchisors require you to sell specials at very low prices, you may find yourself losing a great deal of money on those sales. Tough times lead to low prices, price wars, and lower profits. For example, Smart Money evaluated a Baskin Robbins 31 Cent Scoop Night and found franchisees reported they lost roughly $1.45 a scoop! Subway's $5.00 Footlongs and McDonald's Dollar Menu have also proven financially challenging for a number of their franchisees.

Voluntary chain Organization (consortium) formed by individual wholesalers or retailers to gain purchasing power and other economies of scale

ACTION STEP 60

Investigate Franchisors and Franchisees

Once you have completed basic research through secondary sources and online research, it will be time to reach out directly to the franchisees and franchisors. Make sure you have read through the franchise packet and if possible, the firm's FDD before you venture out. If you do not have the firm's FDD, read through the FDD overview in the appendix. Use the questions throughout the chapter, especially those in Figure 14.3 and the questions that follow, as you explore franchising by interviewing franchisors and franchisees:

1. **Franchisors:** Leave your checkbook at home and interview at least three franchisors. Here are some questions to start you off:
   What is included in the franchise fee?
   What is the duration of the agreement?
   How can the agreement be bought back?
   What separates the top performers from the lower performers?
   What are the franchises long-term goals and plans?
   How are you dealing with social media and your franchisees?
   Can you give me a few examples of how you handled failing franchisees?
   What are the royalty fees and other assessments?
   What level of training and service can I expect?
   Under what circumstances have you terminated franchisees or not renewed leases?
   Is the territory well defined?
   Under what circumstances can the franchisor change the territory?
   What is the turnover rate of the franchisees?
   Are you planning any major technology/equipment upgrades? If so, what costs will be involved?
   How much help can I expect with advertising and promotion?
   What skills do you think are necessary to be successful?

(continued)

10. Freedom of association amongst franchisees may be discouraged by franchisors. Thus, look for a franchise that believes in the strength and success of their franchisees and encourages its franchisees to grow profitably together.

11. Noncompete clauses may be part of your contract. If you work hard but choose to terminate your contract or are terminated by the franchisor, you may not be able to compete as an independent business owner in a similar business.

12. In 38 states, franchisees have no "private right of action" and thus are required to go to the government if the franchisor violates FTC rules.

13. Beware of "ground-floor" franchise opportunities; it is risky to be an early franchisee. A franchisor offering such an "opportunity" would be experimenting with *your money.* You want to buy a recognized brand name, a proven Business Plan, excellent field support, and experience that demonstrates the particular franchise will work in your location. Many services and products do not transfer easily to another part of the country. A Honey Baked Ham franchisee was surprised to find sales in his Arizona franchise did not replicate those of the Southern state franchisees he had spoken with. Upon opening, he discovered that people loved the product in the West, but primarily for holidays; whereas franchisees in the South were able to capture more consistent sales throughout the year.

14. Voluntary chains such as True Value and Ace hardware stores are often a more desirable option to purchasing a franchise. Members of **voluntary chains** remain independent and pay no royalty or franchise fee. Look for more such organizations in the near future.

15. The management and owners of the franchise should be *thoroughly* investigated as occasionally new franchisors have questionable backgrounds. Hiring professionals to conduct research will be money well spent. Do *not* neglect this step.

Complete Action Step 60 to expand your franchising knowledge. You may find your dream business! As you continue exploring franchises, ask if you can work in one of the franchises for one to two weeks to get a feel for daily operations, responsibilities, managing employees, and following rules. You may not be comfortable operating by the rules and regulations set down by franchisors; many entrepreneur-types are not. Nonetheless, it makes good sense to check out franchise opportunities—especially those in your selected industry—because the search will give you a better picture of the marketplace and your franchise competition if you decide to venture out on your own.

In Chapter 13 we presented checklists for evaluating established businesses you are considering. Many of those questions are applicable to new and established franchises as well. The answers to all of the questions presented in Chapters 13 and 14 will help you generate franchise profiles and make an informed and wise decision. In franchising, you are not only investigating the actual franchise you are purchasing, but the franchisor as well. In fact, if purchasing from an area developer you should complete due diligence on them as well. After reading the entire chapter, complete Action Step 61, which summarizes your thoughts and research.

Once you have selected a franchise, they will vet you just as you have vetted them. As you have asked them difficult questions, they too should ask you hard questions. Remember you need to fit into their organization and they want to make sure you are a good fit. Do not be surprised if they ask you to take personality tests to help with their assessment. While you are determining the strength of their organization, they will be analyzing your personal and financial strengths as well. If both parties believe there is a good fit, you will be asked to come to a Discovery Day, where potential franchisees are invited to headquarters to meet with the various departments and for both parties to evaluate if they should move forward.

Legal Assistance

If after all of your research you want to move forward and have not yet hired an attorney, *now* is the time. We cannot emphasize enough the importance of using an experienced franchise attorney. To locate a franchise attorney, contact the International Franchise Association's Council of Franchise Suppliers or AAFD, and network with colleagues and other franchisees. If you have any friends or family members who own franchises, ask them to also review the FDD as well. They may spot issues and concerns based on their franchise experience, which may save you money and heartache.

According to Kay Marie Ainsley and Michel H. Seid, franchise consultants, "Regardless of what has been said or implied during your discussions with the franchisor, or with other franchisees in the system, as you go through the approval process, what is written in the contract *will* rule your relationship with the franchisor. The value of having an attorney review a franchise contract lies not in their ability to beat up the franchisor and 'get a better deal' for you, but in their ability to make sure you fully understand what you are getting into when you sign the contract. They can explain the different provisions, compare the provisions in the contract you are about to sign to what are considered 'best practices' in the industry, and tell you how the courts have interpreted similar provisions in other cases. *Everything* in the franchise agreement is important."

■ PROCESS INVOLVED IN PURCHASING A FRANCHISE

If you have explored and investigated franchising and believe it is the right fit for you, and if you have worked through the Action Steps, the decision process truly begins. After contacting the franchise and prequalification, you will need to complete your due diligence (as suggested above) by researching the franchisor, franchisees, and profit potential. Continue by completing Action Step 60. Remember the franchisor performs due diligence on you as well. You want to buy a franchise, which is "awarded" to you, not sold to you.

When analyzing the franchise packet, recognize that you are reading primarily advertising to sell you on the franchise. Try to read between the lines. Many of the packets will include an application for additional information, such as Subway's shown in Figure 14.6. We have used Subway as our example because we know there are few readers who are unfamiliar with their sandwiches and salads, which are served in more than 35,800 outlets in over 80 countries.

If the franchise is large, a local sales manager or area developer will contact you after reviewing your application. You will meet to discuss capital requirements and available locations further. Spend time and ask the questions we have presented throughout the chapter and those that have arisen from your discussions with franchisees. Inside the franchisor's packet, you will find information on capital requirements like those provided in Figure 14.7, which highlights Subway's requirements for their traditional restaurants.

Contact the American Franchisee Association, IAFD, and AAFD to determine if there is a national/local association of franchisees for your selected franchise. If so, contact them and delve as deeply as necessary, and for as long as you need to, until all your questions are answered. The more contact you have with franchisees, the better equipped you will be to make a final buying decision. As recommended earlier in the chapter, attempt to find a franchisee that will allow you to shadow him or her in their franchise for one to two weeks, or as long as

(continued)

If I aspire to own several franchises, can you provide me with a few examples of people who own multiple franchises and how they accomplished this?

2. **Franchisees:** Now interview as many franchisees as you can, to determine the day-to-day life of a franchisee. Try to ascertain a clear understanding of the financial potential of owning and operating a franchise. Assess the franchisees true working relationship with their franchisors. When interviewing franchisees make sure you interview several from each of the following categories: successful, new, those with like backgrounds, those with 5 years' experience, those with 10 years' experience, those for sale, and closed franchisees. Try the following questions and many others within the chapter. In addition, each interview will lead you to form additional questions you should be asking.

What do you wish you would have known before purchasing the franchise?

Are you happy with the support and training you receive?

What problems are the hardest for you to deal with in the business?

How helpful was the franchisor in your site selection, lease negotiation, financing, and opening?

Are there any issues for you or your fellow franchisees with protected territories?

What would you change if you could within the franchise structure?

Who are your strongest competitors? And how is the franchisor helping your respond to the competition?

Are you able to hire, train, and retain competent employees?

What is your employee turnover rate?

How many hours a week did you work the first year and how many do you work now?

What do you think it takes to be successful franchise operator?

Were start-up costs what you anticipated?

How long did it take your franchise to become profitable?

Is your income what you anticipated? Try to talk real dollars and real profit. If one hesitates ask, "I was making $60,000 before, do you think I will be able to replace my past income within two years?" *And most importantly:* **Would you do it again**?

figure **14.6**

Subway Application for Additional Information

SUBWAY®

Application for Additional Information

In addition to requesting additional information, this application is used for purchasing a new franchise, an additional franchise, or the purchase and transfer of an existing store. The filing of this form does not obligate the applicant to purchase or the franchisor to sell a franchise or location.
Complete in full and do not use abbreviations. Please print clearly or type.

OFFICE USE ONLY

DA Name _____
DA # _____
Sales Manager _____
Disclosed Date _____

YOUR PERSONAL INFORMATION

Date _____ Where did you hear about the SUBWAY® franchise? _____

Name _____ Date of Birth _____

U.S. Citizen? ☐ Yes ☐ No

Tax ID/Social Security Number* _____ Gender ☐ Male ☐ Female

Other names you are known by _____ Are you of legal age ? ☐ Yes ☐ No

U.S. Permanent Resident? ☐ Yes ☐ No

| Have you ever been convicted of a felony or its equivalent? Yes ☐ No ☐ | Have you ever been associated directly or indirectly with terrorist activities? Yes ☐ No ☐ | Has a judgment been filed against you or have you been involved in any litigation proceeding within the last 5 years? Yes ☐ No ☐ | (If yes, on a separate sheet of paper provide the following for each proceeding: names of the parties involved, date filed, court where filed and nature of the proceeding.) |

Telephone (Home) _____ (Fax) _____ (Mobile) _____
Area code / country & city code   Area code / country & city code   Area code / country & city code

Residence Address _____ Apartment/Suite _____

City _____ State/Province _____ Zip/Postal Code _____

Country _____ Email address _____

SPOUSE PERSONAL INFORMATION *(Use a Separate Application for Partners)*

Spouse's Name _____ Date of Birth _____

U.S. Citizen? ☐ Yes ☐ No

Tax ID/Social Security Number* _____ Gender ☐ Male ☐ Female

Other names you are known by _____ Are you of legal age in your State/Province/Residence Area? ☐ Yes ☐ No

U.S. Permanent Resident? ☐ Yes ☐ No

| Have you ever been convicted of a felony or its equivalent? Yes ☐ No ☐ | Have you ever been associated directly or indirectly with terrorist activities? Yes ☐ No ☐ | Has a judgment been filed against you or have you been involved in any litigation proceeding within the last 5 years? Yes ☐ No ☐ | (If yes, on a separate sheet of paper provide the following for each proceeding: names of the parties involved, date filed, court where filed and nature of the proceeding.) |

EDUCATIONAL BACKGROUND

Highest Education Achieved	Schools Attended City State Country	Years	Grade or Degree Attained
☐ College Degree or higher ☐ Some College ☐ High School ☐ GED ☐ Didn't Complete High School	_____		

BUSINESS INFORMATION *(Complete All Questions)*

☐ Self Employed   ☐ Employed by _____

No. Years _____ Nature of Business _____

Title _____ Describe Position _____

Address _____

City _____ State/Province _____ Zip/Postal Code _____ Country _____

Telephone (Bus.) _____ Telephone (Alt.) _____
Area code / country & city code   Area code / country & city code

Select Your Business Experience Level
☐ Restaurant Management
☐ Other Business Management
☐ Restaurant Non Management
☐ No Business Experience
May we contact you at work? ☐ Yes ☐ No

List all restaurant & food service businesses in which you have an ownership interest:
_____
_____
_____

FINANCIAL INFORMATION *(Please List Figures in US Dollars)*

Income from current occupation $ _____ /year

Income from other sources $ _____ /year

Please explain other income _____

Personal Bank(s) /Branch   Address

_____
_____
_____

Individual Liquid Assets (Cash, Stocks, etc.)   a)$ _____
Individual Fixed Assets (Home, Car, etc.)   b)$ _____
Individual Total Assets   (a + b) c)$ _____
Individual Liabilities (Mortgages, Loans, etc.)   d)$ _____
Your Individual Total Net Worth (c – d) e)$ _____
Excluding any financing listed below

Would this business be your sole income source?   Yes ☐ No ☐
Is there other financing not included in (e) above?   Yes ☐ No ☐
If yes, how much financing is available? $ _____

*Optional for additional information purposes but required to begin the process of the purchase and transfer of an existing location. Also note: it will be required prior to the purchase of a new franchise.
SUBWAY® is a registered trademark of Doctor's Associates Inc. ©2011 Doctor's Associates Inc.

APPLICATION ©2011 Doctor's Associates Inc.

(continued)

—————— figure **14.6**

Subway Application for Additional Information *(continued)*

REFERENCES *(Excluding Relatives)*

Name _____

Address _____

Telephone _____
(area code/country & city code)

Name _____

Address _____

Telephone _____
(area code/country & city code)

Name _____

Address _____

Telephone _____
(area code/country & city code)

RESTAURANT OPERATIONS

If qualified, when will you invest in a franchise?
☐ Now ☐ Within 6 months ☐ 6 months - 1 yr.
☐ Over 1 yr.

How involved will you be in operating the franchise?
☐ 0% Not involved at all
☐ 50% Somewhat involved
☐ 100% Completely Involved

In what country would you like to open your SUBWAY® restaurant?:
(If different from your country of residence**)

Estimated training date should you choose to invest: _____

PARTNERS *(All partners need to fill out a separate application and if listed, must be named on any Franchise Agreement executed in connection with this Application.)*

Will you have partner(s)? ☐ Yes ☐ No
If not, you may skip this section. Otherwise, please complete all relevant sections below:

Partner's Name _____
First, last, middle initial
☐ Active ☐ Silent   %Ownership ____ ☐ Male ☐ Female

Partner's Name _____
First, last, middle initial
☐ Active ☐ Silent   %Ownership ____ ☐ Male ☐ Female

Partner's Name _____
First, last, middle initial
☐ Active ☐ Silent   %Ownership ____ ☐ Male ☐ Female

Partner's Name _____
First, last, middle initial
☐ Active ☐ Silent   %Ownership ____ ☐ Male ☐ Female

No one may contribute money toward the franchise purchase unless they are a partner listed on the Application, who will be named on the franchise agreement and pass training. One exception will be if the money is contributed by first of kin or grandparent of the candidate, so long as the money is in the account when we verify the candidates information; and so long as the contributor provides us with a letter indicating their relationship to the candidate and the amount of money contributed toward the franchise.

Submit your completed application in 1 of 3 convenient ways listed below:
Online: http://www.subway.com/apply
Fax: +1.203.783.7336
Mail: Attn: SUBWAY Franchise Sales
Franchise World Headquarters, 325 Bic Drive, Milford, CT 06461, USA

NO POSTAGE
NECESSARY
IF MAILED
IN THE
UNITED STATES

BUSINESS REPLY MAIL
FIRST-CLASS MAIL   PERMIT NO. 16   MILFORD CT

POSTAGE WILL BE PAID BY ADDRESSEE

SUBWAY® FRANCHISE SALES
FRANCHISE WORLD HEADQUARTERS, LLC
325 BIC DRIVE
MILFORD CT 06461-9857

Fold on dotted lines, with address on outside, this panel on back, tape shut, (do not staple) and mail

---

**In order to purchase a SUBWAY® franchise in the US, the franchisee must be a citizen or permanent resident of the US.
I understand that the granting of a franchise is at the sole discretion of the Franchisor (Doctor's Associates Inc. or its affiliate).

I understand that any information I receive from the Franchisor or from any employee, agent or franchisee of the Franchisor or its affiliate is highly confidential ("Confidential Information"), has been developed with a great deal of effort and expense to the Franchisor, and is being made available to me solely because of this application. I agree that I shall treat and maintain all Confidential Information as confidential, and I shall not, at any time, without the express written consent of the Franchisor, disclose, publish, or divulge any Confidential Information to any person, firm, corporation or other entity. or use any Confidential Information, directly or indirectly, for my own benefit or the benefit of any person, firm, corporation or other entity, other than for the benefit of the Franchisor.

I authorize the Franchisor or its designee to procure an investigative consumer report. a general background search and an investigation in accordance with anti-terrorism legislation, such as the USA Patriot Act and Executive Order 13224 enacted by the US Government (collectively referred to as "Investigations"). I understand that these Investigations may reveal information about my background, character, general reputation, mode of living, association with other individuals or entities, creditworthiness, litigation history and job performance (collectively referred to as "Investigation Data"). I understand that, upon written request, within a reasonable period of time, I am entitled to additional information concerning the nature and scope of these Investigations. I hereby release any representative of the Franchisor or its affiliate, a credit bureau, security consultant or other investigative service provider selected by the Franchisor, its affiliates, officers, agents, employees, and/or servants (collectively referred to as the "Investigator") from any liability arising from the preparation of these Investigations.

This authorization for release of information includes but is not limited to matters of opinion relating to Investigation Data. I authorize all persons, schools, companies, corporations, credit bureaus, law enforcement agencies or other investigative service providers to release such information without restriction or qualification to the Investigator. I voluntarily waive all recourse and release them from liability for complying with this authorization. This authorization/release shall apply to this as well as any future request for these Investigations by the above named individuals or entities. I authorize that a photocopy or facsimile of this release be considered as valid as the original.

I agree that I will settle any and all previously unasserted claims, disputes or controversies arising out of or relating to my application or candidacy for the grant of a SUBWAY® franchise from Franchisor, pursuant to the laws of Connecticut, USA* and by binding arbitration only. The arbitration shall be administered by an arbitration agency, such as the American Arbitration Association ("AAA") or the American Dispute Resolution Center, in accordance with its administrative rules including, as applicable, the Commercial Rules of the AAA and under the Expedited Procedures of such rules or under the Optional Rules For Emergency Measures of Protection of the AAA. I agree that arbitration will be held in Bridgeport, Connecticut, USA*, conducted in English and decided by a single arbitrator.

Everything that I have stated in this application is true and I understand that the information provided by me will be relied upon by the Franchisor. In accordance with anti-terrorist legislation, I understand that I will not be approved to purchase a franchise if I have ever been a suspected terrorist or associated directly or indirectly with terrorist activities. I read, understand, and agree to all of the above. Additionally, I understand that the Franchisor may require me to pass a standardized Math and English exam. I understand that I will be required to provide proof of amounts listed as Liquid Assets above by providing copies of my bank statement s for the past three (3) months as verification.

Date _____ Applicant's Signature (required) _____

Date _____ Spouse's Signature (required) _____

SUBWAY® is a registered trademark of Doctor's Associates Inc. ©2011 Doctor's Associates Inc.

Application © 2011 Doctor's Associates

Source: *https://www.subway.com/AdditionalInfoApp/index.aspx.*

figure **14.7**

Subway Franchise Capital Requirements

DAI USA
Effective: 5/2011
US Dollars

Franchise Capital Requirements

Traditional Restaurants

GENERAL BREAKDOWN FOR :	LOWER COST	MODERATE COST	HIGHER COST	METHOD/ WHEN DUE
INITIAL FRANCHISE FEE	$ 15,000	$ 15,000	$ 15,000	LUMP SUM Upon signing franchise agreement
REAL PROPERTY **	$ 2,000	$ 5,000	$ 12,000	LUMP SUM Upon signing intent to sublease
LEASEHOLD IMPROVEMENTS	$ 59,500	$102,100	$134,500	AS INCURRED Pro rata during construction
EQUIPMENT ***	$ 4,500	$ 6,500	$ 7,500	LUMP SUM Before equipment is ordered
SECURITY SYSTEM *(Not including monitoring costs)*	$ 2,000	$ 3,500	$ 6,000	LUMP SUM When you place order
FREIGHT CHARGES *(Varies by location)*	$ 3,000	$ 3,750	$ 4,500	LUMP SUM When you place order or on delivery
OUTSIDE SIGNS	$ 2,000	$ 4,000	$ 8,000	LUMP SUM When you place order
OPENING INVENTORY	$ 4,000	$ 4,750	$ 5,500	LUMP SUM Within one week of opening
INSURANCE	$ 800	$ 1,500	$ 2,500	AS INCURRED Before opening
SUPPLIES	$ 500	$ 900	$ 1,300	AS INCURRED Before opening
TRAINING EXPENSES *(Including travel and lodging)*	$ 2,500	$ 3,500	$ 4,500	AS INCURRED During training
LEGAL & ACCOUNTING	$ 1,000	$ 2,000	$ 3,500	LUMP SUM Before opening
OPENING ADVERTISMENT	$ 2,500	$ 3,250	$ 4,000	LUMP SUM Around opening
MISC. EXPENSES *(Business License, utility deposit, small equip. & surplus capital)*	$ 4,000	$ 6,000	$ 8,000	AS INCURRED As required
ADDITIONAL FUNDS - 3 MONTHS	$ 12,000	$ 26,000	$ 42,000	LUMP SUM As required
ESTIMATED TOTAL INVESTMENT *	**$115,300**	**$187,750**	**$258,800**	

*NON-TRADITIONAL

** This amount is the estimated deposit of 2 months rent payable upon signing the Intent to Sublease.

*** If you do not select the equipment leasing program or it is not available, you should substitute the costs for Equipment Lease Security Deposit with $49,500 to $72,000.

THESE FIGURES ARE ESTIMATES OF THE COMPLETE INVESTMENT IN SETTING UP A SUBWAY®RESTAURANT AND OPERATING IT FOR 3 MONTHS. IT IS POSSIBLE TO EXCEED COSTS IN ANY OF THE AREAS LISTED ABOVE.

Some costs will vary in relation to the physical size of the restaurant. A lower cost restaurant is one that would require fewer leasehold improvements, less seating and fewer equipment expenditures. Moderate and higher costs restaurants may require extensive interior renovations, extensive seating and additional equipment. If you are purchasing a franchise for another location opportunity, such as a non-traditional, satellite or school lunch program location, the above listed capital requirements may vary and could be substantially lower depending upon the necessary equipment you must acquire or changes in leasehold improvements you must make. The above figures do not include extensive exterior renovations.

SUBWAY®is a registered trademark of Doctor's Associates Inc. ©2011 Doctor's Associates Inc.

Source: "Subway: Franchise Capital Requirements Traditional Restaurants," US Requirements, page 1, from *http://www.subway. com/subwayroot/Own_a_Franchise/PDFs/Capital_Req_US_Canada.pdf* (Accessed date 11/09/2012).

you need to better understand the operation, before handing over any fees to the franchisor. Knowing what goes on in a franchise on a daily basis is essential before committing your funds, blood, sweat, and tears. After shadowing a franchisee and exploring your financing options, complete Action Step 61.

If your experience working in the franchise proves to you that you want to purchase a franchise, work with the franchisor to determine the best site or area for you. They should provide you with demographic, geographic, and psychographic information to support the numbers required for a successful franchise in selected areas. Deposits may be required before the site-selection process begins. If you are beginning to look at offices or retail space, involve your attorney immediately.

An accountant should also be called in to review material and point out financial issues that need to be discussed with the franchisor. Your accountant, if he or she has franchise experience, may help you assess the financial possibilities and feasibility of the venture and will help you compare it to other options. The financial information you have gained from your franchisee interviews should also be shared at this point with your accountant.

With the information from the franchise's Business Plan in hand, along with your in-depth research, it is time now for you to develop a Business Plan to fit your potential location and particular target market. Go through the text from the very beginning and rework the relevant Action Steps to develop your own Business Plan for your particular franchise.

With the advice of your accountant, attorney, past and current franchisees, and banker, you are finally ready to negotiate with the franchisor to complete the sale. If your financing is not in place at this time, you need to contact lenders as discussed in Chapter 9. You may be able to receive some financing from the SBA, the franchise itself (if available, it will stated in Item 10 of the FDD), and specialized leasing agreements. Make sure the amount of capital you borrow includes not only your start-up needs (see Figure 14.7) but also a cushion for unforeseen items, as well as for working capital. Specialized brokers work in conjunction with franchisors to help franchisees obtain financing.

Franchisors oftentimes have preferred lenders who they have established relationships with and who have vetted their franchise. Thus, these lenders are ready, willing and able to lend to potential franchisees.

In addition, the use of 401(K)/IRA funds to fund franchises is growing as several major players have entered the market in this area. We urge you to consider very carefully the use of retirement funds in funding your ventures. One franchisee, close to retirement, invested his retirement savings in a reputable franchise and for four years worked daily in the business to not earn any income and lost over $200,000. His retirement looks much bleaker today. Whereas, the media paints a very positive spin on the failure rate of franchises, that rate is highly disputed by many franchisees and their lawyers.

With home equity lines in place to support their venture many have found those equity lines closed as the value of their homes declined and thus were unable to continue financing working capital for their business ventures.

Once you have negotiated your contract, you may be on your own; or you may have a strong franchise organization behind you, helping you with site selection, store design, training, advertising, marketing, and possibly a grand-opening celebration. The story does not end upon opening—it has just begun! **Good luck!**

A Franchising Success Story

Susan Moore and her husband were lucky when it came time to investigate franchises; they had a source of inside information right in the family. Corporate support, which varies greatly among franchisors, was more important than brand-name recognition to Susan and her husband and the franchise they selected excelled in this area.

ACTION STEP 61

Summarize Your Insights and Research

After you have perused several information packets from various franchisors, completed your Internet research, contacted past and present franchisees, and completed your personal assessment, write up your responses to the following questions. Seeing your thoughts on paper will help your final decision-making and make it easier for you to discuss your plans with others.

1. What do you like about franchising?
2. What do you dislike about franchising?
3. What additional information do you need?
4. Which franchise is for you? Why?
5. Can you make the amount of money you desire from this one franchise?
6. If not, could owning multiple franchise locations provide you with enough income?
7. What will you like most and least about owning this franchise?
8. Can you raise the working capital and investment funds you need? (Refer back to Chapters 8 and 9.)
9. Will you like running the day-to-day operation, or are you still in love with the idea of "owning a business" and "being your own boss"?
10. Where do you see this franchisor in five years?
11. Where do you see yourself and your particular franchise in five years?
12. Will you be able to sell this business easily?
13. Will you be allowed to hire a manager to take over day-to-day responsibilities if you so desire? (Some contracts do not allow absentee ownership.)
14. Can you grow in this business?
15. How responsive has the franchisor been to change in the marketplace?
16. Are you creating wealth or just replacing your job?
17. What questions still remain?

Don't be afraid to share your feelings with others: "I love this franchise because …" or "This franchise packet gives me the shakes because …"

"Three years ago, my husband had to travel a lot in his job, and I was working very hard for a large company. While we were both drawing good salaries, we felt we had what it took to succeed on our own but wanted support. We decided to go the franchising route.

We were both interested in the printing industry, and we chose a medium-sized national chain that seemed to have a franchise package we could live with. My brother had been with the franchisor for three years, in the Pacific Northwest area, and he was making a good living.

While we were interested in the quick-print industry, we weren't experts, so the two weeks of intense training was incredibly valuable. In addition, corporate helped us with site selection, market analysis, negotiating the lease, and the layout and design of our shop. There are so many details to think of when you're starting a business; it's very helpful to have experts take over some of the tasks.

Another good feature of this franchise is that corporate will allow you to finance up to 80 percent of your start-up costs. This particular franchise can run as high as $250,000 up front, so that helped us.

We opened a second shop last January, and both stores are doing nicely. We're developing a reputation for being on time in an industry known for being perpetually late."

■ BUYING AN EXISTING FRANCHISE

Turnover of existing franchises may happen due to divorce, health issues, retirement, relocation, franchisor issues, potential road construction, legal changes, or unhappiness of the owners, and these changes may provide an excellent way for you to enter the franchising world. Due diligence of both the franchisor and the franchise for sale should be undertaken as rigorously as if you were purchasing a new franchise location. Along with the information in this chapter, conduct the due diligence suggested in Chapter 13 for ongoing businesses and develop a Business Plan using the Action Steps.

Most franchise agreements require the new franchisee to sign a new franchise agreement rather than taking over the existing franchisee's agreement. Also, expect a transfer fee and possible training fees. The franchisor may also require you to upgrade or renovate the location. Determine the cost before proceeding. Most agreements also state the transferee must be approved by the franchisor who will evaluate your reputation, business skills, and financials.

Purchasing an existing franchise will shorten the required time to full operation; and if the business is currently successful, positive cash flow should come much quicker for you. You also will not have opening expenses and may be able to purchase used equipment at a reasonable price.

You may inherit the current employees, which may or may not be positive. If you are purchasing a retail establishment, shop the store frequently to assess the quality of the current employees. If they are outstanding, you will be a very lucky business owner. Also, if the business has been operating for several years, financial data should be available for you and your accountant to assess. Follow Myron's experience below.

Two Wins, One Loss

Michael Long completed a Regional Occupational Program (ROP) in health care and then earned his personal training certificate and worked at several health clubs for a few years. When he was 24, his great uncle died and left him $100,000. Feeling flush with cash, he considered buying a house or taking a trip around the world, but his parents encouraged him to purchase a franchise. Looking around, he realized his passion for fitness would be best realized if he purchased the Workout Now franchise for his town. Michael opened the fitness center two months later in a strip center.

After successfully operating one franchise for two years, he was offered two more within a 40-mile radius. Seeing this as a way to increase his income substantially, Michael decided to purchase both franchises. One of the store's exercise studios had been losing money, but Michael felt he would be able to turn it around shortly.

Michael recognized after operating all three centers for another year that he was spending over 50 percent of his time at the losing studio and was afraid his time spent there was beginning to affect the other studios. Try as he would, he couldn't make money on the third center. He called the franchisor and explained that the one loser was draining too much of his time, energy and capital, and that he needed assistance in unloading it. The franchisor found several prospective buyers and together they chose the one they thought was the best. Michael now devotes all his time to working with his winners.

■ BUYING INTO A NEW FRANCHISE

Buying a franchise in a system, which is less than two years old, should be considered very carefully. Remember, the main reasons to buy a franchise are to purchase a system and a well-known name, and with little history and experience these may be in short supply. With a franchise, you are hoping to purchase a blueprint not a sketch. Your return on investment may take longer and the training and support may not be as effective or even in place. Investigate in great depth the franchisors and their experience in the industry and in franchising. Also, assess if the product or service is one that can be easily replicated. Do not follow a fad, which will be out of fashion or favor shortly, as the lease you will sign will be for the long term . Even if the franchise goes belly up, your lease payments will be due.

For those *experienced* in franchising, you will be better able to assess the franchisor and the system and may not need extensive support and training. Also, you may be more likely to benefit from the advantages of a new franchise—availability of prime locations, area franchises, flexibility of terms, and a ground floor opportunity. Do your due diligence and you just may find an opportunity you can grow with.

■ THE OTHER SIDE OF FRANCHISING: REASONS FOR NOT PURCHASING

If, after reading this chapter and exploring franchising, you are not convinced this is the correct path for you, you will join the many other entrepreneurs who have decided against buying a franchise. Whether rightly or wrongly, here are some of the reasons they have given:

1. I know the business as well as they do.
2. My name is as well-known as theirs.
3. Why pay a franchise fee?
4. Why pay a royalty fee and advertising fee?
5. My individuality would be stifled.
6. I don't want others to tell me how to run my business.
7. I don't want a ground-floor opportunity where I'd be the guinea pig.
8. It felt like I would have been committed for the rest of my life.
9. There were restrictions on selling out.
10. If I didn't do as I was told, I would lose my franchise.
11. The specified hours of business did not suit my location or desires.
12. The franchisor's promotions and products did not fit my customers' needs or tastes.
13. They offered no territory protection.
14. I would not be in control of my business.

But wait: maybe you do not want to own a franchise, but you have already developed a winning business formula; maybe you can become a franchisor yourself. Many entrepreneurs have done this. This is another reason to learn all you can about franchising now.

■ CAN YOU FRANCHISE YOUR IDEA AND BECOME THE FRANCHISOR?

Paul and Lori Hogan have built a network of more than 900 Home Instead franchises (see Passion feature) throughout the United States and abroad, providing caregivers to the elderly, allowing them to remain independent. From their first office in Paul's mother's house in 1994, they knew they had a successful formula and could meet a growing need for home-care assistance. With previous experience in franchising, they searched out passionate franchisors interested in caring for others as they built Home Instead. Their focus on a rapidly growing market has propelled them to be named one of the top 100 franchise companies by *Entrepreneur*, and Mr. Hogan was named Entrepreneur of the Year by *Franchising World* magazine. Their success is incredible; according to *Franchising World*, the Hogans built "one of the first organizations to apply the franchising model to the home-care industry and take that concept international."

While Home Instead has been quite successful, according to Francorp, a consulting firm in Olympia Fields, IL, the odds do not favor successfully franchising your business: "Fewer than 1 percent of franchise ideas ever get off the ground." Francorp suggested in an *Inc.* article, "Too Much Too Soon," that before you think of franchising, you first ask yourself the following questions:

1. Can someone learn to operate your business in three months or less?
2. How profitable are you? To attract high-quality franchisees, a franchise needs to generate at least $500,000 in annual revenue and earn the owner an income of at least 15 percent.

Consider reading books by Fred DeLuca, the founder of Subway, and articles by other major franchisors. Learning from their experience can be an excellent first step. Also, take time to meet with others who have started franchises—both the successful and the unsuccessful.

One former franchisor Josie Rietkerk, advises that franchising takes a substantial amount of money to start up, with no payoff guarantees, and recommends building a successful and profitable business model and replicating it several

PASSION

Former Marine and Army Reservist Changes Path

Home Instead Senior Care franchisee, Steve Boos, has always followed his heart in business, starting when he worked in the paper industry for a company that was focused on reducing waste in paper manufacturing. So it's not surprising that a stint in the Army Reserves and a year in Iraq drastically changed his career path.

"Being deployed for a year kind of changes your outlook on life," Boos said. "So when I came back, I started looking at some different opportunities."

Boos' wife had worked with the elderly before becoming a stay-at-home mom, and she was familiar with the services that Home Instead provided. When Boos returned from Iraq and the couple began looking into franchise opportunities, Home Instead was one of the franchises they contacted.

"We talked to a lot of current owners of Home Instead Senior Care franchises and went to Omaha (Home Instead's headquarters). It was just a great feel—not only the company but also their mission. It felt like a good fit for me," Boos said.

Boos, who had no experience with home health or senior care before becoming a Home Instead Senior Care franchisee, says his military training (he was active duty in the Marine Corps in the late 1980's before joining the Reserves in 2000) helped him to become a successful franchisee.

"We all have our strengths and weaknesses." Boos said. "My strength is that I can follow a diagram or an outline. I'm not the most creative mind. With Home Instead, they invented the process. If you follow the process, you'll do well."

Source: Veterans Report 2011 by Franchise Business Review. Retrieved from *www.franchise businessreview.com/content/veterans-Report-2011* (Accessed March 12, 2012). Reprinted with permission.

times before attempting to sell any franchises. Also, consider the time and effort entailed in developing your franchisees, and be careful not to provide additional concessions and finances to help them financially beyond what is reasonable.

Mark Siebert, CEO of iFranchise Group in Homewood, IL, warns potential franchisors, "If you truly love that small store of yours, prepare for a tearful farewell. You won't be a retailer anymore. You'll be advertising, marketing, selling, and serving the needs of your franchisees by providing them with operations manuals, training tools, and other assistance. It requires a different skill set."

Keep your idea simple and make sure you can train franchisees within a short period of time. Depending on the type of business, franchisees may only have two or three days' time to learn the business. In addition, consider the amount of time that will be expended to assist the franchisees, not only in their start-up phase but also in the first year of operation. Personnel, as well as personal and financial resources, can be drained by demanding and unsuitable franchisees. Because of this, selecting your early franchisees is incredibly important for initial success. During the start-up phase, you just want to sell franchises; but do not get caught up in the selling, because it is the *success* of the franchises that will grow your business—not just the numbers.

Franchisors need to be aware that not all franchise ideas are transferable to other physical locations. Also, you need to make sure the concept can be replicated and is not dependent on the product or economic cycle. In addition, the success of many businesses is based on the personality of the owners and the employees. For a franchise, the success must not be dependent on the owner's personality but on the systems and the franchise's products or services and the business model.

Before becoming a franchisor, consider if you are willing to fulfill primarily the needs of your franchisees rather than the needs of your customers directly. Being a franchisor means working with many different personalities and setting up systems, operations, and training. In addition, you must be willing to watch others grow "your baby." Be forewarned there are many consultants on the prowl for companies who think they can be the next Subway, and they will do their best to convince you that you are that next company.

■ FRANCHISING TRENDS AND FINAL FRANCHISING THOUGHTS

As you look for the right franchise opportunity, bear in mind that the best opportunity may lie with a young franchise that has proven its concept, has 50 to 60 winners, and is looking for growth in an area with which you are familiar. Many of these franchises currently are capitalizing on providing services such as home health care, fast-food, tutoring, diet and fitness coaching, cleaning, handyman services, and child centered activities.

Also, one of the most important elements in evaluating a franchisor is to assess whether they continually change and update their products and services to meet the changing marketplace. One of the strengths of a strong franchise should be a marketing research department that continually scans the environment to determine what steps will be necessary to capitalize on economic, social, technological, and demographic changes. Select an innovative franchisor. Be sure to discuss with franchisees how their franchisor responds to change.

If you are really interested in making money as a franchisee, research becoming an area franchisee, where your territory could be as small as a section of town or as large as several states. Many individuals with strong business backgrounds have found area franchises to be quite lucrative. If you truly believe in the company's concept and have experience, explore the possibility of an area franchise.

Another growing trend in franchising today is the operation of multiple franchises housed and operated under the same roof. To research such franchise opportunities, interview key people at several multiple-franchise operations. Save yourself time, money, and maybe even some heartache by spending time visiting several successful and unsuccessful multiple-franchise operations.

With tight credit and cautious investors, corporations are offering an array of business franchise models under the same brand. For example, Doc Popcorn offers full-scale stores for an investment up to $150K, mall kiosks for $100K, and mobile carts for a $70K investment. Thus opening up opportunities for many individuals today who would like to start small.

Selling franchises is a numbers game. You, the potential franchisee, are a "lead." You will be told what you want to hear. If you have a few business skills and perhaps some business experience, then your chances of succeeding are far greater as a franchisee. A franchisor with a well-developed Business Plan will keep you on track. Ask to see it. Even if the franchisor has a well-developed Business Plan, you also need to complete one for your particular franchise location.

The key here is gut feeling. Look at franchising as an option—an example to learn from and maybe start with—and then, if you desire in the future, blend that knowledge and experience into a unique business that explores the gaps exposed in Chapters 2 and 3.

Please note that during 2013, possible major legal changes may come to bear in regards to franchisee and franchisor relationships. Currently, the California state legislature is debating major legal changes and if instituted other states may adopt the changes.

If you are not ready to be totally on your own yet, or you want assurance and support, franchising may be the way for you to begin. With minimal financial investment, another alternative may be network marketing discussed in Figure 14.8, which presents both the pros and cons of multilevel marketing.

figure **14.8**

Network Marketers: Pros or Cons?
Microsoft Small Business Center

Network marketing adheres to a fundamental tenet: Lotions, potions and a slew of other products can be better sold face-to-face, without stores or middlemen.

The industry got its start in the early 1900s, and became popular in recent years through companies such as Amway. Network marketers sold door to door for years, with varying degrees of success.

The Internet era hasn't done anything to change this. However, the web has revolutionized some marketing and distribution practices within the industry. It has made it faster and less costly for legitimate network-marketing companies to get the attention of potential customers.

Unfortunately, the Internet also has made it easier for illegal companies — mostly the skilled perpetrators of pyramid schemes and related scams — to get in the face of consumers as well. Many of these scam artists portray themselves as honest network marketers.

If you are interested in this high-risk but potentially lucrative industry, read on. You'll find some background on network marketing, as well as eight tips to help you distinguish a legitimate business opportunity from a fraud.

Amway spearheaded industry growth
First, some background on network marketing, which is also known as multilevel marketing (many people use the terms interchangeably).

  Among its founding principles:

- A direct selling process lets distributors of certain products "educate" consumers more successfully (and more economically) on the products' merits than catchy TV ads or fancy store displays.

- Customers who are sold on a certain product can be motivated to sell it themselves and to recruit others to become sellers as well (forming a business "pyramid" of sorts over time).

- Sellers will have an incentive to sell and to recruit others, as they'll be paid commissions both on their own sales and their recruits' sales. In other words, the earlier you get in to the network, the more money you can make.

- Last, but not least, success is not guaranteed, and only the best products and services — and the best network marketers — will survive in the business.

(continued)

figure 14.8

Network Marketers: Pros or Cons?
Microsoft Small Business Center *(continued)*

Founded in 1959, Amway has built a multibillion-dollar business on these basic premises. In the late 1970s, it successfully fought off claims by the federal government that it was an illegal pyramid scheme. In prevailing in court, Amway proved the key test of a legitimate business — that even the last person recruited into its networks can make money. (In a pyramid scheme, large numbers of people at the bottom end up paying money to only a few people at the top.)

Today, legitimate network marketing companies span the globe, with several hundred in the United States, including recognizable names such as Avon, Mary Kay, NuSkin, Unicity Network (formerly Rexall), and Herbalife. The products they sell range from vitamins and weight-loss plans to skin-care lotions to software and even dental insurance. The Direct Selling Association (DSA) represents network marketers and other companies who sell directly to consumers.

"Technology a Two-Edged Sword"

How pervasive is fraud in the industry? More pervasive than ever before, say many industry experts, although the Federal Trade Commission does not have statistics to quantify the impact. "I can tell you that, in the last 10 years, with the growth of the Internet, we have seen a significant growth in the number of apparent pyramid schemes," says Jim Kohm, the FTC's assistant director of marketing practices.

The low cost of entry into the industry long has encouraged scam artists. But the Internet has enabled them to market their schemes to consumers as successfully as it has legitimate network marketers, Kohm says. "Technology has proven to be a two-edged sword," notes Keith Laggos, an Amway veteran and industry expert who publishes *Money Maker's Monthly* (*www.mmmonthly.com*).

8 Fraud Detectors

So how can you tell a scam or a shady business from a legitimate money-making opportunity? Here are eight things to consider before you take the plunge.

1. **Make sure that a solid product or service figures prominently in the business.** Sounds simple, but in many pyramid schemes, the product or service is a mere "fig leaf" to an illegal source of revenue — often the signup or membership fees required just to join a network. (Most will never see their money again.) Be convinced the product or service is not a gimmick or a throwaway, but one you'd buy yourself. A related scam, the Ponzi scheme, involves no products at all, but rather promises of investment or insurance windfalls. Most network marketers do charge a nominal signup fee of $30 to $60. But if there is no product being sold, keep your money — don't be swayed by the "benefits" of becoming part of a network.

2. **Confirm that the commission structure is supported by product sales.** Note that you are not becoming an "employee," but rather an independent business operator earning sales commissions. In illegal businesses, you can sell well but have your commissions diluted by other costs or obligations. For example, the FTC in 2000 shut down a Las Vegas-based company operating in eight states, because it required participants to pay excessively for seminars and desk space. Only a handful ever made any money.

3. **Don't pay more than $500 in initial "buy-in" costs.** Most network marketing companies require you to buy a certain amount of product to get started. If joining the company means you have to buy $500 in products or services, or if you see excessive product inventory costs, period, watch out. And again, if you are asked to fork over money without getting any product at all, flee as fast as you can.

4. **Beware of high earnings claims.** Many convicted pyramid schemers have been charged with misrepresenting the potential earnings of participants. You should expect reasonable commissions and growth opportunities, but nothing grandiose. Be wary of inordinate product and earnings hype. A rule of thumb: If it sounds too good to be true, it probably is.

5. **Don't participate unless the company is willing to buy back inventory.** Many scams—and some legitimate businesses—will refuse to buy back the leftover inventory you've purchased, even if you decide within a year that network marketing is not for you. In its membership requirements, the DSA mandates that network marketers be willing to buy back unused inventory, for at least 90 percent of the sale price, within a year of the sale.

6. **Find out if the network marketer is a DSA member.** The nine-decade-old association is the closest thing to a governing body for network marketers. The Direct Sales Association has about 150 U.S. member companies and some 50 others undergoing an intense application process for membership, says Joseph Mariano, executive vice president and legal counsel. All members are listed on its website. While less than half the U.S. network marketers are members, if the company you're interested in is a member, that's a good sign.

7. **Find out how long the company has been in business.** At least 90 percent of all network marketers fail within three years. About 80 percent fail within the first year, notes Bill Rodgers, a veteran Seattle-area network marketer who served as president of the Mercer Island Chamber of Commerce. If the company you're interested in has been around for more than three years, it is likely not only legitimate, but viable.

8. **Do your due diligence.** While you want to stay away from scam artists, you also want to avoid wasting time and money with a loser company. In Rodgers' own guidelines for assessing network marketing opportunities, he comments:

   "The FTC has been quick to identify and act on the companies engaging in illegal practices. Unfortunately, it takes a number of people to be swindled before the problem surfaces."

Source: *http://www.microsoft.com/smallbusiness/resources/marketing/privacy-spam/network-marketers-pros-or-cons.aspx*, (Accessed April 20, 2008).

■ SUMMARY

There are two good reasons to consider buying a franchise: If the brand name is respected, you will already be positioned in the marketplace; and if the franchisor is strong, you will inherit a Business Plan that works. Examine the franchise's appeal with consumers carefully; you want a marketing boost from the name. Depending on the franchise, you may also receive other services for your money; for example, you may receive help with site selection, interior layout, and vendor connections, but the main thing you are buying is brand-name recognition. Earnings claims are not legal unless they appear in the Franchise Disclosure Document.

Just as if you were investigating an ongoing, independent business, study the opportunity thoroughly. Examine the financial history, and compare what you would make if you purchased the franchise to what you would make if you invested the same money elsewhere or started a similar business without the franchisor's backing.

Know what drives the business and what factors are important for operating a potential franchise. The territory size you purchase and its demographics in relation to the product or service will help to determine your success and profitability. Information in Chapters 4 and 6 on demographics and site selection should be reviewed. In addition, all the appropriate Action Steps should be completed as you investigate possible franchise opportunities.

Listen to the wisdom and expertise of your accountant, broker, lawyer, and fellow franchisees, but also listen to your heart and your wallet. You want to purchase a franchise and buy into a culture that you want to be part of for a long time, and one you want to grow into an asset you can sell at some point.

Your strengths and skills should match those of the most successful franchisees. Buying a franchise does not ensure success. The ultimate responsibility for the success or failure of the business lies with the franchisee. Along with a name brand, you are purchasing a system to follow. Follow it carefully.

■ THINK POINTS FOR SUCCESS

- Avoid ground-floor opportunities. "Grow with us" should signal *caveat emptor* ("let the buyer beware").
- Talk to franchisees, especially those who have left the system. Franchisees who have left the fold are listed in the FDD. Keep in mind; current franchisees sometimes receive a finder's fee, so they may not be totally honest with a potential buyer.
- Remember you are purchasing a job, and you *have* to do it their way, not your way.
- The franchisor gets a percentage of gross sales for advertising and royalty fees whether the franchisee is profitable or not.

- Consider carefully whether you really need the security blanket of a franchise.
- Read the proposed agreements carefully. They are airtight, favor the franchisor, and are usually nonnegotiable.
- Ask yourself if you can be comfortable relinquishing your independence.
- If you like to break rules, be creative, and stretch things to the limit, do not buy a franchise—you will very likely end up in court.

■ KEY POINTS FROM ANOTHER VIEW

Franchise Matchmakers' Real Clients

Kelly K. Spors

Start shopping for a franchise to buy, and you'll likely soon realize there are hundreds to choose from—some with flashy names like "Extreme Pita" or "Pilates Joe" that you've probably never heard of.

It's no wonder so many aspiring franchisees feel they need help choosing the right franchise. Just be careful where you turn.

There's a thriving industry of so-called franchise brokers, referral networks, or consultants offering prospective franchisees free help finding a franchise system that meets their needs. All these brokers—including bigger operations like FranChoice, FranNet, and the Entrepreneur's Source—essentially do the same thing: They interview prospective franchisees and recommend a short list of supposedly compatible franchises.

Conflict of Interest

But what's often lost in all this "free help" is a screaming conflict of interest: Brokers get paid by the franchise systems that want to be promoted to potential franchisees—not by you.

The extensive interviewing process "gives a prospect a sense of false assurance that the broker is really working for them," says Michael Seid, a West Hartford, Connecticut, franchise adviser. In reality, "the broker's job is to bring as many good leads to the franchisors it represents as possible."

And there's great financial incentive to do just that. Brokers, Mr. Seid says, often make flat commissions of around $20,000, or 50 percent of the franchise fee, for every prospect who buys a franchise they recommended. They generally negotiate their commissions with each franchise system separately, so they might even get more money by recommending one over another.

Another potential drawback to using a broker, he adds, is that some represent only a small group of franchise companies—sometimes fewer than 10. So prospective franchisees may assume brokers are giving them recommendations from a vast pool of options, when they're only pitching the same five franchises again and again. There are no federal requirements for the brokers to disclose the franchises they represent or their compensation, though some states may carry their own disclosure rules.

A 2007 survey by Franchise Update Media Group, an industry resource, found that 14 percent of franchise sales were initiated through brokers. Some franchise systems that use brokers heavily, however, get more than 30 percent of their leads through them, industry experts say.

What the Brokers Do

Here's how the broker relationship usually works: A prospective franchisee hears about a broker through an acquaintance or a website and arranges a call or face-to-face meeting. The broker interviews the prospective franchisee and sometimes administers personality tests to gauge what kind of franchise system is best suited for that person. The interview process often involves questions about lifestyle needs, interests, managerial experience, risk tolerance, and finances.

The broker then provides a list of three or four franchises for the prospect to further examine. The broker doesn't finalize sales for franchises, but instead leads clients their way.

Many brokers say that despite being paid by the franchises they promote, they only represent systems they've thoroughly vetted and believe are financially sound. The valuable service they can offer, they say, is the ability to help prospective franchisees home in on what they want in a franchise.

Kim and Rich Paul of Bel Air, MD, originally thought they wanted to buy a fast-food franchise. But after four hours of phone consultations with a FranChoice broker last year, they realized they preferred a franchise in which they didn't need to have employees or a storefront, one allowing them a more flexible schedule. "Using a broker was probably the best thing we did, because we really didn't know what we wanted," says the 51-year-old Mr. Paul.

After researching the four franchises the broker recommended, the Pauls bought a V2K window-treatment service franchise with $59,500 in start-up costs.

Marc Kiekenapp, a Scottsdale, AZ broker who represents six franchise systems, including LA Sunset Tan and Right At Home, says brokers can also offer clients more details about the franchises they represent, how they operate, and what to expect.

Many of his prospects are referred to him by franchisors wanting to make sure franchisee candidates really understand the business and are well suited before signing up. He provides more information about the franchise and then, if clients are interested, they fly out to the franchisor's headquarters and perform their own due diligence to ensure the franchise really feels like a good fit.

Still, some say the inherent conflict of interest makes the value of using brokers questionable. Mr. Seid estimates that only a few hundred of 1,500 to 2,000 U.S. franchise systems work with brokers. Moreover, some of the best-known ones, like McDonald's, don't.

Careful Approach

Prospective franchisees hoping to use brokers may want to work with several to get the widest pool of possibilities, says Mark Siebert, chief executive of iFranchise Group, a Homewood, Illinois, franchisor consultant.

They should also ask brokers questions to discover how many franchise systems they represent, the fees they get paid, and how they conduct due diligence on the franchises they recommend.

Source: Kelly K. Spors, "Franchise Matchmakers' Real Clients." Reprinted with permission of WSJ.com, Copyright © 2008 Dow Jones & Company, Inc. All Rights Reserved Worldwide. License numbers 3042121216040 and 3042121044098.

■ ACTION STEPS

■ KEY TERMS

Image_Source/iStockphoto.com

Pull Your Plan Together
Launch with Passion

Learning Objectives

- Gather all your information and Action Steps together to build one coherent Business Plan; which will become a portable showcase for your business and more importantly an ever-evolving guide.

- Review the advantages and disadvantages of Business Plan software and using outside help to complete the plan.

- Review a sample Business Plan to discover how one pair of entrepreneurs defined, developed, and planned for their business.

- Understand that words talk. However, numbers show it can be done.

- Develop the Notes section for your financial plan.

- Recognize the importance of providing all back-up data for your readers.

- Launch your finished Business Plan with passion and hard work.

You may be closer to completing your Business Plan than you think. If you have completed the Action Steps in the preceding chapters, you already possess the major components of your plan. If you have not, return to Chapter 1 and work through the necessary Action Steps.

Through the past chapters, you have found gaps in the market, researched your Target Customer, defined your business, developed marketing and promotional ideas, and completed basic financial research and projections. As you develop your Business Plan using the Action Steps you have completed, you may recognize areas that need further attention and research.

As you have developed more knowledge of the market and realized that in some cases the market has changed, revise your Action Steps accordingly. Chapter 15 now provides you with the structure to put your facts, figures, ideas, dreams, passion, and intuition into a workable plan.

Your Business Plan could be one of the most important documents you will ever pull together. If you need to start your business immediately, consider using the Fast-Start Business Plan in Appendix A. Particularly if your business is less complex and has very low capital needs and low risk, this may be the alternative for you.

If you are completing a Business Plan for a high-tech company and seeking venture capital and angel investors, you will need to access additional Business Plans, as the specific requirements may go beyond what is covered in the basic Business Plan presented in this text.

For high-tech products, lenders and investors are most interested in how you plan to introduce a new concept and where specifically you will locate the early adopters for your product. Also, they will look at sales responses as you tested the market.

For new ventures, the traditional channels of distribution may not work for your product, and you will therefore need to develop and substantiate how you will develop a new distribution method. Be sure you are able to answer the question, "How will you generate income and profits?" Investors will also focus on past accomplishments of the major players.

With a completed Business Plan in hand, you will have a document to present to the people who are important to your business: bankers, lenders, relatives, venture capitalists, vendors, suppliers, key employees, friends, the SBA, and others. The plan is portable, so make as many copies as needed to share with people who can help you succeed. E-mail it to contacts across the country, post it on the various Internet sites that link investors with entrepreneurs, or possibly enter it into Business Plan Competitions.

Planning is hard work. You will stay up nights, lose lots of sleep, and miss too many meals; but in the end, you will have saved time. Just as a pilot would not consider flying without a flight plan, neither should you consider a business venture without a Business Plan.

Occasionally, on completion of the plan, you may decide that the costs—in terms of money, time, effort, stress, and risk—are not justified. If this happens to you, congratulations! You have learned a valuable lesson, and it has only cost you time, not money. And you have learned how to research and write a Business Plan, so the next time opportunity knocks you will be ready to act.

Your plan should become a working, breathing, and living document for your business dreams. Share your plan with others; they may have ideas, insights, or recommendations. Listen to their comments with an open ear. Chapter 6 introduced you to networking, and in Chapter 11, we encouraged you to find a mentor. Draw on these resources as well as others; review their input, and revise your plan as necessary.

Business Plan reviewers often ask for further details or back-up data that when added to your plan, will make it stronger and more effective. Sometimes, we become so close to our Business Plan that we omit important and relevant details and information.

■ PREPARING TO WRITE YOUR BUSINESS PLAN

It is now time for your passion to come to the forefront and spill out into every section of your Business Plan. If your plan does not shout passion and confidence, you cannot expect your Business Plan readers to read further than the executive summary. Before you begin, gather in one place all your completed Action Steps and back-up data. Outline your plan, fill in the information from your Action Steps, refine the plan, ask knowledgeable people to review your plan, refine further, and prepare to present the plan to potential investors or lenders. Ask yourself, "Is it profitable to go forward with this plan both for the short term and for the long term?"

Remember, your reader will look at where you are now, where you are going, and how you are going to get there. Planning is an ongoing process. Your Business Plan is a road map, but it should be one for a fast-growing area where new roads and new opportunities and challenges constantly present themselves.

If you are a creative thinker, chances are your thought processes do not always follow a linear sequence. That is great—it will help you as an entrepreneur. Nonetheless, the Action Steps in this chapter do follow a linear sequence: the sequence of the parts of a completed Business Plan. This is a matter of convenience—you will see an example of each part as it would appear in the finished product. Bear in mind, however, that we do not expect you to write each part sequentially. Also, depending on the type of business you are starting, several areas may be much more relevant than the other areas.

The best way to begin writing a Business Plan is to start with the material with which you feel most comfortable. For example, if you really enjoyed interviewing and researching Target Customers, you might begin with "Market and Target Customers."

In this chapter, the Action Steps will serve as a checklist for keeping track of which parts of the plan you have written. For example, in practice you would probably write the cover letter last, but that is the first Action Step we present. Think of the writing of this first cover letter as a valuable exercise. After completing Chapter 15 and your Business Plan, rewrite your cover letter. The more cover letters you write, the easier it becomes to write them effectively.

To jump-start your Businss Plan writing skills, review the plans for Yes, We Do Windows (Appendix A) and Annie's (Appendix B). In addition to these plans, search online to access a wide selection of sample Business Plans. Bplans is one of the best sites, offering more than 500 plans. Even if one of their plans does not exactly fit your business idea or model, you will have an idea of the Business Plan format for your particular type of business.

The example we have provided in the text is for an entrepreneurial training facility; if you are opening a restaurant, Internet business, or manufacturer, the outline and requirements may be different, and you should adjust your plan accordingly. Thus, you may need to add additional sections to your Business Plan. Also, different parts of the Business Plan will need to be emphasized. In Annie's plan, she focused on the retail store aspect and her wide experience in retailing as she tried to can a foothold into Sea World. If you are developing a product or service which has not been offered before, your reader will require background on your test markets and your business and revenue models.

Three-Part Structure: Words, Numbers, and Appendices

Your Business Plan tells the world what kind of business you are in and where you are going. Even if you are not seeking funding, *you* need to know where you are going! For ease of handling, divide your plan into two sections, and provide the needed documentation in appendices at the end.

In Section I, use *words:* Introduce your strategies for marketing and management. Try to hook your reader with the excitement of creating a business, assessing the competition, designing a marketing plan, targeting customers, finding the right location, and building a team—all those human things that most people can relate to, even if they are not in business. Clearly point out your firm's uniqueness and ability to compete and handle change.

In Section II, present *numbers:* projected income statements, cash flows, web analytics, break-even points, and balance sheets. This section is aimed primarily at bankers, credit managers, venture capitalists, vendors, small-business investment companies, and commercial-credit lenders. Projected income statements for three to five years are usually included in the appendix. Numbers should be accessible to the reader who is searching for the bottom line.

Support Sections I and II with *appendices.* This is where you place résumés, maps, diagrams, photographs, tables, reprints from industry journals, letters from customers and vendors, credit reports, personal financial statements, traffic studies and counts, bids from contractors, and other documentation that demonstrates the viability and profitability of your plan.

Note that in most cases, material in the appendices comes from existing sources. You are not stating anything new here; you are merely supporting what you have already said.

Appendices vary for each type of business; for that reason, sample appendices are not included in this book. If you followed and completed the Action Steps in the previous chapters, you will have in hand most of the components and appendices you will need to write a winning Business Plan.

Business Plan Software

Freeware, shareware, and "payware" for business planning are widely available. Business Plan software serves as a guide. Only through completing an incredible amount of work, such as you have done through the Action Steps, will you be able to "fill in the blanks" of a software program.

We strongly suggest you do not use these programs until all your research and planning are complete—and note they are not necessary to complete a plan. If you choose to use the software, be careful not to make your plan look like a "me too" plan. You and your business are unique and you must sell that uniqueness throughout your plan.

Business Plan Pro, BizPlan Builder, and BizPlan are three of the leading software programs. The software programs either have a wizard-driven interface or are packages, which include Microsoft Word and Excel documents to customize. Shortening your time in actually completing the presentation of your research and financials into a very presentable professional document is one of the main reasons to use a program.

Using charts and graphics throughout your presentation may make the plan easier to read and the programs can guide you in this area. Many of the programs also provide sample Business Plans online as well as links to research tools. When reviewing plans online, be careful not to copy or follow another's plan. You've done the work, now make *your* plan work for *you*.

Financial forecasting tools allow you to work with "what if" scenarios as you finalize your financials; however, you should have completed these in Chapter 8. Some programs also allow you to import data from Excel, Peachtree, or Quick-Books. Online support and live support are also available with some software vendors as well as tutorials and videos.

There is no one, magic Business Plan program or template that guarantees success. Only your hard work and passion, and an element of luck, can accomplish this.

Outside Assistance in Writing a Business Plan

Many people ask, "Should I hire a pro to write my Business Plan?" Our response is always, "*You* are the pro!" If you do not want to put the time and effort into writing your own Business Plan, it is doubtful that you will have the energy and drive to develop a business. Also, only *you* can put the passion you feel into your plan.

The information you have collected by completing the Action Steps now allows you to complete your Business Plan. We do suggest that on finishing your initial plan, you look for several business owners and possible investors to review it. In addition, attorneys, marketing specialists, accountants, and manufacturing experts may improve your plan with their review; they will show you what areas need additional clarification or support data. Take all of their comments to heart, and rework your plan where necessary.

Hiring a business consultant to refine your plan is acceptable, but do not allow him or her to dream your dream for you. Also, if you do not have total control over input to your plan, you may embarrass yourself by not being able to explain the details of your plan to investors and bankers.

Reminders

Completing a Business Plan helps reduce the risk of failure. No plan can guarantee success, but a well-researched plan will help acknowledge issues, anticipate problems, and determine the resources available to correct them.

Your plan should be easy to read, with each number and figure well documented. Use bullet points, infographics, and appendices to support the plan's strongest points. Be sure there are no typographical errors and that the plan is well written. If you are not comfortable with your writing skills, hire an editor to read and review your plan.

Focus on the potential opportunities the business provides for investors. Tie together—with a clear, consistent message—all elements of the plan. Include possible risks as well; a business without risks does not exist.

ACTION STEP 62

Write a Draft Cover Letter

Address your letter to a specific person who can help your business. Be brief; aim for about 300–600 words. State the reason you are sending the plan. If you are asking for money, tell the person what you want it for, how much you need, and how you will repay the loan. Several well-written paragraphs should be all you need to do this.

You purpose in writing the cover letter is to open the door gently and prepare the way for further negotiations. The cover letter is bait on your hook. If you are contributing funds toward the business, or have already done so, indicate the amount. Most investors and lenders want to see that you are investing your own money and sweat equity.

The tone you are after in this opening move is confident and slightly formal. You want to appear bright, organized, and in control of your venture and ready to capitalize on market needs. Refer to The Entrepreneurs' Hub's letter.

The plan should consist of about 15 to 25 pages, with additional pages for appendices. The plan should be easy to read and visually appealing so that the reader can move quickly through the document. Make the plan easy for your reader to write notes on, and include how the reader can reach you—e-mail, website, mailing address, phone, and so on.

In this chapter, we illustrate the steps involved in completing a Business Plan, along with providing you samples of each step as completed by a hypothetical business, the Entrepreneurs' Hub. The Hub has been in operation for six months and has been self-financed to this point by the owners, who are now seeking to expand and need additional outside financing.

Read through this chapter once and then reread, completing the Action Steps. Action Steps 62 and 63, writing a draft cover letter and executive summary, would normally be completed after Action Steps 64 through 70, but we suggest you complete draft copies of these two documents to jump-start your Business Plan and keep you focused. When you have completed your Business Plan, revise both your cover letter and executive summary.

The Cover Letter

To aim your plan so it will achieve the best possible results, focus your cover letter on each individual reader's interests, needs, and concerns. The cover letter introduces the excitement of your plan and tells the person specifically why you have chosen to send it to him or her. This may be your only shot at making the reader want to review your Business Plan, so make your letter strong—prove you know who you are, where you are going, and how you are going to get there with passion and hard work.

Read the sample cover letter for the Entrepreneurs' Hub:

Sample Cover Letter

47 Dogwood Lane, Suite 108–9
Oak Ridge, TN 37953
Jackson@net.com
(865) 555–5555

June 5, 2012
River Bank
Ms. Nancy Hopp
Vice President, Lending
1400 Market Lane
Knoxville, TN 37944

Dear Ms. Hopp,
Thank you for the insight you shared with me on reviewing my Business Plan. Your thought-provoking questions in the marketing area led me to research additional social media options. In addition, I have revamped the financial section by adding additional notes to the pro formas and reworking several of the figures. Your suggestions and the subsequent changes make our plan stronger. Everyone here at the Entrepreneurs' Hub appreciates the care you took reading over earlier drafts of our Business Plan.

The positive response to our entrepreneurial services over the past six months requires that the school expand to offer additional services to our entrepreneurs. As the economy is in flux, many clients with substantial severance checks and retirement plan funds in hand are reaching out for the dream of owning a business.

Thus, the over-50 market is very strong. In addition, we are seeing a great need amongst the 20–30-year market who are finding it tough to get good jobs in the economy. Many of these individuals with strong skills and good educations look toward entrepreneurship as their best alternative.

To help make their dreams come true as quickly as possible, we provide our *Fast-Start* training using the most popular Business Planning software and website development software in conjunction with our consulting. Most of our clients have a good working knowledge of computers and basic software, but seek advanced training that focuses on their particular entrepreneurial needs.

We feel passionate about our business and our entrepreneurs. We have watched many of our clients develop websites through our e-commerce courses and have aided in the preparation of more than 30 Business Plans to date. We serve not only the start-up businesses in the community, but also have found a market for our services among entrepreneurs whose businesses have been open two to four years, and who are now interested in expanding and taking their businesses to the next level.

Each of the two founders has contributed $100,000 to launch the Entrepreneurs' Hub. We are currently in the market for a loan of $60,000 to be used for tenant improvements and an additional line of credit to assist with cash flow. The location we have in Oak Ridge is built; however, it will require additional Wi-Fi, electrical wiring, furniture, and appropriate lighting to enable us to provide a second meeting room or classroom. We would appreciate your guidance concerning sources of capital available through your bank or additional avenues.

We plan to repay our loan from profits generated over the next three years as we grow to full capacity. For more information, please refer to the financial section.

Again, thank you for your assistance. We couldn't have done it without you.

Cordially,

Danielle Jackson
President

© Cengage Learning

Let us summarize what is good about our sample cover letter. We can see that:

1. The writer is making use of a previous contact.
2. The writer tells the reader—the manager of a bank—that she is in the market for a loan and a credit line. She does not put her on the spot by asking for money. Instead, she asks for advice on where to find sources of capital.
3. The writer shares her passion for her business and her customers' successes with the reader.
4. The writer strikes the right tone. This often requires several revisions.

You can do as well or better—and it is well worth the effort. As you draft your cover letter, remember that the reader may pass judgment on your Business Plan, and on your business acumen, on the basis of the letter. Do you want your small business to appear profitable? Cutting edge? Exciting? Welcoming? If so, your cover letter needs to convey this same impression. A well-written cover letter will make its readers want to become involved in your venture. Action Step 62 will help you write your draft cover letter now. Revise and finalize your cover letter once you have completed your plan. A good cover letter will lead the reader to your Business Plan, and a poor cover letter may be the only thing that is read.

■ ELEMENTS OF A BUSINESS PLAN

The Table of Contents

Our sample table of contents provides a quick overview of a finished Business Plan. In practice, the table of contents is prepared last. Please note, as previously discussed, that the outline for your particular plan may vary. Review online Business Plans that are most similar to your type of business to discover what additional areas need to be covered and also what appendices might be appropriate. Depending on your business, certain areas will be more relevant to your success and should be treated as such in the plan.

Entrepreneurs' Hub

Table of Contents

Executive Summary

*The need for specific appendices varies greatly from Business Plan to Business Plan. For that reason, we have not included sample appendices. As you draft your plan, you will recognize items that require further documentation to substantiate your business strategies; the most logical place for this kind of documentation is in appendices. In addition, include references and names and contact information for the consultants or technical advisors who have assisted you.

© Cengage Learning

■ EXECUTIVE SUMMARY

The executive summary serves as an introduction to the Business Plan. Its function is similar to that of a preface in a book. It is written to 1) acquaint the reader with the subject matter of the material that follows 2) direct the reader's attention to whatever strengths the author (entrepreneur) wants to emphasize 3) define the market and your plan to reach the market and 4) make the reader want to turn the pages and keep reading. Because the executive summary reviews the entire Business Plan, it is usually written last, but we have included it here to help you first focus on the most important parts of your Business Plan.

We want you to write a two- to three-page draft executive summary; and when your plan is completed, revise the original. Pay special attention to the *business description, current position and future outlook, management, uniqueness,* and—if you need financing—*funds sought, how they will be used, when they will be repaid,* and *how they will be repaid.* This summary appears right after the table of contents and should be able to stand on its own.

As a preview to your plan, the executive summary should excite, entice, and draw the reader into the plan. A well-written executive summary captures the reader's attention and makes him or her eager to explore further. Because many readers never go further than the executive summary, it is important to expend a great deal of effort to make your executive summary an excellent selling tool—it may be your only chance to sell your idea.

As you write your executive summary, remember that lenders prefer hard numerical data and facts. Therefore, such phrases as "30 percent return on the original investment" help to paint a picture of good management and expected solid growth for the Entrepreneurs' Hub.

You, too, can write an effective executive summary. Action Step 63 and this section's review will help you decide which facts and numbers portray you and your business venture as credible and promising, and it will also help you summarize these facts in writing. At this point, draft your executive summary. Upon completion of your Business Plan, revise your executive summary.

Executive Summary of Entrepreneurs' Hub

The Entrepreneurs' Hub is a user-friendly, state-of-the-art entrepreneurial training center. We are tapping into the growing need for entrepreneurs to keep abreast of the latest technologies and develop Business Plans. However, the classes and seminars are only part of the business. We believe the added value for our client is providing a center for budding and growing entrepreneurs to dream with others.

We have found that our entrepreneurs thoroughly thrive on personal interaction with others. After each class, we provide drinks and snacks and encourage everyone to meet in our comfortable conference room area. We find that oftentimes clients ask us to keep the doors open till midnight.

Our market area is growing quickly today because of the expansion of the following groups:

- People who are retiring early out of choice or being downsized and starting new businesses
- Entrepreneurs who are ready to expand their current businesses
- Individuals wanting to take advantage of ecommerce and international market opportunities
- Young people who see entrepreneurship as an alternative to working in a corporate world or replacing jobs which they have lost
- People who run businesses part-time in addition to their full-time jobs and are looking to expand
- Individuals seeking franchising opportunities

We market our seminars and services exclusively to current entrepreneurs and those dreaming of entrepreneurship. In addition to the software training classes we offer, we will be presenting specialized seminars in writing Business Plans, website development and design, marketing with social media, and graphic design. Instructors will always incorporate the students' business ideas into each class. The Entrepreneurs' Hub's sophisticated, smart classroom provides hands-on education and support. We also adapt packaged software to meet each participant's needs.

We are currently operating with one classroom and a conference room and hope to add an additional classroom within the next six months. This expansion will allow us to attain sales over $600,000 by the end of the fiscal year. At that time, our pretax profits will have reached over $150,000.

According to our research and experience, entrepreneurs have an insatiable appetite for education and the support of fellow entrepreneurs. They generally have strong computer backgrounds and are attending our classes for advanced training, support, and advice. We anticipate an annual sales growth rate of 30 percent over the next three years.

Our competitors have recently declined, as many individuals have learned to master standard software, and the traditional software training schools have served their purpose. We are inclined to believe our competition is now the traditional educational system and their offerings as well as the many online offerings . We hope to capitalize on our distinct differences from area school offerings and online by providing a warm, nurturing environment where individuals can grow their businesses surrounded by others. We acknowledge many individuals enjoy online only classes. However, we are seeking those who want person to person feedback in a live setting.

We will contract with marketing consultants, attorneys, financial advisors, and accountants to provide specialized courses at our center, including:

- Patent, copyright and trademark protection
- Selling to federal and state government entities
- Product testing
- Pricing strategies

ACTION STEP 63

Write a Draft Executive Summary

Imagine you have three to five minutes to explain your business venture to a complete stranger. This gives you an idea of what information you need to include in your executive summary. Answer the following questions: What is the problem? Why is your product/service the right solution? Who is the target market and has the product/service been tested? Where will you reach your target market? When will you launch the product/service? How will you make money? Your business model and revenue model will need to be explained in the summary.

Limit yourself and practice explaining your venture to friends, colleagues, potential customers, and strangers. Ask them to raise questions, and use their questions to guide you as you revise and hone your presentation.

When you are satisfied with your oral summary, type it up. It should not exceed two to three typed pages. (The Entrepreneurs' Hub's executive summary that serves as our example was less than one single-spaced page.) This may constitute a very small portion of your Business Plan, but it may be the most important part. Refine your executive summary again after completing your Business Plan and after each presentation.

Many of you will be posting video presentations and you can use the same information to develop your online presence. Make the reader or listener exclaim, "Tell me more!"

Throughout the past six months, we have demonstrated that we offer superior training at competitive prices. Our plans for the future include developing additional training centers. Research and customer surveys indicate that we have just begun to tap the ever-increasing need for entrepreneurial education and services.

Danielle Jackson will continue to focus on sales and marketing in addition to developing and teaching courses with Robert Wojchik. Curriculum for more than 20 courses has been developed, with another 10 courses in development. As the needs of our students change, we will be able to adapt accordingly. Robert Wojchik will also manage the technical aspects of keeping the hardware and software up to date and the computers functioning.

We are seeking funding of $60,000 to cover the remodeling costs required to equip an additional classroom. Funds will also be used for license fees, Wi-Fi, furniture, and equipment costs for our second classroom. The appendix contains contractor, computer, and furniture estimates. We plan to purchase refurbished classroom furniture; many businesses have gone under, so excellent buys are available at potential cost savings of $15,000 to $20,000.

Bank loans will be paid back from the operating profits of the business over the next three years.

© Cengage Learning

SECTION I: DESCRIPTION OF THE BUSINESS

How well do you know your business? You need to prove it with words and numbers. By the time your reader finishes reading your Business Plan, you should have an ally on your side. To give you a sample to follow, we provide key sections from the Business Plan for the Entrepreneurs' Hub, a business that is seeking financing for remodeling and equipment expenses. Regardless of whether your business is ongoing or just starting up, the goals of Section I and II are the same: to demonstrate that you know your business and that you are a winner.

A. COMPANY ANALYSIS AND SERVICES

Include your unique qualifications, company history, and past accomplishments in this section. Review how the Entrepreneurs' Hub tackled this part. The Hub is likely to receive its funding because the writer of the plan proves that the business is a winning concern. The writer has:

- Let the facts speak for themselves
- Supported all claims with numbers
- Avoided hard-sell tactics
- Refused to puff-up the product
- Projected a positive future

The writer does a terrific selling job. Now it is your turn. Complete Action Step 64 after reviewing the Entrepreneur Hub example.

Business Description of Entrepreneurs' Hub

The Entrepreneurs' Hub is an entrepreneurial center in Oak Ridge, Tennessee, near the growing area of West Knoxville. The vast number of scientists and engineers in the area from the University of Tennessee, Tennessee Valley Authority, and the U.S. Department of Energy's Oak Ridge facilty make it ripe for entrepreneurial activity. In addition, we want to tap into the large medical community.

Students are drawn to our teaching method because we provide hands-on experience, and we incorporate their business ideas into our seminars and software usage. In addition, our entrepreneurs are busy, thus our two-hour classes are packed with relevant information and are very fast paced.

ACTION STEP 64

Describe Your Company, Product, and Services

Excite your reader about your business; excitement is contagious. Investors love hot ideas.

If this is a start-up, explain your product or service fully. What makes it unique? What industry is it in? Where does the industry fit in the big picture? Pull in the relevant information from your past Action Steps.

Mention numbers whenever you can. Percentages and dollar amounts are more meaningful than words like *lots* and *many*.

If this is an ongoing business, your records of sales, costs, and profit and loss will substantiate your need for money. Keep the words flowing and the keyboard smoking. You need to convince the reader to continue reading.

With our Fast-Start entrepreneurial program, a 12-session program presented in 6 weeks, each student will produce a finalized Business Plan that has been reviewed by one of the owners as well as by fellow classmates. We will use Internet postings of Business Plans for students to review and comment on through our secure server. We will help our students who are seeking funding to find the appropriate sources. As some of our students will be accessing crowd funding and crowd sourcing to grow their businesses quickly, we will offer specialized training by outside experts. We plan to have a Business Plan competition at the end of each Fast-Start program.

Our center will provide resources for patent and copyright protection, as many of the entrepreneurs will require legal assistance in this area. In addition, lawyers well versed in Internet law will be available at reduced fees to help our clients through an ever-changing and ever-challenging quagmire of developing laws.

Most of our seminars and training will be offered in either two-hour classes or four-hour weekend classes. In contrast, the average college course—which emphasizes concepts, rather than hands-on experience—takes 12 to 18 weeks. Our price is $100 for most two-hour courses and $200 for four-hour classes.

Our entrepreneurs are very busy and have requested short classes. In addition, we will limit our FastStart program, at $1,250 for 6 weeks, to 20 students, so that students build working relationships with their classmates. Our hope is for these relationships to continue after the formal 6-week class has ended. We will make every effort to encourage this through social media and meeting times at our facility. We want all our clients to feel once they have taken a course with us that they are part of the Entrepreneur's Hub's family.

Entrepreneurs' Hub will have free monthly meetings for all Fast-Start graduates, with speakers and time for feedback and support on current issues and projects. If we see the need, we may open the center up once a week for additional time when our students can work together.

As a service business, we sell seats, skills, support, and information. We constantly survey our current customers for additional classes and services they would like to see offered. One area we hope to offer in the future is having a web designer and graphic artist available who can work directly with clients. We would have space available on Monday evenings to provide this service, and the experts could make appointments to work with our clients on a fee basis.

We are open Tuesday through Friday from 1 to 10 p.m. and Saturdays from 8 a.m. to 5 p.m. This schedule allows us to offer single-day, four-hour courses, as well as short, two-hour evening courses, thus maximizing the use of our facility. Seminars and guest speakers will be offered at least monthly.

The Entrepreneurs' Hub is in the business of jump-starting an individual's Business Plan and increasing productivity by providing the following:

- Assistance with writing Business Plans, loan proposals, marketing plans, and employee manuals
- Developing nonprofit organizations and social entrepreneurship ventures
- Web analytics training
- Assistance with selling through Amazon, eBay, etc.
- Advice on self-publishing and selling online
- Assistance with developing infographics
- Training for sales-force automation, manufacturing, and inventory control software
- Tips for effectively using social media such as Facebook, Twitter, LinkedIn, and others
- Additional proposed seminars are listed in the appendix

Our equipment is top quality. Our staff combines excellent training skills with attention to entrepreneurs and their needs. We have launched a solid start-up with a plan to continue our growth and success.

© Cengage Learning

■ B. INDUSTRY AND MARKET OVERVIEW AND TARGET CUSTOMERS

Knowledge is power, especially in the Information Age. The Entrepreneurs' Hub— a service business—capitalizes on expert knowledge to define the marketplace. In the same way, if your research is sound, your niche will be evident in your writing. Depending on your business, this area could be divided in to two sections.

ACTION STEP 65

Describe the Market and the Target Customers

Bring all your marketing research into this section from past Action Steps, and wow your reader with a picture of your Target Customers just sitting there waiting for your product or service. Provide any back-up research data in the appendix.

Use your industry research from the Action Steps in Chapters 2–4 to give your reader an overview of the industry. The reader needs to know the size of the market, trends in the marketplace, how the industry is segmented, where the industry is headed, and what specific part of the market you are aiming your product or service toward. In addition, briefly discuss any technological advances that are changing the industry and how you will capitalize on these changes. Address economic, social, legal, and global changes that may affect the industry and your target market.

Prove to your reader that you understand the market and are meeting a customer need. Discuss market segmentation. Define your Target Customers in great detail. Provide research data to back up your assumptions on demographics, psychographics, market size, web analytics and buying patterns. Return to your Action Steps from Chapter 4 to assist you in describing your Target Customers.

The reader should have a clear idea as to how your product or service will be capable of capturing a unique position in the marketplace. An in-depth explanation should be provided in the competition section of your Business Plan.

Complete Action Step 65 to show that you know the industry and your Target Customers. Review what the Business Plan for the Entrepreneurs' Hub says about its industry and Target Customers. Be sure to use secondary sources—documents, tables, and quotes—to give this section credibility. The following industry and market review is minimal. However, for many entrepreneurs this section will need to focus on changes within an industry and how your firm will accommodate those changes.

Industry/Market Overview and Target Customers of Entrepreneurs' Hub

Industry and Market Overview

Today's seminar and classroom offerings for entrepreneurs are limited primarily to community colleges and universities. In addition, several national organizations offer one-day and weekend entrepreneurial boot-camp programs, as many entrepreneurs need to learn programs and develop their Business Plans quickly and expect to be productive in a short time.

Computers and software can be your best friends, but only if you learn how to maximize their capabilities. The Hub is on the cutting edge of providing services and training focused solely on entrepreneurs.

Target Customers

Geographically, our target area encompasses Knoxville, Oak Ridge, and Harriman. Realistically, most of our customers originate within a 25-mile radius of our location. We are looking ahead to possible future expansion throughout Tennessee over the next five years. Memphis and Chattanooga are two areas we are especially interested in exploring.

Anderson County's population is expected to grow an additional 10 percent over the next 5 years. Our entrepreneurial students are primarily college educated, 23 to 60, with annual incomes of $40,000 to $150,000. Our area has one of the highest concentrations of PhDs in the United States.

Several of the leading scientists and researchers from the Oak Ridge National Laboratory have taken our business-planning courses, developed excellent Business Plans, and are currently seeking funding. The Tennessee Valley Authority employs a large group of engineers and biological scientists, many of whom are interested in developing their expertise into profit-making ventures, with several looking at green technologies.

We hope to also reach individuals who are social entrepreneurs. In addition, several students have expressed interest in developing nonprofit organizations where they offer items for sale to directly support their nonprofits.

Our entrepreneurs, split fairly evenly between manufacturing, service, and retailing businesses, are dreamers first and foremost—our job is to help make their dreams come true as quickly as possible. We have found through our experience that entrepreneurship can be very lonely, because others may not be dreaming the same dream. We hope to reduce the loneliness.

All our sales and marketing efforts are tracked, which aids us in refining our Target Customer profile and focusing our marketing efforts on the strongest and most profitable markets.

© Cengage Learning

■ C. COMPETITIVE ANALYSIS

ACTION STEP 66

Obviously, if you know who your competitors are and how they fail to meet market needs, you are well on your way to developing your niche. You need to persuade the reader that your competitive tactics are well developed and will be effective. Reread Chapters 4 and 5 and review your Action Steps.

If your competitive strength derives from patents, copyrights, or trademarks, include information about them in this area. Copies of any patents or copyrights received or pendings should appear in the appendix with your attorney contact information.

How tough do your competitors look? As you read the Hub's assessment of its competition, note that the writer takes a cool, objective look at the competition. She does not belittle them, and she certainly does not underestimate them. The Hub's plan leaves no doubt that management is exploiting a market gap ignored by the competition: entrepreneurial training.

This is more than a matter of writing skill. Early on, the entrepreneurs who founded the Hub did the right research, so they could make decisions ahead of time—just as you were asked to do in the earlier chapters.

How will you handle your competition? Your readers will expect you to provide an honest appraisal of each of your major competitors. Now you are ready to complete Action Step 66.

Describe Competitors

1. Briefly profile the businesses that compete with you directly. Be objective as you assess their operations.
2. What are their strengths? Weaknesses? What can you learn from them?
3. What makes your product or service unique in the eyes of your customers?
4. After you have described your competitors, indicate how you are going to ace them out of the picture or develop a niche you can own by presenting your competitive positioning strategy. Provide primary and secondary research back-up data in the appendix.

Competitive Analysis of Entrepreneurs' Hub

We hope to capitalize on the need for *entrepreneurial training*, which our competitors are not currently providing. On reviewing our competitors, we discovered that major players in the industry have developed specific niches in the marketplace. A brief review of our two major competitors follows:

- **Roane State Community College:** Headquartered in Harriman, Tennessee, serving a seven-county area of East Tennessee. Their classroom facility in Oak Ridge, Tennessee, offers primarily traditional classes, although recently they have begun to offer online and hybrid classes to meet the needs of busy students. They do not focus on entrepreneurial programs, but occasionally they offer a small-business class. We do recognize the school could possibly compete with us directly if they were to begin offering more short-term or online classes, but we do not see this happening in the near future. Most of our students have told us that completing classes in a short period of time is their primary goal. Classes at Roane State cost approximately $400 per semester for 48 classroom hours. Thus, our cost of $1,250 for our Fast-Start 30-hour program is definitely more costly than our competitors; however, our clients have told us they are willing to pay this amount as it will bring them to market faster than a 16-week class. Also, our class size is half that of Roane State classes.
- **University of Tennessee (UT):** Excellent large university located in Knoxville with easy freeway access. Courses are primarily taught in a traditional classroom manner with an approximate cost of $1000 each. Being close to a leading research and teaching institution will provide our Hub and its students with highly trained experts in many different fields, which we will hire for short presentations and seminars. We are hoping to bring in experts at an approximate cost of $300 to $600 per evening seminar. We may not always make a profit on these specialized classes, but we hope to at least break even. At this time, their extension program does not appear to be offering any entrepreneurial training.
- **SBA Office in Knoxville:** Occasional classes are offered at the SBA office, but these are infrequent; we hope that the office will actually feed students to us, and we are developing a relationship with the director.

Our business is geared to offer $100 and $200 classes. The Fast-Start program charge will be $1,250. We will also offer our monthly meetings, with speakers and support, at $30 per evening. Fast-Start graduates will be able to attend for free. Again, we are stressing constant support from peers and advisors.

Our two main competitors must seek approval for all new classes and this gives us a great advantage in hopping on the latest trends as we can start new classes very quickly.

© Cengage Learning

ACTION STEP 67

Describe Marketing Strategy Work Through the Four Ps

1. Now that you have profiled your Target Customers and assessed your competition, take time to develop the thrust of your marketing strategy. Which techniques will reap the most cost-effective responses? And encourage repeat business and positive word of mouth?

2. Because pricing is such an important consideration, you might start with what your Target Customers see as a good value, and then develop your marketing mix (4 P's + participation) further. Prepare back-up data for the appendix.

■ D. MARKETING STRATEGY

Now it is time to describe your marketing strategy and pull together the work on your Action Steps from Chapters 4–7. You will be highlighting the four *Ps*: *price, product, promotion,* and *place + the fifth "p"—participation*. The reader wants to understand how your firm will position itself in the marketplace. Also, demonstrate how you plan to retain your customers and you will impress readers with your forethought.

The marketing strategy excerpt from the Entrepreneurs' Hub's Business Plan demonstrates a carefully reasoned approach, and it describes conscious marketing policies that will help this small business be competitive. If you were to read a Business Plan in which the writer does not demonstrate this care and deliberation, how much faith would you have in the writer's business abilities?

Note that the Entrepreneurs' Hub uses a four-pronged approach to reaching the public. This business understands the importance of finding a good promotional mix.

In your Business Plan, include distribution channels, selling methods, and public relations. If your firm has plans to sell products or services internationally, discuss those plans in this section. Present a list of potential customers or clients and a sales forecast. If these are extensive, present them briefly in the body, and add further information in the appendices. Action Step 67 will help you refine your marketing strategy.

If you have been in business, make sure you include results from past marketing actions. Numbers speak loudly!

Marketing Strategy for Entrepreneurs' Hub

We use a wide range of strategies to let our customers know about our class offerings, including targeted mailers, special promotions, Internet advertising, social media, personal selling, and networking. We are in the productivity and information business, and toward that end, we have developed a highly interactive and responsive Internet site that will provide a community for budding Knoxville-area entrepreneurs.

A new entrepreneur will be highlighted each week on our site, and we will send out weekly tweets and emails and ask our readers to forward them to their entrepreneurial friends. New class offerings and speakers will also be posted. In addition, we are considering posting, at our clients' request, Business Plans online for potential angel investors to review.

Networking

Each owner belongs to four professional organizations within a 25-mile radius. In addition, each owner has joined a local chamber of commerce organization to network. Both owners have also joined separate BNI networking groups and have found them to contain a wealth of contacts and students. The owners serve as guest speakers to civic and educational organizations as often as possible. A discount program will be designed for entrepreneurs in venture-training programs, such as SBDCs. As we grow, we hope to offer scholarships for several students each year as well.

Radio Program

We plan to host and sponsor a 10-minute talk show each morning during drive time on a local radio station, KBIC. Our show will be called "The Entrepreneurs' Hub." We hope that by highlighting our website and programs on the show, as well as providing advice and encouragement, entrepreneurs will listen and then contact us for further information.

Personal Selling

Fortunately, our owners have experience and talent in the area of personal selling. Each owner spends 5 to 15 hours per week talking with potential entrepreneurs and responding to e-mails. In addition, phone selling is an important aspect of our business. Converting phone and e-mail queries into sales is a major goal of each person. Logging all calls and e-mails and making sure they are followed up on in a timely matter is essential for our success. Hub training programs are being developed for local stores, such as Staples and Office Max, to offer at a discount to their business customers.

Creative Promotions/Free Ink

We will sponsor a yearly Business Plan competition for the Junior Achievement (JA) chapters in the Oak Ridge/Knoxville area. In addition, we will sponsor Business Plan competitions for our clients each year. The prizes will include classes at our center and a small college scholarship for the JA winner. We hope to offer the Business Plan competition in conjunction with Roane State Community College or the University of Tennessee. Once a month we will have special speakers on site free for our current and potential clients as well as speakers where there will be a $30 charge. It is hoped that these will be promoted in the *Knoxville Business Journal*, *Knoxville Sentinel*, and the *Oak Ridge News* and through social media.

© Cengage Learning

■ E. FACILITY LOCATION AND OPERATIONS

The next part of your Business Plan concerns location, site selection, and physical facilities. Review your work from Chapter 6 now.

If you are planning a retail store or distributorship, this area is critical and should include extensive research data to back up your site-selection decision. Discuss the accessibility and visibility of the site and the demographics and psychographics of the surrounding population. Download graphics from the many online databases showing roads, competition, and potential customers for support data, which should be placed in the appendix but referenced in the text.

If you are in manufacturing, explain thoroughly your site selection, which may be based on energy costs, employee costs, and governmental incentives. In addition, provide your facility layout and information on equipment to help support your operations plan. Provide supporting data in the appendix.

For a retail business that will be located in a shopping center or strip center, discuss the retail market mix and how it will help draw customers into your store. Drawings of the actual facility and store layout may help your reader visualize the store as well. Use professional quality photographs to enhance your Business Plan.

You need to paint an attractive picture of your business site and, at the same time, keep your reader interested by inspiring confidence in your choice. Location takes a tremendous amount of analysis. The Entrepreneurs' Hub writer gives himself a subtle pat on the back by describing the lease arrangements and by identifying the need for a second classroom.

Your plan will become very real when you showcase your physical facility. The operational plan, which supports your financial numbers, should clearly represent how you see the growth of your business. Read how the Entrepreneurs' Hub shows off its location, and complete Action Step 68.

ACTION STEP 68

Show Off Your Facility, Location, and Operations

The great thing about a location is that it is so *tangible*. A potential lender can visit your site and get a feel for what is going on. Bankers often visit a client's business site if the Business Plan is to be considered further. That is good news for you, because now the banker is on your turf. Clean up the place before your banker arrives; make it shine!

1. In this section, you want to persuade potential lenders to visit your site. Describe what goes on there. Use photographs, diagrams, and illustrations to make the facility as real to the reader as possible.
2. If you have a manufacturing facility, discuss how you selected the building and equipment. You may need to discuss utility costs, insurance issues, employment costs, and possibly workers' compensation.
3. If your business will be operating in shifts, you may want to discuss those issues here as well.

Facility and Operations of Entrepreneurs' Hub

The Entrepreneurs' Hub has secured a five-year lease at 47 Dogwood Lane, Oak Ridge, Tennessee. The facility is all on the ground floor and occupies 2,000 square feet. The area, which is zoned for business use, is near a hotbed of high technology and entrepreneurial activity. Within a 20-mile radius of the facility are three growing industrial parks, where there are many start-ups we hope to reach out to.

Our location has easy freeway access, is close to the rapidly growing West Knoxville area, and offers well-lit and abundant parking.

During our lease negotiations, we persuaded the landlord to make extensive improvements to the interior and to spread the cost out over the term of the lease. The décor—blue carpet, white walls, and gray furniture—gives the effect of a solid, logical, somewhat plush business-learning environment.

The building is currently divided into five areas: a reception and lounge area (150 square feet), a director's office (150 square feet), a classroom (600 square feet), a conference room (500 square feet), and a seldom used storage area (600 square feet).

The principals envision the storage area as a future second classroom (see diagram in the appendix) and are requesting funds to expand into this area. Each classroom will have 20 networked computers, comfortable chairs, printers, and video screens.

© Cengage Learning

■ F. MANAGEMENT AND PERSONNEL

Management will make or break a small business. You are a member of the management team, and you want this Business Plan to inspire confidence in your investors by highlighting your winning team. Review your work from Chapter 11 now. Many plan reviewers read the management section first especially if you are in technology.

If you have a high-tech business, the team and its past successes will be key, and therefore this section should be placed at the beginning of the Business Plan. Investors want to have confidence not only in the business idea but also in the team that will take the concept to reality. Now is the time to discuss the legal form of business you have chosen. Include applicable agreements and legal papers dealing with partnerships or corporations in the appendix.

Read how the Entrepreneurs' Hub introduced their management team. The Hub's team demonstrates balance, diversity, experience, some interesting track records, and the will to succeed. Danielle Jackson's experience in training and entrepreneurship combined with Robert Bennett's extensive curriculum development are strong selling points.

Highlight the balance and experience of your team with short résumés. Longer and more detailed résumés should be included in the appendix. The reader looks for financial, marketing, technical and operational skills, and management and entrepreneurial experience. In addition, many readers will focus on the teams' people skills.

The Hub was wise to include short résumés of the directors. In this case, the background of the directors enhances the balance of the team. All have admirable depth in their business careers, sharing over 45 years of experience in the corporate and entrepreneurial worlds.

The listing of the legal counsel, accounting firm, insurance broker, and advertising agency also adds to the impression of solid business practices. Nothing is more important than the people who will make your business successful. Present their pedigrees and focus on their track records and accomplishments as you complete Action Step 69.

For a start-up business, you are peering into the future with confidence—completing informal job analyses for key employees who will help you to succeed. For an ongoing business, you need to list your present employees and anticipate your future personnel needs. If you currently employ five people but want to indicate growth, try projecting how many jobs you will be creating in the next three years. Describe the work environment you plan to implement as you grow your business. Discuss what steps you will take to retain your employees as well.

When you start thinking about tasks and people to accomplish them, review your work from Chapter 11. Preparing this part of your plan is important, because it gives you one more chance to analyze job functions before you begin interviewing, hiring, and paying benefits—all of which are very expensive.

ACTION STEP 69

Introduce Your Management Team and Personnel

Use this section to highlight the *positive* qualities of your management team. Focus on quality first—accomplishments, education, training, flexibility, imagination, tenacity. Be sure you weave in experience that relates to your particular business.

Remember—dreamers make terrific master builders, but they may make lousy managers. Your banker knows this, and potential investors will sense it. A great team can help you raise money, and the key to a great team is balance. Describe the kinds of people you will need as employees and how they fit into your plan. What skills will they need? How much will you have to pay them? Will there be a training period? If so, how long will it be? What fringe benefits will you offer? How will you handle overtime?

Most importantly, describe the work environment and company culture you hope to create. Review your goals from Chapter 1 and incorporate them.

Provide short résumés for each of the major players, and highlight their past successes. Full résumés should be placed in the appendix.

If you have not yet written job descriptions, do that now. Job descriptions will help you avoid potential problems with the people who work for you, although they are not necessary for your Business Plan.

Note that the Entrepreneurs' Hub provides a very brief rundown of the personnel situation. In describing their lean operation, the owners who run the Hub keep their job descriptions lean. They demonstrate good sense when they express a commitment to hold down operating costs. Their decision reflects business discipline and foresight. If you were a potential investor in this business, you would appreciate some tight purse strings and sweat equity.

Every person on your team is important. Action Step 69 will help you to describe the kinds of people you will need and how you will help them become productive.

Management and Personnel of Entrepreneurs' Hub

Owners

Danielle Jackson was born in Shaker Heights, Ohio, in 1970. She earned her BS degree in industrial engineering at Purdue University. After graduation, she spent eight years in the Marine Corps, where she was a flight instructor and check pilot. While in the service, Jackson completed her MBA at the University of California in Irvine.

Following military service, Jackson was employed as a pilot for United Airlines for five years. Wanting a change, she purchased a firm exporting software and sold it four years later for $3 million. Serving on regional training committees and as a director of a local Small Business Development Center, she recognized a need for a for-profit center for entrepreneurial support and training.

Robert Wojchik was born in Dallas, Texas, in 1980. He has a BS degree in information science from the University of Oklahoma. After graduation, he worked for Procter and Gamble for several years. For two years he worked developing curriculum and training materials and presented classes for Microsoft and Oracle. For the past two years, he has worked to develop specialized small-business programs for Microsoft. His vast exposure to entrepreneurs and software knowledge are an invaluable asset to the Entrepreneurs' Hub training center.

Directors

Cheryl Hughes Smith, born in Corpus Christi, Texas, in 1983, has an MBA from Harvard and a law degree from the University of Texas at Austin. Smith is a partner in Smith, Jones, and Schultz, a Knoxville law firm. She is the author of numerous journal articles in the field of small-business tax planning as well as the author of the leading small-business tax planning blog.

Phil Carpenter was born in Duluth, Minnesota, in 1975. He graduated from Purdue University with a BS in management and a minor in operations management. Carpenter then worked for a large accounting firm for five years before attending Indiana University for his MBA. His research projects during his master's program focused on entrepreneurship. He is currently a professor of business at Roane State Community College, a general partner in two businesses, and a small-business consultant. He has published and lectured widely in the area of small business.

Other Available Resources

The Entrepreneurs' Hub has retained the legal firm of Farney and Shields and the accounting firm of Hancock and Associates. Our insurance broker is Sharon Mandel of Fireman's Fund. Public relations will be handled by Friend and Associates.

Personnel

During our first six months of operation, we had one full-time employee, but we have found that an additional employee is necessary to facilitate our expansion and to serve our customers properly. Additional instructors for specialized seminars will be hired on a contract basis. We need to run a lean operation, and the owners are willing to put in additional sweat equity.

© Cengage Learning

■ G. EXIT STRATEGY

As discussed in Chapter 12, many readers of your plan will be interested in your exit strategy. The more money involved, the more likely they will want to know your particular plans. The Entrepreneurs' Hub founders plan on continuing for at least five years in their business.

> ### Exit Strategy of Entrepreneurs' Hub
>
> After we build out our Oak Ridge location, we hope to build two additional locations in Tennessee over the next five years. On successful completion, and when we are able to show a strong profit in each center, we plan to sell all three training facilities, either to the managers running the individual centers or to one entrepreneur wishing to run a small chain of centers.

© Cengage Learning

■ SECTION II: FINANCIAL SECTION

Good Numbers

The financial section is the heart of your Business Plan. It is aimed at lenders—bankers, credit managers, venture capitalists, vendors, SBICs, commercial-credit lenders—people who think and dream in numbers. Lenders are skeptics by trade; they will not be swayed by the enthusiasm of your writing in Section I, so your job now is to make your numbers do the talking. This is easier than you might believe, since you are prepared.

In Chapter 8 you projected cash flow and income. You have tested your numbers on real lenders in the real world. If you have not already done so, you need to organize your numbers into standard instruments:

1. Pro forma income and cash-flow statements, pricing scenarios, and so on
2. Balance sheet

Examples from the Entrepreneurs' Hub will serve as models for you; adapt them to suit your business type. The idea is to know where every dime is going. You need to show when you will make a profit and in so doing appear neat, orderly, in control, and conservative. You will know you have succeeded when a skeptical lender looks up from your Business Plan and says, "You know, these numbers look good."

Good Notes

One way to spot a professional lender is to hand over your Business Plan and watch to see which sections he or she reads first. Most lenders first study the notes that accompany income and cash-flow projections. Knowing this allows you to prepare accordingly. Use these notes to explain to potential lenders how you generated your numbers (for example, "Advertising is projected at 5 percent of sales") and to explain specific entries (for example, "Leased Equipment—monthly lease 6,000 charge for computer equipment"). Make these notes easy to read with headings that start your readers off in the upper left-hand corner and march them down the page, step by step, to the bottom line. Some projections use tiny footnotes on the same page. We recommend *large* notes on a separate page with a "Notes" heading. Notes are important, so they should be big.

Creating your Business Plan takes a lot of time. It is only natural for you to hope that lenders will read it, become enthusiastic, and ask questions. The notes to your plan help you accomplish that, even if you have not yet started up and the numbers are projections into the future.

If your business has been going for some time, a detailed financial history should be included. For those seeking funding, the financial statements will be significant. You need to describe which type of funding you are seeking and include specific details on how that funding will be used and repaid.

ACTION STEP 70

Project Your Income Statement and Cash Flow

What you are driving at here is *net profit*—what is left in the kitty after expenses—for each month and for the year.

First, figure your *sales and cost of goods sold.* The first big bite out of that figure is the *cost of goods sold.* (In a service business the big cost is labor.) Subtracting that gives you a figure called *gross margin.*

Now add up all your *expenses*—rent, utilities, insurance, and so on—and subtract them from gross margin. This gives you your *net profit before taxes.* Subtract taxes to arrive at your net profit after tax.

In some cases, the income statement and cash-flow statement can be combined as one. In other instances, two separate statements will be used. Either format is usually acceptable.

Completing your financial statements requires business finance and accounting knowledge.

A. PROJECTED INCOME

Your next task is to put together your projected income statement, also called a *profit and loss statement.* With the information you have gathered so far, it should not be too difficult. In fact, it will be enjoyable if the numbers look good. If they do not, reconsider before you commit.

Review the Entrepreneurs' Hub's projected income statement and the careful documentation of items (Table 15.1). Action Step 70 will help you project your own monthly profits and losses for 12 months. You should also include a projected income statement for the next two to five years for your business. Although a cash-flow projection has not been included for the center, many lenders will require one. Annie's Business Plan in Appendix B provides a cash flow statement. Refer back to the numbers and scenarios you prepared back in Chapter 8 and revise and place them into your Business Plan.

B. BALANCE SHEET

Professional lenders look at your balance sheet, also called a statement of financial position, to analyze the state of your finances at a given point in time. They are looking at liquidity, which shows how easily your assets can be converted into cash, and capital structure—what sources of financing have been used, how much was borrowed, and so on. Professional lenders use such factors to evaluate your ability to manage your business.

The Entrepreneurs' Hub (see Table 15.2) did not provide notes to its balance sheets because in their case, no notes were needed. All the entries in the balance sheet should make sense. Explain any unusual figures clearly so the reader has no questions or feels uncertain about the number you have provided. Complete Action Step 71 to help you prepare and include a balance sheet in your Business Plan.

Action Step 71 is the last Action Step for Chapter 15. It is the end, yes, but also the beginning. However, now you need to return to the beginning of the chapter and revise you cover letter (Action Step 62) and your executive summary (Action Step 63).

All our best wishes go with you as you embark on your great adventure. We hope that this book and its Action Steps have convinced you that you can achieve success—whatever it means to *you*—and have *fun* at the same time. Good luck! Work smart and enjoy your adventure with passion.

ACTION STEP 71

Complete Your Balance Sheet

A balance sheet is a snapshot of your financial position at a certain point in time.

1. Add up your business assets. For convenience, divide these into *current* (cash, notes receivable, etc.), *fixed* (land, equipment, buildings, etc.), and *other* (intangibles like patents, royalty deals, copyrights, goodwill, contracts for exclusive use, etc.). You will need to depreciate fixed assets that wear out. As value, show the net of cost minus the accumulated depreciation.
2. Add up your liabilities. For convenience, divide these into *current* (accounts payable, notes payable, accrued expenses, interest on loans, etc.) and *long-term* (trust deeds, bank loans, equipment loans, balloons, etc.).
3. Subtract liabilities from assets.

You now have a picture of your business net worth. Are you in the red or in the black?

Ending Thoughts

Top 7 Myths About Starting a Business

From our experience consulting to entrepreneurs, start-ups, and small businesses over the past 10 years, we've gained much exposure to the realities of starting and growing businesses. We thought it would be interesting—and hopefully instructive—to lay out some of the myths and assumptions of aspiring entrepreneurs.

1. **It is all dependent on hard work.** Hard work is an absolutely necessary, but not sufficient, condition for starting and growing a business. It is the given, but without a solid Business Plan and compelling value proposition for customers and partners, all of the hard work in the world will be for naught. The world is filled with

table 15.1

Entrepreneurs' Hub's Pro Forma Income Statement

	Total	1st Month	2nd	3rd	4th	5th
SALES REVENUE	$607,329.22	$46,570.00	$47,268.55	$47,977.58	$48,697.24	$49,427.70
EXPENSES						
1. Advertising - 7%	$42,513.05	$3,259.90	$3,308.80	$3,358.43	$3,408.81	$3,459.94
2. Licenses/fees - 6%	$36,439.75	$2,794.20	$2,836.11	$2,878.65	$2,921.83	$2,965.66
3. Payroll Taxes - 10%	$4,159.20	$346.60	$346.60	$346.60	$346.60	$346.60
4. Salaries	$38,126.00	$3,466.00	$3,466.00	$3,466.00	$3,466.00	$3,466.00
5. Bank Charges - 0.4%	$18,219.88	$1,397.10	$1,418.06	$1,439.33	$1,460.92	$1,482.83
6. Dues and Subscriptions	$600.00	$50.00	$50.00	$50.00	$50.00	$50.00
7. Insurance	$18,000.00	$1,500.00	$1,500.00	$1,500.00	$1,500.00	$1,500.00
8. Janitorial - 0.7%	$4,251.30	$325.99	$330.88	$335.84	$340.88	$345.99
9. Office Supplies - 3.5%	$21,256.52	$1,629.95	$1,654.40	$1,679.22	$1,704.40	$1,729.97
10. Phone/Cable - 3%	$18,219.88	$1,397.10	$1,418.06	$1,439.33	$1,460.92	$1,482.83
11. Professional Fees	$12,000.00	$1,000.00	$1,000.00	$1,000.00	$1,000.00	$1,000.00
12. Rent	$46,680.00	$3,890.00	$3,890.00	$3,890.00	$3,890.00	$3,890.00
13. Repairs & Maint. - 3%	$18,219.88	$1,397.10	$1,418.06	$1,439.33	$1,460.92	$1,482.83
14. Travel & Entertain - 1%	$6,073.29	$465.70	$472.69	$479.78	$486.97	$494.28
15. Interest - 9%	$5,400.00	$450.00	$450.00	$450.00	$450.00	$450.00
16. Utilities - 3.0%	$18,219.88	$1,397.10	$1,418.06	$1,439.33	$1,460.92	$1,482.83
17. Misc. Expense - 3.0%	$6,443.93	$1,397.10	$425.42	$431.80	$438.28	$444.85
18. Lease Equipment	$24,000.00	$2,000.00	$2,000.00	$2,000.00	$2,000.00	$2,000.00
19. Contract Instructors (3)	$96,567.05	$7,200.00	$7,344.00	$7,490.88	$7,640.70	$7,793.51
20. Depreciation	$12,000.00	$1,000.00	$1,000.00	$1,000.00	$1,000.00	$1,000.00
TOTAL EXPENSES	$450,855.60	$36,363.84	$35,747.12	$36,114.51	$36,488.14	$36,868.13
NET INCOME BEFORE TAXES	$156,473.61	$10,206.16	$11,521.43	$11,863.07	$12,209.10	$12,559.57

Notes for Pro Forma Income Statement

Sales Revenue: Approximately 20 Fast-Start workshops sold at $1,250 each (income spread over 6 weeks), 80 Saturday workshops at $200 each, 110 weeknight workshops at $100 each, and misc. Seminar income

Advertising: Based on 7% of sales

Licenses/fees: Software license fees estimated at 6% of sales

Payroll Taxes: 10% of salaries

Salaries: 2 full-time secretarial employees earning $9 per hour

Bank Charges: 75% of sales will be charged to credit cards at a cost of 4% of sales.

Dues and Subscriptions: Subscriptions for owners and classrooms

Insurance: Quote provided by our insurance broker, Sharon Mandel of Fireman's Fund

Janitorial: Cleaning will be provided by janitorial service for less than the normal rate as the owner has traded janitorial services for software training.

Office Supplies: 3.5% of sales

overworked, overstressed, and not terribly successful small-business people who struggle not because of lack of appropriate effort, but rather for lack of appropriate planning.

2. **If your product or service is compelling enough, customers will beat a path to your door.** Unless you are building a business based upon intellectual property and/or technology that provides and creates a competitive advantage and compelling customer value proposition, the early success of your business will be based as much on your ability to market and sell your product and service as it will on the product or service offering itself. Remember: In a capitalistic marketplace there is *no* distinction between value and perceived value.

3. **If your product or service is compelling enough, investors will beat a path to your door.** Those who identify themselves as prospective investors in earlier-stage, small companies are mostly *inundated* with investment opportunities. As such, no matter how good and unique your business opportunity, there is always a strong, initial prejudice against investment that needs to be overcome.

4. **It is all about you.** The myth of the charismatic, "do and be everything" entrepreneur is just that—a myth. Any and all companies of value are great teams, much more than they are the by-product of one highly talented individual. The best entrepreneurs and business leaders inspire the mission, values, and philosophy of a company by their own example. This inspiration is then communicated to all of the business' stakeholders—employees, customers, investors, partners, vendors, and its wider community.

table 15.1

Entrepreneurs' Hub's Pro Forma Income Statement (continued)

6th	7th	8th	9th	10th	11th	12th
$50,169.12	$50,921.65	$51,685.48	$52,460.76	$53,247.67	$54,046.39	$54,857.08
$3,511.84	$3,564.52	$3,617.98	$3,672.25	$3,727.34	$3,783.25	$3,840.00
$3,010.15	$3,055.30	$3,101.13	$3,147.65	$3,194.86	$3,242.78	$3,291.42
$346.60	$346.60	$346.60	$346.60	$346.60	$346.60	$346.60
$3,466.00	$3,466.00	$3,466.00	$3,466.00	$3,466.00	$3,466.00	$3,466.00
$1,505.07	$1,527.65	$1,550.56	$1,573.82	$1,597.43	$1,621.39	$1,645.71
$50.00	$50.00	$50.00	$50.00	$50.00	$50.00	$50.00
$1,500.00	$1,500.00	$1,500.00	$1,500.00	$1,500.00	$1,500.00	$1,500.00
$351.18	$356.45	$361.80	$367.23	$372.73	$378.32	$384.00
$1,755.92	$1,782.26	$1,808.99	$1,836.13	$1,863.67	$1,891.62	$1,920.00
$1,505.07	$1,527.65	$1,550.56	$1,573.82	$1,597.43	$1,621.39	$1,645.71
$1,000.00	$1,000.00	$1,000.00	$1,000.00	$1,000.00	$1,000.00	$1,000.00
$3,890.00	$3,890.00	$3,890.00	$3,890.00	$3,890.00	$3,890.00	$3,890.00
$1,505.07	$1,527.65	$1,550.56	$1,573.82	$1,597.43	$1,621.39	$1,645.71
$501.69	$509.22	$516.85	$524.61	$532.48	$540.46	$548.57
$450.00	$450.00	$450.00	$450.00	$450.00	$450.00	$450.00
$1,505.07	$1,527.65	$1,550.56	$1,573.82	$1,597.43	$1,621.39	$1,645.71
$451.52	$458.29	$465.17	$472.15	$479.23	$486.42	$493.71
$2,000.00	$2,000.00	$2,000.00	$2,000.00	$2,000.00	$2,000.00	$2,000.00
$7,949.38	$8,108.37	$8,270.54	$8,435.95	$8,604.67	$8,776.76	$8,952.30
$1,000.00	$1,000.00	$1,000.00	$1,000.00	$1,000.00	$1,000.00	$1,000.00
$37,254.58	$37,647.60	$38,047.32	$38,453.84	$38,867.29	$39,287.79	$39,715.45
$12,914.54	$13,274.05	$13,638.16	$14,006.92	$14,380.38	$14,758.60	$15,141.63

© Cengage Learning

Professional Fees: Estimates received from our attorneys, Farney and Shields, and our accounting firm of Hancock and Associates
Rent: Based on $2.57 per square foot
Repairs and Maintenance: 3% of sales
Travel and Entertainment: 1% of sales; includes dues for professional and service organizations
Utilities: 3% of sales; based on discussions with utility providers and past experience
Misc. Indirect Expense: 3% of sales
Lease Equipment: Set monthly rate estimate provided by vendors
Contract Instructors: Three instructors each working 60 hours per month at $40 per hour
Interest: 9% per year on $60,000; 12 payments per year
Depreciation: Depreciation charges estimated by accountant

5. **The government is your friend.** We are constantly astounded by the regulatory and paperwork maze that a start-up company needs to negotiate and constantly monitor to both start and maintain a business. It is a significant time, money, and energy drain that detracts from the main value-creation intent of a new business. Our best advice in this regard—as resources are available—is to find competent legal and accounting counsel, to both advise upon and outsource the regulatory burden, so you can focus on business building.
6. **The government is your enemy.** Having said the above, in the mixed economy in which we live, government revenue opportunities on a local, state, federal, and international level have never been greater for small business. While slow, meandering, and confusing to approach, governments have much to recommend them as clients and customers, not the least of which is that once sold, government clients pay well and are not bad debt risks. A somewhat trite but very important credo to remember when selling to governments, even more so than in business, is that "it is not as much what you know but who you know."
7. **It is only worth doing if you become the next Google.** The vast majority of small businesses will always remain just that—small businesses. The odds of starting a business and have it become the next Google or a publicly traded company are very, very small. While we would never discourage entrepreneurs for aiming for the stars, it is also important to have success metrics grounded in probability. An expectation of a minimum of two years of very, very hard work with little financial return—but with a lot of learning (and some fun hopefully as well) involved is a good starting point. From this first milestone, then and only then should there start to be an expectation of significant wealth building. Find that balance between the long-term vision and the Monday morning action plan—and success, while not guaranteed, is very likely.

Source: Jay Turo, *http://www.growthink.com* (Accessed February 20, 2008).

table 15.2

The Entrepreneurs' Hub's Balance Sheet

Balance Sheet	ACTUAL (After first 6 months)
Current Assets	
Cash	$13,970
Books/Materials	$2,500
Total Current Assets	$16,470
Leasehold Improvements	$81,000
Furniture	$15,100
Equipment	$40,600
Total Fixed Assets	$146,700
Other Assets	
License	$25,000
TOTAL ASSETS	$178,170
Debt and Equity	
Current Debt	
Accounts Payable	$7,060
Accrued Wages	$2,500
Loan Payment	0
Total Current Debt	$9,560
Long-Term Debt	
Bank Loan	0
TOTAL DEBT	$9,560
Equity	
Owners' Net Worth	$168,610
TOTAL DEBT AND EQUITY	$178,170

Source: Jay Turo, *http://www.growthink.com* (Accessed February 20, 2008).

■ EPILOGUE

Act on What You Know

Well, do you feel like you are ready? You are. You have thoroughly researched your product or service, your industry, your Target Customers, your competition, your marketing strategy, and your location. You have discovered how to prepare for surprises you cannot afford; how to handle numbers; how to pursue financing; when and why you should incorporate; how to build a winning team; and whether you should buy an ongoing business, become a franchisee, or strike out on your own. And you have written it all up in a showcase: your winning Business Plan.

■ SUMMARY

It has been a long haul. When you visit vendors, bankers, and potential lenders, take your portable showcase, your Business Plan, to speak for you and demonstrate to all that you have a blueprint for success.

Begin writing by starting with the material you feel most comfortable with. Once you have completed one portion of the plan, the other parts will fall into place more easily. Fortunately, your work in earlier chapters has prepared you for each section.

Make sure your Business Plan has answered the following questions:

- What is your mission?
- How are you going to market your product or service?
- Who is going to purchase your product or service?
- How will you reach your Target Customers?
- What makes your firm unique?
- What is your business model?
- What is you revenue model?
- How will you support the financial needs of your growing firm?

After you have completed the plan, rewrite your cover letter and executive summary, highlighting the most relevant information and data for your readers. Remember the plan you have written is a working document to be constantly revised. *Good luck and go forth with passion!*

■ THINK POINTS FOR SUCCESS

- The executive summary should read like advertising copy. Keep revising it until it is tight and convincing. But do not exaggerate.
- Section I should generate enthusiasm for your business.
- Section II should substantiate the enthusiasm with numbers.

- Be sure footnotes sufficiently explain the numbers in your financial statements.
- Do not inflate numbers to impress.
- Use your Business Plan as a road map to success.

- Your Business Plan is a working, living document; revise it every 3, or 12 months depending on the volatility in your industry.

■ KEY POINTS FROM ANOTHER VIEW

Entrepreneur Essentials

Serial entrepreneur, Harvard MBA and former Utah Entrepreneur of the Year, Gary L. Crocker, advises entrepreneurs to look at the following issues as they build their businesses.

Provide Passion and Energy

A sense of urgency and the capacity to radiate passion, commitment, and vision with others are absolutely necessary. Few survive without these traits no matter how strong their Business Plan. Founders often loose that sense of urgency once they get a little funding and feel secure. The first infusions of capital are *just* the start of any venture.

Don't Allow Politics Inside

Small ventures cannot sustain infighting and politics. Every minute needs to be productive and every person is responsible for moving the venture forward. Lead from the top and don't allow people to care more about their position in the company than the company itself.

Don't Let Money Cause You to Lose Focus

After receiving funding, don't lose focus on your original Business Plan and attempt to branch out too quickly. Focus again on your business and be sure that you can describe your business to someone in one sentence stressing what makes you unique.

"Look yourself in the mirror before you go to someone with your Business Plan, and apply the one sentence rule. Crisply and succinctly define what your core competence is, what differentiates you, and what make you fundable to a potential investor or to potential employees whose lives will be your moral responsibility."

Structure Decisions so One Bad One Doesn't Destroy

Remember entrepreneurs are calculated risk takers, not wild characters but ones who "want to make things work". Thus, they develop contingency plans and provide resources to take action if something doesn't go as expected.

Share with Those Who Help You Build Your Business

Make sure employees understand their relative importance and the fundamental contributions they make to the venture. Link your employees' "quantifiable performance and behavior" to economic rewards. "Don't toss around equity—it is sacred and is the ultimate motivator."

Communicate Your Mission and Vision Often and with Consistency

"People need to be reminded on a personal basis clearly, briefly, and often of what your vision is for the entity. Don't do it via e-mail. Walk around and make sure that you personally communicate your sense of mission and objectives."

Be Humble

Realistically assess your "organization's skills and competencies." Also, be honest and pragmatic when assessing competitors' strengths. Humbly judge exactly where you and others stand. "Entrepreneurs who survive learn from other people's mistakes, not just their own."

■ ACTION STEPS

Image_Source/iStockphoto.com

Appendix A

Fast-Start Business Plan

The Fast-Start Plan allows you to start *now*—a good option if you have been in business before and know the footwork of entrepreneurship, if you are developing an app, or if you are starting a low-entry cost business—especially on the Internet. With the Fast-Start Plan, you are using the business as a probe into the marketplace.

You can start quickly, because you have an instinct for beating out the competition. You also have a sense of the market and a good feel of the business you are starting.

The Fast-Start Plan is *not* a substitute for preparing a full-fledged plan. Thus, use the Fast-Start Plan for a specific venture that is easy to start and carries minimal financial risk. Also use it for a business that is breaking new ground, where there is little data available and speed to the market is imperative. Or use the Fast-Start Business Plan if you need money now and have a good idea.

In addition, to check out a business idea quickly, you can prepare a Fast-Start Business Plan and then complete a full-fledged plan if the Fast-Start Plan looks promising, or if the business grows quickly and needs additional financing. Read through the Yes, We Do Windows Business Plan at the end of Appendix A before you begin writing your Fast-Start Plan.

If you are going it alone with money you can afford to lose ($1,000; $5,000; $10,000; $100,000), and if the loss of that money will not jeopardize your loved ones and make wolves howl at your door, the Fast-Start Plan may work for you; or it may work if you just want to try out an idea before exploring the business idea further.

If other people are involved—investors, bankers, advisors, company officers—then return to Chapter 15 and write a comprehensive plan that will provide a blueprint to follow month by month through the first year.

Gather up all the information from your past action steps. You can develop the Fast-Start plan on your own; or for additional assistance, use one of the online Business Plan templates discussed in Chapter 15.

■ QUICK CHECKLIST

Below is a quick checklist for implementing the Fast-Start Plan:

1. Can you afford to lose your dollar investment? How much money can you afford to lose at the slots in Reno or Las Vegas or Atlantic City? Can you lose $100? $500? $1,000? $25,000? More? What is your deductible on your car insurance, your boat insurance, or your major medical insurance? Write down the amount you can afford to lose. If you have excess money to speculate with, then the Fast-Start Plan may be for you.
2. How easy is it to enter this business? Is it easy to talk to other owners? Are role models in abundance? Do the prospective customers have a clear understanding of the goods and services provided? Examples of businesses with

easy entry include window washing, auto detailing, landscape maintenance, arts and crafts, selling on eBay, Etsy or Craigslist, opening a store on Shopify, vacation pet sitting, consulting, graphic arts, and writing apps.

3. Can you start this business on a part-time basis? Starting part-time decreases your risk. You have a chance to prove the business and see how much you really like it. Keep a running tally of customer responses, but keep your other job and the income and possible benefits it provides.

4. How tough is it to gather needed data to formulate a Fast-Start Business Plan? In breaking new ground, be careful and be creative and take risks! In such a venture, the market is not clearly defined. There are very few competitors. Pricing is not clear, so you must make certain you have a market out there that is willing to pay. Sometimes this takes time, so make sure you have enough capital to hold you over as you dive into unknown territory. Be frugal. The opportunities though are endless. Pinterest sold to Facebook for $1 billion 18 months after being formed! Work hard. Be creative. Take chances!

5. Can you start using only your own funds? Bill Gates, the founder of Microsoft, could use the Fast-Start Plan for a business start-up costing billions. A single parent of two with rent and a car loan can afford much less. Be honest with yourself. Be honest with your family.

■ STRUCTURING YOUR PLAN

Use these questions and all of the Actions Steps you have completed to complete your Fast-Start Plan:

- How do you describe your business?
- What business are you really in?
- Who is your competition and how are they doing?
- What is your pricing strategy?
- Who is your Target Customer?
- How will you market your product or service?
- What makes your product or service more compelling than your competitors?
- How will you get paid and how will you make money?
- What are your start-up costs?
- What are your sales goals for the first three months?
- What is your break-even point?
- What are your operating expenses for the first three months?
- If you crash and burn, what can you salvage for cash?
- What have you forgotten?

■ A GREAT DREAM CAN EQUAL A GREAT BUSINESS

It's late, and the family has gone to bed. The house is quiet. The pets are snoozing. And in your head, a dream is brewing.

Your dream has given you a jump-start into a new world, a business of your own. Now you need to add in the details and make it happen.

You want to be proud of being in business. You want to care. You want your customers to care. People love to do business with people who care about what they are doing. When people take pride in a job well done, it shows.

■ WHO ARE MY TARGET CUSTOMERS?

Who will receive the biggest benefit from your business? Who can pay the price? Who can you affordably target and reach? Where do they live? What sites do they frequent? What is their income range? What do they need? What work do they do? Are they married, single, divorced, or retired?

Do women outnumber men? What is the average age? What cars do they drive? How are the customers dressed? How expensive are their shoes? Do they use cash? Debit? Credit? How expensive are the items they are buying?

To profile your customers, become a marketplace detective. Practice; study the customers that buy from your competitors. If on the Internet, see who "Likes" your competitors or posts reviews. Check out potential customers Pinterest pages.

Practice trains your new eyes to consider the person as a prospect. Always remember you are meeting your customers' needs not yours! Sell benefits not products or services!

■ HOW CAN I CONNECT WITH MY CUSTOMERS?

Before you spend a bundle on Internet advertising, or three months knocking on doors of houses along Golf Course Drive, take time to refine your message.

What image do you want to project? How do you want the marketplace to perceive your product or service? What position do you want to assume among your competitors? How soon and what steps will you take to begin?

Once you answer these questions, design your business card. Use a name and a logo that offers an insight into your business. If you are starting an auto-detailing business, use something along the lines of "On-Time Quality Service." If you are thinking of house cleaning, try: "Only Sparkle!" Business cards are inexpensive memory seeds, handy reminders, and often your most cost-effective advertising. Be sure to include your website address.

Once your business cards and website are done, research ways of reaching your customers. Do they gather at church, school, Starbucks, football games, or Little League games? Where do they gather on the Net? What do they read, watch, and listen to?

Could you reach them best through blogs, websites, billboards, door hangers, or sandwich boards on the street? What can you afford? Match that amount with the most effective communications channels and most importantly take risks and be creative. Your business is young and you need to get noticed.

For almost all businesses at the beginning, positive word of mouth propels the business forward fastest. Your current customers are your best promotional tools, and encouraging them to spread the word on your behalf is the cheapest and most effective way to promote your business. Remember, bad word of mouth travels even faster so correct any customer issues *immediately*. Social media today can launch your business but it can also sink it like the Titanic.

Stay visible. If your Target Customers gather in groups, try to reach them there. Attend their meetings. Get on their list of speakers. Give a demonstration. Hand out business cards. Offer something for free!

If you must find your customers one at a time, spend a few hours each day knocking on doors. Telephone prospects. Work your mailing list. If you use mail contacts, be sure you do phone follow-ups.

Join the local chamber of commerce. If you are lucky, your chamber will run a short piece about you, the newcomer, in their newsletter. Stay visible at chamber meetings. Do not get pushy with your business cards, but have them handy. Join professional associations and local networking groups.

While you are connecting with customers, do not overlook organizations that might act as your sales force. For example, let us say you have found a school where the parents' group is trying to raise funds to support an athletic endeavor. Put together a flyer for students to take home. In return for each sale from the flyer, your business will donate 10 to 15 percent to the fund-raising group. Consider the donation a part of your promotional budget.

■ WHO ARE MY COMPETITORS?

How do you find them? If you are hunting for retailers or restaurant owners, hop in your car and drive around. Eat in the restaurants. Shop at the stores. Continue to network with your friends and neighbors if you are looking at a local business.

If you are starting an Internet or distribution business, network your way to reviews and information on the Internet. Check out blogs, other websites, Twitter, LinkedIn, Pinterest, and online customer reviews (take these with a grain of salt, since firms are rewarding customers for positive reviews, they need to be looked at skeptically).

If you are manufacturing a product, buy all your competitors' products and use them. Give them to your friends, have them compare. But realize your friends will probably be biased. So you might want to test with other potential customers.

What can you learn from your competitors? Each will probably have one or two elements at which they excel; look hard to find those elements, and *never* discount your competitors' strengths. Your goal is to find an area where *you* will excel.

Once you find your competitors, take a closer look. Were they easy to find? How visible was their advertising? As you study their advertising strategy, what kind of a customer profile can you draw? Are they spending a lot on their advertising? Are they working on a shoestring?

What can you tell from their pricing? Are prices firm or negotiable? Are they high? Low? Competitive? Which Target Customers will purchase at these prices? Who will get shut out? Do your competitors understand the marketplace? Is their pricing structure positioned properly?

Are your competitors zeroed in on a specific Target Customer, or are they using the shotgun approach? Profile the Target Customer of your competitors. Later you will be profiling your customer, and you may want to find a niche that is not being served.

Which of your competitors are successful? Can you tell why? Which are just hanging in there? Why? If a business has been operating for some time, there is a good chance the owner is doing something right. What is it? Nose around. What customer benefits do they offer? Fast service? Quality work? Free delivery? Low prices?

Take the time to talk with the customers of your competitors. Are they satisfied? If not, why not? How do they see the competition? What image does the competition project? How do customers feel about price, quality, and timeliness?

Even the most successful business overlooks something. Find out what your competitors missed. Are they overlooking a market segment? Can *you* reach that overlooked market? Are they sloppy with their advertising? Are their services actually limited? Is inventory sparse? Is their service poor? Thousands of businesses have been built on the weaknesses of the competition.

Take time to chat with competitors outside your area. Is there a gap no one has thought to close? If there is, you may be on your way faster than you thought!

■ HOW MUCH SHOULD I CHARGE?

Find out what is important to the customers. It is probably time, dependability, quality, convenience, prestige, price, or some combination of those. Learn to see the value of your product or service through your customers' eyes. Answer the questions: What is most important to your customers? How can you best meet their needs?

Pricing is *one* key. Do not be misled by thinking you can whisk customers away from established competitors by charging less for the same thing. It did not work for now-bankrupt department stores, and it will not work for you.

■ WHAT ARE MY START-UP COSTS?

List everything that you need to open your business. Do not worry if the list would cost a bundle. You are brainstorming at this point. The key here is not to overlook anything. A visit to your competitors will add ideas to your list. An interview with an owner will trigger new items.

When you are chatting with businesspeople, ask questions: What software do you find most helpful? What was the cost of start-up inventory? What items are essential to start this type of business? When your list is fat, add price tags to each item.

In the beginning, borrow everything you can. When you have to purchase, buy used. Although used equipment might be scratched or dented, you stand to save 50 to 90 percent. Check Craigslist and eBay. Talk with potential suppliers—they usually know someone who is going out of business. You can find good deals from an owner who is folding or upgrading.

When you start purchasing, check the large discount stores. If one company in your area can supply most of your needs, focus on trying to get a package deal, and develop a long-term relationship.

You should also consider leasing your equipment. As your business grows and your leases expire, decide whether to replace by buying new or used. Leasing provides you a lot of up-front flexibility, because you are able to hold on to your capital a little longer. Time now to be realistic and frugal. Divide your start-up list into two columns: Column 1 contains items that are absolutely necessary. Column 2 contains "nice-to-haves."

Check Column 1. Is there anything you can borrow from home, parents, or friends? Scrape to the bottom of the barrel here. Your goal is to cut costs so you will have cash to *run* the business. Many entrepreneurs sink themselves before they even open their doors by thinking it is necessary to have the latest and best. There will be plenty of time for that type of thinking later, but only if you are conservative at the beginning.

■ WHAT ARE MY SALES GOALS FOR THE FIRST THREE MONTHS?

How much would you like to sell the first month, the second, and the third? How much product can you sell with the cash you have for inventory? Or, what level of services can you provide with the time you have available? How much, if any, do you have available to pay others? What is a realistic target for your new business?

Sales goals provide the information you need to forecast your variable expenses, which are those expenses forced to change in relation to sales volume. If you are selling a product or service, sales goals will allow you to estimate the cost of goods sold.

Sales goals provide the driving force for you and your team. They help you focus on your target for the month. When the month is finished, compare how you did with your initial sales goals. Did you make it? If not, why not? Did you exceed your goal by 25 percent? Why? What worked well? What did not? What is selling? What is profitable? Who is buying? As you evaluate, decide how to improve each subsequent month. Revamp.

To chart a reasonable sales goal, focus on three factors:

1. **The weight of your marketing program:** Do you plan a wide-area campaign? Will you start by calling on friends and neighbors, counting on

them to spread the word? How much energy are you putting into this? Will you start full time? Will you keep your job? If you are in school, will you stay enrolled?

2. **The experience of entrepreneurs in businesses like yours who operate in a noncompeting area:** How much effort does Entrepreneur A have to put out to make a $100 sale in his or her area?

3. **The capacity you have to deliver the product or service:** What do you need to make this venture go? If it costs you $500 for materials to build one custom table, and you only have $500 worth of capital, then you will be limited to building one table at a time.

Or let us say you are starting a part-time business detailing automobiles. Detailing one automobile takes three hours. In addition, driving to the clients, collections, and scheduling take approximately one hour per car. Your maximum sales activity per week will be based on the number of hours you can devote to your business after you put in your hours at your full-time job, if you are still employed. If you can devote 24 hours a week your potential gross income would be:

$$24/4 = 6 \text{ autos per week maximum sales volume}$$
$$\text{Your charge per auto} = \$120$$
$$6 \times \$120 = \$720 \text{ per week potential gross income}$$

Make a list of your friends and relatives. Find out how many of them have their cars detailed. Add the repeat factor. How often do they want detailing— once a month, once every quarter, or once a year? When your list is finished, and you have 72 prospects, recognize that you may have a realistic shot at 18 of those prospects. For your business, that is enough for a start-up.

As a wise entrepreneur, you know that your first few jobs will take longer than later ones. You are new, and you are learning the business, so you must make sure you do a superb job so you can count on referrals. You have four prospects who want monthly detailing, and six more want it quarterly. Start with these 10 prospects and your business is underway!

■ YOUR TO-DO LIST

Now that your plan is complete, it is time to follow through. The next step is to finalize your to-do list and begin. You need this list for at least three reasons:

1. It provides steps to follow.
2. It keeps you on target.
3. It provides realistic goals.

■ YOUR TURN NOW!

The key to any business, and to any Business Plan, is how well you understand the needs of your Target Customer *and* the need to make a profit. Find an itch that is not being scratched, and you can ace your competitors.

First read the Yes, We Do Windows Business Plan that follows, and then gather your Action Steps already completed. Then develop your own Fast-Start Plan and you will become the entrepreneur you know you can be.

Once you write your own Fast-Start Plan, keep it handy, and refer to it often and continually update and revise. Remember although we say it is road map, it is one of a fast growing community with lots of changes!

Use it to keep your business on track in those early months of operation. When you have been in business for three months, use your Fast-Start Plan as a launching pad for your next nine months of operation. For your second year, write a full-fledged Business Plan.

May your Business Plan, along with hard work, sweat, long hours, willingness to risk, creativity, and passion, lead to your success.

Congratulations and forge ahead!

■ YES, WE DO WINDOWS

Fast-Start Business Plan

1. Business Description
2. Competition
3. Target Customers
4. Marketing Plan
5. Pricing
6. Start-up Costs
7. Sales Goals and Expenses (three months)
8. To-do List

1. Business Description   Providing sparkling clean windows that allow homeowners to enjoy their home, protect their investment, and deepen their pride of ownership utilizing only eco-friendly, fragrance-free products.

A home is a person's most expensive investment. Many homes today in my target market are supported by dual-income and single family households and few of these homeowners have the time or desire to do their own window cleaning.

2. Competition and My Strengths   At this time, there are five window cleaning services listed in my area Yellow Pages—three franchisees and two independents. The marketing research I undertook by making phone calls to my competitors and talking with potential customers indicated there was room for another professional window cleaning firm in the area.

A few of the firms contacted for services did not return calls, were rude, and were unable to provide phone bids. My research shows three of these operations are not reliable according to former clients. Although, one independent operating as a one-man shop is very reliable; this operation will be my major competitor. As not to cannibalize on his business and acknowledging there is an ample market available, I will try not to compete in the exact same neighborhoods as he does.

Research shows window cleaning services and pricing offered by the competitors are very similar. Thus, I have decided I will not compete on price but will try hard to offer exceptional, timely, guaranteed and professional service. Most window cleaners are in and out of business quickly and do not present a professional image. Thus, I plan to present a very professional appearance at all times; always wearing a clean shirt with my company name and logo, driving an immaculate truck with professional signage, and placing professional signs in each yard as I clean the windows. I will be using eco-friendly products which none of my local competitors offer.

My research also shows several of my competitors do not clean windowsills and tracks, and thus these services will be added in my business. In addition, all screens will be removed and scrubbed. Clients will be charged for these additional services.

Evaluating the competition has given my start-up a real advantage. Since I will be doing all the work myself, I can continue to gather customer data as I work. Many clients mentioned they were uncomfortable with different people working on their homes at each service. Since I will do all the work myself for at least six months, this will definitely be a competitive advantage at the beginning; this also will be one of my marketing focuses at start-up.

As I add employees, I will introduce my employees to the clients and will work with them at the beginning. Since my neighborhoods are very dense and close together I will be able to check their work each day to assure consistency and good work.

A home is a private place. It is a place where one goes to escape from the day. One does not want it invaded by strangers. My plan is to expand only when I find the right employees.

I see two additional "musts" for my business: 1) bids must be firm, and 2) phone skills must be customer-oriented with calls returned within a few hours and e-mails followed through on as quickly as possible. The image I hope to present is: "I aim to please. I'm interested in servicing your home and making you and your windows shine on a continuing basis."

3. Target Customers I am focusing my business on 10 large subdivisions. Within each of these subdivisions there are approximately five to seven floor plans. When clients call for a bid, I will be able to ask them the model of their home and provide a quick estimate based on their information.

The majority of my clients will be dual-career or female-headed households with one to two children. Clients are primarily upper-middle class in this area with incomes of $100–150K. Spare time is at a premium and is reserved for recreation and entertainment. Homeowners drive primarily small SUVs and sedans. The homeowners take great pride in their homes and are very concerned with keeping up with their neighbors.

4. Marketing Plan
- I will maintain an image of high visibility and professionalism. My white truck with blue lettered signs will be washed weekly. All signs on the truck will be kept in perfect condition. My equipment and ladders will all be kept in excellent condition.
- All my advertising will be in navy blue and white. Business cards are blue with white lettering. On the reverse side is a list of my services. Whenever I hand out a business card I aim to gain one in return. Data from these cards will be placed in to my data base immediately for further marketing efforts.
- My attire will include a white shirt with my navy blue logo, navy blue pants and white tennis shoes.
- All my work equipment will be maintained in perfect shape so I present a professional image at all times.
- I acknowledge that I must compete with individuals operating illegally who offer bids 20 to 40 percent lower than the reputable licensed and bonded window cleaners. My challenge will be to turn this problem into an advantage rather than a disadvantage. Thus, clients will be presented with copies of my business license and proof of insurance and bonding. In addition, my insurance firm has a one-page statement that clearly delineates possible financial and legal consequences of using unlicensed businesses operating illegally and I will attach the statement to each bid. I will provide references for each of the neighborhoods where I serve.
- For the first three months, I will spend approximately three to four hours each weekend walking the neighborhoods with door hangers announcing my services. Also, while walking the neighborhoods on the weekend in my uniform, I hope to meet and talk with many of the homeowners who will be working in their yards or playing with their children. I will be giving away a small eco-friendly glass cleaner they can keep in their cars. As people respond to the door hangers, I will continue my market research by asking the following: Whom did you use in the past? What did you like or dislike about their services? What additional services would you like?
- I will purchase my domain name for my website where I will have an online calculator that will provide potential clients quick estimates. In addition, there

will be a scheduling calendar onsite as well. I would like to set up a PayPal and Square accounts to accept payments online and onsite as well.

- I will contact each client within 24 hours after I have completed my services and clear up any problems immediately. As I believe word of mouth will be my best marketing tool, I will do everything to keep my clients satisfied. After the first window cleaning, I will attach a photo of their home in my thank you emails. Hopefully, they might post the photo online and spread the word.
- I will contact each client every three months to try to develop repeat clientele.
- Company signs with my phone number will be displayed on client's property while window cleaning takes place.
- I will purchase small ads in targeted neighborhood association newsletters and will also post small ads on their association websites. These ads are very inexpensive and aimed directly at my clients. Hopefully, they will go online to access a quote or call me.
- I will also donate window cleaning services for my daughter's private school on a monthly basis, hoping my efforts will be mentioned in the PTA newsletter.
- I will join a very successful BNI networking group, which meets on a weekly basis. All members are required to market others' businesses.

5. Pricing   Pricing will be competitive and within close range of my major competitors. I will not compete on price with the illegal operators.

Basic Rates for Window Cleaning	Fees
Windows-in and out/tracks/sills	
Plain	$4–$8 per window
Sliding Glass Doors	$5 per door
French Doors	$7 per door
Screens	$1 per screen
Mirrors	$4 each
Chandeliers	quote upon request
Car windows (inside and out)	$10 sedan/$20 SUV
Average cost per home	$120.00–$150.00

6. Start-up Costs

Insurance (car and business)	700
Truck*	
Bond (initial cost)	750
Ladders	350
Legal advice (1 hour)	150
Bookkeeper advice (2 hours)	100
Supplies	300
Signs for truck	295
Advertising	1,000
Cell phone with Internet access/scheduler	500
P.O. Box per month—first and last month	40
Networking group (initiation fee)**	300
Fictitious business name filing	85
City business license	155
Used desk and chair	375
Supplies and file system	50
Computer accounting and billing software***	195
Bank account (order checks)	125
Total Estimated Start-up Expenses	5,470

*I currently own a white 2010 Ford truck in excellent condition (no payment).

**Networking weekly meetings will cost $80.00 a month.

***Currently own computer and printer.

7. Sales Goals and Expenses, First Three Months I plan to work six days per week for the first three months. I plan to work Monday through Friday completing window cleaning jobs and Saturday will be devoted to marketing and managing the business. I am assuming the first month that I will complete 20 window cleaning jobs, the second month 30, and the third month 40, at an average of $135.00 each.

table **A.1**

Proforma Income Statement— Yes, We Do Windows

| | **Sales Goals and Expenses** | | |
	1st Month	**2nd Month**	**3rd Month**
Sales (1)	2700	4050	5400
Expenses:			
Gas (2)	400	500	600
Maintenance (3)	160	160	160
Insurance (4)	125	125	125
Phone (5)	100	100	100
Advertising (6)	200	400	600
Supplies (7)	200	300	400
Credit Card (8)	300	300	300
Network lunches	80	80	80
P.O. Box	40	40	40
Miscellaneous	200	400	600
Expense Total	1805	2405	3005
Gross Profit	895	1645	2395

© Cengage Learning

Assumptions for Table A.1
1. Average customer $135 (20 – 1st month, 30 – 2nd month, 40 – 3rd month).
2. Gas, ($400 – 1st month, $500 – 2nd month, $600 – 3rd month)
3. Maintenance—mainly a reserve for tires, repairs, oil changes, $40 per week.
4. Auto and business liability, $1,500 per year
5. Apple iPhone cell phone charges (currently own iPhone)
6. Approximately $200 for ads in association newsletters and websites and door hangers
7. Approximately $10 per job
8. Credit card payment for start-up expenses (used $4,000 of cash on hand for expenses and cash advance of $3,000, which I intend to pay back before the end of the year).

8. To-Do List

1. Talk with experienced window cleaners out of my area to confirm my ideas and gather new ideas.
2. Stay organized.
3. Choose a business name.
4. File for fictitious business name.
5. Determine specific geographical area to service and get home models and number of windows, doors for each to put on website for quotes.
6. Setup PayPal account and setup account on Square to accept credit card payments on my iPhone.
7. Check out several banks as fees and services vary. Set up business checking account.
8. Locate, evaluate, and select suppliers and order initial supplies.
9. Check city and county business license regulations and apply.
10. File for a federal ID number—needed by all employers for future.
11. Locate an insurance agent and purchase insurance.
12. Set up a meeting with an accountant/bookkeeper to help set-up Quicken.

13. Complete advertising for association newsletters and websites.
14. Join a discount warehouse club.
15. Order business cards, door hangers, thank you notes, and yard signs.
16. Set up P.O. Box
17. Record all income and expenses and mileage daily.
18. Meet with attorney for an hour to determine if there are any legal issues that I need to consider.
19. Network with friends and relatives; encourage them to spread the word about my new business via social media. Post on my own Facebook and LinkedIn accounts.
20. Order magnetic signs for vehicles.
21. Purchase accounting and billing software.
22. Arrange bond.
23. Obtain *Tax Guide for Small Business* (IRS Publication 334).
24. Obtain *Taxpayers Starting a Business* (IRS Publication 583).
25. Obtain *IRS's Tax Calendar for Small Business.*
26. Join International Window Cleaners Association.
27. Develop website and social media plan.
28. Finish Fast-Start Business Plan.
29. **Start Washing Windows!**

Additional steps previously taken:

1. Completed market research.
2. Reviewed personal financial situation.
3. Reduced all personal/family expenses.
4. Acquired credit score information and dealt with issues.
5. Reviewed health, auto, liability, and business insurance needs.
6. Increased credit line on credit card from $5,000 to $10.000.

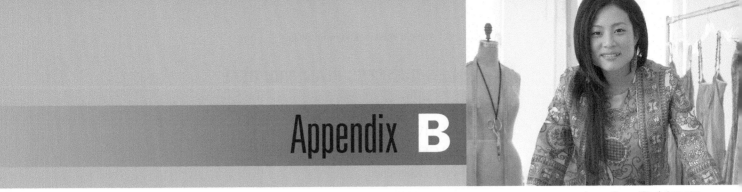

Image_Source/iStockphoto.com

Appendix B

Annie's Business Plan Proposal

■ COVER LETTER FOR ANNIE'S

Business Plan Proposal for Specialty Chocolates and Candy Concession at Sea World

Annie's
27898 Palm Tree Lane
Escondido, CA 92677

Oct. 1, 2012

Sea World
Ms. Janet Wilkes
2 Sea World Drive
San Diego, CA 92888

Dear Ms. Wilkes,

We are pleased to offer our proposal to operate a chocolate and candy concession at Sea World with an August opening date. With 17 years of retailing experience throughout San Diego, and our excellent reputation as a provider of one of the largest selections of candies and chocolates, we believe Annie's will be an excellent addition to Sea World's concession offerings.

Annie's is thrilled to offer your national and international tourists the opportunity to shop at San Diego's finest chocolate and candy store. Sea World's long and successful run as one of the premiere attractions in San Diego offers Annie's a great opportunity to expand our business.

Our firm is self-financed, and our strong balance sheet allows Annie's to expand into Sea World without outside financing. Thus we will be able to open within 8 weeks following proposal acceptance.

On review of our proposal, please contact us to clarify any points. We look forward to a long and profitable association with Sea World.

Sincerely,

Casey Johnson
President (Annie's)

■ ANNIE'S BUSINESS PLAN PROPOSAL

Business Plan Contents

EXECUTIVE SUMMARY

MANAGEMENT AND STAFFING

    Retail Experience

    Management

    Staffing Plan

    Exit Strategy

STORE OVERVIEW

    Floor Plan

    Visual Presentation

    Products

MARKETING

    Retail Trends

    Customer Service Philosophy/Programs

    Marketing Plan

STORE OPERATIONS

    Stocking

    Logistics and Frequency of Deliveries

    Facility Maintenance Plan

FINANCIAL MANAGEMENT and FINANCIALS

    System of Internal Controls

        Sales and Cash Receipts

        Inventory and Accounts Payable

    Projected Rental Revenue

    Capital Investment

    Projected Income and Cash-Flow Statement

APPENDIX

Note: Due to the fact this Business Plan is a proposal for operating a ficticious concession within Sea World, primary emphasis is on store operations, experience, and product. Location is clearly defined, marketing is limited primarily to in-store promotions, and competition is limited to other concessionaires, none of whom are direct competitors.

■ EXECUTIVE SUMMARY

Annie's specialty shop will feature fine chocolates and candy as a concessionaire for Sea World. Annie's unique stores strive to create an atmosphere that is entertaining and fun for the customer to browse and shop in, upscale yet casual, and a place where employees enjoy working. We are known to provide high-quality, fresh products and intimate customer service. Annie's owners like it when people get excited in their stores and remember Annie's as a place that they want to return to. As owners, we are customer-driven and love retailing.

We have been successful candy retailers for the past 17 years and believe we do an excellent job selling bulk candy, chocolates, and candy gift packages. Few other operations offer such a complete selection of confections from hundreds of manufacturers under one roof. Many of the items offered for sale are very different and unusual. Because of this wide selection, Annie's is able to offer many different price points to meet the needs of most customers. Your customers will also consider our candies and chocolates ideal gifts.

Our proposal for a candy concession at Sea World comes after thorough research into the make-up of the other vendors and our belief that Annie's will complement the other stores and not cannibalize sales. Candy is considered an "extra," one that tourists and families gladly splurge on during their vacations. Many visitors will pass our store as they exit Sea World and will want something sweet before they get on the road back to their homes or hotels.

Upon Sea World's acceptance of our proposal, we could be open within eight weeks. Our strong balance sheet and available cash on hand will allow us to act immediately. Annie's staff will thoroughly train our Sea World store staff in our other stores prior to opening in Sea World. On opening day, we will offer trained personnel ready and willing to serve Sea World's customers with our legendary customer service.

Our creative store layout is designed to accommodate a large number of customers at one time, and at the busiest times of the day and year, we will be able to operate two computer registers. Through our 17 years in business, we have refined our store layout to best serve our customers and employees.

We believe our retail experience, strong balance sheet, excellent reputation throughout the Southern California area, and tasty chocolate product offerings will be a wonderful addition to Sea World.

■ MANAGEMENT AND STAFFING

Retail Experience and History

Since its inception in 1995, Annie's has been a successful retailer of bulk candy and chocolates, top-of-the-line gourmet boxed chocolates and truffles, domestic and foreign product lines, sugar-free and gluten-free products, novelty and nostalgia candies, dried fruit gifts, gourmet food gifts, gift baskets, Kosher confections, difficult-to-find items, seasonal merchandise, and related gift items that complement the packaged food products. Annie's is well known by consumers in Southern California as having the largest and most complete selection of confections in the area at our five store locations.

Through the years as owners, we have identified the best sources for over 2000 **SKUs**. We not only know where and how to purchase the merchandise, we also know, for each item, the turnover when reasonably priced, the shelf life, and the gross margin. We know how to purchase in both large and small quantities, depending on the candy, the weather, the store location, and the time of year. We know which vendors are able to keep freight costs under control and pack without excessive damage. Our company "cherry picks" the best from many distributors and manufacturers. We also carry nearly the entire line of those suppliers who do an excellent job; for example, Lindt, Joseph Schmidt, Asher's, Ghiradelli, Goelitz, Laymon, and so on.

SKU Stock Keeping Unit, code to identify product

Annie's does not manufacture any of its own chocolates. Although in the store, employees dip strawberries and other fresh and/or glazed fruit, Oreo cookies, pretzels, Rice Krispie treats, Gummi bears, and so on in chocolate. Sometimes employees make gift baskets for holidays and special events, and the customers have great fun watching this and purchasing these great gifts.

Our five store locations throughout Southern California include Dana Point, Carlsbad, Fallbrook, Escondido, and downtown San Diego. We have opened one store every other year with our own funds. All stores are profitable, and we have more than 30 employees on the payroll.

Annie's opened in 1995 as an LLC in Escondido, California. The principal owner and manager of our company is Casey Johnson whose three adult children, Troy, Samantha, and Max, all play major roles in the management and daily operations of the business. Annie's owns the service mark and trademarks.

Management

1. Casey Johnson (see résumé) began working in her aunt's 15,000-square-foot retail department store business at the age of 13. Through the years working in this third-generation business, she learned many of the fine details of operating a successful retail business.

   Casey worked her way through the ranks at several retail chains such as Sears and The Gap. In addition, she completed her undergraduate degree in economics at the University of California in Santa Barbara. After 20 years working for others, Casey opened Annie's in 1995. Casey Johnson serves as a guest lecturer at several colleges and is a frequent guest speaker at retail association meetings.

2. Troy Johnson is currently site manager. He monitors inventory levels, develops staffing schedules, deals with day-to-day operational issues, and supervises personnel. He worked for several years as a shift supervisor for the Cheesecake Factory. He has been actively involved in all aspects of Annie's since its inception.

3. Samantha Johnson, an English graduate of Indiana University, helped develop all Annie's operation manuals. With six years of retail experience at Hallmark, K-Mart, and Nordstrom, Samantha brought wide exposure to various training methods and store layout and design. She is also responsible for all advertising and social media.

4. Max Johnson holds an Information Management degree from UC Riverside. His primary focus with Annie's has been computer operations and information systems. He has assisted with all new store start-ups.

If awarded this concession, Casey Johnson will oversee overall operations of the business. Troy Johnson will provide on-site management under the close supervision of Casey Johnson. Other company members may also provide on-site management and support with members of the company reporting directly to Casey Johnson. Max Johnson will assist with store start up. Day and evening charge persons will be hired and trained.

Staffing Plan

1. Organizational chart for proposed operations:
   a. Casey Johnson: Responsible for the overall operations and management of the concession.
   b. Troy Johnson: Responsible for on-site, 24-hour management and supervision of the concession. Reports to Casey Johnson.
   c. Casey, Troy, and Samantha Johnson: Consultation and support.
   d. Day charge person (to be hired), reporting to Troy Johnson.
   e. Evening charge person (to be hired), reporting to Troy Johnson.
   f. A minimum of six additional sales people will be hired initially.
2. Staffing plan: There will be two employees to service the customers at all times. During busy seasons, there will be three to four employees. This number includes the charge person.
3. Résumés: see Business Plan Appendix.

Exit Strategy

Casey Johnson and her children will continue to run Annie's as a family company for the next 5 to 10 years, at which time Casey plans to step back from day to day operations and turn over the business to her children. The company has been developed to support and provide a good living for the entire family. Each of the children enjoys retailing and finds opening and running new stores an exciting part of the business. Casey and her family hope to grow Annie's to 10 stores within the next 5 years.

■ STORE OVERVIEW

Floor Plan

A Ghirardelli merchandising tower will be near the right front window and a floor-standing sucker rack near the left window. These may be moved to other areas of the store periodically. Window displays will be seasonal and kept low to enhance visibility into the store. As the customers enter the store, they will face an 8-foot curved glass chocolate showcase merchandised with truffles, turtles, pecan rolls, English toffee, and similar chocolate items. On both sides of the chocolate case will be various packaged candies.

Both the right and left walls will be mirrored. Along the lower right wall will be acrylic Jelly Belly dispensers. Above these dispensers will be staggered glass shelves to display gift items. Along the back wall will be custom-made acrylic bulk candy bins. Gift items will be displayed along the top shelves of these bins, and the rear wall will be painted white. Neon will be installed across the rear wall above the bulk candy. Across from the bulk candy bins, on the back side of the service counter, will be shelves for novelty candy items and bins filled with taffy along the top shelf.

The left wall will have open cabinet shelves, the highest at 36 inches, for boxed chocolates. Above these shelves will be staggered glass shelves for displays of gift items. In the center of this wall will be an 8-foot section of custom slat wall to hang packaged items.

The service counter will be in the center of the store. There will be a 6-foot long, 36-inch high, flat glass counter showcase on both the right and left sides of the service area. The left side will hold sugar-free chocolates, and the right side will hold fudge and other bulk chocolates. A center island will be used to do chocolate dipping, to construct baskets, and so on. There will be one register and one scale on each side of the service counter.

Behind the rear wall of the store is the required hand sink, three-basin sink, mop sink, water heater, microwave, small refrigerator, and shelving. It is estimated that this area is approximately 140 square feet.

Floor Space

Approximately 250 square feet of retail floor space is allocated to merchandise fixtures. Based on this area, the square footage for each category follows:

1. Bulk candy: 84 sq. ft
2. Bulk chocolates: 38 sq. ft
3. Edible gifts: 66 sq. ft
4. Sugar-free and/or fat-free items: 15 sq. ft
5. Nonedible gifts: 10 sq. ft
6. Novelty candy: 37 sq. ft

However, because there are multiple levels of shelves, the percentage of products carried to actual square footage would be quite different. For example, the right wall would have 22 square feet of Jelly Belly Bean fixtures; but above the beans, there would be 4 levels of glass shelves, with approximately 15 square feet for each level, for packaged gift items. It is estimated that 90 percent of all revenue would be from edible food and gift products and less than 10 percent from nonedible gift products. Aisles would be 5 feet wide to allow for wheelchair access, backpacks, and comfortable movement for customers.

See detailed floor plan drawings in the appendix.

Visual Presentation of Merchandise

The colorful world of candy always lends itself to great displays and store designs. The stores are merchandised and decorated to reflect the numerous holidays and seasons throughout the year. The summer season is followed by fall, Halloween (great fun!), Thanksgiving, Hanukah, Christmas, Valentine's Day (the prettiest), St. Patrick's Day, Easter, Mother's Day, graduation, Memorial Day, Independence Day, and Labor Day. Colors and store decor are changed to match these events and holidays. Organdy and other beautiful ribbons are used to dress up packages and displays, and gift-wrap paper is changed to match the seasons and holidays.

In addition, we would love to work with Sea World to develop and customize products to highlight special events at Sea World such as the Pole to Pole Fun Run or Summer Nights.

With the exception of very high-turnover products and products that are always carried, few single items are purchased in large quantities. Rather, many different items are purchased in smaller quantities, thus giving the customer a wider selection of products to choose from, and giving the company the ability to bring in new merchandise and change displays often. Most importantly, this ensures freshness of the products.

Unique gift items are incorporated into the merchandising themes. Many times the company purchases their own supplies to create these unusual gifts. For example, the employees may take small watering cans painted with sunflowers, insert cello bags printed with sunflowers, fill the bags with bulk lemon drops, and tie a silk sunflower into the organdy bow, or attach a small plush item or sunflower button doll. All of the Easter baskets sold by Annie's are custom made.

Bulk chocolates, including sugar-free items, are sold from the chocolate cases. Through the years, the company has identified those items that are in high demand and those companies who manufacture the best products. Annie's knows who makes the best truffles, the best turtles, the best honeycomb, and so on.

The bulk candy bins are very colorful; the customers love them—and they generate nice revenue. The bins will be segmented by types of candy: licorice, sour, gummi, sugar-free, and so on. Approximately 10 percent of the bulk bin space is allocated to candies that have a lower demand, such as horehound lumps and Bit O' Honey. Annie's believes that they maintain a competitive edge by carrying some of these more difficult-to-find items.

Individual shelves within the store may be merchandised with different themes; for example, all sea-item gifts, or all teacher gifts, or all dried-fruit packages. A certain shelf, for example, may be merchandised with the Shamu theme, including such items as suckers and stick candy with a Shamu on them, plush Shamus, and Shamu mugs filled with black and white Jelly Bellies. Product displays are changed frequently, so things do not become boring.

Products

The product lists in the appendix are examples of many products we carry; they are arranged by merchandise category. Not all items are carried at all times; new companies, such as Joseph Schmidt, never repeat their seasonal packaging from year to year, and they frequently change their product lines. Annie's is vigilant about staying on top of the market.

There are six major merchandise categories:

1. Bulk candy in self-serve bins
2. Bulk chocolates in the chocolate cases
3. Packaged, edible gift items (boxed chocolates, mugs filled with candy, etc.)
4. Sugar-free and/or fat-free items (incorporated throughout the store)
5. Nonedible gift items (collectible plush bears, candy dishes, candy tins, etc.)
6. Packaged novelty candy (War Heads, Pop Rocks, etc.)

Estimate of approximate quantities:

1. Bulk candy: 175 bins including 18 taffy and 54 Jelly Belly bins
2. Bulk chocolates: 500 different pieces
3. Edible gifts: 500 to 600 different items
4. Sugar-free items: 100 different items
5. Nonedible gifts: 200 different items
6. Packaged novelty: 300 to 400 different items

Pricing

Most packaged and gift items are now street priced at a 39 to 42 percent margin, which is monitored on the computer with every invoice. Since this was done, the average ticket increased, perhaps because customers feel they can afford to purchase more. Customers are happier now, product turnover is higher, and the problems with transferring product among stores have decreased significantly.

Estimate of price ranges:

1. Bulk candy: $1.79 per 1/4 lb.
2. Bulk chocolates: $2.98 per 1/4 lb. to $4.98 per 1/4 lb., average $3.98 per 1/4 lb.
3. Edible gifts: $1 to $150, average $10 to $30 range
4. Sugar-free and/or fat-free items: Same as 1, 2, and 3 above
5. Nonedible gifts: $1 to $150, average $10 to $30 range
6. Packaged novelty candy: $0.99 to $25, average $1 to $3 each

■ MARKETING

Retail Trends

To keep abreast of retail trends, Annie's frequently attends the following trade shows:

1. The International Fancy Food Show—twice yearly
2. The Philadelphia Candy Show
3. The LA Gift Show
4. The Denver Gift Show
5. The Oasis Gift Show
6. The New York Gift Fair
7. The Seattle Coffee Fest

Annie's subscribes to trade journals and is in constant communication with both vendors and customers. Annie's staff frequently visits all competitors to monitor prices and look for new items.

Customer Service Philosophy/Programs

The customer service goal of Annie's is to meet customer needs in the most efficient and pleasant manner possible. The employees are expected to do whatever is necessary to make the purchase easy for the customer. This may mean gift wrapping a package, wrapping an item in bubble wrap so that it does not break, holding an item for a customer, or processing a special order.

Returns are processed cheerfully, efficiently, and without question. The customer is offered replacement merchandise or a refund. A refund/complaint form is completed, and all employees have the authority to process refunds so that the customer is taken care of immediately.

Customers are often in a hurry and like their purchases processed quickly. This requires employees who are well-trained, know the merchandise, and are swift, accurate, helpful, friendly, and courteous, especially under pressure. Annie's occasionally employs mystery shoppers and uses this feedback for coaching employees. Feedback on employee behavior is solicited from regular customers, employees from other businesses, business acquaintances, and friends whenever possible. Annie's business card is always out on the counter for customers who wish to call or email.

Employees are taught the following concepts of customer service:

1. Always, whenever possible, acknowledge the customer as they enter the store.
2. Offer assistance but also respect customers' wishes to be left alone.
3. Smile—all the time.
4. Do not ignore customers or turn your back on them.
5. Do not talk or gossip among yourselves when customers are in the store.
6. Do not talk badly about any customer, especially in front of other people, not even outside of work hours.
7. Do not complain about anything, or talk about personal problems, religion, or politics to customers or among yourselves when customers are in the store. Save this chatter for after hours, when you are away from the workplace.
8. Try to never leave a customer once you are engaged in a transaction.
9. Process refunds and/or complaints cheerfully and efficiently. Never argue. Listen and hear the customer out. Resolve the problem on the spot whenever possible.
10. Always say thank you.
11. No talking or texting on cell phone during work hours, only on breaks and not in the store.
12. The customer is your real boss, so treat each customer accordingly.

Employees are taught about candy and chocolate, because they are expected to be knowledgeable and conversant. They are also taught how to gift-wrap, tie bows, construct gift baskets, dip chocolate, process special orders, and process charges. They are trained to handle cash accurately. They all learn how to process shipments from invoices and price products.

White aprons, red shirts with our blue logo, navy pants, and name tags are required at all times.

Marketing Plan

1. Entertainment retail: Most customers find it very entertaining just to browse the store. Employees dip chocolate-covered strawberries, caramel apples, and other items where customers can watch. Customers like to watch the employees mold chocolate items, such as Easter Bunnies. They also tend to stand and watch gift baskets being made.

2. Employees often dress up as a Mr. Jelly Belly, as a witch at Halloween, or an Easter Bunny at Easter, and so on.
3. Controlled food sampling is used to promote sales.

■ STORE OPERATIONS

Stocking

Food products will be stored in the shop, and nonfood items will be stored in the storeroom. The storeroom area is inadequate and unsafe for storing food products that are not sealed in cans or glass bottles. The temperature is too warm, and it would be nearly impossible to have adequate pest control. There are storage shelves under the bulk candy bins, under the chocolate bins, and under the service counters. There is limited storage area near the sinks.

During slow periods or off hours, employees will replenish bulk candy bins and other products. Each candy bin is removable and can be replaced with a bin that is full. Employees will do pricing and stocking daily during quiet periods. During busy periods, such as Christmas, Valentines, and Easter, an employee will be brought in to adjust the price of merchandise and replenish shelves. All items will be individually priced, even if bar coded.

The owners may find it necessary to rent off-site storage. If this occurs, a part-time stocker will be hired to accept deliveries at the off-site location and price merchandise before transporting it to the store. During hot weather, merchandise will be transported only at night.

Logistics and Frequency of Deliveries

1. Delivery schedule of new goods: Most goods are delivered by UPS or similar common carrier. UPS can deliver daily. These shipments are generally not very large, and the on-site manager will be responsible for coordinating deliveries. Large freight shipments will come in approximately every 10 days and may have to go to off-site storage for processing. Most manufacturers only ship out UPS on Monday or Tuesday, so product does not sit in a UPS warehouse over the weekend.
2. Replenishment of on-site stock: Par levels are established for items that are carried all the time (e.g., malt balls). Orders are placed at least weekly and more often if needed. Seasonal items are replenished only if they turn over quickly and early. It is impossible to order replacement candy late into the holiday season. While stores are selling Christmas, the manufacturers are processing Valentine's orders, and so on.

Facility Maintenance Plan

1. Policy for maintenance and repairs: A preventative maintenance program will be implemented for the refrigerated chocolate case and the under-counter refrigerator per manufacturer's recommendations. All repairs will be made in a timely manner and as needed.
2. Frequency of cleaning: Glass shelves are cleaned several times a day. Employees mop the floors several times day as well. Floors are professionally cleaned monthly. Windows are washed weekly and touched up daily. The store is dusted daily. It is management's expectation that the store be kept spotless.
3. Disposal of trash: Trash is emptied at least eight times per day and sometimes more often.

4. Replacement of equipment, displays, fixtures, and flooring: No replacement is anticipated during the life of this lease. If the need occurs, items will be replaced accordingly.

■ FINANCIAL MANAGEMENT AND FINANCIALS

System of Internal Controls Sales and Cash Receipts

a. Computer registers—Two point-of-sale computer terminals, which are capable of recording sales by stock-keeping units (SKUs), will be used. They will be equipped with sales-totalizer counters for all sales categories; the counters are locked, constantly accumulating, and cannot be reset. Beginning and ending sales-totalizer counter readings will be recorded daily.

b. Sales will be entered into one of five departments:
   Bulk Candy (self-serve out of the bins)
   Chocolates/Candy (all other food and/or items containing food)
   Nonfood Gifts
   Gift Certificates
   Shipping Costs

c. Sales transactions will be cash, debit or credit card. No personal checks will be accepted. Debit/credit cards will be processed through one of two terminals for electronic authorization and capture. All transactions will be entered into the computer terminals.

d. At the end of each day, the daily journals (Z tapes) will be removed from the registers and placed with the cash receipts for the day. A $200 bank will be left in each register, and a coin bank of $300 will be maintained on the premises. Each morning, for the previous day, Troy Johnson or his designee will prepare the night-drop deposit and deposit it at the bank.

e. The information from the daily journal tapes will be entered onto the weekly sales summary form. At the end of each week, the weekly totals will link to the monthly sales summary form. All Z tapes and any other paper transactions pertinent to the gross and/or net sales for each day (void slips, refund forms, cash paid-out receipts, employee discount receipts, credit card batch slips, deposit slips, etc.) will be attached together by day and stored by month in the storeroom.

f. Weekly and monthly records will be faxed to the CPA, who will prepare the monthly compiled financial statements for the location. The original Z tapes and other paper transactions will be submitted to the CPA, who will prepare the annual audited sales report. Once returned by the CPA, the original Z tapes and report forms will be stored in the storeroom.

g. The CPA performing the annual audit will review the system of internal controls semiannually.

h. Gross sales will only be offset by customer refunds, voids (documented employee errors during sales transactions), shipping expenses when an item is shipped for a customer (customer will only be charged actual cost of shipping), and Annie's employee discounts.

i. Annie's employees are allowed a 30 percent discount on all purchases daily and a 50 percent discount on Christmas Eve and Easter Sunday. All employee purchases will be entered into the registers by management. The sales receipt will be initialed by the manager and the employee and placed with the daily cash receipts. If management is not available, purchases will be documented in a Tab Book and paid for by the employee at a later date. Employees will not be allowed to ring up their own purchases.

j. Sea World employees will be allowed a discount of 10 percent on any total sale of $5 or more. The employee must be in uniform or be able to show proof that he or she is an employee. The person receiving the discount must write where he or she works on the receipt and sign it. This receipt is placed with the daily cash receipts.

k. Employees are not allowed to make change from the register without a sale. There is no exception to this rule. Change is also only made up to the amount of cash tendered to complete the transaction.

l. Cash is bled from the cash drawers at frequent intervals throughout the day and transferred to a locked, built-in cash-drop drawer.

m. Voids: The cash register receipt tape showing the void will be stamped with the void stamp and initialed by the person making the error. Sometimes the customer just changes his or her mind after a sale is rung up. This is also treated as a void. The void slips are placed with the daily cash receipts.

n. Refunds/Returns: The refund/return form will be completed. The customer must present the merchandise and proof of purchase. The receipt will be attached to the refund/return form. If the item was charged, a credit will be processed. If the customer paid cash, a cash refund will be given. If there is no proof of purchase, but it can be determined that it was a valid purchase from Annie's, a refund will still be given. If the customer eats the merchandise and then attempts to get a refund, the request will be denied.

o. Discounts: It is not anticipated that any promotional discounts will be given.

p. Keys: One set of Annie's storeroom keys will be kept on a large key ring in the store, and a key log will be used. One set of keys will also be issued to Casey Johnson and Troy Johnson. Store keys will be issued to those hired to open and close the store. Delivery people and others will never be left unattended in the storeroom.

q. Secret Shoppers: To be used periodically. Employees will be informed of this when they are hired. Also, video cameras may be installed.

Inventory and Accounts Payable

a. Shipments will be checked at delivery for evidence of damage. Any damage will be documented with the carrier. Shipments will be checked against the packing slip/invoice. Internal damage and/or shortages will be documented and the vendor notified immediately.

b. Extensions on all invoices, including computer-generated invoices, will be checked before payment. Amounts for damaged merchandise will be deducted from payment.

c. COD shipments are not accepted by Annie's under any circumstances. It is anticipated that all purchases will be paid for by check or credit card and not by cash on hand.

d. All invoices for payment are to be approved by Casey Johnson. Checks will be prepared and signed by Casey Johnson or other management in her absence. Invoices will be paid when due and stored by month of payment in Annie's storeroom.

e. Inventory counts will be completed monthly.

f. A review of the actual cost of physical inventory will be compared to the inventory on the financial statement. Any significant variations will be investigated, especially for theft of inventory.

g. Transfer of inventory among Annie's locations will be documented, at cost, on a duplicate transfer form. A copy of each transfer form will be kept at both the sending and receiving store. These forms will be stored in Annie's storeroom.

■ ANNIE'S PROJECTED RENTAL REVENUES AND ANNUAL MINIMUM GUARANTEE

Proposer's Name	Annie's
Store Concept	Full line bulk and packaged chocolates, novelty candy, related gift-packaged fancy food, gift baskets, related gifts, bulk candy
Merchandising Theme	Fine chocolates and candy

Established Tenant Rental Rate: 12.5% of gross sales

Projected Gross Sales ($)		Percentage Rent	Projected Rental Revenues	Rental Revs. Per Sq. Ft.
A. Year 1	$600,000	12.5%	$75,000	$71.43
B. Year 2	$660,000	12.5%	$82,500	$78.57
C. Year 3	$726,000	12.5%	$90,750	$86.43
D. Year 4	$798,600	12.5%	$99,825	$95.07
Total/ 4 years	$2,784,600		$348,075	

© Cengage Learning

■ ANNIE'S ESTIMATED CAPITAL INVESTMENT

I. Retail Opportunity

A. Proposer's Name	Annie's
B. Store Concept:	Full line bulk and packaged candy and chocolates, related gift-packaged fancy foods, gift baskets, and gifts
C. Merchandising Theme	Fine Chocolates and Candy

II. Proposer's Estimated Capital Investment

A. Architectural and Engineering Fees		$5,000
B. Equipment, Furnishings, and Fixtures(1)(2)		$20,000
C. Leasehold Improvements(2)		$40,000
D. Working Capital		$15,000
E. Initial Inventory		$25,000
F. Improvements Completion Bond		$2,500
G. Total Investment (Sum of II-A. through II-F.)		$107,500

III. Source of Investment

A. Amount Financed	$75,000	70%
B. Cash	32,500	30%
C. Total Investment (III-A.+ III-B.) (Should equal II-G. above)	$107,500	100%

IV. Facility Improvements/ Sq. Ft. (II-B.+II-C.)/I-D.	$57.14

© Cengage Learning

(1) Items removable at end of lease term.
(2) The sum of these two categories (Equipment, Furnishings, and Fixtures and Leasehold Improvements) shall not be less than $55 per square foot.

■ ASSUMPTIONS USED IN DEVELOPING INCOME AND CASH FLOW PROJECTIONS

1. Statistics for this store are similar to the statistics for other stores in similar locations.
2. Five-year historical sales record for the former See's candy concession.
3. Current monthly sales should closely parallel historical record of former See's candy concession.
4. Growth projections provided by owner.
5. Historical record of growth.
6. Current economic growth.
7. Price increases in product over time.
8. U.S. Department of Commerce Confectionery Report shows a steady, consistent increase in per-capita consumption of candy (in pounds) since 1984.
9. Confection sales are predominantly impulse purchases; therefore, the higher the foot traffic, the higher the sales.

■ ANNIE'S APPENDIX*

A. Balance Sheet
B. Break-Even Analysis
C. Store Layout
D. Facility Design
E. Complete Store Design Details
F. Résumés
G. Legal References
H. Business References
 I. Product Lists
 J. Market Research Statistics

*(Appendices A-J would be provided to Sea World but are not included in the text.)

ANNIE'S

Projected Annual Income and Cash-Flow Statement for Proposed Store

Proposer's Name   Annie's
Store Concept   Packaged and bulk confections and related gift and food items
Merchandising Theme   Fine chocolates and candy

© Cengage Learning

Category	Year 1 Amount	Year 1 % of Gross Sales	Year 2 Amount	Year 2 % of Gross Sales	Year 3 Amount	Year 3 % of Gross Sales	Year 4 Amount	Year 4 % of Gross Sales
Gross Sales	$600,000.00		$660,000.00		$726,000.00		$798,600.00	
Cost of Goods	$216,000.00	36%	$237,600.00	36%	$261,360.00	36%	$287,496.00	36%
Gross Profit	$384,000.00	64%	$422,400.00	64%	$464,640.00	64%	$511,104.00	64%
Operating Expenses:								
Salaries/Wages/Benefits	$84,000.00	14.0%	$92,400.00	14.0%	$101,640.00	14.0%	$11,804.00	14.0%
Utilities and Telephone	$1,200.00	0.2%	$1,320.00	0.2%	$1,452.00	0.2%	$1,597.00	0.2%
Maintenance/Cleaning/Supplies	$14,400.00	2.4%	$15,840.00	2.4%	$17,424.00	2.4%	$19,166.00	2.4%
Insurance	$6,000.00	1.0%	$6,600.00	1.0%	$7,260.00	1.0%	$7,986.00	1.0%
Marketing/Advertising	$6,000.00	1.0%	$6,600.00	1.0%	$7,260.00	1.0%	$7,986.00	1.0%
Licensing Fees	$18,900.00	3.2%	$20,790.00	3.2%	$22,869.00	3.2%	$25,156.00	3.2%
Rent	$75,000.00	12.5%	$82,500.00	12.5%	$90,750.00	12.5%	$99,825.00	12.5%
General and Administration	$36,000.00	6.0%	$39,600.00	6.0%	$43,560.00	6.0%	$47,916.00	6.0%
Interest Expense	$9,600.00	1.6%	$9,600.00	1.5%	$9,600.00	1.3%	$9,600.00	1.2%
Other Misc. Expenses	$1,800.00	0.3%	$1,980.00	0.3%	$3,630.00	0.5%	$3,993.00	0.5%
Total Expenses	$252,900.00	42.2%	$277,230.00	42.1%	$305,445.00	42.1%	$335,029.00	42.0%
Depreciation	$7,600.00	1.3%	$7,600.00	1.3%	$7,600.00	1.3%	$7,600.00	1.3%
Net Income	$123,500.00	20.6%	$137,570.00	20.8%	$151,595.00	20.9%	$168,475.00	21.1%
Add Back: Depreciation	$7,600.00		$7,600.00		$7,600.00		$7,600.00	
Cash Flow From Operations	$131,100.00		$145,170.00		$159,195.00		$176,075.00	
Beginning Cash Balance	$10,000.00		$131,100.00		$251,170.00		$385,365.00	
Plus: Cash Flow from Operations	$131,100.00		$145,170.00		$159,195.00		$176,075.00	
Minus: Debt Service (Principal Only)	$10,000.00		$25,000.00		$25,000.00		$15,000.00	
Minus: On-Going Annual Capital Expenditures	$—		$—		$—		$—	
Ending Cash Balance Available to Proposer	$131,100.00		$251,170.00		$385,365.00		$546,440.00	

Source: See list of assumptions made to create these sales projections and figures on the previous page.

Appendix C

Image_Source/iStockphoto.com

Forms, Forms, Forms

1. Family Budget
2. Personal Financial Statement
3. Application for Employer Identification Number: SS-4
4. Profit or Loss from Business: Schedule C
5. Net Profit from Business: Schedule C-EZ
6. Self-Employment Tax: Schedule SE
7. Employment Eligibility Verification: Form I-9
8. Application for Business Loan: SBA Form 4
9. Franchise Disclosure Document: An Overview

FAMILY BUDGET

TAXES
    Federal Tax   _____
    State Tax   _____
    Social Security/Medicare   _____

HOUSING
    Rent/Mortgage Payments   _____
    Property Taxes   _____
    Repairs/Maintenance   _____
    Furniture/Household Goods   _____
    Insurance   _____
    Association Fees   _____

TRANSPORTATION
    Loan/Lease Payment (s)   _____
    Gas/Oil   _____
    Maintenance/Tires/Washing _____
    Licenses/Taxes   _____
    Public Transportation/ZipCar _____
    Insurance   _____

FOOD
    Home   _____
    Away
        Breakfast   _____
        Lunch   _____
        Dinners   _____
    Other (coffee/vending)   _____

UTILITIES
    Electricity   _____
    Gas   _____
    Phone (cell and landline)   _____
    Water/Garbage   _____
    Internet   _____
    Cable   _____

PERSONAL
    Clothing   _____
    Personal Care (haircuts/makeup) _____
    Health Insurance   _____
    Disability Insurance   _____
    Medical Bills   _____
    Dental/Eye Care   _____
    Prescriptions and OTC   _____
    Entertainment   _____
    Vacations (total/12)   _____
    Christmas Gifts, etc. (total/12) _____
    Child Care   _____
    Alimony/Child Care   _____
    Children (expenses/classes, etc.) _____
    Hobbies   _____
    Education Expenses   _____
    Monthly Memberships   _____
    Gifts (total/12)   _____
    Subscriptions/Books   _____
    Computer software/hardware _____
    Other   _____

CREDIT CARDS/LOANS
    Student   _____
    Credit card (s)   _____
    Other   _____

SAVINGS
    Retirement   _____
    Emergency Fund   _____
    Other   _____

OTHER
    Charitable Contributions   _____
    Vet Bills/Dog Food/Kennel Fees _____
    Misc. (Describe)   _____
    Misc. (Describe)   _____
    Misc. (Describe)   _____

TOTAL EXPENSES   _____

© Cengage Learning 2014

If you will keep track of EVERY dollar you spend each month, you will know what these figures truly are. It will be very hard to determine how much money you can allocate to you business unless you have tracked your income and expenses. Use Websites like Mint and LearnVest to track your expenses for a minimum of three months.

Most entrepreneurs need to be frugal. So, find out what you are spending and then work diligently to decrease each category you can.

OMB APPROVAL NO. 3245-0188
EXPIRATION DATE: 8/31/2011

PERSONAL FINANCIAL STATEMENT

U.S. SMALL BUSINESS ADMINISTRATION

As of _____ , _____

Complete this form for: (1) each proprietor, or (2) each limited partner who owns 20% or more interest and each general partner, or (3) each stockholder owning 20% or more of voting stock, or (4) any person or entity providing a guaranty on the loan.

Name	Business Phone
Residence Address	Residence Phone

City, State, & Zip Code

Business Name of Applicant/Borrower

ASSETS	(Omit Cents)	LIABILITIES	(Omit Cents)
Cash on hand & in Banks	$_____	Accounts Payable	$_____
Savings Accounts........................	$_____	Notes Payable to Banks and Others.............	$_____
IRA or Other Retirement Account	$_____	(Describe in Section 2)	
Accounts & Notes Receivable	$_____	Installment Account (Auto)	$_____
Life Insurance-Cash Surrender Value Only....	$_____	Mo. Payments $_____	
(Complete Section 8)		Installment Account (Other)	$_____
Stocks and Bonds	$_____	Mo. Payments $_____	
(Describe in Section 3)		Loan on Life Insurance	$_____
Real Estate..........................	$_____	Mortgages on Real Estate	$_____
(Describe in Section 4)		(Describe in Section 4)	
Automobile-Present Value..................	$_____	Unpaid Taxes	$_____
Other Personal Property...................	$_____	(Describe in Section 6)	
(Describe in Section 5)		Other Liabilities	$_____
Other Assets	$_____	(Describe in Section 7)	
(Describe in Section 5)		Total Liabilities.........................	$_____
		Net Worth	$_____
Total	$_____	**Total**	$_____

Section 1. Source of Income		**Contingent Liabilities**	
Salary	$_____	As Endorser or Co-Maker	$_____
Net Investment Income	$_____	Legal Claims & Judgments..................	$_____
Real Estate Income	$_____	Provision for Federal Income Tax.............	$_____
Other Income (Describe below)*...........	$_____	Other Special Debt	$_____

Description of Other Income in Section 1.

*Alimony or child support payments need not be disclosed in "Other Income" unless it is desired to have such payments counted toward total income.

Section 2. Notes Payable to Banks and Others. (Use attachments if necessary. Each attachment must be identified as a part of this statement and signed.)

Name and Address of Noteholder(s)	Original Balance	Current Balance	Payment Amount	Frequency (monthly,etc.)	How Secured or Endorsed Type of Collateral

SBA Form 413 (10-08) **Previous Editions Obsolete**

This form was electronically produced by Elite Federal Forms, Inc.

Federal Recycling Program   Printed on Recycled Paper

(tumble)

Section 3. Stocks and Bonds. (Use attachments if necessary. Each attachment must be identified as a part of this statement and signed).

Number of Shares	Name of Securities	Cost	Market Value Quotation/Exchange	Date of Quotation/Exchange	Total Value

Section 4. Real Estate Owned. (List each parcel separately. Use attachment if necessary. Each attachment must be identified as a part of this statement and signed.)

	Property A	Property B	Property C
Type of Property			
Address			
Date Purchased			
Original Cost			
Present Market Value			
Name & Address of Mortgage Holder			
Mortgage Account Number			
Mortgage Balance			
Amount of Payment per Month/Year			
Status of Mortgage			

Section 5. Other Personal Property and Other Assets. (Describe, and if any is pledged as security, state name and address of lien holder, amount of lien, terms of payment and if delinquent, describe delinquency)

Section 6.   Unpaid Taxes.   (Describe in detail, as to type, to whom payable, when due, amount, and to what property, if any, a tax lien attaches.)

Section 7.   Other Liabilities.   (Describe in detail.)

Section 8.   Life Insurance Held.   (Give face amount and cash surrender value of policies - name of insurance company and beneficiaries)

I authorize SBA/Lender to make inquiries as necessary to verify the accuracy of the statements made and to determine my creditworthiness. I certify the above and the statements contained in the attachments are true and accurate as of the stated date(s). These statements are made for the purpose of either obtaining a loan or guaranteeing a loan. I understand FALSE statements may result in forfeiture of benefits and possible prosecution by the U.S. Attorney General (Reference 18 U.S.C. 1001).

Signature: Date: Social Security Number:

Signature: Date: Social Security Number:

PLEASE NOTE: The estimated average burden hours for the completion of this form is 1.5 hours per response. If you have questions or comments concerning this estimate or any other aspect of this information, please contact Chief, Administrative Branch, U.S. Small Business Administration, Washington, D.C. 20416, and Clearance Officer, Paper Reduction Project (3245-0188), Office of Management and Budget, Washington, D.C. 20503. **PLEASE DO NOT SEND FORMS TO OMB.**

Source: US Small Business Administration (SBA.gov).

Form **SS-4** (Rev. January 2010) Department of the Treasury Internal Revenue Service	**Application for Employer Identification Number** **(For use by employers, corporations, partnerships, trusts, estates, churches, government agencies, Indian tribal entities, certain individuals, and others.)** ▶ **See separate instructions for each line.** ▶ **Keep a copy for your records.**	OMB No. 1545-0003 EIN

Type or print clearly.

1 Legal name of entity (or individual) for whom the EIN is being requested

2 Trade name of business (if different from name on line 1)	**3** Executor, administrator, trustee, "care of" name

4a Mailing address (room, apt., suite no. and street, or P.O. box)	**5a** Street address (if different) (Do not enter a P.O. box.)
4b City, state, and ZIP code (if foreign, see instructions)	**5b** City, state, and ZIP code (if foreign, see instructions)

6 County and state where principal business is located

7a Name of responsible party	**7b** SSN, ITIN, or EIN

8a Is this application for a limited liability company (LLC) (or a foreign equivalent)? . . . .   ☐ Yes   ☐ No   **8b** If 8a is "Yes," enter the number of LLC members . . .   ▶

8c If 8a is "Yes," was the LLC organized in the United States? . . . .   ☐ Yes   ☐ No

9a **Type of entity** (check only one box). **Caution.** If 8a is "Yes," see the instructions for the correct box to check.

☐ Sole proprietor (SSN) _____
☐ Partnership
☐ Corporation (enter form number to be filed) ▶_____
☐ Personal service corporation
☐ Church or church-controlled organization
☐ Other nonprofit organization (specify) ▶_____
☐ Other (specify) ▶

☐ Estate (SSN of decedent) _____
☐ Plan administrator (TIN) _____
☐ Trust (TIN of grantor) _____
☐ National Guard   ☐ State/local government
☐ Farmers' cooperative   ☐ Federal government/military
☐ REMIC   ☐ Indian tribal governments/enterprises
Group Exemption Number (GEN) if any ▶

9b If a corporation, name the state or foreign country (if applicable) where incorporated	State	Foreign country

10 **Reason for applying** (check only one box)

☐ Started new business (specify type) ▶ _____
☐ Hired employees (Check the box and see line 13.)
☐ Compliance with IRS withholding regulations
☐ Other (specify) ▶

☐ Banking purpose (specify purpose) ▶_____
☐ Changed type of organization (specify new type) ▶_____
☐ Purchased going business
☐ Created a trust (specify type) ▶_____
☐ Created a pension plan (specify type) ▶_____

11 Date business started or acquired (month, day, year). See instructions.	**12** Closing month of accounting year
13 Highest number of employees expected in the next 12 months (enter -0- if none). If no employees expected, skip line 14.	**14** If you expect your employment tax liability to be $1,000 or less in a full calendar year **and** want to file Form 944 annually instead of Forms 941 quarterly, check here. (Your employment tax liability generally will be $1,000 or less if you expect to pay $4,000 or less in total wages.) If you do not check this box, you must file Form 941 for every quarter. ☐

Agricultural	Household	Other

15 First date wages or annuities were paid (month, day, year). **Note.** If applicant is a withholding agent, enter date income will first be paid to nonresident alien (month, day, year) . . . . ▶

16 Check **one** box that best describes the principal activity of your business.   ☐ Health care & social assistance   ☐ Wholesale-agent/broker
☐ Construction   ☐ Rental & leasing   ☐ Transportation & warehousing   ☐ Accommodation & food service   ☐ Wholesale-other   ☐ Retail
☐ Real estate   ☐ Manufacturing   ☐ Finance & insurance   ☐ Other (specify)

17 Indicate principal line of merchandise sold, specific construction work done, products produced, or services provided.

18 Has the applicant entity shown on line 1 ever applied for and received an EIN?   ☐ Yes   ☐ No
If "Yes," write previous EIN here ▶

Third Party Designee	Complete this section **only** if you want to authorize the named individual to receive the entity's EIN and answer questions about the completion of this form.	
	Designee's name	Designee's telephone number (include area code) ( )
	Address and ZIP code	Designee's fax number (include area code) ( )

Under penalties of perjury, I declare that I have examined this application, and to the best of my knowledge and belief, it is true, correct, and complete.   Applicant's telephone number (include area code)   (   )

Name and title (type or print clearly) ▶

Signature ▶   Date ▶   Applicant's fax number (include area code)   (   )

For Privacy Act and Paperwork Reduction Act Notice, see separate instructions.   Cat. No. 16055N   Form **SS-4** (Rev. 1-2010)

Do I Need an EIN?

File Form SS-4 if the applicant entity does not already have an EIN but is required to show an EIN on any return, statement, or other document. [1] See also the separate instructions for each line on Form SS-4.

IF the applicant...	AND...	THEN...
Started a new business	Does not currently have (nor expect to have) employees	Complete lines 1, 2, 4a–8a, 8b–c (if applicable), 9a, 9b (if applicable), and 10–14 and 16–18.
Hired (or will hire) employees, including household employees	Does not already have an EIN	Complete lines 1, 2, 4a–6, 7a–b (if applicable), 8a, 8b–c (if applicable), 9a, 9b (if applicable), 10–18.
Opened a bank account	Needs an EIN for banking purposes only	Complete lines 1–5b, 7a–b (if applicable), 8a, 8b–c (if applicable), 9a, 9b (if applicable), 10, and 18.
Changed type of organization	Either the legal character of the organization or its ownership changed (for example, you incorporate a sole proprietorship or form a partnership) [2]	Complete lines 1–18 (as applicable).
Purchased a going business [3]	Does not already have an EIN	Complete lines 1–18 (as applicable).
Created a trust	The trust is other than a grantor trust or an IRA trust [4]	Complete lines 1–18 (as applicable).
Created a pension plan as a plan administrator [5]	Needs an EIN for reporting purposes	Complete lines 1, 3, 4a–5b, 9a, 10, and 18.
Is a foreign person needing an EIN to comply with IRS withholding regulations	Needs an EIN to complete a Form W-8 (other than Form W-8ECI), avoid withholding on portfolio assets, or claim tax treaty benefits [6]	Complete lines 1–5b, 7a–b (SSN or ITIN optional), 8a, 8b–c (if applicable), 9a, 9b (if applicable), 10, and 18.
Is administering an estate	Needs an EIN to report estate income on Form 1041	Complete lines 1–6, 9a, 10–12, 13–17 (if applicable), and 18.
Is a withholding agent for taxes on non-wage income paid to an alien (i.e., individual, corporation, or partnership, etc.)	Is an agent, broker, fiduciary, manager, tenant, or spouse who is required to file Form 1042, Annual Withholding Tax Return for U.S. Source Income of Foreign Persons	Complete lines 1, 2, 3 (if applicable), 4a–5b, 7a–b (if applicable), 8a, 8b–c (if applicable), 9a, 9b (if applicable), 10, and 18.
Is a state or local agency	Serves as a tax reporting agent for public assistance recipients under Rev. Proc. 80-4, 1980-1 C.B. 581 [7]	Complete lines 1, 2, 4a–5b, 9a, 10, and 18.
Is a single-member LLC	Needs an EIN to file Form 8832, Classification Election, for filing employment tax returns and excise tax returns, or for state reporting purposes [8]	Complete lines 1–18 (as applicable).
Is an S corporation	Needs an EIN to file Form 2553, Election by a Small Business Corporation [9]	Complete lines 1–18 (as applicable).

[1] For example, a sole proprietorship or self-employed farmer who establishes a qualified retirement plan, or is required to file excise, employment, alcohol, tobacco, or firearms returns, must have an EIN. A partnership, corporation, REMIC (real estate mortgage investment conduit), no nprofit organization (church, club, etc.), or farmers' cooperative must use an EIN for any tax-related purpose even if the entity does not have empl oyees.

[2] However, do not apply for a new EIN if the existing entity only (a) changed its business name, (b) elected on Form 8832 to chan ge the way it is taxed (or is covered by the default rules), or (c) terminated its partnership status because at least 50% of the total interests in partners hip capital and profits were sold or exchanged within a 12-month period. The EIN of the terminated partnership should continue to be used. See Regulations section 3 01.6109-1(d)(2)(iii).

[3] Do not use the EIN of the prior business unless you became the "owner" of a corporation by acquiring its stock.

[4] However, grantor trusts that do not file using Optional Method 1 and IRA trusts that are required to file Form 990-T, Exempt Or ganization Business Income Tax Return, must have an EIN. For more information on grantor trusts, see the Instructions for Form 1041.

[5] A plan administrator is the person or group of persons specified as the administrator by the instrument under which the plan is operated.

[6] Entities applying to be a Qualified Intermediary (QI) need a QI-EIN even if they already have an EIN. See Rev. Proc. 2000-12.

[7] See also *Household employer* on page 4 of the instructions. **Note.** State or local agencies may need an EIN for other reasons, for example, hired employees.

[8] See *Disregarded entities* on page 4 of the instructions for details on completing Form SS-4 for an LLC.

[9] An existing corporation that is electing or revoking S corporation status should use its previously-assigned EIN.

Source: *http://www.irs.gov/pub/irs-pdf/fss4.pdf/IRS.*

SCHEDULE C
(Form 1040)

Department of the Treasury
Internal Revenue Service (99)

Profit or Loss From Business
(Sole Proprietorship)

▶ **For information on Schedule C and its instructions, go to** *www.irs.gov/schedulec.*
▶ **Attach to Form 1040, 1040NR, or 1041; partnerships generally must file Form 1065.**

OMB No. 1545-0074

20**12**

Attachment
Sequence No. **09**

Name of proprietor

Social security number (SSN)

A Principal business or profession, including product or service (see instructions)

B Enter code from instructions
▶

C Business name. If no separate business name, leave blank.

D Employer ID number (EIN), (see instr.)

E Business address (including suite or room no.) ▶

City, town or post office, state, and ZIP code

F Accounting method: **(1)** ☐ Cash **(2)** ☐ Accrual **(3)** ☐ Other (specify) ▶

G Did you "materially participate" in the operation of this business during 2012? If "No," see instructions for limit on losses ☐ Yes ☐ No

H If you started or acquired this business during 2012, check here ▶ ☐

I Did you make any payments in 2012 that would require you to file Form(s) 1099? (see instructions) ☐ Yes ☐ No

J If "Yes," did you or will you file required Forms 1099? ☐ Yes ☐ No

Part I   Income

1	Gross receipts or sales. See instructions for line 1 and check the box if this income was reported to you on Form W-2 and the "Statutory employee" box on that form was checked ▶ ☐	**1**	
2	Returns and allowances (see instructions)	**2**	
3	Subtract line 2 from line 1	**3**	
4	Cost of goods sold (from line 42)	**4**	
5	**Gross profit.** Subtract line 4 from line 3	**5**	
6	Other income, including federal and state gasoline or fuel tax credit or refund (see instructions)	**6**	
7	**Gross income.** Add lines 5 and 6 ▶	**7**	

Part II   Expenses   Enter expenses for business use of your home only on line 30.

8	Advertising	**8**		**18**	Office expense (see instructions)	**18**	
9	Car and truck expenses (see instructions)	**9**		**19**	Pension and profit-sharing plans	**19**	
				20	Rent or lease (see instructions):		
10	Commissions and fees	**10**		**a**	Vehicles, machinery, and equipment	**20a**	
11	Contract labor (see instructions)	**11**		**b**	Other business property	**20b**	
12	Depletion	**12**		**21**	Repairs and maintenance	**21**	
13	Depreciation and section 179 expense deduction (not included in Part III) (see instructions)	**13**		**22**	Supplies (not included in Part III)	**22**	
				23	Taxes and licenses	**23**	
				24	Travel, meals, and entertainment:		
14	Employee benefit programs (other than on line 19)	**14**		**a**	Travel	**24a**	
15	Insurance (other than health)	**15**		**b**	Deductible meals and entertainment (see instructions)	**24b**	
16	Interest:			**25**	Utilities	**25**	
a	Mortgage (paid to banks, etc.)	**16a**		**26**	Wages (less employment credits)	**26**	
b	Other	**16b**		**27a**	Other expenses (from line 48)	**27a**	
17	Legal and professional services	**17**		**b**	**Reserved for future use**	**27b**	

28	**Total expenses** before expenses for business use of home. Add lines 8 through 27a ▶	**28**	
29	Tentative profit or (loss). Subtract line 28 from line 7	**29**	
30	Expenses for business use of your home. Attach **Form 8829.** Do **not** report such expenses elsewhere	**30**	
31	**Net profit or (loss).** Subtract line 30 from line 29.		
	• If a profit, enter on both **Form 1040, line 12** (or **Form 1040NR, line 13**) and on **Schedule SE, line 2.** (If you checked the box on line 1, see instructions). Estates and trusts, enter on **Form 1041, line 3.** • If a loss, you **must** go to line 32.	**31**	

32	If you have a loss, check the box that describes your investment in this activity (see instructions).
	• If you checked 32a, enter the loss on both **Form 1040, line 12,** (or **Form 1040NR, line 13**) and on **Schedule SE, line 2.** (If you checked the box on line 1, see the line 31 instructions). Estates and trusts, enter on **Form 1041, line 3.**
	• If you checked 32b, you **must** attach **Form 6198.** Your loss may be limited.

32a ☐ All investment is at risk.
32b ☐ Some investment is not at risk.

For Paperwork Reduction Act Notice, see your tax return instructions.   Cat. No. 11334P   **Schedule C (Form 1040) 2012**

Schedule C (Form 1040) 2012
Page **2**

Part III   **Cost of Goods Sold** (see instructions)

33	Method(s) used to value closing inventory:	**a** ☐ Cost	**b** ☐ Lower of cost or market	**c** ☐ Other (attach explanation)

34   Was there any change in determining quantities, costs, or valuations between opening and closing inventory?
If "Yes," attach explanation . . . . ☐ **Yes**   ☐ **No**

35	Inventory at beginning of year. If different from last year's closing inventory, attach explanation . . .	**35**	
36	Purchases less cost of items withdrawn for personal use	**36**	
37	Cost of labor. Do not include any amounts paid to yourself	**37**	
38	Materials and supplies	**38**	
39	Other costs	**39**	
40	Add lines 35 through 39	**40**	
41	Inventory at end of year	**41**	
42	**Cost of goods sold.** Subtract line 41 from line 40. Enter the result here and on line 4	**42**	

Part IV   **Information on Your Vehicle.** Complete this part **only** if you are claiming car or truck expenses on line 9 and are not required to file Form 4562 for this business. See the instructions for line 13 to find out if you must file Form 4562.

43   When did you place your vehicle in service for business purposes? (month, day, year)   ▶ _____ / _____ / _____

44   Of the total number of miles you drove your vehicle during 2012, enter the number of miles you used your vehicle for:

a Business _____   **b** Commuting (see instructions) _____   **c** Other _____

45   Was your vehicle available for personal use during off-duty hours? . . . . ☐ **Yes**   ☐ **No**

46   Do you (or your spouse) have another vehicle available for personal use? . . . . ☐ **Yes**   ☐ **No**

47a   Do you have evidence to support your deduction? . . . . ☐ **Yes**   ☐ **No**

b   If "Yes," is the evidence written? . . . . ☐ **Yes**   ☐ **No**

Part V   **Other Expenses.** List below business expenses not included on lines 8–26 or line 30.

48	**Total other expenses.** Enter here and on line 27a	**48**	

Schedule C (Form 1040) 2012

Source: *http://www.irs.gov/pub/irs-pdf/f1040sc.pdf /IRS*.

SCHEDULE C-EZ
(Form 1040)

Department of the Treasury
Internal Revenue Service (99)

Net Profit From Business
(Sole Proprietorship)

▶ **Partnerships, joint ventures, etc., generally must file Form 1065 or 1065-B.**
▶ **Attach to Form 1040, 1040NR, or 1041.** ▶ **See instructions on page 2.**

OMB No. 1545-0074

2011

Attachment
Sequence No. **09A**

Name of proprietor

Social security number (SSN)

Part I   General Information

You May Use Schedule C-EZ Instead of Schedule C Only If You:

- Had business expenses of $5,000 or less.
- Use the cash method of accounting.
- Did not have an inventory at any time during the year.
- Did not have a net loss from your business.
- Had only one business as either a sole proprietor, qualified joint venture, or statutory employee.
- Did not receive any credit card or similar payments that included amounts that are not includible in your income (see instructions for line 1a).

And You:

- Had no employees during the year.
- Are not required to file **Form 4562,** Depreciation and Amortization, for this business. See the instructions for Schedule C, line 13, to find out if you must file.
- Do not deduct expenses for business use of your home.
- Do not have prior year unallowed passive activity losses from this business.

A   Principal business or profession, including product or service

B   Enter business code (see page 2)
▶

C   Business name. If no separate business name, leave blank.

D   Enter your EIN (see page 2)

E   Business address (including suite or room no.). Address not required if same as on page 1 of your tax return.

City, town or post office, state, and ZIP code

F   Did you make any payments in 2011 that would require you to file Form(s) 1099? (see the Schedule C
instructions) . . . . ☐ **Yes**   ☐ **No**

G   If "Yes," did you or will you file all required Forms 1099? . . . . ☐ **Yes**   ☐ **No**

Part II   Figure Your Net Profit

1a	Merchant card and third party payments. For 2011, enter -0-	**1a**	
b	Gross receipts or sales not entered on line 1a (see instructions) . .	**1b**	
c	Income reported to you on Form W-2 if the "Statutory Employee" box on that form was checked. **Caution.** See Schedule C instructions before completing this line	**1c**	
d	Total of lines 1a, 1b, and 1c. If any adjustments to line 1a, you **must** use Schedule C (see instructions)	**1d**	
2	**Total expenses** (see page 2). If more than $5,000, you **must** use Schedule C	**2**	
3	**Net profit.** Subtract line 2 from line 1d. If less than zero, you **must** use Schedule C. Enter on both **Form 1040, line 12,** and **Schedule SE, line 2,** or on **Form 1040NR, line 13** and **Schedule SE, line 2** (see instructions). (If you entered an amount on line 1c, **do not** report the amount from line 1c on Schedule SE, line 2.) Estates and trusts, enter on **Form 1041, line 3**	**3**	

Part III   Information on Your Vehicle. Complete this part **only** if you are claiming car or truck expenses on line 2.

4   When did you place your vehicle in service for business purposes? (month, day, year) ▶ _____ .

5   Of the total number of miles you drove your vehicle during 2011, enter the number of miles you used your vehicle for:

a   Business _____   **b**   Commuting (see page 2) _____   **c**   Other _____

6   Was your vehicle available for personal use during off-duty hours? . . . . ☐ **Yes**   ☐ **No**

7   Do you (or your spouse) have another vehicle available for personal use? . . . . ☐ **Yes**   ☐ **No**

8a   Do you have evidence to support your deduction? . . . . ☐ **Yes**   ☐ **No**

b   If "Yes," is the evidence written? . . . . ☐ **Yes**   ☐ **No**

For Paperwork Reduction Act Notice, see your tax return instructions.   Cat. No. 14374D   **Schedule C-EZ (Form 1040) 2011**

Instructions

 Before you begin, see General Instructions *in the 2011* Instructions for Schedule C. *Also, the IRS has created a page on IRS.gov for information about Schedule C-EZ, at www.irs.gov/schedulecez. Information about any future developments affecting Schedule C-EZ (such as legislation enacted after we released it) will be posted on that page.*

You can use Schedule C-EZ instead of Schedule C if you operated a business or practiced a profession as a sole proprietorship or qualified joint venture, or you were a statutory employee and you have met all the requirements listed in Schedule C-EZ, Part I.

For more information on electing to be taxed as a qualified joint venture (including the possible social security benefits of this election), see *Husband-Wife Qualified Joint Venture* in the instructions for Schedule C. You can also go to IRS.gov, enter "qualified joint venture" in the search box, and select "Election for Husband and Wife Unincorporated Businesses."

Line A

Describe the business or professional activity that provided your principal source of income reported on lines 1a-1d. Give the general field or activity and the type of product or service.

Line B

Enter the six-digit code that identifies your principal business or professional activity. See the instructions for Schedule C for the list of codes.

Line D

Enter on line D the employer identification number (EIN) that was issued to you and in your name as a sole proprietor. If you are filing Form 1041, enter the EIN issued to the estate or trust. Do not enter your SSN. Do not enter another taxpayer's EIN (for example, from any Forms 1099-MISC that you received). If you are the sole owner of a limited liability company (LLC), **do not** enter on line D the EIN issued to the LLC, if any. **If you do not have an EIN, leave line D blank.**

You need an EIN only if you have a qualified retirement plan or are required to file an employment, excise, alcohol, tobacco, or firearms tax return, are a payer of gambling winnings, or are filing Form 1041 for an estate or trust. If you need an EIN, see the Instructions for Form SS-4.

Line E

Enter your business address. Show a street address instead of a box number. Include the suite or room number, if any.

Line F

See the instructions for line I in the instructions for Schedule C to help determine if you are required to file any Forms 1099.

Line 1a—1d

For 2011, the IRS has deferred the requirement to report the amount of merchant card and third party network payments received. Therefore, enter zero on line 1a and report all gross receipts on line 1b, including income reported to you on Form 1099-K. Also include on line 1b amounts you received in your trade or business that were properly shown on Form 1099-MISC. If the total amounts that were reported in box 7 of Forms 1099-MISC are more than the total you are reporting on line 1b, attach a statement explaining the difference. You must show all items of taxable income actually or constructively received during the year (in cash, property, or services). Income is constructively received when it is credited to your account or set aside for you to use. Do not offset this amount by any losses.

You may not enter amounts on both lines 1b and 1c of Schedule C-EZ; if both lines apply, you may not file Schedule C-EZ and must report each amount on a separate Schedule C.

Line 2

Enter the total amount of all deductible business expenses you actually paid during the year. Examples of these expenses include advertising, car and truck expenses, commissions and fees, insurance, interest, legal and professional services, office expenses, rent or lease expenses, repairs and maintenance, supplies, taxes, travel, the allowable percentage of business meals and entertainment, and utilities (including telephone). For details, see the instructions for Schedule C, Parts II and V. You can use the optional worksheet below to record your expenses. Enter on lines **b** through **f** the type and amount of expenses not included on line **a.**

If you claim car or truck expenses, be sure to complete Schedule C-EZ, Part III.

Line 3

Nonresident aliens using Form 1040NR should also enter the total on Schedule SE, line 2, if you are covered under the U.S. social security system due to an international social security agreement currently in effect. See the Schedule SE instructions for information on international social security agreements.

Line 5b

Generally, commuting is travel between your home and a work location. If you converted your vehicle during the year from personal to business use (or vice versa), enter your commuting miles only for the period you drove your vehicle for business. For information on certain travel that is considered a business expense rather than commuting, see the Instructions for Form 2106.

Optional Worksheet for Line 2 (keep a copy for your records)

a	Deductible meals and entertainment (see the instructions for Schedule C, line 24b)	a	
b	_____	b	
c	_____	c	
d	_____	d	
e	_____	e	
f	_____	f	
g	**Total.** Add lines **a** through **f.** Enter here and on line 2	g	

Schedule C-EZ (Form 1040) 2011

Source: *www.irs.gov/pub/irs-pdf/f1040sce.pdf/IRS.*

SCHEDULE SE
(Form 1040)

Department of the Treasury
Internal Revenue Service (99)

Self-Employment Tax

▶ Information about Schedule SE and its separate instructions is at *www.irs.gov/form1040.*

▶ **Attach to Form 1040 or Form 1040NR.**

OMB No. 1545-0074

20**12**

Attachment
Sequence No. **17**

Name of person with **self-employment** income (as shown on Form 1040)

Social security number of person
with **self-employment** income ▶

Before you begin: To determine if you must file Schedule SE, see the instructions.

May I Use Short Schedule SE or Must I Use Long Schedule SE?

Note. Use this flowchart **only if** you must file Schedule SE. If unsure, see *Who Must File Schedule SE* in the instructions.

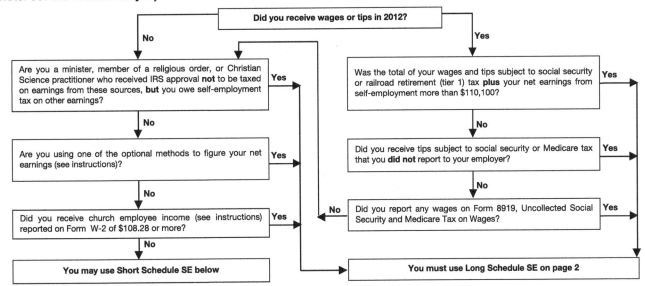

You may use Short Schedule SE below

You must use Long Schedule SE on page 2

Section A—Short Schedule SE.   Caution. Read above to see if you can use Short Schedule SE.

1a	Net farm profit or (loss) from Schedule F, line 34, and farm partnerships, Schedule K-1 (Form 1065), box 14, code A	**1a**		
b	If you received social security retirement or disability benefits, enter the amount of Conservation Reserve Program payments included on Schedule F, line 4b, or listed on Schedule K-1 (Form 1065), box 20, code Y	**1b**	(	)
2	Net profit or (loss) from Schedule C, line 31; Schedule C-EZ, line 3; Schedule K-1 (Form 1065), box 14, code A (other than farming); and Schedule K-1 (Form 1065-B), box 9, code J1. Ministers and members of religious orders, see instructions for types of income to report on this line. See instructions for other income to report	**2**		
3	Combine lines 1a, 1b, and 2	**3**		
4	Multiply line 3 by 92.35% (.9235). If less than $400, you do not owe self-employment tax; **do not** file this schedule unless you have an amount on line 1b . . . . ▶	**4**		

Note. If line 4 is less than $400 due to Conservation Reserve Program payments on line 1b, see instructions.

5 Self-employment tax. If the amount on line 4 is:

• $110,100 or less, multiply line 4 by 13.3% (.133). Enter the result here and on **Form 1040, line 56,** or **Form 1040NR, line 54**

• More than $110,100, multiply line 4 by 2.9% (.029). Then, add $11,450.40 to the result.
Enter the total here and on **Form 1040, line 56,** or **Form 1040NR, line 54** **5**

6 Deduction for employer-equivalent portion of self-employment tax.

If the amount on line 5 is:

• $14,643.30 or less, multiply line 5 by 57.51% (.5751)

• More than $14,643.30, multiply line 5 by 50% (.50) and add $1,100 to the result.

Enter the result here and on **Form 1040, line 27,** or **Form 1040NR, line 27** **6**

For Paperwork Reduction Act Notice, see your tax return instructions.   Cat. No. 11358Z   **Schedule SE (Form 1040) 2012**

Schedule SE (Form 1040) 2012   Attachment Sequence No. **17**   Page **2**

Name of person with **self-employment** income (as shown on Form 1040)	Social security number of person with **self-employment** income ▶

Section B—Long Schedule SE

Part I   Self-Employment Tax

Note. If your only income subject to self-employment tax is **church employee income,** see instructions. Also see instructions for the definition of church employee income.

A   If you are a minister, member of a religious order, or Christian Science practitioner **and** you filed Form 4361, but you had $400 or more of **other** net earnings from self-employment, check here and continue with Part I . . . . ▶ ☐

1a	Net farm profit or (loss) from Schedule F, line 34, and farm partnerships, Schedule K-1 (Form 1065), box 14, code A. **Note.** Skip lines 1a and 1b if you use the farm optional method (see instructions)	**1a**	
b	If you received social security retirement or disability benefits, enter the amount of Conservation Reserve Program payments included on Schedule F, line 4b, or listed on Schedule K-1 (Form 1065), box 20, code Y	**1b**	( )
2	Net profit or (loss) from Schedule C, line 31; Schedule C-EZ, line 3; Schedule K-1 (Form 1065), box 14, code A (other than farming); and Schedule K-1 (Form 1065-B), box 9, code J1. Ministers and members of religious orders, see instructions for types of income to report on this line. See instructions for other income to report. **Note.** Skip this line if you use the nonfarm optional method (see instructions)	**2**	
3	Combine lines 1a, 1b, and 2	**3**	
4a	If line 3 is more than zero, multiply line 3 by 92.35% (.9235). Otherwise, enter amount from line 3 **Note.** If line 4a is less than $400 due to Conservation Reserve Program payments on line 1b, see instructions.	**4a**	
b	If you elect one or both of the optional methods, enter the total of lines 15 and 17 here . .	**4b**	
c	Combine lines 4a and 4b. If less than $400, **stop;** you do not owe self-employment tax. **Exception.** If less than $400 and you had **church employee income,** enter -0- and continue ▶	**4c**	

5a	Enter your **church employee income** from Form W-2. See instructions for definition of church employee income . . .	**5a**			
b	Multiply line 5a by 92.35% (.9235). If less than $100, enter -0-			**5b**	
6	Add lines 4c and 5b			**6**	
7	Maximum amount of combined wages and self-employment earnings subject to social security tax or the 4.2% portion of the 5.65% railroad retirement (tier 1) tax for 2012			**7**	
8a	Total social security wages and tips (total of boxes 3 and 7 on Form(s) W-2) and railroad retirement (tier 1) compensation. If $110,100 or more, skip lines 8b through 10, and go to line 11	**8a**			
b	Unreported tips subject to social security tax (from Form 4137, line 10)	**8b**			
c	Wages subject to social security tax (from Form 8919, line 10)	**8c**			
d	Add lines 8a, 8b, and 8c			**8d**	
9	Subtract line 8d from line 7. If zero or less, enter -0- here and on line 10 and go to line 11 . ▶			**9**	
10	Multiply the **smaller** of line 6 or line 9 by 10.4% (.104)			**10**	
11	Multiply line 6 by 2.9% (.029)			**11**	
12	**Self-employment tax.** Add lines 10 and 11. Enter here and on **Form 1040, line 56,** or **Form 1040NR, line 54**			**12**	
13	**Deduction for employer-equivalent portion of self-employment tax.** Add the two following amounts. • 59.6% (.596) of line 10. • One-half of line 11. Enter the result here and on **Form 1040, line 27,** or **Form 1040NR, line 27**	**13**			

Part II   Optional Methods To Figure Net Earnings (see instructions)

Farm Optional Method. You may use this method **only** if **(a)** your gross farm income[1] was not more than $6,780, **or (b)** your net farm profits[2] were less than $4,894.

14	Maximum income for optional methods	**14**	
15	Enter the **smaller** of: two-thirds (²/₃) of gross farm income[1] (not less than zero) **or** $4,520. Also include this amount on line 4b above	**15**	

Nonfarm Optional Method. You may use this method **only** if **(a)** your net nonfarm profits[3] were less than $4,894 and also less than 72.189% of your gross nonfarm income,[4] **and (b)** you had net earnings from self-employment of at least $400 in 2 of the prior 3 years. **Caution.** You may use this method no more than five times.

16	Subtract line 15 from line 14	**16**	
17	Enter the **smaller** of: two-thirds (²/₃) of gross nonfarm income[4] (not less than zero) **or** the amount on line 16. Also include this amount on line 4b above	**17**	

[1] From Sch. F, line 9, and Sch. K-1 (Form 1065), box 14, code B.

[2] From Sch. F, line 34, and Sch. K-1 (Form 1065), box 14, code A—minus the amount you would have entered on line 1b had you not used the optional method.

[3] From Sch. C, line 31; Sch. C-EZ, line 3; Sch. K-1 (Form 1065), box 14, code A; and Sch. K-1 (Form 1065-B), box 9, code J1.

[4] From Sch. C, line 7; Sch. C-EZ, line 1; Sch. K-1 (Form 1065), box 14, code C; and Sch. K-1 (Form 1065-B), box 9, code J2.

Schedule SE (Form 1040) 2012

Source: *http://www.irs.gov/pub/irs-pdf/f1040sse.pdf/IRS.*

OMB No. 1615-0047; Expires 08/31/12

Department of Homeland Security
U.S. Citizenship and Immigration Services

Form I-9, Employment Eligibility Verification

Read instructions carefully before completing this form. The instructions must be available during completion of this form.

ANTI-DISCRIMINATION NOTICE: It is illegal to discriminate against work-authorized individuals. Employers CANNOT specify which document(s) they will accept from an employee. The refusal to hire an individual because the documents have a future expiration date may also constitute illegal discrimination.

Section 1. Employee Information and Verification *(To be completed and signed by employee at the time employment begins.)*

Print Name: Last	First	Middle Initial	Maiden Name

Address *(Street Name and Number)*	Apt. #	Date of Birth *(month/day/year)*

City	State	Zip Code	Social Security #

I am aware that federal law provides for imprisonment and/or fines for false statements or use of false documents in connection with the completion of this form.

I attest, under penalty of perjury, that I am (check one of the following):

☐ A citizen of the United States

☐ A noncitizen national of the United States (see instructions)

☐ A lawful permanent resident (Alien #) _____

☐ An alien authorized to work (Alien # or Admission #) _____
until (expiration date, if applicable - *month/day/year*) _____

Employee's Signature   Date *(month/day/year)*

Preparer and/or Translator Certification *(To be completed and signed if Section 1 is prepared by a person other than the employee.) I attest, under penalty of perjury, that I have assisted in the completion of this form and that to the best of my knowledge the information is true and correct.*

Preparer's/Translator's Signature	Print Name

Address *(Street Name and Number, City, State, Zip Code)*	Date *(month/day/year)*

Section 2. Employer Review and Verification *(To be completed and signed by employer. Examine one document from List A OR examine one document from List B and one from List C, as listed on the reverse of this form, and record the title, number, and expiration date, if any, of the document(s).)*

List A	OR	List B	AND	List C
Document title: _____		_____		_____
Issuing authority: _____		_____		_____
Document #: _____		_____		_____
Expiration Date *(if any):* _____		_____		_____
Document #: _____				
Expiration Date *(if any):* _____				

CERTIFICATION: I attest, under penalty of perjury, that I have examined the document(s) presented by the above-named employee, that the above-listed document(s) appear to be genuine and to relate to the employee named, that the employee began employment on *(month/day/year)* _____ and that to the best of my knowledge the employee is authorized to work in the United States. (State employment agencies may omit the date the employee began employment.)

Signature of Employer or Authorized Representative	Print Name	Title

Business or Organization Name and Address *(Street Name and Number, City, State, Zip Code)*	Date *(month/day/year)*

Section 3. Updating and Reverification *(To be completed and signed by employer.)*

A. New Name *(if applicable)*	B. Date of Rehire *(month/day/year) (if applicable)*

C. If employee's previous grant of work authorization has expired, provide the information below for the document that establishes current employment authorization.

Document Title: _____	Document #: _____	Expiration Date *(if any):* _____

I attest, under penalty of perjury, that to the best of my knowledge, this employee is authorized to work in the United States, and if the employee presented document(s), the document(s) I have examined appear to be genuine and to relate to the individual.

Signature of Employer or Authorized Representative	Date *(month/day/year)*

LISTS OF ACCEPTABLE DOCUMENTS
All documents must be unexpired

LIST A	LIST B	LIST C
Documents that Establish Both Identity and Employment Authorization	**Documents that Establish Identity**	**Documents that Establish Employment Authorization**
	OR	AND

LIST A	LIST B	LIST C
1. U.S. Passport or U.S. Passport Card	1. Driver's license or ID card issued by a State or outlying possession of the United States provided it contains a photograph or information such as name, date of birth, gender, height, eye color, and address	1. Social Security Account Number card other than one that specifies on the face that the issuance of the card does not authorize employment in the United States
2. Permanent Resident Card or Alien Registration Receipt Card (Form I-551)		2. Certification of Birth Abroad issued by the Department of State (Form FS-545)
3. Foreign passport that contains a temporary I-551 stamp or temporary I-551 printed notation on a machine-readable immigrant visa	2. ID card issued by federal, state or local government agencies or entities, provided it contains a photograph or information such as name, date of birth, gender, height, eye color, and address	3. Certification of Report of Birth issued by the Department of State (Form DS-1350)
4. Employment Authorization Document that contains a photograph (Form I-766)	3. School ID card with a photograph	4. Original or certified copy of birth certificate issued by a State, county, municipal authority, or territory of the United States bearing an official seal
	4. Voter's registration card	
5. In the case of a nonimmigrant alien authorized to work for a specific employer incident to status, a foreign passport with Form I-94 or Form I-94A bearing the same name as the passport and containing an endorsement of the alien's nonimmigrant status, as long as the period of endorsement has not yet expired and the proposed employment is not in conflict with any restrictions or limitations identified on the form	5. U.S. Military card or draft record	
	6. Military dependent's ID card	5. Native American tribal document
	7. U.S. Coast Guard Merchant Mariner Card	
	8. Native American tribal document	6. U.S. Citizen ID Card (Form I-197)
	9. Driver's license issued by a Canadian government authority	
	For persons under age 18 who are unable to present a document listed above:	7. Identification Card for Use of Resident Citizen in the United States (Form I-179)
6. Passport from the Federated States of Micronesia (FSM) or the Republic of the Marshall Islands (RMI) with Form I-94 or Form I-94A indicating nonimmigrant admission under the Compact of Free Association Between the United States and the FSM or RMI	10. School record or report card	8. Employment authorization document issued by the Department of Homeland Security
	11. Clinic, doctor, or hospital record	
	12. Day-care or nursery school record	

Illustrations of many of these documents appear in Part 8 of the Handbook for Employers (M-274)

Form I-9 (Rev. 08/07/09) Y Page 5

Source: *www.uscis.gov/files/form/i-9.pdf /USCIS.*

OMB Approval No. 3245-0016
Expiration Date:11/30/2012

U.S. Small Business Administration
APPLICATION FOR BUSINESS LOAN

Individual	Full Address

Name of Applicant Business	Tax I.D. No. or SSN

Full Street Address of Business	Tel. No. (inc. Area Code)

City	County	State	Zip	Number of Employees (Including subsidiaries and affiliates)

Type of Business	Date Business Established	At Time of Application _____

Bank of Business Account and Address	If Loan is Approved _____
	Subsidiaries or Affiliates _____ (Separate from above)

Use of Proceeds: (Enter Gross Dollar Amounts Rounded to the Nearest Hundreds)	Loan Requested		Loan Requested
Land Acquisition		Payoff SBA Loan	
New Construction/ Expansion Repair		Payoff Bank Loan (Non SBA Associated)*	
Acquisition and/or Repair of Machinery and Equipment		Other Debt Payment (Non SBA Associated)	
Inventory Purchase		All Other	
Working Capital (Including Accounts Payable)		Total Loan Requested	
Acquisition of Existing Business		Term of Loan - (Requested Mat.)	_____ Yrs.

CURRENT AND PREVIOUS SBA AND OTHER GOVERNMENT DEBT: Complete the chart below if you, your business, any principal of your business, any affiliate of your business, any other business currently owned by a principal, or any business previously owned by you or a principal of your business has received or applied for any direct or guaranteed financial assistance from the Federal Government, including student loans and disaster loans. All current, previous, and pending Government debt must be listed, including loans that have been paid in full or those that resulted in a loss to the Government. (Note: Loans that resulted in a loss to the Government include loans that were charged off, compromised, or discharged as a result of bankruptcy. The amount of the loss is the outstanding principal balance of the loan that the Government had to write off after all collection activities (including compromise) were finalized.)

Name of Agency / Agency Loan #	Borrower's Name	Original Amount of Loan	Date of Application	Loan Status	Outstanding Balance	Amount of Loss to the Gov't.
#		$			$	$
#		$			$	$
#		$			$	$

ASSISTANCE: Did you commit to pay -- or have you paid -- anyone (including the lender) to assist you in either obtaining this loan (such as a broker, consultant or referral agent) or in preparing the application or application materials for this loan (such as a loan packager)?   Yes [   ]   No[   ]
If "yes," complete SBA Form 159 (7a) - (Fee Disclosure Form and Compensation Agreement) for each party that was paid or will be paid.)

NOTE: The estimated burden completing this form is 12.0 hours per response. You will not be required to respond to collection of information unless it displays a currently valid OMB approval number. Comments on the burden should be sent to U.S. Small Business Administration, Chief, AIB, 409 3rd St., S.W., Washington, D.C. 20416 and Desk Office Small Business Administration, Office of Management and Budget, New Executive Office Building, room 10202 Washington, D.C. 20503.   OMB Approval (3245-0016). PLEASE DO NOT SEND FORMS TO OMB.   SUBMIT COMPLETED APPLICATION TO LENDER OF CHOICE.

SBA Form 4 (9-09) Previous Edition Obsolete   Page 1

ALL EXHIBITS MUST BE SIGNED AND DATED BY PERSON SIGNING THIS FORM

BUSINESS INDEBTEDNESS: Furnish the following information on all outstanding installment debts, contracts, notes, and mortgages payable. Indicate by an asterisk (*) items to be paid by loan proceeds and reason for paying them. (Present balance should agree with the latest balance sheet submitted).

To Whom Payable	Original Amount	Original Date	Present Balance	Rate of Interest	Maturity Date	Monthly Payment	Security	Current or Past Due
Acct. #	$		$			$		
Acct. #	$		$			$		
Acct. #	$		$			$		
Acct. #	$		$			$		
Acct. #	$		$			$		

MANAGEMENT (Proprietor, partners, officers, directors all holder of outstanding stock - 100 % of ownership must be shown). Use separate sheet if necessary.

Name and Social Security number and Position/Title	Complete Address	% Owned		*Gender
			*Veteran Status Veteran Yes ☐ No ☐ If yes, service-disabled? Yes ☐ No ☐	
Race*: Amer. Ind./Alaska Native ☐ Asian ☐ Black/Afr.-Amer. ☐ Native Haw./Pacific Islander ☐ White/Cauc.☐ Ethnicity *Hisp./Latino ☐ Not Hisp./Latino ☐				
			*Veteran Status Veteran Yes ☐ No ☐ If yes, service-disabled? Yes ☐ No ☐	
Race*: Amer. Ind./Alaska Native ☐ Asian ☐ Black/Afr.-Amer. ☐ Native Haw./Pacific Islander ☐ White/Cauc.☐ Ethnicity *Hisp./Latino ☐ Not Hisp./Latino ☐				
			*Veteran Status Veteran Yes ☐ No ☐ If yes, service-disabled? Yes ☐ No ☐	
Race*: Amer. Ind./Alaska Native ☐ Asian ☐ Black/Afr.-Amer. ☐ Native Haw./Pacific Islander ☐ White/Cauc.☐ Ethnicity *Hisp./Latino ☐ Not Hisp./Latino ☐				
			*Veteran Status Veteran Yes ☐ No ☐ If yes, service-disabled? Yes ☐ No ☐	
Race*: Amer. Ind./Alaska Native ☐ Asian ☐ Black/Afr.-Amer. ☐ Native Haw./Pacific Islander ☐ White/Cauc.☐ Ethnicity * Hisp./Latino ☐ Not Hisp./Latino ☐				

*This data is collected for statistical purpose only. It has no bearing on the credit decision. Disclosure is voluntary. One or more boxes for race may be selected.

For Guaranty Loans please provide an original and one copy (Photocopy is Acceptable) of the Application Form and all Exhibits to the participating Lender. For Direct Loans submit one original copy of the application and Exhibits to SBA.

1. Submit SBA Form 912 (State of Personal History) for each proprietor (if sole proprietorship), partner (if a partnership), and by each officer, director, and owner of 20% or more of the company's stock (if a corporation, limited liability company or development company).

2. If your collateral consists of (A) Land and Building, (B) Machinery and Equipment, (C) Furniture and Fixtures, (D) Accounts Receivable, (E) Inventory, (F) Other, please provide an itemized list that contains serial and identification numbers for all articles that had an original value greater than $5,000. Include a legal description of Real Estate offered as collateral. Label it Exhibit A.

3. Furnish a signed current personal balance sheet (SBA Form 413 may be used for this purpose) for (1) each proprietor; or (2) each limited partner who owns 20% or more interest and each general partner; or (3) each stockholder owning 20% or more of voting stock. Include the assets and liabilities of the spouse and any minor children.

Also, include the tax i.d. number [EIN or Social Security Number (SSN)] Label it Exhibit B.

4. Include the financial statements listed below: a,b,c for the last three years; also a,b,c, and d as of the same date, - current within 90 days of filing the application; and statement e, if applicable. **All** information must be signed and dated. (a) Balance Sheet; (b) Profit and Loss Statement (if not available, explain why and substitute Federal income tax forms); (c) Reconciliation of Net Worth; (d) Aging of Accounts Receivable and Payable (summary); (e) Projection of earnings for at least one year where financial statements for the last three years are unavailable or when SBA requests them, Label it Exhibit C. (Contact SBA for a referral if assistance with preparation is wanted.)

5. Provide a brief history of your company and a paragraph describing the expected benefits it will receive from the loan. Label it Exhibit D.

6. Provide a brief description similar to a resume of the education, technical and business background for all the people listed under Management. Label it Exhibit E.

7. Submit the names, addresses, tax I.D. number (EIN or SSN), and current personal financial statement of any co-signers who are not otherwise affiliated with the business and any guarantors for the loan not covered by 3. above. Exhibit F.

8. Include a list of any machinery or equipment or other non-real estate assets to be purchased with loan proceeds and the cost of each item as quoted by the seller. Include the seller's name and address. Exhibit G.

9. Have you or any officer of your company ever been involved in bankruptcy or insolvency proceedings?   [   ] Yes [   ] No
If yes, please provide the details as Exhibit H.

10. Are you or your business involved in any pending lawsuits?
[   ] Yes   [   ] No   If yes, provide the details as Exhibit I.

11. Do you or your spouse or any member of your household, or anyone who owns, manages, or directs your business or their spouses or members of their households work for the Small Business Administration, Small Business Advisory Council, SCORE or ACE, any Federal Agency, or the participating lender? [   ] Yes [   ] No If yes, please provide the name and address of the person and the office where employed.
Label this Exhibit J.

12. Does your business, its owners of majority stockholders own or have a controlling interest in other businesses?   [   ] Yes [   ] No
If yes, please provide their names and the relationship with your company along with financial data requested in question 4.   Label this Exhibit K.

13. Do you buy from, sell to, or use the services of any concern in which someone in your company has a significant financial interest?
[   ] Yes [   ] No If yes, provide details on a separate sheet of paper. Exhibit L.

14. Is your business a franchise? [   ] Yes [   ] No If yes, include a copy of the franchise agreement and a copy of the FTC disclosure statement supplied to you by the Franchisor. Label this Exhibit M.

CONSTRUCTION LOANS ONLY

---

15. Include as a separate exhibit the estimated cost of the project and a statement of the source of any additional funds. Label this Exhibit N.

16. Provide copies of preliminary construction plans and specifications. Label this as Exhibit O. Final plans will be required prior to disbursement.

EXPORT LOANS

---

17. Does your business currently export, or will it start exporting, pursuant to this loan (if approved)?   Check here: [   ] Yes [   ] No

18. If you answered yes to item 17, what is your estimate of the total export sales this loan would support? $ _____

19. Would you like information on Exporting?
Check here: [   ] Yes [   ] No

COUNSELING/TRAINING

---

20. Have you received counseling or training from SBA (e.g., SCORE, ACE, SBDC, WBC, etc.)?   Check here: [   ] Yes [   ] No

---

SUBMIT COMPLETED APPLICATION TO LENDER OF CHOICE.

AGREEMENTS AND CERTIFICATIONS

AGREEMENTS

By signing below you agree to the following:

(a) Agreements of non-employment of SBA Personnel. I agree that if SBA approves this application I will not, for at least two years, hire as an employee or consultant anyone that was employed by the SBA during the one year period prior to the loan disbursement.

(b) Waiver of Claims. As consideration for any Management, Technical, and/or Business Development Assistance that may be provided, I waive all claims against SBA and its consultants.

(c) Criminal Background. I authorize the SBA's Office of Inspector General to request criminal record information about me from criminal justice agencies for the purpose of determining my eligibility for assistance under the Small Business Act.

(d) Reimbursement of Expenses. I agree to pay for or reimburse SBA for the cost of any surveys, title or mortgage examinations, appraisals, credit reports, etc., performed by non-SBA personnel provided I have given my consent.

(e) Reporting. I agree to report to the SBA Office of the Inspector General, Washington, DC 20416 any federal government employee who offers, in return for any type of compensation, to help get this loan approved.

READ THE FOLLOWING CAREFULLY -- FALSE STATEMENTS ARE SUBJECT TO CRIMINAL PROSECUTION:

If you knowingly make a false statement, you can be fined up to $250,000 and/or imprisoned for not more than five years under 18 USC 1001; if submitted to a Federally insured institution, under 18 USC 1014 by Imprisonment of not more than twenty years and/or a fine of not more than $1,000,000.

CERTIFICATIONS:

By signing below you certify as to the following:

(a) **All information in this Application and the Exhibits is true and complete to the best of your knowledge.**   You understand that this information is being submitted to a lender and SBA so they can decide to make a loan or give a loan guaranty, and that the lender and SBA are relying on this information.

(b) You have not paid anyone employed by the Federal Government for help in getting this loan. You understand that you do not need to pay any other third-party for assistance in locating a lender or preparing this Application or Exhibits, and **you certify that you will disclose all parties that were paid for such assistance**   to the Lender and will complete the SBA Form 159 for all such persons.

(c) I have read a copy of the "Statements Required By Law And Executive Order," which is attached to this application and agree to comply with the requirements in this Notice.

If Applicant is a proprietor or general partner, sign below.

By: _____

_____

If Applicant is a Corporation, sign below:

_____
Corporate Name and Seal   Date

By: _____
              Signature of President

Attested by: _____
              Signature of Corporate Secretary

Other than the person that signed on page 3, each Partner, each Stockholder owning 20% or more, and each Guarantor must sign below. In addition, if a husband and wife collectively own 20% or more of a company, each spouse must also sign. No one should sign more than once.

Business Name: _____

APPLICANT'S CERTIFICATION

READ THE FOLLOWING CAREFULLY -- FALSE STATEMENTS ARE SUBJECT TO CRIMINAL PROSECUTION:

If you knowingly make a false statement, you can be fined up to $250,000 and/or imprisoned for not more than five years under 18 USC 1001; if submitted to a Federally insured institution, under 18 USC 1014 by Imprisonment of not more than twenty years and/or a fine of not more than $1,000,000.

By signing below you certify as to the following:

(a) You have reviewed (1) the responses to the question about debt on page 1 of the application; (2) the responses to questions 11,12, and 13 (application-page 3), and (3) any financial statement that you were required to complete as Exhibit B or F to the application and certify that as to you personally all information in this Application and Financial statement is true and complete to the best of your knowledge.   You acknowledge that this information is being submitted to a lender and SBA so they can decide to make a loan or give a loan guaranty, and that the lender and SBA are relying on this information.

(b) You have read a copy of the "Statements Required By Law and Executive Order," which is attached to this application and agree to comply with the requirements in this Notice.

_____   _____
Signature   Date
Check all that apply: [ ] guarantor   [ ] owner-indicate percentage owned: [   ]   [ ] partner-indicate whether [ ] general or [ ] limited

_____   _____
Signature   Date
Check all that apply: [ ] guarantor   [ ] owner-indicate percentage owned: [   ]   [ ] partner-indicate whether [ ] general or [ ] limited

_____   _____
Signature   Date
Check all that apply: [ ] guarantor   [ ] owner-indicate percentage owned: [   ]   [ ] partner-indicate whether [ ] general or [ ] limited

_____   _____
Signature   Date
Check all that apply: [ ] guarantor   [ ] owner-indicate percentage owned: [   ]   [ ] partner-indicate whether [ ] general or [ ] limited

_____   _____
Signature   Date
Check all that apply: [ ] guarantor   [ ] owner-indicate percentage owned: [   ]   [ ] partner-indicate whether [ ] general or [ ] limited

_____   _____
Signature   Date
Check all that apply: [ ] guarantor   [ ] owner-indicate percentage owned: [   ]   [ ] partner-indicate whether [ ] general or [ ] limited

_____   _____
Signature   Date
Check all that apply: [ ] guarantor   [ ] owner-indicate percentage owned: [   ]   [ ] partner-indicate whether [ ] general or [ ] limited

Source: *http://www.sba.gov/content/application-business-loan.*

■ THE FRANCHISE DISCLOSURE DOCUMENT: AN OVERVIEW

Updated 2010

Disclosure Obligations A Federal Trade Commission (FTC) Rule and the laws in 15 states (commonly referred to as the "Registration States") require franchisors to provide a disclosure document to prospective franchisees before granting a franchise. This "Franchise Disclosure Document" or "FDD" is a document designed to give a prospective franchisee detailed information about the proposed franchise investment.

An Overview of the Required Disclosures

The Franchise Rule identifies 23 items that must be addressed in the Franchise Disclosure Document. The 23 disclosure items of the FDD cover the franchisor, the franchised system, the parties' contractual relationship and other obligations of the parties. Specifically, the FDD must include the following information:

Item 1—The franchisor must describe its business, its business experience and the franchise offered. The franchisor also must provide information about its corporate parents, predecessors and affiliates and their business experience. In addition, information must be disclosed about regulations specific to the franchisor's industry.

Item 2—The franchisor must include employment history for the last five years for directors, principal officers, general partners, trustees and other executives who will have management responsibility in connection with the sale or operation of the franchise. Franchise brokers do not need to be disclosed.

Item 3—The franchisor must disclose certain prior and pending litigation (as well as certain administrative and criminal actions) filed against the franchisor, any predecessor, any affiliate that offers franchises under the franchisor's principal trademark, the persons identified in Item 2 and any parent who guarantees the franchisor's performance. The franchisor must also disclose actions that it initiated against franchisees in the last fiscal year that were material to the franchise relationship (such as royalty collection suits).

Item 4—The franchisor must disclose any bankruptcy filings in the last 10 years involving the franchisor, any predecessor, any affiliate, any parent and any person identified in Item 2.

Item 5—The franchisor must disclose any payments that the franchisee is required to make to the franchisor or its affiliates prior to opening and any conditions under which these fees are refundable.

Item 6—The franchisor must disclose all other isolated or recurring fees that the franchisee is required to pay to the franchisor or its affiliates.

Item 7—The franchisor must estimate the initial investment that the franchisee must make to begin operations of the franchised business.

Item 8—The franchisor must identify any goods or services that the franchisee is required to purchase or lease from sources designated or approved by the franchisor or based upon the franchisor's specifications. The franchisor also must make other disclosures regarding suppliers, such as stating whether (and precisely how) the franchisor or its affiliates will derive income from the franchisee's purchases from approved suppliers. Purchasing or distribution cooperatives also must be disclosed.

Item 9—The franchisor must list the franchisee's principal obligations under the franchise and related agreements.

Item 10—The franchisor must describe any financing offered directly or indirectly to the franchisee by the franchisor or its affiliates, and any consideration received by the franchisor or its affiliates as a result of the placement of financing.

Item 11—The franchisor must describe the services it is contractually obligated to provide to the franchisee, including pre-opening and ongoing assistance. In addition, the franchisor must describe the process for selecting a location for the franchisee's business; the typical length of time between contract signing and unit opening; the franchisor's advertising programs; general information about computer system requirements; and the franchisor's training programs.

Item 12—The franchisor must describe any exclusive territory granted to the franchisee and warn the franchisee about intra-brand competition if the franchisee does not receive an exclusive territory. The franchisor also must disclose whether it has established, or may establish, another distribution outlet for products or services under the same trademark or whether its affiliates have established or may establish other franchises or distribution outlets for similar products or services under a different trademark. The franchisor must disclose any rights it or its affiliates have to use alternative channels of distribution within the franchisee's territory and any right of the franchisee to use alternative channels of distribution to make sales outside its territory.

Item 13—The franchisor must provide information about the principal trademarks and service marks to be licensed to the franchisee and any limitations on the franchisee's use of these marks. The franchisor must provide a specific warning if its principal trademarks have not been registered with the United States Patent and Trademark Office (USPTO).

Item 14—The franchisor must disclose information regarding any patents, copyrights, confidential information or trade secrets material relevant to the franchise.

Item 15—The franchisor must disclose whether the franchisee must personally participate in the operation of the franchised business.

Item 16—The franchisor must disclose any restrictions on the goods or services offered by the franchisee, any restrictions on the customers to whom the franchisee may sell goods or services and whether the franchisor has the right to change the types of goods and services that the franchisee is authorized to offer.

Item 17—The franchisor must disclose information about the franchise relationship, including the term, modification, termination, renewal and transfer of the franchise and dispute resolution. The franchisor also must describe what the term "renewal" means in the system and whether franchisees could be required to sign a renewal contract with materially different terms and conditions.

Item 18—If a public figure endorses or recommends the purchase of the franchise or the public figure is used in the franchise name or logo, the franchisor must disclose the compensation given to that public figure, the extent of the public figure's involvement in the management of the franchisor and the total investment by the public figure in the franchisor.

Item 19—If a franchisor wants to provide "financial performance representations" (FPRs) to a franchisee—information about potential sales, expenses or profits—the franchisor must include that information in this Item. Whether or not the franchisor provides FPRs, it must include certain admonitions in this Item.

Item 20—The franchisor must provide certain statistical information regarding franchised and company-owned outlets for the preceding three-year period. This information includes data regarding the number of outlets; transfers, cancellations and terminations; re-acquisitions by the franchisor; and projected new openings. The franchisor also must disclose contact information for current franchisees and certain former franchisees, and make certain disclosures regarding franchisee associations and any confidentiality agreements that franchisees may have signed in the preceding three years.

Item 21—The franchisor must include audited balance sheets as of the end of its last two fiscal years and statements of operations of stockholders' equity and of cash flow for its last three fiscal years. The financial statements must be prepared according to generally accepted accounting principles (GAAP). The franchisor may use its parent's consolidated financial statement and must include the parent's financial statement if the parent has post-sale performance obligations or guarantees the franchisor's performance.

Item 22—The franchisor must include a copy of every contract that the prospective franchisee will or may be required to sign.

Item 23—The franchisor must include two copies of an acknowledgement of receipt to be signed by the prospective franchisee (one for the franchisee and one for the franchisor).

The Franchise Rule allows the franchisor to provide disclosure electronically. Under the Rule, franchisors must update their disclosure document annually, within 120 days after the close of the company's fiscal year.

What Is a Franchise?

Given the disclosure obligations imposed on franchisors, it is important to understand what constitutes a "franchise." Although the definition varies by jurisdiction, as a general rule, a business will be considered a franchise and be subject to pre-sale registration and disclosure obligations if it meets three criteria:

1. The franchisee's business is identified or substantially associated with the franchisor's trademark or commercial symbol.
2. The franchisor exerts sufficient control over the franchisee's business or there is interdependence between the franchisee's business and the franchisor's system. There are three alternative tests used for this element. First, the Federal Trade Commission uses the "significant control" or "significant assistance" test, which is applicable in the majority of the states. This test focuses on the franchisor's level of control or assistance over the franchisee's entire business. Second, under the "marketing plan" test, which is used by several states, a franchise exists when the franchisor prescribes a marketing plan that the franchisee must follow. Third, under the "community of interest" test, which is used in a smaller number of states, a franchise exists when there is a sufficient level of interdependence between the franchisee and the franchisor.
3. The franchisee is obligated to pay money to the franchisor or its affiliates for the right to engage in the business. Almost any monies paid to the franchisor or its affiliates can satisfy this element, except for the purchase of inventory at *bona fide* wholesale prices.

Some jurisdictions exclude from registration and disclosure certain business relationships that meet the definition of a franchise. Examples of excluded relationships are general partnerships, employment relationships, fractional franchises (where the franchisee has experience in the franchised business and the new franchised business will account for less than 20% of the franchisee's total sales) and certain large investments or large franchisees.

A number of states only require certain franchisors to provide disclosure, but do not require registration. The most common registration exemption is for a franchisor whose net worth exceeds a certain level (generally $5 million) and who is experienced in the franchised business.

Since the definition of a "franchise" and the applicable exclusions and exemptions vary, a business relationship may be considered a franchise in some jurisdictions, but not in other jurisdictions.

Franchising Services

Wiley Rein LLP represents franchisors on matters for which they require expert legal services. We can:

- Determine whether your business concept is a franchise. If it is a franchise, but you would prefer to avoid the registration/disclosure requirements, we can help you modify the business concept to avoid coverage by the franchise laws, if possible, or to take advantage of applicable exclusions.
- Work with you to develop franchise and related agreements that will permit the growth of your concept while allowing you to maintain control.
- Seek federal registrations for your trademarks, and provide assistance in maintaining and protecting those marks.
- Prepare the disclosure document and provide guidance on how to use it.
- Prepare and file all franchise registrations, amendments and renewals, or seek exemptions from registration, in all applicable states.
- If you are a U.S. franchisor, assist you in developing your franchise concept abroad; if you are a foreign franchisor, assist you in bringing your franchise concept to the United States.
- Help you understand your contract rights and obligations and the statutory restrictions that apply to the franchise relationship, including transfers and contract renewals.
- Represent you in any proceedings brought by federal or state franchise regulators.
- Guide you in terminating the relationship with a franchisee without violating statutory restrictions.
- Represent you in litigation or arbitration proceedings with a franchisee.

For more information, please contact *Franchise Group* Chair *Bob Smith* at 202.719.4481.

This is a publication of Wiley Rein LLP and should not be construed as legal advice or a legal opinion on any specific facts or circumstances. The contents are intended for general informational purposes. You are urged to consult your lawyer concerning your own situation and any specific legal questions.

Source: "The Franchise Disclosure Document: An Overview Updated 2010 ," Wiley Rein LLC, from *http://www.wileyrein.com/publications.cfm?sp=articles&id=971*, (Accessed April 13, 2012). Reprinted with permission.

index

Image_Source/iStockphoto.com